Frommer's®
Boston

28th Edition

by Marie Morris

John Wiley & Sons, Inc.

Published by:
JOHN WILEY AND SONS, INC.
111 River St.
Hoboken, NJ 07030-5774

ISBN 978-1-118-28757-6 (paper); 978-1-118-33365-5 (ebk); 978-1-118-33142-2 (ebk);
978-1-118-33479-9 (ebk)

Editor: Matthew Brown
Production Editor: Jana M. Stefanciosa
Cartographer: Andy Dolan
Photo Editor: Richard Fox, Alden Gewirtz
Design by Vertigo Design
Layout, Graphics & Prepress by Wiley Indianapolis Composition Services

Front cover photo: Durgin Park Market, Boston ©Richard Nowitz /
National Geographic Image Collection / Alamy Images
Back Cover Photos, left to right: "Man at the Wheel House" Fisherman Statue, Gloucester, MA
©Ken Cedeno; Public Gardens with swan boats in distance ©Ken Cedeno; Sailboats,
Harvard Bridge, Cambridge, Boston, Massachusetts ©Vince DeWitt

For information on our other products and services or to obtain technical support, please contact
our Customer Care Department within the U.S. at 877/762-2974, outside the U.S. at 317/572-3993
or fax 317/572-4002.

Wiley also publishes its books in a variety of electronic formats. Some content that appears in print
may not be available in electronic formats.

Manufactured in China

53902169

5   4   3   2   1

CONTENTS

List of Maps vi

1 THE BEST OF BOSTON 1

The Most Unforgettable Boston Experiences 3

The Best Food & Drink Experiences 3

The Best Family Experiences 5

The Best Free & Dirt-Cheap Things to Do 6

The Best Ways to See Boston Like a Local 7

The Best Shopping Experiences 8

The Best Boston-Area Museums 10

The Best Outdoor Activities 11

2 BOSTON IN DEPTH 13

Boston Today 15

The Making of Boston 16

When to Go 26

BOSTON CALENDAR OF EVENTS 27

Responsible Tourism in Boston 32

3 BOSTON NEIGHBORHOODS & SUGGESTED ITINERARIES 34

City Layout 35

Neighborhoods in Brief 36

Iconic Boston 43

SUGGESTED EVENING ITINERARIES 49

Boston with Kids 51

Boston for Art Lovers 53

4 EXPLORING BOSTON 54

Boston's Top 20 Sights & Attractions 55

LET'S MAKE A DEAL 58

The Waterfront 59

The North End 61

WELCOME TO THE NORTH END 61

North Station/Science Park 62

Faneuil Hall Marketplace 64

Government Center 64

Downtown Crossing 65

Beacon Hill 65

Charlestown 68

South Boston Waterfront/ Seaport District 68

Chinatown/Theater District 70

The South End 70

The Back Bay 70

Kenmore Square 74

The Fenway 74

Dorchester 77

Jamaica Plain 78

Brookline 79

Cambridge 80

The Freedom Trail 86

Parks & Gardens 102

Organized Tours 104

MISSING THIS WOULD BE A CRIME 111

Especially for Kids 113

Outdoor Activities 117

A VACATION IN THE ISLANDS 120

Sights & Attractions by Theme
Index 124

5 STROLLING AROUND BOSTON 126

WALKING TOUR 1: THE BACK BAY 127

*WALKING TOUR 2: THE
WATERFRONT* 133

*WALKING TOUR 3: HARVARD
SQUARE* 138

6 WHERE TO EAT 148

Best Bets 149

The Waterfront 150

The North End 154

*WEEKDAY BREAKFAST & WEEKEND
BRUNCH* 159

Faneuil Hall Marketplace & the
Financial District 159

Downtown Crossing 161

Beacon Hill 162

Chinatown/Theater District 162

YUM, YUM, DIM SUM 164

The South End 166

The Back Bay 169

QUICK BITES & PICNIC PROVISIONS 171

Kenmore Square &
the Fenway 172

*THE GREAT OUTDOORS:
ALFRESCO DINING* 174

Cambridge 175

Practical Matters: The
Restaurant Scene 185

Restaurants by Cuisine 187

7 SHOPPING 189

The Waterfront 190

The North End 190

Faneuil Hall Marketplace 190

Government Center & the
Financial District 190

Downtown Crossing 191

Beacon Hill 191

South Boston Waterfront
(Seaport District) 191

The South End 191

The Back Bay 191

Kenmore Square 192

The Fenway 192

Cambridge 192

Malls & Markets 194

Shopping A to Z 196

*AN ARTSY STROLL ALONG
NEWBURY STREET* 198

Practical Matters: The
Shopping Scene 215

8 ENTERTAINMENT & NIGHTLIFE 216

The Performing Arts 217
The Bar Scene 229
The Club & Music Scene 235

The Gay & Lesbian Scene 241
Alternative Entertainment 243
Spectator Sports 245

9 WHERE TO STAY 251

Best Bets 252
WHAT YOU'LL REALLY PAY 253
The Waterfront & the North End 254
North Station 259
Faneuil Hall Marketplace &
    Government Center 260
The Financial District &
    Downtown Crossing 261
Beacon Hill 263
Charlestown 265
South Boston Waterfront
    (Seaport District) 265

Chinatown/Theater District 267
The South End 269
The Back Bay 270
FAMILY-FRIENDLY HOTELS 274
Kenmore Square 279
Outskirts & Brookline 279
Cambridge 281
At & Near the Airport 287
Practical Matters: The
    Hotel Scene 288

10 SIDE TRIPS FROM BOSTON 292

Lexington 293
Concord 299
Marblehead 308
Salem 313
Gloucester 320

A WHALE OF AN ADVENTURE 321
NORTH SHORE BEACHES 329
Rockport 330
Plymouth 335
THE ADAMS FAMILY 336

11 PLANNING YOUR TRIP TO BOSTON 343

Getting There 344
LET'S MAKE A DEAL 345
Getting Around 348

Special-Interest Trips & Tours 355
FAST FACTS: BOSTON 356

INDEX 369

Accommodations Index 374

Restaurant Index 375

LIST OF MAPS

Boston's Changing Shoreline 17

Boston Orientation 38

Iconic Boston 44

Boston With Kids & Boston for
 Art Lovers 52

Boston Attractions 56

Walking Tour 1: The Back Bay 129

Walking Tour 2: The Waterfront 135

Walking Tour 3: Harvard Square 141

Boston Restaurants 152

North End Restaurants 157

Cambridge Restaurants 177

Back Bay Shopping 193

Boston After Dark 218

Cambridge After Dark 223

Boston Hotels 256

Cambridge Hotels 283

Boston & Surrounding Areas 295

Lexington 297

Concord 301

Marblehead 309

Salem 315

Gloucester 323

Rockport 331

Plymouth 337

ABOUT THE AUTHOR

Marie Morris grew up in New York and graduated from Harvard, where she studied history. She has worked for Newser.com, *02138* magazine, the *Boston Herald*, *Boston* magazine, and the *New York Times*. She's the author of *Frommer's Boston Day by Day* and *Boston For Dummies*, and she covers Boston for *Frommer's New England* and *Frommer's New England Day by Day*. She lives in Boston, not far from Paul Revere.

ACKNOWLEDGMENTS

Heartfelt thanks to Kelly Regan, Matthew Brown, Maureen Clarke, Ian Skinnari, Andrea Kahn, Ashley Skibicki, and everyone else at Frommer's who overcame numerous obstacles to get this book into your hands. To Peggy Hartmann; Michael Dobler; Andrea Rasmussen; David Wallace; Lauren Goldberg; Susan Steinway; Jim McCormack; Sue Costello; Jeff Keffer; Tim and Chetna Naimi; Jody Kelman; Rob Nabors; and Emma, Timothy, Kathryn, and Jeff Bradley, many thanks for your hearty appetites and strong opinions. And special thanks to Lisa, Ethan, and Will Freudenheim, my favorite adventurers.

DEDICATION

This edition of *Frommer's Boston* is dedicated to former frommers.com Senior Editor Jason Clampet (www.skift.com), who inspired us to show Beantown in its best light.

HOW TO CONTACT US

In researching this book, we discovered many wonderful places—hotels, restaurants, shops, and more. We're sure you'll find others. Please tell us about them, so we can share the information with your fellow travelers in upcoming editions. If you were disappointed with a recommendation, we'd love to know that, too. Please write to:

Frommer's Boston, 28th Edition

John Wiley & Sons, Inc. • 111 River St. • Hoboken, NJ 07030-5774

ADVISORY & DISCLAIMER

Travel information can change quickly and unexpectedly, and we strongly advise you to confirm important details locally before traveling, including information on visas, health and safety, traffic and transport, accommodation, shopping and eating out. We also encourage you to stay alert while traveling and to remain aware of your surroundings. Avoid civil disturbances, and keep a close eye on cameras, purses, wallets and other valuables.

While we have endeavored to ensure that the information contained within this guide is accurate and up-to-date at the time of publication, we make no representations or warranties with respect to the accuracy or completeness of the contents of this work and specifically disclaim all warranties, including without limitation warranties of fitness for a particular purpose. We accept no responsibility or liability for any inaccuracy or errors or omissions, or for any inconvenience, loss, damage, costs or expenses of any nature whatsoever incurred or suffered by anyone as a result of any advice or information contained in this guide.

The inclusion of a company, organization or website in this guide as a service provider and/or potential source of further information does not mean that we endorse them or the information they provide. Be aware that information provided through some websites may be unreliable and can change without notice. Neither the publisher or author shall be liable for any damages arising herefrom.

FROMMER'S STAR RATINGS, ICONS & ABBREVIATIONS

Every hotel, restaurant, and attraction listing in this guide has been ranked for quality, value, service, amenities, and special features using a **star-rating system.** In country, state, and regional guides, we also rate towns and regions to help you narrow down your choices and budget your time accordingly. Hotels and restaurants are rated on a scale of zero (recommended) to three stars (exceptional). Attractions, shopping, nightlife, towns, and regions are rated according to the following scale: zero stars (recommended), one star (highly recommended), two stars (very highly recommended), and three stars (must-see).

In addition to the star-rating system, we also use **seven feature icons** that point you to the great deals, in-the-know advice, and unique experiences that separate travelers from tourists. Throughout the book, look for:

🎁　Special finds—those places only insiders know about

💬　Fun facts—details that make travelers more informed and their trips more fun

☺　Kids—Best bets for kids and advice for the whole family

📷　Special moments—those experiences that memories are made of

✋　Overrated—Places or experiences not worth your time or money

✎　Insider tips—great ways to save time and money

🏷　Great values—where to get the best deals

The following **abbreviations** are used for credit cards:

AE	American Express	**DISC**	Discover	**V**	Visa
DC	Diners Club	**MC**	MasterCard		

TRAVEL RESOURCES AT FROMMERS.COM

Frommer's travel resources don't end with this guide. Frommer's website, **www. frommers.com**, has travel information on more than 4,000 destinations. We update features regularly, giving you access to the most current trip-planning information and the best airfare, lodging, and car-rental bargains. You can also listen to podcasts, connect with other Frommers.com members through our active-reader forums, share your travel photos, read blogs from guidebook editors and fellow travelers, and much more.

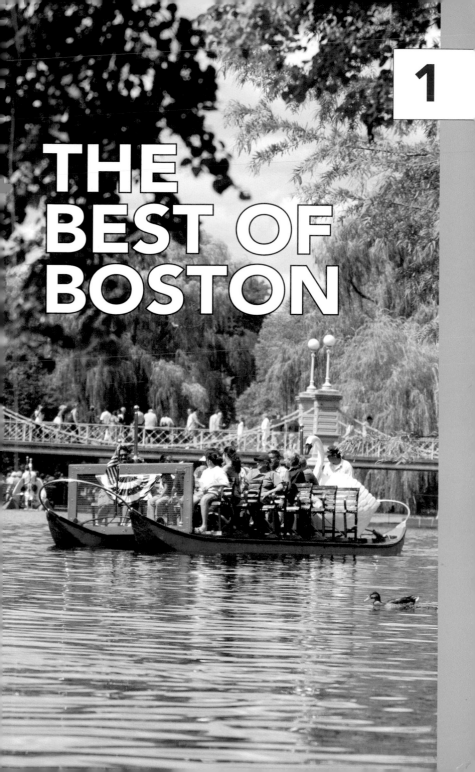

1

THE BEST OF BOSTON

One of the oldest American cities, Boston packs a lot into a small footprint, with its wealth of historic attractions, shopping options for every budget, diverse culture, terrific dining, lovely scenery, and plenty of sports (for watching or doing). It's a crowded, welcoming destination—even areas choked with sightseers are in or near residential neighborhoods, and countless locals are former students who attended one of the many excellent colleges nearby. With so much to offer, Boston is perfect for both a quick visit and a longer stay.

Things to Do   Bostonians walk everywhere. They stroll the galleries of the **Museum of Fine Arts** and the **Institute of Contemporary Art,** the banks of the **Charles River,** the ever-changing **Rose Kennedy Greenway,** and the lively streets of **Harvard Square.** Then they take a break in the **Public Garden** for a ride on a **Swan Boat,** at **Fenway Park** for a **Red Sox** game, or at a restaurant for local seafood. One top historic attraction is a walking tour—the **Freedom Trail**—and two favorite neighborhoods are pedestrian-friendly **Beacon Hill** and the **North End.**

Shopping   Its shops, boutiques, galleries, markets, and malls make the Boston area the most interesting retail destination in New England. **Newbury Street** and **Boylston Street** are perfect for window-shopping as well as for buying; they're in the heart of the **Back Bay,** where high-profile chains thrive alongside only-in-Boston retailers. **Faneuil Hall Marketplace** has a similar blend, but the gems of commerce are the neighborhoods, including **Beacon Hill** and the **South End** in Boston, and **Harvard Square** and **Porter Square** in **Cambridge.**

Restaurants & Dining   Favorites such as New England clam chowder, Boston baked beans, Boston cream pie, and Samuel Adams beer are just part of the dynamic dining scene. Trends are less significant than seafood from nearby waters, local produce, and price points fit for both students and special occasions. Head to **the North End** for Italian, to **the South End** for the hottest bistros, and to **Cambridge** for a mix of upscale, ethnic, and budget-friendly options.

Nightlife & Entertainment   Classical music is the headliner, harmonizing with rock, folk, and jazz. The legendary Boston Symphony Orchestra and beloved Boston Pops play at **Symphony Hall;** across the river, Cambridge's **Central Square** is home to the best live-music scene in New England. Add top-notch comedy and improv, throw in the wild variety of student performances, and you may not even notice that local club culture—thanks largely to the 2am curfew—leaves something to be desired.

PREVIOUS PAGE: **A Swan Boat in the Public Garden.**

THE most unforgettable BOSTON EXPERIENCES

o **A Sky Full of Fireworks:** The Fourth of July fireworks flash over the Charles River; Boston greets the New Year with First Night pyrotechnics that flare above the Common in the early evening and the Inner Harbor at midnight. See "Boston Calendar of Events," in chapter 2.

o **A Ride on a Duck:** Board an amphibious Duck boat (on Huntington Ave. near the Prudential Center, at the Museum of Science, or near the New England Aquarium) for a sightseeing ride that includes a dip in the river—for the boat, not for you. See p. 105.

o **A Visit to Beacon Hill:** The quintessential Boston neighborhood comes complete with Federal-style homes lining cobblestone streets and overlooking stately parks. Wear good walking shoes, and let your imagination run wild. See "Beacon Hill," p. 37.

o **A Day at the Museum of Fine Arts:** The MFA is one of the best art museums in the world. The whole place overflows with breathtaking works, including a surprising number of masterpieces so familiar that seeing them is like running into an old friend on the street. See p. 75.

o **An Afternoon Red Sox Game:** Since 1912, baseball fans have made pilgrimages to Fenway Park, the "lyric little bandbox of a ball park" (in John Updike's words) off Kenmore Square. Soak up the atmosphere and bask in the sun. See p. 246.

o **A Walk Around the North End:** Boston's Little Italy (but don't call it that!) has an old-world flavor you won't want to miss. Explore the shops on Salem Street, and be sure to stop for coffee and a pastry at a Hanover Street *caffè*. See "Welcome to the North End," on p. 61.

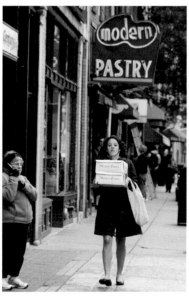

o **A Newbury Street Safari:** From the genteel Arlington Street end to the cutting-edge Massachusetts Avenue end, Boston's legendary shopping destination is 8 blocks of pure temptation: galleries, boutiques, jewelry and gift shops, and more. See chapter 7.

THE best FOOD & DRINK EXPERIENCES

o **Drink,** 348 Congress St., Fort Point (© **617/695-1806**). High-end watering hole meets mad scientist's lab. Amateur mixologist Rachel Maddow (the MSNBC

Modern Pastry is a time-tried favorite for Italian treats on the North End.

host who occasionally instructs Jimmy Kimmel on cocktail culture) calls Drink the best bar in Boston, if not the country. See p. 233.

o **Hamersley's Bistro,** 553 Tremont St. (© 617/423-2700). Established and innovative, adventurous and comfortable, Hamersley's is both a neighborhood favorite and a can't-miss special-occasion place. Julia Child encouraged chef-owner Gordon Hamersley to open the restaurant and became a loyal customer—need I say more? See p. 166.

o **Legal Sea Foods,** 255 State St. (© 617/742-5300), and other locations. Like the culinary equivalent of a medical specialist, Legal's does one thing and does it exceptionally well. It's a chain for a great reason: People can't get enough of the freshest seafood around. See p. 151.

o **Mr. Bartley's Burger Cottage,** 1246 Massachusetts Ave., Cambridge (© 617/354-6559). Trends in food and fashion come and go, and Harvard Square sees them all. Luckily, the neighborhood has a place that puts the "comfort" in comfort food. Bartley's is famous for its juicy burgers, incredible onion rings, and a down-to-earth atmosphere that's increasingly rare in these parts. See p. 178.

o **Pizzeria Regina,** 11½ Thacher St. (© 617/227-0765). With its jampacked dining room and fiery oven, Regina's looks like Hollywood's idea of a pizza joint. After one bite of the slightly smoky, crispy yet chewy crust, you'll be sending Martin Scorsese to the back of the line. See p. 158.

o **Samuel Adams Brewery,** 30 Germania St., Jamaica Plain (© 617/368-5080). One of the best craft beers in the country got its start in Boston, and brewery tours are a fascinating way to see how that delicious "Sam" gets into your glass. You must be 21 years old.

o **Union Oyster House,** 41 Union St. (© 617/227-2750). Wise guys sneer about all the tourists, but the Union Oyster House is popular with both visitors and locals. Dating to 1826, it's a good place for traditional New England food, including oysters shucked while you watch. See p. 160.

Legal Sea Foods.

Pizzeria Regina is popular with both Bostonians and out-of-towners.

THE best FAMILY EXPERIENCES

○ **A Visit to Faneuil Hall Marketplace:** Street performers, crowds from all over the world, the food court, restaurants, bars, and shops make Faneuil Hall Marketplace (you'll also hear it called Quincy Market) Boston's most popular destination. It's conveniently located across the street from the harbor, where a stroll along the water can help your crew decompress. See p. 195.

○ **An Exploration of the Museum of Science:** Your kids will revel in the displays and exhibits that cram every branch of science and inquiry into this enormous and child-accessible institution. See p. 62.

○ **An Excursion to the Public Garden:** A perfect retreat during or after a busy day of sightseeing. Ride a Swan Boat, visit with the Mallard family of *Make Way for Ducklings* fame, admire the real birds, and marvel as the bickering ends and the whole family chills out. See p. 103.

○ **A Trip to the Boston Children's Museum:** The hands-on exhibits, noisy galleries, and overall air of discovery and excitement make this excursion catnip for the elementary-school set. See p. 114.

○ **A Thrill "Ride":** The Mugar Omni Theater (at the Museum of Science) and the 3-D Simons IMAX Theatre (at the New England Aquarium) offer intrepid visitors hair-raising experiences from the safety of a comfortable auditorium. Most of the large-format films concentrate on the natural world. See p. 62 for the Mugar Omni Theater and p. 60 for the Simons IMAX Theatre.

○ **A Tour of Fenway Park:** The creaky, cramped home of the Boston Red Sox, which opened in

The Van de Graaff generator at the Museum of Science.

Ted Williams and his teammates welcome visitors outside Fenway Park.

1912, is a baseball shrine that entrances visitors. Adolescents too cool to admit that they're having fun at other attractions tend to drop any pretense of boredom here, and younger kids unabashedly love it. The parents saving a bundle by not paying for game tickets tend to agree. See p. 248.

o **A Spell in Salem:** A 12-year-old of my acquaintance—now a college graduate who still cringes when I tell this story—returned from a visit to Salem proclaiming that he wanted to become a witch. Manageable size, interesting attractions, an impressively handsome historic district, and plenty of space for running around make the Witch City a great choice for an all-ages day trip. See chapter 10.

THE best FREE & DIRT-CHEAP THINGS TO DO

o **Picnic by the Water:** Head for the harbor or river, relax on a park bench or patch of grass, turn off your phone, and enjoy the spectacular scene. Whether it's sailboats or ocean liners, sea gulls or scullers, there's always something worth watching. My favorite spot is Sargent's Wharf, on the edge of the North End, but it's just one of thousands of pleasant spots. See chapter 6.

o **Visit a Museum:** Schedule your visit to take advantage of free or reduced admission. The **USS *Constitution* Museum** is free all the time; the **Museum of Fine Arts** is free after 4pm Wednesday; the **Institute of Contemporary Art** is free after 5pm Thursday; and the **Children's Museum** costs just $1 after 5pm on Friday. See chapter 4.

o **Ride on a Swan:** A Swan *Boat*, that is. The engagingly low-tech vessels ply the waters of the Public Garden lagoon at a stately pace, allowing an up-close view of the barely wild wildlife that flourishes in the heart of the city. For a family of four, a ride costs all of 8 bucks. See p. 103.

Sargent's Wharf overlooks Boston Harbor.

- **Take a Ranger-Led Tour:** The National Park Service is such a good use of tax money. Free and cheap tours of historic attractions all over eastern Massachusetts elevate a visit to a park, a house, a neighborhood, or even a government installation (the Charlestown Navy Yard) from good to great. See chapters 4 and 10.

- **Relish a Vicarious Thrill:** Without so much as lacing up a sneaker, you can participate in the world-famous Boston Marathon. Stretch a little. Drink plenty of fluids. Claim a piece of sidewalk with a front-row view of the course. Cheer as the runners thunder past. Then put your feet up—you must be exhausted. See p. 249.

- **Check Out a College Concert or Show:** Countless student groups just want an attentive audience, and the free or cheap admission can pay off in the long run. Imagine the credit card commercial: "Ability to say you recognized the talent of [insert name of big star] in a student production? Priceless." See chapter 8.

THE best WAYS TO SEE BOSTON LIKE A LOCAL

- **Stroll (or Jog) Along the River:** The bike path that hugs both shores of the Charles accommodates pedestrians, runners, and in-line skaters as well as cyclists. The Esplanade (adjacent to the Back Bay) features both people-watching and gorgeous trees and shrubs; the Cambridge side has abundant seating and fabulous views of the Boston skyline. See chapters 4 and 5.

- **Check Out a Farmers' Market:** Besides delicious fruits and vegetables, farmers' markets in eastern Massachusetts ply everything from gourmet chocolate to artisan bread to hand-crafted jewelry. See p. 195.

Jogging on the Esplanade with the Prudential Tower in the background.

- **Visit the Top of the Prudential Tower:** At the Prudential Center Skywalk, you'll see Boston like a local, all right—a middle-school student on a field trip. It's a local rite of passage, but kids of all ages from around the world love the 50th-floor views and interactive displays. See p. 73.

- **Have Dinner at a Neighborhood Hangout:** Skip the special-occasion restaurant and enjoy a casual meal with after-work regulars who arrive on foot. Neighborhood joints with excellent food include the South End Buttery, in Boston, and Redbones, in Somerville. See chapter 6.

- **Walk Around the Arnold Arboretum:** You may not see a single other out-of-towner at this gorgeous park. It's open and enjoyable year-round, but most appealing in moderate weather. See p. 103.

- **Cheer for a College Sports Team:** From September to May, local schools field dozens of teams. Many are nationally ranked (and charge admission), but many more are just fun to watch (and free). Ever been to a field hockey game or a crew race? See p. 246.

THE best SHOPPING EXPERIENCES

- **Every Bookstore in the Boston Area:** Bookworms from around the world flock to Boston and Cambridge, with their award-winning independent shops, well-stocked chain outlets, and special-interest businesses catering to every appetite. See chapter 7.

- **Barbara Krakow Gallery,** 10 Newbury St., fifth floor, Back Bay (① 617/262-4490). Despite a handful of notable venues, the refrain that haunts the Boston arts scene is "nice, but it's better in New York." Barbara Krakow runs one of the few galleries that gives New Yorkers the inferiority complex. See p. 197.

- **Black Ink,** 101 Charles St., Beacon Hill (① 617/723-3883), and 5 Brattle St., Cambridge (① 617/497-1221). A funky desktop trinket, a retro toy, a beautifully designed kitchen gadget, a gorgeous card—you may not come out of these little treasure chests with what you went in looking for, but you'll almost certainly find something you love. See p. 211.

- **Converse,** 348 Newbury St., Back Bay (☏ **617/424-5400**). Founded in suburban Malden in 1908, the athletic-shoe manufacturer is a local brand with an international presence. If you don't see exactly the right pair of sneakers, you can create your own. See p. 206.
- **Galería Cubana,** 460 Harrison Ave., South End (☏ **617/292-2822**). It's not the easiest place to find, but this amazing gallery captures the experience of visiting Cuba without a single bit of red tape. See p. 197.
- **International Poster Gallery,** 205 Newbury St., Back Bay (☏ **617/375-0076**). One of the high points of a visit to Newbury Street is a stop here. If you have any interest in graphic design or contemporary art—heck, if you've ever taped a magazine cover to the wall over your desk—you'll find something wonderful here. See p. 198.
- **John Lewis, Inc.,** 97 Newbury St., Back Bay (☏ **617/266-6665**). The exquisite craftsmanship—executed on the premises by John Lewis himself—makes this jewelry store a favorite among several generations of Bostonians in the know. If you see nose prints on the front window, they might be mine. See p. 205.
- **Joie de Vivre,** 1792 Massachusetts Ave., Cambridge (☏ **617/864-8188**). Somewhere amid the thoughtful selection of inventive gifts, toys, cards, jewelry, and inspiring tchotchkes is just the right gift (for someone else or for yourself). Finding it is more than half the fun. See p. 211.
- **Upstairs Downstairs Antiques,** 93 Charles St., Beacon Hill (☏ **617/367-1950**). Even when I don't wind up buying something here, I come away inspired by the layout of the well-edited merchandise and the knowledge of the helpful staff. See p. 197.

The International Poster Gallery.

Upstairs Downstairs Antiques.

THE best BOSTON-AREA MUSEUMS

- **Concord Museum:** Always informative, never overwhelming, this thoughtfully organized museum shows and tells visitors enough about the town's history to help them make the most of a visit. See p. 301.

- **The Institute of Contemporary Art:** Literally and figuratively a trip—it's on the South Boston waterfront and unlike any other cultural institution in Boston—the ICA is a blast. The architecture is amazing; be sure you walk around to the back of the building, which juts out *above* Boston Harbor. See p. 69.

- **Isabella Stewart Gardner Museum:** The Gardner is a magnificent repository of art and nature in a building that's as impressive as anything hanging on the walls. Modeled on a Venetian *palazzo,* the original 1903 structure centers on a glorious plant-filled atrium; the 2011 addition is a contemporary showpiece. See p. 74.

- **John F. Kennedy Presidential Library and Museum:** The exhibits here capture the personality of the library's charismatic namesake through video, artifacts, photos, documents, and more. A visit will help you understand why the Camelot era remains so compelling half a century later. See p. 77.

- **Museum of Fine Arts:** See "The Most Unforgettable Boston Experiences," above.

- **Peabody Essex Museum:** Yes, it's possible to spend a day in Salem without giving witches more than a passing thought. All by itself, the Peabody Essex is worth a trip to the North Shore. Check ahead for information about special exhibitions, or just take in the marvels of the permanent collections. See p. 316.

The Institute of Contemporary Art offers gorgeous views of Boston.

THE best OUTDOOR ACTIVITIES

o **A Ride Across the Harbor:** The commuter ferry that connects Long Wharf and the Charlestown Navy Yard is a treasure concealed in plain sight. You might notice the boat traffic on the Inner Harbor as you make your way around downtown; for just $1.70, you can be part of it. See chapter 4.

o **An Island Excursion:** The Boston Harbor Islands National Recreation Area is something of a hidden secret, just offshore but a world away. Start at the visitor center, on the Rose Kennedy Greenway, before venturing to a destination so accessible and interesting that you won't believe how uncrowded most of it is. See chapter 4.

o **An Interlude at a Cafe:** Outdoor seating in a place with great people-watching is a good idea, right up there with fire and the wheel. A passing parade of shoppers and students (on Newbury St. and in Harvard Sq.) is more interesting than suits and ties (downtown and the rest of the Back Bay), but if the

The atrium at the Isabella Stewart Gardner Museum.

THE BEST OF BOSTON

The Best Outdoor Activities

The ferry ride connecting Long Wharf and the Charlestown Navy Yard.

breeze and the iced cappuccino are cool, what's not to like? See chapter 6.

o **A Free Concert:** The Boston area's cultural scene has no real off season. During the summer, many musicians and musical groups take their acts outside—to parks, plazas, and even a barge (behind the Boston Harbor Hotel). Plan well and you can enjoy music alfresco almost every night. See chapter 8.

o **A Walk Back in Time:** Head for Concord to experience nature as Henry David Thoreau did in the mid–19th century. Through a nearly magical combination of circumstances, Walden Pond looks much as it did when the author and naturalist lived there from July 1845 through September 1847. See chapter 10.

o **A Seaside Saunter:** Gorgeous Marblehead is a quintessential

Sidewalk dining along Newbury Street.

New England town, with crooked lanes leading down to a broad harbor jammed with yachts, sailboats, and fishing vessels. Great shopping, good food, interesting architecture, arresting scenery, and plenty of places to sit and watch the waterborne action make it one of my favorite destinations anywhere. See chapter 10.

BOSTON
IN DEPTH

W
hat draws visitors to Boston? Some come for the historic attractions and great museums, others for seafood and shopping, still others for the top-notch music scene and world-famous sports teams. Conventiongoers, vacationing families, and fall foliage "leaf peepers" flock to Boston, the main gateway to New England and its magnificent scenery. And parents of high school students checking out the area's dozens of colleges often find Boston so engaging that they keep returning long after their kids graduate.

You probably already have some connection—a relative studying here, a neighbor who dreams of qualifying for the Boston Marathon, a child who won't rest until she goes on a whale watch, a co-worker who always wears a Red Sox cap, a friend who's getting into genealogical research. Even if you don't, you'll find Boston a uniquely enjoyable destination, compact in size yet boasting a virtually inexhaustible supply of activities and diversions. The interests that draw you here can monopolize your schedule, but you'll have a better experience if you make some room for serendipity—on your schedule and in your attitude.

Boston is a living landmark that bears many marks of its Colonial heritage, but where it's theoretically possible (this is just an observation) to spend days without going near anything built before 1960, or even going outdoors. Pick out a suitcase that has room for your walking shoes and get ready for your own adventure.

Written in Stone

All over Boston, you'll see plaques commemorating long-gone people, events, and even places ("On this site stood . . ."). Each one tells a little story, in both its text and its context. A plaque commemorating the first Catholic Mass in Boston (on School St. near Washington St., across the street from the Freedom Trail) doesn't seem like a big deal now, but in a Puritan city, toleration of "popery" couldn't have come easily. On Commercial Street near Hull Street, a marker (pictured here) describes the Molasses Flood of 1919, during which 2 million gallons of raw molasses spilled out of a ruptured storage tank into the streets, killing 21 people.

The story recalls the days when manufacturing and industry dominated the area that's now the residential North End and scenic waterfront. Look around as you walk around—history is everywhere, just waiting for you to discover it.

PREVIOUS PAGE: **The Rose Fitzgerald Kennedy Greenway.**

BOSTON TODAY

Boston embodies nearly 4 centuries of contrasts and contradictions—blue blood and blue collar, Yankee and Irish, Brahmin banker and budget-conscious student. The city is home to the country's first public school and to a problematic educational system. A onetime hotbed of abolitionism, it retains an intractable reputation for racism; a proud seaport, it faces a harbor reclaimed from crippling pollution only recently. Boston traditionally was known as an insular city whose obsessions were "sports, politics, and revenge." In the 21st century, it's evolved into a magnet for students and intellectuals from all over the world, and an icon of liberalism and tolerance (it's the capital of the first U.S. state to make same-sex marriage legal). The Boston area is a hotbed of innovation, its economy slowed but not crippled by the recession of the mid-2000s. Cambridge and the South Boston waterfront are home to high-tech leaders of all sizes in every field, from gaming to genetic engineering. Downtown Boston is continuing to evolve, with the parks of the mile-long Rose Kennedy Greenway (which replaced an ugly elevated highway) gaining in popularity among locals and visitors alike.

Today you'll find a metropolis of some 618,000 at the heart of the Greater Boston area, which encompasses 83 cities and towns that are home to 4.5 million people. The hospitals and medical centers are among the best in the world, and healthcare was a hot topic long before the state took a leading role in the country's ongoing debate on the issue. Education and tourism are pillars of the local economy, which has mirrored national trends (positive and negative) in unemployment statistics. The real-estate market is relatively strong, and the city is one of the most expensive places in the country to live—and to visit, if you don't budget carefully.

As they have for more than a century, immigrants—Irish, eastern European Jewish, Italian, Portuguese, African American, Latino, and West Indian—flock to the Boston area. In the last quarter-century, the Asian and Latino populations have soared.

The pre–Big Dig Central Artery slicing through the city.

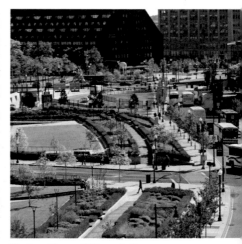

The Rose Fitzgerald Kennedy Greenway.

Whatever their origins, most Bostonians share at least a passing interest in sports. ("How about those Red Sox?" is a favorite conversational gambit all over town.) The Boston Bruins won the 2011 Stanley Cup, the franchise's first NHL title in 39 years; in 2008, the Celtics won their NBA-record 17th championship. The New England Patriots triumphed in the Super Bowl in 2002, 2004, and 2005—only to find that their third title was virtually a footnote. Three months earlier, in October 2004, the Red Sox won the World Series for the first time since 1918. Many Sox fans believe that victory ended a curse, and they point to the Sox's 2007 Series crown as evidence.

Pro sports are only part of the story, though: In a region with an enormous student population, college athletics are a big deal, too. In fact, eastern Massachusetts sometimes feels like one big campus. You've probably heard that Boston is a college town, but you may not realize just how true that is until you're out and about, tripping over chattering postadolescents nearly everywhere.

To get a sense of present-day Boston, hit the streets. All over town, you'll find traces of the groups, institutions, and events that shaped Boston's history and created the complex city you see today.

THE MAKING OF BOSTON

Permanently settled in 1630, Boston was named for the hometown of some of the Puritans who left England to seek religious freedom in the New World. They met with little of the usual strife with the natives, members of the small, Algonquian-speaking Massachuset tribe that roamed the area. The natives grew corn on some harbor islands but made their homes farther inland.

In 1632, the little peninsula known to the Indians as Shawmut became the capital of the Massachusetts Bay Colony, and the population soon increased rapidly because of the great Puritan migration. Thanks to its excellent location on a deep, sheltered harbor, Boston quickly became a center of shipbuilding, trading, and fishing. All these years later, fresh-caught seafood remains an important element of the local cuisine.

The only thing more important than commerce was religion, and the Puritans exerted such a strong influence that their legacy survives to this day. A concrete reminder is Harvard College's original (1636) mission: preparing young men to be ministers. In 1659, Boston's town fathers officially banned Christmas (the town children apparently had second thoughts—records show that the holiday was back in favor by the 1680s). A fictional testament to 17th-century Boston's narrow-mindedness is Nathaniel Hawthorne's classic novel *The Scarlet Letter* (1850). The grave of Elizabeth Pain, the reputed model for protagonist

The indigenous Algonquians.

Boston's
Changing Shoreline

0   1/2 mi
0   1/2 km

CHARLESTOWN

former
Prison Point Bay

former
Millers River

**EAST
BOSTON**

CAMBRIDGE

former
Mill Pond

**NORTH
END**

former
West Cove

former
Great Cove

*Charles
River*

**BEACON
HILL**

Boston   Harbor

**FINANCIAL
DISTRICT**

BACK   BAY

former
South Cove

former
Back Bay

former
South Bay

**SOUTH
BOSTON**

*Since the first permanent English settlers
arrived in the Boston area in 1630, land rec-
lamation projects have added over 1,000
acres to the city's land area. This map
shows the growth of the city from its original
shorelines to the present day.*

■ Original land area, 1630
■ Additions by 1850
■ Additions by 1900
□ Present day

—— Modern street network

**SOUTH
END**

17

Hester Prynne, is in the King's Chapel Burying Ground, on the Freedom Trail. And in 1692, religious extremism and mass hysteria led to the incidents now known as the Salem Witch Trials, which gripped the Boston suburb and continue to inform politics and popular culture to this day.

The Road to Revolution

England began exerting tighter control over its colonies as early as the 1680s. Over the years, laws increasing taxes and restricting trading activities led to trouble. The situation came to a head after the French and Indian War (known in Europe as the Seven Years' War) ended in 1763, as "No taxation without representation" became a rallying cry for the colonists.

In 1768, British troops occupied Boston, and rising tension led to violence. In the Boston Massacre of 1770, five colonists were killed in a scuffle with the redcoats. The first to die was a former slave named Crispus Attucks. The site, represented by a circle of cobblestones, sits on what is now State Street, and the colonists' graves are nearby, in the Granary Burying Ground on Tremont Street.

In December 1773, three British ships laden with tea sat at anchor in Boston Harbor (roughly where present-day Atlantic Ave. meets the Evelyn Moakley Bridge), waiting for their cargo to be unloaded. Before that could happen, the rabble-rousing Sons of Liberty, stirred up after a spirited public meeting at what's now the Old South Meeting House, boarded the ships and dumped 342 chests of tea into the harbor. The antitax protest, soon known as the "Boston Tea Party," endures today as the inspiration for one of the most divisive movements in modern American politics. You can visit replicas of the vessels at the Boston Tea Party Ships & Museum, on the Fort Point Channel; the meetinghouse stages a re-creation of the inflammatory rally every December.

In response to the Tea Party, the British closed the port until the tea was paid for and forced Bostonians to house the soldiers who began to flood the community. They soon numbered 4,000 in a town of 16,000. Mutual distrust ran high—Paul Revere wrote of helping form "a committee for the purpose of watching the movements of the British troops." In 1775, when the royal commander in Boston, Gen. Thomas Gage, learned that the colonists were accumulating arms and ammunition, he dispatched men to destroy the stockpiles. They departed

The Boston Massacre.

The Boston Tea Party.

from what's now Charles Street, between Boston Common and the Public Garden, to cross the Charles River.

A lantern signal soon illuminated the steeple of the Old North Church, alerting Revere to their route—the "two if by sea" made famous nearly a century later by Cambridge resident Henry Wadsworth Longfellow in his 1861 poem **"Paul Revere's Ride"** ("Listen my children and you shall hear / Of the midnight ride of Paul Revere"). The historically outlandish account of the events of April 18 and 19, 1775, is a must if you plan to walk the Freedom Trail or visit Lexington and Concord. For an obsessive and fascinating book-length look at the same critical 48-hour period, check out **Paul Revere's Ride,** by David Hackett Fischer. You'll find a broader perspective on the city's early history in **Paul Revere and the World He Lived In,** an engaging look at Boston before, during, and after the Revolution by Esther Forbes (also the author of the children's classic *Johnny Tremain*).

Revolution & the New Nation

Troops marched from Boston toward Lexington and Concord late on April 18, 1775. On their "midnight ride," William Dawes and Revere alerted the colonists that the British soldiers were on the march. Just north of Harvard Square,

You Can't Spell *Boston* Without *Snob*

I come from good old Boston,
The home of the bean and the cod,
Where the Lowells talk to the Cabots,
And the Cabots talk only to God.
>—attributed to John Collins Bossidy
>and Samuel C. Bushnell, ca. 1905

And the accent! . . . When a real Boston man used to approach me uttering sounds like those of a brick-throated bullfrog it used to occur to me that if the Cabots really had the ear of the Almighty, He must bitterly have regretted that He ever invented the vocal organs of humanity.
>—Ford Madox Ford, *Return to Yesterday*, 1932

horseshoes embedded in the sidewalk show part of Dawes's route. The riders mobilized the local militia companies, or minutemen. The next day, some 700 British soldiers under Maj. John Pitcairn emerged victorious from a skirmish in Lexington. The troops and militia clashed on the town common, a public area that's still known as the "Battle Green." Later that day, the colonists routed the soldiers at Concord near the North Bridge (a replica now stands in its place), forcing them to retreat to Charlestown.

The redcoats took almost an entire day to make the trip, along the route now marked battle road. You can cover it in a car in about a half-hour. Thanks in no small part to Longfellow, Lexington and Concord are closely associated with the beginning of the Revolution. In the early stages, military activity left its mark all over eastern Massachusetts, particularly in Cambridge. So many royalist sympathizers, or Tories, lived on one stretch of Brattle Street that it was called "Tory Row." When the tide began to turn, George Washington made his headquarters on the same street (in a house later occupied by Longfellow, which is now a National Park Service site). On nearby Cambridge Common is the spot where Washington took command of the Continental Army on July 3, 1775.

The British won the Battle of Bunker Hill in Charlestown on June 17, 1775, but at the cost of half their forces. (Win a trivia contest by knowing that the battle actually took place on Breed's Hill.) The redcoats abandoned Boston the following March 17. On July 4, 1776, the Continental Congress

One of the lanterns that signaled Paul Revere.

The luxurious homes on Louisburg Square, in the heart of Beacon Hill, surround a private park.

adopted the Declaration of Independence. Although many Bostonians fought in the 6-year war that followed, Boston itself saw no more battles.

After the war, Boston again became a center of business. Fishing, whaling, and trade with the Far East dominated the economy. Exotic spices and fruits, textiles, and porcelain from the other side of the world were familiar luxuries in Boston and nearby Salem. The influential merchant families who became known as Boston Brahmins spearheaded a cultural renaissance that flourished even after the War of 1812 ravaged international shipping, ending Boston's commercial heyday. As banking and manufacturing rose in importance, Boston took a back seat to New York and Philadelphia in size and influence. But the city became known for its intellectual community and its fine art and architecture, including the luxurious homes you see today on Beacon Hill.

The "Athens of America": 19th-Century Boston

In 1822, Boston became a city. From 1824 to 1826, Mayor Josiah Quincy oversaw the landfill project that moved the waterfront away from Faneuil Hall. The market building constructed at that time, which still stands, was named in his honor. It's at Dock Square, one of many locations all over the city where hilltops were lopped off and deposited in the water, transforming the coastline and skyline. In the 19th century, landfill work tripled the city's area, creating badly needed space. The largest of the projects, started in 1835 and completed in 1882, was the transformation of the Back Bay from mud flats and marshes into the elegant neighborhood you see today.

By the mid-1800s, Ralph Waldo Emerson, Oliver Wendell Holmes, Henry Wadsworth Longfellow, Nathaniel Hawthorne, Bronson Alcott, Louisa May Alcott, John Greenleaf Whittier, Walt Whitman, Henry David Thoreau, and even Charles Dickens (briefly) and Mark Twain (more briefly) had appeared on the literary scene in the city sometimes known as the "Athens of America." William Lloyd Garrison

> ### Welcome to "the Hub"
>
> *Boston State-house is the hub of the solar system. You couldn't pry that out of a Boston man if you had the tire of all creation straightened out for a crowbar.*
>
> —Oliver Wendell Holmes, Sr., *The Autocrat of the Breakfast-Table*, 1858

published the weekly *Liberator* newspaper, a powerful voice in the antislavery movement. Boston became an important stop on the Underground Railroad, the secret network the abolitionists developed to smuggle runaway slaves into Canada. The Black Heritage Trail (p. 65) passes by a number of sites related to the Railroad.

During the Civil War (1861–65), abolitionist sentiment dominated Boston—to such a degree that only names of members of the Union Army appear on the rolls listing the war dead in Harvard's Memorial Hall, which is open to the public. Massachusetts's contributions to the war effort included enormous quantities of firearms, shoes, blankets, tents, and men.

Walden **author and Massachusetts native Henry David Thoreau.**

Black abolitionist Frederick Douglass, a former member of the Massachusetts Anti-Slavery Society, helped recruit the 54th and 55th Massachusetts Colored Regiments. The movie *Glory* tells the story of the 54th, the first army unit made up of free black soldiers, and its white commander, Col. Robert Gould Shaw. The regiment's memorial, a gorgeous bas-relief by Augustus Saint-Gaudens, stands on Boston Common opposite the State House.

The railroad boom of the 1820s and 1830s and the flood of immigration that began soon after had made New England an industrial center. Then as now, Boston was the region's unofficial capital. Before and after the Civil War, immigrants from Ireland poured into the city, the first ethnic group to do so in great numbers since the French Huguenots in the early 18th century. Signs reading NO IRISH NEED APPLY became scarce as the new arrivals gained political power, and the first Irish mayor was elected in 1885.

By that time, Boston's class split was a chasm, with the influx of immigrants adding to the social tension. The Irish led the way and were followed by Italian, Portuguese, and eastern European Jewish immigrants. Each group had its own neighborhoods, houses of worship, schools, newspapers, and livelihoods that intersected only occasionally with "proper" society. A small but concrete example: The birthplace of Rose Fitzgerald—later Rose Kennedy, matriarch of the political dynasty—is in the North End, an Irish stronghold at her birth in 1890 that soon became a predominantly Italian neighborhood.

Even as the upper crust was sowing cultural seeds that would wind up enriching everyone—the Boston Symphony, the Boston Public Library, and the Museum of Fine Arts were established in the second half of the 19th century—its prudish behavior gained Boston a reputation for making snobbery an art form. *The Proper Bostonians* is an entertaining, perceptive nonfiction look at this era. It's an early (1947) work by well-known animal-rights activist Cleveland Amory, himself a Boston blueblood. In 1878 the censorious Watch and Ward Society was founded (as the New England Society for the Suppression of Vice), and the phrase "banned in Boston" soon became well known. In 1889, the private St. Botolph Club removed John Singer Sargent's portrait of Isabella Stewart

- *Johnny Tremain*, by Esther Forbes, is a fictional boy's-eye-view account of the Revolutionary War era. The book vividly describes scenes from the Revolution, many of which take place along the Freedom Trail.

- *Make Way for Ducklings*, by Robert McCloskey, tells the story of Mrs. Mallard and her babies on the loose in the Back Bay. After your kids fall for this book (and they will), you can thrill them with a trip to the Public Garden, home to bronze statues representing the family.

- *The Trumpet of the Swan*, by E. B. White, also uses the Public Garden as a waterfowl playground. After reading it, a turn around the lagoon on a Swan Boat (p. 103) is mandatory.

- *We're Off to Harvard Square*, by Sage Stossel, is a delight, written in sprightly verse and beautifully illustrated. It's intended for 9- to 12-year-olds, but younger kids and adults will like it, too.

Gardner from public view because her dress was too tight. (It's now at the museum that bears her name.)

The 20th Century

The Boston Brahmins could keep their new neighbors out of many areas of their lives, but not politics. The forebears of the Kennedy clan had appeared on the scene—John F. "Honey Fitz" Fitzgerald, Rose's father, was elected mayor in 1910—and the city slowly transformed yet again as WASPs and Catholics struck an uneasy truce. Fitzgerald's successor, James Michael Curley, helped inspire Edwin O'Connor's 1956 novel (and the 1958 Spencer Tracy film) about machine

The *Make Way for Ducklings* **sculpture in the Public Garden.**

politics in Boston, **The Last Hurrah.** Curley (1874–1958) also served as governor, as a U.S. Representative, and twice as a federal inmate who did time for fraud. You can see two statues of the famous/infamous politician in the park on Union Street across North Street from Faneuil Hall. By the time Honey Fitz's grandson John Fitzgerald Kennedy was elected to the U.S. Senate, in 1952, Boston was in the midst of another transformation.

World War II had bolstered Boston's Depression-ravaged industrial economy, and the war's end touched off an economic transformation. Shipping declined, along with New England's textile, shoe, and glass industries, at the same time that students on the GI Bill poured into area colleges and universities. MIT grads in particular helped spark the rise of the local high-tech economy. It remains a worthy competitor for Silicon Valley, with diverse elements including defense contractors, software leaders, biotech and venture capital firms, and more.

The postwar baby boom and the international social upheaval of the 1960s hit the Boston area hard. In the mid-1970s, Boston proper was the center of a

---

 ## Boston on the Big Screen

The best Boston movies combine compelling stories and local settings, even when most of the filming takes place elsewhere (as with *The Social Network* [2010]). Complicating matters, the Boston accent is easy to recognize yet nearly impossible to imitate accurately—and if you don't believe me, watch a bad Boston movie with a local and try to hear the dialog over the laughter. A selection of the more successful efforts:

o **Fever Pitch** (2005): A 103-minute video valentine to Boston and the Red Sox. Many scenes were filmed at Fenway Park, and the ending had to be reshot after the Sox won the World Series in 2004 for the first time in 86 years. The script is clichéd but captures the maniacal-fan persona with alarming accuracy. Bonus: The soundtrack is terrific.

o **The Friends of Eddie Coyle** (1973): A gritty gangster flick based on a brilliant novel by federal prosecutor George V. Higgins.

o **Gone Baby Gone** (2007) and **The Town** (2010): Ben Affleck's justly acclaimed directing debut and his thrill-a-minute follow-up.

o **Good Will Hunting** (1997): Co-stars Ben Affleck and Matt Damon grew up in Cambridge and wrote the Academy Award–winning screenplay together. This is the Boston movie to see if you have time for just one. (Try to ignore Robin Williams's unfortunate brogue.)

o **Love Story** (1970): So sappy! So pretty! A classic tearjerker set mostly in Cambridge and Boston. Yes, that's Tommy Lee Jones as one of Oliver's Harvard roommates.

o **The Perfect Storm** (2000): Sebastian Junger's nonfiction account of a Gloucester fishing boat caught in historically bad weather is positively gripping. The movie version, though heavy on the special effects, will change the way you look at seafood on a menu.

o **The Verdict** (1982): A classic courtroom drama. No crazy accents, but a great screenplay by David Mamet (based on Barry Reed's novel) and superb performances by Paul Newman and an outstanding supporting cast.

Cambridge natives Ben Affleck and Matt Damon, stars and screenwriters of *Good Will Hunting.*

school-busing crisis. Sparked by a court-ordered school desegregation plan enacted in 1974, it touched off riots, violence, and a white boycott. ***Common Ground: A Turbulent Decade in the Lives of Three American Families,*** by J. Anthony Lukas, is the definitive account of the busing crisis and a fascinating portrait of a city in transition.

In pop culture, the 1970s and 1980s were the heyday of local rock, with Boston (the band), the Cars, and the J. Geils Band leading the pack. The piece of music perhaps most closely associated with the city is the Standells' "Dirty Water." Released in 1966, it was written by the band's producer after he was mugged on the Massachusetts Avenue bridge, which connects Boston and Cambridge "down by the banks of the river Charles." And Boston's pop-culture touchstone of the late 20th century is a TV comedy that performed so poorly in its first season that NBC nearly canceled it. ***Cheers*** (1982–1993) was based on a local pub then called the Bull & Finch, and the show became so popular that the original bar changed its name and a spin-off opened in Faneuil Hall Marketplace (p. 229).

The 21st Century

The turn of the century saw Boston emerging as an increasingly "hot" destination. Downtown was in the midst of a $15-billion highway-construction project with a cute nickname (the Big Dig) and a great legacy; by 2007, the new Rose Fitzgerald Kennedy Greenway had transformed the look of a mile-long swath of downtown. After some 50 years overshadowed by an ugly elevated interstate (the road now runs through a tunnel), pedestrians can walk right to the edge of the cleaned-up harbor. During that half-century, Boston largely shed its reputation for insularity and became known as one of the "most European" American cities.

Change in the state tax code in 2005 and 2007 helped make Massachusetts an increasingly popular movie backdrop. ***The Departed*** (2006), which won the Academy Award for Best Picture, helped the Bay State establish its Hollywood reputation, and the films produced since then have ranged from forgettable to classic (see "Boston on the Big Screen," above). At press time, we're eagerly awaiting **R.I.P.D.,** a supernatural thriller starring Ryan Reynolds and Jeff Bridges, and—well, awaiting the Adam Sandler vehicle *That's My Boy.*

It's not all parks and paparazzi, of course—for instance, the Catholic Church's sex-abuse scandal came to light in the Boston Archdiocese, a major presence in this predominantly Catholic area. And the crime spree mounted by James "Whitey" Bulger—whose capture in 2011 after 16 years on the run made international headlines—was a black eye for local and federal law enforcement. (*Black Mass,* by Dick Lehr and Gerard O'Neill, is the definitive nonfiction take on Bulger.) Meanwhile, social divisions were fading. In 2003, the Massachusetts Supreme Judicial Court ruled that not allowing same-sex couples to marry violated the state constitution, institutionalizing an attitude that had already taken hold outside the courtroom. The typical reaction to legal gay marriage was, more or less, What's the big deal? The election of Deval Patrick, who in 2006 became the second African American since Reconstruction (after Virginia's Douglas Wilder) elected governor, inspired similar sentiments.

Thanks in no small part to the college students who clog rapid transit and drive property values out of sight—and who stick around after graduation, keeping the cutting edge nice and sharp—Boston continues to grow and change. A time traveler from the 18th or even 17th century would recognize some parts of the physical city. Its attitude and spirit might be unfamiliar to a visitor from as recently as 20 years ago.

WHEN TO GO

Boston attracts throngs of visitors year-round. Between April and November, the city sees hardly any slow times. Make reservations as early as possible if you plan to visit during busy periods; at really popular times, all of eastern Massachusetts seems to book up.

The area is especially busy during college graduation season (May and early June) and major happenings (see "Boston Calendar of Events," below). Spring and fall are popular times for conventions. Families pour into the area in July and August, creating long lines at many attractions. Summer isn't the most expensive time to visit, though: Foliage season, from mid-September to early November, when many leaf-peepers stay in the Boston area or pass through on the way to other New England destinations, is a huge draw. December is less busy but still a convention time—look for weekend bargains.

The "slow" season is January through March, when many hotels offer great deals, especially on weekends. However, this is when unpredictable weather plagues the Northeast, often affecting travel schedules, and when some suburban attractions close for the winter.

Climate

You've probably heard the saying about New England weather: "If you don't like it, wait 10 minutes." Variations from day to day or morning to afternoon (if not minute to minute) can be enormous. You can roast in March and freeze in June, shiver in July and sweat in November. Dressing in layers is always a good idea.

Spring and fall are the best bets for moderate temperatures, but spring (also known as mud season) is brief. It doesn't usually settle in until early May, and snow sometimes falls in April. Summers are hot, especially in July and August, and can be uncomfortably humid. Fall is when you're most likely to catch a comfortable run of dry, sunny days and cool nights. Winters are cold and usually snowy—bring a warm coat and sturdy boots.

Boston Calendar of Events

The **Greater Boston Convention & Visitors Bureau** (www.bostonusa.com; ✆ **888/733-2678** or 617/536-4100) operates a regularly updated hot line that describes ongoing and upcoming events. The **Mayor's Office of Arts, Tourism & Special Events** (www.cityof boston.gov/arts; ✆ **617/635-3911**) can provide information about specific happenings. If you're planning at the last minute; the arts sections of the daily *Boston Globe* and *Boston Herald* are always packed with ideas.

For an exhaustive list of events beyond those listed here, check **http://events. frommers.com**, where you'll find a searchable, up-to-the-minute roster of what's happening in cities all over the world.

JANUARY

Martin Luther King, Jr., Birthday Celebration, various locations. Events include musical tributes, gospel concerts, museum displays and programs, readings, speeches, and panel discussions. Check special listings in the *Globe* for specifics. Third Monday in January.

Boston Wine Festival, Boston Harbor Hotel and other locations. Tastings, classes, lectures, receptions, and meals provide a lively liquid diversion throughout winter. Check ahead (www.boston winefestival.net; ✆ **888/660-9463**) for details. January to early April.

FEBRUARY

African-American History Month, various locations. Programs include special museum exhibits, children's activities, concerts, films, lectures, discussions, readings, and tours of the Black Heritage Trail led by National Park Service rangers (www.nps.gov/boaf; ✆ **617/742-5415**). All month.

Chinese New Year, Chinatown. The dragon parade (which draws a big crowd no matter how cold it is), fireworks, and raucous festivals are part of the celebration. Special programs take place at the **Children's Museum** (www.bostonkids. org; ✆ **617/426-8855**). For more details, visit **www.chinatownmain street.org**. Depending on the Chinese

lunar calendar, the holiday falls between January 21 and February 19. In 2013, it's February 10; in 2014, January 31.

School Vacation Week, various locations. The slate of activities includes special exhibitions and programs, plays, concerts, and tours. Contact individual attractions or check the *Globe* for information on programs and extended hours. Third week of February.

MARCH

St. Patrick's Day Celebrations, various locations. Concerts, talks, special restaurant menus, and other offerings celebrate the heritage of one of the country's most Irish-American cities. Note that the parade, along Broadway in

Chinese New Year.

27

St. Patrick's Day.

South Boston, is not a city-sponsored event; the organization that runs it is private and therefore free to bar any group it wants to from marching. That includes gays and, at least once in recent years, antiwar veterans. March 17; parade is on the closest Sunday.

APRIL

Big Apple Circus (www.bigapplecircus. org; ☎ 800/922-3772), City Hall Plaza, Government Center. The New York–based "one-ring wonder" performs in a heated tent with all seating less than 50 feet from the ring. Proceeds support the Boston Children's Museum. Early April to mid-May.

Red Sox Opening Day, Fenway Park. Even if your concierge is a magician, this is an extremely tough ticket. Check ahead (www.redsox.com; ☎ 877/733-7699) when tickets go on sale in December. If you can't get tickets to Opening Day, try to see the 10am game on **Patriots' Day,** the third Monday in April. The early start allows spectators to watch the Boston Marathon afterward. Early and mid-April.

Swan Boats Return to the Public Garden. Since their introduction in 1877, the Swan Boats (www.swanboats.com; ☎ 617/522-1966) have been a symbol of Boston. Like real swans, they go away for the

winter. Saturday before Patriots' Day (Apr 15, 2013; Apr 16, 2014).

Patriots' Day, North End, Lexington, and Concord. Festivities commemorate and reenact the events of April 18 and 19, 1775. Lanterns glow in the steeple of the **Old North Church** (www.oldnorth.com; ☎ 617/523-6676). Participants dressed as Paul Revere and William Dawes ride from the North End to Lexington and Concord to warn the minutemen that "the regulars are out" (not that "the British are coming"—most colonists considered themselves British). Musket fire rings out on the Battle Green in Lexington and then at the North Bridge in Concord. For information on reenactments and other events, check the websites of the **Paul Revere House** (www.paulreverehouse.org; ☎ 617/523-2338) and the **Battle Road Committee** (www.battleroad.org). For information about the riders' destinations, where the festivities traditionally include pancake breakfasts, contact the **Lexington Chamber of Commerce Visitor Center** (www.lexingtonchamber.org; ☎ 781/862-1450) or the **Concord Chamber of Commerce** (www.concordchamberof commerce.org; ☎ 978/369-3120). See chapter 10 for information on visiting both towns. Third Monday of April (Apr 15, 2013; Apr 16, 2014).

Boston Marathon, Hopkinton, Massachusetts, to Boston. International stars and local amateurs join in the world's oldest and most famous marathon (www.bostonmarathon.org). Competitors start in stages, with the first setting out at 9am. Cheering fans are welcome until the last weekend warriors stagger across the Boylston Street finish line in the late afternoon. Third Monday of the month (Apr 15, 2013; Apr 16, 2014).

Freedom Trail Week, various locations in Boston, Cambridge, Lexington, and Concord. This is a school vacation week, with plenty of crowds and diversions. Family-friendly events include tours,

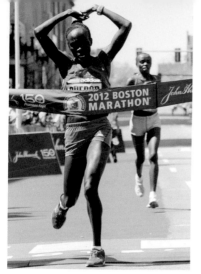

The Boston Marathon.

concerts, talks, and other programs related to Patriots' Day, the Freedom Trail, and the American Revolution. Third week of April.

Independent Film Festival of Boston, various locations. Features, shorts, and documentaries by international filmmakers make up the schedule for this increasingly buzz-worthy event. Check ahead (www.iffboston.org) for the schedule. Late April to early May.

Lilac Sunday, Arnold Arboretum, Jamaica Plain. The arboretum (www.arboretum.harvard.edu; ℰ **617/524-1717**) allows picnicking only once a year, on Lilac Sunday. From sunrise to sunset, wander the grounds and enjoy the sensational spring flowers, including more than 400 varieties of lilacs in bloom. Mid-May.

Street Performers Festival, Faneuil Hall Marketplace. Everyone but the pigeons gets into the act as musicians, magicians, jugglers, sword swallowers, and artists strut their stuff. Late May.

Boston Pride Parade, South End to Government Center (www.bostonpride.org; ℰ **617/262-9405**). The largest gay pride march in New England is the highlight of a weeklong celebration of diversity. The parade, on the second weekend of the month, starts in the South End and ends at City Hall Plaza, where the Boston Pride Festival takes place. Early June.

Dragon Boat Festival, Charles River near Harvard Square, Cambridge

Boston Pride Parade.

(www.bostondragonboat.org). Teams of paddlers synchronized by a drummer propel boats with dragon heads and tails as they race 1,640 feet. The winners go to the national championships; the spectators go to a celebration of Chinese culture and food on the shore. Second or third Sunday of June.

Cambridge River Festival (www.cambridgeartscouncil.org; ✆ **617/349-4380**), Memorial Drive from John F. Kennedy Street to Western Avenue. A salute to the arts, the festival incorporates live music, dancing, children's activities, crafts and art exhibits, and international food on the banks of the Charles River. Mid-June.

JULY

Boston Harborfest, downtown, the waterfront, and the Harbor Islands. The city puts on its Sunday best for the Fourth of July, a gigantic weeklong celebration of Boston's maritime history. Events surrounding Boston Harborfest (www.bostonharborfest.com; ✆ **617/227-1528**) include concerts, children's activities, cruises, fireworks, the Boston Chowderfest, guided tours, talks, and USS *Constitution*'s turnaround cruise. Beginning of the month.

Boston Pops Concert & Fireworks Display, Hatch Shell, on the Esplanade. Spectators start showing up at dawn (overnight camping is not permitted) to stake out a good spot on the lawn and spend all day waiting for the sky to get dark enough for fireworks. Others show up at the last minute—the Cambridge side of the river, near Kendall Square, and the Longfellow Bridge are good spots to watch the spectacular aerial show. The program includes the *1812 Overture*, with real cannon fire and church bells. For details, check the website (www.july4th.org). July 4.

Puerto Rican Festival & Parade, Franklin Park. This 3-day event, instituted in 1967, is part street fair, part cultural celebration, with plenty of live music and traditional food. The highlight of the final day is a lively parade. For details, search **Festival Puertorriqueño** on Facebook. Late July.

AUGUST

Italian-American Feasts, North End. These weekend street fairs begin in July and end in late August with the two biggest: the Fisherman's Feast and the Feast of St. Anthony. The sublime (fresh seafood prepared while you wait, live music, dancing in the street) mingles with the ridiculous (carnival games, tacky T-shirts, fried-dough stands) to leave a lasting impression of fun and indigestion. Visit **www.fishermansfeast.com** or **www.saintanthonysfeast.com** for a preview. Weekends throughout August.

August Moon Festival, Chinatown. A celebration of the harvest and the coming of autumn, the festival includes dragon and lion dances during the parade through the crowded streets, and demonstrations of crafts and martial arts. It's also an excuse to stuff yourself with tasty mooncakes. For details, visit **www.chinatownmainstreet.org**. Mid-August.

SEPTEMBER

Cambridge Carnival International, Kendall Square, Cambridge (www.cambridgecarnival.org; ✆ **617/863-0476**). This Caribbean-style celebration of diversity and unity features live music, ethnic food, kids' activities, and a parade of costumed revelers. Sunday after Labor Day.

Boston Film Festival (www.bostonfilmfestival.org; ✆ **617/523-8388**), various locations. Independent films continue on the festival circuit or make their premieres, sometimes following a lecture by an actor or filmmaker. Most screenings are open to the public without advance tickets. Mid-September.

OCTOBER

Salem Haunted Happenings, various locations. Parades, parties, a special commuter-rail ride from Boston, fortune-telling, cruises, and tours lead up to a ceremony on Halloween. Contact **Destination Salem** (© 877/725-3662) or check the website (www.haunted happenings.org) for specifics. All month.

Oktoberfest, Harvard Square, Cambridge. This immense street fair is a magnet for college students, families, street performers, musicians, and crafts vendors. Sponsored by the Harvard Square Business Association (www.harvardsquare.com; © 617/491-3434). Second Sunday of October.

An Evening with Champions, Bright Athletic Center, Allston. World-class ice skaters and promising local students stage two or three performances to benefit the Jimmy Fund, the children's fundraising arm of the Dana-Farber Cancer Institute. Sponsored by Harvard's **Eliot House** (www.aneveningwithchampions.org; © 617/942-1392). Mid-October.

Boston Book Festival, Copley Square. An indoor/outdoor event that draws top national and local authors and big crowds. The area in front of the Boston Public Library fills with bookworms and vendors, while speeches and panel discussions take place in Trinity Church and other nearby venues. Check ahead (www.bostonbookfest.org; © 617/252-3240) for specifics and tickets, or just show up. Mid- to late October.

Head of the Charles Regatta, Boston and Cambridge. High school, college, and postcollegiate rowing teams and individuals—some 4,000 in all—race in front of tens of thousands of fans along the banks of the Charles River and on the bridges spanning it. The Head of the Charles (www.hocr.org; © 617/868-6200) has an uncanny tendency to coincide with a crisp, picturesque weekend. Late October.

NOVEMBER

Thanksgiving Celebration, Plymouth (www.visit-plymouth.com; © 800/872-1620). Plymouth observes the holiday with a "stroll through the ages," highlighting 17th- and 19th-century Thanksgiving preparations in historic homes. Menus at **Plimoth Plantation,** which re-creates the colony's first years, include a buffet and a Victorian Thanksgiving feast. Reservations (www.plimoth.org; © 800/262-9356 or 508/746-1622) are accepted beginning in June. Thanksgiving Day.

DECEMBER

The Nutcracker, Opera House, Boston. Boston Ballet's annual holiday extravaganza is one of the country's biggest and best. This is *the* traditional way to expose young Bostonians (and visitors) to culture, and the spectacular sets make it practically painless. Buy tickets (www.bostonballet.org; © 617/695-6955) as soon as you plan your trip, ask whether your hotel offers a *Nutcracker* package, or cross your fingers and check when you arrive. Thanksgiving weekend through late December.

Boston Tea Party Reenactment, Old South Meeting House (www.oldsouthmeetinghouse.org; © 617/482-6439) and Tea Party Ship and Museum, Congress Street Bridge (www.bostonteapartyship.com; © 617/338-1773). Chafing under British rule, American colonists rose up on December 16, 1773, to strike a blow where it would cause real pain—in the pocketbook. A re-creation of the preparty rally at the meetinghouse is a lively all-ages audience-participation event. By the time you read this, the museum should have reopened after extensive renovations; check ahead for details. Mid-December.

Black Nativity, Media Arts Center, Roxbury Community College, 1234 Columbus Ave. (www.blacknativity.org; © 617/585-6366). Poet Langston Hughes wrote the "gospel opera," and a cast of more than 100 brings it to life. Mid-December.

Christmas Revels, Sanders Theatre, Cambridge. This multicultural celebration of the winter solstice features the holiday customs of a different culture each year. Themes have included 17th-century Europe, American folk traditions, and Victorian England. Be ready to sing along. For information and tickets, contact the **Revels** (www.revels.org; ✆ **617/972-8300**). Last 2 weeks of the month.

First Night, Back Bay and the waterfront. This is the original arts-oriented, no-alcohol, citywide New Year's Eve celebration. It begins in the early afternoon and includes a parade, ice sculptures, art exhibitions, theatrical performances, and indoor and outdoor entertainment. Some attractions require tickets, but for most you just need a First Night button, available for less than $20 at visitor centers and stores around the city. Fireworks

Poetry 101 (Degrees)

Check the Boston weather forecast by looking up at the short column of lights on top of the old John Hancock building in the Back Bay. (The new Hancock building is the 60-story glass tower next door.) It has its own poem: *Steady blue, clear view / flashing blue, clouds due / steady red, rain ahead / flashing red, snow instead.* During the summer, flashing red means that the Red Sox game is canceled.

light up the sky above Boston Common just before 7pm and over Boston Harbor at midnight. For details, contact **First Night** (www.firstnight.org; ✆ **617/542-1399**) or check the newspapers when you arrive. December 31.

Boston's Average Temperatures & Rainfall

	JAN	FEB	MAR	APR	MAY	JUNE	JULY	AUG	SEPT	OCT	NOV	DEC
TEMP. (°F)	30	31	38	49	59	68	74	72	65	55	45	34
TEMP. (°C)	−1	−1	3	9	15	20	23	22	18	13	7	1
PRECIP. (IN.)	3.8	3.5	4.0	3.7	3.4	3.0	2.8	3.6	3.3	3.3	4.4	4.2

Public Holidays

Banks, government offices, post offices, schools, and many stores, restaurants, and museums close on the following legal national holidays: January 1 (New Year's Day), the third Monday in January (Martin Luther King, Jr., Day), the third Monday in February (Washington's Birthday), the last Monday in May (Memorial Day), July 4 (Independence Day), the first Monday in September (Labor Day), the second Monday in October (Columbus Day), November 11 (Veterans' Day/Armistice Day), the fourth Thursday in November (Thanksgiving Day), and December 25 (Christmas). The Tuesday after the first Monday in November is Election Day, a federal government holiday in presidential-election years (every 4 years, including 2012).

Massachusetts state offices close for **Patriots' Day** on the third Monday in April.

RESPONSIBLE TOURISM IN BOSTON

The Boston area is a hotbed of eco-awareness. True, it's not Europe, or even California, but residents and visitors have a smaller-than-usual carbon footprint almost by accident—driving in the area is such a headache that ditching the car makes sense for both the environment and your sanity.

Before you leave home, visit the website of the **Greater Boston Convention & Visitors Bureau** (www.bostonusa.com/visit) and click "Boston Insider" to get the latest info about the bureau's Eco-friendly Traveler program. Here you'll find information about eco-aware attractions along with lists of hotels and restaurants that are certified green or working toward that status.

Many Boston-area commuters get to work on foot, by public transit, or by bike. Most subway stations and some bus stops have receptacles for recycling the newspaper. Cambridge has been relatively hospitable to bicyclists for years, and Boston has some dedicated lanes and a bike-share program—but riding alone is a safe option only for experienced riders. If you're not a two-wheel commuter at home, consider taking a guided tour (p. 110).

Zipcar originated in Cambridge; your membership in the car-sharing service entitles you to use vehicles all over the Boston area, including locations at the end of most subway lines.

The **Chefs Collaborative** (www.chefscollaborative.org; ℂ **617/236-5200**) is a Boston-based nonprofit dedicated to "changing the sustainable food landscape"; its website has a search function that locates member restaurants. The **Green Restaurant Association** (www.dinegreen.com) maintains a regularly updated list of members, which includes **Taranta Cucina Meridionale** in the North End (p. 155) and Cambridge's **UpStairs on the Square** (p. 175). Carbon-neutral Taranta even uses corn-based-polymer drinking straws.

The industry-leading **Lenox Hotel** (p. 271) was one of the first American hotels to offer a towel reuse program and boasts an impressive portfolio of initiatives and awards—in a luxurious property that makes sustainability matter-of-fact rather than inconvenient. The Lenox is part of the Saunders Hotel Group, a leader in green awareness in the hospitality business. The **Comfort Inn & Suites Boston/Airport** (p. 287) is the firm's other Boston-area property. They have plenty of company: Virtually all of the chain lodgings in the area, and their independent competitors, are on the bandwagon. The **Colonnade Hotel Boston** (p. 270) and the **Seaport Hotel** (p. 266) are particularly green.

Awareness of the importance of recycling is nothing radical in New England, where one of the best-known sayings is "Use it up, wear it out, make it do, or do without." Massachusetts is among the national leaders in the campaign to reduce the use of disposable shopping bags, and Boston has single-stream recycling for household trash. To learn more about green initiatives, visit the Department of Environmental Protection's website at **www.mass.gov/dep**. Learn more about Boston's Environmental and Energy Services initiative at **www.cityofboston. gov/environmentalandenergy**.

In addition to the resources for the Boston area listed above, see **www. frommers.com/tips** for more tips on responsible travel.

3

BOSTON NEIGHBORHOODS & SUGGESTED ITINERARIES

L iving near the Freedom Trail, I meet my beloved *Frommer's Boston* readers all the time. The cheerful ones are going from place to place at a reasonable pace, exploring areas and subjects that interest them, and not fretting over a rigid checklist. The unhappy ones are obsessively following a jampacked schedule, saying "ought" and "should" a lot, and generally acting as though a visit to this fascinating city is a chore, rather than an opportunity.

The first group sounds better, right? Read on for strategies that can help you organize your schedule and still have a great time in Boston. These itineraries include sightseeing destinations, snack and meal suggestions, shopping pointers, and dinner-and-a-movie alternatives. Public transit is the most time- and cost-effective way to navigate the Boston area; consider budgeting for a taxi back to the hotel after your final stop of the afternoon, so you'll have some energy for evening fun. **Two important tips: Wear comfortable shoes,** and **don't ignore the breaks** built into each itinerary, which can help you feel more like a relaxed insider and less like a participant in a scavenger hunt.

Unless otherwise indicated, turn to chapter 4 for descriptions of the recommended attractions and activities. For an introduction to some of Boston's most interesting neighborhoods, see below.

CITY LAYOUT

When Puritan settlers established Boston in 1630, it was one-third the size it is today. Much of the city reflects the original layout, a seemingly haphazard plan that can disorient even longtime residents. Legend has it that the street pattern originated as a network of cow paths, but it owes more to 17th-century London and long-gone property lines. Old Boston abounds with alleys, dead ends, one-way streets, streets that change names, and streets named after extinct geographical features. On the plus side, every "wrong" turn **downtown,** in the **North End,** or on **Beacon Hill** is a chance to see something interesting that you might otherwise have missed.

The most prominent feature of downtown Boston is the five-sided park known since the 1630s as **Boston Common.** Its borders are 1-block-long Park Street (an important subway interchange), and Beacon, Charles, Boylston, and Tremont streets. **Washington Street,** which runs southwest from Boston City Hall all the way to the Rhode Island border, is the most "main" street downtown. Another important street is **Massachusetts Avenue,** or, as it's usually called, "Mass. Ave.," which stretches 9 miles, from Roxbury through the South End, the Back Bay, Cambridge, and Arlington, to Lexington.

Nineteenth-century landfill projects transformed much of the city, altering the shoreline and creating the **Back Bay,** where the streets proceed in orderly

PREVIOUS PAGE: **Costumed guides lead tours along the Freedom Trail.**

parallel lines (and even go in alphabetical order, starting at the Public Garden: Arlington, Berkeley, Clarendon, Dartmouth, Exeter, Fairfield, Gloucester, and Hereford, followed by Mass. Ave.). The adjacent **South End** is the only other central neighborhood laid out in anything close to a grid pattern.

In general, there's no rhyme or reason to the street pattern, compass directions are virtually useless, and there aren't enough street signs. The best way to find an address is to call ahead and ask for directions, including landmarks, or leave extra time for wandering around. If the directions involve a T stop, be sure to ask which exit to use—most stations have more than one.

NEIGHBORHOODS IN BRIEF

These are the areas visitors are most likely to frequent. When Bostonians say **"downtown,"** they usually mean the first seven or eight neighborhoods defined here; there's no "midtown" or "uptown." Especially downtown, the neighborhoods are so small and close together that the borders are somewhat arbitrary. Whether you're picking a hotel or just planning a lunch date, the important distinction is downtown vs. the Back Bay vs. Cambridge—not, for example, the Waterfront vs. the adjacent Financial District.

Neighborhoods outside central Boston include South Boston, East Boston, Dorchester, Roxbury, West Roxbury, Hyde Park, Roslindale, and Jamaica Plain. With a couple of exceptions (noted here), Boston is generally safe, but you should always take the precautions you would in any large city, especially at night. *Note:* I include some compass points here to help you read your map, but that's not how the locals will give you directions: They typically just point.

THE WATERFRONT This narrow area runs along the Inner Harbor, on **Atlantic Avenue** and **Commercial Street** from the Charlestown Bridge (on N. Washington St.) to South Station. Once filled with wharves and warehouses, today it abounds with luxury condos, marinas, restaurants, and offices. Also here are the New England Aquarium and embarkation points for harbor cruises and whale-watching expeditions. The **Rose Kennedy Greenway** roughly parallels the coast for a mile from South Station to North Station. In this central neighborhood, the hotels are luxurious and expensive.

THE NORTH END Crossing the Rose Kennedy Greenway as you head east toward the Inner Harbor brings you to one of the city's oldest neighborhoods. Home to waves of immigrants in the course of its history, it was predominantly Italian for most of the 20th century. It's now less than half Italian-American; many newcomers are young professionals who walk to work in the Financial District. Nevertheless, you'll still hear Italian spoken in the neighborhood, and find a wealth of Italian restaurants, *caffès,* and shops. The main streets are **Hanover Street** and **Salem Street.** The Fairmont Battery Wharf is the only full-size hotel in this busy, convenient area.

NORTH STATION Technically part of the North End but just as close to Beacon Hill, this area around **Causeway Street** is home to the **TD Garden** (sports and performance arena), **North Station,** and many nightspots and restaurants. The neighborhood—sometimes called the West End or the Bulfinch Triangle—gets safer by the day, but wandering alone here late at night is not a good idea. Lodgings in this handy neighborhood run the gamut from dirt-cheap to pricey; rates soar during major events at the Garden.

FANEUIL HALL MARKETPLACE   Employees aside, Boston residents tend to be scarce at Faneuil Hall Marketplace (also called Quincy Market, after its central building). An irresistible draw for out-of-towners and suburbanites, this cluster of restored market buildings—bounded by the Waterfront, the North End, Government Center, and **State Street**—is the city's most popular attraction. You'll find restaurants, bars, a food court, specialty shops, and Faneuil Hall itself. **Haymarket,** a stone's throw away on **Blackstone Street,** is home to an open-air produce market on Fridays and Saturdays. The business-focused hotels here are plush and expensive, with weekend deals often available, especially in the winter.

GOVERNMENT CENTER   Here, stark, modern design breaks up Boston's traditional architecture. Flanked by Beacon Hill, Downtown Crossing, and Faneuil Hall Marketplace, Government Center is home to state and federal offices, City Hall, and a major T stop. Its most prominent feature, the red-brick wasteland of City Hall Plaza, lies between **Congress** and **Cambridge streets.** Neighborhood hotels range in age and style but not much in price, which is generally high.

THE FINANCIAL DISTRICT   Bounded loosely by Downtown Crossing, **Summer Street, Atlantic Avenue,** and **State Street,** the Financial District is the banking, insurance, and legal center of the city. Aside from some popular after-work spots, it's generally quiet at night and on weekends. As in nearby neighborhoods, lodgings here tend to be well appointed and costly.

DOWNTOWN CROSSING   The intersection that gives Downtown Crossing its name is at **Washington Street** where **Winter Street** becomes **Summer Street.** The Freedom Trail runs along one edge of this shopping and business district between Boston Common, Chinatown, the Financial District, and Government Center. Most of the neighborhood hops during the day and slows down in the evening, but it's getting livelier thanks to the increasing presence of theatergoers and students from Emerson College and Suffolk University. Accommodations here are dorms, posh condos, and elegant hotels, without much middle ground.

BEACON HILL   Narrow tree-lined streets, brick and cobblestone alleyways, and architectural showpieces, mostly in Federal style, make up this largely residential area in the shadow of the State House. Two of the loveliest and most exclusive spots in Boston are here: Mount Vernon Street and Louisburg (pronounced "Lewis-burg") Square. Bounded by Government Center, Boston Common, the Back Bay, and the river, Beacon Hill is where you'll find Massachusetts General Hospital. **Charles Street,** which divides the Common from the Public Garden, is the main street of Beacon Hill. Other important thoroughfares are **Beacon Street,** on the north side of the Common, and **Cambridge Street.** The major hotels tend to be expensive; try a B&B agency (p. 290) if you want the pretty surroundings at a lower price.

CHARLESTOWN   One of the oldest areas of Boston is where you'll see the Bunker Hill Monument and USS *Constitution* ("Old Ironsides"). Gentrification has brought some diversity to what was once an almost entirely white residential neighborhood, but pockets remain that have earned their reputation for insularity. Lodgings are on or near the water in a busy area that's some distance from the major downtown attractions.

Boston Orientation

The Chinatown Gate, a traditional *paifang* (archway).

SOUTH BOSTON WATERFRONT/SEAPORT DISTRICT Across the Fort Point Channel from the Waterfront neighborhood, this area is home to the convention center, the Seaport Boston World Trade Center, the Institute of Contemporary Art, the Fish Pier, a federal courthouse, the Boston Children's Museum, one end of the Ted Williams Tunnel, and a lot of construction. The ICA and a scattering of restaurants make this area increasingly inviting, but it's still not quite a nonconvention destination; at slow times, the business-focused hotels here sometimes offer great bargains. **Seaport Boulevard** and **Northern Avenue** are the main drags. The area closest to the channel, where redevelopment is forcing out artists who live and work in renovated warehouses, is often called simply **Fort Point.**

CHINATOWN/THEATER DISTRICT One of the largest Chinese communities in the country is a small area jammed with Asian restaurants, groceries, and gift shops. Chinatown comprises the area between Downtown Crossing and the Massachusetts Turnpike extension. The main street is **Beach Street.** The heart of the Theater District is at **Tremont** and **Stuart streets** (three performance spaces are on Washington St., closer to Downtown Crossing); be careful here at night after the crowds thin out. Accommodations in this area tend to be either reasonably priced (and a great deal for such a convenient location) or swank (and pricey for a neighborhood that's still somewhat gritty).

THE SOUTH END Cross **Stuart Street** or **Huntington Avenue** heading south from the Back Bay, and you'll find yourself in a landmark district packed with Victorian row houses and little parks. The South End has a large gay community and some of the city's best restaurants. In the 1980s and 1990s, **Tremont Street** (particularly the end closest to downtown) gained a cachet that it hadn't known for almost a century. **Washington Street** and **Harrison Avenue** are up-and-coming destinations for diners and shoppers. Long known for its ethnic, economic, and cultural diversity, the neighborhood is now thoroughly gentrified nearly all the way to Mass. Ave. With just a hotel and a hostel, the South End isn't a major player in the lodging market, but a B&B agency (p. 290) may find you a deal not far from the pricier Back Bay. ***Note:*** Don't confuse the South End with South Boston, on the other side of I-93.

THE BACK BAY Fashionable since its creation out of landfill more than a century ago, the Back Bay abounds with gorgeous architecture and chic shops. It lies between the Public Garden, the river, Kenmore Square, and either **Huntington Avenue** or **St. Botolph Street,** depending on who's describing it. Students dominate the area near

> ## Mass(achusetts) Ave(nue)
>
> One of the most important streets in Boston and Cambridge is Massachusetts Avenue, but almost no one calls it that. Bostonians— who reputedly talk faster than any other Americans (including New Yorkers!)—say "Mass. Ave." Similarly, Boston has "Comm. Ave." (Commonwealth Avenue) and "Dot Ave." (Dorchester Avenue).

Mass. Ave. but grow scarce as property values soar near the Public Garden. Back Bay hotels range from basic to superluxurious. Major thoroughfares include **Boylston Street,** which starts at Boston Common and runs into the Fenway; largely residential **Beacon Street** and **Commonwealth Avenue** (say "Comm. Ave."); and boutique central, **Newbury Street.** Access to Cambridge isn't the greatest, but there's so much to do here that you may not care.

KENMORE SQUARE AND BROOKLINE The landmark white-and-red Citgo sign that dominates the skyline above the intersection of **Commonwealth Avenue, Beacon Street,** and **Brookline Avenue** tells you that you're

The Back Bay's Victorian architecture.

approaching Kenmore Square. Its shops, bars, restaurants, and clubs attract students from adjacent Boston University. The Hotel Commonwealth, the most prominent lodging option, lends a touch of class to a generally rowdy neighborhood, which gets even busier when the Red Sox are in town and baseball fans pour into the area on the way to historic Fenway Park, 3 blocks away. Just outside Kenmore Square is the border with **Brookline,** a prosperous suburb known as the birthplace of President John F. Kennedy and the hometown of talk-show host Conan O'Brien.

Cambridge is filled with funky shops.

THE FENWAY Between Kenmore Square and the Longwood Medical Area, the Fenway neighborhood encompasses Fenway Park, the Museum of Fine Arts, the Isabella Stewart Gardner Museum, and innumerable students. Boston University, Northeastern University, and Harvard Medical School are just the largest educational institutions in and near the Fenway. Hotels here court hospital business; the location is somewhat inconvenient if you'll be spending a lot of time elsewhere. The **Fenway** is also the name of a road that winds through the area, at one point bordering a park confusingly named the Back Bay Fens. The area's southern border is **Huntington Avenue,** the honorary "Avenue of the Arts" (or, with a Boston accent, "Otts"), where you'll find the Christian Science Center, Symphony Hall (at the corner of Mass. Ave.), and the MFA. Parts of Huntington can be a little risky, so if you're leaving the museum at night, hail a cab or take the Green Line, and try to travel in a group.

CAMBRIDGE Boston's neighbor across the Charles River is a separate city. The areas you're likely to visit lie along the MBTA Red Line. **Harvard Square** is a magnet for students, sightseers, and well-heeled shoppers. It's an easy walk along Mass. Ave. southeast to **Central Square,** a gentrifying area dotted with ethnic restaurants and clubs; a short stroll away is boho **Inman Square,** a stronghold of independent businesses. North along shop-lined Mass. Ave. from Harvard Square is **Porter Square,** a mostly residential neighborhood with quirky retail outlets of the sort that once characterized Harvard Square. Around **Kendall Square** you'll find MIT and many technology-oriented businesses. Hotels are relatively few and relatively pricey; check a B&B agency (p. 290) if you're on a budget, and don't expect bargains during major events at Harvard and MIT.

Neighborhoods in Brief

BOSTON NEIGHBORHOODS & SUGGESTED ITINERARIES

ICONIC BOSTON

Every trolley-tour company in town (p. 106) boasts that it can show visitors the city in a single day, which is technically true. If you just want to *see* as much as possible as quickly as possible, climb aboard. A more fulfilling way to explore Boston is to schedule fewer activities—using a tour, if you so choose, for an overview and point-to-point transportation—and spend some quality time on each one. Even a single day can give you a taste of what makes this city such a popular destination; below I offer 1-, 2-, and 3-day plans that focus on experiences unique to Boston. You won't have time for full immersion, but you can touch on some singular destinations and experiences. You'll begin with the downtown area, home to the city's oldest and most historic neighborhoods. ***Day 1 start:*** *Boston Common (Red or Green Line to Park St.), 15 State St. (Orange or Blue Line to State), or Faneuil Hall (Green or Blue Line to Government Center).*

1 The Freedom Trail ★★★

Following the whole 2.5-mile Freedom Trail (p. 86) can consume the better part of a day, but several options that concentrate on the downtown part of the walk take 2 hours or so. Your goal is to cover—at whatever pace suits you, as carefully or as casually as you like—the first two-thirds of the trail, from **Boston Common** through **Faneuil Hall.** Start at the Boston Common Visitor Information Center with a pam-

Guides in period costumes lead tours along Boston's famous Freedom Trail.

phlet describing the self-guided tour or with the audio tour available from the Freedom Trail Foundation, or opt for a guided tour (p. 87).

2 Faneuil Hall Marketplace ★★

The combination of retail, dining, street performers, and history makes indoor-outdoor Faneuil Hall Marketplace an insanely popular tourist destination. See chapter 7 for shopping pointers, or just grab a seat on a bench and enjoy some great people-watching.

3 Quincy Market 🍵 ★★

The main level of Faneuil Hall Marketplace's central building, **Quincy Market,** is a gigantic food court. You can eat at the marketplace, but I suggest crossing Atlantic Avenue and enjoying your snack or lunch with a glorious view. Stake out a seat overlooking the marina next to Christopher Columbus Waterfront Park (next to the Marriott, on the side opposite the New England Aquarium). If you'd rather eat indoors, head to **Durgin-Park ★★★**, 340 Faneuil Hall Marketplace (*©* **617/227-2038;** p. 160), or across the street to **Union Oyster House ★**, 41 Union St. (*©* **617/227-2750;** p. 160).

Iconic Boston

Boston Inner Harbor

The Freedom Trail

DAY ONE ●
1   The Freedom Trail
2   Faneuil Hall Marketplace
3a Quincy Market ☕
3b Durgin Park ☕
3c Union Oyster House ☕
4   Paul Revere House
5   The North End
6a Mike's Pastry
6b Caffè Vittoria ☕
6c Caffè dello Sport ☕
7   The Waterfront

DAY TWO ●
8   Museum of Fine Arts
9a Legal Sea Foods ☕
9b Jasper White's Summer Shack ☕
10 Boston Duck Tour
11 Newbury Street
12 Public Garden
13 Beacon Hill

DAY THREE ●
14 Museum of Science
15 John F. Kennedy Presidential Library & Museum
16a Mr. Bartley's Burger Cottage ☕
16b Border Café ☕
17 Harvard Square and Harvard University
18a JP Licks ☕
18b Lizzy's ☕
19 Harvard University Museums
20 Mount Auburn Cemetery

The interior of the Old North Church.

4 Paul Revere House ★★★

My favorite Freedom Trail stop is a little 17th-century home overlooking a picturesque cobblestone square. See p. 97.

5 The North End ★★★

The Freedom Trail continues here with another famous Paul Revere hang-out, the fascinating **Old North Church ★**. But there's more to this historic neighborhood than just history. The city's "Little Italy" (locals don't call it that) is a great place for wandering around. See p. 61.

6 Hanover Street ☕

Coffee outlets throughout the city serve good espresso and cappuccino; the North End adds an authentic Italian accent. Pair your caffeine with a fresh-baked pastry at a bakery or *caffè*, and take in the scene on the North End's main drag. Top choices: **Caffè Vittoria,** 296 Hanover St. (☏ **617/227-7606**), **Mike's Pastry,** 300 Hanover St. (☏ **617/742-3050**), and **Caffè dello Sport,** 308 Hanover St. (☏ **617/523-5063**). See p. 154.

7 The Waterfront

Now downtown Boston's small size pays off: In almost any direction, the gorgeous harbor is a short stroll from the North End. As the day winds down, you can take a **sightseeing cruise ★★** (p. 107) from Long Wharf or Rowes Wharf—though a **ferry** ride from Long Wharf to Charlestown and back may be better for your schedule and budget. If cruises aren't for you or are out of season, explore the **New England Aquarium ★** (p. 59) or the **Boston Children's Museum ★★** (p. 114). Another option is to head for the nearby Seaport District (also known as the South Boston

Waterfront) and visit the **Institute of Contemporary Art ★★** (p. 69). It's a 20- to 30-minute walk or 10-minute cab ride.

Or—it's not the Waterfront, but bear with me—abandon the sightseeing after the Paul Revere House and go **shopping** in the Back Bay, starting with a stroll along Newbury Street (see chapter 7).

One Singular Sensation

On a 1-day visit, consider concentrating on just **one or two things** that you're most excited about, plus a good meal or two. If what really gets you going is the Museum of Fine Arts, the Museum of Science, Newbury Street's art galleries and boutiques, the Boston Harbor Islands, or even a day trip (see chapter 10), you have a good excuse for not doing more—and for a return trip to Boston!

Finally, head back to the hotel to wash off the day's grime, then pick something fun from the "Suggested Evening Itineraries," below.

On **Day 2,** explore beyond downtown and investigate subjects other than history. The Back Bay, Beacon Hill, and other destinations contrast invitingly with the Colonial extravaganza of the Freedom Trail. If possible, book a Duck Tour in the afternoon, but don't worry if you can't—this is a flexible itinerary. Start your day at the Museum of Fine Arts.

8 Museum of Fine Arts ★★★

Be at the museum (T: Green Line E to Museum of Fine Arts or Orange Line to Ruggles) when it opens at 10am. Check the website beforehand to help structure your visit, and consider taking the first guided tour of the day, which begins at 10:30am. The museum has a cafeteria, cafe, and restaurant, but I'd suggest saving your appetite for the next stop. See p. 75.

9 Shops at Prudential Center 🍵

One of my favorite branches of **Legal Sea Foods ★★★** (p. 151) is here, on the main level off Boylston Street. If you prefer something lighter, visit the nearby food court. Or walk 5 minutes to the Back Bay branch of **Jasper White's Summer Shack ★★**. See p. 181.

10 Boston Duck Tour ★★★

This is the most entertaining motorized way to see the city. On a reconditioned World War II amphibious landing vehicle, you see the top attractions, pick up some historical background, and take a ride on the Charles River. See p. 105.

A Boston Duck Tour vessel navigates the city.

Duck Tours don't operate from January through March (unless they're needed for a Patriots Super Bowl victory parade) or on weekdays in December. An excellent alternative is a **Boston Symphony Orchestra ★★★** or **Boston Pops ★★** concert at Symphony Hall (p. 227), a short walk from either the MFA or the Prudential Center.

The Public Garden.

11 Newbury Street

Newbury Street offers the best shopping in New England (see chapter 7). It's also architecturally fascinating (see "Walking Tour 1: The Back Bay," in chapter 5). One block away, Boylston Street also offers excellent shopping.

12 Public Garden ★★★

Newbury Street begins across Arlington Street from the most beautiful park in Boston. The Public Garden (p. 103) is lovely year-round—a visit will brighten up even the grayest off-season day—and the *Make Way for Ducklings* sculptures (p. 23) are always delightful. In warm weather, leave time for a **Swan Boat ride** (p. 103).

13 Beacon Hill ★★★

The most picturesque neighborhood in town is a festival of red brick, cobblestones, and gorgeous architectural details. **Charles Street,** the main thoroughfare, is a lively shopping destination with a refreshing lack of chain stores. Wander on your own (see p. 65 for pointers) or seek out a guide—on summer weekdays, a **Boston By Foot** tour starts at 5:30pm.

"Suggested Evening Itineraries," below, can help you plan the rest of your day.

On **Day 3,** you'll probably want to venture beyond Boston proper. (If not, you can easily extend the suggestions for the first 2 days to fill a third—for instance, complete the Freedom Trail or return to the Museum of Fine Arts, where admission is good for two visits within 10 days.) This itinerary may look skimpy, but it's packed with interesting activities. Begin by picking a morning destination.

14 Museum of Science ★★★

If you prefer science over history or want to stay close to downtown, head to the museum (T: Green Line to Science Park). Otherwise, you're off to Dorchester (T: Red Line to JFK/UMass, then free shuttle bus) to see the:

SUGGESTED evening ITINERARIES

If you're traveling as a family, you may be checking the TV listings for your evening plans. If not—or if you booked a babysitter—here are some suggestions. See chapter 6 for restaurant reviews and chapter 8 for nightlife listings.

- Dinner in the North End, and coffee and dessert at a *caffè*. Afterward, enjoy the view from Copp's Hill Terrace, between Charter and Commercial streets overlooking the harbor, or take in a show at the Improv Asylum. Wind down with a drink at the Cheers bar at Quincy Market.

- Dinner at Legal Sea Foods in the Prudential Center, followed (or preceded) by a visit to the 50th-floor Prudential Center Skywalk or a drink in the lounge at Top of the Hub, on the 52nd floor. If heights aren't your thing, lift a glass at the Bar at Taj Boston.

- Summer only: Assemble a picnic and head to the Hatch Shell for music or a movie, to Boston Common for a play, or to City Hall Plaza for a concert.

- Winter only: A Boston Symphony Orchestra or Boston Ballet performance, then a late supper at Brasserie Jo or dessert at Finale.

- Dinner at the Legal Sea Foods across from the New England Aquarium, then a stroll along the harbor. Hit the North End or the food court at Faneuil Hall Marketplace for dessert.

- Dinner at Brasserie Jo, then a Huntington Theatre Company

performance or music at Wally's Cafe (or both).

- Dinner at the Boston location of Jasper White's Summer Shack, a stroll on Newbury Street, and a nightcap at the Bristol Lounge in the Four Seasons Hotel.

- Shopping at the Coop or the Harvard Book Store, then dinner at Mr. Bartley's Burger Cottage. Contemplate Harvard Yard from the Widener Library steps, and finish up with ice cream at JP Licks or Lizzy's, or with a show at Club Passim (or both).

- Dinner at the East Coast Grill or Oleana, followed by music at Scullers Jazz Club, the Regattabar, or Ryles Jazz Club.

- Dinner at Baraka Café, ice cream at Toscanini's, and music at the Middle East or T. T. the Bear's Place.

- A movie at the Kendall Square Cinema before or after dinner at Hungry Mother or Oleana, then music at the Cantab Lounge.

- Dinner at Redbones or Johnny D's Uptown Restaurant & Music Club, and a show at Johnny D's or the Somerville Theater.

15 John F. Kennedy Presidential Library and Museum ★★

Although they're very different, both of these museums are well worth a trip and a full morning. The Museum of Science (p. 62), with its wealth of hands-on exhibits, is a great destination for families; adults and older kids who have studied American history can't get enough of the Kennedy Library (p. 77). Both museums open at 9am, and both have cafeterias, but I recommend that you wait to have lunch in Harvard Square.

16 Eat Like a College Kid

My favorite Harvard Square lunch destinations are casual places where sightseers fit right in. **Mr. Bartley's Burger Cottage ★★**, 1246 Massachusetts Ave. (© **617/354-6559;** p. 178), is my top choice anywhere for onion rings, not to mention great burgers. It's closed Sunday. The **Border Café,** 32 Church St. (© **617/864-6100;** p. 178), serves terrific Tex-Mex specialties.

17 Harvard Square & Harvard University

I consider these two entities one big stop because the school couldn't exist without the neighborhood, and vice versa. Allow some time to wander around and enjoy the gentrified-boho atmosphere. Take a tour, which begins at the university's Information Center, or head out on your own (see "Walking Tour 3: Harvard Square," in chapter 5). "The Square" is also a fun **shopping** destination (see chapter 7).

18 Ice Cream

Harvard Square is home to some of the best ice-cream shops in this ice-cream-obsessed part of the world. **JP Licks,** 1312 Massachusetts Ave. (© **617/492-1001**), and **Lizzy's,** 29 Church St. (© **617/354-2911**), are equally delicious, so check the daily specials if you can't decide. Take your treat to Harvard Yard.

19 Harvard University Museums ★★

The Harvard Museum of Natural History and the adjacent Peabody Museum (p. 82) are equally welcoming to kids and adults. Until sometime

Mr. Bartley's Burger Cottage.

One of Mount Auburn Cemetery's eye-catching monuments.

in 2013, highlights of the collections of the Harvard Art Museums (p. 81) are on display at the Sackler Museum while the institution's other buildings undergo renovation. (That means a relatively short visit, which may suit you just fine.) All of the university museums close at 5pm.

If the weather's fine, you may prefer to point yourself toward:

20 Mount Auburn Cemetery ★★

A short distance from Harvard Square, Mount Auburn Cemetery is a gorgeous, fascinating destination. See p. 84.

When you've had enough, head back to the hotel. Stay in and order room service, or dress up for one of the "Suggested Evening Itineraries," above.

BOSTON WITH KIDS

My best advice for seeing Boston with the family is unconventional: Skip the Freedom Trail. Ignore me if your offspring are old enough and interested enough to suggest the trail on their own. The other 99.9% can plan on two big activities and some well-earned downtime.

1 Museum of Science ★★★

Be there when the museum (T: Green Line to Science Park) opens, at 9am, and know where you're going. Use the website to find can't-miss exhibits and the schedule for the Omni theater and planetarium. The dining options here are good, but if you can hold out, wait to eat lunch. See p. 62.

2 Faneuil Hall Marketplace ☕

Even the pickiest kids can find something they like at **Quincy Market;** mix and match with more sophisticated adult options. In fine weather, **Christopher Columbus Waterfront Park** (see "Iconic Boston" stop 3, above) is a great picnic spot with both a playground and a fountain.

3 New England Aquarium ★

Check the schedule for feeding the seals in the New Balance Foundation Marine Mammal Center (at the back of the main level), and plan around them. *Tip:* Don't try to visit the aquarium and the Children's Museum (see below) in one afternoon. Split up if your kids vary widely in age, or plan a return trip to the attraction you skip today.

4 Boston Children's Museum ★★

Kids under 10 love this museum, where crowds fluctuate depending on school vacation and day-camp schedules. Let larger groups pass you, and you'll have better access to the exhibits.

5 Greenway pushcarts ☕

In spring, summer, and fall, the Rose Kennedy Greenway boasts an enticing variety of snack options, from barbecue to cupcakes. In a pinch, there's a 7-Eleven at 70 East India Row (enter from Atlantic Ave. at Milk St.; ☎ **617/227-9534**).

Boston With Kids & Boston for Art Lovers

BOSTON WITH KIDS ●
1 Museum of Science
2 Faneuil Hall Marketplace 🛍
3 New England Aquarium
4 Boston Children's Museum
5 Greenway pushcarts 🛍
6 Rose Kennedy Greenway

BOSTON FOR ART LOVERS ●
1 Institute of Contemporary Art
2 Newbury Street
3 Café G 🍽
4 Isabella Stewart Gardner Museum
5 Museum of Fine Arts

6 Rose Kennedy Greenway ★★

The most child-friendly parts of the mile-long Greenway are near places you've already visited. Ride the seasonal carousel (across from Faneuil Hall Marketplace, near Cross St.), check out the displays at the adjacent Boston Harbor Islands Pavilion, frolic in the Rings Fountain (at Milk St.), or just explore the art and sculpture as you unwind and plan your evening.

BOSTON FOR ART LOVERS

This itinerary works best on Wednesday, Thursday, or Friday, when extended hours at the Museum of Fine Arts mean you can really make a day of it. If possible, steer clear of weekends, especially when a high-profile show at the MFA is drawing big crowds. The ICA closes most Mondays, and the Isabella Stewart Gardner Museum closes every Tuesday; both museums stay open late on Thursday. All three museums schedule occasional evening concerts, which you may want to check out (or avoid). **Note:** These stops are somewhat interchangeable—if you're staying near the Fenway or the Seaport District, feel free to adjust accordingly.

1 Institute of Contemporary Art ★★

Be at the ICA (T: Silver Line SL1/SL2 to World Trade Center) when it opens, at 10am. If you're coming from another neighborhood and the weather allows, walk to the Seaport District from downtown, savoring the sensation of having fun while other people head to the office.

2 Newbury Street

Stop in the Back Bay for an optional but enjoyable look at New England's best-known collection of art galleries. See chapter 7 for pointers on exploring, and don't forget to look above street level.

3 Café G ☕

Plan around the schedule of museum tours when you make your lunch reservation. The celebrated restaurant at the Gardner Museum is open until 4pm (8pm on Thurs). It's closed on Tuesday.

4 Isabella Stewart Gardner Museum ★★

Already a landmark, the Gardner Museum became twice as architecturally interesting in 2012, when a new wing designed by Renzo Piano opened. Even if you don't take a tour, plan on some time outdoors, where you can see how the museum's two largest artifacts—the original building and the addition—interact.

5 Museum of Fine Arts ★★★

The Art of the Americas wing, the newest part of the MFA, is usually crowded. Check the website before you visit, and target some older galleries, which you may have almost to yourself. Jazz up your visit with a few minutes of fantasizing that you're enjoying your own private collection.

4

EXPLORING
BOSTON

Whether you want to immerse yourself in the Colonial era or just cruise around the harbor, you can do it—and plenty more—in Boston. Throw out your preconceptions of the city as an open-air history museum (although that's certainly one of the guises it can assume), and allow your interests to dictate where you go.

It's possible but not advisable to take in most of the major attractions in 2 or 3 days if you don't linger anywhere too long. For a more enjoyable, less rushed visit, plan fewer activities and spend more time on them. For descriptions of suggested itineraries, see chapter 3.

Visitors in 2013 will be able to see the rejuvenated **Boston Tea Party Ships & Museum** (p. 68). This attraction, which formerly featured a single ship, closed after a fire in 2001. The museum doubled in size for the 2012 reopening, and it now has a historically accurate total of three ships (new and overhauled replicas) floating alongside. Also in 2013, the **Harvard Art Museums** (p. 81) will be wrapping up a huge renovation project that has closed two of the three museums since 2008. Check for exhibits related to the reopening, slated for 2014.

The recent economic downturn has adversely affected many attractions. Admissions fees and hours in this chapter are current at press time, but by the time you visit, establishments that rely on corporate and government support may cost a bit more or keep shorter hours. Prices for activities that use fuel, such as tours and cruises, are subject to changes or surcharges depending on the fluctuating energy market. If you're on a tight schedule or budget, check ahead.

BOSTON'S TOP 20 SIGHTS & ATTRACTIONS

Paring down this list was so difficult that I cheated a little—the Freedom Trail's 19 points of interest appear here as two attractions (the trail itself and the Paul Revere House). To make walking the trail easier, its stops are listed in order in a separate section that begins on p. 86.

Given the difficulty and expense of parking, the best way to reach Boston's most popular attractions is **on foot** or by **public transportation.** To maximize your enjoyment, try to visit during relatively slow times. If possible, especially in the summer, sightsee on weekdays; if you're traveling without children, aim for periods when Massachusetts schools are in session. And if you're in town on a July or August weekend, resign yourself to lines and crowds.

For tips on planning your visit to Boston, especially if you're short on time, see the "Iconic Boston" itinerary in chapter 3.

- **Boston Children's Museum.** See p. 114.
- **Boston Duck Tours.** See p. 105.
- **Boston Tea Party Ships & Museum.** See p. 68.

PREVIOUS PAGE: **A bell on the USS** *Constitution.*

Abiel Smith School **14**
African Meeting House **14**
Boston Athenæum **16**
Boston Children's Museum **24**
Boston Public Library **8**
Boston Tea Party Ship & Museum **23**
Faneuil Hall Marketplace **18**
Fenway Park **1**
Foster's Rotunda **21**
Gibson House Museum **9**
Independence Wharf **22**
Institute of Contemporary Art **26**
Isabella Stewart Gardner Museum **2**
John Adams Courthouse **17**
Massachusetts Historical Society **4**
Moakley Federal Courthouse **25**

Mary Baker Eddy Library /
    Mapparium **6**
Museum of African American
    History **14**
Museum of Fine Arts **3**
Museum of Science **10**
New England Aquarium **20**
Nichols House Museum **15**
Otis House Museum **13**
Paul Revere House **19**
Skywalk Observatory at the
    Prudential Center **7**
Sports Museum of New England
    (TD Garden) **11**
Symphony Hall **5**
The West End Museum **12**

Boston Attractions

- **Faneuil Hall Marketplace.** See p. 64.
- **Fenway Park.** See p. 246.
- **The Freedom Trail.** See p. 86.
- **Harvard University.** See p. 81.
- **Institute of Contemporary Art.** See p. 69.
- **Isabella Stewart Gardner Museum.** See p. 74.
- **John F. Kennedy Presidential Library and Museum.** See p. 77.
- **Longfellow House–Washington's Headquarters National Historic Site.** See p. 83.

 LET'S MAKE A deal

As you plan your sightseeing, consider these money-saving options. Check their respective websites for info about buying each pass.

If you concentrate on the included attractions, a **CityPASS** (www.citypass.com; ✆ **888/330-5008**) offers great savings. It's a booklet of tickets (so you can go straight to the entrance) to the Museum of Fine Arts, Museum of Science, New England Aquarium, Skywalk Observatory at the Prudential Center, and either the Harvard Museum of Natural History or the Old State House Museum. The price represents a 49% savings for adults who visit all five, and it feels like an even better deal on a steamy day when the line at the aquarium is long. At press time, the cost is $46 for adults, $29 for children 3 to 11, subject to change as admission prices rise. The passes, good for 9 days from first use, also include discounts at other local businesses.

The main competition for CityPass is the **Go Boston Card** (www.goboston card.com; ✆ **800/887-9103**). The original Go Boston Card includes admission to 59 Boston-area and New England attractions, plus dining and shopping discounts, a guidebook, and a 2-day trolley pass. If you strategize wisely, this card can be a deal, but make sure you understand the logistics. It costs $60 for 1 day, $80 for 2 days, $120 for 3 days,

$165 for 5 days, and $195 for 7 days, with discounts for children and winter travelers (some of the included businesses close in the winter). The **Go Select Boston** pass covers a single admission to two or more of the 39 included attractions and is good for 30 days. The price varies with the options you choose.

If you're a Bank of America or Merrill Lynch credit or debit card holder, the **Museums on Us** program gets you into cultural institutions around the country free on the first full weekend of each month. Participating establishments in eastern Massachusetts are the Museum of Fine Arts and the Harvard Museum of Natural History. Visit http://museums.bankofamerica.com for details. On **"Free Fun Fridays"** in the summer, the Massachusetts-based Highland Street Foundation (www.highlandstreet.org) foots the bill for admission to cultural institutions around the state. Check the website for specifics.

The MBTA's 7-day **LinkPass** (www.mbta.com; ✆ **877/927-7277** or 617/222-4545) can be a bargain—but only if you plan to use public transit often enough. See p. 351.

A Note on Online Ticketing

Many museums and other attractions sell tickets online, subject to a service charge, through their websites or an agency. This can be handy, but it can also cost you some flexibility and perhaps some money.

If there's any chance that your plans will change, make sure you **understand the refund policy** before you enter your credit card info—you may not be able to return or exchange prepaid tickets.

○ **Massachusetts Institute of Technology.** See p. 84.

○ **Mount Auburn Cemetery.** See p. 84.

○ **Museum of African American History.** See p. 67.

○ **Museum of Fine Arts.** See p. 75.

○ **Museum of Science.** See p. 62.

○ **New England Aquarium.** See p. 59.

○ **Paul Revere House.** See p. 97.

○ **Public Garden/Swan Boats.** See p. 103.

○ **Skywalk Observatory at the Prudential Center.** See p. 73.

THE WATERFRONT

This long, skinny neighborhood is home to the **New England Aquarium,** the **Rose Kennedy Greenway,** and docks where ferry rides and sightseeing cruises originate. For sightseeing suggestions, see "Walking Tour 2: The Waterfront," in chapter 5.

New England Aquarium ★ ☺ AQUARIUM   This complex is home to more than 30,000 fish and aquatic mammals, and at busy times, it seems to contain at least that many people. In July and August, try to make this your first stop of the morning, especially on weekends. Pause as you enter to visit with the **Atlantic harbor seals,** which frolic in a free outdoor enclosure just past the ticket booth.

Inside, **penguins** from three continents greet visitors as they enter. The focal point of the aquarium is the four-story, 200,000-gallon **Giant Ocean Tank.** A four-story spiral ramp encircles the tank, which contains a replica of a Caribbean coral reef and an assortment of sea creatures that seem to coexist amazingly well. Part of the reason for the peace might be that scuba divers feed the sharks twice a day. The **Shark and Ray Touch Tank** is a 25,000-gallon enclosure that lets visitors get up close and personal with the animals. At the **Edge of the Sea** exhibit, visitors can touch the sea stars, sea urchins, and horseshoe crabs in the tide pool. Other exhibits show off tropical sea creatures, freshwater specimens, denizens of the Amazon, and marine life in the Gulf of Maine. The **Medical Center** is especially involving: It's a working veterinary hospital where you can sometimes see marine animals that ran into trouble in New England waters and had to be rescued. (The aquarium is one of the most important facilities on the East Coast for marine-animal rescue; visit the team blog at **http://rescue.neaq.org** for information about recent activities.) Behind the

Eyes in the Skies

For a smashing view of the airport, the harbor, and the South Boston waterfront, stroll along the harbor or Atlantic Avenue to Northern Avenue. On either side of this intersection are buildings with free observation areas. Be ready to show an ID to gain entrance. The space on the 14th floor of **Independence Wharf,** 470 Atlantic Ave., is open daily from 11am to 5pm. Across the way is **Foster's Rotunda,** on the ninth floor of 30 Rowes Wharf, in the Boston Harbor Hotel complex. It's open Monday to Friday from 11am to 4pm.

building, fronting the harbor, the sheltered, open-air **New Balance Foundation Marine Mammal Center** is home to lively, curious fur seals.

The **Simons IMAX Theatre ★★★**, which has its own building, hours, and admission fees, is worth planning for, too. Its 85×65-foot screen shows 3-D films with digital sound that concentrate on the natural world as well as 3-D versions of recent Hollywood releases. It's an impressive experience.

I suggest starting your day here because you'll want to spend at least half a day, and huge afternoon crowds can make getting around painfully slow. Discounts are available when you combine a visit to the aquarium with an IMAX film or a **whale watch** (p. 109). Also consider investing in a Boston CityPass or Go Boston Card (see the "Let's Make a Deal" box, above); they allow you to skip the ticket line, which can be uncomfortably long, and the price may represent a savings on the steep admission charge.

Central Wharf (Milk St. and Old Atlantic Ave.). www.neaq.org. **𝄢 617/973-5200.** Admission $23 adults, $21 seniors, $16 children 3–11, free for children 2 and under and for those visiting only the outdoor exhibits, cafe, and gift shop. July to Labor Day Sun–Thurs 9am–6pm, Fri–Sat and holidays 9am–7pm; day after Labor Day to June Mon–Fri 9am–5pm, Sat–Sun and holidays

The four-story tank at the heart of the New England Aquarium.

9am–6pm. Simons IMAX Theatre: ℂ **866/815-4629.** Tickets $10–$13 adults, $8–$11 seniors and children 3–11. Daily from 9:30am. Closed Thanksgiving and Dec 25 and until noon Jan 1. T: Blue Line to Aquarium.

THE NORTH END

The **Paul Revere House** and the **Old North Church,** both stops on the Freedom Trail (p. 86), are in the North End. The historic neighborhood, which

 WELCOME TO THE north end

The Paul Revere House and the Old North Church are the best-known buildings in the **North End ★★★**, Boston's "Little Italy" (although locals *never* call it that). Home to natives of Italy and their assimilated children, numerous Italian restaurants and private social clubs, and many historic sites, this is one of the oldest neighborhoods in the city. It was home in the 17th century to the **Mather family** of Puritan ministers, who certainly would be shocked to see the merry goings-on at the festivals and street fairs that take over different areas of the North End on weekends in July and August.

The Italians and their descendants (and the yuppie neighbors who have crowded many of them out since the 1980s) are only the latest immigrant group to dominate the North End. In the 19th century, this was an Eastern European Jewish enclave, and later an Irish stronghold. In 1890, President Kennedy's mother, Rose Fitzgerald, was born on Garden Court Street and baptized at St. Stephen's Church on Hanover Street.

Modern visitors might be more interested in a Hanover Street *caffè,* the perfect place to have coffee or a soft drink and

feast on sweets. **Mike's Pastry ★★**, 300 Hanover St. (www.mikespastry.com; ℂ **617/742-3050**), is a bakery that does a frantic takeout business and has tables where you can sit down and order one of the confections on display in the cases. The signature item is cannoli (tubes of crisp-fried pastry filled with sweetened ricotta cheese); the cookies, cakes, and other pastries are excellent, too. You can also sit and relax at **Caffè Vittoria** or **Caffè dello Sport,** on either side of Mike's.

Before you leave the North End, stroll down toward the water and see whether there's a **bocce** game going on at the courts on Commercial Street near Hull Street. The European pastime is both a game of skill and an excuse to hang around and shoot the breeze—in Italian and English—with the locals (mostly men of a certain age). It's so popular that the neighborhood has courts both outdoors, in the Langone Playground at Puopolo Park, and indoors, at the back of the adjacent Steriti Rink, 561 Commercial St.

retains an Italian-American flavor even as the area becomes more diverse, is an attraction in its own right.

NORTH STATION/SCIENCE PARK

The best pedestrian access to the **Museum of Science** (which is technically its own neighborhood, with its own T stop) is from the North Station area. One end of the **Rose Kennedy Greenway** is here, as are two small special-interest museums, the **Sports Museum of New England** and the **West End Museum.**

Museum of Science ★★★ ☺ MUSEUM For the ultimate pain-free educational experience, head to the Museum of Science. The demonstrations, experiments, and interactive displays introduce facts and concepts so effortlessly that everyone winds up learning something. Take a couple of hours or a whole day to explore the permanent and temporary exhibits, most of them hands-on and all of them great fun.

Among the 700-plus exhibits, you might meet a dinosaur or a live butterfly, find out how much you'd weigh on the moon, or climb into a space module. Activity centers and exhibits focus on fields of interest—natural history (with live animals), computers, the human body—while others take an interdisciplinary approach. **Investigate!** teaches visitors to think like scientists, formulating questions, finding evidence, and drawing conclusions through activities such as strapping on a skin sensor to measure reactions to stimuli or sifting through an archaeological site. **Beyond the X-Ray** explores medical-imaging techniques and allows would-be diagnosticians to try to figure out what's ailing their "patients." The **Science in the Park** exhibit introduces the concepts of Newtonian physics through familiar objects such as playground equipment and skateboards. Temporary exhibits change regularly, and just about any **major touring show** (national or international) that focuses on a scientific topic stops here. One upcoming exhibit is **Mammoths and Mastodons: Titans of the Ice Age** (Oct 7, 2012–Jan 13, 2013).

The separate-admission **theaters** are worth planning for. Even if you're skipping the exhibits, try to see a show. If you're making a day of it, buy all your tickets at once, because shows sometimes sell out. The **Mugar Omni Theater ★★★**, which shows IMAX movies, is an intense experience, bombarding you with images on a five-story domed screen and digital sound. The engulfing sensations and steep pitch of the seating area will have you hanging on for dear life, whether the film is about (for example) tornadoes, whales, or risk-taking. Features change every 4 to 6 months. The **Charles Hayden Planetarium ★★**, which reopened in 2011 after extensive renovations, is now a high-def theater capable of "immersive video" in addition to a great introduction to astronomy. The domed venue has a state-of-the-art digital optics system that allows visitors to see thousands of stars in configurations as much as 10,000 years old, and to experience an astronaut's-eye-view of the earth.

The museum has a terrific gift shop, with toys and games that promote learning without lecturing. The ground-floor Riverview Cafe offers spectacular views of the skyline and the Charles River. **Tip:** There's a parking garage on the premises, but it's on a busy street, and entering and exiting can be harrowing; take the T.

Science Park, off O'Brien Hwy. on bridge btw. Boston and Cambridge. www.mos.org. ℂ **617/723-2500.** Admission to exhibit halls $21 adults, $19 seniors, $18 children 3–11, free for

The Museum of Science.

children 2 and under; to Butterfly Garden or 3-D Digital Cinema (available only with exhibit hall admission) $5 adults, $4.50 seniors, $4 children 3–11. Admission to Mugar Omni Theater or planetarium $9 adults, $8 seniors, $7 children 3–11, free for children 2 and under. Discounted combination tickets available. July 5 to Labor Day Sat–Thurs 9am–7pm, Fri 9am–9pm; day after Labor Day to July 4 Sat–Thurs 9am–5pm, Fri 9am–9pm. Check ahead for extended hours during school vacations. Closed Thanksgiving and Dec 25. T: Green Line to Science Park.

Sports Museum of New England MUSEUM New England sports fans enjoy this museum, on the fifth and sixth floors of the TD Garden arena. It celebrates local teams and athletes of all ages, especially the Celtics and Bruins, who play in this building. You'll see Red Sox legend Ted Williams's locker, a penalty box from the old Boston Garden, and film highlights of the action there— which you watch while squirming on hard wooden seats rescued from the "old barn." Visit the website to download an audio tour. The museum closes unpredictably, depending on the arena schedule; always call ahead. ***Note:*** Visitors may not bring large bags, including backpacks and briefcases, into the arena.

In the TD Garden, 100 Legends Way (Causeway St. at Canal St.). www.sportsmuseum.org. ✆ **617/624-1234** (info line) or 617/624-1235. Admission $10 adults, $5 seniors and children 10–18, free for children 9 and under. Daily 10am–4pm. Closed during events; check ahead. T: Green or Orange Line to North Station.

The West End Museum MUSEUM One victim of the urban-renewal craze that swept the Northeast in the 1950s was the West End. The small, crowded neighborhood superficially resembled the nearby North End, which became predominantly Italian in the 19th century; the West End was notably more diverse. The regularly changing exhibits at this little museum celebrate the gone-but-not-forgotten neighborhood. Take a guided tour if it's offered during your visit to get a sense of what the city lost when the West End nearly disappeared. Check the website for information about guided walking tours.

150 Staniford St. (at Lomasney Way, near Causeway St.). www.thewestendmuseum.org. © **617/723-2125.** Free admission. Tues–Fri noon–5pm; Sat 11am–4pm. T: Green or Orange Line to North Station.

FANEUIL HALL MARKETPLACE

The Freedom Trail crosses through the marketplace, connecting **Faneuil Hall** (p. 95) to downtown and the North End. At the east end of the complex, cross the street to reach the Rose Kennedy Greenway.

Faneuil Hall Marketplace ★★ ☺ MARKET   Since Boston's most popular attraction opened in 1976, cities all over the country have imitated the "festival market" concept. Each complex of shops, food counters, restaurants, bars, and public spaces reflects its city, and Faneuil Hall Marketplace is no exception. Its popularity with visitors and suburbanites is so great that you might understandably think the only Bostonians here are employees.

The marketplace includes five buildings—the central three-building complex is on the National Register of Historic Places—set on brick and stone plazas that teem with crowds shopping, eating, performing, cheering for performers, and people-watching. In warm weather, it's busy from early morning until well past dark. **Quincy Market** (you'll also hear the whole complex called by that name) is the three-level Greek revival–style building at the center of the marketplace. It reopened after extensive renovations on August 26, 1976, 150 years after Mayor Josiah Quincy opened the original market. The **South Market building** reopened on August 26, 1977, the **North Market building** on August 26, 1978.

The central corridor of Quincy Market is the food court, where you can find anything from a fresh-shucked oyster to a full Greek dinner to sweets of all sorts. On either side of this building, under glass canopies, are full-service restaurants and bars—including one that replicates the set of the TV show *Cheers*—as well as pushcarts that sell everything from crafts created by New England artisans to hokey souvenirs. In the plaza between the **South Canopy** and the South Market building is an **information kiosk,** and throughout the complex you'll find a mix of predictable chain stores and unique shops (see chapter 7). On warm evenings, the tables that spill outdoors from the restaurants and bars fill with people. One constant since the year after the market—the *original* market—opened is **Durgin-Park** ★★★ (p. 160), a traditional New England restaurant.

The original **Faneuil Hall** ★ gets lost in the shuffle, but it's worth a visit. The first floor holds a National Park Service Visitor Center. See p. 95 for a full description.

Btw. North, Congress, and State sts. and John F. Fitzgerald Surface Rd. www.faneuilhall marketplace.com. © **617/523-1300.** Marketplace Mon–Sat 10am–9pm; Sun noon–6pm. Mon–Thurs closing time may be earlier in winter. Food court opens earlier; bars and some restaurants close later. T: Green Line to Government Center, Orange Line to Haymarket or State, or Blue Line to Aquarium or State.

GOVERNMENT CENTER

Boston City Hall, the ugly building looming above the T stop that gives this neighborhood its name, is Government Center's main architectural feature.

Street performers at Faneuil Hall Marketplace.

Nearby are three **Freedom Trail** (p. 86) stops: **King's Chapel and Burying Ground,** the **Old State House Museum,** and the **Boston Massacre Site.**

DOWNTOWN CROSSING

The **Freedom Trail** (p. 86) starts here, on **Boston Common.** It continues with **Park Street Church,** the **Granary Burying Ground,** the site of the **First Public School** and the **Benjamin Franklin Statue,** the **Old Corner Bookstore Building,** and the **Old South Meeting House.** Elsewhere in this congested neighborhood, you'll find decent shopping, office workers, and students from Emerson College and Suffolk University.

BEACON HILL

The **Massachusetts State House** (p. 88), the second stop on the Freedom Trail, occupies the peak of Beacon Hill. In this gorgeous neighborhood, you'll find the **Black Heritage Trail,** the **Museum of African American History,** the **Boston Athenæum,** and two lovely historic homes, the **Otis House** and the **Nichols House Museum.**

The 1.5-mile **Black Heritage Trail ★★** covers sites on Beacon Hill that preserve the history of 19th-century Boston. The neighborhood was the center of the free black community, and the trail links stations of the Underground Railroad, homes of famous citizens, and the first integrated public school in the city. You can take a free 2-hour guided tour with a ranger from the National Park Service's **Boston African American National Historic Site** (www.nps.gov/boaf; ✆ **617/742-5415**). Tours start at the **Shaw Memorial** (Memorial to Robert Gould Shaw and the Massachusetts 54th Regiment), on Beacon Street across from the State House. They're available Monday through Saturday from Memorial

LEFT: The Shaw Memorial on Beacon Hill across from the State House. RIGHT: The Boston Athenæum.

Day to Labor Day, and by request at other times; call ahead for a reservation. Or go on your own, using a brochure (available at the Museum of African American History and the Boston Common and Faneuil Hall visitor centers) that includes a map and descriptions of the buildings. The only buildings on the trail that are open to the public are the **African Meeting House** and the **Abiel Smith School,** which make up the **Museum of African American History** (p. 67). Check ahead for special programs year-round.

From the State House, **Beacon and Mount Vernon streets** run downhill to commercially dense **Charles Street,** but leave some time for wandering. You might see the former homes of Louisa May Alcott (10 Louisburg Sq.), Henry Kissinger (1 Chestnut St.), Julia Ward Howe (13 Chestnut St.), Edwin Booth (29A Chestnut St.), and Robert Frost (88 Mount Vernon St.). Residents of the 22 homes around **Louisburg Square** (pronounced "Lewis-burg") are the only ones with keys to the lovely park in the middle.

Boston Athenæum ★ LIBRARY   Both a private library and an art gallery, the Athenæum gives outsiders an insider's perspective on proper Boston society—including the impulse to reach out to the community through arts and culture. In other words, it may sound stuffy, but it isn't. The city's leading families founded the Athenæum in 1807 to make "the great works of learning and science in all languages" available to members. They added the arts component in 1827, and artwork now fills the building. Docent-led **tours** (offered twice weekly, by reservation only; ✆ **617/227-0270,** ext. 279) show off the Palladian-inspired sandstone building, replete with soaring galleries and hideaway nooks, that backs up to the Granary Burying Ground. Completed in 1849 and expanded in 1913–15, it was extensively renovated around the turn of the 21st century. The Athenæum mounts exhibits in the compact **art gallery** on the first floor—the only part of the building regularly open to the public. It also schedules lectures, readings, concerts, and, on rare occasions, viewings of the library's most famous holding: an 1847 volume bound in the author's skin.

10½ Beacon St. www.bostonathenaeum.org. ☏ **617/227-0270.** Free admission. Year-round Mon and Wed 9am–8pm, Tues and Thurs–Fri 9am–5:30pm; Sept–May Sat 9am–4pm. Free tours (reservations required) Tues and Thurs 3pm. Closed Sat June–Aug, Sun, and major holidays year-round. T: Red or Green Line to Park St.

Museum of African American History ★★ MUSEUM   In Revolutionary War–obsessed New England, the history of the black community that thrived in Boston from early Colonial times often gets overlooked, with some notable exceptions. The final stop on the **Black Heritage Trail** (p. 65), this museum is one of those exceptions, presenting a comprehensive look at the history and contributions of blacks in Boston and Massachusetts. It occupies the **Abiel Smith School** (1834), the first American public grammar school for African-American children, and the **African Meeting House,** 8 Smith Court. Changing and permanent exhibits use art, artifacts, documents, historic photographs, and other objects—including many family heirlooms—to explore an important era in the country's history. The oldest standing black church in the United States, the meetinghouse opened in 1806. William Lloyd Garrison founded the New England Anti-Slavery Society in this building, where Frederick Douglass made some of his great abolitionist speeches. Once known as the "Black Faneuil Hall," it also schedules lectures, concerts, and church meetings.

46 Joy St. www.maah.org. ☏ **617/725-0022.** Admission $5 adults, $3 seniors and youths 13–17, free for children 12 and under. Mon–Sat 10am–4pm. Closed Jan 1, Thanksgiving, and Dec 25. T: Red or Green Line to Park St., Red Line to Charles/MGH, or Blue Line to Bowdoin (weekdays only).

Nichols House Museum ★ HISTORIC HOME   A stroll around Beacon Hill leaves many visitors pining to know what the stately homes look like inside. This grand residence is one of the only places to satisfy that curiosity. The 1804 home, designed by celebrated architect Charles Bulfinch, holds beautiful antique furnishings, art, carpets, and tapestries collected by several generations of the Nichols family. Its most prominent occupant, Rose Standish Nichols (1872–1960), was a suffragist and a pioneering landscape designer. Her legacy includes not just family heirlooms but objects from her many travels that she brought back to the thoroughfare that author Henry James (who lived at no. 131) reputedly called "the only respectable street in America."

55 Mount Vernon St. www.nicholshousemuseum.org. ☏ **617/227-6993.** Admission $8, free for children 12 and under. Apr–Oct Tues–Sat 11am–4pm; Nov–Mar Thurs–Sat 11am–4pm; tours every 30 min. T: Red or Green Line to Park St.

Otis House ★★ HISTORIC HOME   Legendary architect Charles Bulfinch designed this gorgeous 1796 mansion for his friends Harrison Gray Otis, an up-and-coming young lawyer who later became mayor of Boston, and his wife, Sally. The restoration was one of the first in the country to use computer analysis of paint, and the result was revolutionary: It revealed that the walls were drab because the paint had faded, not because the colors started out dingy. Furnished in the style to which a wealthy family in the young United States would have been accustomed, the Federal-style building is a colorful, elegant treasure. Guided tours (the only way to see the property) discuss the architecture of the

The Otis House.

house and post-Revolutionary social, business, and family life, and touch on the history of the neighborhood.

Tip: Historic New England owns and operates the Otis House and dozens of other historic properties throughout the region. Contact the organization (www.historicnewengland.org; © **617/227-3956**) for information on its properties, visiting hours, and admission fees.

141 Cambridge St. (entrance on Lynde St.). www.historicnewengland.org. © **617/994-5920.** Guided tour $8 adults, $7 seniors, $4 students. Wed–Sun 11am–4:30pm; tours every 30 min. T: Blue Line to Bowdoin (weekdays only), Green or Blue Line to Government Center, or Red Line to Charles/MGH.

CHARLESTOWN

One of Boston's oldest neighborhoods, Charlestown is home to the final stops on the Freedom Trail (p. 86). The **USS *Constitution*** and its **museum** are at the **Charlestown Navy Yard,** and the **Bunker Hill Monument** is a short but steep walk away.

SOUTH BOSTON WATERFRONT/ SEAPORT DISTRICT

This rapidly evolving area is better known to conventiongoers than to many Bostonians. Here you'll find the **Institute of Contemporary Art,** the **Boston Children's Museum** (p. 114), and (on and near a bridge to downtown), the **Boston Tea Party Ships & Museum.**

Boston Tea Party Ships & Museum ★ MUSEUM   After more than a decade out of commission, this institution reopened in 2012 with more of everything, including twice as much museum space. The museum commemorates and explores the December 1773 Colonial uprising, one of the early acts of rebellion that led to the American Revolution (and inspired the modern movement of the same name). Through performances by reenactors, interactive exhibits, films, and displays of historic artifacts—including a vial of the tea that the rebellious colonists chucked into the harbor—the museum tells the story. Even more exciting: Visitors can explore full-size replicas of two of the three merchant ships raided during the original Tea Party (another is under construction). Check ahead for details; construction was wrapping up at press time, and management was planning a full slate of living-history programs, as well as food service in an 18th-century "tavern."

Congress St. Bridge (btw. Dorchester Ave. and Sleeper St.). www.bostonteapartyship.com. ℂ **855/TEA-1773** (832-1773). Check ahead for admission and hours. T: Red Line to South Station; walk north on Atlantic Ave. 1 block (past Federal Reserve Bank), turn right onto Congress St., then walk 1 long block to bridge.

Institute of Contemporary Art ★★ MUSEUM The city's first new art museum in nearly a century, the endlessly fascinating ICA is a work of art in its own right. The cantilevered building—designed by the New York firm Diller Scofidio + Renfro, whose work on this landmark project helped boost its growing reputation—juts out above the harbor, affording dizzying views of the water, the waterfront, and the airport. Besides making the museum an instant landmark, the architecture reflects the institution's curatorial philosophy that art is inseparable from everyday life, rather than a singular experience reserved for special occasions and field trips. The ICA showcases 20th- and 21st-century art in every imaginable medium, including film and video, music, literature, and dance. Opened in 2006, the 65,000-square-foot museum gives the institution the space it needs to create a permanent collection for the first time since its founding (under a different name) in 1936. Visitors have already enjoyed works by Louise

Bourgeois and Anish Kapoor that wouldn't have fit in (literally or figuratively) elsewhere in Boston, and the schedule of events, concerts, films, and other activities is a joy for anyone with even a passing interest. The cafe overlooks the water and offers outdoor seating in fine weather. The gift shop, the **ICA Store,** stocks a good mix of souvenirs and creative designs.

100 Northern Ave. (off Seaport Blvd. at E. Service Rd.). www.icaboston.org. ℂ **617/478-3100.** Admission $15 adults, $13 seniors, $10 students, free for children 17 and under and those visiting only the cafe. Free to all Thurs after 5pm and to families (up to 2 adults with children 12 and under) last Sat of month Jan–Nov. Sat–Sun, Tues–Wed, and some Mon holidays 10am–5pm; Thurs–Fri 10am–9pm. T: Silver Line SL1/SL2 bus to World Trade Center.

The Institute of Contemporary Art.

CHINATOWN/THEATER DISTRICT

At the edge of Chinatown you'll find one end of the **Rose Kennedy Greenway.** The little park holds a fountain, tables for chess players and snackers (there's often a food truck here), and plantings that evoke the Asian landscape.

THE SOUTH END

One of Boston's most diverse neighborhoods is also one of its largest. There are no museums or other major attractions here, but fans of Victorian architecture can't stay away. Turn to chapter 6 for dining suggestions, then budget extra time to explore the neighborhood's broad main streets (especially Tremont and Washington sts.), which intersect narrow side streets graced with pocket parks and

fountains. The intersection of Clarendon and Tremont streets, not far from the Orange Line Back Bay station, is the part of the South End you're most likely to see if you're not out exploring. This is the area where businesses and restaurants surround the **Boston Center for the Arts** (p. 227). The BCA's **Cyclorama** building (the interior is dome-shaped), at 539 Tremont St., is listed on the National Register of Historic Places.

The Cyclorama at the BCA.

THE BACK BAY

Architecture and shopping (not necessarily in that order) are two favorite reasons to visit the Back Bay. Another is the **Public Garden** (p. 103), which is delightful year-round and even more fun in warm weather, when the **Swan Boats** circle the adorable lagoon. Victorian style predominates in this neighborhood; the **Gibson House Museum** is a good destination if you're curious about the interiors of the lovely buildings. Another good place to start exploring is Copley Square, where the main branch of the **Boston Public Library** faces Trinity Church. For more information, see "Walking Tour 1: The Back Bay," in chapter 5.

Boston Public Library LIBRARY The central branch of the city's library system is an architectural and intellectual monument. The original 1895 building, a National Historic Landmark designed by Charles F. McKim, is an Italian Renaissance–style masterpiece that fairly drips with art. The **lobby doors** are the work of Daniel Chester French (who also designed the Abraham Lincoln statue in the memorial in Washington, the *Minute Man* statue in Concord, and the John Harvard statue in Cambridge). The **murals** are by John Singer Sargent and Pierre Puvis de Chavannes, among others. Visit the lovely **courtyard ★** or peek at it from a window on the stairs. The adjoining addition, of the same height and material (pink granite), was designed by Philip Johnson and opened in 1972.

Strolling around the Back Bay is a great way to spend an afternoon.

Ask the staff at the information desk about changing exhibits. The **Courtyard** restaurant serves lunch Monday through Friday and afternoon tea Wednesday through Friday, and the **Map Room Café** is open Monday through Saturday 9am to 5pm.

Free **Art & Architecture Tours** (www.bpl.org/central/tours.htm) begin Monday at 2:30pm; Tuesday and Thursday at 6pm; and Wednesday, Friday, and Saturday at 11am, with an additional tour October through May on Sunday at 2pm. Visit the website and click "Brief Walking Tour of the McKim Building" for more information. Call © 617/536-5400, ext. 2216, to arrange group tours.

700 Boylston St., Copley Sq. www.bpl.org. © **617/536-5400.** Free admission. Mon–Thurs 9am–9pm; Fri–Sat 9am–5pm; Sun 1–5pm. Closed Sun June–Sept and legal holidays. T: Green Line to Copley.

Gibson House Museum HISTORIC HOUSE   The Gibson House is an 1859 brownstone that embodies the word "Victorian." Forget you've ever heard the phrase "less is more"—the ornate furnishings and abundant accessories offer a compelling look at the domestic life of a socially prominent family in the then new Back Bay neighborhood. You'll see decorations of all kinds, including family photos and portraits, petrified-wood hat racks, a sequined red-velvet pagoda for the cat, a Victrola, and an original icebox. Check ahead for the schedule of lectures and other special events.

137 Beacon St. www.thegibsonhouse.org. © **617/267-6338.** Admission $9 adults, $6 seniors and students, $3 children 11 and under. Tours on the hour Wed–Sun 1–3pm. Closed Jan 1, July 4, Thanksgiving, and Dec 25. T: Green Line to Arlington.

Mary Baker Eddy Library/Mapparium ☺ LIBRARY   The Mary Baker Eddy Library, a research center with two floors of interactive exhibits, aims to explore ideas such as liberty and spirituality through history, with a central role for Mary Baker Eddy, the founder of Christian Science. The most intriguing artifact is the **Mapparium** ★, a unique hollow globe 30 feet across. A work of

The Boston Public Library's central branch.

both art and history, it consists of a bronze framework that connects 608 stained-glass panels. Kids especially like the weird acoustics—the nonporous surfaces of the globe distort sound—and the chance to "journey to the center of the earth." As you cross the glass bridge just south of the equator, you'll see the political divisions of the world from 1932 to 1935, when the three-story-high globe was constructed.

The Gibson House Museum's beautiful period pieces.

The Mapparium at the Mary Baker Eddy Library.

World Headquarters of the First Church of Christ, Scientist, 200 Massachusetts Ave. www.mbe library.org. ℂ **888/222-3711** or 617/450-7000. Admission $6 adults; $4 seniors, students, and children 6–17; free for children 5 and under. Tues–Sun 10am–4pm. Closed federal holidays. T: Green Line E to Symphony; Green Line B, C, or D to Hynes Convention Center; or Orange Line to Massachusetts Ave.

Massachusetts Historical Society 🖋 LIBRARY   The oldest historical society in the United States is an important research library. It caters to specialists, but anyone can enjoy the rotating exhibits, which draw on the society's massive collections of artifacts, documents, photographs, and more. Many are available for online browsing, but do try to visit—the 1899 building is an architectural treasure. Check ahead for the schedule of tours, talks, lectures, and other events. 1154 Boylston St. (btw. Ipswich St. and the Fenway). www.masshist.org. ℂ **617/536-1608.** Free admission. Gallery: Mon–Sat 10am–4pm. Reading room: Mon–Fri 9am–4:45pm (until 7:45pm Thurs); Sat 9am–4pm. T: Green Line B, C, or D to Hynes Convention Center.

Skywalk Observatory at the Prudential Center ★★ ☺ OBSERVA-TORY   The enclosed observation deck on the 50th floor of the Prudential Tower offers a 360-degree view of Boston and far beyond. You can see for miles, even (when it's clear) as far as the mountains of New Hampshire to the north and the beaches of Cape Cod to the south. Away from the windows, interactive audiovisual exhibits chronicle the city's history, and two short films screen in the on-site theater. Also here are fascinating exhibits, including video presentations about refugees, on the history of immigration to Boston. The admission price includes a narrated audio tour, available in versions targeted to adults and children. Call before visiting, because the space sometimes closes for private events. 800 Boylston St. (at Fairfield St.). www.topofthehub.net/skywalk.php. ℂ **617/859-0648.** Admission $14 adults, $12 seniors and college students with ID, $9 children 12 and under. Apr–Oct daily 10am–10pm; Nov–Mar daily 10am–8pm. T: Green Line E to Prudential.

The Skywalk Observatory at the Prudential Center.

KENMORE SQUARE

The Back Bay, the Boston University campus, and the baseball-saturated area surrounding **Fenway Park** meet at this busy intersection. For information about visiting Fenway, see p. 248.

THE FENWAY

The so-called Avenue of the Arts (Huntington Ave.) gets its nickname from the numerous cultural institutions in this neighborhood, notably the **Museum of Fine Arts** and the **Isabella Stewart Gardner Museum.**

Isabella Stewart Gardner Museum ★★ MUSEUM The Gardner Museum is an exquisite blend of old and new. The original 1903 building, which resembles a 15th-century Venetian palace, gained a wing designed by internationally renowned architect Renzo Piano in 2012. Founder Isabella Stewart Gardner's will forbids changing the arrangement of the museum's content, so the dramatic glass-and-brick addition is the most significant physical change the institution has ever experienced. Check ahead for information about introductory talks and guided tours (free with admission), which are interesting whether or not you visited the original museum.

Gardner (1840–1924) was a fascinating character. She was an incorrigible individualist long before strong-willed behavior was acceptable for women in polite Boston society, and her legacy is a treasure for art lovers. "Mrs. Jack" designed her exquisite museum herself and filled it with European, American, and Asian paintings and sculptures, many chosen with the help of her friend and protégé Bernard Berenson. You'll see works by Titian, Botticelli, Raphael,

The Isabella Stewart Gardner Museum.

Rembrandt, Matisse, and Mrs. Gardner's friends James McNeill Whistler and John Singer Sargent. Titian's magnificent *Europa*, which many scholars consider his finest work, is one of the most important Renaissance paintings in the United States.

The original building, which opened to the public after Mrs. Gardner's death, also holds a glorious hodgepodge of furniture and architectural details imported from European churches and palaces. The *pièce de résistance* is the magnificent skylit **courtyard**, filled year-round with fresh flowers grown by the museum's horticultural staff. The new wing holds gallery space and a concert hall, and gives visitors a closer look at the greenhouses. It also contains the excellent cafe and gift shop.

280 the Fenway. www.gardnermuseum.org. ℂ **617/566-1401.** Admission $15 adults, $12 seniors, $5 college students with ID. Free for children 17 and under and adults named Isabella with ID. Wed and Fri–Mon 11am–5pm; Thurs 11am–9pm. Closed July 4, Thanksgiving, and Dec 25. T: Green Line E to Museum of Fine Arts.

Museum of Fine Arts ★★★ ☺ MUSEUM   One of the world's great art museums, the MFA works nonstop to become even more accessible and interesting. It can be overwhelming, so even a little planning before you set out will be time well spent. Take advantage of the excellent website to preview the collections, noting pieces and periods that especially interest you.

The quarter-million-square-foot **Art of the Americas Wing ★★★**, which opened in 2010, is home to some of the museum's highest-profile works. They include Childe Hassam's *Boston Common at Twilight,* Gilbert Stuart's 1796 portrait of George Washington, John Singleton Copley's 1768 portrait of Paul Revere (which looks suspiciously like the Samuel Adams beer logo), and several Luminist masterpieces by Fitz Henry Lane. *The Passage of the Delaware,* an enormous, dramatic painting by Thomas Sully in a 17-foot-wide frame, had been in storage for over a century before being installed here. The wing, designed by Sir Norman

Spotlight on Sargent

One of the signature installations in the Museum of Fine Arts' Art of the Americas Wing is a beloved portrait by John Singer Sargent, *The Daughters of Edward Darley Boit.* The four little girls—their mother was Mary Louisa Cushing Boit, the subject of a Sargent portrait hanging nearby—are depicted in the family apartment in Paris, alongside two huge Japanese vases. The painting hangs on Level 2 of the new wing, next to those very same vases.

Sargent (1856–1925) is a significant presence at the MFA. He created the murals in the **Ruth and Carl J. Shapiro Rotunda,** at the top of the grand staircase inside the Huntington Avenue entrance. Installed in 1921, the mythology-themed work proved so popular that the museum commissioned Sargent to create the adjacent **Colonnade Murals.** In 1925, the night before he was to sail from London to Boston to supervise the installation of the final section, Sargent died in his sleep.

Foster of Foster + Partners, also holds works from the pre-Columbian period through the mid-1970s, from both North and South America.

To focus exclusively on American art would be to miss out on some of the most magnificent holdings. The MFA is known for its **Impressionist ★★★** paintings (including one of the largest collections of Monets outside of Paris), Asian and Old Kingdom Egyptian collections, classical art, Buddhist temple, and fashion arts. Favorites include Renoir's *Dance at Bougival,* a bronze casting of Edgar Degas's sculpture *Little Dancer,* and Gauguin's *Where Do We Come From? What Are We? Where Are We Going?* There are also outstanding holdings of prints, photographs, furnishings, and decorative arts.

The museum is particularly welcoming to children, who can launch a scavenger hunt, admire the mummies, and participate in family-friendly programs scheduled year-round (and extra offerings during school vacations).

None of this comes cheap: The MFA's adult admission fee (which covers two visits within 10 days) is among the highest in the country. A Boston CityPass or Go Boston Card (see the "Let's Make a Deal" box on p. 58) is a bargain if you plan to visit enough of the other included attractions.

The grand entrances from Huntington Avenue and the Fenway are the main points of public access; after disembarking from the Green Line, walk back about half a block to begin your visit. Pick up a floor plan (available in eight languages) at the Sharf Information Center. Free **guided tours** (daily except Mon holidays) include an introduction to the collections (daily 10:30am and 1:30pm; Wed also 6:15pm) plus numerous other topics. For more in-depth information about selected topics, download a multimedia guide ($6) to your smartphone. The sprawling complex encompasses four dining options—a cafeteria, two cafes, and a fine-dining restaurant—two excellent gift shops, and two auditoriums.

Special exhibitions scheduled to coincide with the lifespan of this book include **Ori Gersht: History Repeating** (through Jan 6, 2013), **Cats to Crickets: Pets in Japan's Floating World** (through Feb 18, 2013), and **Art of the White Mountains** (through July 7, 2013).

465 Huntington Ave. www.mfa.org. 📞 **617/267-9300** or 617/369-3395 (tour info). Admission $22 adults, $20 students and seniors, $10 children 7–17 on school days 10am–3pm (otherwise free), free

ABOVE: **John Singleton Copley's portrait of Paul Revere.** LEFT: **The MFA's Art of the Americas Wing.**

for children 6 and under. Admission good for 2 visits within 10 days. Voluntary contribution ($22 suggested) Wed 4–9:45pm. Free admission to Museum Shop, library, and restaurants. Sat–Tues 10am–4:45pm; Wed–Fri 10am–9:45pm. Closed Jan 1, Patriots' Day, July 4, Thanksgiving, and Dec 25. T: Green Line E to Museum of Fine Arts or Orange Line to Ruggles.

DORCHESTER

Dorchester is a big deal for American history aficionados: the John F. Kennedy Presidential Library & Museum is here. In another part of the enormous neighborhood, you'll find the family-oriented **Franklin Park Zoo** (p. 116).

John F. Kennedy Presidential Library and Museum ★★ ☺ LIBRARY/ MUSEUM   The Kennedy era springs to life at this dramatic library, museum, and educational research complex overlooking Dorchester Bay. It captures the 35th president's accomplishments and legacy in video and sound recordings and fascinating displays of memorabilia and photos. Far from being a static experience, it changes regularly, with temporary shows and reinterpreted displays that highlight and complement the permanent installations. Through November 2013, the museum will be celebrating the 50th anniversary of the Kennedy presidency; check ahead for observances during your visit.

You begin with a 17-minute film narrated by John F. Kennedy—it's eerie for a moment, then perfectly natural. Through skillfully edited audio clips, he discusses his childhood, education, war experience, and early political career. Then you enter the museum to spend as much time as you like on each exhibit. Starting with the 1960 presidential campaign, the displays immerse you in the era. The galleries hold campaign souvenirs, film of Kennedy debating Richard Nixon

The John F. Kennedy Presidential Library and Museum.

and delivering his inaugural address, a replica of the Oval Office, gifts from foreign dignitaries, letters, documents, and keepsakes. There's a film about the Cuban Missile Crisis and displays on Attorney General Robert F. Kennedy, First Lady Jacqueline Bouvier Kennedy, the civil rights movement, the Peace Corps, the space program, and the Kennedy family. As the tour winds down, you pass through a darkened chamber where news reports of John Kennedy's assassination and funeral play. The final room, the soaring glass-enclosed pavilion that is the heart of the I. M. Pei design, affords a glorious view of the water and the Boston skyline.

More JFK

For details about visiting President Kennedy's birthplace in suburban Brookline, see p. 79.

Columbia Point. www.jfklibrary.org. 🕐 **866/JFK-1960** or 617/514-1600. Admission $12 adults, $10 seniors and students with ID, $9 youths 13–17, free for children 12 and under. Surcharges may apply for special exhibitions. Daily 9am–5pm (last film begins at 3:55pm). Closed Jan 1, Thanksgiving, and Dec 25. T: Red Line to JFK/UMass, then take free shuttle bus (every 20 min.). By car, take Southeast Expressway (I-93/Rte. 3) south to exit 15 (Morrissey Blvd./JFK Library), turn left onto Columbia Rd., and follow signs to free parking lot.

JAMAICA PLAIN

Although it's off the beaten tourist track, Jamaica Plain is worth a trip if you have time. In "JP," you'll find the **Arnold Arboretum** (p. 103) and a vibrant, culturally diverse community. About 10 minutes on foot from the arboretum—walk along Centre Street, the neighborhood's busy main drag, and turn left on Pond Street— is **Jamaica Pond.** The pond and its banks are a community hub that's especially pleasant in good weather, when people walk, run, skate, fish, picnic, and sunbathe. Many of the 19th-century mansions overlooking the pond date to the days

Jamaica Pond.

when families fled the oppressive heat downtown and moved to the "country" for the summer. The Orange Line Forest Hills and Green Street stops are the neighborhood's main transit access points.

BROOKLINE

Like Cambridge, Brookline is a major suburb that gets lumped together with Boston but has its own appeal. Here you'll find a presidential birthplace, the John F. Kennedy National Historic Site, and plenty of good shopping and dining. Another National Park Service site in Brookline is accessible only by prearranged guided tour (tours are free and book up quickly). To visit the **Frederick Law Olmsted National Historic Site,** known as "Fairsted," 99 Warren St. (www. nps.gov/frla; © **617/566-1689**), make a reservation as soon as you start planning your trip to Boston. Check the website for information about ranger-led walking tours of areas designed by Olmsted, the pioneering landscape architect.

John F. Kennedy National Historic Site HISTORIC HOME   The 35th president's birthplace is a modest 1909 house in a quiet residential neighborhood. The president's mother, Rose Fitzgerald Kennedy, collected many of the items on display and helped with the restoration; the current configuration is her recollection of the house's appearance around 1917, when "Jack," her second child, was born. The tour, led by a National Park Service ranger, explores the future president's formative years. If you miss the last guided tour, ask about the self-guided option, which is available in English, French, German, Japanese, and Spanish. Ranger-led walking tours of the neighborhood take place several times each weekend.

83 Beals St. (½ block from Harvard St.). www.nps.gov/jofi. © **617/566-7937.** Admission, house tours, and walking tours free. Late May to Oct Wed–Sun 9:30am–5pm; last house tour at 3pm. Call ahead to double-check hours and tour schedules, especially early and late in the season.

The John F. Kennedy National Historic Site.

Closed Nov to mid-May. T: Green Line C to Coolidge Corner, then walk 4 blocks north on Harvard St. and turn right.

CAMBRIDGE
Harvard Square

Boston and Cambridge are so closely associated that many people believe they're the same place—a notion that both cities' residents and politicians are happy to dispel. Cambridge is a separate city, with a number of appealing attractions and a fun, youthful vibe that sets it apart from its (relatively) more serious neighbor. Cantabrigians are often considered more liberal and better educated than Bostonians—an idea that, if you bring it up, can get you involved in a lively discussion. For help in organizing your time, see "Walking Tour 3: Harvard Square," in chapter 5.

For a good overview, begin at the main Harvard T entrance. Follow my Harvard Square walking tour, or set out on your own. At the **information booth** (© 617/497-1630) in the middle of Harvard Square, at the intersection of Massachusetts Avenue, John F. Kennedy Street, and Brattle Street, trained volunteers dispense maps and brochures and answer questions Monday through Friday from 9am to 5pm, Saturday and Sunday from 1 to 5pm. The website of the **Cambridge Office for Tourism** (www.cambridge-usa.org), which operates the booth, lists organized excursions and features a tour of its own; the narration is available for download for $5.

Whatever you do, spend some time in **Harvard Square.** It's a hodgepodge of college and high school students, professors and instructors, commuters, street performers, and sightseers. Stores and restaurants line all three streets that spread out from the center of the square and the streets that intersect them. If you follow **Brattle Street** to the residential area just outside the square, you'll

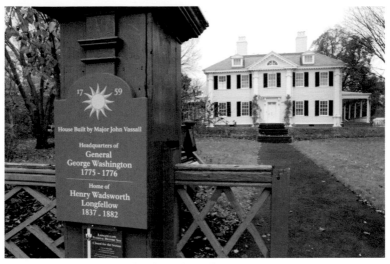

The buildings along "Tory Row" have housed many famous Americans.

arrive at a part of town known as **"Tory Row"** because many residents were loyal to King George during the Revolution.

HARVARD UNIVERSITY

Free student-led tours of the Harvard campus leave from the **Events & Information Center** in Holyoke Center, 1350 Massachusetts Ave. (www.harvard.edu/visitors; ✆ **617/495-1573**). They operate during the school year twice a day on weekdays and once on Saturday, except during vacations, and during the summer four times a day Monday through Saturday. Call or surf ahead for times; reservations aren't necessary. The Information Center is open Monday through Saturday 9am to 5pm and has maps, illustrated booklets, and self-guided walking-tour directions in nine languages, as well as a bulletin board where flyers publicize campus activities.

Harvard Art Museums MUSEUM While two of the three institutions that make up the university's internationally renowned art museum are under renovation, the **Arthur M. Sackler Museum** is showing highlights from all three collections. Special exhibitions complement **Re-View,** an overview of objects drawn from the

You never know what you may see when you visit Harvard Square.

Spending time in the Harvard Art Museums.

quarter-million works in the Harvard Art Museums' impressive repository. You'll see pieces from the modern and contemporary, Asian, and Islamic collections. The **Fogg Museum** and the **Busch-Reisinger Museum** are scheduled to reopen in 2014, when the museums reunite in a single state-of-the-art facility; architect Renzo Piano is leading the renovation and expansion.

485 Broadway. www.harvardartmuseums.org. ☎ **617/495-9400.** Admission $9 adults, $7 seniors, $6 students, free for children 18 and under; free to Massachusetts residents until noon Sat. Tues–Sat 10am–5pm. Closed major holidays. T: Red Line to Harvard, cross Harvard Yard diagonally from the T station and exit onto Quincy St., turn left, and walk to the next corner. Or turn your back on the Coop and follow Massachusetts Ave. to Quincy St., then turn left and walk 1 long block to Broadway.

Harvard Museum of Natural History and Peabody Museum of Archaeology & Ethnology ★ ☺ MUSEUM

These fascinating museums house the university's collections of items and artifacts related to the natural world. Just about everyone finds something interesting here, be it a 42-foot-long prehistoric marine reptile skeleton, the largest turtle shell in the world, an exploration of climate science, or a Native American artifact.

HMNH's best-known collection is the world-famous **Glass Flowers ★★★**, 3,000 models of more than 840 plant species devised between 1887 and 1936 by the German father-and-son team of Leopold and Rudolph Blaschka. You may be skeptical, but it's true: They look real. Children love the museum's **zoological collections ★★**, where dinosaurs share space with preserved and stuffed insects and animals that range in size from butterflies to whales. The evolution exhibition makes a great introduction. Arthropods—insects, centipedes, spiders, and other creepy-crawlies—have their own multimedia installation. The **mineralogical collections** are the most specialized but can be just as compelling as the rest, especially if gemstones hold your interest.

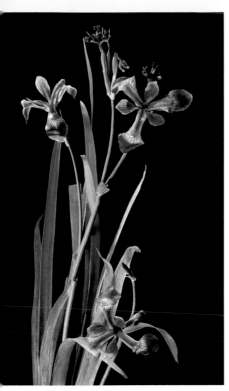
The incredibly lifelike glass flowers at the Harvard Museum of Natural History.

The adjacent **Peabody Museum of Archaeology & Ethnology** ★ boasts the **Hall of the North American Indian,** where 500 artifacts representing 10 cultures are on display. Photographs, textiles, pottery, and art and crafts of all ages and descriptions fill the galleries, spanning six continents and countless years.

One of the university's most popular attractions, this complex is also a world-famous academic resource; interdisciplinary programs and exhibitions tie in elements of all the associated fields. Check ahead for special events, including family programs and lectures by celebrated scientists, during your visit.

Harvard Museum of Natural History: 26 Oxford St. www.hmnh.harvard.edu. ☎ **617/495-3045.** Peabody Museum: 11 Divinity Ave. www.peabody. harvard.edu. ☎ **617/496-1027.** Admission to both $9 adults, $7 seniors and students, $6 children 3–18, free for children 2 and under. Check website for free hours for Massachusetts residents. Daily 9am–5pm. Closed Jan 1, Thanksgiving, Dec 24–25. T: Red Line to Harvard. Cross Harvard Yard, keeping John Harvard statue on right. Exit Harvard Yard; facing the Science Center, bear right as you cross the plaza. First left is Oxford St.

Longfellow House–Washington's Headquarters National Historic Site ★ HISTORIC HOME   This lovely yellow mansion was the longtime home of Henry Wadsworth Longfellow (1807–82). The poet first lived here as a boarder in 1837. When he and Fanny Appleton married, in 1843, her father made the house a wedding present. The furnishings and books in the stately 1759 home are original to Longfellow, who lived here until his death, and to his descendants. During the siege of Boston in 1775–76, the house served as the headquarters of Gen. George Washington, with whom Longfellow was fascinated. On a tour—the only way to see the house—you'll learn about the history of the building and its famous occupants.

105 Brattle St. (at Longfellow Park). www.nps.gov/long. ☎ **617/876-4491.** House tours $3 adults, free for children 15 and under. House June–Oct Wed–Sun 10am–4:30pm; tours at 10:30 and 11:30am, and 1, 2, 3, and 4pm. Closed Nov–May. Gardens and grounds daily dawn to dusk. T: Red Line to Harvard, then 10-min. walk on Brattle St.

Kendall Square

East Cambridge is a high-tech wonderland, which makes perfect sense when you see it on a map—MIT is everywhere.

MASSACHUSETTS INSTITUTE OF TECHNOLOGY (MIT)

The public is welcome at the Massachusetts Institute of Technology campus, 2 miles or so from Harvard Square, across the Charles River from Beacon Hill and the Back Bay. Visit the **Information Office,** 77 Massachusetts Ave. (© **617/ 253-4795**), to take a free guided tour (weekdays at 11am and 3pm) or to pick up a copy of a self-guided walking tour. At the same address, the **Hart Nautical Galleries** (Tues–Fri 10am–5pm) contain ship and engine models that illustrate the development of marine engineering.

MIT's campus is known for its art and architecture. The excellent **outdoor sculpture** collection includes works by Picasso and Alexander Calder, and notable modern buildings include designs by Frank Gehry, Eero Saarinen, and I. M. Pei. Gehry designed the **Stata Center** (http://web.mit.edu/evolving/buildings/stata), a curvilinear landmark on Vassar Street off Main Street. Fumihiko Maki, a Pritzker Prize winner, designed the **Media Lab** complex, 20 Ames St. (at Amherst St.).

To get to MIT, take the MBTA Red Line to Kendall/MIT. The scenic walk from the Back Bay takes you along Massachusetts Avenue over the river straight to the campus. By car from Boston, cross the river at the Museum of Science, Cambridge Street, or Massachusetts Avenue and follow signs to Memorial Drive, where you can usually find parking during the day.

MIT Museum ☺ MUSEUM   Engaging holography displays and robots are the hallmarks of the MIT Museum, where you'll also find works in more conventional media, such as kinetic sculpture. But the focus isn't art—it's the role of science and technology in society, explored through practical applications such as medical devices and gorgeous documents such as historic architectural plans. Little kids aren't the target audience, but middle-schoolers and their older siblings will have a blast with activities and programs geared to them. Be sure to check out the entertaining gift shop.

Tip: The **List Visual Arts Center** (http://web.mit.edu/lvac; © **617/253-4680**), home to MIT's contemporary art collections, is about 5 minutes away— and it's free. Head to the Wiesner Building, 20 Ames St. (btw. Main and Amherst sts.), Tuesday through Sunday from noon to 6pm (until 8pm on Thurs).

265 Massachusetts Ave. (Building N51, at Front St.). http://web.mit.edu/museum. © **617/253-5927.** Admission $9 adults; $4 seniors, students, and children 5–17; free for children 4 and under. Free after 5pm 2nd Fri of each month. Daily 10am–5pm (July–Aug Thurs until 7pm; year-round 2nd Fri of each month until 8pm). Closed major holidays. T: Red Line to Central, then 10-min. walk.

West Cambridge

Largely a posh residential neighborhood, the westernmost part of Cambridge is home to **Mount Auburn Cemetery.** It's accessible by bus and car, but try to leave time for a walk along elegant **Brattle Street.** As long as you're in an exploring mood, note that the banks of the Charles River are nearby.

Mount Auburn Cemetery ★★ CEMETERY   Three important Colonial burying grounds—Granary, King's Chapel, and Copp's Hill—are in Boston (see "The Freedom Trail," below), but the most famous cemetery in the area is in Cambridge.

Mount Auburn Cemetery, the final resting place of many well-known Americans, is also famous simply for existing. Dedicated in 1831, it was the first of the

The Mount Auburn Cemetery.

country's rural, or garden, cemeteries. The establishment of burying places removed from city centers reflected practical and philosophical concerns: Development was encroaching on urban graveyards, and the ideas associated with Transcendentalism and the Greek revival gave communing with nature precedence over organized religion. Since the day it opened, Mount Auburn has been a popular place to retreat and reflect.

Visitors to this National Historic Landmark find history and horticulture coexisting with celebrity. The graves of Henry Wadsworth Longfellow, Oliver Wendell Holmes, Julia Ward Howe, and Mary Baker Eddy are here, as are those of Charles Bulfinch, James Russell Lowell, Winslow Homer, Transcendentalist leader Margaret Fuller, and abolitionist Charles Sumner. In season you'll see gorgeous flowering trees and shrubs (the Massachusetts Horticultural Society had a hand in the design).

Stop at the **visitor center** in Story Chapel (daily 9am–4pm Apr–Oct; closed Sun Nov–Mar and year-round during burials) for an overview and a look at the changing exhibits, or ask at the office or front gate for brochures and a map. You can rent an audio tour ($7; a $15 deposit is required) and listen in your car or on a portable player; there's a 60-minute driving tour and two 75-minute walking tours. Note that animals and recreational activities such as jogging, biking, and picnicking are not allowed.

The **Friends of Mount Auburn Cemetery** conducts workshops and lectures and coordinates walking tours; call the main number for topics, schedules, and fees.

580 Mount Auburn St. (at Brattle St.). www.mountauburn.org. ☏ **617/547-7105.** Free admission. May–Sept daily 8am–7pm; Oct–Apr daily 8am–5pm (call ahead in spring and fall to check closing time). T: Red Line to Harvard, then 25-min. walk on Brattle St. or bus no. 71 or 73. By car (5 min.) or on foot, take Mount Auburn St. or Brattle St. west from Harvard Square; just after they intersect, gate is on the left.

The Harborwalk and Walk to the Sea

The **Harborwalk** ★★ is a path that traces 47 miles of Boston's shoreline, allowing public access to multimillion-dollar views of the water. In theory, it extends from East Boston to Dorchester; in practice, the pathway isn't continuous. Distinctive royal blue signs with a white logo and text point the way along the Harborwalk, which is an ideal route to take from downtown to the Institute of Contemporary Art, on the South Boston waterfront. The ambitious project has been in the works since 1984 and is more than three-quarters complete. Learn more by visiting the website, **www.boston harborwalk.com**, which features a map and a free downloadable audio tour.

Intersecting the Harborwalk is the 1-mile **Norman B. Leventhal Walk to the Sea** ★ (www.walktothesea.com), which begins on Beacon Street in front of the State House and ends at the tip of Long Wharf. It tracks 4 centuries of Boston history with compelling narration on freestanding trail markers; visit the website to download a map and get more information. The Walk to the Sea makes an excellent compromise if you don't have the time or energy to tackle the whole Freedom Trail or Black Heritage Trail, both of which it intersects.

THE FREEDOM TRAIL

A line of red paint or red brick on the sidewalk, the 2.5-mile **Freedom Trail** ★★★ links 16 historic sites, many of them associated with the Revolution and the early days of the United States. The route cuts across downtown and the North End on the way to Charlestown. Markers identify the stops, and plaques point the way from one to the next. For a map of the Freedom Trail, see the inside front cover of this book.

This section lists the stops on the trail in the customary order, from Boston Common to the Bunker Hill Monument. It's important to remember that this is the *suggested* route, laid out after a local journalist cooked up the idea in 1958. Nobody's checking on you. You don't have to visit every stop or even go in order—you can skip around, start in Charlestown and work backward, visit different sights on different days, or even omit some sights. Here's a suggestion: If you find yourself sighing and saying "should" a lot, take a break. That goes double if you're traveling with children.

A hard-core history fiend who peers at every artifact and reads every plaque can easily spend 4 hours along the trail. A family with restless kids will probably appreciate the enforced efficiency of a free 90-minute ranger-led tour. Tours leave from the **Boston National Historical Park Visitor Center,** inside Faneuil Hall, Congress Street at North Street (www.nps.gov/bost; ✆ **617/242-5642**).

The excursions cover the "heart" of the trail, from the Old South Meeting House to the Old North Church. From Patriots' Day through late June and September through November, they begin weekends at 10am and 2pm, weekdays at 2pm only. From late June through August, starting times are daily at 10 and 11am and 2pm. The first-come, first-served tours are limited to 30 people (rangers distribute stickers starting 30 min. before tour time) and not available in bad weather. No tours December through mid-April.

Informative costumed guides lead visitors along the historic Freedom Trail.

The nonprofit **Freedom Trail Foundation** (www.thefreedomtrail.org; ✆ 617/357-8300) is an excellent resource as you plan your visit. The foundation's costumed **Freedom Trail Players** lead 90-minute tours of the trail ($13 adults, $11 seniors and students, $7 children 6–12, with a discount for buying online). Buy tickets online, allowing time to explore the interactive website. It lists a plethora of other activities, including a pub crawl (participants must be 21 or older) and holiday stroll.

Tip: The best time to start on the trail is in the morning. During the summer and fall, aim for a weekday if possible. Try not to set out later than midafternoon, because attractions will be closing and you'll run into the evening rush hour.

Boston Common PARK/GARDEN   In 1634, when their settlement was just 4 years old, the town fathers paid the Rev. William Blackstone £30 for this property. In 1640 it was set aside as common land. The 45 or so acres of the country's oldest public park have served as a cow pasture, a military camp, and the site of hangings, protest marches, and visits by dignitaries. The **Frog Pond** makes a pleasant spot to splash around in the summer and skate in the winter. At the Boylston Street side of the Common is the **Central Burying Ground,** where you can see the grave of famed portraitist Gilbert Stuart. There's also a bandstand where you might take in a free concert or play, and many beautiful shade trees.

Although the city refurbished it recently, the Common still seems run-down (especially compared to the gorgeous Public Garden), but it buzzes with activity all day. You might see a demonstration, a musical performance, a picnic lunch—almost anything other than a cow. Cows have been banned since 1830, which seems to be one of the few events related to the Common that isn't commemorated with a plaque.

One of the loveliest markers is on this route; head up the hill inside the fence, walking parallel to Park Street. At Beacon Street is the **Shaw Memorial ★★★**, designed by Augustus Saint-Gaudens to celebrate the deeds

Boston Common.

(indeed, the very existence) of Col. Robert Gould Shaw and the Union Army's **54th Massachusetts Colored Regiment,** who fought in the Civil War. You might remember the story of the first American army unit made up of free black soldiers from the movie *Glory*.

To continue on the Freedom Trail: Cross Beacon Street.

Btw. Beacon, Park, Tremont, Boylston, and Charles sts. Visitor information center: 148 Tremont St. www.bostonusa.com. *C* **888/733-2678** or 617/536-4100. Mon–Fri 8:30am–5pm; Sat 9am–5pm. Center closed Sun. T: Green or Red Line to Park St.

Massachusetts State House GOVERNMENT BUILDING   Boston is one of the only American cities where a building whose cornerstone was laid in 1795 (by Gov. Samuel Adams) can be the "new" anything. Nevertheless, this is the new State House, as opposed to the Old State House (see below). The great Federal-era architect Charles Bulfinch designed the central building of the state capitol, and in 1802 copper sheathing manufactured by Paul Revere replaced the shingles on the landmark dome. Gold leaf now covers the dome; during World War II blackouts, it was painted black. The state legislature, or Massachusetts General Court, meets here. The House of Representatives congregates under a wooden fish, the **Sacred Cod,** as a reminder of the importance of fishing to the local economy. Take a self-guided tour, or call ahead to schedule a conducted tour.

Whether or not you go inside, be sure to study some of the many statues outside. Subjects range from **Mary Dyer,** a Quaker hanged on the Common in 1660 for refusing to abandon her religious beliefs, to President **John F. Kennedy.** The 60-foot monument at the rear (off Bowdoin St.) illustrates Beacon Hill's original height, before the top was hacked off to use in 19th-century landfill projects.

To continue on the Freedom Trail: Walk down Park Street (which Bulfinch laid out in 1804) to Tremont Street.

The "new" Massachusetts State House.

Beacon St. at Park St. www.malegislature.gov/Engage/StateHouseTours. $\textcircled{C}$ **617/727-3676.** Mon–Fri 9am–5pm. Free tours Mon–Fri 10am–3:30pm. T: Green or Red Line to Park St., or Blue Line to Bowdoin (weekdays only).

Park Street Church CHURCH Famed author Henry James called this 1809 structure with a 217-foot steeple "the most interesting mass of bricks and mortar in America." The church has accumulated an impressive number of firsts: The first Protestant missionaries to Hawaii left from here in 1819; the prominent abolitionist William Lloyd Garrison gave his first antislavery speech here on July 4, 1829; and "America" ("My Country 'Tis of Thee") was first sung here on July 4, 1831. You're standing on **"Brimstone Corner,"** named either for the passion of the Congregational ministers who declaimed from the pulpit or for the fact that gunpowder (made from brimstone) was stored in the basement during the War of 1812. This was part of the site of a huge granary (grain storehouse) that became a public building after the Revolutionary War. In the 1790s, the sails for the USS *Constitution* ("Old Ironsides") were manufactured in that building.

To continue on the Freedom Trail: Walk away from the Common on Tremont Street.

Listen Up: The Audio Freedom Trail

A 2-hour tour narrative commissioned by the **Freedom Trail Foundation** (www.thefreedomtrail.org; $\textcircled{C}$ **617/357-8300**) includes interviews, sound effects, and music that help bring the sites to life. "Walk Into History" costs $15 (credit cards only); buy it as an MP3 download, or rent a handheld digital audio player, for use with or without headphones, that can be picked up at the Boston Common Visitor Center, 148 Tremont St. (and dropped off there or at several other locations).

1 Park St. www.parkstreet.org/tours. $\textcircled{C}$ **617/523-3383.** Tours late June to Aug Tues–Fri 9am–4pm, Sat 9am–3pm, and by appointment. Sun services year-round 8:30 and 11am, and 4pm. T: Green or Red Line to Park St.

Granary Burying Ground ★ CEMETERY This graveyard, established in 1660, was once part of Boston Common. You'll see the graves of patriots **Samuel Adams, Paul Revere, John Hancock,** and **James Otis;** merchant **Peter Faneuil;** and Benjamin Franklin's parents. Also buried here are the victims of the **Boston Massacre**

(see below) and the wife of Isaac Vergoose, who is believed to be **"Mother Goose"** of nursery rhyme fame. Note that gravestone rubbing, however tempting, is illegal in Boston's historic cemeteries.

To continue on the Freedom Trail: Turn left as you leave the cemetery and continue 1½ blocks on Tremont Street. En route to King's Chapel, you'll pass a 21st-century phenomenon: Suffolk University's **Studio 73,** in the lobby of 73 Tremont St. and visible from the sidewalk. Local news station NECN conducts live interviews in the high-definition TV facility, which it shares with Suffolk broadcast journalism and communications students.

Tremont St. at Bromfield St. Daily 9am–5pm (until 3pm in winter). T: Green or Red Line to Park St.

King's Chapel and Burying Ground CHURCH/CEMETERY

Architect Peter Harrison sent the plans for this Georgian-style building from Newport, Rhode Island, in 1749. Rather than replacing the existing wooden chapel, the granite edifice was

Park Street Church.

constructed around it. Completed in 1754, it was the first Anglican church in Boston. George III sent gifts, as did Queen Anne and William and Mary, who presented the communion table and chancel tablets (still in use today) before the church was even built. The Puritan colonists had little use for the royal religion; after the Revolution, this became the first Unitarian church in the new nation. Today, the church conducts Unitarian Universalist services using the Anglican Book of Common Prayer. It schedules public concerts (p. 226) every Tuesday at 12:15pm and some Sundays at 5pm.

The **burying ground** ★★, on Tremont Street, is the oldest in the city; it dates to 1630, 56 years before the congregation was organized. Among the scary Colonial headstones (winged skulls are a popular decoration) are the graves of **John Winthrop,** the first governor of the Massachusetts Bay Colony; **William Dawes,** who rode with Paul Revere; **Elizabeth Pain,** the reputed model for Hester Prynne in Nathaniel Hawthorne's novel *The Scarlet Letter;* and **Mary Chilton,** the first female colonist to step ashore on Plymouth Rock.

To continue on the Freedom Trail: Follow the trail back along Tremont Street and turn left onto School Street.

58 Tremont St. www.kings-chapel.org. (C) **617/523-1749.** Chapel: Summer Sun 1:30–4pm; Mon and Thurs–Sat 10am–4pm; Tues–Wed 10–11:15am and 1:30–4pm. Year-round Sat 10am–4pm. Check website for up-to-date spring and fall hours. Closed to casual tourists during religious

The Granary Burying Ground, final resting place of many famous New Englanders.

services. $2 donation suggested. Services Sun 11am, Wed 12:15pm. Burying ground: Daily 8am–5:30pm (until 3pm in winter). T: Green or Blue Line to Government Center.

First Public School/Benjamin Franklin Statue MONUMENT/MEMORIAL A colorful folk-art **mosaic** embedded in the sidewalk marks the site of the first public school in the country. Founded in 1634, 2 years before Harvard College, the school educated Samuel Adams, Benjamin Franklin, John Hancock,

King's Chapel and Burying Ground.

and Cotton Mather. The original building (1645) was demolished to make way for the expansion of King's Chapel, and the school moved across the street. Other alumni include Charles Bulfinch, Ralph Waldo Emerson, George Santayana, Arthur Fiedler, and Leonard Bernstein. Now called Boston Latin School, the prestigious institution later moved to the Fenway neighborhood and started admitting girls.

Behind the fence in the courtyard to your left is the **Benjamin Franklin statue,** the first portrait statue erected in Boston (1856). Franklin was born in Boston in 1706 and was apprenticed to his half-brother James, a printer, but they fought constantly. In 1723, Benjamin ran away to Philadelphia. Plaques on the base of the statue describe Franklin's numerous accomplishments. The lovely granite Second

LEFT: **The Benjamin Franklin statue near the site of the first public school.** RIGHT: **The Old Corner Bookstore was a key component of America's early literary and publishing scene.**

Empire–style building behind the statue is **Old City Hall** (1865), designed by Arthur Gilman (who laid out the Back Bay) and Gridley J. F. Bryant. The administration moved to Government Center in 1969, and the building now houses commercial tenants.

To continue on the Freedom Trail: Follow School Street to Washington Street.

School St. at City Hall Ave. (btw. Tremont and Washington sts.). T: Blue or Orange Line to State.

Old Corner Bookstore Building ARCHITECTURE Built in 1718, this building stands on a plot of land that was once home to the religious reformer Anne Hutchinson, who was excommunicated and expelled from Boston in 1638 for heresy. In the 19th century, the brick building held the publishing house of Ticknor & Fields, which effectively made this the literary center of America. Publisher James Fields, known as "Jamie," counted among his friends Henry Wadsworth Longfellow, James Russell Lowell, Henry David Thoreau, Ralph Waldo Emerson, Nathaniel Hawthorne, and Harriet Beecher Stowe.

To continue on the Freedom Trail: Turn right and walk 1 block.

3 School St. T: Blue or Orange Line to State.

Old South Meeting House ★ HISTORIC SITE Look for the beautifully restored clock tower that tops this religious and political gathering place, best known as the site of an important event that led to the Revolution. On December 16, 1773, a restive crowd of several thousand, too big to fit into Faneuil Hall, gathered here. They were waiting for word from the governor about whether three ships full of tea—priced to undercut the cost of smuggled tea and to force the colonists to trade with merchants approved by the Crown—would be sent back to England from Boston. The ships were not, and revolutionaries haphazardly disguised as Mohawks cast the tea into the harbor. The meetinghouse

The Old South Meeting House.

commemorates that uprising, the **Boston Tea Party.** You can even see a vial of the tea.

Originally built in 1669 and replaced by the current structure in 1729, the building underwent extensive renovations in the 1990s. In 1872, a devastating fire that destroyed most of downtown stopped at Old South, a phenomenon considered evidence of the building's power. The exhibit **Voices of Protest** tells the story of the events that unfolded here.

The meetinghouse frequently schedules speeches, readings, panel discussions, and children's activities, often with a Colonial theme. Each December, it stages a reenactment of the debate that led to the Tea Party—it's especially fun for kids, who can participate in the heated debate. Check ahead for schedules.

To continue on the Freedom Trail: Exit through the gift shop and look across Milk Street to see **Benjamin Franklin's birthplace.** In a little house at 17 Milk St., Franklin was born in 1706, the 15th child of Josiah Franklin. The house is long gone, but look across at the second floor of what's now 1 Milk St. When the building went up after the Great Fire of 1872, the architect guaranteed that the Founding Father wouldn't be forgotten: A bust and the words BIRTHPLACE OF FRANKLIN adorn the facade.

Now backtrack on Washington Street (passing Spring Lane, one of the first streets in Boston and originally the site of a real spring) and follow it to State Street.

310 Washington St. www.osmh.org. ✆ **617/482-6439.** Admission $6 adults, $5 seniors and students with ID, $1 children 6–18, free for children 5 and under. Freedom Trail ticket (with Old State House and Paul Revere House) $13 adults, $3 children. Daily Apr–Oct 9:30am–5pm; Nov–Mar 10am–4pm. Closed Jan 1, Thanksgiving, Dec 24–25. T: Blue or Orange Line to State St.

Old State House Museum ★ MUSEUM   Built in 1713, this brick structure served as the seat of Colonial government before the Revolution and as the state capitol until 1798. From its balcony, the Declaration of Independence was first read to Bostonians on July 18, 1776. In 1789, President George Washington reviewed a parade from here. The exterior decorations are particularly interesting—the clock was installed in place of a sundial, and the gilded lion and unicorn are reproductions of the original symbols of British rule that were ripped from the facade and burned the day the Declaration of Independence was read.

LEFT: **The Old State House Museum.** RIGHT: **The site of the Boston Massacre.**

Inside is the **Bostonian Society's museum** ★ of the city's history. The society was founded in 1881 to save this building, which was badly deteriorated and, incredibly, about to be sold and shipped to Chicago. Two floors of exhibits focus on the role of the city and the building in the Revolution and the events that led to it—a Paul Revere print depicting the Boston Massacre and tea from the Boston Tea Party are on view—but this experience is hardly a static history lesson. A multimedia presentation explains the Boston Massacre, an interactive display helps recount the story of the building, and changing exhibits focus on other topics, such as the Great Fire of 1872, using vintage photographs and artifacts from the society's collections. Explore on your own or take a 20-minute guided tour; check the website for times.

To continue on the Freedom Trail: Leave the building, turn left, and walk half a block.

206 Washington St. www.bostonhistory.org. ✆ **617/720-1713,** ext. 21. Admission $7.50 adults, $6 seniors and students, $3 children 6–18, free for children 5 and under. Freedom Trail ticket (with Old South Meeting House and Paul Revere House) $13 adults, $3 children. July–Aug daily

 A Revolutionary App

The Bostonian Society, which runs the Old State House Museum, collaborated with Wellesley College on **Mapping Revolutionary Boston,** a website and free iPhone app that delves deep into the events of the 1760s and 1770s. It's a brilliant use of mapping software, allowing visitors (and residents) to learn more about the events that led to the Revolutionary War even as they explore the modern city. Download it from the App Store or visit www.revolutionaryboston.org.

Faneuil Hall.

9am–6pm; Feb–June and Sept–Dec daily 9am–5pm; Jan daily 9am–4pm. Closed Jan 1, first week of Feb, Thanksgiving, Dec 25. T: Blue or Orange Line to State.

Boston Massacre Site MONUMENT/MEMORIAL A ring of cobblestones marks the location of the skirmish that helped consolidate the spirit of rebellion in the colonies. On March 5, 1770, angered at the presence of royal troops in Boston, colonists threw snowballs, garbage, rocks, and other debris at a group of redcoats. The soldiers panicked and fired into the crowd, killing five men. Their graves, including that of Crispus Attucks, the first black man to die in the Revolution, are in the Granary Burying Ground.

To continue on the Freedom Trail: Turn left onto Congress Street and walk down the hill, covering 1 long block. Faneuil Hall will be on your right.

State St. at Devonshire St. T: Blue or Orange Line to State.

Faneuil Hall ★ HISTORIC SITE Built in 1742 (and enlarged using a Charles Bulfinch design in 1805), this building was a gift to Boston from prosperous merchant Peter Faneuil. This "Cradle of Liberty" rang with speeches by orators such as Samuel Adams—whose statue stands outside the Congress Street entrance—in the years leading to the Revolution. Abolitionists, temperance advocates, and suffragists also used the hall as a pulpit. The upstairs is still a public meeting and concert hall. Downstairs is the visitor center for the downtown part of the **Boston National Historical Park.** It has exhibits focusing on Boston history and—in keeping with the nearly 3-century history of retail in this space—a bookstore.

National Park Service rangers give **free historical talks** every half-hour from 9am to 5pm in the second-floor auditorium. On the top floor is a small museum that houses the weapons collection and historical exhibits of the **Ancient and Honorable Artillery Company of Massachusetts.**

Trail Mix

Faneuil Hall Marketplace is a great spot for a break. Time your walk right, and it can be the starting point of a picnic lunch. Visit the **Quincy Market** food court for takeout, then head across the Rose Kennedy Greenway toward the water. **Christopher Columbus Waterfront Park** (pictured), on the left-hand side of the Marriott Long Wharf hotel, is a popular place to picnic, watch the action at the marina, and play in the playground. On this section of the Greenway, a **carousel** operates in the summer.

Back on the trail, as you walk from Faneuil Hall to the Paul Revere House, you'll find yourself in the midst of **Haymarket.** On Friday and Saturday, the bustling open-air market on North, Blackstone, and Hanover streets consists of stalls piled high with produce, seafood, and flowers. Shoppers aren't allowed to touch anything they haven't bought, a rule you might learn

from a hollering vendor or a cutthroat customer. It's a great scene and a favorite with photographers.

To continue on the Freedom Trail: Leave Faneuil Hall, cross North Street, and follow the trail through the "Blackstone Block." These buildings, among the oldest in the city, give a sense of the scale of 18th- and 19th-century Boston. In the park at the corner of North and Union streets are two sculptures of legendary Boston mayor (and Congressman, and federal prisoner) **James Michael Curley,** the inspiration for the protagonist of Edwin O'Connor's *The Last Hurrah.* Beyond the sculptures, you'll see six tall glass columns arranged parallel to Union Street. Pause here.

Dock Sq. (Congress St. and North St.). www.nps.gov/bost. (C) **617/242-5642.** Free admission. Daily 9am–5pm; no public access during special events. T: Green or Blue Line to Government Center, or Orange Line to Haymarket.

The New England Holocaust Memorial ★★ MONUMENT/MEMORIAL

Erected in 1995, these six glass towers designed by Stanley Saitowitz spring up in the midst of attractions that celebrate freedom, reminding us of the consequences of a world without it. The pattern on the glass, which at first appears merely decorative, is actually six million random numbers, one for each Jew who died during the Holocaust. As you pass through, pause to read the inscriptions.

To continue on the Freedom Trail: Follow Hanover Street across the Rose Kennedy Greenway to reach the North End, which begins at Cross Street. Take Hanover Street 1 block to Richmond Street, passing the post office on your right. Turn right, go 1 block, and turn left.

The New England Holocaust Memorial.

Union St. btw. North and Hanover sts. www.nehm.org. ✆ **617/457-8698.** T: Orange or Green Line to Haymarket.

Paul Revere House ★★★ HISTORIC HOME   One of the most pleasant stops on the Freedom Trail, this two-and-a-half-story wood structure presents history on a human scale. Revere (1734–1818) was living here when he set out for Lexington on April 18, 1775, a feat immortalized in Henry Wadsworth Long-fellow's poem "Paul Revere's Ride" ("Listen my children and you shall hear / Of the midnight ride of Paul Revere"). The house holds neatly arranged and identi-fied 17th- and 18th-century furnishings and artifacts, including the famous Revere silver, considered some of the finest anywhere. The oldest house in down-town Boston, it was built around 1680, bought by Revere in 1770, and put to a number of uses before being turned into a museum in 1908.

The thought-provoking tour is self-guided, with staff members around in case you have questions. The format allows you to linger on the artifacts that hold your interest. Revere and his two wives had a total of 16 children—he called them "my lambs"—and he supported the family with a thriving silversmith's trade. At his home, you'll get a good sense of the risks he took in the run-up to the Revolutionary War. Across the courtyard is the home of Revere's Hichborn cous-ins, the **Pierce/Hichborn House ★.** The 1711 Georgian-style home is a rare example of 18th-century middle-class architecture. It's suitably furnished and shown only by guided tour (usually twice a day at busy times). Contact the Paul Revere House for schedules and reservations.

A new **Education and Visitor Center,** in an 1835 building adjoining the house, should be open by the time you visit. The center will give visitors with dis-abilities access to the second floor of the Revere House.

Before you leave North Square, look across the cobblestone plaza at **Sacred Heart Church.** It was established in 1833 as the Seamen's Bethel, a church that ministered to the mariners who frequented the area. Wharves ran

Paul Revere's house.

up almost this far in Colonial days; in the 19th century, this was a notorious red-light district.

To continue on the Freedom Trail: The trail leaves the square on Prince Street and runs along Hanover Street past Clark Street. Before turning onto Prince Street, take a few steps down Garden Court Street and look for no. 4, on the right. The private residence was the birthplace of Rose Fitzgerald, later Rose Kennedy, President John F. Kennedy's mother.

19 North Sq. www.paulreverehouse.org. ℂ **617/523-2338.** Admission $3.50 adults, $3 seniors and students, $1 children 5–17, free for children 4 and under. Freedom Trail ticket (with Old South Meeting House and Old State House) $13 adults, $3 children. Apr 15–Oct daily 9:30am–5:15pm; Apr 1–14 and Nov–Dec daily 9:30am–4:15pm; Jan–Mar Tues–Sun 9:30am–4:15pm. Closed Jan 1, Thanksgiving, and Dec 25. T: Green or Orange Line to Haymarket, Blue Line to Aquarium, or Green or Blue Line to Government Center.

⊙ Church Chat

One surefire way to announce yourself as an out-of-towner is to pause on Hanover Street between Prince and Fleet streets and proclaim that you see the Old North Church. The first house of worship you see is **St. Stephen's,** the only Charles Bulfinch–designed church still standing in Boston. St. Stephen's is perhaps best known as the church where **Rose Fitzgerald Kennedy,** President John F. Kennedy's mother, was baptized (in 1890), and where her funeral took place

(in 1995). The church was Unitarian when it was dedicated in 1804. The next year, the congregation bought a bell from Paul Revere's foundry for $800; it's still in use. The building's design is a paragon of Federal-style symmetry. St. Stephen's became Roman Catholic in 1862. During refurbishment in 1964 and 1965, it regained its original appearance, with clear glass windows, white walls, and gilded organ pipes. It's one of the plainest Catholic churches you'll ever see.

The Paul Revere statue in James Rego Square.

James Rego Square (Paul Revere Mall) PARK/GARDEN A pleasant little brick-paved park also known as "the Prado," the mall holds a famous equestrian statue of Paul Revere—a great photo op. Take time to read some of the **tablets** ★ on the left-hand wall that describe famous people and places in the history of the North End.

To continue on the Freedom Trail: Walk around the fountain and continue to Salem Street, heading toward the steeple of the Old North Church.

Hanover St. at Clark St. T: Green or Orange Line to Haymarket.

Old North Church ★ CHURCH Look up! In this building's original steeple, sexton Robert Newman hung two lanterns on the night of April 18, 1775, to signal Paul Revere that British troops were setting out for Lexington and Concord in boats across the Charles River, not on foot. We know that part of the story in Longfellow's words: "One if by land, and two if by sea." (***Trivia bonus:*** Newman was a great-grandson of George Burroughs, one of the victims of the Salem witch trials of 1692.)

Officially named Christ Church, this is the oldest church building in Boston (1723). The design is in the style of Sir Christopher Wren. The 190-foot spire, long a reference point for sailors, appears on navigational charts to this day.

Members of the Revere family attended this church; their plaque is on pew 54. Famous visitors have included presidents James Monroe, Theodore Roosevelt, Calvin Coolidge, Franklin D. Roosevelt, and Gerald R. Ford; and Queen Elizabeth II. Markers and plaques appear throughout; note the bust of George Washington, reputedly the first memorial to the first president. The **gardens** ★ on the north side of the church (dotted with more plaques) are open to the public. On the south side of the church, volunteers maintain an 18th-century garden.

Free presentations that introduce the self-guided tour begin periodically during open hours year-round. For a more complete look at the church, take a **Behind the Scenes tour** ($8 adults, $6 seniors and students, $5 children 16 and under). The tour includes visits to the steeple and the crypt. It's offered on weekends in June, daily from July through October and from December 25 through January 1, and the rest of the year by appointment. Tickets are available in the gift shop.

To continue on the Freedom Trail: Cross Salem Street onto Hull Street and walk uphill toward Copp's Hill Burying Ground. On the left you'll pass 44

LEFT: **The Old North Church (of "one if by land, two if by sea" fame).** RIGHT: **Copp's Hill Burying Ground.**

Hull St., a fine example of the phenomenon known as the "spite house." The 10-foot-wide private residence is the narrowest house in Boston.

193 Salem St. www.oldnorth.com. ℭ **617/523-6676.** Admission $3 voluntary donation. Jan–Feb Tues–Sun 10am–4pm; Mar–May daily 9am–5pm; June–Oct daily 9am–6pm; Nov–Dec daily 9:30am–4:30pm. Closed to visitors Thanksgiving, Dec 25. Services (Episcopal) Sun 9 and 11am, Thurs 6pm. T: Orange or Green Line to Haymarket.

Copp's Hill Burying Ground ★ CEMETERY   The second-oldest cemetery (1659) in the city is the burial place of Cotton Mather and his family, Robert Newman, and Prince Hall. Hall, a prominent member of the free black community that occupied the north slope of the hill in Colonial times, fought at Bunker Hill and established the first black Masonic lodge. The highest point in the North End, Copp's Hill was the site of a windmill and of the British batteries that destroyed the village of Charlestown during the Battle of Bunker Hill on June 17, 1775. Charlestown is clearly visible (look for the masts of the USS *Constitution*) across the Inner Harbor. No gravestone rubbing is allowed.

To continue on the Freedom Trail: Follow Hull Street down the hill to Commercial Street (be careful crossing Commercial at the dangerous intersection with Hull) and follow the trail to North Washington Street, then across the bridge to Charlestown. Signs and the trail lead to the Charlestown Navy Yard.

Off Hull St. near Snowhill St. Daily 9am–5pm (until 3pm in winter). T: Green or Orange Line to North Station.

USS Constitution ★★ ☺ HISTORIC SITE   **"Old Ironsides,"** one of the U.S. Navy's six original frigates, never lost a battle. The 30-minute tour, led by an active-duty sailor in an 1812 dress uniform, is an excellent introduction to an era when the future of the new nation was anything but certain. The ship was constructed in the North End from 1794 to 1797 at a cost of $302,718, using bolts, spikes, and other fittings from Paul Revere's foundry. As the United States built its naval and military reputation, the *Constitution* played a key role, battling French privateers and Barbary pirates, repelling the British fleet during the War of 1812, participating in 33 engagements, and capturing 20 vessels. The frigate earned its nickname during a battle on August 19, 1812, when shots from HMS *Guerriere* bounced off its thick oak hull as if it were iron.

Retired from combat in 1815, the *Constitution* was rescued from destruction when Oliver Wendell Holmes's poem "Old Ironsides" launched a preservation movement in 1830. The frigate was completely overhauled for its bicentennial in 1997, when it sailed under its own power for the first time since 1881, drawing international attention. Tugs tow the *Constitution* into the harbor every **Fourth of July** for its celebratory "turnaround cruise," and for occasional events around the harbor. If you see TV helicopters circling over the water, wander down and take a look.

Adjacent to the ship in Building 5, National Park Service rangers staff the **Navy Yard Visitor Center** (www.nps.gov/bost; ℂ 617/242-5601) and give free 1-hour guided tours of the base.

To continue on the Freedom Trail: Walk straight ahead to the museum entrance.

Charlestown Navy Yard. www.history.navy.mil/ussconstitution. ℂ **617/242-7511.** Free tours. Apr–Sept Tues–Sun 10am–6pm; Oct Tues–Sun 10am–4pm; Nov–Mar Thurs–Sun 10am–4pm. Year-round tours every half-hour until 30 min. before closing. Closed Jan 1, Presidents' Day, Thanksgiving, and Dec 25. T: Ferry from Long Wharf (Blue Line to Aquarium), or Green or Orange Line to North Station, then a 10-min. walk.

USS Constitution Museum ★ ☺ ✦ MUSEUM   Just across from the vessel, the museum features engaging participatory exhibits that allow visitors to hoist a sail, fire a cannon, swing in a hammock, and learn about life onboard the ship during the War of 1812. The interactive computer displays and naval artifacts appeal to visitors of all ages. A favorite exhibit looks at the frigate from a compelling and relevant perspective: that of a sailor. The museum's collections include more than 3,000 items, arranged and interpreted to put them in context, and staff members and volunteers conduct interesting talks (I've seen one every time I've been in the galleries) that expand on the exhibits. In February and March, special displays and activities focus on ship models.

To continue on the Freedom Trail: Follow the trail up Constitution Road, crossing Chelsea Street, and continue to the Bunker Hill Monument. A more interesting, slightly longer route runs from Chelsea Street and Rutherford Avenue (back where you entered Charlestown) across City Square Park and up Main Street to Monument Street.

Off First Ave., Charlestown Navy Yard. www.ussconstitutionmuseum.org. ℂ **617/426-1812.** Free admission; suggested donation $4 adults, $2 children. Apr–Oct daily 9am–6pm; Nov–Mar daily 10am–5pm. Closed Jan 1, Thanksgiving, and Dec 25. T: Ferry from Long Wharf (Blue Line to Aquarium), or Green or Orange Line to North Station, then a 10-min. walk.

Bunker Hill Monument MONUMENT/MEMORIAL   The 221-foot granite obelisk, a landmark that's visible from miles away, honors the memory of the colonists who died in the Battle of Bunker Hill on June 17, 1775. The rebels lost the battle, but nearly half the British troops were killed or wounded, a loss that contributed to their leaders' decision to abandon Boston 9 months later. The Marquis de

The Bunker Hill Monument.

Lafayette, the celebrated hero of the American and French revolutions, helped lay the monument's cornerstone in 1825. He is buried in Paris under soil taken from the hill. A punishing flight of 294 steps—imagine your worst Stairmaster experience, then imagine not being able to quit in the middle—leads to the top of the monument. It's not a can't-miss experience unless you're traveling with children you'd like to tire out. There's no elevator, and although the views of the harbor and the Zakim–Bunker Hill Bridge are good, the windows are quite small.

Across the street is the excellent **Battle of Bunker Hill Museum ★**. The small ranger-staffed museum, at the corner where Monument Avenue enters Monument Square, holds dioramas, a cyclorama mural, and other exhibits about the battle and the community.

Monument Sq., Charlestown. www.nps.gov/bost. 🕿 **617/242-5641.** Free admission. Monument daily 9am–4:30pm (until 5:30pm July–Aug). Museum daily 9am–5pm (until 6pm July–Aug). T: Orange Line to Community College, 10-min. walk.

 Trailing Off

If you don't feel like retracing your steps at the end of the Freedom Trail, you have two public-transit options. Return to the Charlestown Navy Yard for the **ferry** to Long Wharf, which leaves every half-hour from 6:45am to 8:15pm on weekdays (every 15 min. 6:45–9:15am and 3:45–6:45pm), and every half-hour on the quarter-hour from 10:15am to 6:15pm on weekends. The 10-minute trip costs $2 (or show your 7-day LinkPass), and the dock is an easy walk from "Old Ironsides." Alternatively, walk to the foot of the hill; on Main Street, take **bus no. 92 or 93** toward Haymarket (Green or Orange Line).

PARKS & GARDENS

Green space is an important part of Boston's appeal, and the public parks are known for their beauty. The world-famous **Emerald Necklace,** Frederick Law Olmsted's vision for a loop of green spaces, runs through the city.

The best-known park, for good reason, is the spectacular **Public Garden ★★★**, bordered by Arlington, Boylston, Charles, and Beacon streets. Something lovely is in bloom at the country's first botanical garden at least half the year. The spring flowers are particularly impressive, especially if your visit happens to coincide with the first really warm days of the year. It's hard not to enjoy yourself when everyone around you seems ecstatic just to be seeing the sun.

For many Bostonians, the official beginning of spring coincides with the return of the **Swan Boats ★★** (www.swanboats.com; ℂ **617/522-1966**). The pedal-powered vessels—the attendants pedal, not the passengers—plunge into the lagoon on the Saturday before Patriots' Day, the third Monday of April. The surrounding greenery and placid water help lend a 19th-century aura to the attraction, which the Paget family has operated since 1877. Although the Swan Boats don't move fast, they will transport you. They operate daily from 10am to 5pm in the summer, daily from 10am to 4pm in the spring, and weekdays noon to 4pm and weekends 10am to 4pm from the day after Labor Day to mid-September. The cost for the 15-minute ride is $2.75 for adults, $2 for seniors, and $1.50 for children 2 to 15.

Hey There, You with the Stars in Your Eyes

Two local colleges have on-campus observatories that allow the public a look at the skies above Boston—through a telescope. This is a good evening activity for high school students as well as adults. The Coit Observatory at **Boston University,** 725 Commonwealth Ave. (www.bu.edu/astronomy/events; ℂ **617/353-2630**), throws open its doors on most Wednesdays, year-round. The **Harvard College Observatory,** 60 Garden St. (www.cfa.harvard.edu/events; ℂ **617/495-9059**), schedules a lecture and quality time with a telescope on the third Thursday of each month.

The most spectacular garden in town, the **Arnold Arboretum,** is in Jamaica Plain.

Arnold Arboretum ★★ PARK/GARDEN   Legendary landscape architect Frederick Law Olmsted designed the Arnold Arboretum as part of the Emerald Necklace, the chain of parks that extends from Boston Common to Franklin Park. Founded in 1872, the arboretum, a National Historic Landmark, is one of the oldest parks in the United States. Its 265 acres contain more than 15,000 ornamental trees, shrubs, and vines from all over the world. In the spring, blossoming dogwood, azaleas, and rhododendrons are everywhere, and the air fills with the dizzying scent of hundreds of varieties of lilacs, for which the arboretum is especially famous. This is definitely a place to take a camera—but not food. Lilac Sunday, in May, is the only time the arboretum allows picnicking. Call or visit the website for information about educational programs.

125 Arborway, Jamaica Plain. www.arboretum.harvard.edu. ℂ **617/524-1718.** Arboretum daily dawn to dusk. Visitor center Mon–Fri 9am–4pm; Sat 10am–4pm; Sun noon–4pm. Closed major holidays. T: Orange Line to Forest Hills, then follow signs (about 10 min.). Check website for driving directions.

ORGANIZED TOURS

Orientation Tours

GUIDED WALKING TOURS   Even if you usually prefer to explore on your own, I heartily recommend a walking tour with **Boston By Foot ★★** (www.boston byfoot.org; ℂ **617/367-2345**). From April to October (the full schedule starts in May), the nonprofit educational corporation conducts historical and architectural tours that focus on particular neighborhoods or themes. The rigorously trained guides are volunteers who encourage questions. Buy tickets ($12 adults, $8 children 6–12) from the guide; reservations are not required. The 90-minute tours take place rain or shine. On the last Sunday of each month, a special tour ($15) covers a particular subject or area such as Art Deco design or Harvard Square. In addition, the company offers themed holiday strolls and year-round group tours.

Note: All excursions from Faneuil Hall start at the statue of Samuel Adams on Congress Street.

The **Heart of the Freedom Trail** tour starts at Faneuil Hall daily at 10am and also Friday through Monday at 2pm. Tours of **Beacon Hill** begin at the foot of the State House steps on Beacon Street weekdays at 5:30pm, weekends at 2pm. **Boston Underfoot** looks at subterranean technology, including the subway and the relocation of the Central Artery. It starts at Faneuil Hall Sunday at 1pm and costs $14 (including subway fare). Other tours include the **North End, Victorian Back Bay, Literary Landmarks,** and the **Dark Side of Boston.** Check the website for details and meeting places.

Trademark Tours (www. trademarktours.com; ℂ **855/455-8747**), the brainchild of some entrepreneurial Harvard grads, offers an insider's perspective on Harvard Square. Two student guides lead each of the 70-minute tours, which cost $10 per person. The company also leads tours of MIT and the Freedom Trail.

For information about other guided walking tours of the **Freedom Trail** (with a costumed

Behind the Scenes at the BSO

From October through early May, free volunteer-led tours of **Symphony Hall,** 301 Massachusetts Ave. (www.bso.org; click "Plan Your Visit"; ℂ **617/638-9390**), take visitors all around the landmark building and relate the Boston Symphony Orchestra's fascinating history. The 1-hour tours take place on some Mondays, Wednesdays, and Saturdays; check the website for dates and times. E-mail **bsav@bso.org** to request a slot, then meet in the lobby at the Massachusetts Avenue entrance. For information about performances, see p. 222.

4

EXPLORING BOSTON | Organized Tours

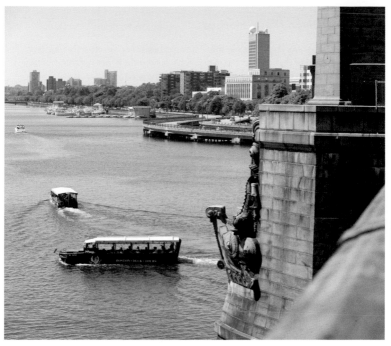

The Boston Duck Tours give you a unique perspective on the city.

Freedom Trail Player, or free with a National Park Service ranger), see the section "The Freedom Trail," on p. 86.

"DUCK" TOURS   The most unusual and enjoyable way to see Boston is with **Boston Duck Tours** ★★★ (www.bostonducktours.com; © **800/226-7442** or 617/267-3825), offered from late March through November and on the first 3 weekends of December. The tours are pricey but great fun. Sightseers board a "duck," a reconditioned World War II amphibious landing craft, behind the Prudential Center on Huntington Avenue or at the Museum of Science. The 80-minute narrated tour begins with a quick but comprehensive jaunt around the city. Then the duck lumbers down a ramp, splashes into the Charles River, and goes for a spin around the basin. Fun!

Tickets, available at the Prudential Center, Museum of Science, and New England Aquarium, are $33 for adults, $27 for seniors and students, $22 for children 3 to 11, and $10 for children 2 and under. Tours run every 30 or 60 minutes from 9am to 30 minutes before sunset, and they usually sell out. Discounted (by $2–$4) 55-minute tours leave from the New England Aquarium starting at 3pm daily from June through August and on weekends in April, May, September, and October. Timed tickets go on sale 30 days ahead online, in person, and by phone; same-day in-person sales start at 8:30am (9am at the aquarium). Reservations are accepted only for groups of 20 or more. No tours late December through mid-March.

⊙ Moon River, Moon Harbor

Fire up the camera as you approach the water. Every **bridge** that crosses the river between Boston and Cambridge affords an excellent perspective. If your travels take you to the area around the Esplanade or Kendall Square (T: Red Line to Charles/MGH or Kendall/MIT), wander out onto the **Longfellow Bridge,** especially at twilight—the views of the river are splendid, and if you hit it just right, the moon appears to shine out of the Hancock Tower.

In warm weather, check the time of moonrise and stroll down to the plaza at the end of **Long Wharf** (T: Blue Line to Aquarium). The full moon seems to rise out of the Boston Harbor Islands, and because it's so close to the horizon, it

looks huge. For astronomical reasons, this only works in the summer, but boy, is it cool.

TROLLEY TOURS   The ticket vendors who clamor for your business wherever tourists gather will claim that no visit is complete without a day on a trolley. Sometimes that's true. If you're unable to walk long distances, are short on time, or are traveling with children, a narrated tour on a trolley (actually a bus chassis with a trolley body) can be a good idea. You can get an overview of the city before you focus on specific attractions, or use the all-day pass to hit as many places as possible in 8 hours or so. **Note:** In some neighborhoods, notably the North End, trolleys stop some distance from the attractions—don't believe a ticket seller who tells you otherwise. Because Boston is so pedestrian-friendly, a trolley tour isn't the best choice for the able-bodied and unencumbered making a long visit, but it can save time and effort. For those who are physically able, I can't say this enough: *Climb down and look around.*

The business is very competitive, with various firms offering different stops and add-ons in an effort to distinguish themselves from the rest. All cover the major attractions and offer informative narratives and anecdotes in their 90- to 120-minute tours; most offer free reboarding if you want to visit the attractions. Each tour is only as good as its guide, and quality varies widely—every few years a TV station or newspaper runs an "exposé" of the wacky information a tour guide is passing off as fact. If you have time, you might chat up guides in the waiting area and choose the one you like best.

Trolley tickets cost $25 to $44 for adults, $16 or less for children. Most companies offer online discounts and reservations, and you may find discount coupons at visitor information centers and hotel-lobby brochure racks. Boarding spots are at hotels, historic sites, and tourist information centers. Busy waiting areas are near the New England Aquarium, the Park Street T stop, and the corner of Boylston Street and Charles Street South, across from Boston Common. Each company paints its cars a different color. They include orange-and-green **Old Town Trolley Tours** (www.trolley tours.com/boston; ℂ **888/910-8687** or 617/269-7010), red **Beantown Trolley** vehicles (www.beantowntrolley.com; ℂ **800/343-1328** or 781/ 986-6100), silver **CityView Trolleys** (www.cityviewtrolleys.com; ℂ **617/ 363-7899**), and yellow-and-green **Upper Deck Trolley Tours** (www. bostonsupertrolleytours.com; ℂ **877/343-8257** or 617/742-1440).

Sightseeing Cruises

Take to the water for a taste of Boston's rich maritime history or a daylong break from walking and driving. You can cruise around the harbor or go all the way to Provincetown. The **sightseeing cruise ★★** season runs from **April through November,** with spring and fall offerings often restricted to weekends. Check websites for discount coupons before you leave home. If you're traveling in a large group, call ahead for information about reservations and discounted tickets. And if you're prone to seasickness, check the size of the vessel for your tour before buying tickets; larger boats provide more cushioning and comfort than smaller ones.

Before taking a cruise just for the sake of taking a cruise, weigh the investment of time and money against your interests. Especially if kids are along, you may be better off with an excursion that targets a destination—the Charlestown Navy Yard (see the box "On the Cheap," adjacent), the Boston Harbor Islands (see the box "A Vacation in the Islands," on p. 120), or Boston Light (see the box "A Lighthouse Tour," below)—than with a pricey narrated cruise.

The largest company is **Boston Harbor Cruises,** 1 Long Wharf (www.bostonharborcruises. com; ℂ **877/733-9425** or 617/ 227-4321). Ninety-minute **historic sightseeing cruises,** which tour the Inner and Outer harbors, depart from Long Wharf May through August daily and on weekends in September at 11am and 1 and 3pm, with extra excursions at busy times. Tickets are $23 for adults, $21 for seniors, and $19 for children 4 to 12; tickets for the sunset cruise (6 or 7pm) cost $1 more. The 45-minute **USS *Constitution* cruise** takes you around the Inner Harbor and docks at the Charlestown Navy Yard so that you can go ashore and visit "Old Ironsides." Tours leave Long Wharf daily April through November hourly from 10:30am to 4:30pm, and on the hour from the Navy Yard from 11am to 5pm. The cruise is $18 for adults, $16 for seniors, and $14 for children. Check the website for other offerings, including dining cruises and a 5-hour excursion that passes a dozen lighthouses.

The **Charles Riverboat Company** (www.charlesriverboat.com; ℂ **617/621-3001**) offers 60-minute narrated cruises from the CambridgeSide Galleria mall daily May through October. Tours of the **lower Charles River basin** start six times daily between 10am and 4:15pm. Tickets cost $15 for adults, $13 for seniors, and $8 for children 2 to 12. The company's other

On the Cheap

You don't have to take a tour to take a cruise. The MBTA runs a **ferry** that connects Long Wharf, next to the New England Aquarium, and the Charlestown Navy Yard. It costs $2, is included in the MBTA's 7-day LinkPass, and makes a good final leg of the Freedom Trail.

North America's oldest lighthouse, **Boston Light ★★**, is the only one in the country that's still staffed (by the Coast Guard). Built on **Little Brewster Island** in 1716, it fell to the British in 1776 and was rebuilt in 1783. Excursions to the 102-foot lighthouse include a narrated cruise that passes two other lighthouses, 90 minutes to explore the island, and a chance to climb the 76-step spiral staircase to the top (you must be at least 50 in. tall). The 3½-hour ranger-led tours operate on weekends from mid-June to late September; meet at the Boston Harbor Islands Pavilion visitor center, on the Rose Kennedy Greenway across from Faneuil Hall Marketplace. Tickets cost $39 for adults, $35 for seniors and students, $29 for children 3 to 11, free for children 2 and under. Only 48 people may take each tour; reservations are strongly recommended (www.boston harborislands.com/tour-lighthouse; ✆ 617/223-8666). Visit the website for information about a tour of Boston Harbor that concentrates on three lighthouses and includes a visit to Little Brewster, but not a lighthouse climb.

offerings include architectural tours of Boston Harbor and the river basin, and sunset cruises on the river. Check the website for details and reservations.

DAY TRIPS Two companies serve **Provincetown ★★★**, at the tip of Cape Cod. On a day trip, you'll have time for world-class people-watching, strolling around the novelty shops and art galleries, lunching on seafood, and—if you're quick—a trip to the famous beaches. However, you'll have to forgo the hopping gay nightlife scene unless you've planned a longer excursion. (For in-depth coverage of Provincetown and other Cape Cod locales, consult *Frommer's Cape Cod, Nantucket & Martha's Vineyard*.)

Bay State Cruise Company (www.provincetownfastferry.com; ✆ **877/783-3779** or 617/748-1428) operates high-speed and conventional service to Provincetown. High-speed service takes half as long and costs almost twice as much as the conventional excursion, which is a time-honored New England tradition that's especially popular with families. Trips leave from the Seaport World Trade Center Marine Terminal, 200 Seaport Blvd. To get to the pier, take the Silver Line bus from South Station to the World Trade Center stop, the $10 water taxi (www.citywatertaxi.com; ☏ **617/422-0392**) from locations around the harbor, or a regular taxi (when you reserve your cruise, ask the clerk for the best way to reach the pier from your hotel).

Fast ferry service on the *Provincetown III* takes 90 minutes and operates three times a day from mid-May to mid-October. The round-trip fare is $83 for adults and $62 for children 3 to 12, plus $6 each way for your bike. Reservations are recommended. **M/V *Provincetown II*** sails Saturday only from July through early September. It leaves at 9am for the 3-hour trip to Provincetown. The return leg departs at 3:30pm, giving you 3½ hours for shopping and sightseeing in P-town. The same-day round-trip fare is $46 for adults, free for children 11 and under (reservations are required). Bringing a bike costs $6 extra each way.

Boston Harbor Cruises, 1 Long Wharf (www.bostonharborcruises. com; ☏ **877/733-9425** or 617/227-4321), operates catamarans that make the trip in just 90 minutes. They operate from mid-May through mid-October, two or three times a day between early June and Labor Day weekend, and less often early and late in the season. The round-trip fare is $83 for adults, $73 for seniors, and $63 for children 4 to 12.

Whale-Watching

For info about whale-watching trips from Cape Ann, see the box titled "A Whale of an Adventure" on p. 321.

The **New England Aquarium** (www.neaq.org; ☏ **617/973-5206;** p. 59) runs **whale watches ★★** daily from mid-April through late October and on weekends in early April. You'll travel several miles out to sea to Stellwagen Bank, the feeding ground for the whales as they migrate from Newfoundland to Provincetown. Enthusiastic naturalists narrate and identify the whales, many of which they call by name. Allow 3 to 4 hours. Tickets are $45 for adults, $35 for children 3 to 11, $18 for children 2 and under. Reservations are strongly recommended; you can buy tickets online, subject to a service charge.

With its onboard exhibits and vast experience, the aquarium offers the best whale watches in Boston. If they're booked, try **Boston Harbor Cruises** (www.bostonharborcruises.com; ☏ **877/733-9425** or 617/227-4321), which operates up to four trips a day on its two high-speed catamarans, trimming the excursion time to 3 hours total.

Specialty Tours

Two excellent resources to investigate before you leave home are the **Boston Center for Adult Education** (www.bcae.org; ☏ **617/267-4430**) and the **Cambridge Center for Adult Education** (www.ccae.org; ☏ **617/547-6789**). Multiple-week courses are the norm, but both schools also schedule single-day classes that last 2 hours or longer. The expert-led offerings include walking tours (often with a focus on local architecture), cooking classes and wine tastings, and workshops about everything from poetry to gardening. Prices start at $30, and preregistration is required.

The **French Cultural Center** (www.frenchculturalcenter.org; ℭ 617/912-0400) offers cooking classes as well as intensive language instruction.

FOR HISTORY BUFFS Historic New England ★ (www.historicnewengland.org; ℭ 617/994-5920) offers a 2-hour walking tour of Beacon Hill on Saturday afternoons, plus excursions that concentrate on other areas and topics—surf ahead for specifics and schedules. Beacon Hill tours begin at the Otis House, 141 Cambridge St. Prices start at $12, which includes a house tour, and reservations are recommended.

The **Cambridge African American Heritage Trail** focuses on significant sites in the history of the city's large black community. To buy the guide ($2), visit the office on the second floor of 831 Massachusetts Ave., download an order form from the website, or send a check for $3.50 (includes shipping) to the **Cambridge Historical Commission,** 831 Massachusetts Ave., Cambridge, MA 02139 (www.cambridgema.gov/historic; click "History and Links"; ℭ 617/349-4683).

A map of the self-guided tour created by the **Boston Irish Tourism Association** (www.irishheritagetrail.com; ℭ 617/696-9880) is available at the Boston Common and Prudential Center visitor centers. Check the website for an interactive map with pop-ups describing the sites, and information about guided tours.

FOR ARCHITECTURE BUFFS Check ahead for information about architectural tours with the **Charles Riverboat Company** (p. 107) and walking tours and classes with the **Boston Center for Adult Education** or **Cambridge Center for Adult Education** (see above).

FOR CRIMINAL-JUSTICE MAJORS Free guided tours of the **John Joseph Moakley U.S. Courthouse,** 1 Courthouse Way, South Boston, show off the waterfront building's dramatic architecture and introduce visitors to the workings of the justice system. You may even see part of a trial. Docents from **Discovering Justice** (www.discoveringjustice.org; ℭ 617/748-4185) lead the 1-hour tours, which are available to individuals and groups by appointment only Tuesday, Wednesday, and Friday throughout the year (reserve 2 weeks in advance). Children must be 10 or older.

The courthouse is on Fan Pier, off Northern Avenue across Fort Point Channel from the Coast Guard building at 408 Atlantic Ave. You can walk from downtown or take the Silver Line bus from South Station to the Courthouse stop, 1 block away. To enter the building, adults must show two forms of ID (one of which must have a photo), and everyone must temporarily surrender his or her cellphone. *Tip:* You don't have to take a tour to enter—local office workers often visit the second-floor cafeteria, which has decent food and a breathtaking view.

FOR PEDAL PUSHERS A group bicycle tour covers more in 2½ to 3 hours than you could ever see on foot. Among the numerous and diverse offerings of **Urban AdvenTours,** 103 Atlantic Ave. (www.urbanadventours.com; ℭ 800/979-3370 for tickets, or 617/670-0637 for info) are a tour that focuses on historic neighborhoods and landmarks, and another that traces the harbor and the Charles River. You can also request a customized special-interest excursion. Prices for daytime tours begin at $50 per person and include bicycle and helmet rental. You can also rent bikes, which can be

missing **THIS WOULD BE A CRIME**

A bailiff at the adjacent Suffolk County Courthouse tipped me off to the wonders of the **John Adams Courthouse** ★★. (I was a juror, but thanks for asking.) One of the most beautiful buildings in Boston, the courthouse is also among the city's most interesting destinations. Constructed between 1886 and 1894, expanded in 1910, and extensively renovated around the turn of the 21st century, it recalls an era when public buildings were more like cathedrals.

The courthouse is the suitably impressive home of the Supreme Judicial Court, or SJC, the highest court in the Massachusetts system and the oldest (1692) appellate court in the Western Hemisphere. The French Second Empire facade of the courthouse conceals an unbelievably elaborate interior dripping with frescoes, moldings, paintings, and sculptures. They surround a soaring central space, the Great Hall, which sits beneath a richly decorated vaulted ceiling. The galleries on either side of the lowest level hold exhibits relating to history and the courts; **John Adams: Architect of American Government** will be on display during your visit.

The public is welcome to look around, or to attend a court session if one is going on. The building is open Monday through Friday from 9am to 5pm; guards will screen you and your bags before you enter. The entrance is at 1 Pemberton Sq., hidden in plain sight behind the curving Center Plaza complex on Cambridge Street, across from City Hall Plaza and the Government Center T stop. Head to the second floor and ask for a brochure from the helpful staff of the **Public Information Office** (www.mass.gov/courts/sjc; ✆ **617/557-1114**), or arrange in advance to take a 1-hour tour with **Discovering Justice** (www.discoveringjustice.org; ✆ **617/748-4185**).

picked up at the North End shop (off the Rose Kennedy Greenway near Faneuil Hall Marketplace) or delivered to your hotel or any other location.

FOR SHUTTERBUGS The unusual offerings of **PhotoWalks** (www.photowalks. com; ℂ 617/851-2273) combine narrated walking tours with photography tips. On a 90-minute stroll around Beacon Hill, the Back Bay, or another picturesque area, visitors learn to look at Boston from (literally) a different angle—that of a creative photographer. Adults pay $30, children 10 to 17 (with a paying adult) $15. Tours run several times a week from April through October, and by appointment during the winter. For tickets, call ℂ **800/979-3370.**

FOR FILM & TV FANS **On Location Tours** (www.screentours.com; ℂ 212/683-2027) are walking tours and bus excursions that look at Boston on the silver and small screens—a busy undertaking now that there's film production going on all over the place. Guides offer regularly updated info about numerous movies and TV shows, always including (of course) *Cheers.* Passengers on the 3-hour bus tours ($40) can watch clips on TV screens in the vehicle, which adds an interesting dimension to the experience. The 90-minute Boston Movie Mile walking tours ($24) are seasonal (Apr–Oct) and concentrate on Beacon Hill and the Back Bay. Check start times and meeting points when you make reservations, which are strongly recommended.

FOR HORROR-MOVIE FANS **Ghosts & Gravestones** (www.ghostsandgrave stones.com; ℂ **617/269-3626**) covers burial grounds and other shiver-inducing areas in a trolley and on foot, with a guide dressed as a gravedigger. The 90-minute tour starts at dusk on weekends in April, May, and early November, and nightly from Memorial Day weekend through October. It costs $40 for adults, $37 for seniors and students, $25 for children 4 to 12. Children 3 and under are not allowed, and the company cautions that the tour might not be suitable for kids 12 and under. Reservations are required.

FOR FOODIES A neighborhood resident offers **North End Market Tours ★** (www.bostonfoodtours.com; ℂ **617/523-6032**), 3-hour excursions that stop at many of the shops in the legendary Italian-American stronghold. Tours ($50) include product tastings, cooking tips, and plenty of local lore. The same company offers 3½-hour **Chinatown Market Tours;** the price ($65) includes a dim sum lunch. Visit the website to register and pay in advance.

A cooking or wine-tasting class makes an excellent, if pricey, break from shopping and sightseeing. Resources to check out before you leave home include: **Boston University's Seminars** in the Arts and Culinary Arts (www.bu.edu/foodandwine; ℂ 617/353-9852), the **Cambridge School of Culinary Arts** (www.cambridgeculinary.com; ℂ 617/354-2020), the **Boston Vegetarian Society** (www.bostonveg.org; ℂ 617/424-8846), the **Elephant Walk** restaurant (www.elephantwalk.com/classes; ℂ 617/285-0410; p. 173), and the **Bristol Lounge,** in the Four Seasons Hotel, 200 Boylston St. (www.fourseasons.com/boston/dining; click "Events and Promotions"; ℂ 617/338-4400).

Winter visitors can check ahead for classes during the **Boston Wine Festival** (www.bostonwinefestival.net; ℂ **888/660-9463;** p. 27). Another resource for wine lovers is the **Boston Wine School** (www.bostonwine school.com; ℂ **617/784-7150**).

ESPECIALLY FOR KIDS

What can the children do in Boston? A better question might be, what *can't* they do? Just about every major attraction either is designed to appeal to kids or easily adapts to do so.

The following attractions are covered extensively elsewhere; here's the boiled-down version for busy parents.

Destinations that offer something for every member of the family include the **Boston Tea Party Ships & Museum** (𝄋 855/TEA-1775 [832-1775]; p. 68); **Faneuil Hall Marketplace** (𝄋 617/338-2323; p. 64); the **Museum of Fine Arts** (𝄋 617/267-9300; p. 75), which offers special weekend and after-school programs; and the **USS** *Constitution* **Museum** (𝄋 617/426-1812; p. 101).

Hands-on exhibits and large-format films are the headliners at the **New England Aquarium** (𝄋 617/973-5200; p. 59), where you'll find the Simons IMAX Theatre, and at the **Museum of Science** (𝄋 617/723-2500; p. 62), home to the Mugar Omni Theater as well as the Hayden Planetarium.

You might get your hands on a baseball at a **Red Sox game** (p. 246) or the **Sports Museum of New England** (𝄋 617/624-1234; p. 63).

The allure of seeing people the size of ants draws young visitors to the **Sky-walk Observatory at the Prudential Center** (𝄋 617/859-0648; p. 73). And they can see actual ants—although they might prefer the dinosaurs—at the **Har-vard Museum of Natural History** (𝄋 617/495-3045; p. 82).

Older children who have studied modern American history will enjoy a visit to the **John F. Kennedy Presidential Library and Museum** (𝄋 617/929-4523; p. 77). Middle-schoolers who enjoyed Esther Forbes's *Johnny Tremain* will probably get a kick out of the **Paul Revere House** (𝄋 617/523-2338; p. 97). Young visitors who have read Robert McCloskey's classic *Make Way for Ducklings* will relish a visit to the **Public Garden** (p. 103), and fans of E. B. White's *The Trumpet of the Swan* certainly will want to ride on the **Swan Boats**

 More Kid Stuff

For more suggestions, check (or let the kids check) elsewhere in this book. Chapter 8 lists nightlife destinations for all ages. Before night falls (and sometimes afterward), the whole family can have a great time at the **Hard Rock Cafe** (food and music), **Club Passim** (folk music), *Shear Madness* (audience-participation theater), **Blue Man Group** (performance art), and the **Puppet Showplace Theater.**

Turn to chapter 7 for shopping recommendations—**Black Ink,** the **Boston Bead Company,** the **CambridgeSide Galleria** mall, and the area's numerous **college bookstores** can be almost as fun as all-toy stores.

Finally, check chapter 10 for information about day trips. Fun destinations include **Salem, Plymouth,** and (for *Little Women* fans) **Concord.**

(© **617/522-1966;** p. 103). Considerably less tame (and much longer) are **whale watches** (p. 109).

Boston Harbor Cruises, 1 Long Wharf (www.bostonharbor cruises.com; © **877/733-9425** or 617/227-4321;), offers a cruise called **Codzilla,** which it bills as a "high-speed thrill boat ride." It leaves Long Wharf daily from mid-May through early October; from the shore, you may be able to hear delighted screaming. Tickets cost $27 for adults, $25 for seniors, and $23 for children 4 to 12; reservations are recommended.

The walking-tour company **Boston By Foot ★★** (p. 104) offers **"Boston By Little Feet"** for children 6 to 12 years old. The 1-hour walk gives a child's-eye view of the architecture along the Freedom Trail, and of Boston's role in the American Revolution. Children must be accompanied by an adult, and a map is provided. Tours run from May through October and begin at the statue of Samuel Adams on the Congress Street side of Faneuil Hall. They begin Friday and Saturday at 10am and Sunday at 2pm, rain or shine. The cost is $8 per person.

Blue Hills Trailside Museum ☺

At the foot of Great Blue Hill, a 20-minute drive south of Boston, this museum is fun for all ages, and especially popular with the under-10 set. Here you'll see replicas of the natural habitats found in the area, displays about Native Americans, and live animal exhibits. Resident animals include a bald eagle, owls, honeybees, otters, snakes, opossum, and turtles. Children can feed the ducks and turkeys. Other activities include climbing the lookout tower and hiking around the 7,500-acre Blue Hills Reservation recreation area. Check ahead for the schedule of weekend programs, which might include a live animal presentation, outdoor excursion, or another activity. Special events and family programs change with the seasons; call ahead to register.

The Blue Hills Trailside Museum focuses on the natural world.

1904 Canton Ave., Milton. www.massaudubon. org. © **617/333-0690.** Admission $3 adults, $2 seniors, $1.50 children 2–12, free for children 1 and under and Mass Audubon Society members. Museum: Thurs–Sun and Mon holidays 10am–5pm. Trails: Daily dawn to dusk. By car, take I-93 S. to exit 2B (Rte. 138 N.).

Boston Children's Museum ★★ ☺

As you approach this wonderful museum, look for the 40-foot-high red-and-white milk bottle out front—and for children and their chronological-adult companions racing each other to the

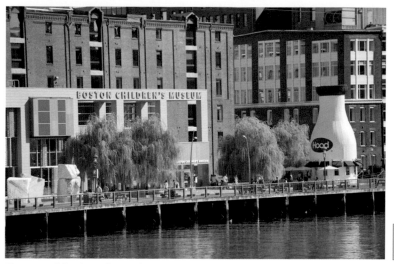

The giant milk bottle out front makes the Boston Children's Museum easy to spot.

entrance. The under-11 set is the target audience for this delightful museum, but it appeals to the little kid in everyone.

As they explore, beginning in the glass-enclosed lobby, young visitors can stick with their adults or wander on their own, learning, doing, and role-playing. A three-story-high structure, the **New Balance Climb,** incorporates motor skills and problem-solving; kids work their way through while adults watch from the stairs. Other favorite hands-on exhibits include physical experiments (such as creating giant soap bubbles) in **Science Playground** and getting creative with **Johnny's Workbench,** a souped-up version of puttering in the garage. You can explore **Boston Black,** which celebrates the city's black history and culture, and the **Japanese House,** a two-story residence from Kyoto, one of Boston's sister cities. Children under 4 and their caregivers have a special room, **Play-Space,** that's packed with toys and activities; kids 3 to 5 can learn basic science skills in **Peep's World,** based on the PBS program *Peep and the Big Wide World.*

Check ahead for information about traveling exhibitions and for special events as the museum, the second-oldest children's museum in the country (only Brooklyn's is older), celebrates its centennial in 2013.

The museum occupies a converted wool warehouse, and is a certified green building right down to the toilets; visit the website to learn more, and be sure to check out the excellent gift shop.

308 Congress St. (Museum Wharf), at Sleeper St., on Fort Point Channel. www.boston childrensmuseum.org. ☏ **617/426-6500.** Admission $12 adults, seniors, and children 1–15; free for children under 1; Fri 5–9pm $1 for all; Sat–Thurs after 4pm $6 for all. Sat–Thurs 10am–5pm; Fri 10am–9pm. Closed Thanksgiving, Dec 25, and until noon Jan 1. T: Red Line to South Station; from South Station walk north on Atlantic Ave. 1 block (past Federal Reserve Bank), turn right onto Congress St., then walk 2 blocks (across bridge). Or Silver Line to Courthouse; walk toward downtown and turn left at Fort Point Channel.

Lowland gorillas are just some of the many animals you'll encounter at the Franklin Park Zoo.

Franklin Park Zoo 😊 ZOO   This enjoyable, engaging attraction is in an outly-ing neighborhood of Boston; animal-mad families won't mind the cab ride or trek on public transit. The centerpiece is the **Tropical Forest** exhibit, a sprawling complex that houses more than 50 species of animals. Here you might have a close encounter with a Western lowland gorilla (Little Joe, who made interna-tional headlines by literally going over the wall in 2003, is secure in a redesigned enclosure) or see a pygmy hippo. Kids find the hands-on **Franklin Farm** both entertaining and educational. **Tigers, lions,** and **giraffes** (with their zebra friends) have their own turf, as do the zoo's 400 budgies (parakeets). The **Seren-geti Crossing** and **Outback Trail** exhibits assemble species from their respec-tive continents—African zebras, ibex, and ostriches; and Australian kangaroos, emus, and cockatoos.

Allow half a day or longer for a visit, and try to budget for a cab ride in at least one direction. Franklin Park is 40 minutes from downtown by subway and bus, and the walk from the main gate and parking area to the entrance is fairly long.

1 Franklin Park Rd. www.franklinparkzoo.org. ✆ **617/541-LION (5466).** Admission $16 adults, $13 seniors, $10 children 2–12, free for children 1 and under; $10 for all 1st Sat of the month before noon. Apr–Sept Mon–Fri 10am–5pm, Sat–Sun and holidays 10am–6pm; Oct–Mar daily 10am–4pm. Closed Thanksgiving and Dec 25. T: Orange Line to Forest Hills or Red Line to Andrew, then no. 16 bus to main entrance, or a $15 cab ride from central Boston.

OUTDOOR ACTIVITIES

The state **Department of Conservation & Recreation,** or DCR (www.state. ma.us/dcr; ✆ **617/626-1250**), oversees outdoor activities on public lands through its divisions of Urban Parks & Recreation and State Parks & Recreation. The incredibly helpful website includes descriptions of properties and activities, and has a planning area to help you make the most of your time.

Beaches

The beaches in Boston proper are not worth the trouble. Besides being bone-chilling, Boston Harbor water periodically flunks health and safety tests, especially after heavy rains. If you want to swim, book a hotel with a pool. If you want the sand-between-your-toes experience, visit the North Shore or Walden Pond in Concord. See chapter 10 or consult the DCR (see the introduction to this section) for information on suburban beaches.

Biking

Despite Boston's recent push to be more welcoming to cyclists, out-of-towners who are anything less than expert are better off exploring the area's numerous bike paths than braving the city streets. If you do stay in Boston, consider taking a tour (see "For Pedal Pushers," p. 110)—the supervision of a guide experienced with the city's terrifying traffic is well worth the money. At the very least, wear a helmet—a shocking number of local cyclists don't.

The bike-sharing program **New Balance Hubway** (www.thehubway.com; ✆ **855/4HUBWAY** [448-2929]) has solar-powered stations on sidewalks and

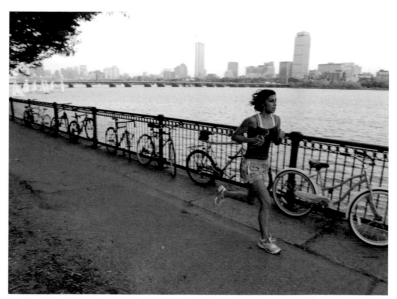

The Dr. Paul Dudley White Charles River Bike Path is popular with both joggers and cyclists.

curbs in Boston, Cambridge, Brookline, and Somerville. The Hubway, which operates in spring, summer, and fall, charges as little as $5 for a 24-hour membership. Activate the system using a credit card at a kiosk (find one using the map on the website). The system is designed for quick hops from station to station; if you need a bike for longer than an hour or so, consult one of the businesses listed below.

Rental shops require you to show a driver's license or passport and leave a deposit using a major credit card. Daily flat rates run $30 to $65. **Urban AdvenTours** (see "For Pedal Pushers," p. 110) and **MyBike,** 516 E. Second St., South Boston (www.mybike.com; ℂ **617/202-9720**), will deliver to your hotel. Urban AdvenTours also operates a seasonal rental kiosk on Boston Common, near the Park Street T stop.

Other local shops include **Back Bay Bicycles,** 366 Commonwealth Ave., near Massachusetts Avenue (www.backbaybicycles.com; ℂ **617/247-2336**); **Cambridge Bicycle,** 259 Massachusetts Ave., near MIT (www.cambridgebicycle. com; ℂ **617/876-6555**); and **Ferris Wheels Bike Shop,** 66 South St., Jamaica Plain (www.ferriswheelsbikeshop.com; ℂ **617/524-2453**).

State law requires that children 16 and under wear helmets. Bicycles are forbidden on buses and the Green Line at all times and during rush hours on the other lines of the subway system and commuter rail. For additional information, including the lowdown on other laws and a calendar of events, check out **MassBike** (www.massbike.org; ℂ **617/542-2453**) as well as **Bike Safe Boston** (www.bikesafeboston.com) and **Boston Bikes** (www.cityofboston.gov/bikes).

Dr. Paul Dudley White Charles River Bike Path ★ MULTIUSE TRAIL This 18-mile loop covers both sides of the Charles River. Note that there's heavy vehicular traffic at nearly every crosswalk along the way. Bikers share the path with joggers and in-line skaters, especially in Boston near the Esplanade and in Cambridge near Harvard Square. The DCR (see the introduction to this section) maintains the path. Along the Charles River, from Science Park (near the Museum of Science) to suburban Watertown and back. T: Green Line to Science Park or Arlington, or Red Line to Kendall/MIT, Harvard, or Central.

Memorial Drive ★ ☺ MULTIUSE TRAIL On summer Sundays from 11am to 7pm, a flat 1½-mile stretch of "Mem Drive" closes to cars. It's also popular with pedestrians and in-line skaters, and can get quite crowded. Along the Charles River, from Western Ave. (near Central Sq.) to the Eliot Bridge, west Cambridge. T: Red Line to Harvard or Central.

Minuteman Bikeway ★★ MULTIUSE TRAIL An 11-mile rail trail, the bikeway is lovely, but stay alert—it crosses a number of busy streets as it passes through Cambridge, Arlington, Lexington, and Bedford. This is a wonderful way for experienced cyclists to reach the historic sites in Lexington (see chapter 10). From Alewife station, Cambridge, to Bedford Freight House, 120 South Rd., Bedford. www.minutemanbikeway.org. T: Red Line to Alewife.

Pierre Lallement Bike Path MULTIUSE TRAIL From the edge of the Back Bay, this 5-mile path runs through the South End and Roxbury along the route of the MBTA Orange Line to Boston's largest park. From outside the Copley Place mall, Dartmouth St. btw. Huntington and Columbus aves., to Franklin Park, Dorchester. T: Orange Line to Back Bay or Massachusetts Ave.

Golf

Golf courses dot the Boston suburbs. The concierge at your hotel should be able to suggest a suitable course and help you arrange transportation. The **Massachusetts Golf Association** (www.mgalinks.org; ℂ **800/356-2201** within Massachusetts, or 774/430-9100) represents more than 400 golf courses around the state and has a searchable online database. Getting a decent tee time on a weekend can be difficult for an out-of-towner; if possible, opt for lower prices and smaller crowds on weekdays. Many courses offer discounts for juniors, seniors, and anyone teeing off in the late afternoon.

One of the best public courses in the area, **Newton Commonwealth Golf Course,** 212 Kenrick St., Newton (www.sterlinggolf.com; ℂ **617/630-1971**), is a challenging 18-hole Donald Ross design. It's 5,305 yards from the blue tees, par is 70, and greens fees are $30 on weekdays, $37 on weekends.

Within the city limits is the legendary 6,009-yard **William J. Devine Golf Course,** in Franklin Park, Dorchester (www.cityofbostongolf.com; ℂ **617/265-4084**). As a Harvard student, Bobby Jones sharpened his game on the 18-hole, par-70 course, which is managed by the city parks department. Greens fees are $40 on weekdays, $45 on weekends.

Less challenging but with more of a neighborhood feel is the 9-hole, par-35 **Fresh Pond Golf Course,** 691 Huron Ave., Cambridge (www.freshpondgolf. com; ℂ **617/349-6282**). The 3,161-yard layout adjoins the Fresh Pond Reservoir, and there's water on four holes. It charges $23, or $33 to go around twice, on weekdays; $26 and $38, respectively, on weekends and holidays.

Gyms

If your hotel doesn't have a health club, your best bet is to ask the concierge or front-desk staff to recommend one nearby; you may receive a pass good for free or discounted admission. Guests at the **Ritz-Carlton, Boston Common,** have the use of the over-the-top facilities at the 100,000-square-foot Sports Club/LA, which is otherwise closed to nonmembers. Other hotels with good health clubs include the **Boston Harbor Hotel,** the **Charles Hotel,** the **Four Seasons Hotel,** the **Hilton Boston Logan Airport,** the **InterContinental Boston,** and the **Royal Sonesta Hotel** (see chapter 9).

The "Y" (www.ymcaboston.org) offers the best combination of facilities and value; each of these locations has a pool, gym, weight room, and fitness center. The **Wang YMCA of Chinatown,** 8 Oak St. W., off Washington Street (ℂ **617/426-2237**), is convenient to downtown and charges $15 for a 1-day pass. The **Huntington Avenue YMCA,** 316 Huntington Ave. (ℂ **617/536-7800**), near Symphony Hall, charges $10.

There are eight **Boston Sports Clubs** (www.bostonsportsclubs.com) in the city and more than a dozen in nearby suburbs; a guest pass costs $30 and is good for 1 to 30 days. If you're a Sports Clubs Network member at home (in New York, Philadelphia, or Washington), check to see whether your plan includes access to the Boston-area locations.

A day pass costs $20 at women-only, no-pool **Healthworks** (www.healthworks fitness.com), which has well-equipped facilities in the Back Bay at 441 Stuart St.

Majestic ocean views, hiking trails, historic sites, rocky beaches, nature walks, campsites, and picnic areas abound in New England. To find them all together, head east (yes, east) of Boston to the **Boston Harbor Islands** (www.boston harborislands.org; ☏ **617/223-8666**). The national park area's unspoiled beauty is a welcome break from the urban landscape, and the islands are not well known, even to many longtime Bostonians. Of the 34 islands and peninsulas that dot the Outer Harbor, at least a half dozen are open for exploring, camping, swimming, and more. Bring a sweater or jacket. Plan a day trip or even an overnight trip, but note that only Georges and Spectacle islands have fresh water, and management strongly suggests bringing your own.

Ferries run to **Georges Island** and **Spectacle Island.** Georges Island has a visitor center, museum, refreshment area, fishing pier, picnic area, and wonderful views of Boston's skyline. It's home to Fort Warren (1833), which held Confederate prisoners during the Civil War and may have a resident ghost. You can investigate on your own or take a ranger-led tour. **Spectacle Island,** which opened to the public in 2006, holds more than 3 million cubic yards of material dug up during the Big Dig—then sealed, covered with topsoil, and landscaped to allow recreational use. It's home to 5 miles of hiking trails, a beach, and an eco-friendly visitor center with a cafe. (**Thompson Island,** home of Thompson Island Outward Bound, is accessible to the public by ferry on summer Sun only.)

Allow at least half a day, longer if you plan to take the inter-island shuttle (summer only) to **Bumpkin, Grape, Lovells,** or **Peddocks islands,** all of which have picnic areas and campsites.

Admission to the islands is free. **Boston's Best Cruises** (www.bostons bestcruises.com; ☏ **617/222-6999**) runs ferries to Georges Island (30 min.) and Spectacle Island (20 or 45 min.) from Long Wharf. Tickets are for sale online and at the kiosks at the **Boston Harbor Islands Pavilion** visitor center, on the Rose Kennedy Greenway across from Faneuil Hall Marketplace. Round-trip tickets cost $15 for adults, $11 for seniors, $9 for children 4 to 11, free for children 3 and under, $43 for families (two adults, two kids); the inter-island shuttle is free. Cruises depart daily on the hour from 9am to 5pm (6pm on

(☏ **617/859-7700**), and in Cambridge at the Porter Square Shopping Center, 35 White St. (☏ **617/497-4454**).

Hiking

For information about hiking in state parks and forests, visit **www.massparks.org**. The **Appalachian Mountain Club** (www.outdoors.org; ☏ **617/523-0722**) organizes recreational activities for people of all ages throughout the Appalachian region. Explore the website, bearing in mind that some locations in New Hampshire, Rhode Island, and even Maine are closer to the greater Boston area than places in western Massachusetts. The **Boston Harbor Islands** offer great hiking; circling the largest island, Peddocks, takes half a day. See the box, "A Vacation in the Islands," above.

weekends) from mid-June through Labor Day weekend, with shorter hours in the spring and fall. In the off season, check ahead for winter wildlife excursions (scheduled occasionally).

A public-private National Park Partnership administers the **Boston Harbor Islands National Recreation Area** (www.nps.gov/boha). For more information, chat up the park rangers at the Boston Harbor Islands Pavilion from May through October (it's not staffed in the winter). Or contact the **Friends of the Boston Harbor Islands** (www.fbhi.org; $ℂ$ **617/740-4290**). The Friends coordinate a variety of cruises on and around the harbor throughout the summer and fall; check ahead for details. For information about tours of **Boston Light,** the lighthouse on Little Brewster Island, see the box "A Lighthouse Tour," p. 108.

Ice Skating

The outdoor ice-skating season runs from mid-November to mid-March, weather permitting. Check ahead for open hours and closures for private events.

The rink at the Boston Common **Frog Pond** ★★ (www.bostonfrogpond.com; $ℂ$ **617/635-2120**) is an extremely popular cold-weather destination. It's an open surface with an ice-making system and a clubhouse. Admission is $5 for adults, free for children 13 and under; skate rental costs $8 for adults, $5 for kids. The rink gets unbelievably crowded on weekend afternoons, so try to go in the morning or on a weekday.

Kendall Square Community Skating, 300 Athenaeum St., Kendall Square, Cambridge (www.kendallsquare.org; $ℂ$ **617/492-0941**), is an open rink in a courtyard not far from MIT. It charges $5 for adults, $3 for seniors and

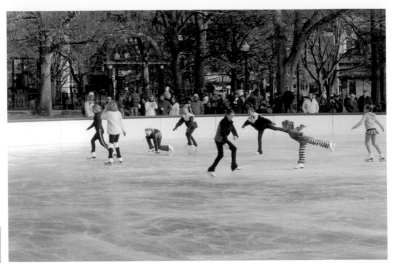
Skating on the Frog Pond is a popular winter activity.

students, $1 for children 13 and under; skate rentals are $8 for adults, $5 for kids. Validated discounted parking is available.

In-Line Skating

A favorite spot for in-line skaters is the **Esplanade,** between the Back Bay and the Charles River. It's part of the bike path that runs to Watertown and back (see "Jogging," below), but after you leave the Esplanade, the pavement isn't totally smooth, which can lead to mishaps. Your best bet is to wait for a Sunday in the summer, when **Memorial Drive ★** near Harvard Square in Cambridge closes to traffic from 11am to 7pm. It's a perfect surface. Unless you're confident of your ability and your knowledge of Boston traffic, stay off the streets.

To rent skates or blades, visit the **Beacon Hill Skate Shop,** 135 Charles St. S. (© **617/482-7400**). It's not on Beacon Hill but near the Theater District, not too far from the Esplanade, and has a knowledgeable staff. Expect to pay about $15 a day. The **InLine Club of Boston**'s website (www.sk8net.com) offers up-to-date event and safety information.

Jogging

The **Dr. Paul Dudley White Charles River Bike Path ★★** is also a jogging route. The 18-mile loop along the water is extremely popular because it's car-free (except at intersections), scenic, and generally safe—but always be aware of your surroundings. Be careful around abutments, where you can't see far ahead. Don't jog at night, try not to go alone, and if you're using headphones, keep the volume low. The bridges that connect Boston and Cambridge allow for circuits of various lengths. Visit the DCR website (www.state.ma.us/dcr) to view a map that gives distances. If the river's not convenient, the concierge or desk staff at your hotel probably can provide a map with suggested jogging routes. As in any other city, stay out of park areas at night.

Kayaking

In addition to offering 2- to 4-hour guided tours, **Charles River Canoe & Kayak,** 500 Broad Canal St., Kendall Square, Cambridge (www.paddleboston. com; *©* **617/965-5110**), rents kayaks, canoes, and stand-up paddleboards by the hour and day. From this location, everyone can explore the Charles River Basin, and qualified paddlers can make arrangements to continue to Boston Harbor. If the free-for-all atmosphere of the harbor doesn't appeal, consider a one-way rental ($10 plus the hourly rate) and an excursion on the river to or from Allston/Brighton, another of the company's five locations. Check the website for details. Rental rates start at $15 per hour (1-hr. minimum), which includes use of a mandatory life jacket. You must be 18 to rent, but children of all ages can participate. Tours cost $55 and up. Reservations for hourly rentals are accepted only for eight or more boats.

Sailing

Sailboats fill the Charles River basin all summer and skim across the Inner Harbor in all but the coldest weather. Your options during a short stay aren't especially cost-effective, but they are fun.

The best deal is with **Community Boating,** 21 David Mugar Way, on the Esplanade (www.community-boating.org; *©* **617/523-1038**). It's on a gorgeous but congested patch of water between the Back Bay and Cambridge's Kendall Square. The oldest public sailing facility in the country offers lessons and boating programs for children and adults from April through November. The fleet includes 13- to 23-foot sailboats as well as windsurfers and kayaks. Experienced visitors pay $75 for a day of sailing or $40 for a day of kayaking. To sail on the harbor, check out the **Boston Sailing Center,** Lewis Wharf (www.bostonsailing center.com; *©* **617/227-4198**). The cheapest membership is $420; skippered charters are available.

Tennis

Public courts are available throughout the city at no charge. Well-maintained courts that seldom get busy until after work are at several spots on the Southwest Corridor Park in the **South End** (there's a nice one near **West Newton St.**). The courts on **Boston Common,** in the **North End** (Commercial and North Washington sts.), and in **Charlesbank Park,** overlooking the river next to the bridge to the Museum of Science, are more crowded during the day. To find the court nearest you, ask the concierge or desk staff at your hotel or visit the DCR website (www.state.ma.us/dcr).

Yoga

The Boston area is home to dozens of studios, and many gyms offer at least a couple of classes a week. The front-desk staff at your hotel can point you to an appropriate yoga studio and may be able to arrange a free or discounted class.

Visit **www.bostonyoga.com** and click "Yoga Classes" for an overview. Well-regarded establishments include **Back Bay Yoga,** 364 Boylston St. (www.back bayyoga.com; ℰ 617/375-9642); **North End Yoga,** 256 Hanover St. (www. northendyoga.com; ℰ 617/227-9642); and **Karma Yoga Studio** (www.karmayoga studio.com), 778 Tremont St., South End (ℰ 617/329-9719), and 1120 Massachusetts Ave., Harvard Square (ℰ 617/547-9642). Hot-yoga aficionados rave about **Baptiste Yoga,** 2000 Massachusetts Ave., Porter Square (www.baron baptiste.com; ℰ 617/661-6565), and **Bikram Yoga Boston** (www.bikramyoga boston.com), 561 Boylston St., Back Bay (ℰ 617/585-6565), 108 Lincoln St., Financial District (ℰ 617/556-9926), and 30 John F. Kennedy St., Harvard Square (ℰ 617/547-9328).

SIGHTS & ATTRACTIONS BY THEME INDEX

AFRICAN-AMERICAN HISTORY

Black Heritage Trail (p. 65)
Museum of African American History (p. 67)
Shaw Memorial (Memorial to Robert Gould Shaw and the Massachusetts 54th Regiment) (p. 87)

AMERICAN REVOLUTION

Boston Massacre Site (p. 95)
Boston Tea Party Ships & Museum (p. 68)
Bunker Hill Monument (p. 101)
Longfellow House–Washington's Headquarters National Historic Site (p. 83)
Freedom Trail (p. 86)
Paul Revere House (p. 97)

AQUARIUM

New England Aquarium (p. 59)

BOATS & SHIPS

Boston Duck Tours (p. 105)
Boston Tea Party Ships & Museum (p. 68)
Swan Boats (p. 103)
USS *Constitution* (p. 100)

BOTANICAL GARDENS

Arnold Arboretum (p. 103)
Public Garden (p. 103)

CEMETERIES & BURYING GROUNDS

Copp's Hill Burying Ground (p. 100)
Granary Burying Ground (p. 89)
King's Chapel and Burying Ground (p. 90)
Mount Auburn Cemetery (p. 84)

CHURCHES

King's Chapel and Burying Ground (p. 90)
Old North Church (Christ Church) (p. 99)
Park Street Church (p. 89)

COLLEGE & UNIVERSITIES

Harvard University (p. 81)
Massachusetts Institute of Technology (p. 84)

COLONIAL BOSTON

Copp's Hill Burying Ground (p. 100)
Granary Burying Ground (p. 89)
King's Chapel and Burying Ground (p. 90)
Massachusetts State House (p. 88)
Old North Church (Christ Church) (p. 99)
Old South Meeting House (p. 92)
Paul Revere House (p. 97)

HISTORIC BUILDINGS

Faneuil Hall/Faneuil Hall Marketplace
(p. 95 and 64)
Fenway Park (p. 246)
Massachusetts State House (p. 88)
Old Corner Bookstore Building (p. 92)
Old South Meeting House (p. 92)

HISTORIC HOUSES

Gibson House Museum (p. 71)
John F. Kennedy National Historic Site
(p. 79)
Longfellow House–Washington's
Headquarters National Historic Site
(p. 83)
Nichols House Museum (p. 67)
Otis House (p. 67)
Paul Revere House (p. 97)

LIBRARIES

Boston Athenæum (p. 66)
Boston Public Library (p. 70)
Mary Baker Eddy Library/Mapparium
(p. 71)
Massachusetts Historical Society
(p. 73)

MONUMENTS & MEMORIALS

Boston Massacre Site (p. 95)
Bunker Hill Monument (p. 101)
First Public School/Benjamin Franklin
Statue (p. 91)
New England Holocaust Memorial
(p. 96)
Shaw Memorial (Memorial to Robert
Gould Shaw and the Massachusetts
54th Regiment) (p. 87)

MUSEUMS

Blue Hills Trailside Museum (p. 114)
Boston Children's Museum (p. 114)

Harvard Art Museums (p. 81)
Harvard Museum of Natural History
(p. 82)
Institute of Contemporary Art (p. 69)
Isabella Stewart Gardner Museum
(p. 74)
John F. Kennedy Presidential Library
and Museum (p. 77)
MIT Museum (p. 84)
Museum of African American History
(p. 67)
Museum of Fine Arts (p. 75)
Museum of Science (p. 62)
Old State House Museum (p. 93)
Peabody Museum of Archaeology &
Ethnology (p. 82)
Sports Museum of New England
(p. 63)
West End Museum (p. 63)
USS *Constitution* Museum (p. 101)

OBSERVATORY

Skywalk Observatory at the Prudential
Center (p. 73)

PARKS & OPEN SPACES

Boston Common (p. 87)
James Rego Square (p. 99)
Public Garden (p. 103)
Rose Kennedy Greenway (p. 134)

WALKING TRAILS

Black Heritage Trail (p. 65)
Freedom Trail (p. 86)

ZOO

Franklin Park Zoo (p. 116)

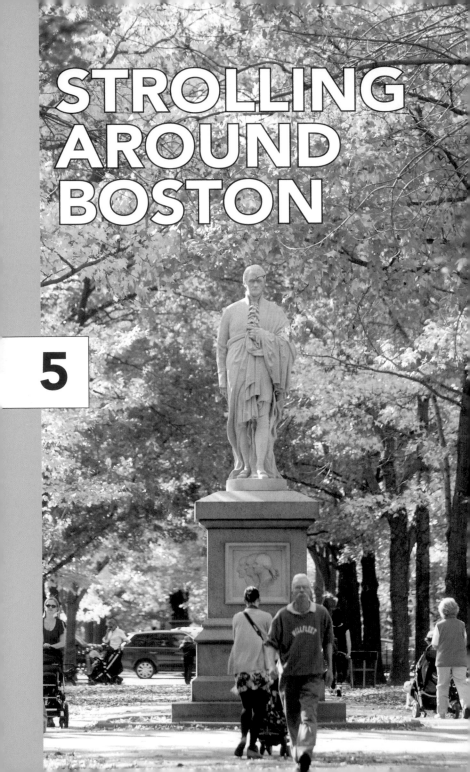

STROLLING AROUND BOSTON

5

Walking is the best way to see Boston. The narrow, twisting streets that make driving such a headache are a treat for pedestrians, who are always close to something worth seeing. The central city is compact—walking quickly from one end to the other takes about an hour—and abounds with historically and architecturally interesting buildings and neighborhoods.

In this chapter you'll find a tour of Boston's **Back Bay,** a walk along Boston's **Waterfront,** and an excursion around **Harvard Square** in Cambridge. For information on Boston's most famous walking tour, the 2.5-mile **Freedom Trail ★★★**, see chapter 4.

Be sure to wear comfortable shoes, and if you're not inclined to pay designer prices for designer water, bring your own bottle and fill it at your hotel.

WALKING TOUR 1: **THE BACK BAY**

START:	**The Public Garden (T: Green Line to Arlington).**
FINISH:	**Copley Square.**
TIME:	**2 hours if you make good time, 3 hours if you detour to the Esplanade, and longer if you do a lot of shopping.**
BEST TIME:	**Any time before late afternoon.**
WORST TIME:	**Late afternoon, when people and cars pack the streets. And don't attempt the detour on July 4th, when concertgoers jam the neighborhood. This walk is mostly outdoors, so if the weather is bad, you may find yourself in lots of shops. You decide whether that makes an overcast day a "best" or "worst" time.**

The Back Bay is the youngest neighborhood in central Boston, the product of a massive landfill project that transformed the city from 1835 to 1882. It's flat, symmetrical, logically designed—the names of the cross streets go in alphabetical order—and a refreshing contrast to downtown Boston's tangled geography.

Begin your walk in the:

1 Public Garden

Before the Back Bay was filled in, the Charles River flowed right up to Charles Street, which separates Boston Common from the Public Garden. On the night of April 18, 1775, British troops bound for Lexington and Concord boarded boats at the edge of the Common ("two if by sea") and set off for Cambridge across what's now the Public Garden.

Explore the lagoon, the trees and other flora, and the statuary. Take a ride on the **Swan Boats** (mid-Apr to mid-Sept), and then make your way

PREVIOUS PAGE: **The Commonwealth Avenue Mall.**

toward the corner of Charles and Beacon streets, staying inside the Public Garden (follow the sound of delighted children).

Here you'll see a 35-foot strip of cobblestones topped with the bronze figures that immortalize Robert McCloskey's book:

2 Make Way for Ducklings

The George Washington statue in the Public Garden.

Installed in 1987 and wildly popular since the moment they were unveiled, Nancy Schön's renderings of Mrs. Mallard and her eight babies are irresistible. Mrs. Mallard is just 38 inches tall, but that doesn't keep people of all ages from climbing on. If you don't know the story of the family's perilous trip to meet Mr. Mallard at the lagoon, ask one of the parents or children you'll find here.

The city bought the site of the Public Garden from private interests in 1824. Planting began in 1837, but it wasn't until the late 1850s that Arlington Street was built and the land permanently set aside.

Cross the lagoon using the tiny suspension bridge—reputedly the smallest in the world—and look for the statue of:

3 George Washington

Unveiled in 1875, this was Boston's first equestrian statue. It stands 38 feet tall and is considered an excellent likeness of the first president of the United States, an outstanding horseman. The artist, Thomas Ball, was a Charlestown native who worked in Italy. Among his students was noted sculptor Daniel Chester French. Pass through the gate onto Arlington Street. This is a good place to detour, before you begin exploring in earnest.

4 Take a Break ☕

Turn right and walk up Arlington Street to Beacon Street. On your right, across the busy intersection, is **Cheers,** 84 Beacon St. (www.cheersboston.com; ☎ **617/227-9605**), originally the Bull & Finch Pub. The food at this tourist magnet is tasty enough, and the bar looks enough like its TV offspring to satisfy all but the most devoted fans (you'll find a replica of the set at the Faneuil Hall Marketplace spinoff).

Alternatively, turn right on Beacon Street and walk 1 long block to Charles Street. You can eat in or pick up food to go at **Panificio,** 144 Charles St. (☎ **617/227-4340**), or indulge in a delicious French-style pastry at **Cafe Vanille,** 70 Charles St. (☎ **617/523-9200**). This street is also a promising place for a shopping break (see chapter 7).

**Walking Tour 1:
The Back Bay**

1 Public Garden
2 *Make Way for Ducklings*
3 George Washington
4a Cheers
4b Panificio
4c Cafe Vanille
5 Arthur Fiedler
6 Commonwealth Avenue
   Mall
7 First Baptist Church
8 Newbury Street
9 Exeter Street Theater
10 Church of the Covenant
11 Boston Museum of
   Natural History
12 Emmanuel Church
13 Arlington Street Church
14 Copley Square
15 Trinity Church
16 Boston Public Library
17 *The Tortoise & Hare*
   at Copley Square

After you've eaten, snacked, or picked up picnic food, backtrack along Beacon Street past Arlington Street to Embankment Road and turn right. Take the Arthur Fiedler Footbridge across Storrow Drive to the Esplanade and proceed forward across another (smaller) bridge. You'll soon see the giant head of:

5 Arthur Fiedler

Installed in 1985, this sculpture by Ralph Helmick consists of sheets of aluminum that eerily capture the countenance of the legendary conductor of the Boston Pops, who died in 1979. The amphitheater that's visible from all over the Esplanade is the **Hatch Shell,** where the Pops perform free in early July. The July 3 performance is a dress rehearsal for the legendary Fourth of July concert.

When you're ready, retrace your steps to the corner of Arlington Street and Commonwealth Avenue. You're looking down the:

6 Commonwealth Avenue Mall

The 8-block mall is the centerpiece of architect Arthur Gilman's design of the Back Bay. The graceful promenade is 100 feet wide (the entire street is 240 ft.) and stretches to Kenmore Square. Elegant Victorian mansions, almost all divided into apartments or in commercial or educational use, line the street. One of the great delights of being a pedestrian in Boston is taking in the details that adorn these buildings, which superficially look very much alike and up close resemble the members of a large, stylish, exceedingly eccentric family. Down the center of the boulevard, an apparently random collection of sculptures adorns the mall. They begin with **Alexander Hamilton,** across Arlington Street from **George Washington.** The most moving sculpture is at Dartmouth Street: The **Vendome Memorial** honors the memory of the nine firefighters who lost their lives in a blaze at the Hotel Vendome in 1972.

Two blocks from the Public Garden, at 110 Commonwealth Ave., at the corner of Clarendon Street, is the:

7 First Baptist Church

Built from 1870 to 1872 of Roxbury puddingstone, it originally housed the congregation of the Brattle Street Church (Unitarian), which had been downtown, near Faneuil Hall.

At Clarendon Street or Dartmouth Street, turn left and walk 1 block to:

8 Newbury Street

Commonwealth Avenue is the architectural heart of the Back Bay, and Newbury Street is boutique central. Take some time to roam around here (see chapter 7 for pointers), browsing in the galleries, window-shopping, and watching the chic shoppers.

Walk down Newbury Street to Exeter Street. At 26 Exeter St. is the building that was once the:

9 Exeter Street Theater

Designed in 1884 as the First Spiritualist Temple, it was a movie house from 1914 to 1984. Once known for the crowds flocking to *The Rocky Horror Picture Show,* it now houses offices and a restaurant.

When you're ready to continue your stroll (or when your credit cards cry for mercy), turn back toward the Public Garden and seek out three of Newbury Street's oldest buildings, starting with the:

10 Church of the Covenant

This Gothic-revival edifice at 67 Newbury St. was designed by Richard Upjohn and completed in 1867. The stained-glass windows—on view to the public only during Sunday services (10:30am)—are the work of Louis Comfort Tiffany.

Across the street, set back from the sidewalk at 234 Berkeley St., is the original home of the:

11 Boston Museum of Natural History

A forerunner of the Museum of Science, it was built according to William Preston's French Academic design. The 1864 structure, originally two stories high, still has its original roof, preserved when the building gained a third floor.

Cross Newbury Street again and continue walking toward the Public Garden. On your left, at 15 Newbury St., is:

12 Emmanuel Church

The first building completed on Newbury Street, in 1862, this Episcopal church ministers by way of the arts, so there might be a concert (classical to jazz, solo to orchestral) going on during your visit. Check ahead (www.emmanuelmusic.org; ✆ 617/536-3356) for schedules.

Now you're almost back at the Public Garden. On your left is the swanky Taj Boston hotel, which until 2007 was known as the original **Ritz-Carlton** (1927).

Turn right onto Arlington Street and walk 1 block. On your right, at 351 Boylston St., is the:

13 Arlington Street Church

This is the oldest church in the Back Bay, completed in 1861. An interesting blend of Georgian and Italianate details, it's the work of architect Arthur Gilman, who laid out this whole neighborhood. Here you'll find more Tiffany stained glass. Step inside (ask at the office for admission to the sanctuary) to see the pulpit that was in use in 1788 when the congregation worshipped downtown on Federal Street.

Follow Boylston Street away from the Public Garden. Two blocks up is:

14 Copley Square

Enjoy the fountain and visit the farmers' market, which operates Tuesday and Friday afternoons from July through November.

Overlooking the square is one of the most famous church buildings in the United States. This is:

15 Trinity Church

H. H. Richardson's Romanesque masterpiece, completed in 1877, is to your left. The church, 206 Clarendon St. (www.trinitychurchboston.org; ✆ 617/536-0944), was built on 4,502 pilings driven into the mud that was once the Back Bay. Brochures and guides are available to help you find your way around a building considered one of the finest examples of church architecture in the country. Tours cost $7 for adults, $5 for seniors and students with ID. The building is open weekdays from 9am to 5pm (until 7pm on Wed), Saturday 9am to 4:30pm, Sunday 7am to 7pm; check the website for the schedule of guided and self-guided tours. Friday organ recitals (p. 226) begin at 12:15pm.

The Copley Square Farmers' Market.

Across Dartmouth Street is the:

16 Boston Public Library

The work of architect Charles Follen McKim and many others, the Renaissance revival building was completed in 1895 after 10 years of construction. Its design reflects the significant influence of the Bibliothèque Nationale in Paris. Wander up the steps to check out the building's impressive interior (p. 70). The celebrated American sculptor **Daniel Chester French** designed the doors.

Head back across the street to Copley Square. In a sense, you've come full circle; as at the Public Garden, you'll see a playful and compelling sculpture by Nancy Schön:

17 The Tortoise and Hare at Copley Square

Designed to signify the end of the **Boston Marathon** (the finish line is on Boylston St. between Exeter and Dartmouth sts.), this work was unveiled for the 100th anniversary of the event in 1996.

From here you're in a good position to set out for any other part of town or to walk a little way in any direction and

The Tortoise and Hare at Copley Square.

continue exploring. Copley Place and the Shops at Prudential Center are nearby, Newbury Street is 1 block over, and there's a Green Line T station at Boylston and Dartmouth streets.

WALKING TOUR 2: **THE WATERFRONT**

START: **Old State House Museum (T: Orange or Blue Line to State).**
FINISH: **John Joseph Moakley U.S. Courthouse.**
TIME: **2–4 hours, depending on how much time you spend in shops and museums.**
BEST TIME: **Mid-morning to early afternoon.**
WORST TIME: **Mid-afternoon or later. Most attractions will be closing, and you'll be wandering through rush-hour traffic.**

One of America's legendary seaports, Boston draws much of its considerable appeal from its proximity to the water. This tour takes you near and along the shoreline of the Colonial town and the modern city.

The same building holds the subway station and your first stop, the:

1 Old State House Museum

The little brick building at 206 Washington St. (www.bostonhistory.org; ✆ 617/720-1713) was erected in 1713, replacing the Boston Town House. Back then, the shore was just a couple of blocks away, and this was a tall building. Exit and turn toward the water (downhill), passing the subway entrance. See p. 93 for details about the museum and the **Boston Massacre Site,** a circle of cobblestones on the sidewalk beneath the balcony.

Down the shallow hill to your left is **Faneuil Hall.** Now landlocked, it stood on the shore before the harbor began to fill with silt and garbage. The filling-in was completed (using earth) and new streets laid out as part of the Quincy Market project of 1826. Ahead of you, sloping gently toward Boston Harbor, is **State Street.** This was King Street until 1784 (fairly late considering the antiroyal sentiment that inspired the change), and it ran right out into the harbor.

With the Old State House at your back, follow State Street toward the water. Note that the 40-story glass skyscraper at the corner of Congress Street, Exchange Place, encloses the facade of its predecessor, the Boston Stock Exchange (1891). On State Street just before Kilby Street, a plaque marks the former site of the:

2 Bunch of Grapes Tavern

Constructed in 1712, the tavern entertained both independence-minded colonists and their royalist counterparts before and during the Revolutionary War. After the British symbols (including the lion and unicorn from the Old State House) were removed from most of the public buildings in town in July 1776, they were made into a bonfire here. The Ohio Company, which settled that state, was formed here in 1786.

Where Kilby Street and Merchants Row meet on either side of State Street, pause and step out of the way of other pedestrians. This is the:

From where he sat on the steps of the Town House, he [Johnny] could look the brief length of King Street which quickly and imperceptibly turned into Long Wharf, running for half a mile into the sea . . . There was not another wharf in America so large, so famous, so rich.
—Esther Forbes, *Johnny Tremain*, 1943

3 Shoreline of Colonial Boston

The construction of Long Wharf began here in 1709. At its greatest, Boston's main wharf was 1,743 feet long and 104 feet wide, extending so far into the harbor that the water at the end was 17 feet deep.

Continue on State Street, crossing Broad Street, developed in 1805–07 as part of a plan to improve the waterfront. Charles Bulfinch helped design 60 of the brick warehouses that stood here, some of which still stand. Pause at the corner of State and India streets and look up at the:

4 Custom House

Construction took a full decade, from 1837–47; the foundation alone, which sits on some 3,000 wooden piles resting on bedrock, took 3 years to build. The tower, added in 1911–15, was for many years the tallest structure in town. The building is now a Marriott timeshare property. Admire the colorful clocks on all four sides of the tower, but don't count on them to tell the correct time.

5 Take a Break ☕

Faneuil Hall Marketplace is a block away. If the weather is fine, head to the enormous food court inside Quincy Market for a snack or meal to go, then take it across the street to the Greenway (see the next stop).

Leave through the archway at the east end of the complex, in Marketplace Center (look for the Gap). Filling the space between the market and the harbor, where traffic on an ugly interstate highway once roared about 20 feet above street level, is the:

6 Rose Fitzgerald Kennedy Greenway

This lovely park occupies 15 acres of prime real estate, arranged like no park you've ever seen before—it's 1 mile long and a block or so wide. The major legacy of the $15-billion Big Dig highway-construction project, this constantly evolving institution already features gorgeous plants and flowers along with dramatic public art. Check the website, **www.rosekennedygreenway.org**, to see whether any events are scheduled during your visit. Formally opened in 2008, the Greenway consists of four sections: North End, Wharf District, Dewey Square, and Chinatown. You're standing in the Wharf District.

Across the way, to your right as you face the harbor, is the Boston Marriott Long Wharf hotel. Cross the John F. Fitzgerald Surface Road, the Greenway, and Atlantic Avenue and step out of the flow of the crowd to take in:

7 Long Wharf

Boston's principal wharf opened for business in 1710. This is the embarkation point for many sightseeing cruises, as well as the MBTA ferry to Charlestown. Even at its busiest, it's not nearly as crowded and frantic as it was in its

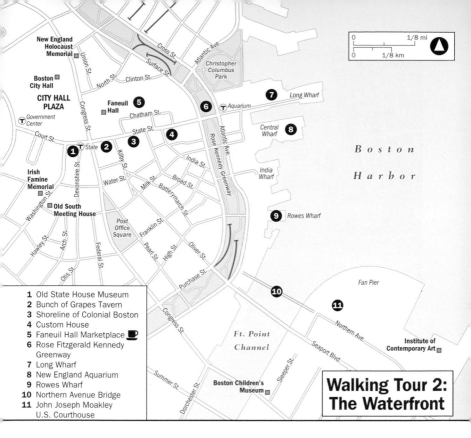

1 Old State House Museum
2 Bunch of Grapes Tavern
3 Shoreline of Colonial Boston
4 Custom House
5 Faneuil Hall Marketplace
6 Rose Fitzgerald Kennedy Greenway
7 Long Wharf
8 New England Aquarium
9 Rowes Wharf
10 Northern Avenue Bridge
11 John Joseph Moakley U.S. Courthouse

Walking Tour 2: The Waterfront

18th- and 19th-century heyday, when Boston was one of the most important American ports. Near the end of the wharf is a granite building, dating from 1846, that was used by Customs appraisers. Now it houses offices and residences. At the very end of the wharf is a small plaza with a spectacular view that encompasses the harbor, the airport, and the Harbor Islands.

Return to the Marriott and stand with the lobby behind you. Walk 1 block (with Legal Sea Foods on your right) on Old Atlantic Avenue to the:

8 New England Aquarium

The aquarium opened in 1969. Peter Chermayeff, then with Cambridge Seven Associates, designed the structure, which echoes the waves of the adjacent harbor. You don't have to buy a ticket to check out the harbor seals, which frolic in an exhibit near the entrance. See the listing on p. 59.

Continue to walk along the waterfront for the equivalent of 2 blocks. On your right, you'll pass the residential Harbor Towers, designed by I. M. Pei and opened in 1971. This is India Wharf, which adjoins your next stop:

9 Rowes Wharf

Turn left as you reach the first redbrick building in this complex and follow the walkway that encircles it, along the water. The hotel-office-residential development bears the name of John Rowe (known as "Merchant" Rowe),

The Rose Fitzgerald Kennedy Greenway has replaced the traffic jams of the Central Artery with a greenery-filled escape.

who donated the Sacred Cod that hangs in the State House. The wharf was constructed after a fire in 1760 and has long been used as a ferry terminal. It's probably better known today for the dramatic arch in the center of the Boston Harbor Hotel (1985), designed by the Chicago architecture firm Skidmore, Owings, and Merrill. Enjoy the peekaboo view of the Greenway through the arch as you walk past the hotel and the boats in the marina and at the docks.

At the end of this little promenade is a short staircase that leads up to the:

10 Northern Avenue Bridge

An iron-turntable bridge built in 1908, the pedestrian-only bridge is a favorite with bridge aficionados—if "through truss swing span" means something to you, make sure you have your camera—and makes a good place to pause and look around. Beneath you is Fort Point Channel, which separates downtown from South Boston. A stone's throw away is the Evelyn Moakley Bridge, the vehicular access point to the Seaport District and an important

---

💬 It's All French to Me

As you explore the Boston area, you may hear the name of sculptor **Daniel Chester French.** French (1850–1931), a New Hampshire native, was responsible for the gorgeous doors on the Dartmouth Street side of the **Boston Public Library,** the statue of **John Harvard** in Harvard Yard, and the **Minute Man** statue near the North Bridge in Concord. If you're not a parochial Bostonian, you probably know him best as the sculptor of the seated Abraham Lincoln in the presidential memorial in Washington.

The striking architecture of the John Joseph Moakley U.S. Courthouse.

piece of the Big Dig. Behind you, at the corner of Atlantic Avenue, is the First District Headquarters of the U.S. Coast Guard. The *Massachusetts,* the first commissioned revenue cutter, was based here. (Revenue cutters were the forerunners of the U.S. Coast Guard.)

Cross the Northern Avenue Bridge. You're on Old Northern Avenue, but the formal address of your destination is 1 Courthouse Way. This is the:

11 John Joseph Moakley U.S. Courthouse

Dedicated in 2001, the courthouse bears the name of a longtime Massachusetts congressman who was instrumental in securing funding for the Big Dig. Henry N. Cobb of Pei Cobb Freed & Partners designed the deceptively plain structure. Follow the Harborwalk around to the back to take in the centerpiece of the design, an 88-foot-tall wall of glass that opens the interior of the courthouse to the harbor. During business hours, the public is welcome to enter the building, take in the dramatic views, and even have a meal or snack overlooking the water in the second-floor cafeteria. You can't bring in your cellphone (the guards in the lobby will take it away and return it as you leave), and adults must show two forms of ID to enter.

The park outside the courthouse makes a good place to plan your next stop. From here, both the **Boston Children's Museum** (p. 114) and the **Institute of Contemporary Art** (p. 69) are within easy walking distance. You can return to the Greenway and work up an appetite by following it south to **Chinatown** or north to the **North End.** Or take public transportation—the Silver Line Courthouse stop is nearby, and South Station is about 15 minutes away on foot—to your next destination.

START:	**Harvard Square (T: Red Line to Harvard).**
FINISH:	**John F. Kennedy Park.**
TIME:	**2–4 hours, depending on how much time you spend in shops and museums; allow an hour for the detour to the Longfellow House–Washington's Headquarters National Historic Site.**
BEST TIME:	**Almost any time during the day. The Harvard Art Museums offer free admission to Massachusetts residents on Saturday morning.**
WORST TIME:	**The last week of May. You might have trouble gaining admission to Harvard Yard during commencement festivities. The ceremony is Thursday morning; without a ticket, you won't be allowed in.**

Popular impressions to the contrary, Cambridge is not exclusively Harvard. In fact, even Harvard Square isn't exclusively Harvard. During a walk around the area, you'll see historic buildings and sights, interesting museums, and notable architecture on and off the university's main campus.

Leave the T station by the main entrance (use the ramp to the turnstiles, then take the escalator) and emerge in the heart of:

1 Harvard Square

Town and gown meet at this lively intersection, where you'll get a taste of the improbable mix of people drawn to the crossroads of Cambridge. To your right is the landmark **Out of Town News** kiosk (✆ **617/354-1441**). It stocks newspapers, magazines, and tons of souvenirs (a selection that reflects the Internet-fueled drop in demand for nonvirtual journalism). At the colorful kiosk in front of you, you can request information about the area. Step close to it so that you're out of the flow of pedestrian traffic and look around.

The store across Massachusetts Avenue is the **Harvard Coop.** The name rhymes with *hoop*—say "co-op" and risk being taken for a Yalie. On the far side of the intersection, at the corner of John F. Kennedy and Brattle streets, is a sign reading dewey, cheetham & howe (say it out loud) on the third floor of the brick building. National Public Radio's *Car Talk* originates here.

Turn around so that the Coop is at your back and walk half a block, crossing Dunster Street. Across the way, at 1341 Massachusetts Ave., you'll see:

2 Wadsworth House

Most of the people waiting for the bus in front of this yellow wood building probably don't know that it was built in 1726 as a residence for Harvard's fourth president—but then, neither do most Harvard students. Its biggest claim to fame is a classic: George Washington slept here.

Cross Mass. Ave., pass through the gate, and continue until you're at the edge of a sweeping lawn crisscrossed with walking paths. This is:

3 Harvard Yard

You're standing in the oldest part of "the Yard." It was a patch of grass with animals grazing on it when Harvard College was established in 1636 to train young men for the ministry, and it wasn't much more when the Continental Army spent the winter of 1775–76 here. Harvard is the oldest college in the country, and it has the most competitive admissions process. If you suggest aloud that it's not the best, you might encounter the attitude that inspired the saying "You can always tell a Harvard man, but you can't tell him much."

Walk forward until you see majestic Johnston Gate on your left and take in the classroom and administration buildings and dormitories that make up the:

4   Old Yard

Just inside the gate stands **Massachusetts Hall.** Built in 1720, this National Historic Landmark is the university's oldest surviving building. First-year students

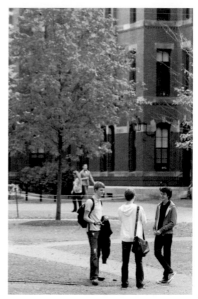

When school is in session, Harvard Yard fills with students.

share "Mass. Hall" with the first-floor office of the university president, whom they traditionally invite upstairs for tea once a year. Across the way is **Harvard Hall,** a classroom building constructed in 1765. Walk along the Yard side of Harvard Hall until you reach matching side-by-side buildings, **Hollis** and **Stoughton halls.** Hollis dates to 1763 (Stoughton "only" to 1805) and has been home to many students who went on to great fame, among them Ralph Waldo Emerson, Henry David Thoreau, and Charles Bulfinch. Almost hidden across the tiny lawn between these two buildings is **Holden Chapel,** a Georgian-style gem completed in 1744. It has been an anatomy lab, a classroom building, and, of course, a chapel, and it is now home to the oldest American college choir, the Harvard Glee Club.

Impressions

One emerged, as one still does, from the subway exit in the Square and faced an old red-brick wall behind which stretched, to my fond eye, what remains still the most beautiful campus in America, the Harvard Yard. If there is any one place in all America that mirrors better all American history, I do not know of it.

—Theodore H. White, *In Search of History,* 1978

Cross the Yard to the building opposite Johnston Gate. This is:

5   University Hall

Designed by Charles Bulfinch and constructed of granite quarried in suburban Chelmsford, the 1813 structure is the college's main administration building. In 1969, students protesting the Vietnam War occupied it.

University Hall is best known as the backdrop of the:

6 John Harvard Statue

This is one of the most photographed objects in the Boston area. Daniel Chester French designed it in 1884.

Walk around University Hall into the adjoining quad. This is still the Yard, but it's the **"New Yard,"** sometimes called **Tercentenary Theater** because the college's 300th-anniversary celebration was held here in 1936. Commencement and other university-wide ceremonies take place here.

On your right is:

7 Widener Library

The centerpiece of the world's largest university library system was built in 1913 as a memorial to Harry Elkins Widener, Harvard class of 1907. Thoroughly debunked legend has it that he

The John Harvard statue.

died when the *Titanic* sank in 1912 because he was unable to swim 50 yards to a lifeboat, and his heartbroken mother donated $2 million for the library on the condition that every undergraduate prove his ability to swim 50 yards. Today the library holds more than three million volumes, including 3,500 rare volumes collected by Harry Elkins Widener himself, on 50 miles of shelves. Don't even think about swiping Harry's Gutenberg Bible. The last person to try, in 1969, gained access from above but couldn't climb out. With the 70-pound Bible in his knapsack, he fell six stories to the courtyard below (and survived).

Horace Trumbauer of Philadelphia designed the library. His primary design assistant was Julian Francis Abele, a student of architecture at the University of Pennsylvania and the first black graduate of L'Ecole des Beaux Arts in Paris. The lobby—which sits within view of the locked memorial room that holds Widener's collection—is not open to the public, but you may be able to talk your way in if you're affiliated (student or staff) with another university; visit

---

💬 Nothing but the Truth

The likeness of **John Harvard** outside University Hall is known as the "Statue of Three Lies" because the inscription reads "John Harvard/Founder/1638." In fact, the college was founded in 1636. Harvard, one of the school's many benefactors, didn't establish it, but did donate money and his library. What's more, this isn't even John Harvard. No portraits of him survive, so the model for the benevolent-looking bronze gentleman was, according to various accounts, either his nephew or a student.

Walking Tour 3: Harvard Square

LAW SCHOOL

Cambridge Common

RADCLIFFE COLLEGE

Old Burying Ground

HARVARD YARD

KENNEDY SCHOOL OF GOVERNMENT

J.F.K. Park

Waterhouse St.

Berkeley St.

Mason St.

Garden St.

Brattle St.

Hilliard St.

Story St.

Mt. Auburn St.

University Rd.

Bennett St.

Appian Wy.

Farwell Pl.

Church St.

Palmer St.

Brattle St.

John F. Kennedy St.

Winthrop St.

South St.

Dunster St.

Holyoke St.

Linden St.

Plympton St.

DeWolfe St.

Bow St.

Mt. Auburn St.

Arrow St.

Massachusetts Ave.

Massachusetts Ave.

Oxford St.

Divinity Ave.

Kirkland St.

Cambridge St.

Sumner Rd.

Broadway

Harvard St.

Ware St.

Prescott St.

Quincy St.

T Harvard

0   1/8 mi
0   1/8 km

1 Harvard Square	**13** Memorial Hall
2 Wadsworth House	**14** Harvard Museum of Natural History
3 Harvard Yard	**15** Science Center
4 Old Yard	**16** Science Center
5 University Hall	**17** Cambridge Common
6 John Harvard Statue	**18** Christ Church
7 Widener Library	**19** Radcliffe Yard
8 Memorial Church	**20** L.A. Burdick Chocolates
9 Sever Hall	**21** Brattle Theatre
10 Carpenter Center for the Visual Arts	**22** Harvard Lampoon Castle
11 Fogg Museum *(closed through 2014)*	**23** John F. Kennedy Park
12 Arthur M. Sackler Museum	

the office to the left of the main entrance. If you're not allowed to take a peek, pause at the top of the outside staircase and turn around to enjoy the view.

Walk down the stairs and across the quad. Facing the library is:

8 Memorial Church

Built in 1931, the church is topped with a tower and weather vane 197 feet tall. You're welcome to look around the Georgian revival–style edifice unless services are going on, or to attend them if they are. Morning prayers run daily from 8:45 to 9am, and the Sunday service is at 11am. Weddings and funerals also take place here. The entrance is on the left. Inside, on the south wall (toward the Yard), panels bear the names of Harvard alumni who

Sever Hall's whispering gallery.

died in the world wars, Korea, and Vietnam. One is Joseph P. Kennedy, Jr., the president's brother, class of 1938.

Facing Widener Library with Memorial Church behind you, turn left toward:

9 Sever Hall

H. H. Richardson, architect of Boston's Trinity Church, designed this classroom building (1880). Surveys of architects and designers consistently name the deceptively simple structure one of the professionals' favorite buildings in the Boston area. Note the gorgeous brickwork that includes rolled moldings around the doors, the fluted brick chimneys, and the arrangement of the windows.

> **○ Pssst . . . Check This Out**
>
> Climb the front steps of **Sever Hall** and scoot to the side of the entrance, out of the way of passing students. The doorway is set in a "whispering gallery." Stand on one side of the arch, station a friend or willing passerby on the opposite side, and speak softly into the facade. Someone standing next to you can't hear you, but the person at the other side of the arch can.

Facing Sever Hall, turn right and go around to the back. The building on your right is Emerson Hall, which appeared in the movie *Love Story* as Barrett Hall, named after the family of Ryan O'Neal's character. Cross this quad and exit through the gate onto Quincy Street.

Turn right and walk about 300 feet. On the other side of the street, at 24 Quincy St., is the:

10 Carpenter Center for the Visual Arts

Art exhibitions occupy the lobby, the Harvard Film Archive shows movies in the basement (pick up a schedule on the main floor), and the concrete-and-glass building is itself a work of art. Opened in 1963, it was designed by the

Swiss-French architect Le Corbusier and the team of Sert, Jackson, and Gourley. It's the only Le Corbusier design in North America.

Backtrack along Quincy Street. Opposite the gate through which you left the Yard is the:

11 Fogg Museum

Founded in 1895, the museum has been at 32 Quincy St. since the building was completed in 1927. The Fogg, the adjacent Busch-Reisinger Museum, and the Sackler Museum (described below) make up the Harvard Art Museums. The Fogg and Busch-Reisinger are scheduled to reopen in 2013 after extensive renovations. Highlights of the excellent collections are on display at our next stop. See p. 81 for details.

Continue on Quincy Street and cross the street to 485 Broadway, the:

12 Arthur M. Sackler Museum

The British architect James Stirling designed the Sackler, which he called "the newest animal in Harvard's architectural zoo." It opened in 1984. The Sackler normally houses the university's spectacular collection of Asian art; at press time, the focus is on a selection of work from the Harvard Art Museums' collections.

Continue on Quincy Street. As you cross Cambridge Street, watch out for confused drivers emerging from the underpass to your left. Filling the block between Cambridge and Kirkland streets is:

13 Memorial Hall

This imposing Victorian structure, known to students as "Mem Hall," was completed in 1874. Enter from Cambridge Street and investigate the hall of memorials, a transept where you can read the names of the Harvard men who died fighting for the Union during the Civil War—but not of their Confederate counterparts. (The name of Col. Robert Gould Shaw, Matthew Broderick's character in the movie *Glory,* is halfway down on the right.) To the right is **Sanders Theatre,** prized as a performance space and lecture hall for its excellent acoustics and clear views. To the left is **Annenberg Hall.** It's a dining hall that's closed to visitors, but you may be able to sneak a look at the gorgeous stained-glass windows. Harvard graduates William Ware and Henry Van Brunt won a design competition for Memorial Hall, which was constructed for a total cost of $390,000 (most of it donated by alumni). The colorful tower is a replica of the original, destroyed by fire in 1956 and rebuilt in 1999.

Facing in the same direction you were when you entered, walk through the transept and exit onto Kirkland Street. Turn left and quickly right, onto Oxford Street. One block up on the right, at 26 Oxford St., you'll see an entrance to the:

14 Harvard Museum of Natural History

Adjoining the **Peabody Museum of Archaeology & Ethnology** at 11 Divinity Ave., the Museum of Natural History entertainingly presents the university's collections and research relating to the natural world. See p. 82 for a full description.

The Science Center is said to resemble a Polaroid camera.

Leave through the back door of 11 Divinity Ave. and look around. Across the street at 6 Divinity Ave. is the **Semitic Museum** (www.semitic museum.fas.harvard.edu; 🕿 **617/495-4631**), where the second- and third-floor galleries hold displays of archaeological artifacts and photographs from the Near and Middle East. Horace Trumbauer, the architect of Widener Library, designed the building next door, 2 Divinity Ave. It's home to the **Harvard-Yenching Library,** a repository of the university's hundreds of thousands of volumes relating to the Far East. For every person who can tell you that, there are several thousand who know this building for the pair of **Chinese stone lions** flanking the front door.

Turn right and return to Kirkland Street, then go right. You'll pass Memorial Hall on your left as you proceed to the intersection of Kirkland and Oxford streets. At 0 Oxford St. is the university's:

15 Science Center

The 10-story monolith is said to resemble a Polaroid camera (Edwin H. Land, founder of the Polaroid Corporation, was one of its main benefactors). The Spanish architect Josep Lluís Sert designed the Science Center, which opened in 1972. Sert, the dean of the university's Graduate School of Design from 1953 to 1969, was a disciple of Le Corbusier (who designed the Carpenter Center for the Visual Arts). On the plaza between the Science Center and the Yard is the **Tanner Rock Fountain,** a group of 159 New England boulders arranged around a small fountain. Since 1985 this has been a favorite spot for students to relax and watch unsuspecting passersby get wet: The fountain sprays a fine mist, which begins slowly and gradually intensifies.

16 Take a Break 🍽

The **main level of the Science Center** is open to the public and has several options if you want a soft drink, gourmet coffee, or sandwich. Go easy on the sweets, though, in anticipation of the next break.

Leave the Science Center through the doors near the fountain and turn right. Keeping the underpass on your left, follow the walkway for the equivalent of 1½ blocks as it curves around to the right. The Harvard Law School campus is on your right. You're back at Massachusetts Avenue. Cross carefully to:

17 Cambridge Common

Memorials and plaques dot this well-used plot of greenery and bare earth. Follow the sidewalk along Massachusetts Avenue to the left, and after a block or so you'll walk near or over horseshoes embedded in the concrete. This is the path William Dawes, Paul Revere's fellow alarm-sounder, took from Boston to Lexington on April 18, 1775. Turn right onto Garden Street and continue following the Common for 1 block. On your right you'll see a monument marking the place where Gen. George Washington took control of the Continental Army on July 3, 1775.

Cross Garden Street and backtrack to Zero Garden St. This is:

18 Christ Church

Peter Harrison of Newport, Rhode Island (also the architect of King's Chapel in Boston), designed the oldest church in Cambridge, which opened in 1760. Note the square wooden tower. Inside the vestibule you can still see bullet holes made by British muskets. At one time troops from Connecticut, who melted down the organ pipes to make ammunition, used the church as their barracks. The graveyard on the Massachusetts Avenue side of the building, the **Old Burying Ground,** is the oldest in Cambridge, dating to 1635. It's the final resting place of nine Harvard presidents as well as many early settlers and at least two black Revolutionary War soldiers.

Facing Christ Church, turn right and follow Garden Street to the next intersection. This is Appian Way. Turn left and take the first right into:

19 Radcliffe Yard

Radcliffe College was founded in 1879 as the "Harvard Annex" and named for Ann Radcliffe, Lady Mowlson, Harvard's first female benefactor. Undergraduate classes merged with Harvard's in 1943, Radcliffe graduates first received Harvard degrees in 1963, and Harvard officially assumed responsibility for educating undergraduate women in 1977. Radcliffe was an independent corporation until 1999; it's now the university's Radcliffe Institute for Advanced Study. The institute's first dean, Drew Gilpin Faust, became the university's first female president in 2007.

After you've strolled around, return to Appian Way, turn right, and walk half a block. You'll emerge on Brattle Street.

A visit to the **Longfellow House–Washington's Headquarters National Historic Site,** 105 Brattle St. (www.nps.gov/long; ✆ **617/876-4491**; p. 83), makes an interesting detour and adds about an hour to your walk. If you don't detour, turn left and continue walking along Brattle Street. Excellent shops (see chapter 7) line both sides of the street.

20 Take a Break 🍵

Sate your sweet tooth with something from the celebrated New Hampshire–based confectioner **L. A. Burdick Chocolates,** 52 Brattle St. (www.burdick chocolate.com; ✆ **617/491-4340**). Burdick's treats are pricey but scrumptious; drinks, available hot or iced, include coffee, tea, and, of course, chocolate. **Crema Cafe,** 27 Brattle St. (www.cremacambridge.com; ✆ **617/876-2700**), serves sandwiches, soups, salads, pastries, and great coffee.

At 40 Brattle St. you'll find the:

21 Brattle Theatre

Opened in 1890 as Brattle Hall, the theater (www.brattlefilm.org; ✆ **617/ 876-6837**) was founded by the Cambridge Social Union and used as a cultural and entertainment venue. It became a movie house in 1953 and gained a reputation as Cambridge's center for art films.

You're now in the **Brattle Square** part of Harvard Square. You might see street performers, a protest, a speech, or more shopping opportunities. Facing Dickson Brothers Hardware, cross Brattle Street, bear right, and follow the curve of the building all the way around the corner so that you're on Mount Auburn Street. Stay on the left-hand side of the street as you cross John F. Kennedy, Dunster, Holyoke, and Linden streets. On your left, between Dunster and Holyoke streets, is **Holyoke Center,** a Harvard administration building designed by Josep Lluís Sert that has commercial space on the ground floor.

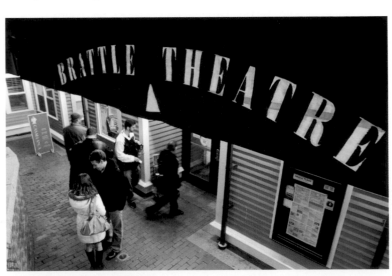

Here's looking at you, Brattle Theatre.

Play It, Sam

The **Brattle Theatre,** one of the oldest independent movie houses in the country, started the *Casablanca* revival craze, which explains the name of the restaurant in the basement.

The corner of Mount Auburn and Linden streets offers a good view of the:

22 Harvard Lampoon Castle

Constructed in 1909, designed by Wheelwright & Haven (architects of Boston's Horticultural Hall), and listed on the National Register of Historic Places, this is the home of Harvard's undergraduate humor magazine, the ***Lampoon.*** The main tower resembles a face, with windows as the eyes, nose, and mouth, topped by what looks like a miner's hat. All five of the building's addresses have been mentioned on *The Simpsons,* which draws many of its writers from the staff. The *Lampoon* and the daily student newspaper, the **Crimson,** share a long history of reciprocal pranks and vandalism.

You'll pass the *Crimson* offices on your right if you detour to the **Harvard Book Store** (turn left onto Plympton St. and follow it up the hill to the corner of Mass. Ave.). Otherwise, cross Mount Auburn Street and walk away from Holyoke Center on Holyoke Place, Holyoke Street, or Dunster Street to get a sense of some of the rest of the campus. The tower directly in front of you sits atop Lowell House, one of a dozen residences for upperclassmen. (First-year students live in and around Harvard Yard.)

Turn right on Winthrop Street or South Street, and proceed to John F. Kennedy Street. Turn left and walk toward the Charles River. On your right at Memorial Drive is:

23 John F. Kennedy Park

In the 1970s, when the search was on for a site for the Kennedy Library, this lovely parcel of land was an empty plot near the MBTA train yard (the Red Line then ended at Harvard). Traffic concerns led to the library's being built in Dorchester, but the **Graduate School of Government** and this adjacent park bear the president's name. Walk away from the street to enjoy the fountain, which is engraved with excerpts from JFK's speeches. This is a great place to take a break and plan the rest of your day.

The Harvard Lampoon Castle.

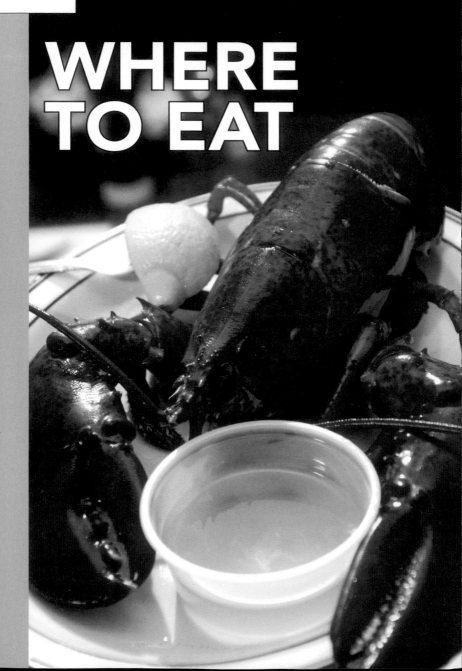

6

WHERE TO EAT

The days when restaurant snobs in Boston complained that they had to go to New York to get a decent meal are long gone. Especially in warm weather, when local produce appears on menus in every price range, Boston-area restaurants are excellent. Celebrity chefs and rising stars spice up the dynamic dining scene, students seek out good value, and traditional favorites—notably seafood—occupy an important niche.

The Italian restaurants of the North End are a classic Boston destination, but the city's hottest restaurant scenes are in the South End and the Fenway. Across the river, Cambridge offers a tasty mix of special-occasion places, neighborhood stalwarts, cheap student hangouts, and diverse ethnic restaurants. Small plates and food trucks are among the national trends that have caught on in the Boston area; meat often hogs the spotlight, but vegetarians and vegans (as well as gluten-sensitive diners) have more options than ever before. And many visitors just want to know where they can get a big lobster. This chapter aims to help every diner find something that hits the spot.

best BETS

- **Best for Families:** The wood-fired brick ovens of the **Bertucci's** chain are magnets for kids' attention, and the pizza that comes out of them is equally enthralling. Picky parents will be happy here, too. There are locations in Boston and Cambridge. See p. 179.

- **Best Value:** Quality is high and prices are reasonable all over Chinatown; **Great Taste Bakery & Restaurant** is an excellent example. You'll do a double-take when the check arrives after a dinner of Afghan favorites at the **Helmand,** in East Cambridge. Yes, you're really that satisfied for that little money. See p. 165 and p. 182.

- **Best Splurge:** South End pioneer **Hamersley's Bistro** has been the best restaurant in Boston's foodiest neighborhood since 1987. In Cambridge, the **East Coast Grill & Raw Bar** is a colorful blur of a place that earns national acclaim for both seafood and barbecue. See p. 166 and p. 180.

- **Most Romantic:** The best restaurant in the North End, **Mamma Maria,** is my unwavering suggestion for anniversary dinners. It serves remarkable regional Italian fare in a spaghetti-and-meatballs neighborhood. Soaring ceilings, colorful decor, and (seasonally) a roaring fire make the atmosphere in the Monday Club Bar at **UpStairs on the Square,** in Harvard Square, perfect for a rendezvous. See p. 154 and p. 175.

- **Best Service:** The **Bristol Lounge** boasts fantastic food, a lovely atmosphere, and an apparently mind-reading waitstaff; it's expensive and totally worth it. See p. 171.

PREVIOUS PAGE: **Fresh lobster is a local specialty.**

Price Categories

Very Expensive	$41 and up
Expensive	$31–$40
Moderate	$20–$30
Inexpensive	Under $20

o **Best Seafood: Legal Sea Foods** is a chain for a great reason: People can't get enough of the freshest fish and shellfish around. There are locations in Boston and Cambridge. See p. 151.

o **Best for Sharing:** Dim sum may be the perfect food for sharing, and Boston's best dim sum is at **Hei La Moon.** Across the river, superb Spanish tapas and luscious sangria make **Dalí** a favorite with groups and families. See p. 164 and p. 180.

o **Best Wine List:** A wine list that suits the tricky cuisine and doesn't break the bank is just one of many things to love about **Market.** The food at **Oleana,** in Cambridge, is equally challenging; the wine list is generally pricey but definitely rises to the occasion. See p. 163 and p. 180.

o **Best for a Business Lunch:** Plenty of deals go down at private clubs and formal restaurants, but that can take hours. Show your local savvy by joining the line at the **Sultan's Kitchen,** in the Financial District. **Clover Food Lab** enjoys similar cachet in Harvard Square and operates multiple trucks that feed hordes of local businesspeople. See p. 160 and p. 178.

o **Best for Vegetarians:** The ideal middle ground for herbivores dining with omnivores, the **Elephant Walk** serves sublime French and Cambodian cuisine. Vegetarians and vegans alike will find flavorful dishes that cater to their needs. There are locations in Boston and Cambridge. See p. 173.

THE WATERFRONT

Restaurants in this neighborhood draw much of their business from hungry tourists, expense-account travelers (including conventiongoers fleeing the Seaport's chain overload), and local office workers in search of a quick lunch that won't ruin their budgets. To join that third group, visit **Clover Food Truck** (p. 178), on the Rose Kennedy Greenway across from South Station (Atlantic Ave. and Summer St.), and see the box "Boston's Food Trucks," below.

The Barking Crab ★ ☺ SEAFOOD   The Barking Crab is a clam shack overlooking the water. That wouldn't be a big deal on the Maine coast or the shores of the Chesapeake Bay, but in downtown Boston, it's beyond cool. This extremely casual restaurant has a busy bar and a clientele of local office workers and families visiting the Boston Children's Museum. The place to be in the summer is at a picnic table on the deck, which might require a wait at busy times; in the off season, the dining room is a cozy oasis. The menu includes the usual clam chowder, fried-seafood plates, and lobsters, with a handful of creative options (such as a yummy crab-cake sandwich) and enough nonseafood dishes to keep vegetarians from starving. The food is fine, and overall quite good, but that's not really the point. This is a *downtown* clam shack—what a concept.

88 Sleeper St. (btw. Northern Ave. and Seaport Blvd.). www.barkingcrab.com. ✆ **617/426-2722.** Reservations accepted only for parties of 6 or more. Main courses $10–$25; sandwiches

$7–$21 (most less than $15); fresh seafood market price. AE, DC, MC, V. Sun–Wed 11:30am–11pm; Thurs–Sat 11:30am–1am. Closed 3 weeks in Jan. T: Red Line to South Station and 10-min. walk or Silver Line to Courthouse; or Blue Line to Aquarium and 10-min. walk.

Legal Sea Foods ★★★ SEAFOOD   This family-owned chain enjoys a well-deserved international reputation for serving only the freshest, best-quality fish and shellfish, processed at its own state-of-the-art plant. No, it's not a secret insider tip—it's better. The menu includes regular selections (haddock, salmon, shrimp, calamari, and lobster, among others), plus whatever looked good that morning, and it's all splendid. The clam and fish chowders are justly famous. Entrees run from grilled fish served plain or with Cajun spices (try the arctic char) to cioppino, an aquarium's worth of seafood in tomato broth. Or splurge on a mammoth lobster. For dessert, the Boston cream pie is so good that you might come back just for that. And the wine list is exceptional—a wine-journalist friend tells me it's the best restaurant-chain list in the country. The flagship location, Legal Harborside, is a three-level space on Northern Avenue in the Seaport District—a hassle to reach, but the only branch with a water view.

255 State St. (1 block from Atlantic Ave.). www.legalseafoods.com. ℭ **617/742-5300.** Reservations recommended. Main courses $11–$19 at lunch, $14–$35 at dinner; lobster market price. AE, DC, DISC, MC, V. Mon–Thurs 11am–10pm; Fri–Sun 11am–11pm. T: Blue Line to Aquarium. Also at the Prudential Center, 800 Boylston St., btw. Fairfield and Gloucester sts. (ℭ **617/266-6800;** T: Green Line B, C, or D to Hynes Convention Center, or E to Prudential); 26 Park Sq., btw. Columbus Ave. and Stuart St. (ℭ **617/426-4444;** T: Green Line to Arlington); Copley Place, 2nd level (ℭ **617/266-7775;** T: Orange Line to Back Bay or Green Line to Copley); at Liberty Wharf, 270 Northern Ave., at D St., South Boston (ℭ **617/477-2900;** T: Silver Line SL1/SL2 bus to Silver Line Way); in the courtyard of the Charles Hotel, 20 University Rd., off Bennett St., Cambridge (ℭ **617/491-9400;** T: Red Line to Harvard); 5 Cambridge Center, off Main St., Cambridge (ℭ **617/864-3400;** T: Red Line to Kendall/MIT); and in the 3 domestic terminals at Logan Airport.

Trade ★ MEDITERRANEAN/INTERNATIONAL   Trade opened in 2011 and already has a loyal clientele of businesspeople, foodies, and chic cocktail hounds drawn to the stylish bar scene. The menu, brainchild of local legend Jody Adams, offers inventive small plates, luscious flatbreads, and appealing sides all the time, plus more substantial main courses at dinner. Lamb sausage flatbread with eggplant and garlic yogurt is a flavor bomb; toothsome clam chowder reminds you why it's a classic; and gingered beets with ricotta salata is a delightful take on the bistro salad cliché. A cavernous space with exposed-brick walls and floor-to-ceiling windows overlooking the Greenway, Trade is loud but (thanks to clever soundproofing) not deafening. This is great food for sharing, served in moderate portions; watch out if you're dining with hearty eaters and not on an expense account, because the bill can mount fast.

540 Atlantic Ave. (at Congress St.). www.trade-boston.com. ℭ **617/451-1234.** Reservations recommended. Lunch main courses $10–$21; dinner main courses $11–$31; small plates $7–$15. AE, MC, V. Mon–Fri 11:30am–5:30pm (lunch menu until 2:30pm); Mon–Thurs 5:30–10pm; Fri–Sat 5:30–11pm; Sun 5:30–9pm; bar menu until 1 hr. later. Validated parking available at dinner. T: Red Line to South Station.

Abe & Louie's **18**
Artú **69**
Bangkok City **6**
The Barking Crab **59**
Ben & Jerry's **14, 20, 40**
Bertucci's **4**
Bond Restaurant & Lounge **62**
Boston Public Library **21**
Brasserie Jo **23**
The Bristol Lounge **45**
Café Jaffa **9**
The Capital Grille **12**
Chacarero **65**
Charlie's Sandwich Shoppe **24**
Chau Chow City **54**
China Pearl **50**
Citizen Public House & Oyster Bar **3**
Coppa **30**
Daily Catch **73**
Davio's Northern Italian Steakhouse **37**
The Elephant Walk **1**
Emack & Bolio's **7**

Fajitas & 'Ritas **66**
Figs **71**
Finale **41**
Fleming's Prime Steakhouse & Wine Bar **42**
Flour Bakery & Cafe **27, 58**
Great Taste Bakery & Restaurant **53**
Grill 23 & Bar **35**
Grotto **67**
Hamersley's Bistro **31**
Hei La Moon **55**
Jacob Wirth Company **48**
Jasper White's Summer Shack **11**
La Verdad Taqueria Mexicana **6**
Legal Sea Foods **16, 22, 44, 72**
The Lounge at Taj Boston **33**
Lobby Lounge at Mandarin Oriental, Boston **17**
Maggiano's Little Italy **43**
Market **47**
McCormick & Schmick's **39**
Miel **60**
Milk Street Cafe **63**
Morton's of Chicago **74**

Orinoco **28**
P. F. Chang's China Bistro **13, 46**
The Paramount **70**
Parish Café and Bar **34**
Peach Farm **52**
Picco Restaurant **32**
Rowes Wharf Sea Grille **61**
Ruth's Chris Steak House **64**
Savenor's Market **38**
Smith & Wollensky **36, 57**
South End Buttery **29**
Stephanie's on Newbury **19**
Swans **38**
Tapéo **10**
Teranga **25**
Toro **26**
Trade **56**
Trader Joe's **8**
Wagamama **15**
Winsor Dim Sum Cafe **51**
Xinh Xinh **49**

Boston Restaurants

see North End Restaurants map

NORTH END

Old North Church

CambridgeSide Galleria

Museum of Science

Science Park

TD Garden/ North Station

North Station

Paul Revere Park

Charlestown Bridge

Commercial St.

Hull St.

Prince St.

Hanover St.

Fleet St.

North St.

Lewis St.

Charles River Reservation

Mass. General Hospital

Charles/MGH

Longfellow Bridge

68

69

Philips St.

Revere St.

Myrtle St.

Pinckney St.

BEACON HILL

Mass. State House

67

Cambridge St.

Bowdoin

New Chardon St.

New Sudbury St.

Boston City Hall

Government Center

Faneuil Hall Marketplace

Christopher Columbus Park

Aquarium

New England Aquarium

Rose Kennedy Greenway

Haymarket

Cross St.

Surface Rd.

Atlantic Ave.

Commercial Ave.

Hatch Shell

70

71

Mt. Vernon St.

Chestnut St.

Beacon St.

Park Street

64

School St.

Water St.

63

Post Office Square

FINANCIAL DISTRICT

62

61

72

73

74

BOSTON COMMON

Winter St.

Washington St.

Hawley St.

Oliver St.

High St.

Congress St.

Purchase St.

60

56

57

59

58

PUBLIC GARDEN

66

West St.

Downtown Crossing

65

Chauncy St.

Ave. de Lafayette

South Station

Summer St.

Seaport Blvd.

33

Commonwealth Ave.

Arlington

34

Boylston St.

see inset

Boylston

Chinatown

Essex St.

CHINATOWN

Beach St.

Kneeland St.

Lincoln St.

South Station

Boston Children's Museum

St. James Ave.

Copley Square

John Hancock Tower

35

36

Park Plaza

Stuart St.

Piedmont St.

Tufts Medical Center

Harrison Ave.

Tyler St.

Hudson St.

Fort Point Channel

Melcher St.

A St.

Isabella St.

Melrose St.

Fayette St.

Oak St.

Back Bay

Back Bay Station

90

Marginal Rd.

Herald St.

Chandler St.

Appleton St.

Warren Ave.

32

E. Berkeley St.

Traveler St.

Albany St.

Dorchester Ave.

South Boston Bypass Rd.

31

Dwight St.

Milford St.

Hanson St.

30

Peters Park

93

1

Broadway

W. 4th St.

29

Washington St.

0   1/4 mi
0   1/4 km

SOUTH END

28

27

Blackstone Square

Franklin Square

25

26

Park Plaza area and Chinatown

Boylston St.

45

Park Plaza

46

Boylston St.

Chinatown

Essex St.

54

CHINATOWN

53

Tremont St.

Lagrange St.

48

49

Beach St.

50

55

38

40

41

43

44

42

Stuart St.

47

52

37

Columbus Ave.

Warrenton St.

Tufts Medical Center

Kneeland St.

Tyler St.

51

Surface Rd.

Beach St.

Lincoln St.

153

Boston's Food Trucks

Like a lot of other dining trends, food trucks conquered New York before sweeping Boston—but Boston has embraced them warmly. You'll find trucks that serve everything from barbecue to vegetarian specialties to Vietnamese sandwiches to cupcakes along the **Rose Kennedy Greenway,** outside the **Boston Public Library** in Copley Square, and next to **Boston City Hall** every day in warm weather and at the **SoWa Open Market** (p. 196) on summer Sundays.

Clover Food Truck (p. 178) originated and has two brick-and-mortar locations in Cambridge, and it's one of the only Boston vendors that's open year-round. Another is **Boston Super Dog,** whose permanent location is a truck at 42 Newmarket Sq., off Mass. Ave., in Roxbury (✆ 617/839-0102; http://bostonsuper dog.com). Grab a cab so you don't have to endure a poky bus ride and long, grim walk before your taste buds reach hot-dog paradise.

THE NORTH END

On weekends, tourists jam Boston's Italian-American enclave, which can get unbearably crowded. If possible, dine here between Sunday and Thursday.

Many of the North End's dozens of restaurants are tiny and don't serve dessert and coffee. Hit the *caffès* for postmeal coffee and pastries in an atmosphere where lingering is welcome. My favorite destinations are **Caffè Vittoria,** 296 Hanover St. (www.vittoriacaffe.com; ✆ 617/227-7606), and **Caffè dello Sport,** 308 Hanover St. (www.caffedellosport.us; ✆ 617/523-5063). **Mike's Pastry,** 300 Hanover St. (www.mikespastry.com; ✆ 617/742-3050), is a bakery that's famous for its bustling takeout business and its cannoli. If you plan to eat in, find what you want in the cases first, then take a seat and order from the server. Or prep for a picnic at **Modern Pastry,** 257 Hanover St. (✆ 617/523-3783; see box, "Go Straight to the Source," below). For gelato, head to **GiGi Gelateria,** 272 Hanover St. (www.gelateriacorp.com; ✆ 617/720-4243), which serves at least two dozen flavors of the Italian frozen treat as well as pastries, coffee, and Italian soft drinks.

Very Expensive

Mamma Maria ★★★ NORTHERN ITALIAN   In a town house overlooking the Paul Revere House, the best restaurant in the North End offers innovative cuisine in a sophisticated, romantic setting. Upscale restaurants are colonizing this old-world neighborhood, with their fashionable bars and noisy dining rooms—but every time someone with a generous budget requests a recommendation, I suggest Mamma Maria (and get raves in return). The menu changes seasonally, featuring superb entrees that are unlike anything else in this neighborhood, except in size—portions are more than generous. Fork-tender *osso buco* is almost enough for two, but you'll want it all for yourself. You can't go wrong with main-course pastas such as sublime lobster *agnolotti* (pasta pockets), and the steaks, chops, and seafood specials (say, grilled yellowfin tuna over squid-ink linguini) are uniformly marvelous. The pasta, bread, and desserts are homemade, and the wine list is excellent.

3 North Sq. (at Prince and Garden Court sts.). www.mammamaria.com. (C) **617/523-0077.** Reservations recommended. Main courses $26–$36. AE, DC, DISC, MC, V. Sun–Thurs 5–10pm; Fri–Sat 5–11pm. Valet parking available. T: Green or Orange Line to Haymarket.

Taranta Cucina Meridionale ★★ SOUTHERN ITALIAN/PERUVIAN
Taranta's menu incorporates the flavors of the chef-owner's native Peru, ingredients you won't see on other Boston menus, and classic Italian preparations. The dining room is typical upscale North End, with an open kitchen and closely spaced tables; ask to sit on the second level if you want more room. Servers are friendly and eager to explain the unusual cuisine. Risk-averse diners can opt for pasta with tomato sauce—a good rendition, but not the reason to come here. Dishes like espresso-crusted filet mignon and grilled trout with Peruvian potatoes and giant lima beans make Taranta a standout. The signature main course is a Flintstones-esque pork chop with a sweet-hot glaze of sugar cane and *rocoto* pepper; it's not unusual to see a whole table of businessmen who resemble NFL linemen ordering it. Desserts are as accomplished as everything else, so try to save room.

210 Hanover St. (btw. Cross and Parmenter sts.). www.tarantarist.com. (C) **617/720-0052.** Reservations recommended. Main courses $19–$36. AE, DC, MC, V. Daily 5:30–10pm. T: Green or Orange Line to Haymarket.

Expensive

Daily Catch ★ SOUTHERN ITALIAN/SEAFOOD   The Daily Catch offers excellent food, chummy service, and very little elbow room. About the size of a large kitchen (it seats just 20), the storefront restaurant packs a wallop—of garlic. The surprisingly varied menu includes an impressive variety of calamari (try it fried, in squid-ink pasta *puttanesca,* or stuffed with bread crumbs, parsley, and garlic) and a tempting selection of broiled, fried, and sautéed fish and shellfish. One of the pickiest eaters I know comes from New York just for the monkfish Marsala. All food is prepared to order, and some dishes arrive still in the frying pan. This isn't fine dining—wine is served in plastic cups—but it's been a favorite since 1973 for a reason.

323 Hanover St. (btw. Richmond and Prince sts.). www.dailycatch.com. (C) **617/523-8567.** Reservations not accepted. Main courses $17–$27. No credit cards. Daily 11:30am–10pm. Validated parking available. T: Green or Orange Line to Haymarket. Also at the Moakley Federal Courthouse, 2 Northern Ave., across the bridge from Atlantic Ave. ((C) **617/772-4400;** reservations recommended at dinner; Mon–Thurs 11am–9:30pm, Fri 11am–10:30pm, Sat noon–10:30pm, Sun 1–9pm; AE, MC, V; T: Red Line to South Station and 10-min. walk or Silver Line SL1/SL2 bus to Courthouse, or Blue Line to Aquarium and 10-min. walk), and 441 Harvard St. (btw. Thorndike and Coolidge sts.), Brookline ((C) **617/734-2700;** reservations not accepted; Mon–Sat 4–10pm, Sun 2–10pm; AE, MC, V; T: Green Line D to Brookline Village).

Neptune Oyster ★ SEAFOOD   Tiny and cramped, Neptune feels like a secret place—or it would, if the 42-seat space weren't so crowded. Superfresh, inventively prepared seafood keeps it busy and loud, and not just with North Enders sick of chicken parm; even in the winter, plan for lunch or an early dinner on a weekday. Check the daily specials, then start comparing oysters from both coasts; Pacific Northwest Kumamotos are my favorite. Main courses include some standards, at least two of which aren't seafood (the burger is excellent), and

Go Straight to the Source

The tiramisu at many North End restaurants comes from **Modern Pastry,** 257 Hanover St. (℃ **617/523-3783**). The surreal, sumptuous concoction ($3.50 a slice at the shop) makes an excellent picnic dessert in the summer. Head 4 blocks down Richmond Street to eat in Christopher Columbus Waterfront Park, off Atlantic Avenue.

dishes that use whatever's freshest. You might find something unfamiliar like cod cheeks, exotic like sea urchin, or familiar like a lobster roll (cold with mayonnaise or hot with butter—quite the dilemma). Neptune is just off the Freedom Trail and easy to find: Look for the oysters on ice in the window and the crowd inside. 63 Salem St. (off Cross St.). www.neptuneoyster.com. ℃ **617/742-3474.** Reservations not accepted. Main courses $16–$35; lobster market price. AE, MC, V. Sun–Thurs 11:30am–9:30pm; Fri–Sat 11:30am–10:30pm. Raw bar closes 1 hr. after kitchen. T: Green or Orange Line to Haymarket.

Moderate

Artú ITALIAN   A neighborhood favorite and a good stop for Freedom Trail walkers, Artú specializes in roasted meats and veggies, bounteous home-style pasta dishes, and (at lunch) tasty sandwiches and pizza. Roast lamb, *penne alla puttanesca,* and chicken stuffed with ham and cheese are all terrific. Panini (sandwiches) are big in size and flavor—the prosciutto, mozzarella, and tomato is sublime, and chicken parmigiana is tender and filling. Originally a little takeout place, Artú now occupies three storefronts, one of which holds a marble-topped bar. It isn't a great place for quiet conversation, especially during dinner in the noisy main room, but it's one of the most reliably satisfying restaurants in the North End.

North End Restaurants

Mamma Maria **16**
McCormick & Schmick's **19**
Mike's Pastry **11**
Modern Pastry **5**
Nebo **1**
Neptune Oyster **3**
Pizzeria Regina **2**
Sultan's Kitchen **23**
Taranta Cucina Meridionale **4**
Union Oyster House **18**
Volle Nolle **14**
Wagamama **21**

Artú **13**
Bertucci's **22**
Caffè dello Sport **12**
Caffè Vittoria **10**
Daily Catch **9**
Durgin-Park **20**
Emack & Bolio's **25**
Galleria Umberto
   Rosticceria **8**
Giacomo's Ristorante **15**
Gigi Gelateria **7**
Il Panino Express **6**
La Summa **17**
Legal Sea Foods **24**

6 Prince St. (btw. Hanover St. and North Sq.). www.artuboston.com. ☏ **617/742-4336.** Reservations recommended at dinner. Main courses $10–$15 at lunch, $15–$24 at dinner; sandwiches $7–$9. AE, MC, V. Mon–Fri 11:30am–11pm; Sat 11:30am–midnight; Sun noon–11pm; bar menu daily until 1am. T: Green or Orange Line to Haymarket. Also at 89 Charles St. (off Pinckney St.), Beacon Hill (☏ **617/227-9023;** Tues 5–9pm, Wed–Sat 11am–10pm, Sun 1–8pm; T: Red Line to Charles/MGH).

Giacomo's Ristorante ★★ ITALIAN/SEAFOOD   The line outside Giacomo's forms early and grows long, especially on weekends. No reservations, cash only, tiny dining room, open kitchen—what's the attraction? Terrific food, generous portions, and the we're-all-in-this-together atmosphere. My dad is a New York ethnic-dining snob, and this is his favorite Boston restaurant. Start with fried calamari, then check out the specials and either take the chef's advice or put together your own main dish from the list of ingredients on the wall. The best suggestion is salmon and sun-dried tomatoes in tomato cream sauce over fettuccine; any dish with shrimp is delectable, too. Nonseafood offerings, such as pumpkin tortellini in sage–mascarpone cheese sauce, are equally appetizing. Service is friendly but incredibly swift, and lingering is not encouraged. Have a heart—people are waiting outside whether it's freezing, sweltering, or pouring.

355 Hanover St. (off Fleet St.). ☏ **617/523-9026.** Reservations not accepted. Main courses $14–$19; specials market price. No credit cards. Mon–Thurs 5–10pm; Fri–Sat 5–10:30pm; Sun

4–10pm. T: Green or Orange Line to Haymarket. Also at 431 Columbus Ave. (btw. Braddock Park and Holyoke St.), South End (𝐂 **617/536-6723;** reservations recommended; Mon–Sat 5–10pm, Sun 5–9:30pm; T: Orange Line to Back Bay).

La Summa ★ SOUTHERN ITALIAN   Because La Summa isn't on a main drag, it maintains a cozy neighborhood atmosphere. Unlike some neighborhood places, it's friendly to outsiders—you'll feel welcome even if your server doesn't greet you by name. La Summa is worth seeking out just for the wonderful home-made pasta and desserts, and the more elaborate entrees are scrumptious, too. You might start with salad, ravioli, or soup. (Our waitress one night didn't know exactly what was in the excellent butternut squash soup because, and I quote, "My mother made it.") Then try any seafood special, *pappardelle e melanzane* (strips of eggplant tossed with ethereal fresh pasta in marinara sauce), hearty risotto, or the house special—veal, chicken, sausage, shrimp, artichokes, *pepperoncini* (pickled hot peppers), olives, and mushrooms in white-wine sauce. Desserts, especially ricotta cheesecake, are terrific.

30 Fleet St. (btw. Garden Court and Moon sts., 1 block from Hanover St.). www.lasumma.com. 𝐂 **617/523-9503.** Reservations recommended on weekends. Main courses $8–$10 at lunch, $13–$24 at dinner. AE, DC, DISC, MC, V. Mon–Wed 4–10:30pm; Thurs–Sat noon–10:30pm; Sun noon–9:30pm. T: Green or Orange Line to Haymarket.

Inexpensive

Galleria Umberto Rosticceria 🍴 ITALIAN   The long, fast-moving line snaking toward the door is your first clue that this cafeteria-style spot just off the Freedom Trail is a bargain. Then you notice that most of the customers are locals and businesspeople, not tourists. Score! You can fill up on a couple of slices of pizza, but for the true Umberto's experience, try *arancini* (a deep-fried rice ball filled with ground beef, peas, and cheese). Calzones filled with various combinations of meats, vegetables, and cheese are wonderful—mmm, salami—and *panzarotti* (mozzarella-stuffed potato croquettes) are tasty and satisfying. Study the cases of food while you wait, and be ready to order when you reach the head of the line. Enjoy a quick lunch and get on with your sightseeing.

289 Hanover St. (btw. Richmond and Prince sts.). 𝐂 **617/227-5709.** All items less than $5. No credit cards. Mon–Sat 10:45am–2:30pm. Closed July. T: Green or Orange Line to Haymarket.

Pizzeria Regina ★★ PIZZA   The line outside Regina's stretches up the street on busy nights, but even at off hours, business is seldom slow. The North End classic and its brick oven have been delighting pizza lovers since 1926. Locals often call for takeout, though if you do that, you'll miss the full experience. Busy waitresses who might call you "dear" weave through the boisterous dining room, shouting orders and questions as they deliver peerless pizza steaming hot from the brick oven—ask for yours well done. (You can also drop in for a slice, weekdays at lunch only.) Let it cool a little before you dig in. Topping options include nouveau ingredients such as sun-dried tomatoes, but that's not authentic. House-made sausage, maybe some pepperoni, and a couple of beers—now, *that's* authentic.

11½ Thacher St. (at N. Margin St.). www.pizzeriaregina.com. 𝐂 **617/227-0765.** Reservations not accepted. Pizza $13–$22. AE, MC, V. Sun–Thurs 11:30am–11:30pm; Fri–Sat 11:30am–12:30am. T: Green or Orange Line to Haymarket.

WEEKDAY breakfast & WEEKEND BRUNCH

Several top hotels serve Sunday brunch buffets of monstrous proportions—outrageous displays that are outrageously expensive. They're nice for a special occasion, but you can have a less incapacitating a la carte experience for considerably less money. Dine on a weekday to get a sense of the neighborhood and mingle with the regulars.

My top choice is in Cambridge: the **S&S Restaurant** (p. 184), a family-run operation that never sends anyone away hungry. In Boston, the **Elephant Walk** (p. 173) and **Hamersley's Bistro** (p. 166) are excellent Sunday brunch destinations. **Charlie's Sandwich Shoppe,** 429 Columbus Ave. (© **617/536-7669**), is a longtime South End favorite not far from the Back Bay—just the right distance to walk off some blueberry-waffle calories; Charlie's is closed Sunday and doesn't accept credit cards. The **Paramount,** 44 Charles St., Beacon Hill (www.paramount boston.com; © **617/720-1152**), is a classic for pancakes and eggs with a side of neighborhood gossip. At the **Centre Street Café,** 669 Centre St., Jamaica Plain (www.centrestcafe.com; © **617/ 524-9217**), natives tough out long weekend waits for strong coffee and delicious specials made (when possible) with local and organic ingredients.

Volle Nolle ★ 👜 SANDWICHES   This little shop is a textbook example of doing one thing exactly right. The menu—written on the chalkboard-painted back wall—focuses on pressed gourmet sandwiches grilled to crispy perfection. The amazing Cubano (pork, ham, Swiss) was my favorite, until I tried the pesto chicken. And the pastrami and Swiss, the tuna with lemon mayonnaise, and the portobello mushroom with mozzarella and roasted red peppers. Too fancy? There's a kids' grilled cheese, as well as salads and a daily soup. Mostly a takeout operation, Volle Nolle has about a dozen seats; grab one and enjoy the parade of neighborhood regulars drawn by the amazing food, friendly service, gourmet chips and soft drinks, and phenomenal chocolate-chip cookies. *Tip:* At press time, Volle Nolle had just landed a beer-and-wine license—check ahead to see whether that means the hours now include dinner.

351 Hanover St. (near Fleet St.). © **617/523-0003.** All items less than $11 (most less than $9). No credit cards. Mon–Sat 11am–4pm. T: Green or Orange Line to Haymarket.

FANEUIL HALL MARKETPLACE & THE FINANCIAL DISTRICT

The key to finding a good meal in these neighborhoods is to follow the crowds of office workers (whose favorites often close on weekends). Or embrace your out-of-towner status and realize that you're going to mingle with tourist crowds sooner or later. The best place to do that is at **Quincy Market,** home to Faneuil Hall Marketplace's giant food court.

The national chain **McCormick & Schmick's Seafood Restaurant** has a branch at Faneuil Hall Marketplace in the North Market Building (© **617/ 720-5522**).

Durgin-Park ★★ ☺ NEW ENGLAND   For huge portions of delicious food and a rowdy atmosphere where CEOs share tables with students, people have poured into Durgin-Park since 1827. Make a reservation and skip the line, which often stretches down the stairs to the first floor of Faneuil Hall Marketplace's North Market building. The food is wonderful—prime rib the size of a hubcap, lamb chops, fried seafood, huge salads, broiled-to-order fish, and juicy roast turkey are sure bets. Boston baked beans are a signature dish, and this is the best place to try them. For dessert, Indian pudding (molasses and cornmeal baked for hours and served with ice cream) is a New England classic. Long known for backtalk from cranky waitresses, Durgin-Park now has friendly, professional service. I've recommended it to numerous jaded residents, and all sounded surprised when they reported that they enjoyed it—even with the plentiful tourists.

340 Faneuil Hall Marketplace. www.durgin-park.com. ☏ **617/227-2038.** Reservations recommended at dinner. Main courses $8–$16 at lunch, $11–$40 at dinner; lobster market price; children's menu $8–$9. AE, DC, DISC, MC, V. Mon–Sat 11:30am–10pm; Sun 11:30am–9pm. Validated parking available. T: Green or Blue Line to Government Center, Green or Orange Line to Haymarket, or Blue Line to Aquarium.

Milk Street Cafe ✦ VEGETARIAN   A cafeteria-style restaurant on the ground floor of an office building probably sounds like something you're trying to get away from. Ignore your instincts and follow the corporate crowds. They're here for fresh and delicious soups, salads, quiches, and sandwiches; a few dishes have fish, but otherwise the Milk Street Cafe is vegetarian. (If you keep kosher, check ahead for details of the restaurant's certification.) I'm not a fan of the pizza here, but the fresh-baked cookies hit the spot. To beat the crowds, come for breakfast or arrive early for lunch, or opt for takeout—the lovely park at Post Office Square is just a couple of blocks away.

50 Milk St. (at Arch St., 2 short blocks from Washington St.). www.milkstreetcafe.com. ☏ **617/542-3663.** Breakfast items $6 or less; lunch items $4–$9. AE, MC, V. Mon–Thurs 7am–3pm; Fri 7am–2:30pm. T: Orange or Blue Line to State, or Red Line to Downtown Crossing.

Sultan's Kitchen ★ TURKISH/MIDDLE EASTERN   Both novel and familiar, the flavorful, reasonably priced food accounts for the long lunchtime lines at Sultan's Kitchen. The Turkish dishes filling the display case are like nothing else in downtown Boston, and the Middle Eastern options have unusual twists (orange zest in the tabbouleh, fava beans in the falafel). I recommend ordering a combination of *meze* (appetizers) and salads—they include *kabak mucveri* (zucchini patties), *saksuka* (roasted spiced eggplant, zucchini, and green peppers), *zeytinyagli enginar* (braised artichoke hearts), just to name a few—and kebabs, available in sandwiches or as part of a plate with rice pilaf and salads. Most of the businesspeople who flock here are either heading back to the office or eating in the small table area. Lucky you can have everything packed up for a picnic on the Rose Kennedy Greenway or at Christopher Columbus Waterfront Park.

116 State St. (at Broad St.). www.sultans-kitchen.com. ☏ **617/570-9009.** Sandwiches $6–$9; main courses $9–$12. AE, DC, MC, V. Mon–Fri 11am–8:30pm; Sat 11am–4pm. T: Orange or Blue Line to State.

Union Oyster House ★ SEAFOOD/NEW ENGLAND   America's oldest restaurant in continuous service (since 1826), the Union Oyster House serves tasty, traditional New England fare to visitors following the adjacent Freedom Trail as well as to savvy locals. They're not looking for anything fancy, and you shouldn't, either—classic preparations account for the restaurant's staying power. At the oyster bar on the lower level of the antique building (a National Historic Landmark "where Daniel Webster drank many a toddy in his day"), try excellent fish chowder, oyster stew, or the cold shellfish sampler to start. Follow with a broiled or grilled dish such as scrod or salmon, or perhaps fried seafood or grilled pork loin. A "shore dinner" of chowder, steamers or mussels, lobster, corn, and potatoes is an excellent introduction to local favorites. For dessert, try ginger-bread with whipped cream. A plaque marks John F. Kennedy's favorite booth (no. 18), where he often sat to read the Sunday papers.

41 Union St. (btw. North and Hanover sts.). www.unionoysterhouse.com. ⓒ **617/227-2750.** Reservations recommended. Main courses $10–$25 (most under $18) at lunch, $19–$34 at dinner; lobster market price; children's menu $6–$12. AE, DC, DISC, MC, V. Sun–Thurs 11am–9:30pm (lunch menu until 5pm); Fri–Sat 11am–10pm (lunch until 6pm). Union Bar daily 11am–midnight (lunch until 3pm, late supper until 11pm). Validated and valet parking available. T: Green or Orange Line to Haymarket.

DOWNTOWN CROSSING

Office workers abound here, along with students from Emerson College and Suffolk University. Expect good value.

Fajitas & 'Ritas ★ TEX-MEX   This colorful, entertaining restaurant is one of the most fun places around. It serves nachos, quesadillas, burritos, and, of course, fajitas—exactly the way you want them. You mark your food and drink selections on a checklist, and a member of the busy staff quickly returns with big portions of tasty food. You can also try barbecue items, such as smoked brisket or pulled pork, or tequila-marinated chicken wings. There's nothing particularly exotic—beef, chicken, shrimp, beans, and so forth—but it's all superfresh, because this place is too busy to let anything sit around for very long. As the name indicates, 'ritas (margaritas) are a house specialty. Primarily a casual business destination at lunch, it's livelier at dinner (probably thanks to the 'ritas) and a

---

 Boston Restaurant Weeks

During **Boston Restaurant Week,** dozens of places serve a three-course prix-fixe lunch for the decimal equivalent of the year—in 2013, $20.13—and many offer dinner for an additional $10 to $13. The third week of August was the original Restaurant Week; it's now 2 weeks, as is the March incarnation. I find the latter less enjoyable because late winter's seasonal ingredients are dull, but the price is right. Popular restaurants book up quickly, so plan accordingly. The

Convention & Visitors Bureau (www.bostonusa.com/restaurantweek; ⓒ **888/733-2678**) lists names of participating restaurants and numbers to call for reservations. Ask whether the menu is set yet, and seek out restaurants that really get into the spirit by offering more than just a couple of choices for each course. If you don't, you're going to experience more chicken, salmon, and begrudging service than anyone deserves.

The Lunch Line

Try to be near Downtown Crossing at lunchtime at least once during your visit and seek out **Chacarero,** 101 Arch St., off Summer Street (www.chacarero.com; (C) **617/542-0392**). It serves other things, but the lines are so long because of the scrumptious Chilean sandwiches, served on house-made bread. Order chicken, beef, or vegetarian, ask for it "with everything"—tomatoes, cheese, avocado, hot sauce, and (unexpected but delicious) green beans—and dig in. The lines move fairly quickly, and for less than $10, you feel like a savvy Bostonian.

perfect stop before or after a movie at the nearby AMC Loews Boston Common theater.

25 West St. (btw. Washington and Tremont sts.). www.fajitasandritas.com. (C) **617/426-1222.** Reservations accepted only for parties of 8 or more. Main courses $6–$10 at lunch, $6–$15 at dinner. AE, DC, DISC, MC, V. Mon–Tues 11:30am–9pm; Wed–Thurs 11:30am–10pm; Fri–Sat 11:30am–11pm; Sun 11:30am—8pm. T: Red or Green Line to Park St., or Red or Orange Line to Downtown Crossing.

BEACON HILL

Artú (p. 156) has a branch at 89 Charles St. ((C) **617/227-9023**). It's open Tuesday from 5 to 9pm, Wednesday through Saturday from 11am to 10pm, and Sunday from 1 to 8pm.

Grotto ★★ ITALIAN   Grotto's subterranean dining room is a cozy retreat, with contemporary art on the exposed-brick walls and busy servers bustling around the small, crowded space. Chef-owner Scott Herritt has fun with seasonal local ingredients, beginning his regularly changing menu with imaginative soups and ending with fruit desserts. The three-course fixed-price dinner is one of the best deals around. You might see crab ravioli with asparagus, almonds, and saffron in the spring; apple-stuffed duck breast in the winter; or spaghetti and meatballs "with Grotto's insanely fabulous tomato sauce" anytime. Hearty gnocchi with braised short ribs, Gorgonzola cheese, and mushrooms is one of the best dishes in Boston. Desserts are indulgent but not overwhelming: A friend who's usually indifferent to sweets devoured banana bread pudding with caramel ice cream. Great—more chocolate cake for me.

37 Bowdoin St. (at Derne St., btw. Cambridge St. and the State House). www.grottorestaurant. com. (C) **617/227-3434.** Reservations recommended at dinner. Main courses $8–$14 at lunch, $21–$29 at dinner; 3-course fixed-price dinner $36. AE, DC, MC, V. Mon–Fri 11:30am–3pm; daily 5–10pm. T: Green or Red Line to Park St., Green or Blue Line to Government Center, or Blue Line to Bowdoin (weekdays only).

CHINATOWN/THEATER DISTRICT

You'll find food from all over Asia in Boston's small, crowded Chinatown, but Chinese food dominates. The most entertaining and delicious introduction to the cuisine is **dim sum** (see "Yum, Yum, Dim Sum," below). At lunch and dinner, many restaurants have a second menu for Chinese patrons (often written in Chinese). You can ask for it or tell your waiter that you want your meal Chinese-style.

If you're serious about sweets, consider ending—or even beginning—your meal at **Finale** (p. 228), 1 Columbus Ave. (www.finaledesserts.com; ✆ 617/423-3184).

The area around Park Square (near Stuart St. and Charles St. S.), between the Theater District and the Public Garden, is a hotbed of upscale national chain restaurants. None of these places offer a unique or even unusual experience, but they're all reliable destinations if you're feeling unadventurous. They include **Fleming's Prime Steakhouse & Wine Bar,** 217 Stuart St. (✆ 617/292-0808); **Maggiano's Little Italy,** 4 Columbus Ave. (✆ 617/542-3456); **McCormick & Schmick's Seafood Restaurant,** 34 Columbus Ave., in the Boston Park Plaza Hotel (✆ 617/482-3999); and **P. F. Chang's China Bistro,** 8 Park Plaza (✆ 617/573-0821).

Very Expensive

Market ★★★ FUSION   Before Jean-Georges Vongerichten was a culinary megastar, he briefly worked in Boston. A quarter-century later, in 2009, he returned in triumph to open Market. It's the creation of a mature talent with an adventuresome spirit: inventive menu, exotic and local ingredients, impeccable service, exceptional wine list, even a superb burger. The food demonstrates why chefs have groupies. Start with foie gras brûlée, a disc of pure richness with a crackly, almost-burnt caramel crust, or a perfectly balanced salad. Main courses show off those local ingredients, with New England seafood in emulsions of Asian spice, citrus, and soy alongside seasonal vegetables, and expertly prepared meat dishes reminding you that you're in a hotel restaurant. I enlisted the pickiest diners I know to help me evaluate Market, and their biggest criticism was that the glass-walled dining room gets somewhat noisy—it's the buzz of happy, satisfied diners.

In the W Boston hotel, 100 Stuart St. (at Tremont St.). www.marketbyjgboston.com. ✆ **617/310-6790.** Reservations recommended. Lunch main courses $21–$33; pizzas and sandwiches $10–$17; 3-course prix fixe $21–$26; dinner main courses $17–$39 (most $21–$33); 5-course prix fixe $62 (whole tables only). AE, DC, DISC, MC, V. Mon–Fri 7–10:30am; Sat–Sun 8–11am; Mon–Fri 11:30am–3pm; Sat–Sun brunch 11:45am–2:30pm; Sun–Thurs 5–10pm; Fri–Sat 5–11pm. Valet parking available. T: Green Line to Boylston.

Expensive

There's a branch of **Legal Sea Foods** (p. 151) at 26 Park Sq., between Columbus Avenue and Stuart Street (www.legalseafoods.com; ✆ 617/426-4444).

Moderate

Jacob Wirth Company GERMAN/AMERICAN   In the heart of the Theater District, "Jake's" has been serving Bostonians since 1868—even before there were theaters here. The wood floor and brass accents give the spacious room the feeling of a saloon, and the menu incorporates traditional pub grub and more contemporary fare. Hearty German specialties include Wiener schnitzel, mixed grills, bratwurst, knockwurst, and potato pancakes; check out the wine-snob-style beer pairings. Daily specials, comfort-food favorites like chicken potpie, and a large variety of sandwiches and salads round out the menu. Service at lunchtime is snappy, but if you want to be on time for the theater, be ready to remind

YUM, YUM, dim sum

Many Chinatown restaurants offer **dim sum,** the traditional midday meal featuring appetizer-style dishes. You'll see steamed buns *(bao)* filled with pork or bean paste; meat, shrimp, and vegetable dumplings; sticky rice dotted with sausage and vegetables; shrimp-stuffed eggplant; spring rolls; sweets such as sesame balls and coconut gelatin; and more. At most restaurants, waitresses wheel carts laden with tempting dishes to your table, and you order by pointing (unless you know Chinese). She then stamps your check with the symbol of the dish, adding about $2 to $3 to your tab for each selection. Unless you order a la carte items from the regular menu or the steam table off to the side in most dining rooms, the total usually won't be more than about $10 to $12 per person. On weekends, the selection is wider than on weekdays, the turnover is faster (which means fresher food), and you'll often see three generations of families sharing large tables.

Looking to confirm a hunch, I asked a Hong Kong native to name Boston's best dim sum restaurant, and we agreed: **Hei La Moon ★★**, 88 Beach St. (www.heilamoon. com; ℰ **617/338-8813**). It opened in 2004 and has since eclipsed a pair of excellent competitors: **China Pearl ★**, 9 Tyler St., 2nd floor (ℰ **617/426-4338**), and **Chau**

Chow City ★, 83 Essex St. (ℰ **617/338-8158**). To order off a sushi-style menu and have dim sum prepared just for you—a good tactic on weekdays—head to **Great Taste Bakery & Restaurant** (p. 165) or **Winsor Dim Sum Cafe,** 10 Tyler St. (ℰ **617/338-1688**).

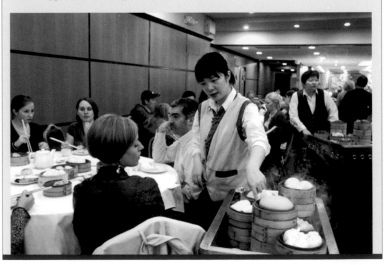

your server. On Friday after 8pm, a live pianist leads singalong night, which has something of a chicken-and-egg connection to the enormous beer selection (20-plus in bottles, even more on tap).

31–37 Stuart St. (btw. Tremont and Washington sts.). www.jacobwirth.com. ℰ **617/338-8586.** Reservations recommended at dinner. Main courses $8–$14 at lunch, $9–$23 (most items less than $20) at dinner; children's menu $6–$7. AE, DC, DISC, MC, V. Sun–Mon 11:30am–9pm; Tues–Thurs 11:30am–11pm; Fri–Sat 11:30am–midnight. Validated parking available. T: Green Line to Boylston or Orange Line to Tufts Medical Center.

Peach Farm ★ SEAFOOD/CANTONESE/SZECHUAN Chinatown's go-to place for fresh seafood is a subterranean hideaway with no notable decor. You won't be looking around much anyway—the service is so fast that just saying "calamari" seems to make spicy dry-fried salted squid appear. Main courses follow almost instantly: messy clams with black-bean sauce, lobster with ginger and scallions, braised chicken or beef hot pot, an emerald-green pile of stir-fried pea-pod stems. Spicy salt shrimp is a specialty; it's not on the menu, but you can ask to have that same spicy salt preparation applied to tender scallops. Both are fantastic. Fair warning to the softhearted: Order the Cantonese classic fresh fish steamed with ginger and scallions, and the waiter brings the poor creature to your table thrashing in a plastic bucket; it reappears moments later, perfectly cooked. Peach Farm is virtually indistinguishable from the other little restaurants that dot Chinatown's narrow streets, except that it's so crowded—savvy locals and celebratory groups fill both dining rooms every night.

4 Tyler St. (off Beach St.). ℂ **617/482-3332.** Reservations recommended for large groups at dinner. Main courses $5–$34 (most items less than $15); fresh seafood market price. MC, V. Daily 11am–3am. T: Orange Line to Chinatown.

Inexpensive

Great Taste Bakery & Restaurant ★ 🦀 CANTONESE/DIM SUM Dim sum served a la carte (see box, "Yum, Yum, Dim Sum," above) first drew me and my friends to Great Taste, and the rest of the food—Hong Kong–style and Chinese-American classics—keeps us coming back. The small, nondescript space gets crowded and loud, which is great if you like to point to the next table and ask your server what your neighbors are eating. Good choices include chow foon with the proper amount of char from the wok, hot pots (listed as "casserole specials"), stir-fried seafood with salt and pepper or spicy salt, and brilliant Chinese broccoli

---

Dining Gluten-Free in Boston & Cambridge

I turned to the parents of young acquaintances who have celiac disease in search of suggestions for Frommer's readers who are in the same boat. Perhaps most important is not forgetting to do what you do at home: Be sure your server knows that a diner or diners at the table can't eat gluten. Good local options include **Davio's** (p. 170), the **Elephant Walk** (p. 173), and **Nebo**, 90 N. Washington St. (www.neborestaurant.com; ℂ 617/723-6326), an Italian restaurant on the edge of the North End. The **Legal Sea Foods** (p. 151) and **Bertucci's**

(p. 179) chains have gluten-free menus. Other dependable choices are branches of two national chains: **P.F. Chang's China Bistro** (www.pfchangs.com), 8 Park Plaza (ℂ 617/573-0821), and in the Prudential Center, 800 Boylston St. (ℂ 617/378-9961); and **Wagamama** (www.wagamama.us), Quincy Market, Faneuil Hall Marketplace (ℂ 617/742-9242); in the Prudential Center, 800 Boylston St. (ℂ 617/778-2344); and 57 John F. Kennedy St., Cambridge (ℂ 617/499-0930).

or pea shoots. This is also a good place to try congee for breakfast. Next door to the dining room is a full-service bakery that offers everything from cookies and tarts to elaborate birthday cakes.

61–63 Beach St. (off Hudson St.). www.bostongreattastebakery.com. ☎ **617/426-6688.** Reservations not accepted. Main courses $5–$16 (most items less than $12); dim sum $2.50–$5. AE, DISC, MC, V. Sun–Thurs 6:30am–10pm; Fri–Sat 6:30am–11pm. T: Orange Line to Chinatown.

Xinh Xinh ★★ VIETNAMESE   One of the best Vietnamese restaurants in the Boston area is this cheery little storefront with an encyclopedic menu and welcoming service. Xinh Xinh (say "Sin Sin") lists close to 200 dishes, from fresh spring rolls to specialties that include beef tripe, pork skin, and various other animal parts. It also offers wonderful appetizers (try the fried spring rolls), numerous vegetarian options, and an extensive beverage menu. My favorite options are *bun*—shredded lettuce, cooked vermicelli, fresh mint, and other toppings with your choice of hot protein, all mixed together—anything with lemon grass chicken, and an exceptional version of traditional beef noodle soup, or *pho*. You can also check the specials board. Best of all, if you can't find something appealing or need help deciding, the helpful staff will step in.

7 Beach St. (at Knapp St., 1 block from Washington St.). ☎ 617/422-0501. Main courses $6–$14 (most less than $11). MC, V. Daily 10am–10pm. T: Orange Line to Chinatown.

THE SOUTH END

Tremont Street from Berkeley to West Brookline is the restaurant row that gave the South End its foodie reputation, but you'll find appealing dining options at every price point all over this sprawling neighborhood.

Very Expensive

Hamersley's Bistro ★★★ FRENCH/AMERICAN   A beloved special-occasion restaurant and neighborhood favorite, Hamersley's put the South End on Boston's culinary map. It opened in 1987 but feels as fresh as the local ingredients all over the menu, which changes seasonally. The dining room has an open kitchen (the tall guy in the Red Sox cap is owner Gordon Hamersley) and lots of sound-muffling soft surfaces, a perfect combination of showy and comfortable—which also describes the vegetarian-friendly food. Deceptively simple roast chicken with garlic, lemon, and parsley is deservedly famous, and I'd cheerfully eat the spicy halibut and clam roast every night. For meat-eaters, grilled skirt steak with anchovy butter and asparagus is a gorgeous combination of flavors. Desserts are among the best in town—try the strawberry shortcake. The enthusiastic, professional staff can help navigate the excellent wine list. There's seasonal outdoor seating.

553 Tremont St. (at Clarendon St.). www.hamersleysbistro.com. ☎ **617/423-2700.** Reservations recommended. Main courses $26–$44. AE, DISC, MC, V. Sun–Thurs 5:30–9:30pm; Fri–Sat 5:30–10pm; Sun brunch 11am–2pm. Closed 1st week of Jan. Valet parking available. T: Orange Line to Back Bay.

Expensive

Coppa ★★ ITALIAN   Coppa sounds almost like a parody. An enoteca that lists farmers' names on its nose-to-tail menu, with a hipster drinks list?

What's Italian for "pretentious"? But crowds and national critics come here for a reason—phenomenal food, served in a casual storefront by staff members who couldn't be nicer, even at crazy-busy times. *Stuzzichini* (bar snacks) and *salumi* (cured meats) share the regularly changing menu with scrumptious pizzas, antipasti, pastas, and main courses, each more flavorful than the last. I crave the squid-ink linguini, chicken-liver mousse, meatballs, sparkling-fresh salads, and every roasted vegetable I've tried—and the condiments and garnishes are just as delectable. Portions of nonpizza dishes are small, which means you can try a wide variety of flavors and textures. It also means a much higher bill than you might expect after a quick look at the menu. Totally worth it.

253 Shawmut Ave. (at Milford St.). www.coppaboston.com. © **617/391-0902.** Reservations recommended. Main courses $9–$22; pizza $14–$16; *salumi* $10; *stuzzichini* $5–$8. AE, MC, V. Mon–Fri noon–11pm; Sat 5–11pm; Sun 11am–3pm (brunch) and 5:30–11pm. T: Silver Line SL4/ SL5 bus to E. Berkeley St., or Orange Line to Back Bay, then 10-min. walk.

Moderate

Orinoco ★ 🍴 VENEZUELAN   Orinoco is a magnet for adventurous diners. The intensely flavorful food isn't necessarily spicy, but it's complex and satisfying. To start, try a delectable *arepa*—a corn patty stuffed with meat, cheese, or both, then grilled—or an empanada (I like the *verde* version, enclosing a savory mushroom mixture). The signature main course is *pabellón criollo*, the national dish of black beans and rice, which Venezuelans serve with shredded beef and plantains. The lunch menu includes salads and sandwiches; the dinner specials change regularly, and if you're lucky, your meal will coincide with beef tenderloin *churrasquito* (with crab *picadillo* and salsa *chimi*). Portions are generous, and sauces inventive and flavorful. If you can't get here for lunch, when it's less crowded than at dinner, consider arriving shortly after 6pm to avoid a long wait. Heading to Cambridge or Brookline is no shortcut—those locations are larger but equally crowded.

477 Shawmut Ave. (at W. Concord St.). www.orinocokitchen.com. © **617/369-7075.** Reservations not accepted. Main courses $5–$14 (most dishes less than $9) at lunch, $13–$19 at dinner. DISC, MC, V. Tues–Sat noon–2:30pm; Tues–Wed 6–10pm; Thurs–Sat 6–11pm; Sun brunch 11am–3pm. T: Silver Line SL4/SL5 bus to Worcester St., or Orange Line to Massachusetts Ave., then 10-min. walk. Also at 56 John F. Kennedy St., Cambridge (© **617/354-6900;** Tues–Sat noon–2:30pm, Tues–Wed 5:30–10pm, Thurs–Sat 5:30–11pm, Sun 11am–3pm for brunch and 5:30–9pm; T: Red Line to Harvard), and 22 Harvard St., Brookline (© **617/232-9505;** Tues–Sat noon–2:30pm, Tues–Wed 5:30–10pm, Thurs–Sat 5:30–11pm, Sun 11am–3pm for brunch and 5:30–9pm; T: Green Line D to Brookline Village).

South End Buttery AMERICAN   A neighborhood hangout on a not-too-busy corner, South End Buttery is primarily a casual cafe and bakery. Scones, croissants, muffins, and other pastries are fresh and wonderful, and the amazing cupcakes put this little place on the map. It's exceedingly popular at breakfast, with long lines of commuters hustling in and out. Lunch—big sandwiches on fantastic bread (try the turkey club), house-made soups that include rib-sticking chili, abundant salads—is a treat, especially if there's room on the sidewalk patio. The counter staff has a reputation for being standoffish, but I've almost always found the service friendly and helpful. At night and during weekend brunch, the back dining room transforms South End Buttery into a full-service comfort-food restaurant that serves bistro favorites to stay or (a popular option in this gentrified neighborhood) to go.

314 Shawmut Ave. (at Union Park St.). www.southendbuttery.com. (C) **617/482-1015.** Reservations recommended at dinner. Cafe items $2.25–$9 (most under $7); soups, sandwiches, and salads $6–$10; brunch items $4–$14; dinner main courses $13–$29 (most under $21). AE, MC, V. Cafe daily 6:30am–8pm. Restaurant Sun–Wed 5:30–10pm; Thurs–Sat 5:30–11pm; Sat–Sun brunch 10am–3pm. T: Orange Line to Back Bay or Silver Line SL4/SL5 bus to Union Park.

Teranga ★★ 🔥 SENEGALESE The unusual food and beverages, reasonable prices, elegant dining room, and friendly service make Teranga ("hospitality" in the Wolof language) one of the best deals in Boston. Chef-owner Marie-Claude Mendy's Senegalese cuisine, with its French and Vietnamese influences, is a marvel. Start with *croquettes de poisson* (fish cakes) or *fataya* (spiced-fish turnovers) rather than *nems* (spring rolls), which are on the doughy side. Main courses are richly spiced but not spicy; any dish with caramelized onions is amazing. My favorites are *thiébou yap* (lamb with mixed vegetables) and *thiou guinar* (chicken stew); vegetarian versions are available. The only thing I've tried that wasn't sublime was the "national dish," *thiébou djeun*; our server warned that the whitefish at the center of the fragrant stew is well done, and she wasn't kidding.

1746 Washington St. (btw. Mass. Ave. and E. Springfield St.). www.terangaboston.com. (C) **617/266-0003.** Reservations not accepted. Main courses $12–$13 at lunch, $14–$17 at dinner. DC, DISC, MC, V. Mon–Sat 11:30am–2:30pm and 5–10:30pm; Sun brunch 11am–2:30pm and dinner 5–10pm. T: Silver Line SL4/SL5 bus to Mass. Ave.

Toro ★ SPANISH/TAPAS The solution to the hassle of dinner at this Barcelona-style tapas bar is simple: Have lunch. Noisy and crowded from the moment it opens in the evening, Toro is busy but pleasant at midday, allowing you to concentrate on the delicious, authentic food. From simple *tortilla española* (potato-and-onion omelet) to the layered flavors of tuna belly with tomato tapenade, hot and cold tapas are three- and four-bite delights. The house special—grilled corn with garlic, lime, pepper, and cheese—is so good that I'd even brave the dinner rush to get it. This is great food for sharing, and the accommodating staff gives good advice about portion sizes. Order more than one *milanesa bocadillo*—a crispy chicken cutlet sandwich with avocado, cheese, refried beans, and chipotle mayonnaise (available at lunch only)—because you're going to want your own.

1704 Washington St. (near E. Springfield St.). www.toro-restaurant.com. (C) **617/536-4300.** Reservations accepted only for parties of 6 or more at lunch and brunch; not accepted at dinner. Tapas $5–$15 at lunch, $8–$16 at dinner; salads and sandwiches $8–$10 at lunch; main courses $15–$38 at dinner. AE, DC, DISC, MC, V. Mon–Fri noon–3pm; Mon–Thurs 5:30–10:15pm; Fri 5:30–11:45pm; Sat 5–11:45pm; Sun 5–10:15pm; Sun brunch 10:30am–2:30pm. Valet parking available at dinner Thurs–Sat. T: Silver Line SL4/SL5 bus to Mass. Ave.

Inexpensive

Flour Bakery & Cafe AMERICAN/BAKERY Flour's claim to fame is out-of-this-world baked goods, but that doesn't account for the lunchtime crowds at all three locations. Chalk those up to the top-notch sandwiches—on house-made breads, of course—soups, and salads. Sandwiches range from grilled cheese and PB&J for kids to curried tuna and roasted lamb with tomato chutney for choosier palates. Show up early or late to get a

Where's the Beef?

Say "Boston," think "seafood," right? Apparently not. Branches of most of the national steakhouse chains dot the city, and they're all at the top of their game—a rising tide lifts all boats, as the seafood folks say. Make a reservation, and have a light lunch.

Local favorites include **Grill 23 & Bar** (p. 170) and **Abe & Louie's,** 793 Boylston St. (www.abeandlouies.com; *C* **617/536-6300**). Devotees of the national chains can choose from the **Capital Grille,** in the Hynes Convention Center, 900 Boylston St. (www.thecapitalgrille.com; *C* **617/262-8900**); **Fleming's Prime**

Steakhouse & Wine Bar, 217 Stuart St. (www.flemingssteakhouse.com; *C* **617/292-0808**); **Morton's of Chicago,** World Trade Center East, 2 Seaport Lane (www.mortons.com; *C* **617/526-0410**); **Ruth's Chris Steak House** (www.ruthschris.com; *C* **800/544-0808**), in Old City Hall, 45 School St.; and **Smith & Wollensky** (www.smithandwollensky.com), 101 Arlington St. (*C* **617/432-1112**), and 294 Congress St. (*C* **617/778-2200**). The **Palm** was on the move at press time; visit www.thepalm.com for information about its relocation from the Back Bay to the Financial District.

---

table, and don't leave without trying something sweet. The cupcakes, macaroons, and "pop tarts" (puff pastry stuffed with jam) are my favorites.
1595 Washington St. (at Rutland St.). www.flourbakery.com. *C* **617/267-4300.** Reservations not accepted. Breakfast items $3–$7; sandwiches $5–$8; baked goods from $1.25. AE, DISC, MC, V. Mon–Fri 7am–9pm; Sat 8am–6pm; Sun 8am–5pm. T: Silver Line SL4/SL5 bus to Rutland St. Also at 12 Farnsworth St. (off Congress St.), Fort Point Channel (*C* **617/338-4333;** Mon–Fri 7am–7pm, Sat 8am–6pm, Sun 9am–4pm; T: Red Line to South Station, then 10-min. walk), and 190 Massachusetts Ave. (at Albany St.), Cambridge (*C* **617/225-2525;** Mon–Fri 7am–8pm, Sat 8am–6pm, Sun 9am–5pm; T: Red Line to Central, then 10-min. walk).

Picco Restaurant ★ PIZZA   This upscale pizzeria serves traditional and gentrified pizza and phenomenal ice cream in an airy space up the street from the Boston Center for the Arts. The pizza menu ranges from Neapolitan (tomato, basil, and cheese) to the "Alsatian variation," topped with a lip-smacking combo of caramelized onions, shallots, bacon, sour cream, roasted garlic, and Gruyère cheese. The crust—a little smoky from the oven, blistered in spots, thin but not crackery—is as good as the toppings. Somewhat unexpectedly, Picco also has great fish tacos and a fantastic wine list. And the ice cream? Some people are here just for that, and everything—including a huge brownie sundae, ice-cream sodas, even a dish of plain old vanilla—is scrumptious. There's outdoor seating in good weather.
513 Tremont St. (btw. Clarendon and Berkeley sts.). www.piccorestaurant.com. *C* **617/927-0066.** Reservations accepted only for parties of 8 or more. Pizza $10 and up; main courses $8–$14. MC, V. Sun–Wed 11am–10pm; Thurs–Sat 11am–11pm. T: Orange Line to Back Bay.

THE BACK BAY

Like many fashionable neighborhoods, the Back Bay abounds with mediocre dining options—but there's plenty of good food here if you know where to look. In addition to pricey special-occasion destinations, you'll find cheaper places that cater to students and shoppers.

Very Expensive

Davio's Northern Italian Steakhouse ★★ STEAKS/NORTHERN ITAL-IAN   A cavernous space with a surprisingly comfortable vibe, Davio's offers robust cuisine in a business-chic setting. It's stylish but not trendy: Owner-chef Steve DiFillippo built the restaurant's excellent reputation on its top-notch kitchen and dedicated staff. Northern Italian cuisine shares the menu with picture-perfect steakhouse offerings and inventive comfort-food sides. The traditional dishes—pasta, homemade sausage, savory soups, out-of-this-world risotto (I'd walk a mile for the lobster version)—are equally superb, making Davio's a great compromise for hard-core carnivores dining with Italophiles. And this is the place to credit (or blame) for the Philly-cheese-steak-spring-roll phenomenon. The exceptional wine list includes some rare and expensive Italian vintages. Despite the open kitchen, the noise level allows for conversation, even at busy times. Bonus, if you're a fan of the New York Yankees: When the Bronx Bombers are in town, at least a few of them often turn up here.

75 Arlington St. (at Stuart St., 2 blocks from the Public Garden). www.davios.com. ℂ **617/357-4810.** Reservations recommended. Main courses $9–$43 at lunch (most less than $25), $17–$51 at dinner; 4-course tasting menu $75. AE, DC, DISC, MC, V. Mon–Fri 11:30am–3pm; Sun–Tues 5–10pm (lounge menu until 11pm); Wed–Sat 5–11pm (lounge menu until midnight). Validated and valet parking available. T: Green Line to Arlington.

Grill 23 & Bar ★ STEAKS/AMERICAN   The best steakhouse in town, Grill 23 is a wood-paneled, glass-walled place with a businesslike ambience. A brief-case-toting crowd fills its two levels—the dining rooms get *very* noisy—and chows down on traditional slabs of beef and chops, traditional steakhouse side dishes, and sophisticated yet traditional desserts. The meat is of the highest quality, humanely raised and expertly prepared. Steak au poivre and lamb chops are perfectly grilled, crusty, juicy, and tender. Fish dishes aren't quite as memorable as the meat offerings, but, hey, it's a steakhouse. The bountiful a la carte sides include out-of-this-world mashed potatoes, mushrooms with pesto, and "Truffle Tots." Desserts are toothsome but don't always include cheesecake. (This is *not* your father's steakhouse!) The service is exactly right for the setting, helpful but not familiar.

161 Berkeley St. (at Stuart St.). www.grill23.com. ℂ **617/542-2255.** Reservations recommended. Main courses $22–$49; Kobe beef $59. AE, DC, DISC, MC, V. Mon–Thurs 5:30–10:30pm; Fri 5:30–11pm; Sat 5–11pm; Sun 5:30–10pm. Valet parking available. T: Green Line to Arlington.

Expensive

For seafood of all sorts, **Jasper White's Summer Shack** (p. 181) has a branch at 50 Dalton St. (ℂ **617/867-9955**), across the street from the Sheraton Boston and the Hynes Convention Center. The excellent tapas restaurant **Tapéo,** 266 Newbury St. (ℂ **617/267-4799**), is owned by the same family as **Dalí** (p. 180).

Brasserie Jo ★★ REGIONAL FRENCH   One of the most discriminating diners I know lit up like a marquee upon hearing that Boston has a branch of this Chicago favorite. The food is classic—house-made pâtés, fresh baguettes, superb shellfish, *salade Niçoise,* Alsatian onion tart, *choucroute,* coq au vin—but never boring. The house beer, an Alsace-style draft, is a good accompaniment. The casual, all-day French brasserie and bar fits well in this neighborhood, where shoppers can always use a break. It's also a good bet before or after a symphony

QUICK BITES & picnic PROVISIONS

If you're walking the Freedom Trail, pick up food at **Faneuil Hall Marketplace** and stake out a bench. Or buy a tasty sandwich in the North End at **Volle Nolle** (p. 159) or **Il Panino Express,** 266 Hanover St. (© **617/720-5720**), and stroll down Fleet or Richmond street toward the harbor. Eat at the park on Sargent's Wharf, behind 2 Atlantic Ave., or in Christopher Columbus Waterfront Park, overlooking the marina (which is also an option if you stocked up at Faneuil Hall Marketplace).

Two neighborhoods abut the Charles River Esplanade, a great destination for a picnic, concert, or movie. In the **Back Bay,** stop at **Trader Joe's,** 899 Boylston St. (© **617/262-6505**), for prepared food. At the foot of **Beacon Hill,** pick up all you need for a do-it-yourself feast at **Savenor's Market,** 160 Charles St. (© **617/723-6328**). Or call ahead for gourmet thin-crust pizza from **Figs,** 42 Charles St. (© **617/742-3447**).

On the Cambridge side of the river, **Harvard Square** is close enough to the water to allow a riverside repast. About 5 minutes from the heart of the Square and well worth the walk, **Darwin's Ltd.,** 148 Mount Auburn St. (www.darwinsltd.com; © **617/354-5233**), serves excellent gourmet sandwiches and salads. Take yours to John F. Kennedy Park, on Memorial Drive and Kennedy Street, or right to the riverbank, a block away. Nowhere near the Charles, there's a branch at 1629 Cambridge St. (© **617/491-2999**), between Harvard and Inman squares.

or pops performance, and popular for business lunches. The noise level can be high when the spacious room is full—have your tête-à-tête near the bar.

In the Colonnade Hotel, 120 Huntington Ave. (at Garrison St., 1 block from W. Newton St.). www.brasseriejoboston.com. © **617/425-3240.** Reservations recommended at dinner. Main courses $10–$24 (most under $20) at lunch, $15–$37 at dinner; *plats du jour* $20–$24. AE, DC, DISC, MC, V. Mon–Fri 6:30am–11pm; Sat 7am–11pm; Sun 7am–10pm; Sat–Sun brunch noon–3pm; bar menu Mon–Sat until midnight, Sun until 11pm. Valet and garage parking available. T: Green Line E to Prudential.

The Bristol Lounge ★★ AMERICAN   The Bristol Lounge is to a regular restaurant as the Four Seasons is to a regular hotel: It looks about the same, but everything is just *better.* Columns and cushy banquettes break up a large space with floor-to-ceiling windows, red-leather accents, and plenty of wood paneling; there's seating in the lively bar and the stylish dining area. The all-day menu extends from pricey breakfast items to tasty bar bites to sophisticated versions of classic dishes. The juicy burgers are famous, the soups and salads depend on what's fresh and seasonal, and the main courses are top-of-the-line comfort food (grilled salmon, roasted chicken, hand-rolled pastas). Desserts are inventive versions of bread pudding, Boston cream pie, and other traditional favorites. In keeping with every other element of a meal here, the service is fantastic.

In the Four Seasons Hotel, 200 Boylston St. (at Hadassah Way, btw. Arlington St. and Charles St. S.). www.fourseasons.com/boston/dining. © **617/338-4400.** Reservations recommended. Main courses $18–$33 at lunch, $20–$35 at dinner; bar menu $8–$27. AE, DC, DISC, MC, V. Mon–Thurs 6:30am–10:30pm; Fri 6:30am–11:30pm; Sat 7am–11:30pm; Sun 7am–10:30pm. Valet parking available. T: Green Line to Arlington.

Moderate

P. F. Chang's China Bistro has a branch in the Prudential Center, 800 Boylston St. (✆ **617/378-9961**).

Bangkok City ★ THAI   In a neighborhood loaded with Thai restaurants, this is my top choice. Tempting aromas and cordial employees greet you as you check out the exotic decor and lengthy menu. Appetizers are the usual dumplings and satays, plus unusual items like "Boston triangles" (tasty fried pork-and-shrimp patties). Entrees range from mild pad thai to blow-your-hair-back curries, with many vegetarian options. The mix-and-match selection of proteins and sauces is larger than at many other Thai restaurants, so you can let your palate's imagination run wild. (Oh, great—now I want some tamarind duck.) *Hot tip:* The friend who steered me to this place comes here just for the zesty salt-and-pepper squid.

167 Massachusetts Ave. (btw. Belvidere and St. Germain sts.). www.bkkcityboston.com. ✆ **617/266-8884.** Reservations recommended before symphony and pops performances. Main courses $7–$10 at lunch, $10–$18 at dinner; whole fish market price. AE, DC, DISC, MC, V. Mon–Sat 11:30am–3pm; Mon–Thurs 5–10pm; Fri 5–10:30pm; Sat 3–10:30pm; Sun 5–10pm. T: Green Line B, C, or D to Hynes Convention Center.

Inexpensive

The Boston Public Library, 700 Boylston St., offers two dining options (www.thecateredaffair.com/bpl; ✆ **617/859-2251**). The **Courtyard** restaurant is open for lunch on weekdays and afternoon tea Wednesday through Friday, and the self-service **Map Room Café** offers meals and snacks Monday through Saturday from 9am to 5pm.

Café Jaffa ✦ MIDDLE EASTERN/MEDITERRANEAN   A long, narrow brick room with a glass front, Café Jaffa looks more like a snazzy pizza place than the excellent Middle Eastern restaurant it is. The reasonable prices, high quality, and large portions draw hordes of students and other thrifty diners for traditional Middle Eastern offerings. I'm a fan of the combo plates and sandwiches—mix-and-match falafel, baba ghanouj, hummus, grape leaves, and more—and *shawarma*, available in a sandwich, on a salad, or as a full dinner (with Greek salad, rice pilaf, and pita bread). Burgers and steak tips are popular, too. For dessert, try the baklava if it's fresh; skip it if not.

48 Gloucester St. (btw. Boylston and Newbury sts.). www.cafejaffa.net. ✆ **617/536-0230.** Main courses $10–$19; sandwiches and salads $7–$10. AE, DC, DISC, MC, V. Mon–Thurs 11am–10:30pm; Fri–Sat 11am–11pm; Sun noon–10pm. T: Green Line B, C, or D to Hynes Convention Center.

KENMORE SQUARE & THE FENWAY

Long pigeonholed (accurately) as a culinary wasteland of limp hot dogs and stale popcorn, the area around Fenway Park now boasts a dining scene that gets more interesting by the day. Before a big night out, remember that most of the Fenway is some distance from the subway, and plan accordingly.

Very Expensive

Island Creek Oyster Bar ★ SEAFOOD   One of the best seafood restaurants in Boston, "ICOB" is also known for its wine list, cocktails, and knowledgeable, courteous service. The oyster selection includes specimens from the actual Island Creek, in suburban Duxbury, and an impressive variety of other options from near and far. The menu changes daily, drawing on a network of fishermen and aquaculturists who help management balance sustainability with customer demand. Between the labor-intensive sourcing and the upscale-hotel setting, don't expect a bargain—but you really do get what you pay for here. When not creating top-notch versions of classics such as lobster rolls and fried clams, the kitchen shows off an innovative streak; signature dishes include oyster sliders (one delectable fried mollusk on a teeny brioche roll) as well as lobster roe noodles. Not feeling fishy? The burger is among the best in town.

In the Commonwealth Hotel, 500 Commonwealth Ave. (at Kenmore St.). www.islandcreek oysterbar.com. **℗ 617/532-5300.** Reservations recommended. Main courses $13–$26 at lunch, $16–$38 (most more than $20) at dinner. AE, DC, DISC, MC, V. Mon–Sat 4–11pm (late-night menu until 1am); Sun 10:30am–10pm (brunch until 3pm, late-night menu until midnight). Check hours before Red Sox home games Apr–Oct. Valet parking available. T: Green Line B, C, or D to Kenmore.

Expensive

Citizen Public House & Oyster Bar ★★ AMERICAN   A cozy space with a long bar and a seasonal patio, Citizen serves comfort food so good that I almost don't care how loud it is. (Very.) Start with feather-light *canederli* meatballs or roasted-tomato soup served with a cute little grilled-cheese sandwich. Main courses are high-end homey, with a lot of seafood and pork options (the logo is a pig); the tuna burger is perfectly dressed up with Asian accents and served almost raw. Vegetarians have their own equally appealing menu. As for the name, Citizen is more public house than oyster bar; the alcohol selection dwarfs the shellfish variety. Options include 75 whiskeys, artisan cocktails, over a dozen beers, and the cult-favorite *digestif* Fernet Branca on tap.

1310 Boylston St. (at Jersey St.). www.citizenpub.com. ℗ **617/450-9000.** Reservations accepted only for parties of 6 or more. Main courses $18–$23. AE, DC, DISC, MC, V. Daily 5pm–1am; Sun brunch 11am–4pm. Validated parking available. T: Green Line B, C, or D to Kenmore, then 10-min. walk.

The Elephant Walk ★★ FRENCH/CAMBODIAN   The menu at this madly popular spot 4 blocks from Kenmore Square is French on one side and Cambodian on the other, but the boundary is porous. Many Cambodian dishes have part-French names, such as *curry de crevettes* (wonderful shrimp curry with vegetables) and *mee siem au poulet,* a tangle of rice noodles, sliced omelet, tofu, chicken, and picture-perfect vegetables. I'd come here just for *loc lac,* fork-tender beef in addictively spicy-hot sauce. On the French side, you'll find *poulet rôti* (roasted chicken) and top-notch pan-seared tuna. The pleasant staff will help if you need guidance. Many dishes are vegetarian, and this is one of the best destinations in the Boston area if you can't have gluten. *Tip:* Sunday brunch, which includes the prettiest omelets I've ever seen, is worth checking out.

THE GREAT OUTDOORS: alfresco DINING

Cambridge is a better destination for outdoor dining than Boston, where an alarming number of tables sit unpleasantly close to busy traffic, but both cities offer agreeable spots to lounge under the sun or stars.

Across the street from the Charles River near Kendall Square, both restaurant patios at the **Royal Sonesta Hotel,** 5 Cambridge Pkwy. (© 617/491-3600), have great views. The hotel's **ArtBar** is casual; **Dante** is fancier. On one of Harvard Square's main drags, **Shay's Pub & Wine Bar,** 58 John F. Kennedy St. (© 617/864-9161), has a small, lively seating area. More peaceful are the patios at **Henrietta's Table** (p. 176) and **Oleana** (p. 180).

On the other side of the river, try the airy terrace at **Miel** (© 617/217-5151), in the InterContinental Boston hotel, which overlooks Fort Point Channel. Most bars and restaurants in **Faneuil Hall Marketplace** offer outdoor seating and great people-watching. In the Back Bay, Newbury Street is similarly diverting; a good vantage point is **Stephanie's on Newbury,** 190 Newbury St. (© 617/236-0990). A popular shopping stop and after-work hangout is the **Parish Cafe and Bar,** 361 Boylston St. (© 617/247-4777), where the sandwich menu is a "greatest hits" roster of top local chefs' creations.

900 Beacon St. (at Park Dr.). www.elephantwalk.com. © **617/247-1500.** Reservations recommended. Main courses $8–$20 at lunch (most items less than $13), $15–$23 at dinner; dinner tasting menu $30 for 3 courses, $34 for 4 courses. AE, DC, DISC, MC, V. Mon–Fri 11:30am–2:30pm; Sun–Thurs 5–10pm; Fri–Sat 5–11pm; Sun brunch 11:30am–2:30pm. Valet parking available at dinner. T: Green Line C to St. Mary's St. Also at 2067 Massachusetts Ave., Porter Sq., Cambridge (© **617/492-6900;** Mon–Fri 11:30am–10pm, Sat–Sun 5–10pm, Sun brunch 11:30am–2:30pm; T: Red Line to Porter).

Moderate

La Verdad Taqueria Mexicana MEXICAN   Let's cut to the chase: The dining room here is a noisy eyesore, the service far from polished, the food a bit pricey (five bucks for chips and salsa, really?), and I couldn't care less. La Verdad serves the best fish tacos in Boston, one of nine outstanding taco options that include grilled skirt steak, *carnitas* (pork), chipotle-stewed chicken, chorizo and sweet potato, and braised pork belly. To start, skip the pricey chips and opt for incredible grilled corn coated in garlic mayonnaise, chile powder, and crumbled *cotija* cheese. To finish, skip dessert—I honestly can't recommend any of them—and order another margarita. Try not to come here before or after a Red Sox game or a big show at the House of Blues, when it's painfully crowded and loud, even in the outdoor seating area.

1 Lansdowne St. (at Ipswich St.). www.laverdadtaqueria.com. © **617/421-9595** (restaurant) or 617/351-2580 (taqueria). Reservations recommended at dinner. Main courses $9–$19 (most under $14). AE, DISC, MC, V. Restaurant daily 5pm–1am. Taqueria daily 11am–1am. T: Green Line B, C, or D to Kenmore, 10-min. walk.

Inexpensive

Tasty Burger ☺ AMERICAN   Boston's take on the faux-retro burger-joint trend is Tasty Burger, in a renovated service station near Fenway Park. The aptly named ⅓-pound burgers come with lettuce and tomato; adding other toppings bumps up the price, but not outrageously. Swapping beef for a turkey or veggie burger is free; other options include chicken sandwiches, hot dogs, and even salads. For hungry teenagers, a single main course may not be enough food, but standard-issue appetites will be happy to round out a meal with a side or two. The "why didn't I think of that" side is the 50/50 mix of French fries and onion rings, and beverage options are extensive. Tasty Burger has a beer-and-wine license, but you may prefer a raspberry lime rickey or a milkshake.

1301 Boylston St. (at Yawkey Way). www.tastyburger.com. **℃ 617/425-4444.** Main courses $4–$7. AE, MC, V. Daily 11am–2am. T: Green Line B, C, or D to Kenmore, then 10-min. walk.

CAMBRIDGE

The dining scene in Cambridge, as in Boston, offers something for everyone, from penny-pinching students to the tycoons many of them aspire to become. The Red Line runs from Boston to Harvard Square, and many of the restaurants listed here are within walking distance of the square; others (including a couple of real finds over the Somerville border) are under the heading "Outside Harvard Square."

Harvard Square & Vicinity

A brilliant idea cooked up by a pair of Harvard Business School students, **Finale** (p. 228), 30 Dunster St. (℃ 617/441-9797), specializes in dessert.

VERY EXPENSIVE

UpStairs on the Square ★★ AMERICAN   Overlooking a little park, UpStairs on the Square is the perfect combination of comfort food and fine dining. It consists of two lovely spaces. The second-floor Monday Club Bar dining room is a relaxed yet romantic space where firelight flickers on jewel-toned walls. The food—unusual salads and sandwiches, pizza (at lunch), fried chicken, inventive pastas, steak with ever-changing versions of potatoey goodness—is homey and satisfying, and the bar is a tweedy Cambridge scene. The top-floor Soirée Room, all pinks and golds under a low, mirrored ceiling, is the place for that big anniversary dinner. The menu is enjoyably old-fashioned, with inventive starters and straightforward main courses (olive oil–poached salmon, pork loin with caraway-roasted bacon). Tasting menus, for vegetarians and carnivores, let the kitchen show off. In both rooms, you'll find outstanding wine selections and desserts.

91 Winthrop St. (at John F. Kennedy St.). www.upstairsonthesquare.com. **℃ 617/864-1933.** Reservations recommended. Monday Club Bar main courses $13–$29; prix-fixe lunch $20. Soirée Room main courses $23–$34; tasting menus $72–$95. AE, DC, DISC, MC, V. Monday Club Bar Mon–Sat 11am–3pm; Sun–Thurs 5–10pm; Fri–Sat 5–11pm (bar open until 1am); Sun brunch 10am–3pm; afternoon tea Sat 2–4pm. Soirée Room Tues–Thurs 5–10pm; Fri–Sat 5:30–11pm. Validated and valet parking available. T: Red Line to Harvard.

EXPENSIVE

There's a **Legal Sea Foods** (p. 151) in the Charles Hotel courtyard, 20 University Rd. (☎ **617/491-9400**).

Henrietta's Table ★★ NEW ENGLAND   Before it was a cliché, "sophisticated comfort food" was a great idea, and Henrietta's Table does it exactly right. Decorated in upscale farmhouse style, the restaurant serves deceptively simple food—baked scrod, roasted chicken, Yankee pot roast, and so on—made with fresh, usually local, often organic provisions. Complementing top-of-the-line meats, fish, and poultry are terrific breads and an impressive variety of gorgeous produce, prepared to let the quality of the ingredients take center stage. I especially enjoy the bounteous salads and tasty desserts, but try any dish with ingredients you like: Mysterious additions aren't a problem here. ***Tip:*** Given a choice, go for lunch over "supper," when service can be scattered and a la carte side dishes can run up the bill. There's seasonal outdoor seating in the pleasant courtyard.

In the Charles Hotel, 1 Bennett St. (at Eliot St.). www.henriettastable.com. ☎ **617/661-5005.** Reservations recommended. Main courses $13–$20 at lunch, $15–$23 at dinner; "yard sale" dinner (Sun–Thurs) $25 for 2 courses, $32 for 3 courses. AE, DC, MC, V. Mon–Fri 6:30–11am; Sat 7–11am; Sun 7–10:30am; daily noon–3pm (Sat a la carte brunch, Sun buffet brunch); daily 5:30–10pm. Valet and validated parking available. T: Red Line to Harvard.

Russell House Tavern ★ NEW AMERICAN   This cavernous gastropub seems to be trying to be all things to (almost) all people, and—somewhat improbably—succeeding. In the heart of Harvard Square, Russell House Tavern is popular with everyone from starving students to picky parents to committed locavores. Try a craft cocktail and some perfect oysters. Split a pizza topped with fantastic house-made sausage. Savor a locally sourced salad or the signature poached-and-deep-fried egg (much better than it sounds). Then dig into short rib "Wellington," a potpie with a lid of puff pastry covering luscious beef, apples, and mushrooms,

---

 ## The Scoop on Ice Cream

No less an expert than Ben Cohen of Ben & Jerry's has described Boston as "a great place for ice cream." That goes for Cambridge, too—residents of both cities famously defy even the most frigid weather to get their fix. I like Cambridge's offerings better: Try **JP Licks,** 1312 Massachusetts Ave. (www.jplicks. com; ☎ 617/492-1001); **Ben & Jerry's,** in the Garage mall, 36 John F. Kennedy St. (www.benjerry.com; ☎ 617/864-2828); or **Lizzy's,** 29 Church St. (www.lizzysice cream.com; ☎ 617/354-2911)—all in Harvard Square. Or try **Christina's,** 1255 Cambridge St., Inman Square (www. christinasicecream.com; ☎ 617/492-7021).

Favorite Boston destinations include **Emack & Bolio's,** 290 Newbury St., Back Bay (www.emackandbolios.com; ☎ 617/536-7127), and 255 State St., across from the New England Aquarium (☎ 617/367-0220); and **JP Licks,** 659 Centre St., Jamaica Plain (☎ 617/524-6740). **Ben & Jerry's** also has stores in Boston at the Prudential Center, 800 Boylston St. (☎ 617/266-0767), 174 Newbury St., Back Bay (☎ 617/536-5456), and 20 Park Plaza, a block from the Public Garden (☎ 617/426-0890). Check the JP Licks and Emack & Bolio's websites for addresses of locations in Somerville and Brookline.

Cambridge Restaurants

Baraka Café **31**
Ben & Jerry's **17**
Bertucci's **10, 32**
Border Café **8**
Christina's **26**
Clover Food Lab **20, 28**
Clover Food Truck **35**
Dalí **24**
Darwin's Ltd. **6, 23**
East Coast Grill & Raw Bar **25**
The Elephant Walk **1**
Finale **19**
The Helmand **36**
Henrietta's Table **11**
Hungry Mother **33**
India Pavilion **30**
Jasper White's Summer
  Shack **2**
Johnny D's Uptown
  Restaurant & Music Club **3**
JP Licks **21**
Legal Sea Foods **11, 34**

Lizzy's **7**
Mr. Bartley's Burger Cottage **22**
Oleana **28**
Orinoco **13**
Porter Exchange **4**
Redbones **5**
Royal Sonesta Hotel **37**
Russell House Tavern **18**
S&S Restaurant **27**
Shay's Pub & Wine Bar **12**
Tealuxe **16**
Upstairs on the Square **15**
Veggie Planet **9**
Wagamama **14**

Harvard Square area

HARVARD
UNIVERSITY

177

or simple grilled fish with yummy garlic-herb mayonnaise. If the menu has a weak spot, it's heavy desserts; the trio of sprightly fruit sorbets is a perky exception. Seating is in the street-level bar, on the patio, or in the huge downstairs dining room. All are loud at busy times.

14 John F. Kennedy St. (at Brattle St.). www.russellhousecambridge.com. ℭ **617/500-3055.** Reservations recommended at dinner. Main courses $9–$14 at lunch, $11–$39 (most less than $25) at dinner; pizzas $10–$13. AE, DC, MC, V. Daily 11am–11pm (late-night menu Sun–Wed until midnight, Thurs–Sat until 1am); brunch Sat–Sun until 4pm. T: Red Line to Harvard.

MODERATE

Border Café TEX-MEX/CAJUN   This Harvard Square hangout has been packing 'em in since 1987 with generous portions of tasty food that goes well with beer and margaritas. Patrons loiter at the bar for hours, enhancing the festival atmosphere. Finally seated, you'll probably have to shout your order. Try an excellent chorizo appetizer, quesadillas (shrimp and crawfish is delectable), tacos, or popcorn shrimp. Fajitas for one or two, sizzling noisily, are a popular choice. The menu features plenty of vegetarian options, and the staff keeps the chips—fried after you order them—and fresh house-made salsa coming. Set aside a couple of hours, get into a party mood, and ask to be seated downstairs if you want to be able to hear your companions. *Tip for parents:* Although there's no children's menu, this place is great for kids, but only if you eat early. (You do that anyway, right?)

32 Church St. (at Palmer St.). www.bordercafe.com. ℭ **617/864-6100.** Reservations not accepted. Main courses $7–$18. AE, MC, V. Daily 11am–11pm. T: Red Line to Harvard.

INEXPENSIVE

Clover Food Lab ★ VEGETARIAN/VEGAN   Clover specializes in local, organic-when-possible vegetarian and vegan-friendly food, but you might not notice. This cheery place lets you feel virtuous without sacrificing flavor or spending a fortune. The regularly changing menu includes soups, salads, rosemary fries, and sandwiches on whole-wheat pita. Chickpea fritter (falafel, basically) is the signature sandwich, but consider barbecued seitan—wheat gluten dressed up with sauce so good, you won't miss the meat. Besides terrific coffee and tea, the drinks menu features delicious fresh-squeezed juices, lemonades, and house-made soda. The brainchild of an MIT and Harvard grad who gave up management consulting to work at Burger King (as research), Clover started as a food truck; it now has multiple vehicles, at MIT and around Boston, and another brick-and-mortar location (at 1075 Cambridge St., outside Inman Sq.). Visit the website or check Twitter (@cloverfoodtruck) to learn more about this eco-conscious, employee-empowering phenomenon. Or just worry about whether there are any cookies left.

7 Holyoke St. (off Mass. Ave.). www.cloverfoodtruck.com. ℭ **617/640-1884.** All items $5 or less. MC, V. Daily 7am–10pm. T: Red Line to Harvard.

Mr. Bartley's Burger Cottage ★★ AMERICAN   Great burgers and incomparable onion rings make Bartley's a perennial favorite with a cross-section of Cambridge. In increasingly generic Harvard Square, it's a beacon of originality. Founded in 1960, this family business is a crowded, high-ceilinged room (there's also a small outdoor seating area) plastered with signs, posters, and memorabilia.

Family-Friendly Restaurants

Like chocolate and champagne, well-behaved children are welcome almost everywhere. Most Boston-area restaurants can accommodate families. Below are some suggestions of kid-friendly dining options.

The nonstop activity and lively crowds at **Durgin-Park** (p. 160) will entrance any child, and parents of picky eaters appreciate the straightforward New England fare. Other good nonchain choices are **Redbones** (p. 182), the **Barking Crab** (p. 150), and the Cambridge location of **Jasper White's Summer Shack** (p. 181), which has a giant lobster tank.

The **Bertucci's** chain of pizzerias (www.bertuccis.com) appeals to children and adults equally, with wood-fired brick ovens that are visible from many tables, great rolls made from pizza dough, and pizzas and pastas that range from basic to sophisticated. There are convenient branches at Faneuil Hall Marketplace, on Merchants Row off State Street (*(C)* **617/227-7889**); at 533 Commonwealth Ave., Kenmore Square (*(C)* **617/236-1030**); and in Cambridge at 21 Brattle St., Harvard Square (*(C)* **617/864-4748**), and 799 Main St. (*(C)* **617/661-8356**), a short walk from Central Square.

Burgers bear the names of local and national celebrities, notably political figures; the names change, but the ingredients stay the same.

Anything you can think of to put on your personal 7 ounces of house-ground beef is available, from American cheese to grilled pineapple. Good meatless dishes include veggie burgers, huge salads, and creamy, garlicky hummus. Bartley's also serves sandwiches and comfort-food dinners, and it's one of the only places around that still serves a real raspberry lime rickey.

1246 Massachusetts Ave. (btw. Plympton and Bow sts.). www.bartleysburgers.com. *(C)* **617/354-6559.** Burgers $10–$14; main courses, salads, and sandwiches $5–$9; children's menu $4–$5. No credit cards. Mon–Sat 11am–9pm. Closed Memorial Day, July 4, Labor Day, Dec 25–Jan 1. T: Red Line to Harvard.

Veggie Planet ★ PIZZA/VEGETARIAN/VEGAN   Don't let the virtuous slant of Veggie Planet's menu put you off—this is tasty, flavorful food that happens to be (mostly) good for you. The subterranean restaurant in the legendary coffeehouse and folk club has an unusual specialty: your choice of organic pizza dough, brown rice, or coconut rice, topped with combinations of ingredients. Some you'd expect to see on pizza—tomatoes, spinach, and cheese, for example; others, like zesty peanut curry or black beans, salsa, and pepper jack cheese, you might not. There's no meat, and dairy only if you want it. Salads, soups, and tasty desserts round out the menu, which features natural and fair-trade soft drinks in addition to beer and wine. Veggie Planet's sister restaurant, **Veggie Galaxy,** 450 Massachusetts Ave. (at Brookline St.), Central Square (www.veggiegalaxy.com; *(C)* **617/497-1513**), is a diner that serves breakfast all day.

In Club Passim, 47 Palmer St. (at Church St., 1 block from Mass. Ave.). www.veggieplanet.net. *(C)* **617/661-1513.** Main courses $7–$11; children's menu $3–$6. No credit cards. Daily 11:30am–10:30pm; Sun brunch until 3pm. T: Red Line to Harvard.

Outside Harvard Square

VERY EXPENSIVE

East Coast Grill & Raw Bar ★★★ SEAFOOD/BARBECUE   Huge portions, a dizzying menu, and funky decor have made the East Coast Grill madly popular since 1985. Just walking into the colorful, noisy restaurant is exciting. The kitchen handles fresh seafood (an encyclopedic variety), barbecue, and grilled fish and meats with equal authority and imagination. To start, consider the raw-bar offerings, or try the sublime fried oysters. The seafood entrees are exceptional—always check the specials board, but consider trying shrimp and scallops served over ginger-garlic noodles with perfect sesame-chile spinach. Barbecue comes on abundant platters in three styles: Texas beef, Memphis spareribs, and North Carolina pork. Vegetarians can opt for the "all-vegetable experience of the day." Desserts are above average, but if you've played your cards right, you won't have room.

1271 Cambridge St. (off Prospect St.), Inman Sq. www.eastcoastgrill.net. *℡* **617/491-6568.** Reservations accepted only Sun–Thurs for parties of 5 or more. Main courses $16–$30; fresh seafood market price. AE, DISC, MC, V. Sun–Thurs 5:30–10pm; Fri–Sat 5:30–10:30pm; Sun brunch 11am–2:30pm. Validated parking available. T: Red Line to Central, then a 10-min. walk on Prospect St., or Red Line to Harvard, then no. 69 (Harvard-Lechmere) bus to Inman Sq.

Oleana ★★ MEDITERRANEAN   The wonderful food and welcoming atmosphere make Oleana, a casual neighborhood place outside Inman Square, one of the best restaurants in the Boston area. The seasonal menu, which features cuisine typical of and inspired by the Mediterranean—not just the usual suspects; Turkey and Armenia figure in—relies on fresh ingredients and unusual flavors. Tempting aromas signal the arrival of striped bass with black garlic–tahini sauce, which might land next to a plate of veal sausage with beans, pumpkin, and feta. A signature offering is the vegetarian tasting menu, which even makes carnivores happy. Portions are generous, and the dessert menu is heavy on house-made ice cream. In warm weather, there's seating on the peaceful patio; it can't be reserved, so try to eat early.

134 Hampshire St. (off Elm St.), Inman Sq. www.oleanarestaurant.com. *℡***617/661-0505.** Reservations recommended (not accepted for patio). Main courses $22–$30; vegetable tasting menu $40. AE, MC, V. Sun–Thurs 5:30–10pm; Fri–Sat 5:30–11pm. Free parking. T: Red Line to Central, then a 10-min. walk.

EXPENSIVE

There's a **Legal Sea Foods** (p. 151) at 5 Cambridge Center, Kendall Sq. (*℡* **617/864-3400**). The **Elephant Walk** (p. 173) has a branch outside Porter Square, at 2067 Massachusetts Ave. (*℡* **617/492-6900**).

Dalí ★★ TAPAS/SPANISH   This festive restaurant is noisy and inconvenient, accepts only limited reservations, and still fills nightly with people cheerfully waiting for a table. The payoff is authentic tapas—little plates of hot or cold creations that burst with flavor. Entrees include excellent paella, but most diners come with friends and explore the tapas offerings. Each is enough for three or four people to have a good-size taste. They include *patatas ali-oli* (garlic potatoes), *albóndigas de salmón* (salmon balls with caper sauce), and *lomito al cabrales* (pork tenderloin with blue cheese), plus monthly specials. The helpful staff sometimes seems rushed but supplies plenty of bread for sopping up juices and sangria for washing it all down. Finish with "ubiquitous flan" or luscious *tarta de chocolates*.

415 Washington St. (at Beacon St.), Somerville. www.dalirestaurant.com. ℭ **617/661-3254.** Reservations recommended; accepted Sun–Thurs until 6:30pm, Fri until 6pm, Sat at 5:30pm. Tapas $4.50–$16 (most less than $10); main courses $24–$26; late-night menu $4.50–$9. AE, DC, MC, V. Mon–Sat 5:30–11pm; Sun noon–11pm. Bar serves food until 12:30am. T: Red Line to Harvard, then follow Kirkland St. to intersection of Washington and Beacon sts. (20-min. walk or $6 cab ride).

Hungry Mother ★ SOUTHERN/CONTEMPORARY AMERICAN Sea-
sonal produce, top-quality pork, plenty of butter—Southern food and French technique are made for each other. They meet at this casual little place, one of the Boston area's most reliable neighborhood restaurants. Hungry Mother's menu changes with the season, emphasizing local and sustainable ingredients. That translates to an unforgettable appetizer of Maine shrimp and grits with chunks of house-made tasso ham, supercrispy cornmeal crusts on green tomatoes and delectable catfish, pork shoulder stewed in bourbon and served with one chewy rib. Desserts are more Southern than French; if sweets aren't your thing, you might be better off with something from the inventive drinks menu. As for the name, it's a happy coincidence—chef and co-owner Barry Maiden is from Virginia, near the state park of the same appellation.

233 Cardinal Medeiros Ave. (at Bristol St., 1 block from Hampshire St.), Kendall Sq. www.hungry mothercambridge.com. ℭ **617/499-0090.** Reservations recommended. Main courses $19–$25; late-night menu $3–$11. AE, DC, DISC, MC, V. Tues–Sun 5–10pm; late-night menu 10pm–12:30am. Validated parking available. T: Red Line to Kendall/MIT, then 10-min. walk.

Jasper White's Summer Shack ★★ ☺ SEAFOOD An enormous space
with a giant lobster tank, the Summer Shack feels like an overgrown seaside clam shack—but nationally renowned chef Jasper White makes it something more. All the basics are here: raw bar, excellent fries, lobster rolls, corn dogs, fantastic tuna burgers, and much more. Turn to the specials and the aptly named "big bucks lobster" section of the menu for foodie favorites like wok-seared lobster with ginger and scallions or steamed mussels in wine-and-herb broth. When it's full, this is one of the loudest restaurants in the Boston area. Arrive early, and ask to sit on the second level; it's just a few steps up, but much quieter.

The Summer Shack in Boston's **Back Bay** is especially popular before and after Red Sox games and symphony performances.

149 Alewife Brook Pkwy. (at Cambridgepark Dr., opposite Alewife Station). www.summer shackrestaurant.com. ℭ **617/520-9500.** Reservations recommended at dinner. Main courses $8–$36 (most $25 or less); sandwiches $5–$15; lobster and specials market price. AE, DISC, MC, V. Mon–Thurs 11:30am–9:30pm (lunch menu until 5pm); Fri 11:30am–10:30pm (lunch menu until 5pm); Sat noon–10:30pm; Sun noon–9pm. Free parking. T: Red Line to Alewife. Also at 50 Dalton St. (at Scotia St., 1 block from Boylston St.), Boston (ℭ **617/867-9955;** Apr–Oct Sun–Wed 11:30am–10pm, Thurs–Sat 11:30am–11pm; Nov–Mar Mon–Wed 5–10pm, Thurs–Fri 5–11pm, Sat 11:30am–11pm, Sun 11:30am–10pm).

MODERATE

Besides being a magnet for music fans, **Johnny D's Uptown Restaurant & Music Club** (p. 237), in Somerville's Davis Square, is a good stop for a meal, especially if you're a vegetarian or want to keep one happy.

Baraka Café ★ ALGERIAN/TUNISIAN/MEDITERRANEAN   On a dull side street off Central Square, Baraka Café is a tiny, aromatic destination for adventurous diners. Flavorful, highly spiced (not necessarily hot) food served in an elaborately decorated dining room makes it a favorite with local foodies. They talk about it as though it's a secret, but one look at the line that forms on weekend evenings tells the truth. The quality of the food outweighs the drawbacks—no alcohol, cash only, tiny dining room, deliberate service. Start with house-made breads and appetizers such as spicy *merguez* sausage and *bedenjal mechoui* (Algerian baba ghanouj, more or less). Main courses include fantastic couscous, fork-tender lamb chops, and eggplant stuffed with a tasty concoction of olives, spinach, scallions, and two cheeses. Be sure to ask about daily specials, which show off the kitchen's considerable abilities better than the limited regular menu.

80½ Pearl St. (at William St., 3½ blocks from Massachusetts Ave.), Central Sq. www.barakacafe. com. 📞 **617/868-3951.** Reservations not accepted. Main courses $5–$9 at lunch, $9–$16 at dinner. No credit cards. Tues–Sat 11:30am–3pm; Tues–Sun 5:30–10pm. T: Red Line to Central.

The Helmand ★★ 🔖 AFGHAN   The Helmand, named for the region and river in Afghanistan, is low-profile yet always crowded. The elegant setting near the CambridgeSide Galleria mall belies the reasonable prices. Afghan food has elements of Middle Eastern, Indian, and Pakistani cuisine, with many vegetarian options; meat is often one element, rather than the centerpiece, of a dish. To start, try baked pumpkin topped with spicy ground meat sauce or *aushak,* "Afghan ravioli" filled with leeks or potatoes with a sauce of either meat or split peas and carrots. The grilled entrees are fine, but I prefer homier dishes such as a larger portion of those irresistible *aushak* or *kourma challow,* an excellent mélange of lamb, potatoes, onion, tomatoes, and green beans. Every meal comes with fluffy bread made fresh in the wood-fired brick oven. Service could be more attentive, but with food this good, that's a minor quibble.

143 First St. (at Bent St.). www.helmandrestaurant.com. 📞 **617/492-4646.** Reservations recommended. Main courses $13–$23. AE, MC, V. Sun–Thurs 5–10pm; Fri–Sat 5–11pm. T: Green Line to Lechmere.

Redbones ★ ☺ BARBECUE   Geographically, this raucous restaurant is in Somerville, but in spirit it's on a Southern back road. Barbecued ribs (Memphis-, Texas-, and Arkansas-style), smoked beef brisket, fried Louisiana catfish, and grilled chicken come with traditional side dishes such as coleslaw and beans. The chummy staff can help you choose sweet, hot, mild, or vinegar sauce. The best nonbarbecue dish is succulent buffalo shrimp, swimming in hot sauce. Portions are large, so pace yourself. Don't miss the appetizers and sides—catfish "catfingers," succotash, corn pudding, and collard greens, just to name a few; if you're with enough other people, the appetizer samplers are a good deal. The only less-than-tasty dish I've ever had here was watery broccoli. The beer selection is huge, and there's valet bike parking. ***Tip:*** Given a choice, sit upstairs—Underbones, downstairs, is a noisy bar.

55 Chester St. (off Elm St.), Somerville. www.redbones.com. 📞 **617/628-2200.** Reservations accepted only Sun–Thurs before 7pm for parties of 10 or more. Main courses $9–$21; sandwiches $6–$11; children's menu $5. AE, MC, V. Mon–Thurs 11:30am–10:30pm; Fri–Sat 11:30am–11pm; Sun 11am–10:30pm (brunch until 4pm); late-night menu daily until 12:30am. T: Red Line to Davis.

In Boston, the only city that has a tea party named after it, the tradition of afternoon tea is alive and well. Reservations are strongly recommended; at the Four Seasons and Taj Boston hotels, they're pretty much mandatory.

The best afternoon tea in town is at the **Bristol Lounge** in the Four Seasons Hotel, 200 Boylston St. (℃ **617/351-2037**). The gorgeous room, lovely view, and courtly ritual elevate scones, pastries, tea sandwiches, and nut bread from delicious to unforgettable. The Bristol serves tea ($28) every day from 3 to 4:15pm.

Taj Boston, 15 Arlington St. (℃ **617/598-5255**), serves tea in the celebrated **Lounge** at 2 and 4pm; it's available Saturday and Sunday in the winter, Friday through Sunday the rest of the year. The price is $25 for tea and pastries, $33 to add sandwiches.

The Langham, Boston, 250 Franklin St. (℃ **617/956-8751**), serves afternoon tea ($31) daily from 3 to 5pm in **Bond Restaurant & Lounge.** The chain's flagship is in London, and as you'd expect, this is a proper British experience. The **Rowes Wharf Sea Grille,** in the Boston Harbor Hotel, 70 Rowes Wharf (℃ **617/856-7744**), serves tea daily from 2:30 to 4pm in a lovely room overlooking the hotel marina. It costs $19 to $30. The Mandarin Oriental, Boston, 776 Boylston St. (℃ **617/535-8800**), serves tea in the **Lobby Lounge** Thursday through Sunday from 2:30 to 4pm. It prices food ($27) and drinks ($6–$9) separately. **Swans** at the Boston Park Plaza Hotel & Towers, 50 Park Plaza (℃ **617/654-1906**), serves tea Friday through Sunday from 3 to 5pm and offers meatless and dairy-free options. The price is $30 to $32 for adults, $17 for children.

Two nonhotel destinations are worth considering. The **Courtyard** restaurant at the Boston Public Library, 700 Boylston St. (℃ **617/859-2251**), serves tea ($23) Wednesday through Friday from 2 to 4pm. And across the river, beloved Cambridge restaurant **UpStairs on the Square** (p. 175), shown here, makes a wonderful destination. Zebra Tea ($28) is a three-tiered wonder that lets the inventive kitchen cut loose on a small scale. Food and drinks are also available a la carte, and the Grand Peppermint Tea ($18) combines minty sweets and a pot of the headliner. Tea is served Saturday and Sunday (Thurs–Sun in Dec) from 2 to 4pm.

And if you just want a well-prepared cuppa, head to Harvard Square, where **Tealuxe,** Zero Brattle St., Cambridge (www.tealuxe.com; ℃ **617/441-0077**), has been delighting tea aficionados since 1996. It serves and sells more than 100 varieties and offers light fare and desserts.

INEXPENSIVE

Clover Food Lab (p. 178) sends a **Clover Food Truck** to MIT, where it parks at 20 Carleton St. (btw. Amherst and Main sts.), weekdays from 8am to 7pm.

The food court on the lower level of the **Porter Exchange mall,** 1815 Massachusetts Ave., Porter Square, is home to half a dozen or so Japanese businesses that attract expats from all over the Boston area. The superauthentic dining options are mostly fast-food counters with small seating areas in front; wander around until you see a dish that strikes your fancy. All open in the late morning and close by 9pm. Start at **Cafe Mami** (© 617/547-9130), but also check out—in rough order of preference—**Sapporo Ramen** (© 617/876-4805), **Tampopo** (© 617/868-5457), and **Ittyo Restaurant** (www.ittyo.com; © 617/354-5944). Afterward, hit **Japonaise Bakery** (www.japonaisebakery.com; © 617/547-5531) for French- and Japanese-style pastries, notably the items that incorporate *azuki* (red bean) cream.

India Pavilion ✦ INDIAN   The oldest Indian restaurant in the Boston area opened in 1979 and remains a favorite for its flavorful cuisine, lunch buffet, and reasonable prices. Among excellent renditions of now-familiar northern Indian favorites—*rogan josh* (lamb in spiced tomato sauce), chicken *tikka masala* (in tomato cream sauce), *saag paneer* (spinach with cheese)—are less common options such as eggplant-based *baingan bharta* and Peshwari nan (stuffed with coconut, almonds, raisins, and apricots). If the latter two dishes don't sound familiar, the house dinners for two and *thaali* (literally, "plate") selections make good introductions. As at most Indian restaurants, vegetarians will be happy here, and so will their carnivore friends.

17 Central Sq. (at Green St.). www.royalbharatinc.com. © **617/547-7463.** Lunch buffet $8; main courses $8–$19 (most less than $14). AE, DC, MC, V. Daily noon–11pm (lunch until 3pm). T: Red Line to Central.

S&S Restaurant ★★ DELI   *Es* is Yiddish for "eat," and this Cambridge classic is as straightforward as its name ("eat and eat"). Founded in 1919 by the great-grandmother of the current owners, it draws huge weekend brunch crowds, and it's worth a visit during the week, too. With lots of light wood and plants, it looks contemporary, but the brunch offerings are huge portions of traditional dishes such as pancakes, waffles, and omelets. The bagels and cinnamon rolls are among the best in the area; you'll also find traditional deli items (corned beef, pastrami, tongue, potato pancakes, and blintzes), yummy house-made corned beef hash, and breakfast anytime. At dinner, comfort food prevails: barbecue, fresh seafood, chicken parmigiana. Be early for brunch, or plan to spend part of your Saturday or Sunday standing around people-watching and getting hungry—I'll be right there with you.

1334 Cambridge St. (at Oak St.; back entrance off Hampshire St.), Inman Sq. www.sandsrestaurant. com. © **617/354-0777.** Main courses $5–$20; brunch main courses $10–$17. AE, MC, V. Mon–Wed 7am–10pm; Thurs–Fri 7am–11pm; Sat 8am–11pm; Sun 8am–10pm; brunch Sat–Sun until 4pm. Free parking; ask cashier for token on weekends. T: Red Line to Harvard, then bus 69 (Harvard-Lechmere) to Inman Sq.; or Red Line to Central, then a 10-min. walk on Prospect St.

PRACTICAL MATTERS: THE RESTAURANT SCENE

RESERVATIONS At restaurants that take reservations, it's always a good idea to make them, particularly for dinner. To make reservations at any hour, visit **www.opentable.com**, which handles many local restaurants. If you strike out, consider eating at the bar. It won't be as comfortable as the dining room, but the food and service tend to be roughly comparable.

WHEN TO DINE Boston-area restaurants are far less busy early in the week than they are Friday and Saturday. If you're flexible about when you indulge in fine cuisine and when you go for pizza and a movie, choose the low-budget option on the weekend and pamper yourself on a weeknight. Note that many chefs have Sunday or Monday (or both) off. If you plan to eat at a particular restaurant to check out a specific chef, call ahead to make sure he or she is working that night.

BARGAINS **Lunch** is an excellent, economical way to check out a fancy restaurant. At higher-end restaurants that offer it (many don't), you can get a sense of the dinner menu without breaking the bank. To get a bargain at dinner, investigate **group-buying sites** such as Groupon (www.groupon.com) and Living Social (www.livingsocial.com). Sign up for Boston alerts when you start planning your trip, and you may land a great deal.

DRESS CODES As you might expect in a city overrun with college students and tourists, just about anything goes. Even at pricier establishments, being clean and neat suffices, but you—and the couple at the next table who just got engaged—will probably feel more comfortable if you change out of the shorts and sneakers you wore all day.

INGREDIENTS At almost every restaurant—trendy or classic, expensive or cheap, American (whatever that is) or ethnic—you'll find seafood on the menu. A quick introduction: **Scrod** or **schrod** is a generic term for fresh white-fleshed fish, usually served in filets. Local shellfish includes Ipswich and Essex **clams,** Atlantic (usually Maine) **lobsters,** Wellfleet and Island Creek **oysters, scallops, mussels,** and **shrimp.**

New England clam chowder.

Fresh oysters.

If you're worried about overfishing, download the Monterey Bay Aquarium's pocket guide to buying and eating fish in the Northeast (www.montereybay aquarium.org).

Lobster ordered boiled or steamed usually comes with a plastic bib, drawn butter (for dipping), a nutcracker (for the claws and tail), and a pick (for the legs). Restaurants price lobsters by the pound; you'll typically pay at least $15 to $20 for a "chicken" (1- to 1¼-lb.) lobster, and more for bigger specimens. If you want someone else to do the work, lobster is available in a "roll" (lobster-salad sandwich), stuffed and baked or broiled, in or over pasta, in a "pie" (casserole), in salad, and in bisque.

Well-made **New England clam chowder** is studded with fresh clams and thickened with cream. Recipes vary, but they *never* include tomatoes. (Tomatoes go in Manhattan clam chowder.) If you want clams but not soup, many places serve **steamers,** or soft-shell clams cooked in the shell, as an appetizer or main dish. More common are hard-shell clams—**littlenecks** (small) or **cherrystones** (medium-size)—served raw, like oysters.

Traditional **Boston baked beans,** which date from Colonial days, when cooking on the Sabbath was forbidden, earned Boston the nickname "Beantown." Durgin-Park (p. 160) does an excellent rendition.

To wash it all down, consider a local beer. The Boston Beer Co., which produces the highly regarded **Samuel Adams** brand, has a brewery in Boston. Numerous bars in the area feature New

Summer Lovin'

The axiom that you should order **oysters** only in months with an *R* in them originates in biology. Summer is breeding season, when the energy that usually goes into bulking up (and making lots of juicy meat) gets diverted to reproduction. To experience the best the oyster has to offer, wait till the weather turns colder.

England microbrews, and some places—including Boston Beer Works (p. 234) and the Cambridge Brewing Company (p. 234)—make their own.

Finally, **Boston cream pie** is golden layer cake sandwiched around custard and topped with chocolate glaze—no cream, no pie.

RESTAURANTS BY CUISINE

AFGHAN
The Helmand ★★ ($$, p. 182)

ALGERIAN
Baraka Café ★ ($$, p. 182)

AMERICAN
The Bristol Lounge ★★ ($$$, p. 171)
Citizen Public House & Oyster Bar ★★ ($$$, p. 173)
Flour Bakery & Cafe ($, p. 168)
Grill 23 & Bar ★ ($$$$, p. 170)
Hamersley's Bistro ★★★ ($$$$, p. 166)
Hungry Mother ★ ($$$, p. 181)
Jacob Wirth Company ($$, p. 163)
Mr. Bartley's Burger Cottage ★★ ($, p. 178)
Russell House Tavern ★ ($$$, p. 176)
South End Buttery ($$, p. 167)
Tasty Burger ($, p. 175)
UpStairs on the Square ★★ ($$$$, p. 175)

BARBECUE
East Coast Grill & Raw Bar ★★★ ($$$$, p. 180)
Redbones ★ ($$, p. 182)

CAJUN
Border Café ($$, p. 178)

CAMBODIAN
The Elephant Walk ★★ ($$$, p. 173)

CANTONESE/SZECHUAN
Great Taste Bakery & Restaurant ★ ($, p. 165)
Peach Farm ★ ($$, p. 165)

DELI
S&S Restaurant ★★ ($, p. 184)

FRENCH
Brasserie Jo ★★ ($$$, p. 170)
The Elephant Walk ★★ ($$$, p. 173)
Hamersley's Bistro ★★★ ($$$$, p. 166)

FUSION
Market ★★★ ($$$$, p. 163)

GERMAN
Jacob Wirth Company ($$, p. 163)

INDIAN
India Pavilion ($, p. 184)

ITALIAN
Artú ($$, p. 156)
Coppa ★★ ($$$, p. 166)
Daily Catch ★ ($$$, p. 155)
Davio's Northern Italian Steakhouse ★★ ($$$$, p. 170)
Galleria Umberto Rosticceria ($, p. 158)
Giacomo's Ristorante ★★ ($$, p. 157)
Grotto ★★ ($$, p. 162)
La Summa ★ ($$, p. 158)
Mamma Maria ★★★ ($$$$, p. 154)
Taranta Cucina Meridionale ★★ ($$$$, p. 155)

MEDITERRANEAN
Baraka Café ★ ($$, p. 182)
Café Jaffa ($, p. 172)
Oleana ★★ ($$$$, p. 180)
Trade ★ ($$$, p. 151)

KEY TO ABBREVIATIONS
$$$$ = Very Expensive $$$ = Expensive $$ = Moderate $ = Inexpensive

MEXICAN

La Verdad Taqueria Mexicana ($$, p. 174)

MIDDLE EASTERN

Café Jaffa ($, p. 172)
Sultan's Kitchen ★ ($, p. 160)

NEW ENGLAND

Durgin-Park ★★ ($$, p. 160)
Henrietta's Table ★★ ($$$, p. 176)
Union Oyster House ★ ($$$, p. 160)

PERUVIAN

Taranta Cucina Meridionale ★★ ($$$$, p. 155)

PIZZA

Bertucci's ($$, p. 179)
Picco Restaurant ★ ($, p. 169)
Pizzeria Regina ★★ ($, p. 158)
Veggie Planet ★ ($, p. 179)

SANDWICHES

Volle Nolle ★ ($, p. 159)

SEAFOOD

Barking Crab ★ ($$, p. 150)
Daily Catch ★ ($$$, p. 155)
East Coast Grill & Raw Bar ★★★ ($$$$, p. 180)
Giacomo's Ristorante ★★ ($$, p. 157)
Island Creek Oyster Bar ★ ($$$$, p. 173)
Jasper White's Summer Shack ★★ ($$$, p. 181)
Legal Sea Foods ★★★ ($$$, p. 151)
Neptune Oyster ★ ($$$, p. 155)
Peach Farm ★ ($$, p. 165)
Union Oyster House ★ ($$$, p. 160)

SENEGALESE

Teranga ★★ ($$, p. 168)

SOUTHERN

Hungry Mother ★ ($$$, p. 181)

SPANISH

Dalí ★★ ($$$, p. 180)
Toro ★ ($$, p. 168)

STEAKS

Davio's Northern Italian Steakhouse ★★ ($$$$, p. 170)
Grill 23 & Bar ★ ($$$$, p. 170)

TAPAS

Dalí ★★ ($$$, p. 180)
Toro ★ ($$, p. 168)

TEX-MEX

Border Café ($$, p. 178)
Fajitas & 'Ritas ★ ($, p. 161)

THAI

Bangkok City ★ ($$, p. 172)

TUNISIAN

Baraka Café ★ ($$, p. 182)

TURKISH

Sultan's Kitchen ★ ($, p. 160)

VEGETARIAN

Clover Food Lab ★ ($, p. 178)
Milk Street Cafe ($, p. 160)
Veggie Planet ★ ($, p. 179)

VENEZUELAN

Orinoco ★ ($$, p. 167)

VIETNAMESE

Xinh Xinh ★★ ($, p. 166)

7

SHOPPING

f you turned straight to this chapter, you're in good company: Surveys of visitors to Boston consistently show that shopping is their most popular activity, beating museum-going by a comfortable margin.

Boston-area shopping represents a tempting blend of classic and contemporary. Boston and Cambridge teem with tiny boutiques and sprawling malls, esoteric bookshops and national chain stores, exclusive galleries and snazzy secondhand-clothing outlets.

This chapter features only-in-Boston businesses as well as national and international names that are worth a visit. I'll point you to areas that are great for shop-hopping and toward specific destinations that are notable for particular items.

THE WATERFRONT

With the exception of **Lannan Ship Model Gallery** (p. 211) and the gift shop at the **New England Aquarium** (p. 59), the Waterfront is not a notable shopping destination.

THE NORTH END

Known for its dozens of Italian restaurants, the North End has a limited but fun retail scene. In addition to Italian foodstuffs, shops on Hanover and Salem streets are worthwhile destinations for jewelry, gifts, and home accessories.

FANEUIL HALL MARKETPLACE

The shops, boutiques, and pushcarts at Boston's busiest attraction sell everything from candles to costume jewelry, sweaters to souvenirs. The only off-premises Museum of Fine Arts gift shop is here, but chain outlets dominate the five-building complex. The marketplace is generally better for people-watching than for serious shopping—but if you're visiting from a place that doesn't have a lot of malls, you may enjoy a look around.

GOVERNMENT CENTER & THE FINANCIAL DISTRICT

Restaurants, bars, and coffee shops take up most of the retail space in these neighborhoods. The business-apparel stalwarts **Brooks Brothers** (p. 203) and **Thomas Pink** (p. 204) are about as exciting as this area gets.

PREVIOUS PAGE: **Newbury Street is popular with shoppers.**

DOWNTOWN CROSSING

The traffic-free pedestrian mall along Washington, Winter, and Summer streets near Boston Common abounds with souvenir pushcarts, cellphone stores, and discount-clothing shops. Some well-regarded chain stores, the **Brattle Book Shop** (p. 201), the **Eddie Bauer Outlet** (p. 209), and the **Windsor Button** shop (p. 200) are here, but unless you have a specific destination, other neighborhoods are better for exploring.

BEACON HILL

Picturesque Charles Street, at the foot of Beacon Hill, is one of Boston's favorite shopping destinations. Best known for top-notch antiques dealers, the main drag and the side streets—be sure to check out River Street, a block away on the flat side of Charles—are also home to excellent gift shops and boutiques.

SOUTH BOSTON WATERFRONT (SEAPORT DISTRICT)

Most of the shopping in this neighborhood—and there isn't much—is in the Fort Point area. Also here are excellent gift shops at the **Institute of Contemporary Art** (p. 69) and the **Boston Children's Museum** (p. 114). **Fort Point Arts Community,** 300 Summer St. (© **617/423-4299;** www.fortpointarts.org), operates a gallery and coordinates numerous events, including open studios twice a year. **Flour Bakery & Cafe** (p. 168) is a good refueling stop.

THE SOUTH END

The South End boasts a great selection of art galleries, quirky gift shops, and chic boutiques. A terrific destination for strolling, shopping, and snacking, it's more spread out than the adjacent Back Bay—be ready to walk. At the edge of the neighborhood, near I-93, is the SoWa district—short for "south of Washington Street." The **SoWa Artists Guild** (www.sowaartistsguild.com) website makes a good introduction to the community. The best time to visit is the first Friday of the month, when guild members with spaces in 450 Harrison Ave. (at Thayer St.) throw open their doors to visitors from 5 to 9pm for **First Friday Open Studios.**

THE BACK BAY

This is the Boston area's premier shopping district. Dozens of upmarket art galleries, shops, and boutiques make Newbury Street the top destination in New England for fine art and if-you-have-to-ask-you-can't-afford-it designer fashion. Long considered Boston's answer to Fifth Avenue or Rodeo Drive, Newbury Street is in some ways a victim of its own success: Rents are so high that many—though not all—of the quirky independent retailers that give a shopping destination much of its zing have been priced out. Parallel Boylston Street is also appealing, but chain stores are crowding out local outlets there, too. Still, a little exploring on both streets can yield some unique finds.

Boylston Street, like Newbury Street, is a mecca for shoppers.

Stretching south from Boylston Street are two high-end malls, the Shops at Prudential Center and Copley Place, linked by an enclosed walkway across Huntington Avenue.

KENMORE SQUARE

Stores in this neighborhood that cater to Boston University students—including a huge **Barnes & Noble** (p. 201)—take a backseat to Red Sox souvenir and memorabilia outlets.

THE FENWAY

The gift shops at the **Museum of Fine Arts** (p. 75) and the **Isabella Stewart Gardner Museum** (p. 74)

Inman Square is a great stop for fans of independent retailers, such as Boutique Fabulous.

probably aren't worth a trip on their own, but budget some time and money for a stop at one or both if you're in the area.

CAMBRIDGE

Harvard Square, with its bookstores and boutiques, is about 15 minutes from downtown Boston by subway. Despite the neighborhood association's efforts, chain stores have swept over "the Square." You'll find a mix of national and regional outlets, including a well-stocked Barnes & Noble, and more than a few persistent independent retailers. For a less generic experience, stroll from Harvard Square along shop-lined Massachusetts Avenue toward Porter Square to the north or Central Square to the southeast. About 10 minutes up Prospect Street from Central Square is Inman Square, home to a number of vibrant independent retailers. East Cambridge has the only suburban-style mall in the immediate

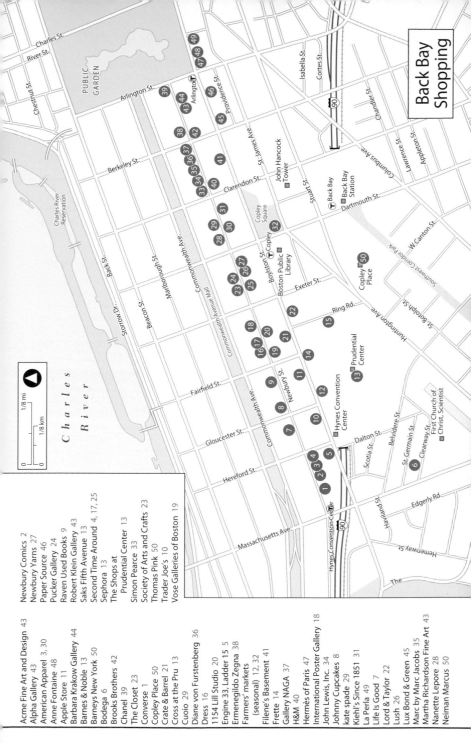

PUBLIC
GARDEN

Charles
River

Acme Fine Art and Design 43
Alpha Gallery 43
American Apparel 3, 30
Anne Fontaine 48
Apple Store 11
Barbara Krakow Gallery 44
Barnes & Noble 13
Barneys New York 50
Bodega 6
Brooks Brothers 42
Chanel 39
The Closet 23
Converse 1
Copley Place 50
Crate & Barrel 21
Cross at the Pru 13
Cuoio 29
Diane von Furstenberg 36
Dress 16
1154 Lill Studio 20
Engine 33, Ladder 15 5
Ermenegildo Zegna 38
Farmers' markets
(seasonal) 12, 32
Filene's Basement 41
Frette 14
Gallery NAGA 37
H&M 40
Hermès of Paris 47
International Poster Gallery 18
John Lewis, Inc. 34
Johnny Cupcakes 8
kate spade 29
Kiehl's Since 1851 31
La Perla 49
Life Is Good 7
Lord & Taylor 22
Lush 26
Lux Bond & Green 45
Marc by Marc Jacobs 35
Martha Richardson Fine Art 43
Nanette Lepore 28
Neiman Marcus 50

Newbury Comics 2
Newbury Yarns 27
Paper Source 46
Pucker Gallery 24
Raven Used Books 9
Robert Klein Gallery 43
Saks Fifth Avenue 13
Second Time Around 4, 17, 25
Sephora 13
The Shops at
Prudential Center 13
Simon Pearce 33
Society of Arts and Crafts 23
Thomas Pink 50
Trader Joe's 10
Vose Galleries of Boston 19

Boston area, the **CambridgeSide Galleria** (see below), as well as the Garment District, a used-and-vintage favorite.

MALLS & MARKETS

Boston Public Market   After years of planning, the city's new permanent market is under construction, with a targeted opening date of spring 2014. While the 30,000-square-foot space is coming together, the Boston Public Market Association operates two seasonal markets that offer a tasty mix of farm products and specialty foods. The **Dewey Square** market, on the Rose Kennedy Greenway at Atlantic Avenue and Summer Street (T: Red Line to South Station), is open on Tuesday and Thursday afternoons from late May through late December. The **City Hall Plaza** market, on Cambridge Street near Boston City Hall (T: Green or Blue Line to Government Center), runs on Monday and Wednesday afternoons from late May through November. Boston Public Market: On the Rose Kennedy Greenway at Hanover St. www.bostonpublicmarket.org. ✆ **617/997-8669.** T: Orange or Green Line to Haymarket.

CambridgeSide Galleria   This three-level mall houses two large department stores—**Macy's** (✆ **617/621-3800**) and **Sears** (✆ **617/252-3500**)—and more than 100 specialty stores. Pleasant but generic, it might be the bargaining chip you need to lure your teenager to the nearby Museum of Science.

There's trendy sportswear at **Abercrombie & Fitch** (✆ **617/494-1338**) and **H&M** (p. 203), electronics at the **Apple Store** (p. 214), casual and dressier clothing at **J. Crew** (✆ **617/225-2739**) and **White House Black Market** (✆ **617/374-6180**), and cosmetics at **Sephora** (p. 200). The mall also has three full-service restaurants, a food court, and seating along a pleasant canal.

Strollers and wheelchairs are available. Open Monday through Saturday from 10am to 9pm, Sunday from noon to 7pm. 100 CambridgeSide Place (btw. Edwin H. Land Blvd. and First St.), Cambridge. www.shopcambridgeside.com. ✆ **617/621-8666.** T: Green Line to Lechmere, or Red Line to Kendall/MIT and free shuttle bus (every 20 min.). Garage parking from $2 per hour.

Copley Place ★   Copley Place has set the standard for upscale shopping in Boston since 1985. Connected to the Westin and Marriott hotels and the Prudential Center, it's a crossroads for office workers, out-of-towners, and enthusiastic consumers. You can while away a couple of hours or a whole day shopping and dining here and at the adjacent Shops at Prudential Center (see below) without ever going outdoors.

Some of Copley Place's 70-plus shops will be familiar from the mall at home, but this is emphatically not a suburban shopping complex that happens to be in the city. You'll see designer boutiques such as **Christian Dior** (✆ 617/927-7577), **Jimmy Choo** (✆ 617/927-9570), and **Louis Vuitton** (✆ 617/437-6519), as well as the Boston branch of **Tiffany & Co.** (✆ 617/353-0222). The anchor department stores are the fashion wonderland **Barneys New York** (✆ 617/385-3461) and Texas-based luxury retailer **Neiman Marcus** (✆ 617/536-3660). Also here is a branch of **Legal Sea Foods** (p. 151).

Open Monday through Saturday from 10am to 8pm, Sunday from noon to 6pm. Some establishments keep longer or shorter hours. 100 Huntington Ave. (at Dartmouth St.). www.simon.com. ✆ **617/262-6600.** Discounted validated parking with purchase. T: Orange Line to Back Bay or Green Line to Copley.

Faneuil Hall Marketplace ★★ The original festival market hall is both wildly popular and widely imitated, and Faneuil Hall Marketplace changes constantly to appeal to visitors as well as locals wary of its touristy reputation. The original part of **Faneuil Hall** (p. 95) dates to 1742. The **Quincy Market Colonnade,** in the central building, houses a gargantuan selection of food and confections. The bars and restaurants always seem to be crowded, and the shopping is terrific if generic.

In and around the five buildings, the shops tend less toward "only in Boston" than toward "only at every mall in the country." **Marketplace Center** and the ground floors of the **North Market** and **South Market buildings** have lots of chain outlets. Most of the unique offerings are under the Quincy Market canopies, where crafts and gifts cram dozens of **pushcarts,** and upstairs and downstairs in the market buildings.

Shop hours are Monday through Saturday from 10am to 9pm (until 7pm Mon–Thurs in winter) and Sunday from noon to 6pm. The Colonnade opens earlier, and most bars and restaurants close later. Btw. North, Congress, and State sts. and Atlantic Ave. www.faneuilhallmarketplace.com. © **617/338-2323.** Discounted validated parking with purchase. T: Green or Blue Line to Government Center or Orange Line to Haymarket.

Farmers' Markets Massachusetts farmers and growers coordinated by the state **Department of Agricultural Resources** dispatch trucks filled with seasonal produce to the heart of the city from late spring through October or November. Depending on the time of year, you'll have your pick of berries, herbs, tomatoes, squash, pumpkins, apples, corn, and more, all fresh and reasonably priced. Most markets also include specialty-food vendors selling everything from fresh pasta to maple syrup. In Boston, you can stop by **Copley Square** (St. James Ave. at Dartmouth St.) on Tuesday or Friday (T: Green Line to Copley or Orange Line to Back Bay), or the **Shops at Prudential Center** (Boylston St. near Gloucester St.) on Thursday (T: Green Line E to Prudential). The Boston Public Market Association (see above) runs the markets at **Dewey Square** and **City Hall Plaza.** In Cambridge, several locations around **Harvard Square** (T: Red Line to Harvard) play host to relatively small markets throughout the week; to see the full range of local produce, head to Parking Lot 5, Norfolk Street and Bishop Allen Drive (1 block from Mass. Ave.), in **Central Square** on nonholiday Mondays (T: Red Line to Central). Multiple locations. www.mass.gov/massgrown and www.massfarmersmarkets.org. © **617/626-1700.**

Greenway Open Market ★ An offshoot of the wildly successful SoWa Open Market (see below), the Greenway market features a similar, smaller variety of crafts, jewelry, art, specialty foods, and more. It operates from late May through October on Saturday only from 11am to 5pm, rain or shine. Rose Fitzgerald Kennedy Greenway, along Atlantic Ave. btw. State and High sts. © **800/403-8305.** www.greenwayopenmarket.com. T: Blue Line to Aquarium or Orange Line to State.

The Shops at Prudential Center ★ The main level of the city's second-tallest tower holds this sprawling complex. It's home to dozens of shops and boutiques, a large **Barnes & Noble** (p. 201), a food court, a post office, and 10 restaurants, including **Legal Sea Foods** (p. 151) and the **Cheesecake Factory.** Also here are Boston's branches of **Saks Fifth Avenue** (p. 208), **Club Monaco** (© **617/262-2658**), and **Sephora** (p. 200), and one of a handful of retail outlets for the upscale office and home accessories that **Levenger** (ℭ **800/ 667-8934** or 617/536-3434; www.levenger.com) calls "tools for serious readers." Vendors sell gifts, souvenirs, and novelty items off carts and kiosks in the arcades, and the Greater Boston Convention & Visitors Bureau operates an **information booth.** The complex has outdoor space if you need some fresh air, and hosts a farmers' market on summer and fall Thursdays.

Hours are Monday through Saturday from 10am to 9pm, Sunday from 11am to 6pm. Restaurant hours vary. 800 Boylston St. (at Fairfield St.); back entrance off Huntington Ave. at Belvidere St. www.prudentialcenter.com. ℭ **800/746-7778.** Discounted validated parking with purchase. T: Green Line E to Prudential, Green Line to Copley, or Orange Line to Back Bay.

SoWa Open Market ★★ This art, crafts, and food (fresh and prepared) market is the place to be on Sundays in the stylish South End. Vendors vary from week to week, but you'll always have the chance to meet talented artists and artisans. The SoWa (short for "South of Washington," a designation that's still catching on) market also plays host to farm stands and food trucks. The neighborhood, which you may not have a chance to explore otherwise, is home to numerous art galleries. In summer (May to mid-Nov), hours are 10am to 5pm on non-holiday-weekend Sundays; in winter, fewer vendors set up and hours are 10am to 2pm. 460 Harrison Ave. (at Thayer St.). www.sowaopenmarket.com. ℭ **800/403-8305.** T: Silver Line SL4/SL5 bus to E. Berkeley St., or Orange Line to Tufts Medical Center or Back Bay, then 15-min. walk.

SHOPPING A TO Z

Here I've singled out establishments that I especially like and neighborhoods that suit shoppers interested in particular types of merchandise. Addresses are in Boston unless otherwise indicated.

Antiques & Collectibles

Bromfield Pen Shop ★ This shop's selection of antique pens will thrill any collector. Whether you're sick of digital communication or looking for a gift, the knowledgeable staff will help make a good match. The shop also repairs pens and sells new ones—including Montblanc, Pelikan, Waterman, and Omas. Also available are Swiss army knives, watches, and business gifts. Closed Sunday. 5 Bromfield St. (off Washington St.). www.bromfieldpenshop.com. ℭ **617/482-9053.** T: Red or Orange Line to Downtown Crossing.

Cambridge Antique Market ★★ 🎁 As you navigate the enormous variety of merchandise spread over five floors (don't forget to check out the basement), you may feel as though you're on a treasure hunt—and really, aren't you? Weekends, especially Saturdays, are when most of the 100-plus dealers are likeliest to be open. Prices are better than in Boston's fancier shops, but the selection is more random. Closed Monday. 201 Monsignor O'Brien Hwy. (at Third St.), Cambridge. www.marketantique.com. ℭ **617/868-9655.** T: Green Line to Lechmere.

Danish Country European & Asian Antiques ★ Owner James Kilroy specializes in Scandinavian antiques dating from the 1700s onward. In this mahogany-heavy neighborhood, the light woods are a visual treat. You'll also see folk art, lovely Mora clocks, Royal Copenhagen porcelain, and antique Chinese furniture and home accessories. 138 Charles St. (btw. Revere and Cambridge sts.). www. europeanstyleantiques.com. ℭ **617/227-1804.** T: Red Line to Charles/MGH.

Upstairs Downstairs Antiques ★★ 🎁   The merchandise in this unexpectedly large store (keep walking toward the back) spans 3 centuries and every price point. You'll find everything from majestic sideboards to delicate teacups to just the right gift—ask a member of the amiable staff for brainstorming help. 93 Charles St. *℗* **617/367-1950.** T: Red Line to Charles/MGH.

Art Galleries

Art galleries dot the city and suburbs, with the greatest concentrations in Boston's Back Bay and South End. Time (yours) and space (mine) preclude my listing galleries in outlying neighborhoods and suburbs, but if your travels take you off the beaten path, look around—soaring rents have driven savvy proprietors to some unexpected locations. For tips on navigating **Newbury Street,** see the box "An Artsy Stroll Along Newbury Street," below.

An excellent way to see artists at work is to visit during neighborhood **open studio** days. Artists' communities throughout the Boston area stage the weekend events once or twice a year. You might be asked for a contribution to a charity in exchange for a map of the studios. Check listings in the *Globe, Herald,* and *Improper Bostonian* or visit **www.cityofboston.gov/arts** for information.

Acme Fine Art   Twentieth-century American art is Acme's raison d'être, and the gallery represents numerous living artists. That means a lively mix of styles and media, with an emphasis on abstraction over figurative works. Closed Sunday and Monday. 38 Newbury St. (btw. Arlington and Berkeley sts.), 4th floor. www.acmefineart.com. *℗* **617/585-9551.** T: Green Line to Arlington.

Alpha Gallery ★★   The Alpha Gallery specializes in contemporary paintings, sculpture, and works on paper, as well as modern master paintings and prints. Established in 1967, this is a family operation: Director Joanna E. Fink is founder Alan Fink's daughter. Closed Sunday and Monday. 37 Newbury St. (btw. Arlington and Berkeley sts.), 4th floor. www.alphagallery.com. *℗* **617/536-4465.** T: Green Line to Arlington.

Barbara Krakow Gallery ★★★   This prestigious gallery, founded in 1964, is as cutting-edge as they come. It specializes in paintings, sculptures, drawings, and prints created after 1945. If you're lucky, the delightfully opinionated owner will be on the premises. Closed Sunday and Monday and all of August. 10 Newbury St. (btw. Arlington and Berkeley sts.), 5th floor. www.barbarakrakowgallery.com. *℗* **617/262-4490.** T: Green Line to Arlington.

Galería Cubana ★★   Galería Cubana shows extraordinary work by contemporary Cuban artists—it's not an underground operation, but the holder of one of the scarce licenses permitting Americans to travel to and trade with the island. Owner Michelle Wojcik, who opened the gallery's first location in Provincetown in 2007, visits three times a year on a quest to build up ties between the U.S. and Cuba through culture. Closed Monday and Tuesday fall through spring; call ahead in summer. 460 Harrison Ave. (at Thayer St.). www.lagaleriacubana.com. *℗* **617/292-2822.** T: Silver Line SL4/SL5 bus to E. Berkeley St., or Orange Line to Tufts Medical Center or Back Bay, then 15-min. walk.

Gallery NAGA ★★   In the neo-Gothic Church of the Covenant, Gallery NAGA exhibits contemporary paintings, photography, and studio furniture, often by New England artists. A stop here is a must if you want to see holography (trust me, you do). Closed Sunday and Monday. 67 Newbury St. (at Berkeley St.). www.gallerynaga.com. *℗* **617/267-9060.** T: Green Line to Arlington.

AN artsy STROLL ALONG NEWBURY STREET

The Boston area's best-known destination for art lovers is **Newbury Street.** New England's equivalent of New York's Madison Avenue, it's home to galleries of all descriptions. As you explore, don't forget to look up—some great businesses thrive at street level, but their upstairs neighbors who pay lower rents can often afford to be more adventuresome. Most galleries are open Tuesday through Saturday or Sunday from 10 or 11am to 5:30 or 6pm. Exhibitions typically change once a month. For specifics, visit individual websites or pick up a copy of the free monthly *Gallery Guide,* available at many businesses along Newbury Street.

If gallery-hopping isn't a habit for you, here's an observation: Galleries can look intimidating, but remember that each one is a business—and a proprietor who keeps a gallery operating in tough economic times is by definition a good businessperson. Gallery owners aren't selling art because they couldn't break into widget sales; they're in the art business because they love it. They welcome browsers and questions that show you've given the art some thought.

For a good overview, plot a course that starts with **Barbara Krakow Gallery** at 10 Newbury St. or at 38 Newbury St., where **Robert Klein Gallery** shares a floor with three other worthy establishments (Acme Fine Art and Design, Martha Richardson Fine Art, and Miller Block Gallery). Your ultimate destination is 238 Newbury St., home of **Vose Galleries of Boston,** which is closer to its 300th anniversary than to its 200th. Stop along the way to check out at least a couple of the other galleries listed in this chapter. Now, that's an "only in Boston" experience.

International Poster Gallery ★★★ 🎁 Yes, posters are art—as you'll see before you even cross the threshold of this extraordinary gallery. It features extensive collections of French, Swiss, Soviet, and Italian vintage posters, and thousands of other posters, including originals from around the world. The enthusiastic, accommodating staff will comb its databases (cyber and cerebral) to help you find the exact image you want, and the website is a great resource. The theme of the works on display changes three or four times a year. Prices start at $50, with most between $500 and $2,500. 205 Newbury St. (btw. Exeter and Fairfield sts.). www.internationalposter.com. 📞 **617/375-0076.** T: Green Line to Copley.

Made in Fort Point ★★ Despite widespread redevelopment, the rapidly changing Fort Point section of the Seaport District remains a thriving artists' community. This retail-and-gallery space is a great place to see what's happening amid the studios-turned-condos and convention crowds. 12 Farnsworth St. (off Congress St.). www.fortpointarts.org/shop. 📞 **617/423-1100.** T: Red Line to South Station, then 10-min. walk.

Martha Richardson Fine Art ★ Contemporary art often seems to hold sway on Newbury Street, but not here—the specialty is 19th- and 20th-century American and European paintings and drawings. You'll see landscapes, still lifes, portraits, and the occasional abstract. Closed Sunday and Monday; open Tuesday by appointment only. 38 Newbury St. (btw. Arlington and Berkeley sts.), 4th floor. www.martharichardsonfineart.com. 📞 **617/266-3321.** T: Green Line to Arlington.

Pucker Gallery ★   The eclectic offerings here include African, Asian, Inuit, and Israeli art; contemporary paintings, prints, drawings, sculpture, and ceramics by regional and international artists; and excellent photographs. The staff is eager to answer questions about the art, which spreads over five floors. 171 Newbury St. (btw. Dartmouth and Exeter sts.). www.puckergallery.com. © **617/267-9473.** T: Green Line to Copley.

Robert Klein Gallery ★★★   For 19th- to 21st-century photography, head here. Among the dozens of artists represented are Diane Arbus, Robert Mapplethorpe, Man Ray, and Ansel Adams. Closed Sunday and Monday. 38 Newbury St. (btw. Arlington and Berkeley sts.), 4th floor. www.robertkleingallery.com. © **617/267-7997.** T: Green Line to Arlington.

Vose Galleries of Boston ★   One of Vose's specialties is Hudson River School paintings—fitting, because the business and the mid-19th-century movement are about the same age. Six generations of Voses have run the oldest family-owned gallery in the United States, which opened in 1841. You'll see works of the Boston School and American Impressionist art among the 18th-, 19th-, and early-20th-century American paintings, as well as contemporary pieces by American realists. Closed Sunday and Monday. 238 Newbury St. (off Fairfield St.). www.vose galleries.com. © **617/536-6176.** T: Green Line to Copley, or Green Line B, C, or D to Hynes Convention Center.

Arts, Crafts & Museum Stores

Museum shops are a wonderful source of unique items, including crafts and games. Particularly good outlets include those at the **Museum of Fine Arts,** the **Museum of Science,** the **Isabella Stewart Gardner Museum,** and the **Institute of Contemporary Art** (see chapter 4), and the **Concord Museum** and **Peabody Essex Museum** (see chapter 10). See "Jewelry," later in this chapter, for information about **Boston Bead Company.**

Cambridge Artists' Cooperative Craft Gallery ★   Top-notch creations fill this three-level space on a Harvard Square side street. The artist-owned-and-operated gallery carries a huge variety of work by American artisans, including jewelry, home accessories, glassware, clothing, gifts, and other handcrafted treasures. It's not cheap—consider the neighborhood—but prices are reasonable given the quality. 59A Church St. (off Brattle St.), Cambridge. www.cambridgeartistscoop. com. © **617/868-4434.** T: Red Line to Harvard.

Newbury Yarns ★   Packed with high-end yarns from all over the globe, Newbury Yarns is a welcoming destination for experts and beginners alike. Check ahead for information about classes and workshops, or drop in to browse the impressive selection and ask the patient, helpful staff for advice. 166 Newbury St. (btw. Dartmouth and Exeter sts.). www.newburyyarns.com. © **617/572-3733.** T: Green Line to Copley.

Paper Source ★★   Gorgeous paper (writing and wrapping), cards, pens, ink, stamps, books, stickers, unusual gifts, and custom invitations make these well-organized stores magnets for anyone with a thing for stationery. Be sure to check out the handmade paper. A craft-loving friend swears by the Boston location of the national chain; I find all three delightful. 338 Boylston St. (off Arlington St.). www. paper-source.com. © **617/536-3444.** T: Green Line to Arlington. 1810 Massachusetts Ave. (at Arlington St.), Cambridge. © **617/497-1077.** T: Red Line to Porter. 1361 Beacon St. (at Webster St.), Brookline. © **617/264-2800.** T: Green Line C to Coolidge Corner.

Society of Arts and Crafts ★★ Contemporary American work is the focus at the oldest nonprofit craft organization in the country. The exquisite jewelry, furniture, home accessories, glass, ceramics, and fiber art range from practical to purely decorative; the second floor holds a gallery that mounts four shows a year. Open Monday by appointment only. The society also sponsors **CraftBoston,** a prestigious juried show that takes place in the spring and before the holidays; check the website for dates and locations. 175 Newbury St. (btw. Dartmouth and Exeter sts.). www.societyofcrafts.org. ✆ **617/266-1810.** T: Green Line to Copley.

TistiK 🎁 Artisans from developing countries, mostly in Latin America, create the merchandise in this dazzling gallery. The ever-changing stock varies widely in style and price; it's mostly women's jewelry, with some gifts and home accessories in the mix. TistiK is worth a visit, if only to see how true the name—Maya for "a warm welcome"—is. 54 Church St. (off Brattle St.), Cambridge. www.shoptistik.com. ✆ **617/661-0900.** T: Red Line to Harvard.

Windsor Button The name doesn't come close to telling the whole story of this 75-plus-year-old business. It's known for its impressive range of yarn and knitting and crochet patterns and accessories; except at the busiest times, the staff is a great resource. Also in stock are thousands of buttons, from utilitarian to ultrafancy, as well as ribbon, trim, notions, and needlework kits. Closed Sunday. 35 Temple Place (btw. Tremont and Washington sts.). www.windsorbutton.com. ✆ **617/482-4969.** T: Red or Green Line to Park St., or Orange Line to Downtown Crossing.

Beauty, Cosmetics & Perfume

Colonial Drug ★★ 🎁 The perfume counter at this family business puts the "special" in "specialize." You can choose from more than 1,000 fragrances—plus cosmetics, soap, shaving necessities, and countless hard-to-find body-care products—with the help of the gracious staff members. They remain unflappable even during Harvard Square's equivalent of rush hour, Saturday afternoon. No credit cards; closed Sunday except in December. 49 Brattle St. (off Church St.), Cambridge. www.colonialdrug.com. ✆ **617/864-2222.** T: Red Line to Harvard.

Kiehl's Since 1851 ★ Lots of retail chains originate in New York, but few of them develop this kind of cult following. Customers wax evangelical over the skin, hair, and body products from Kiehl's, which straddle the line between cosmetics and pharmaceuticals. 112 Newbury St. (off Clarendon St.). www.kiehls.com. ✆ **617/247-1777.** T: Green Line to Copley.

Lush ★★★ Of all the lotions-and-potions purveyors in the Boston area, this is my favorite. It smells great, and the enthusiastic staff is entirely attitude-free. U.K.-based Lush specializes in fresh, organic, natural products, notably "bath bombs" (solid bubble bath) and solid shampoo priced by the pound. 166 Newbury St. (btw. Dartmouth and Exeter sts.). www.lushusa.com. ✆ **617/375-5874.** T: Green Line to Copley. 30 John F. Kennedy St. (off Mt. Auburn St.). ✆ **617/497-5874.** T: Red Line to Harvard.

Sephora ★★ This European phenomenon is a fashionista magnet. You'll find an encyclopedic, international selection of manufacturers and products in well-lit, well-organized spaces overflowing with testers. Everything is self-service, and the staff provides as much help as you want. Shops at Prudential Center, 800 Boylston St. (at Fairfield St.). www.sephora.com. ✆ **617/262-4200.** T: Green Line E to Prudential or Green Line to Copley. CambridgeSide Galleria, 100 CambridgeSide Place, Cambridge. ✆ **617/577-1005.** T: Green Line to Lechmere, or Red Line to Kendall/MIT and free shuttle bus (every 20 min.).

Books, Maps & Stationery

The Boston area is a book-lover's paradise. It's an important stop on most author tours; check the local papers or stop by any store that sells new books for details on **readings and book signings.** See "College Merchandise," below, for information about centrally located college bookstores.

Barnes & Noble ★ This well-stocked branch of the national chain offers both a cafe and plenty of kids' events, and it's the best place in the Back Bay to shop for magazines. Barnes & Noble runs most of the college bookstore operations around town (see "College Merchandise," below). Shops at Prudential Center, 800 Boylston St. (enter from Huntington Ave. at Belvidere St.). www.barnesandnoble.com. ✆ **617/247-6959.** T: Green Line E to Prudential or Green Line to Copley.

Bob Slate Stationer This is the anti-Staples—an old-fashioned business (when was the last time you used the word "stationer"?) that specializes in top-quality pens and pencils, writing paper, greeting cards, art supplies, and office accessories. 30 Brattle St. (btw. John F. Kennedy and Mount Auburn sts.), Cambridge. www. bobslate.com. ✆ **617/547-1230.** T: Red Line to Harvard.

Brattle Book Shop ★★ This marvelous store near Macy's buys and sells used, rare, and out-of-print titles, and second-generation owner Kenneth Gloss does free appraisals. Allow time to check the outdoor carts and shelves for good deals on books of all ages. Closed Sunday. 9 West St. (btw. Washington and Tremont sts.). www.brattlebookshop.com. ✆ **800/447-9595** or 617/542-0210. T: Red or Orange Line to Downtown Crossing, or Green Line to Park St.

Brookline Booksmith ★★★ The huge, varied selection makes this store a polymath's dream. The employees have excellent taste—look for their recommendations. A great gift-and-card section, a small but choice used-book selection in the basement, and tons of events are among the offerings. 279 Harvard St. (btw. Beacon and Green sts.), Brookline. www.brooklinebooksmith.com. ✆ **617/566-6660.** T: Green Line C to Coolidge Corner.

Grolier Poetry Book Shop Packed bookshelves fill this tiny space from floor to high, high ceiling. The shop, founded in 1927, carries just what the name says: only poetry, and lots of it. Closed Sunday and Monday. 6 Plympton St. (off Mass. Ave.), Cambridge. www.grolierpoetrybookshop.org. ✆ **617/547-4648.** T: Red Line to Harvard.

Harvard Book Store ★★★ On the main level of this shop, readers peruse an excellent scholarly selection and discounted bestsellers. Also here is one of just a few dozen Espresso Book Machines in the country, an amazingly cool device that prints and binds paperback books—you choose, from the 3.6-million-title catalog—to order while you wait. The basement is the draw for those in the know: Prices on remainders are good, and used paperbacks (many bought for classes and hardly opened) are discounted 50% off their original prices. Check ahead for information on readings and other special events. 1256 Mass. Ave. (at Plympton St.), Cambridge. www.harvard.com. ✆ **800/542-7323** or 617/661-1515. T: Red Line to Harvard.

Lorem Ipsum Books A well-edited selection of used titles fills this airy space in the heart of Inman Square. The staff is as helpful or hands-off as you like, and the constantly changing stock includes everything from current bestsellers to "Murder & Mayhem." 1299 Cambridge St. (at Oakland St.), Cambridge. www.loremipsum books.com. ✆ **617/497-7669.** T: Red Line to Central, then 10-min. walk on Prospect St.

Porter Square Books ★★ A well-stocked independent bookstore with everything from bestsellers to esoteric academic tomes to a great children's department—it's a dying breed. If they were all run as well as this one, with staffs this helpful and selections this brain-tickling, the species would be anything but endangered. Check ahead for author events. In the Porter Square Shopping Center, 25 White St. (off Mass. Ave.), Cambridge. www.portersquarebooks.com. ✆ **617/491-2220.** T: Red Line to Porter.

Raven Used Books The specialty at these little shops is scholarly titles—an underserved market even in Cambridge and Boston. Both locations carry enough general-interest stock to keep casual browsers engaged while their more academic companions explore. 52B John F. Kennedy St. (near Winthrop St.), Cambridge. www.ravencambridge.com. ✆ **617/441-6999.** T: Red Line to Harvard. 263 Newbury St. (btw. Fairfield and Gloucester sts.). ✆ **617/578-9000.** T: Green Line B, C, or D to Haynes Convention Center.

Schoenhof's Foreign Books ★ The oldest foreign-language bookseller in the country stocks volumes for adults and children in more than 50 languages. It also carries dictionaries and language-learning materials for 700-plus languages and dialects, plus quirky gift items (haven't you always wanted a Hannah Arendt T-shirt?) and translations of children's classics. Closed Sunday except at the beginning of the semester (early Sept and late Jan). 76A Mt. Auburn St. (at Holyoke St.), Cambridge. www.schoenhofs.com. ✆ **617/547-8855.** T: Red Line to Harvard.

WardMaps LLC ★ A ward map shows municipal divisions, usually on a grid and often bound into an atlas. This entrancing shop outside Porter Square carries maps—not just ward maps—and prints in various sizes and conditions, with an especially good selection of 19th-century items. The excellent gift items include posters, coasters, puzzles, mugs, notebooks, and more—printed with, ahem, maps. 1735 Massachusetts Ave. (at Prentiss St.), Cambridge. www.wardmaps.com. ✆ **617/ 497-0737.** T: Red Line to Porter.

Clothing & Accessories
ADULTS

The Back Bay, notably lower Newbury Street, is a can't-miss place for designer fashion and window-shopping. To start exploring, stroll west from the Public Garden and check out **Chanel,** 15 Arlington St., in the Taj Boston (✆ 617/859-0055); **Ermenegildo Zegna,** 39 Newbury St. (✆ 617/424-6657); **Diane von Furstenberg,** 73 Newbury St. (✆ 617/247-7300); **Marc by Marc Jacobs,** 81 Newbury St. (✆ 617/425-0707); **kate spade,** 117 Newbury St. (✆ 617/262-2632); and **Nanette Lepore,** 119 Newbury St. (✆ 617/421-9200). In the Heritage on the Garden complex at Boylston and Arlington streets, in addition to Anne Fontaine (see below), are **Hermès of Paris,** 22 Arlington St. (✆ 617/482-8707), and **La Perla,** 250 Boylston St. (✆ 617/423-5709).

American Apparel A leading light of the antisweatshop movement, American Apparel sells women's and men's T-shirts, underwear, and other fashionable knits—all manufactured in downtown L.A.—that are fun, gorgeous, or both. Sizes run small; try everything on. 138 Newbury St. (off Dartmouth St.). www.american apparel.com. ✆ **617/536-4768.** T: Green Line to Arlington. 330 Newbury St. (btw. Hereford St. and Mass. Ave.). ✆ **617/236-1636.** T: Green Line B, C, or D to Hynes Convention Center. 47 Brattle St. (at Church St.), Cambridge. ✆ **617/661-2770.** T: Red Line to Harvard.

Anne Fontaine ★ This was the first U.S. outlet for the designer's "perfect white blouse collection from Paris." I wanted to laugh, but then I visited—and almost every item *is* a perfect (for one reason or another) white blouse. Prices start at $80. Closed Sunday. Heritage on the Garden, 318 Boylston St. (off Arlington St.). www.annefontaine.com. ✆ **617/423-0366.** T: Green Line to Arlington.

Bodega ★★ This place gets an extra star for being nearly impossible to find: It's the back room of what appears to be a convenience store (stand in front of the Snapple machine and watch what happens). Vintage and limited-edition sneakers are the headliners; add a discriminating selection of bleeding-edge-trendy streetwear—mostly for guys, with some women's accessories and clothing—and you have a destination for hipsters and wannabes from all over Boston and far beyond. 6 Clearway St. (off Mass. Ave.). www.bdgastore.com. ✆ **617/421-1550.** T: Green Line B, C, or D to Hynes Convention Center or Green Line E to Symphony.

Brooks Brothers Would-be "proper Bostonians" head here for blue blazers, gray flannels, seersucker suits, and less conservative business and casual wear for men and women. Brooks is the only place for exactly the right preppy shade of pink button-down oxford shirts—something I've never seen at the outlet stores. The Financial District location is closed Sunday. 46 Newbury St. (at Berkeley St.). www.brooksbrothers.com. ✆ **617/267-2600.** T: Green Line to Arlington. 75 State St. (at Kilby St.). ✆ **617/261-9990.** T: Orange or Blue Line to State.

Crush Boutique ★ The staff at Crush will help dress you from the skin up. The welcoming boutiques feature up-and-coming designers whose work has caught the sharp eyes of the young owners, and the well-edited stock of women's fashion includes plenty of affordable options. 131 Charles St. (btw. Cambridge and Revere sts.). www.shopcrushboutique.com. ✆ **617/720-0010.** T: Red Line to Charles/MGH. 264 Newbury St. (btw. Fairfield and Gloucester sts.). ✆ **617/424-0010.** T: Green Line B, C, or D to Hynes Convention Center.

Dress ★ Think of the verb, not the noun. This airy boutique stocks women's fashion (including dresses), jeans, shoes, and jewelry. Many pieces are the work of designers whose creations aren't available elsewhere in Boston—always the goal on Newbury Street. 221 Newbury St. (btw. Exeter and Fairfield sts.). www.dressboston.com. ✆ **617/424-7125.** T: Green Line to Copley.

1154 Lill Studio ★★ 🎁 Shoppers at this adorable design-your-own-handbag shop have a lot of decisions to make, starting with a big one: instant or delayed gratification? Bags of all sizes are on display; if you don't see *exactly* what you want, customize yours using an impressive variety of fabrics, straps, and linings. Your creation arrives a month or so later, built from scratch just as you imagined it. This is a branch of the Chicago-based minichain. Prices run $28 to $200. 220 Newbury St. (btw. Exeter and Fairfield sts.). www.1154lillstudio.com. ✆ **617/247-1154.** T: Green Line B, C, or D to Hynes Convention Center.

H&M The Swedish discount-fashion juggernaut specializes in cheap, stylish clothing and accessories. The Downtown Crossing store outfits women, men, and kids; the Cambridge branch concentrates on fashions for women (including underwear) and teens of both genders. 350 Washington St. (at Franklin St.). www.hm.com. ✆ **617/482-7001.** T: Red or Orange Line to Downtown Crossing. 100 Newbury St. (at Clarendon St.). ✆ **617/859-3192.** T: Green Line to Copley. CambridgeSide Galleria, 100 CambridgeSide Place, Cambridge. ✆ **617/225-0895.** T: Green Line to Lechmere, or Red Line to Kendall/MIT and free shuttle bus (every 20 min.).

Injeanius ★★ The North End doesn't have a bookstore, but it does have a designer-jean boutique—and it's a really good one. Owner Alison Barnard and her staff will find just the right fit for you in their well-edited selection of high-end denim; the tops, shoes, and bags represent an impressive variety of hard-to-find-in-Boston brands. The nearby sister shop, **Twilight,** 12 Fleet St. (off Hanover St.; 𝄢 **617/523-8008;** www.twilightboutique.com), carries a gorgeous, ever-changing selection of party dresses and accessories. 441 Hanover St. (at Salutation St.). www.injeanius.com. 𝄢 **617/523-5326.** T: Green or Orange Line to Haymarket.

Johnny Cupcakes There's no food in the bakery cases at this adorable shop—just limited-edition, custom-designed T-shirts made in the U.S. Pricey but adorable, they've inspired something of a cult, with clever designs that often play off the cupcake theme. And, yes, there really is a Johnny (but his last name is Earle). 279 Newbury St. (off Gloucester St.). www.johnnycupcakes.com. 𝄢 **617/375-0100.** T: Green Line B, C, or D to Hynes Convention Center.

Life Is Good ★ This popular casual clothing and accessories brand got its start in a Boston suburb with some T-shirts and a van. My sister is a devotee who says: "Really nice colors, fun designs, very comfortable, wears well, great baby stuff." Prices for adult T-shirts start at $25. The company mascot, a stick figure named Jake, adorns many items, doing everything from snowboarding to just kicking back. 285 Newbury St. (btw. Fairfield and Gloucester sts.). www.lifeisgood.com. 𝄢 **617/262-5068.** T: Green Line B, C, or D to Hynes Convention Center.

Looks ★★ A picky postcollegiate clientele has made Looks a favorite in this college town for well over 2 decades. Sophisticated yet comfortable, the women's clothes suit everything from barbecue to boardroom, with an excellent selection of special-occasion fashions. Equally appealing are the eye-catching accessories and jewelry. 11–13 Holyoke St. (btw. Mass. Ave. and Mount Auburn St.), Cambridge. www.looksclothing.com. 𝄢 **617/491-4251.** T: Red Line to Harvard.

Louis Boston Louis (pronounced "Louie's") enjoys a well-deserved reputation for dressing stuffy Bostonians in cutting-edge New York fashions. The ultraprestigious store sells men's designer suits, handmade shirts, silk ties, and Italian shoes; the women's fashions are equally elegant. Louis is one of the few retailers in the Seaport District, where its sleek building overlooks the harbor. On the premises are a full-service salon and a restaurant. Fan Pier, 60 Northern Ave. (off Seaport Blvd.). www.louisboston.com. 𝄢 **617/262-6100.** T: Silver Line SL1/SL2 bus to Court House.

Thomas Pink The London-based haberdasher carries top-quality men's (mostly) and women's dress shirts, both off the rack and made to order. The merchandise is just as lovely and the prices less tic-inducing during periodic sales. And you get to say "haberdasher." The Financial District location closes Sunday. 280 Washington St. (at School St.). www.thomaspink.com. 𝄢 **617/426-7859.** T: Blue or Orange Line to State. Copley Place, 100 Huntington Ave. 𝄢 **617/267-0447.** T: Orange Line to Back Bay.

Wish The interior is stark, the service chilly, the prices high—and the designer fashions unbeatable. Wish is a default destination for an incredible number of stylish Bostonians and suburbanites, not because the labels are unusual but because the selection is so painstaking. *Tip:* The January and July sales are worth waiting for. 49 Charles St. (btw. Chestnut and Mount Vernon sts.). www.wishboston.com. 𝄢 **617/227-4441.** T: Red Line to Charles/MGH.

CHILDREN

Diaper Lab   Oh, those Cambridge hippies, with their cloth diapers. A lot of them are stocking up at this Davis Square shop, which is also a good resource for accessories and a small but choice selection of clothing, toys, and books. Closed Sunday and Monday. 200 Elm St. N. (btw. Russell and Tenney sts.), Cambridge, on the Somerville line. www.diaperlab.com. ℂ **617/764-0192.** T: Red Line to Davis.

Mulberry Road ★   The well-edited selection of apparel and accessories at this delightful boutique is both practical and (beyond the omnipresent Sophie the giraffe) unusual. Merchandise this adorable doesn't come cheap, but then, neither do most things on Newbury Street. 128 Newbury St. (btw. Clarendon and Dartmouth sts.). www.mulberryroad.com. ℂ **617/859-5861.** T: Green Line to Copley.

The Red Wagon ★   Just about everything in this boutique is as cute as a kitten. Busy parents cherish this Beacon Hill mainstay for its wide selection of American and European clothing and shoes (newborn to size 8) and the fact that it's also a well-stocked toy shop—two errands in one stop. 69 Charles St. (off Mount Vernon St.). www.theredwagon.com. ℂ **617/523-9402.** T: Red Line to Charles/MGH.

JEWELRY

Boston Bead Company   The jewelry here will suit you exactly—you make it yourself. Prices for the dazzling variety of raw materials start at 5¢ a bead, findings (hardware) are available, and you can assemble your finery at the in-store worktable. Ready-made pieces are in stock, and the store schedules jewelry-making workshops; check ahead for details. 23 Church St. (btw. Mass. Ave. and Palmer St.), Cambridge. www.bostonbeadcompany.com. ℂ **617/868-9777.** T: Red Line to Harvard.

High Gear Jewelry ★★   The biggest jewelry snob I know invents excuses to visit the North End just to stop in here. The eye-catching shop right on the Freedom Trail carries an impressive selection of reasonably priced costume jewelry, watches, and hair accessories. If you don't see what you want, ask the friendly staff for help—the owner recently turned a pair of pierced earrings into clip-ons for me in a matter of seconds, for no extra charge. Closed Sunday in winter. 204 Hanover St. (off Cross St.). ℂ **617/523-5804.** T: Green or Orange Line to Haymarket.

John Lewis, Inc. ★★★ 🎁   John Lewis's imaginative women's and men's jewelry—designed and made on the premises—suits both traditional and avant-garde tastes. The wide selection of silver, gold, and platinum items and unusual colored stones add to the museum-like shop's appeal. The pieces that mark you as a savvy Bostonian are earrings, necklaces, and bracelets made of hammered metal circles. Closed Sunday and Monday. 97 Newbury St. (off Clarendon St.). www.johnlewisinc.com. ℂ **800/266-4101** or 617/266-6665. T: Green Line to Arlington.

Lux Bond & Green ★★   A family business founded in 1898, Lux Bond & Green is a full-service jeweler with an "only in Boston" feature: The chain is the official Red Sox jeweler. This is the go-to destination for high-end souvenirs (cuff links, Christmas ornaments) as well as memorabilia (autographed baseballs). Closed Sunday. 416 Boylston St. (off Berkeley St.). www.lbgreen.com. ℂ **617/266-4747.** T: Green Line to Arlington.

Topaz ★   Inventive jewelry is the headliner here, with sterling silver and semiprecious stones taking precedence over higher-end materials—but not at the expense of style. The baubles range widely in price and size, from ladylike to borderline gaudy (not that there's anything wrong with that!). You'll also find funky gifts, a well-edited selection of accessories, including lovely leather goods and scarves, and a lively, helpful staff. 11 Dunster St. (off Mass. Ave.), Cambridge. www.topazcambridge.com. *© **617/492-3700.** T: Red Line to Harvard.

SHOES & ACCESSORIES

Also see the listing for **DSW Shoe Warehouse,** under "Discount Shopping," below.

Berk's Shoes ★ "Trendy" doesn't adequately describe the wares at this Harvard Square institution. College students and people who want to look like them come here to seek out whatever's fashionable right this red-hot minute. 50 John F. Kennedy St. (at Winthrop St.). www.berkshoes.com. *© **888/462-3757** or 617/492-9511. T: Red Line to Harvard.

Converse ★★ The Converse store is more than just Chuck Taylors (I was wondering, too). Along with a whole floor of athletic shoes, it carries a good selection of men's and women's sportswear, including jeans. The helpful staff at the second-floor customization bar will trick out your new Chucks just for you. 348 Newbury St. (btw. Hereford St. and Mass. Ave.). www.converse.com. *© **617/424-5400.** T: Green Line B, C, or D to Hynes Convention Center.

Cuoio The enormous selections of designer footwear at these compact boutiques are dream fuel for the truly fetishistic (you know who you are). Be sure to check out the dramatically discounted clearance merchandise. 150 State St. (at India St.). *© **617/742-4486.** T: Blue Line to Aquarium or Green Line to Government Center. 115 Newbury St. (btw. Clarendon and Dartmouth sts.). *© **617/859-0636.** T: Green Line to Arlington.

Helen's Leather Shop ★ Homesick Texans visit Helen's just to gaze upon the boots. Many are handmade from exotic leathers, including ostrich, buffalo, and snakeskin. The shop carries brands such as Lucchese and Tony Lama, along with a large selection of Western apparel for adults and children, leather goods, belts and buckles, and Stetson hats. And it smells great. Closed Tuesday. 110 Charles St. (at Pinckney St.). www.helensleather.com. *© **617/742-2077.** T: Red Line to Charles/MGH.

Moxie ★★ A chic little shop with an unbelievable selection of designer shoes, Moxie may look intimidating, but it really isn't. The welcoming, accommodating staff will help put together an ensemble of accessories (shoes, handbag, jewelry) for any occasion. 51 Charles St. (btw. Chestnut and Mount Vernon sts.). www.moxieboston.com. *© **617/557-9991.** T: Red Line to Charles/MGH.

New Balance Experience ★ A block from the Boston Marathon finish line, the Experience store—the third in the world—shows off New Balance's footwear, running gear, and fashions for men and women. Massachusetts-based New Balance boasts that it's the only athletic-shoe company still manufacturing shoes in the U.S. 583 Boylston St. (btw. Clarendon and Dartmouth sts.). www.newbalance.com/bos. *© **617/266-1583.** T: Green Line to Copley.

Sudo Shoes You may need a minute to figure out why your fellow shoppers are excited, because much of the merchandise here is so fashionable that it's hard to believe it's vegan. The clientele is largely online shoppers thrilled with the opportunity for 3-D browsing—for men's, women's, and kids' footwear—plus the occasional fashionista who doesn't even miss the leather and suede. 1771 Massachusetts Ave. (at Forest St.), Cambridge. www.sudoshoes.com. *© **617/354-1771.** T: Red Line to Porter.

Vibram This is the flagship U.S. outlet for Vibram (say "*Vee*-brum"), the Italian company that inflicted the FiveFingers shoe on your sensitive eyes. Displays let shoppers test the intriguing glove-style footwear on various surfaces, including stones and wood chips. 292 Newbury St. (btw. Gloucester and Hereford sts.). www.vibram fivefingers.com. ℂ **857/263-8508.** T: Green Line B, C, or D to Hynes Convention Center.

VINTAGE & SECONDHAND CLOTHING

Bobby From Boston ★★ Boston's vintage clothing scene tends to be light on men's options, though not on people whining about it. The perfect rejoinder is this off-the-beaten-track shop on the edge of the South End—in 2009, *Esquire* proclaimed it the best in the country for men's vintage. The focus is the 1940s through 1970s, and there's a small selection of women's clothing. Closed Sunday and Monday. 19 Thayer St. (off Harrison Ave.). ℂ **617/423-9299.** T: Silver Line SL4/SL5 bus to E. Berkeley St., or Orange Line to Tufts Medical Center, then 10-min. walk.

Boomerangs ★★ 🎁 The AIDS Action Committee operates this minichain of resale stores; the crown jewel is the "Special Edition" in the chic South End, which stocks women's and men's fashion. Some items are new, but the real finds here are vintage and "gently used." The Central Square location also carries furniture and home accessories, as do the Jamaica Plain and West Roxbury stores (check the website for information). The Special Edition is closed on Monday. 1407 Washington St. (btw. Union Park and Pelham sts.). www.shopboomerangs.com. ℂ **617/456-0996.** T: Silver Line SL4/SL5 bus to Union Park St. or Orange Line to Tufts Medical Center, then 10-min. walk. 563 Massachusetts Ave. (at Pearl St.), Cambridge. ℂ **617/758-6128.** T: Red Line to Central.

The Closet ★★★ This is the not-very-secret weapon of many a chic shopper. One of the Boston area's best consignment shops, it opened in 1979 and offers "gently worn" (not vintage) high-end designer clothing and accessories for women and men at drastically reduced prices. Be sure to check out the shoes and bags. 175 Newbury St. (btw. Dartmouth and Exeter sts.). www.closetboston.com. ℂ **617/536-1919.** T: Green Line to Copley.

The Garment District ★ You're hitting the clubs and you want to look cool, but money is tight. Join the shoppers here, paying great prices for a huge selection of contemporary and vintage clothing, costumes, and accessories. "By the pound" merchandise on the first floor is a steal at $1.50 a pound. And Boston Costume, also on the premises, is *the* place for rental, retail, and vintage costumes, which are available year-round. 200 Broadway (at Davis St.), Cambridge. www.garmentdistrict.com. ℂ **617/876-5230.** T: Red Line to Kendall/MIT.

Kulturez 🎁 Vintage and vintage-y T-shirts appeal to skater dudes, graffiti artists, and the fashion-conscious of both genders. Kulturez features a well-edited selection of apparel, "urban art supplies" (think spray paint), and a friendly vibe—I'm hardly the target audience, but I always feel welcome. In the Garage mall, 36 John F. Kennedy St. (at Mount Auburn St.), Cambridge. www.kulturez.com. ℂ **617/661-3865.** T: Red Line to Harvard.

Oona's Experienced Clothing ★★★ From funky accessories and costume jewelry to vintage dresses nice enough to get married in, Oona's carries a large but choice selection of women's and men's clothing at good prices. The friendly, fashionable Harvard Square stalwart has a branch in Inman Square. 1210 Massachusetts Ave. (near Bow St.), Cambridge. ℂ **617/491-2654.** T: Red Line to Harvard.

Oona's Outpost, 1297 Cambridge St. (at Oakland St.), Cambridge. ✆ **617/661-1967.** T: Red Line to Central, then 10-min. walk on Prospect St.

Second Time Around   Part of an East Coast chain, these consignment stores have a catch-as-catch-can flavor that entrances some shoppers and drives others nuts. The Closet (see listing above) outshines Second Time Around in every regard, but if you're in a bargain-hunting mood, you might find a keeper here. 82 Charles St. (btw. Mount Vernon and Pinckney sts.). www.secondtimearound.net. ✆ **617/227-0049.** T: Red Line to Charles/MGH. 176 Newbury St. (btw. Dartmouth and Exeter sts.). ✆ **617/247-3504.** T: Green Line to Copley. 219 Newbury St. (btw. Exeter and Fairfield sts.). ✆ **617/266-1113.** T: Green Line to Copley. 324 Newbury St. (at Hereford St.). ✆ **617/236-2028.** T: Green Line B, C, or D to Hynes Convention Center.

College Merchandise

The big names are Harvard and BU (you'll see Boston College merchandise on pushcarts downtown, too), but you have literally dozens of other options—the Boston area is home to that many schools. Look like an insider with a souvenir or shirt from **Barnes & Noble at Emerson College,** 114 Boylston St. (http://emerson.bncollege.com; ✆ **617/824-8696;** T: Green Line to Boylston); the **MIT Coop,** 3 Cambridge Center (www.thecoop.com; ✆ 617/499-3200; T: Red Line to Kendall/MIT), and 84 Massachusetts Ave. (✆ 617/499-3240; T: Red Line to Kendall/MIT); the **Northeastern University Bookstore,** 360 Huntington Ave. (http://northeastern.bncollege.com; ✆ 617/373-2286; T: Green Line E to Northeastern); or the **Suffolk University Bookstore,** 148 Cambridge St., Beacon Hill (http://suffolk.bkstr.com; ✆ 617/227-4085; T: Blue Line to Bowdoin [closed weekends] or Green Line to Government Center).

Barnes & Noble at Boston University ★   The BU crest, terrier mascot, or name appears on at least a floor's worth of clothing and just about any other item with room for a logo. The book selection is huge, and the author series brings writers to campus year-round. 660 Beacon St. (at Commonwealth Ave.). http://bu.bncollege.com. ✆ **617/267-8484.** T: Green Line B, C, or D to Kenmore.

The Harvard Coop ★★   The Coop (rhymes with *hoop*), or Harvard Cooperative Society, is student-oriented but not a run-of-the-mill college bookstore. You'll find Harvard-insignia merchandise, stationery, prints, and posters. As at BU, Barnes & Noble runs the sprawling book operation. 1400 Massachusetts Ave. (at Brattle St.), Cambridge. www.thecoop.com. ✆ **617/499-2000.** T: Red Line to Harvard.

Department Stores

Lord & Taylor ★★   Despite the strong New York association, Lord & Taylor is a Boston favorite for special-occasion outfits. Great seasonal sales, superb cosmetics and costume jewelry, and a wide selection of men's and women's sportswear make it a good stop even if you don't need an outfit to wear to a wedding. 760 Boylston St. (at Ring Rd.). www.lordandtaylor.com. ✆ **617/262-6000.** T: Green Line to Copley.

Saks Fifth Avenue ★   A high-end New York favorite noted for its designer fashions, cosmetics, and shoe collections. To avoid the mall crowds, enter from Ring Road. Shops at Prudential Center, 800 Boylston St. (at Fairfield St.), Cambridge. www.saksfifthavenue.com. ✆ **617/499-2000.** T: Red Line to Harvard.

Discount Shopping

City Sports ★   The regional athletic-apparel retailer City Sports carries clothing, footwear, and some sports equipment. The crowded lower level of this store—also a regular retail location—stocks a constantly changing selection of out-of-season merchandise at excellent prices. 11 Bromfield St. (btw. Washington and Province sts.). www.citysports.com. © **617/423-2015.** T: Red or Orange Line to Downtown Crossing.

DSW Shoe Warehouse   Here you'll find two large floors of discounted women's and men's shoes, boots, sandals, and sneakers. Check the clearance racks for the real deals. 385 Washington St. (at Bromfield St.). www.dsw.com. © **617/556-0052.** T: Red or Orange Line to Downtown Crossing.

Eddie Bauer Outlet   Not what you might expect from an outlet—the prices aren't always breathtakingly low (they're lowest during Jan and Aug end-of-season sales), but the quality and selection of casual, outdoorsy clothes and accessories for men and women are generally excellent. 500 Washington St. (at West St.). www.eddiebaueroutlet.com. © **617/423-4722.** T: Red or Orange Line to Downtown Crossing.

Food & Drink

Beacon Hill Chocolates   This shop's artisan creations are a consistently hot topic on the chocoholic grapevine. The special-occasion selections in handmade boxes are as beautiful as they are delicious. Salted caramels are a sublime nonchocolate option, and the gelato, hot chocolate, and coffee drinks are delectable. 91 Charles St. (at Pinckney St.). www.beaconhillchocolates.com. © **617/725-1900.** T: Red Line to Charles/MGH.

J. Pace & Son ★★   The original North End location of this local grocery minichain specializes in imported Italian foodstuffs, including meats and cheeses. This is a great place for hard-to-find olive oils and vinegars, numerous varieties of pasta and dry goods—and excellent sandwiches. Pace's (pronounced *Pah*-chay's) has seating on a small patio across the street from the Rose Kennedy Greenway. 42 Cross St. (off Salem St.). www.jpaceandson.com. © **617/227-9673.** T: Green or Orange Line to Haymarket.

Penzeys ★★   The Wisconsin-based purveyor of spices, herbs, flavorings, and rubs attracts delighted cooks and foodies from miles around (the closest branch

---

 An Outlet Excursion

If you can't get through a vacation without some outlet shopping, the fact that you left the car at home doesn't have to stop you. **Boston Common Coach** (www.bostoncommoncoach.com; © **877/723-3833** or 617/773-2784) and **Brush Hill Tours** (www.brushhilltours.com; © **800/343-1328** or 781/986-6100) offer service from Boston to **Wrentham Village Premium Outlets** (www.premiumoutlets.com/wrentham; © **508/384-0600**), a huge complex about 45 minutes south of downtown. Its dozens of outlet stores include—and this is merely scratching the surface—Anne Klein, Banana Republic, Barneys New York, Coach, Juicy Couture, J. Crew, kate spade, Kenneth Cole, Nike, Polo Ralph Lauren, Reebok, 7 for All Mankind, Tommy Hilfiger, and Versace. Shoppers leave Boston between 9 and 10am. The round-trip fare is $42 to $45 for adults (Brush Hill charges $25 for children 3–11); both companies require reservations.

Fired Up

A good souvenir is something you'd never find anywhere else, and a **Boston Fire Department T-shirt** is a great one. They cost about $15 at most neighborhood firehouses. The handiest for out-of-towners are **Engine 8, Ladder 1,** 392 Hanover St. (at Charter St.), in the North End near the Freedom Trail; **Engine 4, Ladder 24,** 200 Cambridge St. (at Joy St.), on the north side of Beacon Hill; and **Engine 33, Ladder 15,** 941 Boylston St. (at Hereford St.), in the Back Bay near the Hynes Convention Center.

is in Connecticut) with its huge, reasonably priced selection. Getting here is a pain, but it's absolutely worth the trip. 1293 Massachusetts Ave. (at Davis Rd.), Arlington. www.penzeys.com. ☏ **800/741-7787** or 781/646-7707. T: Red Line to Harvard or Porter, then bus no. 77.

Polcari's Coffee ★   Dozens of varieties of coffee beans, half a dozen types of espresso, and a wide tea selection make Polcari's the North End's go-to place for do-it-yourself caffeine (and decaf). The little shop also stocks bulk candy and nuts, spices and herbs, domestic and imported kitchen staples, and numerous cheeses. Best of all, it's a neighborhood favorite—that means great people-watching—with a knowledgeable, friendly staff. Closed Sunday. 105 Salem St. (at Parmenter St.). www. polcariscoffee.com. ☏ **617/227-0786.** T: Green or Orange Line to Haymarket.

Salumeria Italiana ★★   The city's premier Italian grocer caters to picky North Enders and foodies from all over the Boston area. Owner Gaetano Martignetti, the son of the founder, prides himself on his selection of meats, cheeses, olives, olive oils, vinegars, pastas, and more. The store is small, the variety huge. 151 Richmond St. (btw. Hanover and North sts.). www.salumeriaitaliana.com. ☏ **617/523-8743.** T: Green or Orange Line to Haymarket.

Trader Joe's ★   The celebrated California-based retailer stocks a large selection of prepared foods, cheeses, nuts, baked goods, natural and organic products, and other edibles, all at excellent prices. Get a preview on the website or just ask devotees—they can't shut up about it. The Cambridge locations are good stops for picnic provisions if you're driving. The Memorial Drive and Brookline stores sell beer and wine. 899 Boylston St. (at Gloucester St.). www.traderjoes.com. ☏ **617/262-6505.** T: Green Line B, C, or D to Hynes Convention Center. 1317 Beacon St. (off Harvard St.), Brookline. ☏ **617/278-9997.** T: Green Line C to Coolidge Corner. 748 Memorial Dr. (at Riverside Rd., 1 block from Magazine St.), Cambridge. ☏ **617/491-8582.** 211 Alewife Brook Pkwy. (at Concord Ave.), Cambridge. ☏ **617/498-3201.** T: Red Line to Alewife, 10-min. walk.

Gifts & Souvenirs

Boston has dozens of shops and pushcarts that sell T-shirts, hats, and other souvenirs. At the stores listed here, you'll find gifts that say Boston without actually *saying* "Boston" all over them. The online-only merchandise of the **Boston Public**

Library (www.bpl.org) incorporates images from the library's vast holdings, including historic maps, photos, and even sports memorabilia—and you don't have to take up space in your carry-on to get your souvenirs home.

Black Ink ★★★   The wacky wares here defy categorization, but they all fit comfortably under the umbrella of "oh, cool." Stuffed animals, unusual paper clips, and little cookbooks caught my eye recently; greeting cards, desktop accessories, and retro toys are equally appealing. 101 Charles St. (btw. Revere and Pinckney sts.). www.blackinkboston.com. ✆ **617/723-3883.** T: Red Line to Charles/MGH. 5 Brattle St. (off John F. Kennedy St.), Cambridge. ✆ **866/497-1221** or 617/497-1221. T: Red Line to Harvard.

Buckaroo's Mercantile ★   Slightly off the beaten track in Central Square, this place stocks a wild selection of vintage and retro-style contemporary gifts, home accessories, clothing, and gadgets. The wacky stock—I have my eye on a Bettie Page magnet—changes regularly. 5 Brookline St. (at Mass. Ave.), Cambridge. www.buckmerc.com. ✆ **617/492-4792.** T: Red Line to Central.

Front ★   The retail arm of the beloved Bob's Your Uncle gifts, games, and stationery brand, Front (which also carries a discriminating selection of other brands) is a great reason to detour to Fort Point. Owing to the clever toys, home accessories, and colorful novelty items, leaving empty-handed requires more willpower than I can muster. Closed Sunday and Monday. 125 Channel Center St. (off A St.). www.front-online.com or www.bobsyouruncle.com. ✆ **857/362-7289.** T: Red Line to South Station, then 15-min. walk.

Joie de Vivre ★★★ 🎁   When I'm stumped for a present for a person who has everything, I head to this delightful little shop, in business since 1984. Joie de Vivre's constantly changing selection of gifts and toys for adults and sophisticated children is beyond compare. The kaleidoscope collection alone is worth the trip; you'll also find jewelry, postcards, puzzles, music boxes, clocks, puppets, and salt and pepper shakers. 1792 Massachusetts Ave. (at Arlington St.), Cambridge. www.joiedevivre.net. ✆ **617/864-8188.** T: Red Line to Porter.

Lannan Ship Model Gallery 🎁   Fronting the Greenway, this intriguing Financial District shop carries nautical art, marine memorabilia, and a huge selection of ship models. It also schedules occasional auctions. Home accessories—think mermaid candleholders—are surprisingly reasonably priced, and a good excuse to check out a unique business. Closed Sunday except by appointment. 99 High St. (entrance at 185 Purchase St., at Congress St.). www.lannangallery.com. ✆ **617/451-2650.** T: Red Line to South Station.

Museum of Fine Arts Gift Shop ★★   For those without the time or inclination to visit the museum, the satellite shop carries posters, prints, cards and stationery, books, educational toys, scarves, mugs, T-shirts, and reproductions of jewelry in the museum's collections. You might even be inspired to pay a call on the real thing. 3 South Market Building, Faneuil Hall Marketplace. www.mfashop.org. ✆ **617/720-1266.** T: Green or Blue Line to Government Center.

St. Francis Gift & Book Store   Across the street from the Freedom Trail, St. Leonard of Port Maurice Church has a secular feature: a little shop overlooking the church's Peace Garden. In addition to religious merchandise, it carries greeting cards, jewelry, and an extensive selection of books. Proceeds benefit the church and its Franciscan missions. Hanover St. at Prince St. ✆ **617/523-2111.** T: Green or Orange Line to Haymarket.

Shake the Tree ★   Tucked in among the North End's innumerable restaurants is this appealing boutique. It's artsier than a lot of gift shops, with an ever-changing stock of handmade jewelry, clothing, handbags, baby presents, home accessories, candles, and soaps. Check ahead for details of the monthly cocktail party. 67 Salem St. (off Cross St.). www.shakethetreeboston.com. **℃ 617/742-0484.** T: Green or Orange Line to Haymarket.

Home Design, Furnishings & Housewares

The Boston Shaker   This little shop outside Davis Square carries everything for the hipster mixologist except the booze. You'll find glassware, bar accessories, books and magazines, and nonalcoholic cocktail ingredients, from olives to an encyclopedic selection of bitters (celery—who knew?). Check ahead to see whether a class or workshop is taking place during your visit. 69 Holland St. (at Irving St.), Somerville. www.thebostonshaker.com. **℃ 617/718-2999.** T: Red Line to Davis.

Boutique Fabulous ★   The name only partly conveys the fun of exploring this emporium of home accessories, antiques, cosmetics, tableware, memorabilia, greeting cards, vintage fashion, and (in case this isn't implied) offbeat gifts. A visit to Boutique Fabulous is the perfect treat after brunch or dinner in Inman Square—it's open Thursday through Saturday 11am to 10pm, other days until 8pm. 1309 Cambridge St. (at Oak St.), Cambridge. www.boutiquefabulous.com. **℃ 617/864-0656.** T: Red Line to Central, 10-min. walk on Prospect St.

Crate & Barrel ★★   This is wedding-present heaven, packed with contemporary and classic housewares as well as furniture and home accessories. The merchandise, from juice glasses and linen napkins to top-of-the-line knives and roasting pans, includes items to suit any budget. 777 Boylston St. (btw. Exeter and Fairfield sts.). www.crateandbarrel.com. **℃ 617/262-8700.** T: Green Line to Copley. 1045 Massachusetts Ave. (at Trowbridge St.), Cambridge. **℃ 617/547-3994.** T: Red Line to Harvard.

Frette   Maybe a night in a luxury hotel is so restful because many of them use Frette bed and bath linens. The legendary Italian retailer also carries plush bathrobes and nightclothes, adorable baby gifts, and home accessories such as throws and pillows. True, some of them cost as much as a car, but there's no harm in looking—and maybe finding something gorgeous on sale. In the Mandarin Oriental, Boston, 776B Boylston St. (at Fairfield St.). www.frette.com. **℃ 617/267-0500.** T: Green Line to Copley.

Jonathan Adler ★★   I want to party with Jonathan Adler, but I'll settle for robbing a bank and outfitting my apartment with his colorful, contemporary designs. From ceramics to furniture to dog harnesses, this irresistible shop carries everything you need to attain the designer's signature "happy chic." 129 Newbury St. (btw. Clarendon and Dartmouth sts.). www.jonathanadler.com. **℃ 617/437-0018.** T: Green Line to Copley.

Lekker   *Lekker* is Dutch for "tempting," which this striking store certainly is. A perfect fit for the modish South End, it features contemporary home accessories and furniture. Be sure to check out the delightful selection of gifts for adults and children. 1317 Washington St. (at Waltham St.). www.lekkerhome.com. **℃ 877/7-LEKKER (753-5537)** or 617/542-6464. T: Silver Line SL4/SL5 bus to Union Park St., or Orange Line to Back Bay and 10-min. walk.

Marimekko Cambridge   The Finnish design company—you might recognize the bold, colorful prints from the Crate & Barrel catalog—stocks home

Flying Lobsters

Why stop at a postcard when you can send a souvenir lobster? **James Hook & Co.,** 15–17 Northern Ave., at Atlantic Avenue (www.jameshooklobster.com; 𝄐 **617/423-5501;** T: Red Line to South Station or Blue Line to Aquarium), and

Legal Sea Foods, Logan Airport Terminal B and C (http://shop.legalseafoods.com; 𝄐 **800/343-5804,** 617/568-2811, or 617/568-2800; T: Blue Line to Airport), ship live crustaceans overnight.

accessories and linens, textiles, and clothing and accessories for women, children, and men. Closed Sunday except in December. 350 Huron Ave. (at Gurney St.). www.marimekkocambridge.com. 𝄐 **617/354-2800.** T: Red Line to Harvard, then no. 72 bus or 25-min. walk.

Simon Pearce ★   Dramatic designs make Simon Pearce's hand-blown glass and handmade pottery as much art as tableware. The Vermont-based company originated in Ireland, where Pearce learned glass blowing, and has grown into an internationally recognized go-to destination for high-end wedding presents. 103 Newbury St. (at Clarendon St.). www.simonpearce.com. 𝄐 **617/450-8388.** T: Green Line to Copley.

Twelve Chairs   A pair of interior designers run this irresistible shop in a loftlike Fort Point space. Just looking at the gorgeous furniture, lovely home accessories, and sophisticated gifts makes me feel more stylish. What's more, the eco-conscious business chooses merchandise based on "People & Planet Principles." Ask the pleasant staff about the name, which has nothing to do with the Mel Brooks movie or the Russian novel. Closed Monday. 319 A St. (at Melcher St., 1 block from Summer St.). www.twelvechairsboston.com. 𝄐 **617/701-3496.** T: Red Line to South Station, then 10-min. walk.

Music

Cheapo Records   The specialty here is vinyl, but the selection of other formats is nothing to sneeze at. And sneeze you might—it's a tad dusty—as you search for something specific or let serendipity be your guide. If you need help, just ask the staff, whose members are as friendly as they are knowledgeable. 538 Massachusetts Ave. (at Norfolk St.). www.cheaporecords.com. 𝄐 **617/354-4455.** T: Red Line B to Central.

In Your Ear Records ★★   Asked to recommend a used-music store, a DJ friend instantly suggested In Your Ear. These stores, adjacent to Boston University and Harvard, carry huge, constantly changing inventories of CDs, vinyl, DVDs, and even cassettes and eight-track tapes, plus turntables and posters. 957 Commonwealth Ave. (at Harry Agganis Way). www.iye.com. 𝄐 **617/787-9755.** T: Green Line B to Pleasant St. 72 Mount Auburn St. (off Holyoke St.), lower level. 𝄐 **617/491-5035.** T: Red Line to Harvard.

Newbury Comics ★   A quickly adapting survivor of the format revolution, Newbury Comics is a funky local chain that stocks a wide selection of music, gifts, novelty items, posters, T-shirts—and, of course, comics. You'll find video games, DVDs, and new and used CDs of mainstream and cutting-edge music, with lots of independent labels and imports. North Market Building, Faneuil Hall Marketplace. www.newburycomics.com. 𝄐 **617/248-9992.** T: Orange Line to Haymarket, or

Green or Blue Line to Government Center. 332 Newbury St. (btw. Hereford St. and Mass. Ave.). © **617/236-4930.** T: Green Line B, C, or D to Hynes Convention Center. In the Garage mall, 36 John F. Kennedy St., Cambridge. © **617/491-0337.** T: Red Line to Harvard.

Stereo Jack's ★   I love music; I'm not obsessed, but I can recognize people who are, and the staff here qualifies. If you just can't get enough jazz, blues, and R&B (new and used), you'll feel right at home. Call first—Stereo Jack's may be moving during the lifespan of this book. 1686 Massachusetts Ave. www.stereojacks. com. © **617/497-9447.** T: Red Line to Porter.

Technology

Apple Store ★   The glittering glass box across the street from the Prudential Center holds two floors of high-tech toys, with the Genius Bar on the third floor. A madhouse since it opened in 2008, the Boston store is open Monday through Saturday 9am to 10pm, Sunday 11am to 7pm. The smaller Cambridge location keeps mall hours—Monday through Saturday 10am to 9pm, Sunday noon to 7pm. 815 Boylston St. (btw. Fairfield and Gloucester sts.). www.apple.com/retail/boylston street. © **617/385-9400.** T: Green Line to Copley. CambridgeSide Galleria, 100 Cambridge-Side Place, Cambridge. www.apple.com/retail/cambridgeside. © **617/225-0442.** T: Green Line to Lechmere, or Red Line to Kendall/MIT, then free shuttle bus (every 20 min.).

Toys & Games

Also check out most of the shops listed under "Gifts & Souvenirs," the children's specialists in the "Clothing & Accessories" section, and the gift shops at the **Boston Children's Museum, Museum of Science,** and **New England Aquarium** (see "Boston with Kids," in chapter 3).

The Games People Play ★   Just outside Harvard Square, this store carries enough board games (foreign as well as domestic) to outfit every country, summer, and beach house in New England. Also check out the wide selection of puzzles (jigsaw and mechanical), playing cards, Steiff toys, and chess, backgammon, and go sets. 1100 Massachusetts Ave. (at Putnam Ave.), Cambridge. www.thegames peopleplaycambridge.com. © **888/492-0711** or 617/492-0711. T: Red Line to Harvard.

Henry Bear's Park ★★★   This minichain is well into its 4th decade of thrilling Boston-area children and the adults who want to keep them delighted. The toys "promote healthy and positive play," which luckily is a concept that knows no age limit (yes, that yo-yo was for me). Staff members are enthusiastic and helpful, and gift-wrapping is free. In the Porter Square Shopping Center, 25 White St. (off Mass. Ave.), Cambridge. www.henrybear.com. © **617/547-8424.** T: Red Line to Porter. 19 Harvard St. (near Webster Place), Brookline. © **617/264-2422.** T: Green Line D to Brookline Village.

Magic Beans ★   A small local chain with a big reputation, Magic Beans is mostly a baby-gear destination, with terrific toy and gift selections. The locations beyond the Back Bay are a bit out of the way, but hey—the 'burbs are where the kids are. Shops at Prudential Center, 800 Boylston St. (at Fairfield St.). www.mbeans.com. © **617/383-8296.** T: Green Line E to Prudential or Green Line to Copley. 361 Huron Ave. (btw. Chilton and Standish sts.), Cambridge. © **617/300-0171.** T: Red Line to Harvard, then No. 72 bus or 25-min. walk. 321 Harvard St. (at Babcock St.), Brookline. © **617/264-2326.** T: Green Line to Coolidge Corner.

Stellabella Toys ★★   Both retro (lots of wooden toys) and modern (no guns), Stellabella is a welcoming destination for parents and kids alike. It carries everything from baby strollers to craft supplies and costumes for big kids, and the friendly staff can lend a hand if you need help maintaining your status as the cool aunt or uncle. 1967 Massachusetts Ave. (btw. Allen and Beech sts.), Cambridge. www.stellabellatoys.com. ✆ **617/864-6290.** T: Red Line to Porter. 1360 Cambridge St. (btw. Oak and Springfield sts.), Inman Sq., Cambridge. ✆ **617/491-6290.** T: Red Line to Central, then 10-min. walk on Prospect St.

PRACTICAL MATTERS: THE SHOPPING SCENE

OPEN HOURS & DAYS   In major shopping areas, stores usually open at 10am and close at 6 or 7pm Monday through Saturday. On Sunday, most open at noon and close at 5 or 6pm, but some don't open at all. Closing time may be later 1 night a week, usually Wednesday or Thursday. Malls keep their own hours (see "Malls & Markets," above), and some smaller shops open at 11am or later. Open hours and days can vary in winter. Year-round, some businesses—including many art galleries—close on Sunday, Monday, or both.

In short, if a store sounds too good to pass up, call to make sure it's open before you head out.

TAXES & SHIPPING   The United States has no national sales tax, but most states impose their own. Tags and labels show pretax prices. Massachusetts does not charge sales tax on clothing priced below $175 or on food items. The state taxes all other items at 6.25%.

Just about every store will handle domestic shipping for a fee, but if the store is part of a chain that operates in your home state, you'll probably have to pay that sales tax. Be sure to ask.

ENTERTAINMENT
& NIGHTLIFE

8

Countless musicians, actors, and comedians went to college or got their start in the Boston area, and it's a great place to check out rising stars and promising unknowns. You might get an early look at the next Branford Marsalis, Bonnie Raitt, Esperanza Spalding, Louis C.K., or Yo-Yo Ma. And numerous established artists perform at world-renowned Symphony Hall as well as at countless lower-profile venues. Nearly every day of the year, no matter your budget, you'll find someone expressing him- or herself in public, and eager for an audience.

The key is to see Boston's limitations as an opportunity. Even if they stayed open past 2am—which they don't—the city's dance clubs would leave something to be desired. (Flying to New York after work, carousing all night, and taking the first shuttle back the next morning isn't unheard of.) Meanwhile, a rush ticket makes a performance by the Boston Symphony Orchestra cheaper than a nice lunch; the avant-garde theater sensation *Sleep No More* played suburban Brookline before New York; and jazz musicians of all stripes turn up at Wally's, a 50-plus-year-old club. Tap the city's strengths.

For up-to-date entertainment information online, start at **http://events. frommers.com**. The *Boston Globe* offers suggestions at **www.boston.com/ thingstodo/nightlife** and on Twitter (**@bostoncalendar**), where you'll also find the *Phoenix* (**@BostonPhoenix**). The Greater Boston Convention & Visitors Bureau (**www.facebook.com/BostonUSA**) is another good resource. The websites of the agencies listed under "Getting Tickets," below, let you view events by date and location (don't forget to check Cambridge as well as Boston). For variety's sake, I suggest following links or setting up bookmarks and social-media connections to lower-profile sources. At press time, I'm enjoying **www. bostonhospitalityindustry.com**, **@beantownblog**, and **www.facebook.com/ bostoneventsinsider**.

To do low-tech research, consult the daily **Boston Globe,** Friday's **Boston Herald,** and the Sunday arts sections of both papers. Four free publications, available at newspaper boxes around town, publish good nightlife listings: the weekly **Boston Phoenix** and **Weekly Dig,** and the biweekly **Stuff@Night** (a *Phoenix* offshoot) and **Improper Bostonian.**

Tip: The *Phoenix* website (**www.bostonphoenix.com**) archives the alternative weekly's voluminous season-preview issues. Especially before a summer or fall visit, it's an invaluable planning tool.

THE PERFORMING ARTS

Classical music and pre–Broadway theater are Boston's big stars, but just about everyone and everything that isn't a Vegas-style extravaganza—rock and pop

PREVIOUS PAGE: **Everyone at the Faneuil Hall Cheers may not know your name, but fans of the show are always glad they came.**

AMC Loews Boston Common **56**
Bank of America Pavilion **86**
The Bar at Taj Boston **37**
The Beehive **34**
Berklee Performance Center **19**
The Black Rose **78**
Bleacher Bar **9**
BosTix **27, 77**
Boston Beer Works **4, 69**
Boston Center for the Arts **32**
Boston Common
    Coffee Co. **61, 73, 81**
Boston Opera House **59**
Brasserie Jo **25**
Bricco **77**
The Bristol Lounge **42**
Caffe Pompei **72**
Cask 'n Flagon **6**
Charles Playhouse **50**
Cheers **35, 80**
Citi Wang Theatre **53**
Club Café **30**
Colonial Theatre **44**
Commonwealth Shakespeare
    Company **43**
Cutler Majestic Theatre **46**
Davio's Northern Italian
    Steakhouse **39**
DeLux Cafe **31**

Drink **84**
Eastern Standard **7**
Emmanuel Church **36**
Equal Exchange Cafe **67**
The Estate **45**
Finale **41**
The Fours **68**
Fritz **33**
Game On! Sports Cafe **5**
The Grand Canal **70**
Great Scott **1**
Hard Rock Cafe **76**
Hatch Shell **34**
House of Blues Boston **8**
Huntington Theatre Company **17**
Improv Asylum **74**
Isabella Stewart Gardner
    Museum **13**
Jacob Wirth **55**
Jacque's Cabaret **47**
Jasper White's Summer Shack **21**
Jerry Remy's Sports Bar &
    Grill **11, 85**
Jillian's Boston **10**
Kings **22**
King's Chapel **64**
The Littlest Bar **79**
Lyric Stage **29**
Machine **12**

Mr. Dooley's Boston Tavern **80**
Modern Theatre **60**
Museum of Fine Arts **14**
New England Conservatory **16**
Old South Church **26**
Orpheum Theater **62**
Paradise Rock Club **2**
Paramount Center **58**
Pizzeria Regina **71**
Radius **82**
The Red Room @ Cafe 939 **23**
Rise **38**
Royale Boston **52**
Rumor **49**
Shubert Theatre **51**
Silvertone Bar & Grill **63**
South Street Diner **83**
Symphony Hall **18**
TD Garden **66**
Thinking Cup **57**
Top of the Hub **24**
Trident Booksellers & Café **20**
Trinity Church **28**
21st Amendment **65**
Via Matta **40**
Wally's Cafe **15**
Wheelock Family Theatre **3**
Wilbur Theatre **54**

Getting Discount Tickets

Some of the best bargains in town are available at the **BosTix** (www.bostix.org ℭ **617/262-8632**) booths at **Faneuil Hall Marketplace** (T: Green or Blue Line to Government Center, or Orange Line to Haymarket) and in **Copley Square** at the corner of Boylston and Dartmouth streets (T: Green Line to Copley or Orange Line to Back Bay). Check the board or the website for the day's offerings.

Both locations sell half-price same-day tickets to musical and theatrical performances, subject to availability. You must visit in person, and there are no refunds or exchanges. The booths are also Ticketmaster outlets. Both are open Tuesday through Saturday from 10am to 6pm, and Sunday from 11am to 4pm. BosTix also offers full-price advance tickets; discounts on more than 100 theater, music, and dance events; and tickets for trolley tours. *Tip:* Sign up for e-mail updates (you can always unsubscribe after you return home).

An actor friend turned me on to **Goldstar** (www.goldstar.com). Sign up for daily e-mails alerting you to discounts on upcoming events, and act quickly when you see something you like—tickets can sell out fast. **Gilt City** (www.giltcity.com/boston) focuses on special events, which tend to be pricey even with a discount, but the site can be a good intro to high-end entertainment and leisure options.

stars, established and up-and-coming comedians, world-music legends, avant-garde cabaret, and much, much more—originates or eventually plays in the area.

As a rule, the bigger the name, the larger the venue, the pricier the tickets, and the longer the lead time. For an international superstar playing Symphony Hall or the TD Garden, tickets are expensive and sell out weeks or even months ahead. At the other end of this broad spectrum, student performances in campus spaces are free or cheap, and you can decide to attend moments before they begin. Evening performances of all types usually start at 7, 7:30, or 8pm, and curtain time for matinees ordinarily is 1 or 2pm; *always* double-check.

Three neighborhoods—the Theater District and the Fenway in Boston, and Harvard Square in Cambridge—are home to many prominent performing-arts venues, but don't write off an event taking place elsewhere. You might miss out on something great.

Getting Tickets

Some companies and venues sell tickets online or over the phone; many will refer you to a ticket agency. Two major agencies serve Boston: **Ticketmaster** (www.ticketmaster.com; ℭ **800/745-3000** or TDD 800/943-4327) and **Telecharge** (www.telecharge.com; ℭ **800/432-7250** or TTY 888/889-8587). Many smaller venues use independent companies that charge lower fees than their big rivals. Two popular firms are **Brown Paper Tickets** (www.brownpapertickets.com; ℭ **800/838-3006**) and **Eventbrite** (www.eventbrite.com or ℭ **888/810-2063** [tech support]).

To avoid fees—and possible losses if your plans change and you can't get your money back—visit the box office in person. *Tip:* If you wait until the day before or day of a performance, you'll sometimes have access to tickets that were held back for some reason and have just gone on sale.

Classical Music, Opera & Dance

The Boston area's cultural institutions deftly balance the appeal of classics with the excitement of innovation. Even at companies whose names might suggest that nothing new has come along for centuries, you can count on fresh interpretations that make the familiar feel novel.

Founded in 1815, the **Handel and Haydn Society** (www.handeland haydn.org; ℂ **617/266-3605**) uses period instruments and techniques in its "historically informed" orchestral, choral, and opera performances. Tickets cost $20 to $87. H&H gave the American premiere of Handel's ***Messiah*** in 1818 and has made it a holiday tradition since 1854. If you'll be in town in December, check for tickets as soon as you start planning your trip.

Boston Baroque (www.bostonbaroque.org; ℂ **617/484-9200**) is a Grammy-nominated period orchestra with a chamber chorus. Semistaged opera complements orchestral and choral performances, which often feature international guest artists. Tickets cost $29 to $75.

The **Boston Philharmonic Orchestra** (www.bostonphil.org; ℂ **617/236-0999**) is a semiprofessional ensemble with a strong educational component; conductor Benjamin Zander introduces each performance with a talk that includes input from the audience. Tickets run $15 to $90.

The **Boston Lyric Opera** (www.blo.org; ℂ **866/348-9738** or 617/542-6772) mounts one or two classical and one or two contemporary productions per season. Expect to pay $32 to $155.

Best known for its annual production of *The Nutcracker*, **José Mateo Ballet Theatre** (www.ballettheatre.org; ℂ **617/354-7467**) focuses on "culturally relevant" works by artistic director and choreographer Mateo, who founded the company in 1986.

Boston Ballet ★★   One of the top dance companies in the country, Boston Ballet is widely known for its beloved holiday production of *The Nutcracker*, which runs from Thanksgiving to New Year's. During the rest of the season (Oct–May), artistic director Mikko Nissinen slates an eclectic mix of classic story ballets and contemporary works. *Nutcracker* tickets go on sale in early July; for the rest of the season, in September. Performing at the Boston Opera House, 539 Washington St. (at Ave. de Lafayette). www.bostonballet.org. ℂ **617/695-6955.** Tickets $25–$137. Senior, student, and child rush tickets (2 hr. before most performances) $20 cash; not available for Nutcracker. T: Orange Line to Chinatown or Green Line to Boylston.

Boston Pops ★★   "It's nice to eat a good hunk of beef," longtime Boston Pops conductor Arthur Fiedler once said, "but you want a light dessert, too." The Pops are the dessert to the Boston Symphony Orchestra's beef. From early May to early July, tables and chairs replace the floor seats at Symphony Hall, and drinks and light refreshments are served. Under the direction of conductor Keith Lockhart, the Pops play a range of music from light classical to show tunes to popular (hence the name), often with celebrity guest stars of both the Broadway and Top 40 variety. Performances are Tuesday through Sunday evenings. Special holiday performances in December ($27–$125) usually sell out well in advance, but it can't hurt to check; tickets go on sale in late October.

The regular season ends with two **free outdoor concerts at the Hatch Shell** on the Esplanade along the Charles River. The traditional **Fourth of July** concert is a mob scene; the rehearsal the night before is merely very crowded. Both are great fun. Performing at Symphony Hall, 301 Massachusetts Ave. (at Huntington

ENTERTAINMENT & NIGHTLIFE

The Performing Arts

Ave.). www.bso.org. ☏ **617/266-1492,** 617/266-2378 (concert info), or 888/266-1200 (tickets). Tickets $40–$99 for tables, $22–$63 for balcony seats. T: Green Line E to Symphony or Orange Line to Massachusetts Ave.

Boston Symphony Orchestra ★★★ One of the world's greatest symphony orchestras, the BSO was founded in 1881. Its repertoire includes contemporary music, but classical is its great strength. You might want to schedule your trip to coincide with a particular performance or with a visit by a celebrated guest artist.

The season runs from October to April, with performances most Tuesday, Thursday, and Saturday evenings; Friday afternoons; and some Friday evenings. Thirty-minute explanatory talks (included in the ticket price) begin 1 hour and 15 minutes before the curtain rises. If you can't buy tickets in advance, check at the box office for returns from subscribers 2 hours before show time. Except on Saturday, a limited number of same-day **rush tickets** (one per person, cash only) are available. Some Wednesday evening and Thursday morning rehearsals are open to the public. Symphony Hall, 301 Massachusetts Ave. (at Huntington Ave.). www.bso.org. ☏ **617/266-1492,** 617/266-2378 (concert info), or 888/266-1200 (tickets). Tickets $30–$120. Rush tickets $9 (cash only; on sale Fri 10am and Tues, Thurs, and Fri 5pm). Rehearsal tickets $20. T: Green Line E to Symphony or Orange Line to Massachusetts Ave.

Theater

Local and national companies, professional and amateur actors, and classic and experimental material combine to animate the local theater scene. To see what's on, search the Internet or call before you arrive, or check the papers or BosTix (see "Getting Discount Tickets," on p. 220) after you're in town. With rare exceptions, performances are in English.

Boston is one of the last cities for pre-Broadway tryouts, allowing an early look at a classic (or a catastrophe) in the making. It's also a popular destination for touring companies of established hits. The promoter is often **Broadway in Boston** (http://boston.broadway.com; ☏ **866/523-7469** or 617/451-2345). You'll find most of the shows headed to or coming from Broadway in the Theater District, at the **Boston Opera House,** 539 Washington St. (at Ave. de Lafayette; www.bostonoperahouseonline.com; ☏ **617/259-3400**); the **Citi Wang Theatre,** 270 Tremont St. (½ block from Stuart St.); the **Colonial Theatre,** 106 Boylston St. (off Tremont St.); and the **Shubert Theatre,** 265 Tremont St. (½ block from Stuart St.). The **Citi Performing Arts Center** (www.citicenter.org; ☏ **617/482-9393**) operates the Colonial, the Shubert, and the Wang.

 Tanglewood: The BSO Goes to the Berkshires

When the Boston Symphony Orchestra goes away for the summer, it heads to **Tanglewood** (www.tanglewood.org; ☏ **413/637-1600** or 617/266-1492 out of season), in Lenox, Massachusetts, a 2½-hour drive from Boston. Weekend concerts sell out in advance, but tickets to weeknight performances and Saturday morning rehearsals are usually available at the box office. If you can't get a seat inside, bring a blanket and picnic on the lawn. Consult *Frommer's New England* and *Frommer's New England Day by Day* for information about western Massachusetts.

Cambridge After Dark

Johnny D's Uptown Restaurant &
  Music Club **3**
Kendall Square Cinema **34**
Lizard Lounge **4**
The Middle East **28**
Miracle of Science Bar + Grill **29**
Nameless Coffeehouse **8**
Paradise **30**
The Plough & Stars **21**
Regattabar **7**
Ryles Jazz Club **31**
Sanders Theatre **14**
Scullers Jazz Club **20**
Somerville Theater **5**
T.T. the Bear's Place **27**
1369 Coffee House **22**
Toad **2**
The Western Front **19**

Algiers Café & Restaurant **10**
American Repertory Theater **6**
BeanTowne Coffee House **31**
Brattle Theatre **10**
The Burren **1**
Cambridge Brewing Company **32**
Cantab Lounge **23**
Casablanca **10**
Club Oberon **18**
Club Passim **9**
The Comedy Studio **16**
Finale **13**
Flat Top Johnny's **33**
Grafton Street **17**
Green Street **26**
Grendel's Den **11**
Harvard Film Archive **15**
Havana Club **25**
The Hong Kong **16**
ImprovBoston **24**
John Harvard's Brew House **12**

223

Free Shakespeare, Outdoors

The **Commonwealth Shakespeare Company ★★★** (www.commshakes.org; ☎ **617/426-0863**) performs free on Boston Common Tuesday through Sunday nights in late July and early August. Bring a picnic and blanket, rent a chair ($7 or so) if you don't want to sit on the ground, and enjoy the sunset and a high-quality performance. The independent company is about half Equity actors, and the sets, lighting, and costumes are spectacular.

In recent years, the highest-profile Broadway show that originated in the Boston area was *The Gershwins' Porgy and Bess.* It was the work of the **American Repertory Theater,** or ART (pronounced A-R-T), which makes its home at Harvard University's **Loeb Drama Center,** 64 Brattle St. (at Hilliard St.), Cambridge (www.americanrepertorytheater.org; ☎ **617/547-8300**). The ART celebrates innovation, both on the main stage and in the programming of **Club Oberon,** a "theatrical club space"—think performance art, cabaret, and liquor—at 2 Arrow St. (at Mass. Ave.; www.cluboberon.com; ☎ **617/496-8004**). The off-Broadway hit *Sleep No More,* a British production, was a co-creation with the ART. The ART's main local rival for daring, offbeat events is the **Boston Center for the Arts** (see "Major Theaters & Companies," below).

Boston also has its own nationally acclaimed repertory company: The **Huntington Theatre Company,** which performs at the Boston University Theatre, 264 Huntington Ave. (btw. Mass. Ave. and Gainsborough St.; www.huntingtontheatre.org; ☎ **617/266-0800**), books more revivals than the ART and is equally likely to see a show wind up on Broadway.

Emerson College enjoys a rising profile on the local and national arts scene. **ArtsEmerson: The World on Stage** (www.artsemerson.org or www.aestages.org [tickets]; ☎ **617/824-8400**), the umbrella organization for the college's vibrant cultural offerings, offers everything from student films to American and international professional theater companies. It books six performance spaces in the Theater District, including the **Cutler Majestic Theatre,** 219 Tremont St. (btw. Boylston and Stuart sts.), and the **Paramount Center,** 559 Washington St. (btw. West and Avery sts.).

The **Lyric Stage,** 140 Clarendon St. (at Stuart St.; www.lyricstage.com; ☎ **617/585-5678**), mounts contemporary and modern works in an intimate second-floor setting.

The American Repertory Theater's production of *Alice vs. Wonderland* at the Loeb Drama Center.

FAMILY THEATER

Boston's Fenway neighborhood, the nearby suburb of Brookline, and the North Shore suburb of Beverly (about 40 min. from Boston by car) are home to three beloved varieties of family theater.

The Wheelock Family Theatre, 180 The Riverway (near Short St.; www. wheelockfamilytheatre.org; ℂ **617/879-2234**), mounts three productions a year—typically a family musical, a children's play, and an adult comedy or drama—with casts that mix professionals and talented amateurs, children and adults. Check ahead for the suggested minimum age for audience members; not appropriate for children under 3.

The professional puppeteers of the **Puppet Showplace Theatre,** 32 Station St. (off Washington St.), Brookline (www.puppetshowplace.org; ℂ **617/731-6400**), present favorite fables, ethnic legends, and folktales and fairy tales from around the world. The lovely 100-seat theater displays historic puppets and puppet posters, offers puppet-making workshops and other classes, and sells toy puppets. Family performances take place on weekends, with shows for toddlers on weekdays.

Three generations of magicians make up **Le Grand David and His Own Spectacular Magic Company** (www.legranddavid.com; ℂ **978/927-3677**), a nationally acclaimed troupe of illusionists that has delighted families since 1977. The ever-changing 2-hour shows, directed by master magician Marco the Magi, take place on alternating Sunday afternoons at the Cabot Street Cinema Theater, 286 Cabot St., Beverly, and Larcom Theatre, 13 Wallis St., Beverly. A show makes a perfect stop after a sightseeing excursion to the North Shore (see chapter 10).

College Concerts & Theaters

See "Theater," above, for information about the diverse programming of Emerson College's **ArtsEmerson: The World on Stage,** BU's **Huntington Theatre Company,** and Harvard's **American Repertory Theater.** See "Major Theaters & Companies," below, for information about New England Conservatory's **Jordan Hall,** Harvard's **Sanders Theatre,** and Berklee College of Music's **Berklee Performance Center.**

Students and faculty members at two prestigious musical institutions perform frequently during the academic year; admission is usually free. For information, contact the **New England Conservatory of Music,** 290 Huntington Ave. (at Gainsborough St.; www.necmusic.edu/concerts-events; ℂ **617/585-1260**), or the **Longy School of Music of Bard College,** 1 Follen St. (at Garden St.), Cambridge (www.longy.edu, click "Concerts & Events"; ℂ **617/876-0956,** ext. 1500).

The area's other college companies and venues are too numerous to list, but check their websites for a sense of what's on at **Boston University** (www. bu.edu; click "Campus Life," then "Calendars"), **Harvard University** (http:// ofa.fas.harvard.edu), **MIT** (http://arts.mit.edu), **Northeastern University** (www.northeastern.edu/northeasterncreates), and **Suffolk University** (www. suffolk.edu/theatre). Many Suffolk student performances, as well as professional productions, play at the lovingly restored **Modern Theatre,** 525 Washington St. (at Ave. de Lafayette; www.moderntheatre.com; ℂ **617/557-6537**). The 1914 performance space seats 185 for films, readings, and dramatic and musical performances.

Music Under the Sky & Stars

The **Boston Landmarks Orchestra** (www.landmarksorchestra.org; ℂ **617/ 520-2200**) performs at venues around town—often outdoors, and always free—on evenings from July through September (and occasionally the rest of the year). A concert is a great excuse to visit a pretty park and hear some excellent music.

Concert & Performance Series

The starriest names in classical music, dance, theater, jazz, opera, and world music play Boston as part of the **Celebrity Series of Boston** (www.celebrity series.org; ℂ **617/482-2595** [info] or 617/482-6661 [tickets]). It's a subscription series that also offers tickets to individual events.

World Music (www.worldmusic.org; ℂ **617/876-4275**) showcases top-flight musicians, dance troupes, and other performers from around the globe.

The **Museum of Fine Arts** (www.mfa.org/programs/music; ℂ **800/440-6975**) and the **Isabella Stewart Gardner Museum** (www.gardnermuseum. org/music; ℂ **617/278-5150**) schedule concerts year-round. Check ahead for schedules and tickets, which include museum admission. See p. 75 and p. 74 for full museum listings.

FREE (& ALMOST FREE) CONCERTS

Radio stations sponsor free outdoor music all summer. Specifics change frequently, but you can count on hearing oldies, pop, jazz, alternative, rock, and classical music at various venues, including City Hall Plaza, Copley Square, and the Hatch Shell, at lunch, after work, and in the evening. Check the papers when you arrive, listen to a station that sounds good to you, or just follow the crowds.

Four long-running concert series fill historic churches with music at least once a week. Admission to the first two is by free-will offering. At the **Old South Church,** 645 Boylston St. (off Dartmouth St.; www.oldsouth.org; ℂ **617/536-1970**), the choir sings or the hand-bell choir performs at the 11am Sunday service, accompanied by a 7,625-pipe Skinner organ, and a 1-hour jazz service begins at 6pm every Thursday. Across the square, **Trinity Church,** 206 Clarendon St. (btw. Boylston St. and St. James Ave.), in Copley Square (www.trinity churchboston.org; ℂ **617/536-0944**), features 30-minute organ recitals by local and visiting artists on Friday at 12:15pm. And **King's Chapel,** 58 Tremont St. (at School St.), on the Freedom Trail (www.kings-chapel.org; ℂ **617/227-2155**), schedules 30- to 40-minute organ, instrumental, and vocal classical, jazz, and folk performances at 12:15pm on Tuesday, 5pm on some Sundays; $3 donation requested.

Emmanuel Music ★★ Gorgeous Emmanuel Church fills with exquisite music every Sunday from early October through early May. Emmanuel Music's orchestra and chorus perform Bach cantatas during the 10am service. Check ahead for details of evening and chamber performances. Emmanuel Church, 15 Newbury St. (btw. Arlington and Berkeley sts.). www.emmanuelmusic.org. ℂ **617/536-3356.** Free-will offering. T: Green Line to Arlington.

Major Theaters & Companies

Two lovely college venues share the bulk of Boston's classical bookings with **Symphony Hall** (see below): New England Conservatory's **Jordan Hall,** 30 Gainsborough St. (at Huntington Ave.; www.necmusic.edu/concerts-events; ✆ **617/585-1270**), and Harvard University's **Sanders Theatre,** 45 Quincy St. (at Cambridge St.), Cambridge (www.fas.harvard.edu/~memhall; ✆ **617/496-4595**).

The **Hatch Shell,** on the Esplanade (www.mass.gov/dcr/hatch_events. htm; ✆ **617/626-4970;** T: Red Line to Charles/MGH or Green Line to Arlington), is an amphitheater best known as the site of the Boston Pops' Fourth of July concerts. On many summer nights, free music and dance performances and films take over the stage, to the delight of crowds on the lawn.

Bank of America Pavilion   One of the most pleasant venues in the area, this giant white tent encloses a 5,000-seat waterfront pavilion. It schedules pop, rock, country, rap, folk, and jazz on evenings from May through September. Check ahead for information about water transportation. 290 Northern Ave. (at Congress St.), South Boston. www.livenation.com. ✆ **617/728-1600** or 877/598-8497 (Live Nation). T: Waterfront Silver Line bus to Silver Line Way.

Berklee Performance Center   The Berklee College of Music's theater features professional artists (many of them former Berklee students, alumni as well as dropouts), instructors, and students. Offerings are heavy on jazz and folk, with plenty of other options. 136 Massachusetts Ave. (at Boylston St.). www.berkleebpc.com. ✆ **617/747-2261.** T: Green Line B, C, or D to Hynes Convention Center.

Boston Center for the Arts   Multiple performance spaces and an anything-goes booking policy make the BCA a leading venue for contemporary theater, music and dance performances, and visual arts exhibitions. The BCA and the Huntington Theatre Company (see "Theater," earlier in this chapter) are partners in the Calderwood Pavilion, which comprises 350- and 200-seat theaters. 539 Tremont St. (at Clarendon St.). www.bcaonline.org. ✆ **617/426-5000.** T: Orange Line to Back Bay.

Comcast Center   When a mainstream act's summer schedule says "Boston," that often means this bucolic setting about an hour south of town. A sheltered (it has a roof but no sides) auditorium surrounded by a lawn, the Comcast Center features rock, pop, folk, country, and light classical artists. Shows go on rain or shine. 885 S. Main St. (Rte. 140), Mansfield. www.livenation.com. ✆ **508/339-2331** or 800/745-3000 (Ticketmaster).

Orpheum Theatre   Although it's old (1852) and cramped, the Orpheum offers an intimate setting for big-name music and comedy performers. It books top local acts, popular up-and-coming artists, and international icons, recently including Creed, Snow Patrol, and Tori Amos. 1 Hamilton Place (off Tremont St., across from Park Street Church). www.livenation.com. ✆ **617/482-0106** or 800/745-3000 (Ticketmaster). T: Red or Green Line to Park St.

Symphony Hall   Acoustically perfect Symphony Hall, which opened in 1900, is the home of the **Boston Symphony Orchestra** and the **Boston Pops** (see earlier in this chapter). When they're away, top-notch classical, chamber, world, and popular music artists from elsewhere take over. For information on free tours of Symphony Hall, see p. 104. 301 Massachusetts Ave. (at Huntington Ave.). www. bostonsymphonyhall.org. ✆ **617/266-1492** or 888/266-1200 (tickets). T: Green Line E to Symphony or Orange Line to Massachusetts Ave.

ENTERTAINMENT & NIGHTLIFE

The Performing Arts

Dessert Alert

Finale is a little chain of "desserteries"—cafes that serve a mouthwatering variety of glorious desserts in elegant, romantic surroundings. Yes, it's a tad expensive. No, this is not a balanced meal. But the sweet tooths (sweet teeth?) who flock to Finale don't care. The original is in the Theater District at 1 Columbus Ave., in the pointy end of the Park Plaza Building (www.finaledesserts.com; ℭ **617/423-3184;** T: Green Line to Arlington). There's also a branch at 30 Dunster St., Harvard Square (ℭ **617/441-9797;** T: Red Line to Harvard). Finale also serves real food, such as salads and pizzas, but the desserts are the draw.

TD Garden This 19,600-seat facility is home to the Celtics (basketball), the Bruins (hockey), the circus (in Oct), ice shows (at least twice a year), and touring rock and pop artists of all stripes. Concerts at the Garden—"Gah-den," in Bostonian—are in the round or in the arena-stage format. 100 Legends Way (Causeway St.). www.tdgarden.com. ℭ **617/624-1000** (event info) or 800/745-3000 (Ticketmaster). T: Orange or Green Line to North Station.

Wilbur Theatre This historic Theater District venue (it opened in 1914) holds 1,200 for performances by big-name standup comics and touring musical acts. 246 Tremont St. (at Stuart St.). www.thewilburtheatre.com. ℭ **617/248-9700** or 800/745-3000 (Ticketmaster). T: Green Line to Boylston or Orange Line to Tufts Medical Center.

Long-Running Shows

The **Charles Playhouse,** 74 Warrenton St. (off Stuart St.), is home to two beloved long-running shows.

The off-Broadway sensation **Blue Man Group** ★ (www.blueman.com; ℭ **800/BLUE-MAN** [258-3626] or 617/426-6912) began selling out the theater's Stage I as soon as it arrived in 1995. The trio of cobalt-colored entertainers backed by a rock band uses music, percussion, food, and audience members in its ever-changing performances. It's not recommended for children under 8, but older kids will love it. Shows are usually at 8pm Tuesday through Thursday; 7 and 10pm Friday; 2, 5, and 8pm Saturday; and 2 and 5pm Sunday (with extra days and performances during the holidays and school vacations). Tickets are $49 and $73; student rush, when available, for $39 [cash only]) are sold at the box office and through **Ticketmaster** (ℭ **800/982-2787**).

No Smoking; No, Really

Massachusetts state law forbids smoking in all workplaces, including bars, nightclubs, and restaurants.

Shear Madness ★ (www.shearmadness.com; ℭ **617/426-5225**), downstairs on Stage II, is the longest-running nonmusical play in theater history. Since January 1980, the zany "comic murder mystery" has turned the stage into a unisex hairdressing salon—and crime scene. The show's never the same from one performance to the next; one of the original audience-participation productions, the play changes as spectator-investigators question suspects, reconstruct events, and then name the murderer. Performances are Tuesday through Friday at 8pm, Saturday at 6 and 9pm, and Sunday at 3 and 7pm. Tickets ($50, $38 AAA members, $25 student rush when available) are available online and at the box office.

THE BAR SCENE

Bostonians had some quibbles with the TV show *Cheers*, but no one complained that the concept of a neighborhood bar where everybody knows your name was implausible. The bar scene tends to be fairly insular—as a stranger, don't assume that you'll get a warm welcome (except at Cheers, which is full of tourists!). This is one area where you can and probably should judge a book by its cover: If you peek in and see people who look like you and your friends, give it a whirl.

Bars & Lounges

The Bar at Taj Boston ★   The Bar at the Ritz, this lovely space's predecessor, established it as *the* place to go for a classic martini. The cushy seating, crackling fire, impeccable service, and view of the Public Garden have made it a favorite with generations of Bostonians. Open Monday through Saturday 11:30am to 12:30am, Sunday noon to 11:30pm. In the Taj Boston hotel, 15 Arlington St. (at Newbury St.). ✆ **617/536-5700.** T: Green Line to Arlington.

The Beehive   This restaurant and lounge takes up a funky two-level space beneath the Boston Center for the Arts (p. 227). The Beehive schedules live music, usually jazz, every night. Early in the week, the crowd tends toward laid-back and local; weekends see a suburbanite see-and-be-seen scene. 541 Tremont St. (at Clarendon St.). www.beehiveboston.com. ✆ **617/423-0069.** T: Orange Line to Back Bay.

The Bristol Lounge ★★★   This is a perfect choice after the theater, after work, or after anything else. An elegant room with soft lounge chairs, a fireplace, and fresh flowers, it features a fabulous Viennese dessert buffet ($25) on Friday and Saturday from 9pm to midnight. There's live music every evening. Food is available until 11:30pm (Fri–Sat until 12:30am). In the Four Seasons Hotel, 200 Boylston St. (at Hadassah Way, btw. Arlington St. and Charles St. S.). ✆ **617/351-2037.** T: Green Line to Arlington.

Casablanca ★★   Students and professors jam this legendary Harvard Square watering hole, especially on weekends. You'll find an excellent jukebox, excellent Middle Eastern food, and excellent eavesdropping. 40 Brattle St. (btw. Brattle Sq. and Church St.), Cambridge. www.casablanca-restaurant.com. ✆ **617/876-0999.** T: Red Line to Harvard.

Cheers (Beacon Hill)   Originally the Bull & Finch Pub, this onetime neighborhood hangout has embraced its status as a TV icon. A copy of the bar from the set of the long-running sitcom makes a good photo backdrop, and the souvenir selection is impressive. There's food from 11am until late

The familiar exterior of the Beacon Hill Cheers.

evening. 84 Beacon St. (at Brimmer St.). www.cheersboston.com. ℂ **617/227-9605.** T: Green Line to Arlington.

Cheers (Faneuil Hall Marketplace) Blatantly but good-naturedly courting fans of the sitcom, this bar's interior is an exact replica of the *Cheers* TV set. It serves pub fare starting at noon Monday through Thursday, 11am on weekends, and plays dance music on weekend nights. You must be 21 to enter after 9pm. Memorabilia on display includes Sam Malone's Red Sox jacket. Bring a camera. Quincy Market Building, South Canopy, Faneuil Hall Marketplace. www.cheersboston.com. ℂ **617/227-0150.** T: Green or Blue Line to Government Center, or Orange Line to Haymarket.

DeLux Cafe ★★ One of the coolest places in the increasingly gentrified South End, the DeLux is the epitome of a classy dive. The funky decor, selection of microbrews, and veggie-friendly ethnic menu attract a cross-section of the neighborhood. Part of the appeal is the decor, a scrapbook of 20th-century pop culture (posters, photos, postcards, and such)—check out the Elvis shrine. 100 Chandler St. (at Clarendon St.). ℂ **617/338-5258.** T: Orange Line to Back Bay.

Eastern Standard A cavernous brasserie with a mile-long marble bar, Eastern Standard is an all-things-to-all-people destination. It serves food from early morning through late night, offers outdoor seating, and has a hopping bar scene every night during the week and almost all day on weekends. The specialty cocktails are numerous and diverse, and the bartenders know their way around the wine list. On Red Sox game nights, be prepared to stand. In the Hotel Commonwealth, 528 Commonwealth Ave. (at Kenmore St.). www.easternstandardboston.com. ℂ **617/532-9100.** T: Green Line B, C, or D to Kenmore.

Grafton Street Deftly accommodating party-hearty students and demanding Cantabrigians, this Harvard Square veteran is a classy watering hole with a superb beer selection. It's also a busy restaurant, but I prefer a snack or sandwich at the bar to a meal in the dining room. Open weeknights until 1am, weekends until 2am. 1230 Massachusetts Ave. (at Bow St.), Cambridge. www.graftonstreetcambridge.com. ℂ **617/497-0400.** T: Red Line to Harvard.

Grendel's Den ★ A vestige of prefranchise Harvard Square, this cozy subterranean space is *the* place to celebrate a 21st birthday. Recent grads and grad students dominate, but Grendel's has been so popular for so long (since 1971) that it also attracts millennials' parents. The food is tasty, with loads of vegetarian dishes, and the fireplace enhances the comfy atmosphere. 89 Winthrop St. (at John F. Kennedy St.), Cambridge. www.grendelsden.com. ℂ **617/491-1160.** T: Red Line to Harvard.

The Hong Kong This fun hangout is a retro Chinese restaurant on the first floor, a bar on the second floor, and a small dance club (starting at 11pm nightly) on the third floor. It's also the home of the scorpion bowl, a rum-based concoction that has contributed to the destruction of countless Ivy League brain cells. Nevertheless, you might see Harvard football players here. Never mind how I know. 1238 Massachusetts Ave. (at Bow St.), Cambridge. www.hongkongharvard.com. ℂ **617/864-5311.** T: Red Line to Harvard.

Miracle of Science Bar + Grill ★★ A stone's throw from both Central Square and the MIT campus, Miracle of Science is the perfect match for its hipster-geek neighbors. The friendly vibe and decent, if not huge, beer selection make it a popular after-work hangout. The kitchen serves three meals daily—perfect if you've been up all night writing code. The menu is on the chalkboard festooned with what you thought was the periodic table. 321 Massachusetts Ave. (at State St.), Cambridge. www.miracleofscience.us. ☎ **617/686-ATOM** (2866). T: Red Line to Central.

Radius The high-tech bar at this special-occasion restaurant offers almost everything the dining room does—the stylish crowd, the noise, the perfect martinis—without the sky-high food bill. The bar snacks are pricey but worth every penny. 8 High St. (off Summer St.). www.radiusrestaurant.com. ☎ **617/426-1234.** T: Red Line to South Station.

Silvertone Bar & Grill ★ One of the few real hangouts in the Downtown Crossing area, this tiny, subterranean bar attracts a noisy after-work crowd. The dining room is noted for reasonably priced comfort food (try the sublime macaroni and cheese). Closed Sunday. 69 Bromfield St. (off Tremont St.). www.silvertone downtown.com. ☎ **617/338-7887.** T: Red or Green Line to Park St.

Sonsie The Newbury Street version of a neighborhood watering hole, Sonsie is a chic restaurant with a trendy bar scene. Martinis are a specialty. Dress up a little if you want to fit in, or just enjoy the people-watching. 327 Newbury St. (off Hereford St.). www.sonsieboston.com. ☎ **617/351-2500.** T: Green Line B, C, or D to Hynes Convention Center.

Top of the Hub ★★★ Boasting a panoramic view of greater Boston, Top of the Hub is 52 stories above the city; the view is especially beautiful at sunset. The elegant lounge is a favorite with couples out on a big date or celebrating a special occasion. Take a turn around the dance floor, or just enjoy the live jazz and the late-night menu, which features superb desserts. Dress is casual but neat (no jeans). Open Sunday and Monday until midnight, Tuesday through Thursday until 12:30am, Friday and Saturday until 1am. Prudential Center, 800 Boylston St.

 Late-Night Bites

Boston and Cambridge aren't great places to satisfy late-night hunger, but you won't starve, either. Before midnight, especially on weekends, you even have a shot at a good meal: Hit a restaurant (see chapter 6) that keeps long hours. They include **Artú** in the North End; **Brasserie Jo, Davio's, Island Creek Oyster Bar, Jacob Wirth,** and **Jasper White's Summer Shack** in the Back Bay; and **Pizzeria Regina** and **Russell House Tavern** in Cambridge. After midnight or so, the pickings get slim. In the North End, **Bricco,** 241 Hanover St. (btw. Cross and Richmond sts.; www.bricco.com; ☎ **617/248-6800**), serves pizza at the bar until 2am Tuesday through Saturday, and **Caffé Pompei,** 280 Hanover St. (☎ **617/523-9438**), draws club-hoppers and neighborhood shift workers until

3:30am. A number of **Chinatown** restaurants don't close until 3 or 4am. Asking for "cold tea" might—*might*—get you a teapot full of beer.

The 24-hour "dining" scene relies heavily on the microwave ovens in convenience stores, with three notable exceptions. In the North End, **Bova's Bakery,** 134 Salem St. (www.bovasbakeryboston.com; ☎ **617/523-5601**), is a good place to soothe a sweet tooth. On the edge of Chinatown, not far from South Station, is the **South Street Diner,** 178 Kneeland St. (www.southstreetdiner.com; ☎ **617/350-0028**), a '50s-style joint with a wine-and-beer license and a jukebox. Or make like a college student and road-trip to the **International House of Pancakes** at 1850 Soldiers Field Rd. in Brighton (☎ **617/787-0533**).

www.topofthehub.net. ℂ **617/536-1775.** $24 minimum at tables after 8pm. T: Green Line to Copley or Green Line E to Prudential.

21st Amendment   A Beacon Hill standby, this tavern looks like a regular old neighborhood bar and restaurant—unless the Massachusetts legislature is in session. Then it turns into an annex of the State House, just across the street, and the entertainment value of the conversation jumps dramatically. (In case you were absent from class that day, the 21st Amendment repealed Prohibition.) 150 Bowdoin St. (off Beacon St.). www.21stboston.com. ℂ **617/227-7100.** T: Red Line to Park St.

Via Matta   This chic Italian restaurant's equally stylish bar and divine wine list make this a perfect place to recharge after an afternoon of hard work or hard shopping—Newbury Street is 3 blocks away. 79 Park Plaza (Arlington St. and St. James Ave.). www.viamattarestaurant.com. ℂ **617/422-0008.** T: Green Line to Arlington.

Sports Bars

Bleacher Bar ★   The location is irresistible: *under* the Fenway Park bleachers. The most coveted seats—there's a time limit on game days—are adjacent to a large outfield-facing window that's covered with one-way glass when the Red Sox are playing and otherwise open, weather permitting. (I'm told the urinals in the men's room enjoy the same view.) The unimaginative beer menu and decent food are reasonably priced, all things considered—and look, the outfield! 82A Lansdowne St. (btw. Brookline Ave. and Ipswich St.). www.bleacherbarboston.com. ℂ **617/262-2424.** T: Green Line B, C, or D to Kenmore.

Cask 'n Flagon ★   A long fly ball away from Fenway Park, "the Cask," which opened in 1969, is one of the best-known sports bars in this sports-mad city. It's much bigger than it looks from Brookline Avenue, but lines on game days are still comically long. The crowds watching major events on numerous TVs in the memorabilia-crammed bar are large and enthusiastic year-round. 62 Brookline Ave. (at Lansdowne St.). www.casknflagon.com. ℂ **617/536-4840.** T: Green Line B, C, or D to Kenmore.

The Fours ★★   One of Boston's best and best-known sports bars—*Sports Illustrated* says it's the best in the country—the Fours is across the street from the TD Garden. Festooned with sports memorabilia and TVs, it's a madhouse before Celtics and Bruins games—and a promising place to pick up an extra ticket. 166 Canal St. (off Causeway St.). www.thefours.com. ℂ **617/720-4455.** T: Green or Orange Line to North Station.

Game On! Sports Cafe   Yes, it's actually *in* Fenway Park, and no, you can't sneak into the stands. The overgrown sports bar and restaurant boasts the latest techno toys, including high-def TVs and a booming sound system, on two deafeningly loud levels of a onetime bowling alley. On game days, the line stretches out the door. 82 Lansdowne St. (off Brookline Ave.). www.gameonboston.com. ℂ **617/351-7001.** T: Green Line D to Fenway, or B, C, or D to Kenmore.

Jerry Remy's Sports Bar & Grill ★   As a player and broadcaster, Jerry Remy has made his living at Fenway Park for years. This cavernous establishment across the street proves his talent in another business. It's on the expensive side, but the food is tasty, and the sheer number of TVs means you won't miss a play. There's seating on the breezy patio in good weather. 1265 Boylston St. (at Ipswich St.). www.jerryremys.com. ℂ **617/236-7369.** T: Green Line B, C, or D to Kenmore, then 10-min. walk. Also at 250 Northern Ave. (off D St.), Seaport District. www.jerryremysseaport.com. ℂ **617/856-7369.** T: Silver Line SL1/SL2 bus to Silver Line Way.

Cocktail Culture

Like a lot of other trends, the cocktail craze arrived in Boston late and quickly took off. All over town, devoted bartenders and adventuresome drinkers unite to combat the cosmopolitanizing of the American libation. A nationally renowned example of the hard-core cocktail bar is **Drink** ★★, 348 Congress St. (near A St.; www.drinkfortpoint.com; ✆ **617/695-1806**; T: Red Line to South Station). Drink has no menu, just bartenders who chat with you about what you're in the mood for and create something on the spot. Sounds crazy, works perfectly. It's pricey, but you're paying for an evening's entertainment and an enthusiastic guide. Open daily at 4pm. Other destinations where "genever," "elderflower," and "Sazerac" are more than just crossword puzzle answers include **Eastern Standard** (p. 230); **Hungry Mother** (p. 181); and **Green Street,** 280 Green St. (off Magazine St., 1 block from Mass. Ave.; www.greenstreetgrill.com; ✆ **617/876-1655**; T: Red Line to Central).

Irish Bars

The Black Rose   Purists might sneer at the Black Rose's touristy location, but performers don't. Sing along with the authentic entertainment at this jampacked pub and restaurant at the edge of Faneuil Hall Marketplace. You might even be able to make out the tune on a fiddle over the din. 160 State St. (at Commercial St.). www.blackroseboston.com. ✆ **617/742-2286.** Cover $3–$8. T: Orange or Blue Line to State.

The Burren ★   The expatriate Irish community has found the Burren an antidote to homesickness since 1996. There's traditional music in the front room, acoustic rock in the large back room, and good food. Sunday's grunge brunch runs from 11am to 3pm. 247 Elm St. (at Chester St.), Somerville. www.burren.com. ✆ **617/776-6896.** Cover (back room only) $5–$10. T: Red Line to Davis.

The Grand Canal   This atmospheric pub and restaurant boasts an excellent beer selection, good food, a 12-foot TV screen, and Irish or rock cover bands or DJs Friday and Saturday nights. French windows that open to the street make it a popular after-work spot in good weather. The namesake waterway isn't in Venice—it connects Dublin to the Shannon River. 57 Canal St. (btw. New Chardon St. and Valenti Way). www.grandcanalboston.com. ✆ **617/523-1112.** Cover $5 for music. T: Green or Orange Line to Haymarket or North Station.

The Littlest Bar ★   A low-key Financial District hangout with a fine selection of beers and whiskeys, the Littlest Bar is not particularly little. (The nearby original location, however, was minuscule.) Prices are reasonable, the staff is friendly, and one table has a contraption that lets you pour your own beer—though you should really stick to Smithwick's and let the sure-handed bartenders handle the Guinness dispensing. 102 Broad St. (at Wharf St.). www.littlestbar.com. ✆ **617/542-8469.** T: Blue Line to Aquarium.

Mr. Dooley's Boston Tavern ★★   Sometimes an expertly poured Guinness is all you need. If one of the nicest bartenders in the city pours it, and you enjoy it in an authentically decorated room, so much the better. This Financial District spot offers a wide selection of imported beers on tap, live entertainment on weekend nights, and a menu of pub favorites at lunch and dinner. 77 Broad St. (at Custom House St.). www.somerspubs.com. ✆ **617/338-5656.** Cover (Fri–Sat only) $3–$5. T: Orange Line to State or Blue Line to Aquarium.

The Plough & Stars ★ Although it's tiny, the Plough is a huge presence on the local pub scene. A neighborhood hangout during the day, it's a hipster magnet at night. Live music is a regular feature and a big draw, and the kitchen serves lunch (except Mon), dinner, and weekend brunch. 912 Massachusetts Ave. (at Hancock St.), Cambridge. www.ploughandstars.com. *☎* **617/576-0032.** Cover $6 or less. T: Red Line to Central or Harvard.

Brewpubs

Boston Beer Works Across the street from Fenway Park, this cavernous space is frantic before and after Red Sox games. Don't plan to be able to hear anything your friends are saying. It has a full food menu and 16 brews on tap, including excellent bitters and ales. The sweet-potato fries make a terrific snack. Open daily from 11am to 1am. The **North Station** branch, near the TD Garden, is equally loud and has 11 pool tables. Open Sunday through Thursday from 11:30am to midnight, Friday and Saturday from 11:30am to 1am. 61 Brookline Ave. (at Lansdowne St.). www.beerworks.net. *☎* **617/536-BEER.** T: Green Line B, C, or D to Kenmore. 110 Canal St. (btw. Causeway St. and Valenti Way). *☎* **617/896-BEER.** T: Green or Orange Line to North Station.

Cambridge Brewing Company ★ CBC brews its own excellent beers, offering year-round and seasonal selections. The patio is especially pleasant in fine weather, but this place is perennially popular with the techy neighborhood crowd. 100 Kendall Sq., Building 100 (Hampshire St. and Cardinal Medeiros Ave.), Cambridge. www.cambrew.com. *☎* **617/494-1994.** T: Red Line to Kendall/MIT; 10-min. walk.

John Harvard's Brew House ★★ This subterranean Harvard Square hangout, the flagship of the regional chain, pumps out terrific English-style brews in a clublike setting, and prides itself on its food. The brewed-on-the-premises beer selection changes regularly. Order a sampler if you can't decide, and while

---

🎁 Make Some Noise in a Museum

The **Museum of Fine Arts,** 465 Huntington Ave. (www.mfa.org; *☎* **617/267-9300**), becomes a spirited nightlife destination on the first Friday of each month. It courts 20- and 30-somethings with live music, cocktails, food, and mingling; a visit is a good activity for couples and groups alike. MFA First Fridays run from 5:30 to 9:30pm. General admission to the museum ($20) includes the evening event. A similar program, the "Gardner After Hours" series (shown here) at the **Isabella Stewart Gardner Museum,** 280 The Fenway (www.gardnermuseum.org; *☎* **617/566-1401**), takes place on the third Thursday of each month. See p. 75 and p. 74 for museum listings.

you wait, try to find the sports figures in the stained-glass windows. Open Monday through Thursday from 11:30am to 12:30am, Friday and Saturday until 2am, Sunday until midnight, with food service until 11:30pm. 33 Dunster St. (off Mount Auburn St.), Cambridge. www.johnharvards.com. ✆ **617/868-3585.** T: Red Line to Harvard.

THE CLUB & MUSIC SCENE

The Boston-area club scene is multifaceted and constantly changing. As a rule, live music is more compelling than the dance-club scene by several orders of magnitude, but somewhere out there is a good time for anyone, regardless of age, musical taste, or budget. Check the sources listed in the introduction to this chapter for ideas; if you prefer to wait for inspiration to strike after you reach Boston, ask the staff at your hotel and check the daily *Globe,* the Friday *Herald,* the *Phoenix, Stuff@Night,* or the *Improper Bostonian.* If you run across a venue that shares your taste, follow it on Twitter and friend it on Facebook—you may get advance notice about special bookings and deals.

Dance clubs cluster in the Theater District and on nearby **Boylston Place,** off Boylston Street near Boston Common. The center of the local live-music universe is **Central Square** in Cambridge. Rowdy college bars and clubs abound near the intersection of Harvard and Brighton avenues in **Allston** (T: Green Line B to Harvard Ave.). That makes club-hopping easy, but it also means dealing with swarms of teenagers, students, and recent college grads. To steer clear, stick to slightly more upscale and less centrally located nightspots. If you do like teenagers (or you are one), seek out a place where admission is 18- or 19-plus. Policies change regularly, sometimes from night to night, so check ahead.

A night on the town in Boston and Cambridge is brief: Most bars close by 1am, clubs close at 2am, and the T shuts down between 12:30 and 1am. The drinking age is 21; a valid driver's license or passport is required as proof of age, and the law is strictly enforced, especially near college campuses.

Live Music

ROCK & POP

Great Scott ★★ Worth the trek to the student mecca of Allston, Great Scott is a friendly neighborhood bar that happens to be an excellent live-music venue. It books mostly rock bands, usually local, plus DJs. On a busy night you might see four different acts. Open daily from noon to 2am; live shows usually start at

---

⭕ Put Some Salsa on That

The hip-shaking party that is **Havana Club** ★ (www.havanaclubsalsa.com; ✆ **617/312-5550**) makes a great introduction to salsa dancing. Lessons—beginners are welcome—precede 4 hours of nonstop motion accompanied by a DJ or live band. The crowd consists mostly of dance fiends and curious novices of all ages and ethnicities. Havana Club takes place on Friday and Saturday from 10pm to 2am (lessons start at 9pm) at the Greek American Political Club, 288 Green St. (at River St., 1 block from Mass. Ave.), Central Square, Cambridge. Both nights are 21-plus, admission is $12, and the bar is cash only.

9pm. The bar accepts cash only. 1222 Commonwealth Ave. (at Harvard Ave.). www.great
scottboston.com. ☏ **617/566-9014.** Cover $5–$15 (usually $10 or less). T: Green Line B to Harvard Ave.

The Middle East ★★★   The best rock club in the area and one of the best
in New England, the Middle East books an impressive variety of progressive and
alternative artists in two rooms (upstairs and downstairs) every night. Showcasing
top local talent as well as bands with local roots and international reputations, it's
a popular hangout that gets crowded, hot, and *loud.* The club is the heart of a
complex comprising the **Corner,** a former bakery that features acoustic artists
most of the time and belly dancers on Sunday and Wednesday, and **ZuZu,** a
Middle Eastern restaurant that has its own music schedule and gallery space
with rotating art exhibits. Most
shows are 18-plus (ZuZu is
21-plus); the age of the crowd varies with the performer. 472–480 Massachusetts Ave. (at Brookline St.), Central
Sq., Cambridge. www.mideastclub.com.
☏ **617/864-3278** or 866/777-8932
(TicketWeb). Cover $8–$25 (usually $15
or less; ZuZu cover $5 Fri–Sat only). T:
Red Line to Central.

Rock of Ages

Bring your driver's license or passport when
you go club-hopping, no matter how old you
think you look—you must be 21 to drink
alcohol, and the law is strictly enforced.
Most bouncers won't risk a fine or license
suspension, especially at 18-plus shows.

Paradise Rock Club ★   Close
to the Boston University campus, the medium-size Paradise draws enthusiastic,
student-intensive crowds for top local rock and alternative performers. You might
also see national names who want a relatively small venue and others who aren't
ready to headline a big show on their own (lately, Death Cab for Cutie, Mayer

If you love your nightlife raucous, be sure to swing by the Middle East.

Hawthorne, and Garbage). Most shows are 18-plus. 967–969 Commonwealth Ave. (½ block from Pleasant St.). www.thedise.com. ℭ 617/562-8800 or 877/598-8497 for tickets. T: Green Line B to Pleasant St.

Toad ★★ 🥂   Essentially a bar with a stage, this narrow, high-ceilinged space draws a savvy three-generation clientele attracted by local big-name performers—rock, rockabilly, and sometimes blues—and the lack of a cover charge. Toad enjoys good acoustics but not much elbowroom—a plus when restless performers wander into the crowd. 1912 Massachusetts Ave. (at Porter Rd.), Cambridge. www. toadcambridge.com. ℭ 617/497-4950 (info line). T: Red Line to Porter.

T.T. the Bear's Place ★★   A mainstay of the Central Square live-music scene since it opened in 1985, "T.T.'s" has an uncanny knack for booking hot new talent. A friendly, no-frills spot, it generally attracts a young, savvy crowd, but 30-somethings will feel comfortable, too (especially at the twice-a-month '80s dance night). Bookings—three or four per night—range from cutting-edge alternative and roots music to up-and-coming indie-rock acts. New bands predominate early in the week, with more established artists on weekends. Open Sunday to Wednesday until 1am, Thursday through Saturday until 2am. 10 Brookline St. (at Mass. Ave.), Cambridge. www.ttthebears.com. ℭ 617/492-0082, 617/492-2327 (concert line), or 866/777-8932 (TicketWeb). Cover $5–$17. T: Red Line to Central.

ECLECTIC

Johnny D's Uptown Restaurant & Music Club ★★★ 🎁   This family-owned-and-operated establishment is one of the best places in the area for live music. It draws a congenial, low-key crowd for acts on international tours as well as artists who haven't been out of eastern Massachusetts. The music ranges from zydeco to rock, rockabilly to jazz, blues to ska. The veggie-friendly food's good, too; try the weekend jazz brunch. The club, which opened in 1969, is worth a long trip, but it's only two T stops past Harvard (about 15 min. at night). Most shows are 21-plus; some are all ages. Open Monday through Wednesday at 3:30pm, Thursday and Friday at 11am, and weekends at 8:30am (brunch until 2:30pm); food's available Sunday through Wednesday until 10pm, Thursday through Saturday until midnight. *Tip:* Make a dinner reservation, and you're guaranteed a seat for the show. 17 Holland St. (½ block from the center of Davis Sq.), Somerville. www.johnnyds.com. ℭ 617/776-2004 or 617/776-9667 (concert line). Cover $3–$30 (usually $8–$12). T: Red Line to Davis.

Lizard Lounge ★★   In the basement of the Cambridge Common restaurant, this way-cool, cozy-but-not-cramped room features well-known local rock, folk, and jazz musicians who play right out on the floor. It draws a postcollegiate-and-up crowd (Harvard Law School is next door) and serves food until 1am on weekends and midnight on weekdays. Shows daily; doors usually open at 7:30pm. Sunday is poetry night; Monday is open-mic night. 1667 Massachusetts Ave. (at Wendell St.), Cambridge. www.lizardloungeclub.com. ℭ 617/547-0759 (show listings) or 800/838-3006 (Brown Paper Tickets). Cover $5–$15. T: Red Line to Harvard.

The Red Room @ Cafe 939 ★ 🥂   Berklee College of Music students run and often perform at this all-ages club and coffeehouse (in other words, no alcohol), which holds 200 for live music most Wednesday through Saturday nights. It books professionals as well as students; popular acts often sell out. To buy advance tickets without a service fee, or to use your student discount, visit the Berklee Performance Center box office at 136 Massachusetts Ave. Closed

Sunday. 939 Boylston St. (off Hereford St.). www.cafe939.com. ✆ **617/747-2261** (tickets) or 617/747-6038 (coffeehouse). Tickets free to $20; most $12 or less. T: Green Line B, C, or D to Hynes Convention Center.

The Western Front A 30-ish friend raved about this legendary reggae club: "You're never the oldest one there." Open since 1968, it's a casual, friendly spot on a nondescript street south of Central Square. Integrated crowds flock here for world-beat music, blues, jazz, hip-hop, salsa, soca, and especially reggae. Open Thursday through Saturday from 8pm to 2am; live entertainment usually begins at 9pm. 343 Western Ave. (at Putnam Ave., 2 blocks from the Charles River), Cambridge. ✆ **617/492-7772.** Cover $5–$10. T: Red Line to Central.

FOLK

Boston is one of the only cities where folk musicians consistently sell out large venues that usually book rock and pop performers. If an artist you want to see is touring, check ahead for Boston-area dates.

The music listings in Thursday's *Globe* include information about **coffeehouses,** the area's main outlets for folk. One of the oldest (since 1966) and best known, the **Nameless Coffeehouse** (www.namelesscoffeehouse.org; ✆ **617/864-1630**), puts on a show every month or so in the First Parish Church, 3 Church St., Harvard Square, Cambridge. The streets around **Harvard Square** are another promising venue—Tracy Chapman is just one famous graduate of the scene.

Also see the **Lizard Lounge** (p. 237).

Club Passim ★★★ Passim has launched more careers than the mass production of acoustic guitars—Joan Baez, Shawn Colvin, and Tom Rush started out here, and this is where you'll find Arlo Guthrie and Ellis Paul when they're in town. In a basement on a Harvard Square side street, the legendary coffeehouse has nurtured new talent and showcased established musicians since 1958. Patrons who have been regulars since day one mix with college students. There's live music nightly, vegetarian food from **Veggie Planet** (p. 179) until 10:30pm, plus beer, wine, and, of course, coffee. Tuesdays without other bookings are open-mic nights. Open Sunday through Thursday from 11am to 11pm, Friday and Saturday from 11am to midnight. Most shows start at 8pm; on two-show nights, starting times are 7 and 10pm. 47 Palmer St. (at Church St.), Cambridge. www.passimcenter.org. ✆ **617/492-7679.** Cover $5–$40 (most shows $20 or less). T: Red Line to Harvard.

JAZZ & BLUES

Jazz Week (www.jazzboston.org) is a 10-day event in late April and early May at multiple venues. Surf around the website for an introduction to the local scene. The 6-day **Berklee Beantown Jazz Festival** (www.beantownjazzfestival.com), in late September, books top-notch artists into professional venues around Boston and draws tens of thousands of aficionados to Columbus Avenue in the South End for a full weekend afternoon of free outdoor music. Check the website for details.

On summer Thursdays at 6pm, the **Boston Harbor Hotel** (www.bhh.com; ✆ **617/491-2100**) sponsors free performances on the "Blues Barge," behind the hotel (p. 254).

Cantab Lounge ★ Follow your ears to this friendly neighborhood bar, which attracts a lively three-generation crowd. When the door swings open at night, deafening music—usually blues, bluegrass, rock, or jazz—spills out. Downstairs is the Cantab Underground, which has its own schedule, including a poetry slam every Wednesday. 738 Massachusetts Ave. (at Pleasant St.), Cambridge. www.cantab-lounge.com. ℂ **617/354-2685.** Cover $3–$10. T: Red Line to Central.

House of Blues Boston ★★ The House of Blues chain originated in Cambridge, and its Boston-area location is now this enormous space across the street from Fenway Park. It draws large crowds with a stellar slate of touring blues, rock, and pop acts; tickets are for general-admission standing room and for reserved seating. The kitchen serves above-average Southern food (show nights and during Red Sox home games 4–9pm; appetizers 9pm–midnight). 15 Lansdowne St. (btw. Brookline Ave. and Ipswich St.). www.houseofblues.com/boston. ℂ **888/693-2583** or 617/960-8358 (restaurant). Tickets $23–$55 (most shows $40 or less). T: Green Line B, C, or D to Kenmore.

Regattabar ★★ The Regattabar's selection of local and international jazz artists may be the best in the area—I'd give the edge to Scullers Jazz Club (see below), but check both schedules. Cassandra Wilson, the Django Reinhardt All-Stars, and Federico Aubele have appeared recently. The large third-floor room holds about 220. Buy tickets in advance or at the door at least 30 minutes before showtime. Open Tuesday through Saturday and some Sundays, with one or two performances per night. In the Charles Hotel, 1 Bennett St. (at Eliot St.), Cambridge. www.regattabarjazz.com. ℂ **617/661-5000** or 617/395-7757 for tickets. Tickets $15–$35. T: Red Line to Harvard.

Ryles Jazz Club ★ This popular spot, which doubles as a barbecue joint, books a wide variety of excellent blues, jazz, R&B, world beat, and Latin on the main stage and in the Ryles Dance Hall, upstairs. Sunday jazz brunch runs from 10am to 3pm. Open Tuesday through Sunday at 5pm; shows start between 9 and 10pm. 212 Hampshire St. (at Inman St.), Inman Square, Cambridge. www.ryles.com. ℂ **617/876-9330.** Cover for music $10–$20 (usually $15 or less). T: Red Line to Central, then 10-min. walk on Prospect St.

Scullers Jazz Club ★★★ Overlooking the Charles River, Scullers is a lovely, comfortable room with a top-notch sound system. The club, which opened in 1989, books acclaimed singers and instrumentalists—recent notables include Ben E. King, Linda Eder, Big Bad Voodoo Daddy, and the Manhattans. Patrons tend to be more hard-core than the crowds at the Regattabar (above), but it depends on who's performing. Scullers usually schedules two shows a night Tuesday through Saturday; the box office is open Monday through Saturday from 11am to 6pm. Ask about dinner packages ($62–$87 per person), which include preferred seating and a three-course meal. In the DoubleTree Suites by Hilton Boston hotel, 400 Soldiers Field Rd. (at Cambridge St.). www.scullersjazz.com. ℂ **617/562-4111.** Tickets $20–$50. Validated parking available.

Wally's Cafe ★★ This Boston institution, near a busy corner in the South End, opened in 1947. Its New Orleans–style all-about-the-music atmosphere draws a notably diverse crowd—black, white, straight, gay, affluent, indigent. Live jazz, by local ensembles, students and instructors from the Berklee College of Music, and the occasional regional or international star, starts every night at 9pm. Monday is blues night. Open daily until 1:30am. *Tip:* I can't promise anything, but big-name performers in town to play bigger venues have been known to turn up at Wally's afterward. 427 Massachusetts Ave. (off Columbus Ave.). www.wallyscafe.com. ℂ **617/424-1408.** No cover; 1-drink minimum. T: Orange Line to Massachusetts Ave.

Theme a Little Theme

The **Hard Rock Cafe,** 24 Clinton St. (at North St.; www.hardrock.com; ✆ **617/424-7625**), is a fun link in the fun chain—just ask the other tourists all around you. The memorabilia that covers the walls of this cavernous space across the street from Faneuil Hall Marketplace celebrates rock musicians, and the kid-friendly menu features salads, burgers, sandwiches, and barbecue.

Comedy Clubs

The **Wilbur Theatre** (p. 228) books high-profile comics on national tours, as well as music acts. The annual **Boston International Comedy & Movie Festival** (www.bostoncomedyfestival.com; ✆ **617/499-3380**) attracts big-name national performers, local up-and-comers, and films. The popular weeklong event takes place all over town in September; check ahead for schedules and venues.

The Comedy Studio ★★ 🎁 Nobody here is a sitcom star—yet. With a stellar reputation for searching out undiscovered talent, the no-frills Comedy Studio draws a savvy crowd of connoisseurs, college students, and network scouts. It's not just setup–punch line–laugh, either; sketches and improv spice up the standup. Shows are Tuesday ("Mystery Lounge," featuring magicians) through Sunday at 8pm. At the Hong Kong restaurant, 1238 Massachusetts Ave. (at Bow St.), Cambridge. www.thecomedystudio.com. ✆ **617/661-6507.** Cover $8–$12. T: Red Line to Harvard.

Improv Asylum Let the posters that catch your eye on the Freedom Trail draw you back to the North End later for raucous improv and sketch comedy in a subterranean setting. Performances are Tuesday through Sunday evenings and weekend afternoons, and buying tickets in advance is suggested. Recommended for people over 16; you must be 21 to buy alcohol. 216 Hanover St. (off Cross St.). www.improvasylum.com. ✆ **617/263-6887.** Tickets $15–$25; midnight shows and student performances $5–$10. T: Green or Orange Line to Haymarket.

ImprovBoston ★ 🖋 Founded in 1982, ImprovBoston presents pros and amateurs in two spaces—main stage and cabaret—and offers a lengthy list of classes. Standup, storytelling, and student showcases complement the improv and sketch comedy. The 6pm Saturday show is geared for families. Shows run Wednesday through Sunday, and the lobby bar serves beer and wine. 40 Prospect St. (off Mass. Ave.). www.improvboston.com. ✆ **617/576-1253.** Tickets free to $16 (most shows $10 and up). T: Red Line to Central.

Dance Clubs

Most clubs enforce a **dress code** that forbids athletic wear (including game jerseys), sneakers, jeans, Timberland boots, and ball caps—or some combination thereof—on everyone, as well as tank tops on men. Some places require that men wear a shirt with a collar, and a few require a jacket. Check ahead. Club listings in the *Improper Bostonian* and the *Phoenix* are good resources, but a savvy concierge is even better. *Tip:* While you're visiting websites, note that some clubs will let you put your name on the VIP list online. Can't hurt, might help.

The Estate A cavernous space with a balcony overlooking the large dance floor, the Estate attracts a lively 20-something crowd with well-known local DJs and an excellent sound system. The dress code is "dress like you mean it," which appears to equal collared shirts on men and something tight and black on women. The key to jumping the inevitable line is to reserve a table and look sharp. Open Thursday (gay night) through Saturday; check ahead for specifics. 1 Boylston Place (off Boylston St., near Tremont St.). www.theestateboston.com. ✆ **617/351-7000.** Cover $20–$25. T: Green Line to Boylston.

Royale Boston ★★ This onetime hotel ballroom boasts excellent house and techno DJs, a huge dance floor, and a U-shaped balcony that's perfect for checking out the action below. Live music, booked by a New York–based promoter noted for its rock acts, takes good advantage of the sight lines. Check ahead for the schedule of all-ages shows in the early evening. In the Courtyard Boston Downtown/Tremont hotel, 279 Tremont St. (½ block from Stuart St.). www.royaleboston.com. ✆ **617/338-7699.** Cover $15–$25. T: Green Line to Boylston or Orange Line to Tufts Medical Center.

THE GAY & LESBIAN SCENE

The first state to legalize same-sex marriage, Massachusetts enjoys a well-deserved reputation for open-mindedness. Boston and Cambridge—especially the places where out-of-towners are likely to spend time—are gay-friendly destinations. The South End is the area's highest-profile gay neighborhood, and lesbians gravitate toward Porter Square in Cambridge and Jamaica Plain in Boston, but LGBT Bostonians and Cantabrigians live, work, and play all over their respective cities. Throughout eastern Massachusetts, gay couples are no longer remarkable, and families with two mommies or two daddies fit right in. When you're out on the town, do remember that over-the-top PDA probably won't win you many friends—but the same is true for handsy straight couples. Paradoxically, the long-term result of all this inclusion is that bricks-and-mortar non-nightlife businesses catering more or less exclusively to gay and lesbian customers are vanishing.

Bars & Clubs

In addition to the clubs listed here, some mainstream venues schedule a weekly gay night. The particulars here are current at press time, but always check ahead.

Rumor, 100 Warrenton St. (www.rumorboston.com; ✆ **617/422-0045**), features Latin music and the occasional drag show on Wednesday; the **Estate** (above) plays host to **Glamlife** on Thursday; and the **House of Blues Boston** (p. 239) is home to Epic Saturdays. Also check the website of party promoter Chris Harris Presents (www.chrisharrispresents.com).

The **Midway Cafe,** 3496 Washington St., Jamaica Plain (www.midway cafe.com; ✆ **617/524-9038**), schedules women's dance night, featuring "Queer-aoke," every Thursday.

On the first Friday of each month, the Boston chapter of **Guerrilla Queer Bar** (http://bostonguerrilla.com) stages a flash mob–style takeover of a straight bar just for the night. Visit the website to sign up for a notification e-mail. The first and third Sundays of the month mean a men's dance party at **ZuZu** in Cambridge (p. 236).

For up-to-date listings, check the print and online versions of *Bay Windows* (www.baywindows.com), the *Improper Bostonian* (www.improper.com), and the *Phoenix* (www.bostonphoenix.com). Worthwhile websites include www.edge boston.com, www.queeragenda.org, http://boston.gaycities.com, and www.dyke night.com.

Club Café ★★ This fun South End spot draws a chic crowd of men and women for conversation (the noise level is reasonable), dining, live music in the front room, and video entertainment in the back room. Thursday is the busiest night. Open daily until 2am; the restaurant serves Sunday brunch, dinner nightly, and a light lounge menu daily starting at noon. 209 Columbus Ave. (at Berkeley St.). www.clubcafe.com. ℂ **617/536-0966.** T: Green Line to Arlington or Orange Line to Back Bay.

Fritz This popular South End hangout is a neighborhood favorite that serves brunch on weekends. The friendly crowd bonds over sports on the plasma satellite TVs. In the Chandler Inn Hotel, 26 Chandler St. (at Berkeley St.). www.fritzboston.com. ℂ **617/482-4428.** T: Orange Line to Back Bay.

Jacque's Cabaret ★ The only drag venue in town, Jacque's draws a friendly crowd of gay and straight patrons who mix with the "girls" and sometimes engage in a shocking activity—that's right, disco dancing. The eclectic entertainment includes live music (on weekends), performance artists, and, of course, drag shows. Open daily from noon to midnight; no credit cards. 79 Broadway (at Piedmont St.), Bay Village. www.jacquescabaret.com. ℂ **617/426-8902.** Cover $6–$10. T: Green Line to Arlington.

Machine The large dance floor sets Machine apart from the rest of Boston's gay nightlife destinations. Be in the mood to move or to play pool (in a separate room). Thursday is karaoke night. Upstairs is the **Ramrod** (www.ramrod-boston. com; ℂ **617/266-2986**), a leather bar with a strict dress code for the back room. 1254 Boylston St. (at Ipswich St.). www.machine-boston.com. ℂ **617/536-1950.** Cover $10. T: Green Line B, C, or D to Kenmore, then a 10-min. walk.

Paradise Not to be confused with the Boston rock standby (well, you can, but it won't be quite the same experience), this club near MIT attracts an all-ages male crowd. There's a stripper every evening. Monday is karaoke night. Open Sunday through Wednesday until 1am, Thursday through Saturday until 2am. 180 Massachusetts Ave. (at Albany St.), Cambridge. www.paradisecambridge.com. ℂ **617/868-3000.** T: Red Line to Central, then a 10-min. walk.

Rise The only official after-hours club in Boston, Rise attracts both gay and straight patrons who don't want the party to end. The crowd is 18-plus; the two-level venue is alcohol-free; the music is house, electronic, techno, and anything else the DJs think will keep the energy high. Rise is technically members only— check the website for instructions on visiting as a guest. Open Saturday and Sunday, plus some Fridays, 1 to 6am. 306 Stuart St. (at Columbus Ave.). www.riseclub. us. ℂ **617/423-7473.** T: Green Line to Arlington.

Performing Arts & More

LGBT artists are thoroughly integrated into Boston's cultural scene, and mainstream companies and groups schedule gay-themed works and performances with some regularity. The **Boston Center for the Arts** (p. 227) is the most prominent but far from the only institution worth checking out—remember, no less a talent than Michael Tilson Thomas got his big break with the Boston Symphony

Orchestra. The highest-profile gay musical groups in the area are the **Boston Gay Men's Chorus** (www.bgmc.org; ✆ 617/542-7464) and the LGBT-and-friends chorus **Coro Allegro** (www.coroallegro.org; ✆ 617/236-4011).

Boston Pride (www.bostonpride.org) and the **Aids Action Committee** (www.aac.org) are good resources in searching for activities and events, including volunteer opportunities and fancy fundraisers, year-round. If you're athletically inclined, visit www.pridesportsboston.com, or check the "Community" page on the Fritz sports bar's website (see above) for information about the Boston area's gay sports leagues. They include everything from basketball and rugby to bowling and darts.

ALTERNATIVE ENTERTAINMENT

Movies

Free Friday Flicks at the Hatch Shell ★★★ (http://boston.cbslocal.com/flicks; ✆ 617/787-7200) are family-friendly movies that play on a large screen in the amphitheater on the Esplanade. On the lawn in front of the Hatch Shell, hundreds of people picnic until the sky grows dark and the credits roll. The films tend toward recent releases (no big thrill for anyone with young kids and/or decent cable), but the movie is only part of the experience. *Tip:* Bring sweaters in case the breeze off the river grows chilly.

Two superb local revival houses feature lectures and live performances in addition to foreign and classic films: the **Brattle Theatre,** 40 Brattle St., Cambridge (www.brattlefilm.org; ✆ 617/876-6837; T: Red Line to Harvard), and the **Coolidge Corner Theatre,** 290 Harvard St., Brookline (www.coolidge.org; ✆ 617/734-2500; T: Green Line C to Coolidge Corner). The Coolidge also schedules midnight shows. Classic and foreign films are the tip of the iceberg at the quirky **Harvard Film Archive,** 24 Quincy St., Cambridge (http://hcl.harvard.edu/hfa; ✆ 617/495-4700; T: Red Line to Harvard), which also shows student films.

For first-run independent and foreign films, head to the **Kendall Square Cinema,** 1 Kendall Sq., Cambridge (www.landmarktheatres.com; ✆ 617/499-1996; T: Red Line to Kendall/MIT). The best movie theater in the immediate Boston area, it offers discounted parking in the adjoining garage. First- and second-run current releases at discount prices are the usual fare at the **Somerville Theater,** 55 Davis Sq. (www.somervilletheatreonline.com; ✆ 617/625-5700; T: Red Line to Davis), which schedules occasional concerts, too. For mainstream releases, head to the 19-screen **AMC Loews Boston Common,** 175 Tremont St. (at Avery St.; www.amctheatres.com; ✆ 888/262-4386 [show times] or 617/423-5801; T: Green Line to Boylston), which has stadium seating, digital sound, and 3D capability.

Coffeehouses

As in most other American cities, you won't get far without seeing a Starbucks. For coffee and hanging out, the Boston area offers plenty of less generic options. Many are in the North End (see chapter 6); other favorites are listed here. Open hours are generally long and loitering is encouraged—these are good places to bring your laptop or journal.

Algiers Café & Restaurant ★   Middle Eastern food and music, plain and flavored coffees, and the legendary atmosphere make this a classic Harvard Square hangout. Your "quick" snack or drink (try the mint coffee) might turn into a longer stay as the sociologist in you studies the would-be intellectuals. This is a good spot to eavesdrop while you sample terrific soups, sandwiches, homemade sausages, falafel, and hummus. 40 Brattle St. (btw. Brattle Sq. and Church St.), Cambridge. ℭ **617/492-1557.** T: Red Line to Harvard.

BeanTowne Coffee House & Cafe   A splash of the bohemian in a buttoned-up office-retail complex, this is a good stop before or after a film at the Kendall Square Cinema. Order from the extensive beverage menu or the tempting selection of soups, salads, and sandwiches. There's only one problem with this little place—it's too popular. If a table empties, move in fast. It's closed weekends. 1 Kendall Sq. (off Broadway near Cardinal Medeiros Ave.), Cambridge. www.bean townecambridge.com. ℭ **617/621-7900.** T: Red Line to Kendall.

Boston Common Coffee Co. ★★   Most of the other coffee places in the North End are right out of a Scorsese movie. This is a yuppier caffeine-delivery system, with free wireless Internet and a menu of delectable baked goods and hearty sandwiches. It seems a bit incongruous at first, but it's always crowded. The **Downtown Crossing** branch, 515 Washington St. (at West St.; ℭ **617/542-0595**), is popular with shoppers and Emerson College students. The **Financial District** location, 10 High St., off Summer Street (ℭ **617/695-9700**), is frantic on weekdays and closed on weekends. 97 Salem St. (off Parmenter St.). www.boston commoncoffee.com. ℭ **617/725-0040.** T: Green or Orange Line to Haymarket.

Equal Exchange Cafe   Virtuous and delicious, this sunny little spot near the TD Garden serves fair-trade coffee, tea, and hot chocolate. The veggie-friendly food and sweets come from several local vendors, and the drinks from the well-known Equal Exchange co-op, which is based in a Boston suburb. Wi-Fi is free, but seating is scarce at busy times. Open weekdays 7am to 7pm, Saturday 9am to 5pm. 226 Causeway St. (off N. Washington St.). www.equalexchangecafe.com. ℭ **617/372-8777.** T: Green or Orange Line to North Station.

Thinking Cup   Across the street from Boston Common, Thinking Cup serves cult favorite Stumptown coffee, organic teas, tasty sandwiches, and house-made baked goods. The cozy space, decorated with black-and-white photos and vintage newspaper headlines, is a magnet for students and instructors from nearby Emerson College and Suffolk University. 165 Tremont St. (near Avery St.). www.thethinking cup.com. ℭ **617/482-5555.** T: Green Line to Boylston.

1369 Coffee House ★   A long, narrow room with a colorful clientele, the 1369 offers excellent baked goods, a dazzling selection of premium teas and coffees, and great people-watching. There's also a light lunch menu and a pleasant outdoor seating area. The equally enjoyable but less convenient original location is at 1369 Cambridge St. (at Springfield St.), Inman Square (ℭ **617/576-1369**). 757 Massachusetts Ave. (at Pleasant St.), Central Sq., Cambridge. www.1369coffeehouse.com. ℭ **617/576-4600.** T: Red Line to Central.

Trident Booksellers & Café ★★   This Back Bay institution is more than just a cafe. The veggie-friendly menu (including breakfast served all day) complements the free Wi-Fi access, thoughtful book selection, and casual, New Age-y atmosphere. There's patio seating in fine weather. Open 8am to midnight daily.

Alternative Entertainment

ENTERTAINMENT & NIGHTLIFE

338 Newbury St. (btw. Hereford St. and Mass. Ave.). www.tridentbookscafe.com. © **617/267-8688.** T: Green Line B, C, or D to Hynes Convention Center.

Literary Readings & Lectures

The Thursday *Globe* and the *Improper Bostonian* are the best printed sources for listings of readings, lectures, and talks on a wide variety of subjects, often at colleges, libraries, and museums. Many are free or charge a small fee.

Most of the bookstores listed in chapter 7 sponsor author readings; check their websites or in-store displays. Also check the schedules of the **Celebrity Series of Boston** (p. 226), the **John F. Kennedy Jr. Forum** at Harvard's Institute of Politics (http://forum.iop.harvard.edu; © **617/495-1380**), and the **Ford Hall Forum at Suffolk University** (www.fordhallforum.org; © **617/557-2007**).

Pool & Bowling

These establishments aren't the divey hangouts of your misspent youth; they're upscale destinations with prices to match. For pool, expect to pay at least $12 an hour on weekend evenings, with weekday and daytime discounts. Bowlers can count on parting with at least $6 per person per game.

Flat Top Johnny's ★★   I blink like a geisha every time I walk in here—I can't believe such a cool, funky spot is this close to MIT. A spacious, loud room with an impressive beer selection and 12 red-topped pool tables, Flat Top Johnny's has a casual neighborhood feel despite being in an office-retail complex. Open Monday through Wednesday 4pm to 1am, Thursday and Friday noon to 1am, weekends 3pm to 1am. 1 Kendall Sq. (off Broadway near Cardinal Medeiros Ave.), Cambridge. www.flattopjohnnys.com. © **617/494-9565.** T: Red Line to Kendall/MIT.

Jillian's Boston ☺   The 70,000-square-foot Jillian's complex, which anchors the Lansdowne Street strip, offers billiards on 35 tables, an upscale bowling alley (part of the Lucky Strike Lanes chain), a spring break–themed dance club (Tequila Rain), tons of plasma TVs, five full bars, and two restaurants. If you can't scare up some fun here, check your pulse. Open Monday through Saturday from 11am to 2am, Sunday from noon to 2am. Children under 18 accompanied by an adult are admitted before 8pm Monday through Thursday; on weekends after 8pm, Jillian's is 21-plus. 145 Ipswich St. (at Lansdowne St.). www.jilliansboston.com or www.luckystrikeboston.com. © **617/437-0300.** T: Green Line B, C, or D to Kenmore.

Kings ★   In a former movie theater across from the Hynes Convention Center, Kings is a popular destination to bring a date, and it attracts the occasional pro athlete or celebrity. It has 20 bowling lanes (four of them private) and an eight-table billiards room. It's open Monday through Thursday 3pm to 2am, Friday through Sunday 11:30am to 2am; after 6pm, patrons must be at least 21. 50 Dalton St. (at Scotia St., ½ block from Boylston St.). www.backbaykings.com. © **617/266-2695.** T: Green Line B, C, or D to Hynes Convention Center.

SPECTATOR SPORTS

Boston has a well-deserved reputation as a great sports town. Purists know that "Titletown" refers exclusively to Green Bay, Wisconsin, but giddy Bostonians point to the recent successes of the Red Sox, Celtics, Bruins, and New England Patriots in staking their city's claim to the nickname. Boston fans are also passionate about college sports, particularly hockey, in which the Division I schools are fierce rivals.

Tickets for pro teams can be tough or impossible to get, but before you resort to paying a reseller or scalper, try the following: Ask the **hotel concierge** for suggestions, sign up for **TixList** (www.tixlist.com), and visit the **team website** to see whether season ticket-holders' returns are available to the public. Then grit your teeth and check **StubHub** (www.stubhub.com; ☏ **866/788-2482**) and **Ace Ticket** (www.aceticket.com/boston; ☏ **800/697-3287** or 617/783-3333)—or, if you're feeling lucky and don't mind the possibility of being scammed, **Craigslist.**

Beyond the "big four" professional sports and dozens of college options, several lower-profile pro franchises call the Boston area home. Major League Soccer's **New England Revolution** (www.revolutionsoccer.net; ☏ **877/438-7387** or 508/543-8200) plays at Gillette Stadium on Route 1 in Foxboro from March through October. Tickets cost $22 to $44 and are available through **Ticketmaster** (www.ticketmaster.com; ☏ **800/745-3000**).

The **Boston Cannons** (www.bostoncannons.com; ☏ **617/746-9933**) of Major League Lacrosse play at Harvard Stadium from late April through mid-August. Tickets cost $16 and $26 and are available through **Ticketmaster** (www.ticketmaster.com; ☏ **800/745-3000**).

The **Boston Breakers** of Women's Professional Soccer (www.bostonbreakers soccer.com; ☏ **781/619-9339**) play at Dilboy Stadium, off Route 16 in suburban Somerville, from May through July. Tickets cost $12 adults, $10 children 5 to 17, free for children 4 and under. Buy tickets through the website.

Pro & College Sports

BASEBALL

No other experience in sports matches watching a **Boston Red Sox** game at legendary **Fenway Park ★★★**, which celebrated its centennial in 2012. After an 86-year drought, the Sox won the 2004 World Series, and the baseball world was still pinching itself when the team brought home the 2007 crown. Fenway consistently sells out, and tickets remain a precious commodity, sky-high prices notwithstanding.

The season runs from early April to early October (later if the team makes the playoffs). The quirkiness of the oldest park in the major leagues, rich with history and atmosphere, only adds to the mystique. Most seats are narrow and uncomfortable, but also gratifyingly close to the field. A hand-operated scoreboard fronts the 37-foot left-field wall, or "Green Monster." Watch carefully during a pitching change—the left fielder might suddenly disappear into a door in the wall to get out of the sun.

One of the most imaginative management teams in baseball strives to make visiting Fenway worth the big bucks. New sections of seats keep cropping up in previously unused areas of the ballpark, notably including the section *above* the Green Monster. Just outside the park, Yawkey Way turns into a sort of carnival midway for ticket-holders before games, with concession stands, live music, and other diversions. One good stop is the **Xfinity Zone**—sure, Comcast is promoting its telecom products, but it's also offering free long-distance phone calls and Internet access, HD TVs showing Red Sox programming, and, best of all on a steamy day, air-conditioning.

Practical concerns: Compared with its modern brethren, Fenway is tiny. Tickets are the most expensive in the majors—a few upper bleacher seats go for $12, but most are in the $30-to-$99 range, with the best dugout boxes topping $300, and that's *if* you pay face value. They go on sale in December; try to order early. Given a choice between seats in a low-numbered grandstand section—say, 10 or below—and in the bleachers, go for the bleachers. They can get rowdy during night games, but the view is better from there than from deep right field. "Monster" seats cost $165, but they're so popular that they're sold by lottery in batches throughout the season; check the website. A limited number of same-day standing-room tickets ($20–$35) are available before each game, and fans sometimes return presold tickets, especially if a rainout causes rescheduling. It can't hurt to check, particularly if the team isn't playing well; cross your fingers and visit the ticket office. ***Tip:*** The Game Day Ticket Sales office, near Gate E on Lansdowne Street, offers tickets that went unsold for some reason. The doors open 2 hours before game time; lining up is permitted 3 hours before that (but not earlier).

The **Fenway Park ticket office** (www.redsox.com; 🕾 **888/REDSOX6;** T: Green Line B, C, or D to Kenmore, or D to Fenway) is at 4 Yawkey Way, near the corner of Brookline Avenue. Tickets for people with disabilities and in no-alcohol sections are available. Smoking is not allowed in the park.

BASKETBALL

The **Boston Celtics** raised their 17th National Basketball Association championship banner to the rafters of the TD Garden in 2008 after a 22-year dry spell. The team's rejuvenation had made it madly popular even before that triumph, but you can sometimes land surprisingly good (and pricey) seats without much notice. The Celtics play from early October until at least mid-April (later if they make the playoffs). When a top contender or a star player is visiting, getting

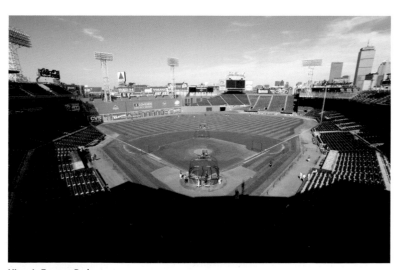

Historic Fenway Park.

Fenway Park tours (www.redsox.com/tours; ✆ **617/226-6666**) take visitors around the legendary ballpark. This is an excellent alternative if your budget or schedule doesn't allow for attending a game. Depending on what's going on at the park, the 50-minute tour may include a walk on the warning track, a stop in the press box, and a visit to the Red Sox Hall of Fame. During the season, tours start on the hour daily from 9am to 5pm (or 3 hr. before game time, whichever is earlier). There are no tours on holidays or before day games. In the winter, hours are shorter and tours may be truncated because of construction (but also cheaper than in the summer); check ahead to avoid disappointment. Admission is $16 for adults, $14 for seniors, $12 for students, active-duty military, and children 3 to 15. Advance individual sales aren't available.

tickets is especially tough. Prices are as low as $10 for some games and top out around $600 (more for floor seats). For information, call the **Garden** (www.nba.com/celtics; ✆ **617/624-1000**); for tickets, contact **Ticketmaster** (www.ticketmaster.com; ✆ **800/745-3000**). To reach the Garden, take the MBTA Green or Orange Line or commuter rail to North Station. *Note:* Spectators may not bring any large bags, including backpacks and briefcases, into the arena.

FOOTBALL

The **New England Patriots** (www.patriots.com; ✆ **800/543-1776**) were playing to standing-room-only crowds even before they won three Super Bowls in 4 years (2002, 2004, and 2005). The Pats play from August through December or January at Gillette Stadium on Route 1 in Foxboro, about a 45-minute drive south of Boston. Tickets ($65–$185) sell out well in advance, often as part of season-ticket packages. Call or check the website for information on individual ticket sales and resales, as well as public-transit options.

Boston College is the state's only Division I-A team. The Eagles, who compete in the Atlantic Coast Conference, play at Alumni Stadium in Chestnut Hill (www.bceagles.com; ✆ **617/552-4622**). The area's FCS (formerly Division I-AA) team is Ivy League power **Harvard University,** Harvard Stadium, North Harvard Street, Allston (www.gocrimson.com; ✆ **617/495-2211**).

HOCKEY

Tickets to see the 2011 Stanley Cup champion **Boston Bruins,** one of the NHL's original six teams, are expensive ($25–$340) but worth it for hard-core fans. For information, call the **TD Garden** (www.bostonbruins.com; ✆ **617/624-1000**); for tickets, contact **Ticketmaster** (www.ticketmaster.com; ✆ **800/745-3000**). To reach the Garden, take the MBTA Green or Orange Line or commuter rail to North Station. *Note:* Spectators may not bring large bags, including backpacks and briefcases, into the arena.

Budget-minded fans who don't have their hearts set on seeing a pro game will be pleasantly surprised by the quality of local **college hockey ★**. Even for sold-out games, standing-room tickets are usually available the night of the game. The local teams regularly hit the national rankings; they include **Boston College,** Conte Forum, Chestnut Hill (www.bceagles.com; ✆ **617/552-4622**);

Boston University, Agganis Arena, 928 Commonwealth Ave. (www.goterriers. com; ☏ **617/353-4628** or 800/745-3000 [Ticketmaster]); **Harvard University,** Bright Hockey Center, North Harvard Street, Allston (www.gocrimson.com; ☏ **617/495-2211**); and **Northeastern University,** Matthews Arena, St. Botolph Street (www.gonu.com; ☏ **617/373-4700**). These four are the Beanpot schools, whose men's teams play a tradition-steeped tournament on the first two Mondays of February at the TD Garden. Women's games don't normally sell out.

HORSE RACING

Suffolk Downs ★, 111 Waldemar Ave., off Route 1A, East Boston (www. suffolkdowns.com; ☏ **617/567-3900;** T: Blue Line to Suffolk Downs, then take shuttle bus or walk 10 min.), is one of the best-run smaller tracks in the country. The legendary Seabiscuit raced here; a marker commemorates his storied career. The live racing season runs from May to November; post time is 12:45pm. The track offers extensive simulcasting options day and night year-round. General admission and general parking for live racing are free. **Note:** The state recently approved casino gambling, which should mean higher purses even if Suffolk Downs doesn't become a slots-and-table-games destination.

Annual Events

BOSTON MARATHON

Every year on Patriots' Day—the third Monday in April—the **Boston Marathon** ★★★ rules the roads from suburban Hopkinton to Copley Square in Boston. Cheering fans line the entire route. An especially nice place to watch is tree-shaded Commonwealth Avenue between Kenmore Square and Mass. Ave., but

The Head of the Charles Regatta.

you'll be in a crowd wherever you stand. The finish line is on Boylston Street in front of the Boston Public Library. For information about watching, ask the staff at your hotel or check the daily papers. For information about qualifying as a runner, contact the **Boston Athletic Association** (www.bostonmarathon.org; ✆ **617/236-1652**).

GOLF TOURNAMENTS

Over Labor Day weekend, the PGA Tour visits the Tournament Players Club of Boston, which is actually in suburban Norton (www.thetpcofboston.com; ✆ **508/285-3200**), for the **Deutsche Bank Championship.** Visit www.deutsche bankchampionship.com or www.pgatour.com for more information. The senior women on the **Legends Tour** (www.thelegendstour.com) stop at Plymouth's **Pinehills Golf Club** (www.pinehillsgolf.com; ✆ **508/209-3000**) in September. Aside from the pro tours, the *Globe* and *Herald* regularly list numerous amateur events for fun and charity.

HEAD OF THE CHARLES

On the third or fourth weekend of October, the **Head of the Charles Regatta ★** (www.hocr.org; ✆ **617/868-6200**) attracts more rowers than any other crew event in the country. Some 4,000 oarsmen and -women of all ages race against the clock for 3 miles from the Charles River basin to the Eliot Bridge in west Cambridge. Hundreds of thousands of spectators line the riverbanks, socializing—it's hard to overstate just how preppy the whole event is—and occasionally watching the action.

9

WHERE TO STAY

Boston hotels are convenient—the central city is so small that nearly every location is a good one—but generally expensive. Lodgings reflect the city's historic character: Decades- and even century-old properties compete with establishments on the cutting edge of 21st-century tech. Rooms vary in size from tiny to enormous. The average room rate is nearly $200, but bargains are often available, particularly at slow times. Including Cambridge and Brookline in your search increases your options. With enough planning and a little luck, you'll almost certainly find a place that suits your needs and taste. At busy times, though, you may need to increase your budget.

best BETS

o **Best for Families:** The **DoubleTree Suites by Hilton Boston** offers two rooms for the price of one, with two TVs and a refrigerator, and the property has a nice pool. The location, straddling Boston and Cambridge, is especially good if you're driving from the west—you leave the turnpike before downtown traffic shatters the peace in the back of the minivan. See p. 280.

o **Best Value:** The **Newbury Guest House** is ideal for travelers who want to take advantage of the Back Bay's excellent shopping. You can't beat the location, right on lively Newbury Street, and room rates even include breakfast. Motorists will want to check out the **MidTown Hotel,** which offers comfortable, no-frills rooms and the cheapest guest parking in the Back Bay. See p. 278 and 278.

o **Best Splurge:** The **Boston Harbor Hotel** has it all: huge rooms, magnificent views, impeccable service, luxurious health club and spa, terrific pool, and a great location adjacent to a marina where you can moor your yacht. Across the river, Cambridge's **Charles Hotel** offers a similar combination of amenities, location, and pampering service (though without the boat accommodations). See p. 254 and 281.

o **Most Romantic:** The intimate atmosphere and elegant furnishings make a suite at the **Eliot Hotel** a great spot for a rendezvous. If you and your beloved need some time apart, close the French doors and maintain eye contact while in separate rooms. In Cambridge, the luxurious rooms at the **Hotel Veritas** feel cozy, not cramped—perfect for cuddling. See p. 270 and 282.

Price Categories	
Very Expensive	$326 and up
Expensive	$226–$325
Moderate	$151–$225
Inexpensive	Under $150

PREVIOUS PAGE: **The Four Seasons Hotel.**

WHAT YOU'LL really PAY

The prices quoted here are rack rates, the maximum a hotel charges. You will probably not pay that much in the Boston area unless you travel at the height of foliage season or during a busy college graduation period. You can typically find deals when booking through the major discounters (Priceline, Hotels.com, Expedia, and Travelocity). During slow times, it's often possible to land a room at an expensive property for the same rate you'd ordinarily pay at a less pricey one. Rack rates at the Lenox Hotel start at $215, for example, but in February 2012, a cursory search of the usual Web discount sites revealed that rooms were available for as much as $98 less.

If you're the gambling type, you can bid for a room on Priceline or Hotwire. In late October 2011—the tail end of foliage season—rooms at the Hyatt Regency Cambridge, where rack rates start at $179, were going for about $100 on Priceline.

Sometimes all you have to do is contact the hotel directly and negotiate. Just by asking, you may be able to make a deal with a reservations clerk to match or beat a price that's available through a discount website.

Another possibility is daily-deal sites like Groupon, LivingSocial, and the like. Hotels use them to move inventory at

slow times, so this is almost exclusively an off-season option.

And remember to check hotel websites for special offers. The Colonnade Hotel Boston offers a 2-night winter weekend deal that lets guests pay the Friday evening temperature in dollars for their room that night—in other words, 32°F at 5pm, $32 for your first night in the room (plus the standard rate for Sat night).

Note: Quoted discount rates almost never include hotel tax. Unless otherwise specified, they don't include breakfast or parking.

- **Best Service:** The **Four Seasons Hotel** is tops not just in Boston but in all of New England. The hotel's your-wish-is-my-command service—which applies to both people and their animal companions—isn't the only reason for that status, but it helps. See p. 271.

- **Best for Business Travelers:** The **Langham, Boston** occupies an unbeatable location in the heart of the Financial District and supplies all the services and amenities a tycoon or would-be tycoon could want. Yes, it's part of a chain, but a small, London-based chain that deserves its great reputation. See p. 261.

- **Best for Travelers with Disabilities:** The **Royal Sonesta Hotel** in Cambridge trains its staff in disability awareness and offers 18 rooms (some of which adjoin standard units) equipped for the hearing, ambulatory, and vision impaired. A wheelchair ramp for use in conference rooms is available. See p. 282. The Westin chain is particularly attentive to the needs of travelers with special mobility needs; check out the **Westin Copley Place Boston** and the **Westin Boston Waterfront.** See p. 276 and 266.

- **Best for Eco-Sensitive Travelers:** Listing hotels that *aren't* on the green bandwagon might be quicker. Boston's **Lenox Hotel, Seaport Hotel,** and **Colonnade Hotel** are especially green but by no means the only earth-friendly properties in town. Every large hotel chain is boosting its environmental awareness, with **Hyatt** and **Kimpton**—parent company of Hotel Marlowe, Nine Zero, and the Onyx Hotel—on the cutting edge.

- **Best Pool:** The **Sheraton Boston Hotel** has a great indoor-outdoor pool with a retractable dome. Cambridge's **Royal Sonesta Hotel** has a similarly enjoyable arrangement. See p. 276 and 282.
- **Best Views:** Several hotels offer impressive views of their immediate surroundings, but for a picture-postcard panorama of Boston and Cambridge, head to the upper floors of the **Westin Copley Place Boston.** If you prefer up-close-and-personal views of Boston Harbor, check out the **Fairmont Battery Wharf,** on the edge of the North End, Boston's Italian-American stronghold. See p. 276 and 254.

THE WATERFRONT & THE NORTH END

Businesspeople and sightseers dominate the hotels in these neighborhoods, between the Rose Kennedy Greenway and Boston Harbor.

BEST FOR   Travelers who want easy access to downtown, the Seaport District (home of the convention center and the Seaport World Trade Center), and the airport.

DRAWBACKS   Touristy atmosphere, distance from the Back Bay and Cambridge, expense (at most properties).

Very Expensive

Boston Harbor Hotel ★★★   Guests at the Boston Harbor Hotel are demanding—and satisfied—business and leisure travelers drawn to its luxurious accommodations, abundant amenities, top-notch service, and great location. Its traditional style distinguishes this hotel from its nearest competitor, the InterContinental Boston. The landmark arch at the center of the 16-story brick hotel-office-condo complex connects the marina off the lobby to the Rose Kennedy Greenway and the Financial District. The plush guest rooms have residential-style mahogany furnishings, work desks, muted jewel-toned walls and fabrics, pillow-top mattresses, marble bathrooms, and abundant business features. Rooms occupy the top nine floors of the 16-story building, and offer sensational views of the harbor or of the skyline and Greenway. Rooms that face downtown are less expensive.

Rowes Wharf (entrance on Atlantic Ave. at High St.), Boston, MA 02110. www.bhh.com. ℂ **800/ 752-7077** or 617/439-7000. Fax 617/330-9450. 230 units. $345–$795 double; from $685 suite. Extra person $50. Children 17 and under stay free in parent's room. Packages available. AE, DC, DISC, MC, V. Valet parking $44; self-parking $40 weekdays, $29 weekends. T: Red Line to South Station or Blue Line to Aquarium. Pets accepted. **Amenities:** 2 restaurants; bar; babysitting; concierge; well-appointed health club & spa; 60-ft. lap pool; room service. *In room:* A/C, TV, CD player, hair dryer, minibar, Wi-Fi (free).

Fairmont Battery Wharf ★★   This luxurious boutique hotel is the only large lodging in the North End. Part of a harborfront hotel-condo complex, it has a residential feel, with large, surpassingly comfortable guest rooms and attentive

Boston Harbor Hotel.

service. The three low-rise buildings enjoy dazzling water views. Businesspeople can walk to the Financial District or take a water taxi from the hotel dock to locations around the harbor. Water transportation helps make up for the main drawback: the distance from the subway. It's hardly burdensome, but it feels long if you've been on your feet sightseeing all day. The trade-off is that the private wharf is a quiet enclave out of range of traffic and the activity at the adjacent Coast Guard station. *Tip:* Members of Fairmont's frequent-guest program, which is free to join, don't pay for Internet access.

3 Battery Wharf (off Commercial St. at Battery St.), Boston, MA 02109. www.fairmont.com/batterywharf. © **800/441-1414** or 617/994-9000. Fax 617/994-9098. 150 units, 104 with shower only. Apr to mid-Nov from $379 double, from $849 suite; mid-Nov to Mar from $279 double, from $749 suite. Children 17 and under stay free in parent's room. Weekend, spa, and other packages available. AE, DC, DISC, MC, V. Valet parking $42. T: Green Line to North Station, Orange Line to Haymarket, or Blue Line to Aquarium and 10-min. walk. Pets accepted ($25 fee). **Amenities:** Restaurant; bar; babysitting; concierge; well-equipped health club; room service; 12,000-sq.-ft. Exhale spa. *In room:* A/C, TV/DVD, CD player, hair dryer, minibar, MP3 docking station, Wi-Fi ($15 per day).

InterContinental Boston ★★ With over-the-top amenities and helpful service, InterContinental earns repeat business from its predominantly corporate clientele. The 21-story glass-sheathed building (the hotel occupies the bottom 12 floors) faces the Rose Kennedy Greenway, a block from the Financial District and not far from the convention center. Guest rooms on the east (back) side overlook Fort Point Channel. All are decorated in polished contemporary style, with plush earth-tone fabrics and pillow-top beds. Rooms are large enough to hold a comfy chaise and oversize work desk, and bathrooms are huge. The spa, health club, dining options, and condos upstairs amplify the residential feel, making the InterContinental a worthy competitor for the nearby Boston Harbor Hotel.

510 Atlantic Ave. (at Pearl St.), Boston, MA 02210. www.intercontinentalboston.com. © **800/424-6835** or 617/747-1000. Fax 617/747-5190. 424 units. $299–$600 double; suites from $800 and

Ames **45**
Anthony's Town House **4**
The Back Bay Hotel **23**
Best Western Plus Boston/The Inn
    at Longwood Medical **5**
Boston Common Hotel &
    Conference Center **21**
Boston Harbor Hotel **51**
Boston Marriott Copley Place **15**
Boston Marriott Long Wharf **48**
The Boston Park Plaza Hotel &
    Towers **27**
Bulfinch Hotel **37**
Chandler Inn Hotel **25**
Charlesmark Hotel **13**
Colonnade Hotel Boston **16**
Comfort Inn & Suites
    Boston/Airport **60**
Copley Square Hotel **14**
Courtyard Boston Brookline **1**
DoubleTree by Hilton Boston
    Downtown **31**
Eliot Hotel **7**
Embassy Suites Hotel Boston at
    Logan Airport **58**

Fairmont Battery Wharf **41**
The Fairmont Copley Plaza **20**
Fifteen Beacon **42**
40 Berkeley **24**
Four Seasons Hotel **28**
Hampton Inn Boston
    Logan Airport **59**
Harborside Inn **47**
Hilton Boston Back Bay **8**
Hilton Boston Financial District **50**
Hilton Boston Logan Airport **56**
Holiday Inn Boston at Beacon Hill **36**
Holiday Inn Boston Brookline **2**
Holiday Inn Express Hotel & Suites
    Boston Garden **39**
Hostelling International—Boston **32**
Hotel Commonwealth **6**
Hotel 140 **22**
Hyatt Harborside **57**
Hyatt Regency Boston
    Financial District **34**
Inn @ St. Botolph **17**
InterContinental Boston **52**
The Langham, Boston **49**
The Lenox Hotel **12**

The Liberty Hotel **35**
Longwood Inn **3**
Mandarin Oriental, Boston **11**
The MidTown Hotel **18**
Millennium Bostonian Hotel **46**
Newbury Guest House **10**
Nine Zero **43**
Omni Parker House **44**
Onyx Hotel **38**
Renaissance Boston Waterfront
    Hotel **55**
Residence Inn Boston Harbor on
    Tudor Wharf **40**
The Revere Boston **29**
The Ritz-Carlton, Boston
    Common **33**
Seaport Hotel **53**
Sheraton Boston Hotel **9**
Taj Boston **26**
W Boston **30**
The Westin Boston Waterfront **54**
The Westin Copley Place
    Boston **19**
XV Beacon **42**

Boston Hotels

way up. Club Lounge access $85. Extra person $35. Children 17 and under stay free in parent's room. Weekend and other packages available. AE, DC, DISC, MC, V. Valet parking $40. T: Red Line to South Station. Pets under 25 lb. accepted ($75 fee). **Amenities:** Restaurant; 2 bars; babysitting; concierge; 24-hr. health club; 45-ft. lap pool; room service; spa. *In room:* A/C, TV, hair dryer, minibar, MP3 docking station, Wi-Fi ($15 per day).

Expensive

Boston Marriott Long Wharf ★★   Steps from the New England Aquarium, the landmark Marriott attracts business travelers with its proximity to the Financial District and families with its pool and central location. It's in great shape following a $30-million renovation completed in 2012. Large and decorated in upscale-chain-hotel style, rooms surround a seven-story atrium. They hold either one king or two double beds (with pillow-top mattresses and down comforters), and a table and chairs by the window. Without any close neighbors, the building gets more natural light than any other downtown lodging except perhaps the Boston Harbor Hotel, which offers a more personalized experience but is generally pricier. Rooms near the water afford good views of the wharves and waterfront; other units overlook the Rose Kennedy Greenway.

296 State St. (at Atlantic Ave.), Boston, MA 02109. www.marriottlongwharf.com. (© **800/228-9290** or 617/227-0800. Fax 617/227-2867. 412 units. Apr–Nov $249–$629 double; Dec–Mar $159–$369 double; year-round $450–$800 suite. Weekend and family packages available. AE, DC, DISC, MC, V. Valet parking $44. T: Blue Line to Aquarium. **Amenities:** Restaurant; lounge; concierge; fitness center; Jacuzzi; indoor pool; room service. *In room:* A/C, TV, fridge, hair dryer, Wi-Fi ($13 per day).

Harborside Inn ★★ 🗡   The Harborside Inn offers an unbeatable combination of location and value; at this price point in this neighborhood, it has no competition. Sightseers are near Faneuil Hall Marketplace and the harbor, and business travelers are near the Financial District. Every room is different from

The Harborside Inn.

the next; each holds a pillow-top queen- or king-size bed. The decor is modern and unfussy with nautical touches—sailboat models and prints, not over-the-top "ahoy, matey." Accommodations on higher floors of the renovated 1858 warehouse have lower ceilings and better views than those closer to street level. Rooms that face out are more expensive but can be noisier; if that's a concern, reserve an interior unit that opens onto the skylit eight-story atrium.

185 State St. (btw. Atlantic Ave. and the Custom House Tower), Boston, MA 02109. www.harbor sideinnboston.com. *©* **617/723-7500.** Fax 617/670-6015. 98 units. $129–$299 double. Extra person $15. Rates may be higher during special events. AE, DC, DISC, MC, V. Off-site parking $29. T: Blue Line to Aquarium, or Blue or Orange Line to State. **Amenities:** Access to nearby health club ($15). *In room:* A/C, TV/DVD, hair dryer, Wi-Fi (free).

NORTH STATION

This neighborhood lies between the North End and Beacon Hill. Causeway Street fronts North Station, a major transit hub that's within easy walking distance of most downtown destinations.

BEST FOR   Access to the TD Garden arena, public transit, and the postcollegiate nightlife scene.

DRAWBACKS   Generally pricey, especially at busy times, and far from scenic. The narrow streets of this neighborhood attract rowdy crowds on weekend nights and after big events at the TD Garden.

Across the street from North Station and the TD Garden, the **Holiday Inn Express Hotel & Suites Boston Garden,** 280 Friend St. (www.hiexpress. com; *©* **888/465-4329** or 617/720-5544), consists of 72 units in a five-story building that was previously a hostel. Rates start at $195 for a double, skyrocketing during major events at the Garden, and include continental breakfast and Wi-Fi. Valet parking costs $39.

Bulfinch Hotel   One block from North Station, the Bulfinch is a leisure-traveler magnet that also attracts thrifty businesspeople with its convenient location and reasonable rates. Every room in the 1904 building is different; they're on the small side, but custom furnishings make good use of the space. Plush fabrics in cool neutrals, flatscreen TVs, and marble bathrooms set off the contemporary, uncluttered design. The best units in the nine-story hotel are executive king suites—actually oversize doubles—in the "nose" of the triangular building, with windows on three sides of the bed. The Onyx, around the corner, is pricier but offers better amenities and service.

107 Merrimac St. (at Lancaster St., 1 block from Causeway St.), Boston, MA 02114. www.bulfinch hotel.com. *©* **877/267-1776** or 617/624-0202. Fax 617/624-0211. 79 units, most with shower only. $169–$399 double; $199–$489 executive king. Children 17 and under stay free in parent's room. Packages, AAA, AARP, military, and long-term discounts available. AE, DC, DISC, MC, V. Parking $30 in nearby garage. T: Green or Orange Line to North Station. Pets accepted ($50 fee). **Amenities:** Restaurant; lounge; concierge; exercise room; room service. *In room:* A/C, TV, hair dryer, high-speed Internet (free).

Onyx Hotel ★   On a relatively quiet side street, this plush boutique hotel is the finest property in a rapidly evolving neighborhood. The 10-story hotel is contemporary in style, decorated in soothing jewel tones with sleek lines and high ceilings that make the decent-size rooms feel even bigger. Each unit in the eco-friendly Kimpton property holds a large work desk. The best accommodations are the top-floor suites, but any room with a floor-to-ceiling window feels like a mini-palace. The nearby Bulfinch is less expensive and offers correspondingly fewer amenities. *Tip:* Sign up for the (free) frequent-guest program, and the hotel waives the Internet access fee.

155 Portland St. (btw. Causeway St. and Anthony Valenti Way), Boston, MA 02114. www.onyx hotel.com. ℂ **866/660-6699** or 617/557-9955. Fax 617/557-0005. 112 units. $209–$349 double. Extra person $25. Children 17 and under stay free in parent's room. Rates include evening wine reception. Weekend, family, and other packages, AAA and AARP discounts available. AE, DC, DISC, MC, V. Valet parking $42. T: Green or Orange Line to North Station. Pets accepted. **Amenities:** Lounge; exercise room; access to nearby health club; room service. *In room:* A/C, TV, hair dryer, minibar, MP3 docking station, Wi-Fi ($10).

FANEUIL HALL MARKETPLACE & GOVERNMENT CENTER

Beacon Hill and the Financial District adjoin these neighborhoods. Faneuil Hall Marketplace is Boston's most popular attraction, and Government Center is an important T stop.

BEST FOR   Proximity to public transit, the harbor, the Rose Kennedy Greenway, and the airport.

DRAWBACKS   Packed with tourists and chain businesses; most lodgings are pricey, except at the slowest times.

Ames ★★   With the most eye-catching interior in town, combining minimalist style and traditional details, the Ames is a hipster magnet—a category that encompasses business and leisure travelers alike. The rehab of Boston's first skyscraper, the 1889 Ames Building, created a wide range of room configurations; all have cushy bedding, work desks, and wood floors, which lend an airy feel even in units that don't have huge windows (the largest windows are on the 3rd, 9th, and 14th floors). The staff is both exceptionally chic and welcoming. The Ames is part of Morgans Hotel Group, and it compares favorably with the boutique-hotel pioneer's best-known properties, the Delano in Miami and New York's Hudson. The Ames's closest competitors, XV Beacon and Nine Zero, attract a more traditional crowd and are generally less expensive.

1 Court St. (at Washington and State sts.), Boston, MA 02108. www.ameshotel.com. ℂ **800/697-1791** or 617/979-8100. Fax 617/979-8101. 114 units. Apr–Nov $550 double, $850 suite; Dec–Mar $200 double, $500 suite. Children 17 and under stay free in parent's room. Rates include continental breakfast. Packages available. AE, DC, DISC, MC, V. Valet parking $42; self-parking $37. T: Green or Blue Line to Government Center or Orange Line to State. **Amenities:** Restaurant; bar; concierge; exercise room; room service. *In room:* A/C, TV, hair dryer, minibar, MP3 docking station, Wi-Fi ($10 per day).

Millennium Bostonian Hotel ★   Across the street from Faneuil Hall Marketplace, this relatively small hotel offers excellent service and features that make it competitive with larger rivals such as the nearby Boston Marriott Long Wharf. It's popular with business travelers who want a break from the convention grind, and with vacationers who appreciate the boutique atmosphere and access to the marketplace and downtown attractions. Guest rooms occupy three brick 19th-century buildings. All cool neutrals and clean lines, they have Frette linens and down comforters on pillow-top beds. Rooms vary in size; in half of them,

French doors open onto small private balconies. My favorites overlook the marketplace, which is lively but not noisy, thanks to good soundproofing.

At Faneuil Hall Marketplace, 26 North St. (off Blackstone St.), Boston, MA 02109. www.millennium hotels.com. © **866/866-8086** or 617/523-3600. Fax 617/523-2454. 201 units. $189–$449 double; $229–$489 superior double; suites from $350 and way up. Extra person $20. Children 17 and under stay free in parent's room. Weekend, spa, family, and other packages available. AE, DC, DISC, MC, V. Valet parking $45. T: Green or Blue Line to Government Center, or Green or Orange Line to Haymarket. **Amenities:** Restaurant; lounge; babysitting; concierge; small exercise room; access to nearby health club ($10); room service. *In room:* A/C, TV, hair dryer, minibar, Wi-Fi ($10 per day).

THE FINANCIAL DISTRICT & DOWNTOWN CROSSING

Hotels in these areas are closer than their Waterfront competitors to the major shopping areas, the start of the Freedom Trail, and the subway to Cambridge.

BEST FOR   Businesspeople and sightseers year-round; winter weekend travelers on a budget.

DRAWBACKS   Generally sleepy at night and on weekends, except where noisy college students gather; some businesses close on Sunday. Weeknight room rates tend to be high.

Very Expensive

The Langham, Boston ★★   In the heart of the Financial District, the Langham is one of the best business hotels in the city. Leisure travelers, who can take advantage of weekend discounts, are near downtown attractions and perhaps a 10-minute walk from public transit. Elegantly decorated in rich jewel tones and large enough to hold a generous work area, the luxurious guest rooms have 153 configurations, including loft suites with two bathrooms. The most desirable rooms in the nine-story building overlook the lovely park in Post Office Square. The Langham's views pale in comparison to the vistas from the best units at the hotel's main competitors, the Boston Harbor Hotel and the InterContinental Boston—but room rates here are generally lower.

250 Franklin St. (at Post Office Sq.), Boston, MA 02110. www.boston.langhamhotels.com. © **800/791-7761** or 617/451-1900. Fax 617/423-2844. 318 units. $185–$495 double; suites from $545 and way up. Extra person $35. Weekend, family, spa, and other packages available. AE, DC, DISC, MC, V. Valet parking $42 Sun–Thurs, $28 Fri–Sat. T: Blue or Orange Line to State, or Red Line to Downtown Crossing or South Station. Pets accepted ($50 fee). **Amenities:** Restaurant and lounge w/DJ on weekends; cafe w/Sun brunch and Sat "Chocolate Bar Buffet" (Sept–June); concierge; state-of-the-art health club & spa; Jacuzzi; 40-ft. indoor pool; room service; sauna. *In room:* A/C, TV, hair dryer, minibar, Wi-Fi ($12 per day).

Nine Zero ★★   This well-located boutique hotel offers a sleek, sophisticated atmosphere and service in the old-school customer-is-always-right mold. Guest rooms and oversize bathrooms contain opulent features, including luxurious linens and toiletries, and extensive business amenities. The 19-story hotel, which opened in 2002, is part of the eco-conscious luxury Kimpton chain. Tucked away on a side street, which cuts down on noise, Nine Zero is 2 blocks from Boston Common and the subway. More traditional XV Beacon and the trendier Ames are the closest competitors. The service at all three is attentive and personal; let style and price guide your choice. *Tip:* Sign up for the frequent-guest program (it's free), and the hotel waives the Internet access fee.

90 Tremont St. (near Bromfield St.), Boston, MA 02108. www.ninezero.com. © **866/906-9090** or 617/772-5800. Fax 617/772-5810. 190 units. $289–$599 double; suites $500 and way up. Packages available. AE, DC, DISC, MC, V. Valet parking $40. T: Red or Green Line to Park St. Pets accepted. **Amenities:** Restaurant; bar; babysitting; concierge; exercise room; access to nearby health club; room service. *In room:* A/C, TV, hair dryer, minibar, MP3 docking station, Wi-Fi ($10 per day).

Expensive

Hilton Boston Financial District ★

The Hilton is the closest hotel in this area to the harbor, and the location, except at the height of rush-hour traffic, is surprisingly quiet. The spacious guest rooms have 9½-foot ceilings, sophisticated decor, and excellent lighting—a desirable feature in this densely packed neighborhood. The 14-story building is near Faneuil Hall Marketplace, but not all that close (by Bostonian standards) to the T. The best units, on the upper floors of the renovated 1928 Art Deco building, afford great views of the harbor and downtown. The Hilton's closest competitor, literally and figuratively, is the Langham, which is less convenient to public transit but has a swimming pool.

89 Broad St. (at Franklin St.), Boston, MA 02110. www.bostonfinancial.hilton.com. © **800/445-8667** or 617/556-0006. Fax 617/556-0053. 362 units. $169–$499 double; weekdays $269–$599 suite. Children 17 and under stay free in parent's room. Weekend, holiday, and family packages available. AE, DC, DISC, MC, V. Valet parking $38. T: Blue or Orange Line to State, or Red Line to South Station. Pets accepted ($75 fee). **Amenities:** Restaurant; bar; concierge; 24-hr. exercise room; room service. *In room:* A/C, TV, hair dryer, minibar, MP3 docking station, Wi-Fi ($15 per day).

Hyatt Regency Boston Financial District ★ 🦅

Your fellow guests at this 22-story hotel are likely to be other conventiongoers during the week, and sightseers and families on weekends. Decorated in soft earth tones, rooms are spacious enough to hold sitting areas, desks, and settees, with Hyatt touches such as pillow-top mattresses and good service. They have cushy upholstery and luxe linens on the king-size or (in about one-quarter of the units) two double beds. The hotel is closer to Downtown Crossing than to the Financial District; it's also convenient to the Greenway, Chinatown, the Back Bay, and Beacon Hill, but the immediate neighborhood is less than scenic. Ask to be on a high floor to get away from construction on adjacent Washington Street. The nearest competitors are the less expensive DoubleTree and the far more expensive Ritz-Carlton.

1 Ave. de Lafayette (off Washington St. btw. West and Avery sts.), Boston, MA 02111. www.regencyboston.hyatt.com. © **800/233-1234** or 617/912-1234. Fax 617/451-0054. 500 units. $179–$469 double; suites from $350 and way up. Extra person $25. Children 17 and under stay free in parent's room. Weekend, family, and other packages available. AE, DC, DISC, MC, V. Valet parking $43; self-parking $32. T: Red or Orange Line to Downtown Crossing, or Green Line to Park St. or Boylston. **Amenities:** Restaurant; bar; babysitting; concierge; health club; 52-ft. indoor saline pool; room service; sauna. *In room:* A/C, TV, hair dryer, minibar, MP3 docking station, Wi-Fi ($10 per day).

Omni Parker House ★ ☺ 🦅

In continuous operation longer than any other hotel in America (since 1855), the Parker House is centrally located on the Freedom Trail across from the nation's oldest burial ground at King's Chapel. With more than 50 room configurations and as great a range of prices, the hotel is

Food for Thought

Yes, this is the Parker House of Parker House roll fame. The rolls (pictured here) were invented (if food is truly "invented") here, as was Boston cream pie.

And that's not the hotel's only claim to fame. JFK proposed to Jackie in the restaurant—the first to hire Emeril Lagasse, fresh out of culinary school. Malcolm X and Ho Chi Minh both worked here, Charles Dickens lived here, and the room that's now Parker's Bar played host to a literary salon called the Saturday Club: Henry Wadsworth Longfellow, Oliver Wendell Holmes, Ralph Waldo Emerson, Nathaniel Hawthorne, and, while he was a resident, Dickens.

popular with families and sightseers, who can cut costs with a weekend deal or "economy single." Kids receive gifts at check-in, and the Freedom Trail suite is decorated like a colonial dwelling and stocked with period costumes and board games. Many of the room layouts aren't large, but even the smallest are regularly refurbished and thoughtfully appointed, in traditional style with cherry furnishings. Bathrooms tend to be small. The closest competitors are the more expensive Ames and Nine Zero; price the Parker House against the Harborside Inn and Holiday Inn Boston at Beacon Hill. *Tip:* Sign up for the free frequent-guest program, and the hotel waives the in-room Internet access fee.

60 School St. (at Tremont St.), Boston, MA 02108. www.omniparkerhouse.com. ℂ **800/843-6664** or 617/227-8600. Fax 617/742-5729. 551 units, some with shower only. $159–$189 economy room; $189–$289 double; $249–$399 suite. Children 17 and under stay free in parent's room. Weekend packages and AARP discount available. AE, DC, DISC, MC, V. Valet parking $40. T: Green or Blue Line to Government Center, or Red or Green Line to Park St. Pets accepted (deposit required). **Amenities:** Restaurant; 2 bars; concierge; exercise room; room service. *In room:* A/C, TV, hair dryer, high-speed Internet ($10/day), minibar, MP3 docking station.

BEACON HILL

The lovely neighborhood between Boston Common and Massachusetts General Hospital is home to many downtown workers; while they walk to the office, visitors can stroll to the waterfront attractions.

BEST FOR   Travelers who prefer a residential atmosphere to downtown's businesslike feel. It's an easy walk to downtown, the Back Bay, the river, and East Cambridge.

DRAWBACKS   Generally pricey; check with a B&B agency (p. 290) for more affordable alternatives.

XV Beacon ★★   Nonstop pampering, high-tech appointments, and outrageously luxurious rooms make this Boston's premier boutique hotel. The meticulously maintained 10-story property has attracted demanding travelers, especially businesspeople and international visitors, since it opened in 2000. The guest rooms, individually decorated in an austere but plush style that's more SoHo than Beacon Hill, contain king- and queen-size beds with Frette linens, surround-sound stereo systems, gas fireplaces, 42-inch flatscreens, and 4-inch TVs in the bathroom. "Studio" units have a sitting area. The hotel even has a seasonal roof deck and hot tub. The Ames and Nine Zero, which are part of fancy chains, are the main competition; this smaller independent property gets the nod from its loyal, high-maintenance fans.

15 Beacon St. (at Somerset St., 1 block from the State House), Boston, MA 02108. www.xvbeacon.com. © **877/982-3226** or 617/670-1500. Fax 617/670-2525. 62 units, some with shower only. From $295 double; from $1,200 suite. AE, DC, DISC, MC, V. Valet parking $44. T: Red or Green Line to Park St., or Green or Blue Line to Government Center. Dogs accepted ($25 MSPCA donation). **Amenities:** Restaurant; bar; babysitting; concierge; exercise room; access to nearby health club ($15); room service. *In room:* A/C, TV, CD player, hair dryer, minibar, MP3 docking station, Wi-Fi (free).

Holiday Inn Boston at Beacon Hill Just off one of Beacon Hill's main streets, this 15-story hotel books mostly leisure travelers and visitors to adjacent Massachusetts General Hospital. Especially appealing to vacationing families is the seasonal outdoor pool. Guest rooms are quite large, with contemporary furnishings and picture-window views of the city, the State House, or the parking structure. (*Tip:* Ask for a room on a high floor, facing Blossom St. if possible.) The building is part of a small retail-office complex with a Whole Foods supermarket, a drugstore, and a handful of shops. The staff is particularly sensitive to the needs of hospital patients and their relatives.

5 Blossom St. (at Cambridge St.), Boston, MA 02114. www.hisboston.com. © **800/465-4329** or 617/742-7630. Fax 617/742-4192. 303 units, some with shower only. $155–$400 double; from $390 suite. Extra person $15. Rollaway $20. Children 17 and under stay free in parent's room. Weekend and corporate packages available. AE, DC, DISC, MC, V. Valet or self-parking $40. T: Red Line to Charles/MGH. **Amenities:** Restaurant; lounge; concierge; executive-level rooms; small exercise room; access to nearby health club ($20); outdoor heated pool; room service. *In room:* A/C, TV, hair dryer, Wi-Fi (free).

The Liberty Hotel ★★ A luxury hotel with top-of-the-line furnishings, next-gen tech, and huge bathrooms, the Liberty used to be the Charles Street Jail. The original 1851 hoosegow now holds the public areas and 18 guest rooms that—despite not having been "guest" accommodations before—are in high demand. Other guest rooms are in a new building, opened in 2007, between the jail and the adjacent hospital. Rooms that face the Charles River (across Storrow Dr., a busy parkway) are preferable to those with a view of the neighborhood; units on higher floors are best. My favorites are corner rooms with a river view from the bathtub. The Liberty's closest competition, XV Beacon, offers more personal service in a less lively neighborhood with fewer dining options.

215 Charles St. (at Cambridge St.), Boston, MA 02114. www.libertyhotel.com. © **617/224-4000.** Fax 617/399-4259. 298 units. $295–$550 double; $600–$1,000 suite. Children 17 and under stay free in parent's room. Weekend and other packages available. AE, DC, DISC, MC, V. Valet or self-parking $42. T: Red Line to Charles/MGH. Small pets accepted. **Amenities:** 2 restaurants; bar; concierge; 24-hr. exercise room; room service. *In room:* A/C, TV, hair dryer, minibar, MP3 docking station, Wi-Fi (free).

CHARLESTOWN

Across the Inner Harbor from the North End, this largely residential area is home to the final stops on the Freedom Trail, the Charlestown Navy Yard, and Bunker Hill Monument.

BEST FOR Travelers with business in Charlestown or east Cambridge, families who want to be near the Freedom Trail, and anyone who needs easy access to downtown (by MBTA ferry, by water taxi, or on foot).

DRAWBACKS Access to the Back Bay and central Cambridge isn't quick or easy; lodging and nightlife options are limited.

Residence Inn Boston Harbor on Tudor Wharf ★★ ✦ The Residence Inn combines the familiar suburban brand and a prime urban location, meaning patrons tend to be business travelers on weeknights and families on weekends. Easy transit access (water taxis stop at the hotel dock) and the included breakfast buffet make this hotel a better deal than many downtown competitors, and a renovation completed in 2012 left the property in tip-top shape. Adjacent to the Charlestown Navy Yard, it consists of studio and one- and two-bedroom suites with full kitchens and plenty of natural light. Even the smallest units are generous in size. Most rooms in the eight-story building enjoy impressive views of either the harbor or the Charles River and the Zakim Bridge. Prices listed here are for 1 to 4 nights; longer stays mean greater discounts.

34–44 Charles River Ave. (½ block from Chelsea St.), Charlestown, MA 02129. www.marriott.com/bostw. ✆ **866/296-2297,** 800/331-3131 (Marriott), or 617/242-9000. Fax 617/242-5554. 168 units. Apr–Nov $189–$399 double; Dec–Mar $129–$269 double. Rates include full breakfast. Children stay free in parent's room. Weekend, family, and other packages from $129 per night. AAA, government, and long-term discounts available. AE, DC, DISC, MC, V. Valet parking $35. T: Blue Line to Aquarium and ferry from Long Wharf to Navy Yard, then 5-min. walk; Green or Orange Line to North Station, then 10-min. walk; or Orange Line to Community College, then 10-min. walk. Pets accepted ($100 fee). **Amenities:** Exercise room; access to nearby YMCA ($8); Jacuzzi; indoor lap pool. *In room:* A/C, TV, hair dryer, kitchen, Wi-Fi (free).

SOUTH BOSTON WATERFRONT (SEAPORT DISTRICT)

This rapidly evolving neighborhood boasts hotels full of business travelers and conventioneers, but no supermarket or drugstore (yet). Silver Line buses make the quick trip to the airport or to South Station, and the Red Line connects South Station to Cambridge.

BEST FOR Access to the Boston Convention and Exhibition Center, Seaport World Trade Center, Institute of Contemporary Art, Boston Children's Museum, and airport.

DRAWBACKS Downtown is some distance by bus and subway or on foot (Faneuil Hall Marketplace, for instance, is at least a 15-min. walk), and access to the Back Bay isn't great. Dining options are expanding but limited, and there's no shopping or entertainment to speak of.

Renaissance Boston Waterfront Hotel ★ Ultra-high-tech features make the Renaissance a favorite with business travelers. Lightning-fast DS-3 Internet access makes each guest room a media hub, with the capability to run everything through the 37-inch HDTV. As you'd expect within walking distance of both the convention center and the World Trade Center, the style is familiar business contemporary, all sleek silhouettes and vibrant colors, with comfy, well-appointed beds. On weekends, expect a predominantly leisure clientele and correspondingly lower prices—which seems only fair, given the location. Higher floors of the glass-clad 21-story building enjoy sensational views of the harbor, a block away, and the downtown skyline.

606 Congress St. (at D St.), Boston, MA 02210. www.renaissanceboston.com. ☎ **888/796-4664,** 800/468-3571, or 617/338-4111. Fax 617/338-4138. 471 units. $169–$499 double; from $459 suite. Children 18 and under stay free in parent's room. Weekend, family, and other packages available. AE, DC, DISC, MC, V. Valet parking $44. T: Red Line to South Station, then Silver Line SL1/SL2 bus to World Trade Center or 20-min. walk. Or water taxi to World Trade Center. **Amenities:** Restaurant; lounge; coffee bar; babysitting; concierge; health club; indoor pool; room service. *In room:* A/C, TV, hair dryer, MP3 docking station, Wi-Fi ($13 per day).

Seaport Hotel ★★ ☺   Across the street from and affiliated with the World Trade Center, the independent Seaport Hotel books up unpredictably, depending on the schedule there and at the nearby convention center. The sophisticated, eco-conscious hotel was designed and built (by Fidelity Investments) to appeal to techno-savvy business travelers. The well-appointed, decent-size rooms have thoughtful features such as pillow-top mattresses and Logan Airport flight information (on the TV). Views from higher floors of the 18-story building are breathtaking. The hotel operates a shuttle to downtown destinations and an electric water taxi. The kid-conscious staff, pool, weekend packages, and proximity to the Boston Children's Museum make this a good choice for families, too.

> **Planning Pointer**
>
> If your trip involves a cultural event—for example, a big museum show or *The Nutcracker*—look into a hotel package that includes tickets. Usually offered on weekends, these deals always save time and often save money.

1 Seaport Lane (btw. Seaport Blvd. and Congress St.), Boston, MA 02210. www.seaportboston.com. ☎ **877/732-7678** or 617/385-4000. Fax 617/385-5090. 426 units. $189–$399 double; $450 and way up suite. Children 16 and under stay free in parent's room. Weekend and family packages available. AE, DC, DISC, MC, V. Valet parking $42 (1 night free for hybrid and electric vehicles); self-parking $32. T: Red Line to South Station, then Silver Line SL1/SL2 bus to World Trade Center or 20-min. walk. Or water taxi to World Trade Center. Pets under 50 lb. accepted. **Amenities:** Restaurant; cafe; lounge; bikes; concierge; well-equipped health club; 50-ft. indoor pool; room service; spa. *In room:* A/C, TV, hair dryer, minibar, MP3 docking station, Wi-Fi (free).

The Westin Boston Waterfront ★★   The only hotel attached to the Boston Convention and Exhibition Center, the Westin offers the chain's abundant amenities, including Heavenly Beds, in its signature contemporary style. The large rooms have plenty of space for oversize work desks, and huge windows showcase the city skyline, the water, or nearby office buildings and construction. Northeast-facing units on higher floors of the 16-story building enjoy panoramas of the action on the harbor, which—notwithstanding the hotel's name—is 2 blocks away. Bathrooms hold the nicest mirrors (huge and backlit) that I've ever seen in a hotel. Access to the convention center is through a weather-protected sky bridge off the enormous lobby, which holds a bar that hops after work on weeknights.

425 Summer St. (at D St.), Boston, MA 02210. www.westin.com. ☏ **800/937-8461** or 617/532-4600. Fax 617/532-4630. 793 units. $259–$599 double; $359 and up suite. Children 17 and under stay free in parent's room. Weekend and family packages available. AE, DC, DISC, MC, V. Valet parking $43; self-parking $33. T: Red Line to South Station, then Silver Line SL1/SL2 bus to World Trade Center. Pets accepted. **Amenities:** 2 restaurants; lounge; bar; coffee shop; concierge; state-of-the-art health club; indoor pool; room service. *In room:* A/C, TV, hair dryer, minibar, Wi-Fi ($13–$19 per day).

CHINATOWN/THEATER DISTRICT

Bordered by Downtown Crossing, Boston Common, the South End, and the Rose Kennedy Greenway, this small area is densely packed and centrally located.

BEST FOR   A compromise if you need easy access to both downtown and the Back Bay, sometimes for less than you'd pay in those areas.

DRAWBACKS   Narrow, congested streets create a gritty atmosphere; the Theater District is crowded before and after performances but deserted late at night.

Very Expensive

The Revere Boston ★   The Revere is the main challenger to the Ames and the nearby W Boston in the city's growing funky-boutique-hotel sector. Opened in 2012 after a $27-million overhaul, the independent hotel boasts a much fresher look—and charges considerably more—than in its previous life as a Radisson. The Ames is in a nicer neighborhood and the W has a higher profile, but the Revere's guest rooms are among the largest in the city; each has a private balcony, sitting area, and oversize work desk. Clad in grays and tans, with punches of neon-bright greens and golds, the style is anything but traditional—an approach that's already paying off in the battle for the image-conscious business and leisure traveler.

200 Stuart St. (at Charles St. S.), Boston, MA 02116. www.reverehotel.com. ☏ **866/673-8373** or 617/482-1800. Fax 617/451-2750. 356 units, some with shower only. $399–$499 double; from $699 suite. Extra person $20. Children 11 and under stay free in parent's room. Packages available. AE, DC, DISC, MC, V. Valet parking $46; self-parking $39. T: Green Line to Arlington or Orange Line to Tufts Medical Center. Pets accepted. **Amenities:** Restaurant; 2 bars; babysitting; concierge; exercise room; access to nearby health club ($35); indoor pool; room service. *In room:* A/C, TV, hair dryer, MP3 docking station, Wi-Fi (free).

The Ritz-Carlton, Boston Common ★   This plush, ultramodern hotel is a magnet for visiting celebrities—the state-of-the-art Sports Club/LA is a powerful draw—as well as for fans of the Ritz-Carlton brand. You don't have to be a movie star for the staff here to treat you like one. The luxurious hotel's guest rooms occupy the 9th through 12th floors of a building a half-block from Boston Common; public spaces are at street level. The good-size guest rooms and huge suites feel residential, with indulgent amenities such as Frette linens, feather duvets, and three phones (one in the large bathroom). You'll pay more for a room with a view of the Common. The hotel's chief rivals, the Four Seasons and the Mandarin Oriental, are in the more desirable Back Bay but have less impressive fitness facilities.

10 Avery St. (btw. Tremont and Washington sts.), Boston, MA 02111. www.ritzcarlton.com. ℂ **800/241-3333** or 617/574-7100. Fax 617/574-7200. 193 units. From $425 double; from $550 Club Level; from $625 suite. Weekend, family, and other packages available. AE, DC, DISC, MC, V. Valet parking $44; self-parking $30. T: Green Line to Boylston. Pets accepted. **Amenities:** Restaurant; bar; babysitting; concierge; club-level rooms; access ($15 per day) to adjoining Sports Club/LA (100,000-sq.-ft. facility w/lap pool, complete spa services, salon, regulation basketball court, 10,000-sq.-ft. weight room, steam rooms, saunas, 5 exercise studios, 4 squash courts); room service. *In room:* A/C, TV, CD player, hair dryer, minibar, MP3 docking station, Wi-Fi ($10 per day).

W Boston ★ The W is a favorite with regular guests who seek out the boutique chain for its signature touches, including serene accommodations, hopping public spaces, and excellent service. They rave about the compact yet indulgent guest rooms, with feather-top mattresses and down comforters, contemporary style, and local flair (Thoreau quotes stenciled on the walls of the huge bathrooms, for example). Also a W hallmark: the congested lobby, with a lively lounge that roars after work. The hotel occupies the first 15 floors of a 27-story hotel-condo glass tower, which opened in 2009. Views, of neon marquees and rooftops, aren't as good as the panoramas from the balconies at the Revere, the W's closest rival. Ask for a room as high as possible to cut down on the noise from the lobby and Theater District traffic.

100 Stuart St. (at Tremont St.), Boston, MA 02116. www.whotels.com. ℂ **877/946-8357** or 617/261-8700. Fax 617/261-8725. 235 units. $259–$579 double; from $439 and way up suite. Weekend, spa, and other packages available. AE, DC, DISC, MC, V. Valet parking $42. T: Green Line to Boylston or Orange Line to Tufts Medical Center. Pets accepted ($125 fee for 1st night, then $25 per night). **Amenities:** Restaurant (Market; p. 163); 2 lounges; bike rental; concierge; well-equipped 24-hr. exercise room; room service; Bliss Spa. *In room:* A/C, TV/DVD, CD player, hair dryer, high-speed Internet ($15 per day), MP3 docking station.

Moderate

DoubleTree by Hilton Boston–Downtown ★ 🐾 This hotel is popular with leisure and business travelers as well as with visitors to the adjacent medical center. It's cheaper than you might think for pleasant accommodations in a very convenient location. The six-story building is a former high school with high ceilings and compact, well-designed rooms decorated in contemporary style. Ask for a unit facing away from busy Washington Street and you'll have a view of the city rather than of Tufts Medical Center, across the street. Don't confuse this hotel with its all-suite corporate sibling on the Charles River (p. 280).

821 Washington St. (at Oak St., 1 block from Stuart St.), Boston, MA 02111. www.hiltonfamily boston.com/downtown. ℂ **800/222-8733** or 617/956-7900. Fax 617/956-7901. 267 units, some with shower only. $139–$299 double; $189–$359 suite. Extra person $10. Children 17 and under stay free in parent's room. Weekend and other packages, AAA, AARP, and military discounts available. AE, DC, DISC, MC, V. Valet parking $40. T: Orange Line to Tufts Medical Center. **Amenities:** Restaurant; lounge; coffee shop; concierge; access to adjoining YMCA w/pool; room service. *In room:* A/C, TV, hair dryer, MP3 docking station, Wi-Fi ($13 per day).

Inexpensive

Hostelling International–Boston Students, youth groups, and other travelers in search of comfortable, no-frills lodging flock to this new hostel, which opened in 2012. Accommodations are dorm-style (all men, all women, or coed), with six beds in most units and shared bathrooms; 22 private units have en suite bathrooms. Public areas in the air-conditioned building include a kitchen, dining room, community room, library, and meeting and workshop space. Linens are provided, or you can bring your own; sleeping bags are not permitted. The enthusiastic staff organizes free and inexpensive cultural, educational, and recreational programs. After a $44-million overhaul of an 1886 landmark building, the six-story structure is officially green—it's one of the first LEED-certified hostels.

19 Stuart St. (off Washington St.), Boston, MA 02116. www.bostonhostel.org. ✆ **888/999-4678** or 617/536-9455. Fax 617/424-6558. 481 beds. Members of Hostelling International–American Youth Hostels $28–$45 per bed, nonmembers $31–$48 per bed; members $70–$130 per private unit, nonmembers $73–$133 per private unit. Children 3–12 half-price, children 2 and under stay free. Rates include continental breakfast. MC, V. T: Orange Line to Tufts Medical Center or Green Line to Boylston. **Amenities:** Coffee shop; Wi-Fi (free). *In room:* A/C, no phone.

THE SOUTH END

The South End extends far beyond Berkeley Street, where you'll find these two lodgings in the most convenient corner of the neighborhood.

BEST FOR   Budget-conscious travelers with business in the adjacent Back Bay; easy access to the South End's excellent restaurants.

DRAWBACKS   Access to Cambridge isn't easy; Berkeley Street is fairly busy all day and into the evening.

Chandler Inn Hotel ★ 🔥   Just 2 blocks from the Back Bay, the Chandler Inn is a bargain with a bonus: the boutique feel. The eight-story building holds small but well-designed rooms, decorated in cool neutrals with splashes of orange and equipped with plasma TVs and marble bathrooms; all have individual climate control. The staff is welcoming and helpful. This gay-friendly hotel books up early for events such as the Boston Marathon and Boston Pride March and for foliage season. Off-season rates are excellent.

26 Chandler St. (at Berkeley St.), Boston, MA 02116. www.chandlerinn.com. ✆ **800/842-3450** or 617/482-3450. Fax 617/542-3428. 56 units. $109–$279 double. Children 11 and under stay free in parent's room. AE, DC, DISC, MC, V. Parking $27 at nearby garage. T: Orange Line to Back Bay. Pets under 25 lb. accepted ($50 fee). **Amenities:** Lounge (Fritz; p. 242); access to nearby health club ($10). *In room:* A/C, TV, hair dryer, MP3 docking station, Wi-Fi (free).

40 Berkeley   This pleasant, convenient hostel and residence consists of dorm-style guest rooms and welcoming public spaces. Accommodations are basic, containing little more than beds, but they're well maintained and comfortable—not plush, but not cells, either. That description might not seem to justify the prices, but check around a little before you turn up your nose, especially if you plan to spend most of your time out and about. Formerly for women only, this erstwhile YWCA now accommodates adults on all seven floors. The well-kept public areas include a 24-hour TV lounge, game room, and patio garden.

40 Berkeley St. (at Appleton St.), Boston, MA 02116. www.40berkeley.com. ✆ **617/375-2524.** Fax 617/375-2525. 200 units, none with bathroom. $50–$80 single; $80–$110 double; $99–$132 triple or quad. Rates include full breakfast. Long-term rates available (2-month minimum). Packages available. MC, V. No parking. T: Orange Line to Back Bay or Green Line to Arlington. **Amenities:** Cafeteria; computer kiosk w/Internet access ($1 per 10 min.). *In room:* No phone, Wi-Fi (free).

THE BACK BAY

Boston's widest variety of lodgings is in this neighborhood, which stretches from the Public Garden past the Hynes Convention Center and incorporates the Esplanade, the recreational area on the Charles River.

BEST FOR   Anyone who wants to be where the action is. The Boston area's best shopping and people-watching is here. Budget-conscious travelers have more options here than in any other centrally located part of town.

DRAWBACKS   Rates can be extremely high, especially during citywide events such as the Boston Marathon. Tour groups overrun the neighborhood year-round, especially during foliage season. The most convenient T access is on the unreliable Green Line. Reaching Cambridge isn't easy or consistently fast (the subway can be as slow as the pokey No. 1 bus).

Very Expensive

Colonnade Hotel Boston ★★ ☺   Adjacent to Copley Place and the Prudential Center, the independently owned Colonnade caters to an international clientele of businesspeople, sightseers, shoppers, and families. It's a welcome alternative to the chain properties that dominate this neighborhood. The 11-story concrete-and-glass hotel has an attentive, gracious staff and large guest rooms decorated in muted earth tones. The sleek residential-style furnishings include pillow-top beds, marble-clad bathrooms, and a round table in place of a desk. Light floods through floor-to-ceiling windows, which open on the bustling Prudential Center or—my preference—the South End's urban patchwork. The seasonal "rooftop resort" and swimming pool are a welcome retreat in warm weather.

120 Huntington Ave. (at Garrison St., 1 block from W. Newton St.), Boston, MA 02116. www.colonnadehotel.com. *C* **800/962-3030** or 617/424-7000. Fax 617/424-1717. 285 units. $229–$459 double; $575 and way up suite. Children 11 and under stay free in parent's room. Weekend, family, and other packages, winter and other discounts available. AE, DC, DISC, MC, V. Parking $38. T: Green Line E to Prudential. Pets accepted. **Amenities:** Restaurant (Brasserie Jo; p. 170); bar; babysitting; concierge; well-equipped exercise room; heated outdoor rooftop pool; room service. *In room:* A/C, TV/DVD, hair dryer, minibar, MP3 docking station, Wi-Fi ($14 per day).

Eliot Hotel ★★   On tree-lined Commonwealth Avenue, this exquisite hotel offers a romantic atmosphere as well as top-notch business features. European-style service and abundant amenities keep both leisure and business travelers returning to the traditional-looking red-brick building a block from the bustle of Newbury Street. Almost every unit is a spacious suite (16 rooms are standard doubles) with a residential feel: subtle geometric and floral patterns on the rugs and upholstery, antique furnishings, down comforters, and marble-clad bathrooms. French doors separate the living rooms and bedrooms in the suites. The hotel is near Boston University and Fenway Park, and across the river from MIT—convenient, but with a getaway feel that distinguishes the Eliot from its closest rival, the Hotel Commonwealth.

370 Commonwealth Ave. (at Mass. Ave.), Boston, MA 02215. www.eliothotel.com. *C* **800/443-5468** or 617/267-1607. Fax 617/536-9114. 95 units, most with shower only. $235–$395 double; $355–$545 1-bedroom suite; $580–$890 2-bedroom suite. Extra person $30. Children 17 and under stay free in parent's room. Packages available. AE, DC, MC, V. Valet parking $36. T: Green Line B, C, or D to Hynes Convention Center. Pets accepted. **Amenities:** Restaurant; sashimi bar;

babysitting; concierge; free access to nearby health club; room service. *In room:* A/C, TV, hair dryer, minibar, MP3 docking station, Wi-Fi ($5 per day).

The Fairmont Copley Plaza ★★   The Copley Plaza is a classic grand hotel, with a regular clientele of leisure and business travelers who expect luxurious lodgings and superior service. Built in 1912, the seven-story Renaissance-revival building faces beautiful Copley Square. The spacious guest rooms underwent a $20 million renovation for the property's centennial, with plush upholstery in cool neutrals complementing dark-wood custom furnishings, including oversize desks and pillow-top mattresses. Rooms that face the square afford better views than those overlooking busy Dartmouth Street, but all beat the views from the hotel's nearest rival, the Lenox. The beautifully restored **OAK Long Bar + Kitchen** began welcoming guests in July 2012 with its wood-fired farm-to-table cuisine, vaulted ceilings, fireplaces, and huge Palladian windows. Inventive weekend packages, hotel history tours, and a resident black Lab guests can take for walks make the eco-conscious Copley Plaza a favorite with generations of Bostonians and visitors. *Tip:* Internet access is complimentary to members of Fairmont's free frequent-guest program.

138 St. James Ave. (btw. Dartmouth St. and Trinity Place), Boston, MA 02116. www.fairmont.com/copleyplaza. ☏ **800/441-1414** or 617/267-5300. Fax 617/267-7668. 383 units. From $289 double; from $899 suite. Extra person $30. Weekend and other packages available. AE, DC, MC, V. Valet parking $42. T: Green Line to Copley or Orange Line to Back Bay. Pets accepted ($25/day). **Amenities:** Restaurant; lounge; concierge; concierge-level rooms; access to nearby health club ($20); exercise room; room service. *In room:* A/C, TV, hair dryer, minibar, MP3 docking station, Wi-Fi ($15/day).

Four Seasons Hotel ★★★   With its exquisite service, beautiful location, elegant guest rooms and public areas, terrific health club, and wonderful restaurant, the Four Seasons is the best hotel in Boston and perhaps in all of New England. The 16-story brick-and-glass building (the hotel occupies eight floors) overlooks the Public Garden. The spacious accommodations feel more like stylish apartments than hotel rooms, with lots of plush fabrics, elaborate moldings, and marble bathrooms. The best, dizzyingly expensive units enjoy vistas of the Public Garden; less pricey rooms at the back of the hotel overlook city streets. The welcoming staff is famously responsive to the needs (and whims) of businesspeople, families, and celebrities. Compared with its main rivals, the Four Seasons beats the Ritz-Carlton on location and the Mandarin Oriental, which doesn't have a pool, on facilities.

200 Boylston St. (at Hadassah Way, btw. Arlington St. and Charles St. S.), Boston, MA 02116. www.fourseasons.com/boston. ☏ **800/819-5053** or 617/338-4400. Fax 617/423-0154. 273 units. $495 double weekdays, $425 double weekends; from $895 1-bedroom suite; from $1,545 2-bedroom suite. Children 18 and under stay free in parent's room. Weekend and family packages available. AE, DC, DISC, MC, V. Valet parking $48. T: Green Line to Arlington. Pets under 25 lb. accepted. **Amenities:** Restaurant and bar (Bristol Lounge; p. 171); babysitting; concierge; health club; Jacuzzi; 24-hr. 44-ft. pool overlooking the Public Garden; room service. *In room:* A/C, TV/DVD, CD player, hair dryer, minibar, MP3 docking station, Wi-Fi ($10 per day).

The Lenox Hotel ★★   The central location makes the Lenox popular with business travelers, and its relatively small size and accommodating staff make it a welcome alternative to the huge convention hotels that dominate this

The Mandarin Oriental.

neighborhood. Those competitors do offer more extensive fitness options, though. The Lenox's spacious, luxurious guest rooms have high ceilings and are large enough to contain sitting areas and Aeron chairs. Custom-designed wood furnishings and marble bathrooms add to the anything-but-generic vibe; rooms on the top two floors of the 11-story building enjoy excellent views. My favorites are the 12 corner units with wood-burning fireplaces. This hotel was one of the first in the country to embrace eco-consciousness, and management's commitment to shrinking its environmental footprint is truly impressive.

61 Exeter St. (at Boylston St.), Boston, MA 02116. www.lenoxhotel.com. © **800/225-7676** or 617/536-5300. Fax 617/236-0351. 214 units, some with shower only. $215–$425 double; $289–$545 junior suite; from $770 1-bedroom fireplace suite. Children 16 and under stay free in parent's room. Corporate, weekend, and family packages available. AE, DC, DISC, MC, V. Valet parking $45. T: Green Line to Copley. **Amenities:** Restaurant; bar; pub; babysitting; concierge; small exercise room; room service. *In room:* A/C, TV, hair dryer, MP3 docking station, Wi-Fi (free).

Mandarin Oriental, Boston ★★ Mandarin Oriental's first New England property, which opened in 2008, courts both international business travelers and devoted shoppers with its great location, sublime service, and top-notch amenities, including an excellent spa. The hotel, a block from Newbury Street, connects to the Prudential Center (and from there to Copley Place and the Hynes Convention Center). Guest rooms are large and luxurious, with Frette linens and color palettes of soft greens and browns; they occupy the fourth through eighth floors of a 14-story building that also holds condos and apartments. In keeping with the Hong Kong–based luxury chain's philosophy, the elegant, peaceful hotel was designed using the principles of feng shui. The Mandarin Oriental's big rivals—the Four Seasons and the InterContinental—have superior fitness facilities, but better access to shopping and dining here may tip the scales for you.

776 Boylston St. (at Fairfield St.), Boston, MA 02199. www.mandarinoriental.com/boston. © **866/796-5475** or 617/535-8888. Fax 617/535-8889. 148 units. Apr–Nov from $445 double; from $1,195 suite; Dec–Mar from $345 double; from $995 suite. Children 16 and under stay free

in parent's room. Weekend, spa, and other packages available. AE, DC, DISC, MC, V. Valet parking $45. T: Green Line to Copley or Green Line E to Prudential. Pets accepted. **Amenities:** Restaurant; lounge; airport transfers ($110); babysitting; concierge; exercise room; access to nearby health club ($35); room service; 16,000-sq.-ft. spa. *In room:* A/C, TV/DVD, hair dryer, minibar, MP3 docking station, Wi-Fi ($15 per day).

Taj Boston ★   With its luxurious accommodations, legendary service, and old-Boston atmosphere, Taj Boston appeals to vacationers and business travelers alike. In a great location overlooking the Public Garden, the beautifully maintained, elegantly appointed guest rooms have dark-wood furnishings, feather duvets, Frette linens, three phones (one in the marble bathroom), and windows that open. You'll pay more for a Public Garden view. The best units are suites, which have wood-burning fireplaces. Taj, an India-based luxury chain, took over the original Ritz-Carlton (1927) in 2007. One of the most traditional lodgings in town, it's competitive with other top-tier hotels on cachet alone. The Mandarin Oriental and archrival Four Seasons have superior fitness facilities—and higher prices.

15 Arlington St. (at Newbury St.), Boston, MA 02116. www.tajhotels.com. ✆ **877/482-5267** or 617/536-5700. Fax 617/536-1335. 273 units. From $249 double; from $399 Club Level or suite. Extra person $20. Children 12 and under stay free in parent's room. Weekend, family, and other packages available. AE, DC, DISC, MC, V. Valet parking $42. T: Green Line to Arlington. Pets under 20 lb. accepted ($150 fee). **Amenities:** Restaurant; bar (p. 229); lounge; babysitting; concierge; club-level rooms; exercise room; room service. *In room:* A/C, TV, hair dryer, minibar, Wi-Fi ($11 per day).

Expensive

The 16 units at the **Inn @ St. Botolph,** 99 St. Botolph St. (at W. Newton St.; www.innatstbotolph.com; ✆ **617/236-8099;** T: Green Line E to Prudential), are so popular that they're almost always booked, but I suggest checking anyway. In a residential neighborhood a block from Huntington Avenue and the Prudential Center, guests pretty much fend for themselves, which is perfect if you like the atmosphere of an upscale B&B but not mingling with the staff and other guests. The lavishly decorated suites have self-catering kitchens (management supplies the breakfast fixings) and Wi-Fi but no other services besides a small exercise room—no parking, bell staff, or restaurant. Rates for a double in high season start at $209.

The Back Bay Hotel ★   Formerly Boston's police headquarters, this luxurious hotel attracts business (weeknight) and leisure (weekend) travelers with its handy location and excellent service. The 1925 limestone-and-brick building gained a wing and two floors before opening in 2004. Decorated in peaceful, muted colors, the large guest rooms have nice touches such as a work area with an ergonomic chair, down comforters, and windows that open but also do a good job of muffling traffic noise. Light sleepers will want to face away from busy Berkeley Street, and perhaps request a room on the second floor, where windows are smaller than elsewhere. This is the only New England property of the Doyle Collection, an Irish chain that's challenging Boston's corporate giants.

350 Stuart St. (at Berkeley St.), Boston, MA 02116. www.doylecollection.com. ✆ **617/266-7200.** Fax 617/266-7203. 225 units, some with shower only. $215–$589 double; $765 jr. suite; $1,390 presidential suite. Extra person $20. Children 12 and under stay free in parent's room.

😊 family-friendly HOTELS

Almost every hotel in the Boston area regularly plays host to children, and many offer special family packages. For more information, see "Family Travel," p. 359. Moderately priced chains have the most experience with youngsters, but their higher-end competitors put on a good show.

Units at the **DoubleTree Suites by Hilton Boston** (p. 280) are a great deal—they have two rooms in which to spread out, and they cost far less than adjoining rooms at any other hotel this nice. Stash breakfast fixings in the in-room refrigerator, then splurge on lunch and dinner.

In the Back Bay, the **Colonnade Hotel Boston** (p. 270) offers a family weekend package that includes parking, breakfast for two adults, up to four passes (for two adults and two children) to an attraction of your choice, and a fanny pack for younger guests that holds sunglasses, a pad and pen, a yo-yo, and a toy duck.

The **Omni Parker House** (p. 262) is on the Freedom Trail and within easy walking distance to the waterfront. Young guests receive a backpack that contains games and toys at check-in, and milk and cookies on the first night of their stay. Parents can request a kit with outlet covers and a night light.

The **Seaport Hotel** (p. 266), near Museum Wharf, offers excellent weekend deals, splendid views of the harbor and airport, underwater music piped into the swimming pool, and even a grandparent-grandchild package.

On the edge of the Back Bay, the **MidTown Hotel** (p. 278) has a seasonal outdoor pool, a limited number of adjoining rooms (so the kids can have their own space), and parking prices that are easy on the family travel budget.

In Cambridge, the **Royal Sonesta Hotel** (p. 282) is around the corner from the Museum of Science and has a large indoor/outdoor pool. It fills the vacation months with Summerfest, which includes free use of bicycles, ice cream, and boat rides along the Charles River. On off-season weekends, the Family Fun package includes four passes to the Museum of Science.

Across the street, **Hotel Marlowe** (p. 284) boasts an excellent location, the welcoming atmosphere that family travelers have come to expect from the Kimpton chain, and special weekend packages.

The riverfront **Hyatt Regency Cambridge** (p. 284) courts families with its pool, bicycle rentals, easy access to the banks of the Charles, and discounted rates (subject to availability) on a separate room for the kids.

Weekend, family, and other packages available. AE, DC, DISC, MC, V. Valet parking $42. T: Orange Line to Back Bay, or Green Line to Arlington or Copley. **Amenities:** Restaurant; Irish bar; coffee and wine lounge; exercise room; room service. *In room:* A/C, TV, CD player, hair dryer, fridge, Wi-Fi (free).

Boston Marriott Copley Place ★ This 38-story tower with something for everyone—complete business facilities, a good-size pool, and direct access to Boston's shopping wonderland—is extremely popular with convention and meeting planners. It's the hotel component of countless package deals. The contemporary-style guest rooms, which were renovated in 2012, are large enough to hold two armchairs or an armchair and an ottoman; they have the chain's signature Revive bedding and down comforters. As at the Back Bay's other lofty lodgings, ask for the highest possible floor and you'll enjoy excellent views. Besides booking hordes of vacationers, this Marriott and the Sheraton Boston are New England's biggest convention hotels; the Sheraton has a better pool, but both are reliable and comfortable enough that you can't go wrong by letting price and frequent-traveler points help you distinguish between them.

110 Huntington Ave. (at Harcourt St.), Boston, MA 02116. www.copleymarriott.com. ℂ **800/228-9290** or 617/236-5800. Fax 617/236-5885. 1,147 units. $159–$499 double; $500 and way up suite. Children 17 and under stay free in parent's room. Weekend and other packages available. AE, DC, DISC, MC, V. Valet parking $46; self-parking $35. T: Orange Line to Back Bay, Green Line to Copley, or Green Line E to Prudential. **Amenities:** Restaurant; bar; concierge; health club; Jacuzzi; indoor pool; room service. *In room:* A/C, TV, fridge, hair dryer, high-speed Internet ($13 per day).

The Boston Park Plaza Hotel & Towers ★

The Park Plaza does a hopping convention and function business and is popular with tour groups. It's in a terrific location a block from the Public Garden, within easy walking distance of the Back Bay, Beacon Hill, and Chinatown. The old-fashioned hotel (built in 1927) completed $5 million in renovations in 2012 and offers modern comforts such as pillow-top beds and flatscreen TVs. The least expensive ("petite") units here are tiny; if you're not a crash-and-dash traveler, just asking at the front desk may get you moved into a larger room. Towers units offer upgraded amenities and terrific views, especially from the higher floors of the 15-story building. The DoubleTree, this hotel's closest competitor, has better fitness offerings, but the eco-conscious Park Plaza is more convenient to the Back Bay.

50 Park Plaza (at Arlington St., 1 block from Boylston St.), Boston, MA 02116. www.bostonparkplaza.com. ℂ **800/225-2008** or 617/426-2000. Fax 617/426-5545. 941 units, some with shower only. $139–$489 double; $279–$3,500 suite. Extra person $25. Children 17 and under stay free in parent's room. Senior discount, weekend, and family packages available. AE, DC, DISC, MC, V. Valet parking $46. T: Green Line to Arlington. Pets accepted. **Amenities:** 6 restaurants; cafe; Irish pub; nightclub; concierge; executive-level rooms; exercise room; room service. *In room:* A/C, TV, hair dryer, high-speed Internet ($10 per day).

Copley Square Hotel ★

If you can manage without full business features and a tricked-out health club, the Copley Square Hotel is a terrific choice. A stone's throw from the Back Bay's convention behemoths, it's an eco-conscious boutique property that primarily courts vacationers. The location and courteous service also appeal to corporate travelers, who find enough business features here to keep them happy. The seven-story 1891 building was gutted and revamped in sleek, contemporary style in 2009. The 19th-century rooms haven't changed in size—"boutique" units are quite snug—but they're exceedingly comfy, with pillow-top beds and cushy linens and upholstery in grays, taupes, and crisp white.

47 Huntington Ave. (at Exeter St.), Boston, MA 02116. www.copleysquarehotel.com. ℂ **800/225-7062** or 617/536-9000. Fax 617/421-1402. 143 units, 38 with shower only. Apr–Oct $249–$549 double, $499–$729 suite; Nov–Mar $159–$299 double, $399–$499 suite. Rates include 24-hr. coffee and tea in lobby, evening glass of wine. Children 18 and under stay free in parent's room. Packages available. AE, DC, DISC, MC, V. Valet parking $43. T: Green Line to Copley or Orange Line to Back Bay. Pets under 30 lb. accepted ($40 fee). **Amenities:** Restaurant; lounge; nightclub;

concierge; exercise room; access to nearby health club ($15); room service. *In room:* A/C, TV, hair dryer, MP3 docking station, Wi-Fi (free).

Hilton Boston Back Bay ★   Across the street from the Hynes Convention Center, the Hilton is primarily a top-notch business hotel; vacationing families like the location and the pool. The large, well-kept guest rooms are furnished in modern style, with oversize work desks and down comforters. Units on higher floors of the 26-story tower enjoy excellent views. Weekend packages, especially in winter, can be a great deal. The atmosphere tends to be considerably calmer than the scene at the Hilton's main competition, the three megahotels attached to the Prudential Center and Copley Place. The closest of those, the Sheraton, is across the street. It's three times the Hilton's size, has a better pool, and books more vacation and function business.

40 Dalton St. (at Belvidere St., off Boylston St.), Boston, MA 02115. www.bostonbackbay.hilton. com. ℂ **800/445-8667** or 617/236-1100. Fax 617/867-6104. 390 units, 66 with shower only. $199–$699 double. Extra person $20. Rollaway $25. Children 17 and under stay free in parent's room. Packages and AAA discount available. AE, DC, DISC, MC, V. Self-parking $41. T: Green Line B, C, or D to Hynes Convention Center. **Amenities:** Restaurant; bar; concierge; well-equipped exercise room; indoor pool; room service. *In room:* A/C, TV, hair dryer, minibar, MP3 docking station, Wi-Fi ($15 per day).

Sheraton Boston Hotel ★★   Its central location, range of accommoda- tions, extensive convention and function facilities, and huge pool make this 29-story hotel one of the most popular in the city with both business and leisure travelers. It offers direct access to the Hynes Convention Center and Prudential Center (which connects to Copley Place). The fairly large guest rooms, deco- rated in sleek contemporary style, contain the chain's signature sleigh beds with pillow-top mattresses. The top floors hold club-level suites, but even standard accommodations on higher floors afford gorgeous views. Because it's so big, the Sheraton often has available rooms when smaller properties are full, but shop around before you book; you may land a better deal elsewhere.

39 Dalton St. (at Scotia St., off Boylston St.), Boston, MA 02199. www.sheraton.com/boston. ℂ **800/325-3535** or 617/236-2000. Fax 617/236-1702. 1,220 units. $209–$409 double; $309 and way up suite. Children 17 and under stay free in parent's room. Weekend packages avail- able. AE, DC, DISC, MC, V. Valet parking $46; self-parking $39. T: Green Line E to Prudential, or B, C, or D to Hynes Convention Center. Dogs under 40 lb. accepted with prior approval. **Amenities:** 3 restaurants; concierge; club-level rooms; well-equipped health club; heated indoor/outdoor pool; room service; sauna. *In room:* A/C, TV, hair dryer, high-speed Internet ($10 per day).

The Westin Copley Place Boston ★★   Towering 36 stories above Copley Square, the Westin attracts business travelers, conventiongoers, sightseers, and shoppers with its great location and solicitous staff. Sky bridges connect to Cop- ley Place and the Prudential Center complex. Like the other hotels in the Pru complex, this is a reliable, well-maintained chain property; it generally has better packages than the Marriott and Sheraton, but price all three before booking. The Westin's spacious guest rooms—all on the eighth floor and higher—have tradi- tional oak and mahogany furniture and the chain's beloved pillow-top mattresses. Junior suites are oversize doubles with generous sitting areas, and one-bedroom suites have one of the most entertaining features around: a queen-size Murphy bed in the living room. You might not notice any of that at first, because the views are spectacular.

10 Huntington Ave. (at Dartmouth St.), Boston, MA 02116. www.westin.com/copleyplace. ℂ **800/937-8461** or 617/262-9600. Fax 617/424-7483. 803 units. $179–$569 double; $239–$599 suite; $999–$3,300 specialty suite. Extra person $25–$50. Weekend packages available. AE, DC, DISC, MC, V. Valet parking $46; self-parking $35. T: Green Line to Copley or Orange Line to Back Bay. Pets accepted. **Amenities:** 3 restaurants; bar; concierge; health club & spa; indoor pool; room service. *In room:* A/C, TV/VCR, hair dryer, minibar, Wi-Fi ($13 per day).

Moderate

Boston Common Hotel & Conference Center ★ 🎁   A limited-service lodging with an old-fashioned air and a helpful staff, this eight-story hotel is a hidden jewel. In an unbeatable location on a dead-end street near Back Bay Station, the former John Hancock Hotel books many groups that use the abundant meeting space. The compact, comfortable guest rooms aren't fancy, but they're well maintained and big enough not to feel claustrophobic; bathrooms, however, are tiny. The closest competitor, the funkier Hotel 140, sometimes beats this hotel on price; winter rates here are fantastic.

40 Trinity Place (off Stuart St.), Boston, MA 02116. www.bostoncommonhotel.com. ℂ **617/933-7700.** Fax 617/933-7709. 64 units. $109–$189 double. Rates include continental breakfast. Extra person $15. Children 17 and under stay free in parent's room. AE, DC, DISC, MC, V. Validated self-parking $27 in nearby garage. T: Orange Line to Back Bay or Green Line to Copley. *In room:* A/C, TV, hair dryer, Wi-Fi (free).

Charlesmark Hotel ★★ ✐   In an excellent location overlooking the Boston Marathon finish line, the Charlesmark has a boutique feel and great prices. The amenities don't challenge the perks at the neighborhood's large hotels, but they'll satisfy most business or leisure travelers. The sleek, contemporary design ingeniously uses custom furnishings to maximize the 1892 building's compact spaces. Guest rooms are small but have pillow-top mattresses and enough space to hold a chair. Rates include breakfast, light refreshments such as bottled water and fruit, and local phone calls, all part of management's policy not to pad your bill with incidentals. The only real drawback is that the building has just one elevator—and if that's your biggest problem, you're doing pretty well.

655 Boylston St. (btw. Dartmouth and Exeter sts.), Boston, MA 02116. www.thecharlesmark.com. ℂ **617/247-1212.** Fax 617/247-1224. 40 units, most with shower only. $129–$249 double. Rates include continental breakfast. Children stay free in parent's room. AE, DC, DISC, MC, V. Self-parking $27 in nearby garage. T: Green Line to Copley. Pets accepted with prior approval. **Amenities:** Lounge; access to nearby health club ($10). *In room:* A/C, TV/DVD, CD player, fridge, hair dryer, Wi-Fi (free).

Hotel 140 ✐   Two short blocks from Copley Square, Hotel 140 is a good deal for the pricey Back Bay. Contemporary-style rooms and bathrooms are on the small side—the tiniest units hold just a full-size bed—but the hotel consistently fills with leisure and thrifty business travelers. It occupies the fifth through eighth floors of a 14-story building; the deli in the lobby serves breakfast and lunch. The hotel opened in 2005 in a renovated former YWCA that dates to 1929. Its main competitor is the Boston Common Hotel, which is more traditional in style.

140 Clarendon St. (at Stuart St.), Boston, MA 02116. www.hotel140.com. ✆ **800/714-0140** or 617/585-5600. 59 units, all with shower only. $119–$339 double. Weekend, theater, and other packages and long-term rates available. AE, MC, V. Self-parking $27 in adjacent garage. T: Orange Line to Back Bay. **Amenities:** Exercise room; access to nearby health club. *In room:* A/C, TV, hair dryer, Wi-Fi (free).

The MidTown Hotel ★ ☺ ✍   This centrally located two-story hotel is a tour-group standby that's popular with families, who like the seasonal pool, and with budget-conscious businesspeople. The boxy white building is on a busy street across from the Prudential Center, within walking distance of Symphony Hall and the Museum of Fine Arts. Rooms are large, bright, and attractively outfitted in no-frills contemporary style; bathrooms are small. Some units have connecting doors that allow families to spread out. The best rooms are at the back of the building, away from Huntington Avenue traffic. The hotel is an oddity in this neighborhood of cushy chain and independent accommodations; even if you score a great rate at one of those properties, do the math to see whether the relatively cheap parking here makes the MidTown a better bargain.

220 Huntington Ave. (at Cumberland St., 1 long block from Mass. Ave.), Boston, MA 02445. www.midtownhotel.com. ✆ **800/343-1177** or 617/262-1000. Fax 617/262-8739. 159 units. $119–$259 double; $139–$279 suite. Extra person $15. Children 17 and under stay free in parent's room. Packages and AAA, AARP, and government discounts may be available. AE, DC, DISC, MC, V. Parking $18. T: Green Line E to Prudential or Orange Line to Massachusetts Ave. Dogs accepted ($30 fee). **Amenities:** Concierge; access to nearby health club ($5–$10); heated outdoor pool. *In room:* A/C, TV, hair dryer, Wi-Fi ($10 per day).

The Newbury Guest House.

Newbury Guest House ★★ ✍
The Newbury Guest House is one of the best bargains in Boston: The well-maintained property offers comfortably furnished, nicely appointed guest rooms at a great price for a terrific location. The largest rooms are the bay-window units, which overlook the lively street; rooms at the back are quieter but face an alley. The Newbury Guest House, which occupies three 1880s brick town houses, opened in 1991 and operates near capacity year-round, drawing business travelers during the week and sightseers on weekends. Reserve early.

261 Newbury St. (btw. Fairfield and Gloucester sts.), Boston, MA 02116. www.newburyguest house.com. ✆ **800/437-7668** or 617/670-6000. Fax 617/670-6100. 32 units, some with shower only. $139–$279 double. Extra person $20. Off-season discounts available. Rates include continental breakfast. Packages available. Rates may be higher during special

events. AE, DC, DISC, MC, V. Parking $20 (reservation required). T: Green Line B, C, or D to Hynes Convention Center. **Amenities:** Restaurant; access to nearby health club ($25). *In room:* A/C, TV, fridge, hair dryer, Wi-Fi (free).

KENMORE SQUARE

Beneath the iconic Citgo sign where Commonwealth Avenue, Beacon Street, and Brookline Avenue meet is Kenmore Square, a landmark for baseball fans.

BEST FOR   Visitors to nearby Fenway Park, Boston University, and the museums and cultural institutions of the Fenway neighborhood.

DRAWBACKS   Unbelievably large, loud crowds during baseball season; college-town atmosphere year-round. Getting to Cambridge is a hassle.

Hotel Commonwealth ★★   This five-story boutique hotel in the heart of Kenmore Square draws a lot of business from nearby Boston University and from local cultural institutions. It boasts extensive business features as well as luxurious amenities such as Frette linens and large marble bathrooms. My favorite guest rooms are the huge Commonwealth units; each has a king bed and a heavy curtain that draws across the center of the room, separating the sleeping area and the "parlor." These rooms overlook the bustling street, outdoor restaurant seating, and the bus station (and attendant traffic) at the center of the square. You might prefer a Fenway room—they're smaller, but they face the legendary ballpark, which lies across the Massachusetts Turnpike.

500 Commonwealth Ave. (at Kenmore St.), Boston, MA 02215. www.hotelcommonwealth.com. © **866/784-4000** or 617/933-5000. Fax 617/266-6888. 150 units. $235–$415 standard double; $265–$485 minisuite or parlor room. Extra person $20. Children 17 and under stay free in parent's room. Packages and AAA discount available. AE, DC, DISC, MC, V. Valet parking $42. T: Green Line B, C, or D to Kenmore. Pets accepted ($125 fee). **Amenities:** 3 restaurants; bar; concierge; exercise room; room service. *In room:* A/C, TV/DVD, hair dryer, minibar, MP3 docking station, Wi-Fi (free).

OUTSKIRTS & BROOKLINE

What Bostonians consider "outskirts" would be centrally located in many larger cities. Brookline starts about 3 blocks west of Boston's Kenmore Square; beyond that are the Boston neighborhoods Allston and Brighton, and to the southwest, past Fenway Park, is the Longwood Medical Area.

BEST FOR   Travelers who want more room and lower prices than properties in other areas generally offer. For those who must drive, parking is generally (but not always) cheaper here than it is elsewhere.

DRAWBACKS   Unless they're sticking near their hotels, sightseers staying in this area essentially become commuters. If you're visiting Cambridge, public transit connections are unwieldy at best.

The 188-unit **Courtyard Boston Brookline,** 40 Webster St. (off Beacon St.), Brookline (www.brooklinecourtyard.com; © **866/296-2296,** 800/321-2211, or 617/734-1393; T: Green Line C to Coolidge Corner), is a well-equipped, conveniently located business hotel. It has a breakfast cafe, indoor pool, exercise room, and shuttle service to the nearby Longwood Medical Area. A double in high season goes for $179 to $399, which includes Wi-Fi; parking costs $24.

The Holiday Inn Boston Brookline, 1200 Beacon St. (at St. Paul St.), Brookline (www.holidayinn.com; ✆ **800/465-4329** or 617/277-1200; T: Green Line C to St. Paul St.), overlooks the trolley tracks just outside Coolidge Corner. The six-story hotel has a restaurant, exercise room, small indoor pool, and shuttle service to the nearby hospitals. Rates for a double start at $169, including Wi-Fi; parking costs $21.

Anthony's Town House   This friendly establishment offers homey, comfortable accommodations with shared bathrooms; it's popular with Europeans and budget-minded Americans. Each floor holds three high-ceilinged rooms furnished in Queen Anne or Victorian style and one bathroom with an enclosed shower. Smaller rooms (one per floor) have twin beds; the large front rooms have bay windows. Two family units hold as many as five people comfortably. Guests have the use of two refrigerators and a microwave, and the staff supplies a DVD player, VCR, hair dryer, or iron on request. The four-story brownstone guesthouse, a family business since 1944, is 1 mile from Boston's Kenmore Square and, by T, about 15 minutes from downtown. It's more convenient than the nearby Longwood Inn, which has private bathrooms. There's no smoking on the premises.

1085 Beacon St. (at Hawes St.), Brookline, MA 02446. www.anthonystownhouse.com. ✆ **617/566-3972.** Fax 617/232-1085. 10 units, none with private bathroom. $78–$108 double; from $125 family room. Extra person $10. Weekly rates and winter discounts available. No credit cards. Limited free parking; off-premises parking $10. T: Green Line C to Hawes St. *In room:* A/C, TV, no phone, Wi-Fi (free).

Best Western Plus Boston/The Inn at Longwood Medical ★   Next to Children's Hospital in the Longwood Medical Area, this eight-story hotel is a good base for those with business at the hospitals. The helpful staff is responsive to the needs of patients and their families. Museums, colleges, and Fenway Park are nearby, and downtown Boston is 20 minutes away by T. The well-maintained guest rooms are quite large and furnished in colorful, contemporary style. Try to stay on the highest floor possible, to enjoy the views and to get away from the busy intersection of Longwood and Brookline avenues. Suites have kitchen facilities that make them a good choice for long-term guests. The hotel adjoins the Longwood Galleria business complex, which has a food court (with Boston's only Dairy Queen) and shops, including a drugstore.

342 Longwood Ave. (at Brookline Ave.), Boston, MA 02115. www.innatlongwood.com. ✆ **800/468-2378** or 617/731-4700, TTY 617/731-9088. Fax 617/731-4870. 161 units. $139–$259 double; from $269 suite. Extra person $15. Children 17 and under stay free in parent's room. Weekend and family packages, hospital and long-term discounts available. AE, DC, DISC, MC, V. Parking $18. T: Green Line D or E to Longwood. **Amenities:** Restaurant; lounge; concierge; access to nearby health club ($8); room service. *In room:* A/C, TV, hair dryer, kitchenette (in 18 units), Wi-Fi (free).

DoubleTree Suites by Hilton Boston ★★ ☺ ✦   This hotel is one of the best deals in town—almost every unit is a two-room suite with a living room, bedroom, and bathroom. Business travelers can entertain and families can spread out, making this a good choice for both. It's near Cambridge and across the street from the Charles River, but not in an actual neighborhood or near the T; shuttle service is available to local destinations. The well-kept suites surround a 15-story atrium. Rooms are large and attractively furnished in upscale-chain-hotel style.

Most bedrooms have a king-size bed (some have two oversize twins) and a writing desk. Each living room contains a full-size sofa bed, dining table, microwave, and refrigerator. The Hyatt Regency Cambridge, the hotel's nearest rival, is slightly more convenient but generally more expensive.

400 Soldiers Field Rd. (at Cambridge St.), Boston, MA 02134. www.hiltonfamilyboston.com/boston. *℃* **800/222-8733** or 617/783-0090. Fax 617/783-0897. 308 units. $129–$309 double. Extra person $10. Children 17 and under stay free in parent's room. Packages and AAA and AARP discounts available. AE, DC, DISC, MC, V. Self-parking $35. T: Red Line to Harvard, then take shuttle bus. Pets accepted with prior approval ($250 deposit). **Amenities:** Restaurant; lounge; excellent Scullers Jazz Club (p. 239); concierge; well-equipped exercise room; Jacuzzi; indoor pool; room service. *In room:* A/C, TV, fridge, hair dryer, MP3 docking station, Wi-Fi ($10 per day).

Longwood Inn   In a residential area 3 blocks from the Boston border, this three-story guesthouse offers comfortable accommodations at modest rates. The homey style suits the Victorian architecture of the building, which has been extensively renovated and is meticulously maintained. Guests have use of a kitchen, common dining room, and patio with tables and chairs. The apartment has a private bathroom, kitchen, and balcony. Tennis courts, a running track, and a playground at the school next door are open to the public. The Longwood Medical Area and Coolidge Corner are within easy walking distance, and public transportation is nearby—not as close as it is to Anthony's Town House, but this property has private bathrooms (one unit's bathroom is across the hall; others are en suite).

123 Longwood Ave. (at Marshall St., 1 block from Kent St.), Brookline, MA 02446. www.longwood-inn.com. *℃* **617/566-8615.** Fax 617/738-1070. 22 units, 4 with shower only. Apr–Nov $129–$154 double; Dec–Mar $94–$129 double. Extra person $5–$10. 1-bedroom apt (sleeps 4-plus) $124–$164. Weekly rates available. AE, DISC, MC, V. Free parking. T: Green Line D to Longwood or C to Coolidge Corner. *In room:* A/C, TV, Wi-Fi (free).

CAMBRIDGE

Across the Charles River from Boston, Cambridge has its own attractions and excellent hotels. Graduation season (May and early June) is especially busy, but campus events can cause high demand at unexpected times, so plan ahead.

BEST FOR   Well-heeled visitors to Cambridge, and travelers to downtown Boston and the South Boston waterfront, which are relatively easy to reach on the T from both the Harvard Square area and East Cambridge.

DRAWBACKS   Access to most other areas of Boston, notably the Back Bay and South End, can be slow, expensive, or both. Budget accommodations are limited, and parking at most hotels is almost as expensive as parking in Boston.

Very Expensive

The Charles Hotel ★★★   Just a block from Harvard Square, the Charles has been *the* place for business and leisure travelers to Cambridge since it opened in 1985. Vacationing families and visiting parents enjoy the same high level of service as Harvard affiliates, business tycoons, and the odd celebrity. The style in the nine-story brick hotel is luxe contemporary country, with custom adaptations of early American Shaker furniture. The austere design contrasts with the swanky amenities in the good-size guest rooms, which have floor-to-ceiling windows, down quilts, and Bose Wave radios; bathrooms contain telephones and TVs (in the mirrors—cool!). The eco-aware Charles rivals the Four Seasons and Boston Harbor Hotel for cachet and amenities; the only other Cambridge hotel with comparable features and service is the Royal Sonesta, which is less convenient and generally less expensive.

1 Bennett St. (at Eliot St., 1 block from Mount Auburn St.), Cambridge, MA 02138. www.charles hotel.com. ⓒ **800/882-1818** or 617/864-1200. Fax 617/864-5715. 294 units. $299–$599 double; $409 and way up suite. Off-season discounts and weekend packages available. AE, DC, MC, V. Valet or self-parking $34. T: Red Line to Harvard. Pets accepted ($50 fee). **Amenities:** 2 restaurants (including Henrietta's Table; p. 176); 2 bars; Regattabar jazz club (p. 239); concierge; free access to adjacent health club w/pool, Jacuzzi, and sauna; room service; adjacent spa. *In room:* A/C, TV/DVD, hair dryer, minibar, Wi-Fi (free).

Hotel Veritas ★ The only boutique hotel in Harvard Square is a lovely, romantic property that makes up for potential drawbacks with thoughtful amenities and great service. Rooms are small but luxurious, with high ceilings and plush residential-style appointments. There's no restaurant or room service, but room rates include bottled water as well as coffee, tea, juice, and soda (available in the lobby). Five blocks from the T, the hotel, which opened in 2010, faces busy Mass. Ave. and has a small, low-key lounge in the lobby; ask for a room at the back of the property (numbers that end in "01" and "02") if street noise is a concern, and request a unit away from the lobby if you need quiet before 11pm.

1 Remington St. (at Mass. Ave.), Cambridge, MA 02138. www.thehotelveritas.com. ⓒ **888/520-1050** or 617/520-5000. Fax 617/520-5004. 31 units, 26 with shower only. $245–$395 double; $595–$795 suite. Children stay free in parent's room. Weekend and other packages available. AE, DC, DISC, MC, V. Valet parking $34. T: Red Line to Harvard. **Amenities:** Lounge; babysitting; concierge; free access to nearby health club. *In room:* A/C, TV, hair dryer, MP3 docking station, Wi-Fi (free).

Royal Sonesta Hotel ★★ ☺ This luxurious hotel is popular with business travelers and with families, who enjoy the huge pool. The CambridgeSide Galleria mall is across the street, the Museum of Science around the corner, and tech-happy Kendall Square 10 minutes away on foot. Even amid all that activity, the hotel feels serene, thanks in part to the helpful staff. Most of the rooms in the 10-story building look out on the river or the city (higher prices are for better views). Everything is custom designed in modern, comfortable style and exceptionally well maintained. The Sonesta's closest rival is Hotel Marlowe, across the street, which offers less extensive fitness options and fewer river views.

40 Edwin H. Land Blvd. (at CambridgeSide Place), Cambridge, MA 02142. www.sonesta.com/ boston. ⓒ **800/766-3782** or 617/806-4200. Fax 617/806-4232. 400 units, some with shower only. $239–$279 standard double; $259–$299 superior double; $279–$319 deluxe double; $339 and up suite. Extra person $25. Children 17 and under stay free in parent's room. Weekend, family, and other packages available. AE, DC, DISC, MC, V. Valet parking $27. T: Green Line to Lechmere, then a 10-min. walk. **Amenities:** Restaurant; cafe w/seasonal outdoor seating; bike rental (seasonal); concierge; well-equipped 24-hr. health club & spa; heated indoor/outdoor pool w/retractable roof; room service. *In room:* A/C, TV, hair dryer, minibar, MP3 docking station, Wi-Fi (free).

Cambridge Hotels

Best Western Hotel Tria **1**
The Charles Hotel **4**
Courtyard Boston Cambridge **8**
DoubleTree Suites by Hilton Boston **7**
Hampton Inn Boston/Cambridge **12**
Harvard Square Hotel **3**
Holiday Inn Express Hotel & Suites **11**
Hotel Marlowe **13**
Hotel Veritas **6**
The Hyatt Regency Cambridge **9**
The Inn at Harvard **5**
Le Méridien Cambridge **10**
Royal Sonesta Hotel **14**
Sheraton Commander Hotel **2**

Expensive

The **Hampton Inn Boston/Cambridge,** 191 Msgr. O'Brien Hwy., at Water Street, Cambridge (www.bostoncambridge.hamptoninn.com; © **800/426-7866** or 617/494-5300; T: Green Line to Lechmere), is a 5-minute walk from the T. Rates at the 114-room hotel start at $249 for a double in high season and include parking (one vehicle per room), buffet breakfast, and Wi-Fi.

Hotel Marlowe ★ ☺   Hotel Marlowe offers abundant amenities for both business and leisure travelers, with easy access to the CambridgeSide Galleria mall, the Museum of Science, the Charles River, and MIT. Rooms in the eight-story building were completely renovated in 2011; they're elegant yet fun, and large enough to hold a work desk and armchair. All have down comforters and three phones (one in the bathroom), and suites have spa tubs. Views are of the river, a small canal, or the landscaped courtyard/driveway off the lobby. The eco-savvy hotel's closest competitor is the Royal Sonesta Hotel, across the street, which has a pool and health club, better river views, and correspondingly higher prices. *Tip:* Sign up for the (free) Kimpton frequent-guest program, and the hotel waives the Internet access fee.

25 Edwin H. Land Blvd. (at Cambridge Pkwy., 1 block from Msgr. O'Brien Hwy.), Cambridge, MA 02141. www.hotelmarlowe.com. © **800/825-7040,** 800/546-7866, or 617/868-8000. Fax 617/868-8001. 236 units, some with shower only. $199–$449 double; from $409 suite. Extra person $25. Rates include morning coffee and tea, evening wine reception, and use of bikes. Children 17 and under stay free in parent's room. Weekend, family, and other packages, AAA and AARP discounts available. AE, DC, DISC, MC, V. Valet parking $30; self-parking $20. T: Green Line to Lechmere or Red Line to Kendall. Pets accepted. **Amenities:** Restaurant; bar; bikes; concierge; exercise room; room service. *In room:* A/C, TV, hair dryer, MP3 docking station, Wi-Fi (free).

The Hyatt Regency Cambridge ★ ☺   Across the street from the Charles River and 10 minutes by car from downtown Boston, the Hyatt Regency books businesspeople on weeknights and vacationers on weekends. It's convenient to Harvard and Kendall squares and Boston University, but not near the subway. The landmark pyramidal building, last renovated in 2010, holds spacious, well-outfitted guest rooms with pillow-top beds. Most rooms face the 16-story atrium, others overlook central Cambridge, and the best enjoy breathtaking views of Boston. Families (see "Family-Friendly Hotels," p. 274) can take advantage of special two-room rates, subject to availability. If you plan to rely on public transit, allow time for the bus or hotel shuttle. The closest competitor is the DoubleTree, which is even farther from public transit but consists of all suites.

575 Memorial Dr. (at Amesbury St., 1 block from the BU Bridge), Cambridge, MA 02139. www.cambridge.hyatt.com. © **800/233-1234** or 617/462-1234. Fax 617/491-6906. 470 units, some with shower only. $129–$359 double; $750–$1,500 suite. Extra person $25. Children 17 and under stay free in parent's room. Weekend packages available. AE, DC, DISC, MC, V. Self-parking $35. T: Red Line to Harvard or Kendall/MIT, then shuttle bus (no luggage permitted) or $6 cab ride. Pets under 25 lb. accepted ($50 fee). **Amenities:** Restaurant with seasonal outdoor seating; lounge; bike rental; concierge; rooftop health club; 75-ft. indoor lap pool; room service; sauna. *In room:* A/C, TV, hair dryer, MP3 docking station, Wi-Fi ($13 per day).

The Inn at Harvard ★★   The Georgian-style red-brick Inn at Harvard, adjacent to Harvard Yard, is popular with university visitors and business travelers. Guest rooms are elegantly decorated in subdued neutrals and have pillow-top beds; each has a work area and Aeron chair. Some units have dormer windows and window seats; the best rooms are on higher floors facing Harvard Street. The four-story skylit atrium holds the "living room," a huge, well-appointed guest lounge that's suitable (in furnishings and volume level) for meeting with a visitor if you don't want to conduct business in your room.

1201 Massachusetts Ave. (at Quincy St.), Cambridge, MA 02138. www.hotelsinharvardsquare.com. © **800/458-5886** or 617/491-2222. Fax 617/520-3711. 111 units, some with shower only. $159–$399 double; $1,500 presidential suite. AAA and AARP discounts available. AE, DC, DISC, MC, V. Valet parking $35. T: Red Line to Harvard. **Amenities:** Restaurant; dining privileges at nearby Harvard Faculty Club; exercise room; room service. *In room:* A/C, TV, hair dryer, Wi-Fi (free).

Le Méridien Cambridge ★　The only sizable lodging close to lively Central Square, this hotel primarily attracts visitors to MIT and the tech-oriented businesses nearby. Rooms are large enough to hold small seating areas and oversize desks, with cushy beds that soften the neutrals of the contemporary decor. The eight-story building encloses a lovely courtyard; units facing inward are preferable to those with street views. The closest competitors are the Sonesta and Marlowe, in East Cambridge—about the same distance from the T, but with easier access to the river—and the Hyatt Regency, which is some distance from the subway but has a pool.

20 Sidney St. (at Green St., 1 block from Mass. Ave.), Cambridge, MA 02139. www.lemeridien. com/cambridge. © **800/543-4300** or 617/577-0200. Fax 617/494-8366. 210 units, 8 with shower only. $199–$419 double; $249–$519 suite. Extra person $20. Children 17 and under stay free in parent's room. Weekend, family, and other packages, AAA and AARP discounts available. AE, DC, DISC, MC, V. Valet parking $32; self-parking $28. T: Red Line to Central. Pets under 50 lb. accepted. **Amenities:** Restaurant; bar; concierge; 24-hr. exercise room; access to nearby health club. *In room:* A/C, TV, CD player, hair dryer, Wi-Fi (free).

Sheraton Commander Hotel ★　University guests, visiting parents, and business travelers make up the bulk of the Sheraton Commander's business. In the heart of Cambridge's historic district, the hotel is exactly what you'd expect of a traditional hostelry within sight of the Harvard campus. Many guest rooms have four-poster beds, and all have Sheraton's signature mattresses and plenty of accents in crimson, Harvard's school color. Ask the pleasant front-desk staff for a room facing Cambridge Common; even if you aren't high up in the six-story building, you'll enjoy a pleasant view. The Sheraton Commander doesn't have the Charles Hotel's cachet and amenities, but it doesn't charge the Charles's prices, either. Plan far ahead if you're visiting during a Harvard event.

16 Garden St. (at Berkeley St., 3 blocks from Mass. Ave.), Cambridge, MA 02138. www.sheraton. com/commander. © **800/325-3535** or 617/547-4800. Fax 617/234-1396. 175 units, some with shower only. $159–$479 double; $354 and way up suite. Extra person $20. Children 17 and under stay free in parent's room. Weekend packages, AAA and AARP discounts available. AE, DC, DISC, MC, V. Valet parking $29. T: Red Line to Harvard. Dogs under 80 lb. accepted. **Amenities:** Restaurant; lounge; concierge; small exercise room; room service. *In room:* A/C, TV, hair dryer, Wi-Fi (free).

Moderate

The 112-unit **Holiday Inn Express Hotel & Suites,** 250 Msgr. O'Brien Hwy., at Sciarappa Street, Cambridge (www.hiexpress.com/boscambridgema; © **888/ 887-7690** or 617/577-7600; fax 617/354-1313), is a limited-services property

10 minutes from the Green Line on a busy street. There's no restaurant, but each room has a fridge and microwave, and a supermarket is a block away. Rates for a double in high season start at $169 and include Wi-Fi, breakfast, and parking—a big plus in Cambridge.

Best Western Plus Hotel Tria ★ ✦   Because of its borderline-suburban location, the Tria usually beats other Cambridge hotels on price, and its standard rooms are as large as some other properties' suites. All are decorated in muted jewel tones, with comfy contemporary furnishings. The building is set back from the busy road, which cuts down on traffic noise. The walking/jogging path and golf course at Fresh Pond, a shopping center, and Whole Foods and Trader Joe's markets are nearby. The T is about 10 minutes away on foot or 5 minutes on the hotel shuttle. Boston lies a 15-minute drive or a 25-minute T ride away; Lexington and Concord are less than a half-hour by car.

220 Alewife Brook Pkwy. (at Concord Ave.), Cambridge, MA 02138. www.hoteltria.com. ✆ **866/333-8742** or 617/491-8000. Fax 617/491-4932. 121 units. Mid-Mar to Oct $149–$299 double; Nov to mid-Mar $119–$199 double. Rates include breakfast. Rates may be higher during special events. Children 16 and under stay free in parent's room. Packages available. AE, DC, MC, V. Parking $12. T: Red Line to Alewife, then a 12-min. walk. Pets accepted; reservation required ($25 fee and $100 deposit). **Amenities:** Restaurant; bar; coffee shop; bikes; exercise room. *In room:* A/C, TV, fridge, hair dryer, Wi-Fi (free).

Courtyard Boston Cambridge ★   This 16-story hotel is popular with visitors to colleges on both sides of the river. It's across the street from the Charles, meaning the views are great but public-transit access isn't. The tasteful but unremarkable Marriott decor includes supercomfy beds but doesn't compete with the killer views through the floor-to-ceiling windows. Prices vary with room size, floor, and view; units on higher floors facing the river enjoy a panorama of the Boston skyline. Even the priciest units generally undercut rates at the posher Hyatt Regency and DoubleTree, the only nearby competitors. The hotel doesn't offer room service, but Trader Joe's and Starbucks are next door. If you're relying on public transit, allow time for the hotel shuttle.

777 Memorial Dr. (at Pleasant St., 1 block from River St.), Cambridge, MA 02139. www.cambridge courtyard.com. ✆ **800/235-6426,** 888/236-2427 (Marriott), or 617/492-7777. Fax 617/492-6038. 203 units. $169–$329 double; $269–$359 suite. Children stay free in parent's room. Weekend, family, and other packages available. AE, DC, DISC, MC, V. Parking $32. T: Red Line to Kendall/MIT or Central, then hotel shuttle or $10 cab ride. **Amenities:** 2 restaurants; lounge; 24-hr. exercise room; indoor pool; room service. *In room:* A/C, TV, hair dryer, Wi-Fi (free).

Harvard Square Hotel ✦   In the heart of "the Square," this six-story brick hotel offers relatively small rooms for relatively low rates—most of the year—that make it the best deal in a pricey location. Visiting parents and budget-conscious business travelers flock here year-round; at busy times, including fall foliage season, room rates spike. In great condition following a $5-million overhaul in 2012, the comfortable accommodations are decorated in muted neutrals with crimson accents and light-wood furnishings that lend an airy feel. Each has a flatscreen TV (important when every inch counts), and some overlook Harvard Square.

110 Mount Auburn St. (at Eliot St.), Cambridge, MA 02138. www.hotelsinharvardsquare.com. ✆ **800/458-5886** or 617/864-5200. Fax 617/492-4896. 73 units, some with shower only. $139–$259 double. Extra person $10. Children 16 and under stay free in parent's room. Packages,

corporate rates, AAA and AARP discounts available. AE, DC, DISC, MC, V. Parking $35. T: Red Line to Harvard. **Amenities:** Dining privileges at Harvard Faculty Club; free access to nearby health club. *In room:* A/C, TV, fridge, hair dryer, Wi-Fi (free).

AT & NEAR THE AIRPORT

Accommodations in this neighborhood range from high-end business hotels to budget chain lodgings, but even the least expensive properties aren't the dirt-cheap motels found near airports in many other parts of the country.

BEST FOR Anyone with an early flight. If you're not staying at the Hilton, make sure that you know the shuttle schedule and that the front-desk staff knows you have a plane to catch.

DRAWBACKS Distance from attractions, relying on the hotel shuttle to get to the subway (except at the Hilton).

The **Embassy Suites Hotel Boston at Logan Airport,** 207 Porter St., at Cottage Street, Boston (www.bostonloganairport.embassysuites.com; ✆ **800/362-2779** or 617/567-5000), is a 273-unit hotel with an indoor pool, exercise room, and business center. Each suite in the 10-story hotel has a living room with a pull-out couch. Room rates, which start at $199, include breakfast and shuttle service to the airport and the Airport T stop; Internet access costs $10 per night.

For moderately priced accommodations, if the Comfort Inn is booked consider the **Hampton Inn Boston Logan Airport,** 2300 Lee Burbank Hwy., Revere (www.hamptoninn.com; ✆ **800/426-7866** or 781/286-5665), on a commercial-industrial strip about 3 miles north of the airport. A free shuttle bus serves the 227-room hotel, which has a pool. Rates start at about $129 for a double and include continental breakfast and parking.

Comfort Inn & Suites Boston/Airport ★ 🗲 The airport lies about 3½ miles south of the well-equipped Comfort Inn, which offers a good range of features for business and leisure travelers. The eight-story hotel, part of the environmentally pioneering Saunders Hotel Group, sits on a hill set back from the road near a busy traffic circle. It has an attentive staff, an indoor pool, and round-the-clock shuttle service. Guest rooms are large, with cherrywood furnishings and unassuming beige decor. Suites are oversize rooms that contain sofa beds, and king suites have refrigerators as well. The somewhat inconvenient location translates to reasonable rates, and the North Shore is easily accessible if you plan a day trip. Revere Beach is about 2 minutes away by car.

85 American Legion Hwy. (Rte. 60), Revere, MA 02151. www.comfortinnboston.com. ✆ **877/485-3600** or 781/485-3600. Fax 781/485-3601. 208 units. $109–$239 double; $139–$279 suite. Rates include continental breakfast. Children 17 and under stay free in parent's room. Senior and AAA discounts available. AE, DC, DISC, MC, V. Free parking. T: Blue Line to Airport; then hotel shuttle. Pets accepted ($25 per night). **Amenities:** Restaurant; lounge; exercise room; indoor pool; room service. *In room:* A/C, TV, hair dryer, Wi-Fi (free).

Hilton Boston Logan Airport ★ Smack in the middle of the airport, the Hilton draws most of its guests from meetings, conventions, and canceled flights. Well equipped for business travelers, it's also a good fallback for vacationers who don't mind commuting to downtown. Guest rooms are large and tastefully furnished (in colors that make me think of business suits), with excellent soundproofing. The best units in the 10-story building afford sensational airport and harbor views. A shuttle bus serves all airport locations, including the ferry dock and subway, and walkways link the building to Terminals A (nearby) and E (farther). The Hyatt Harborside is the closest competition—it's at the edge of the airport, which means less commotion outside, better views, and less convenient T access.

1 Hotel Dr., Logan International Airport, Boston, MA 02128. www.hiltonfamilyboston.com/boston logan. **800/445-8667** or 617/568-6700. Fax 617/568-6800. 599 units. $139–$399 double; from $600 suite. Children 17 and under stay free in parent's room. Packages available. AE, DC, DISC, MC, V. Valet parking $40; self-parking $32. T: Blue Line to Airport, then take shuttle bus. Pets accepted ($25 fee). **Amenities:** Restaurant; pub; coffee counter; health club; Jacuzzi; 40-ft. lap pool; room service. *In room:* A/C, TV, hair dryer, MP3 docking station, Wi-Fi ($10–$18 per day).

Hyatt Harborside ★   Primarily a convention and business destination, this striking waterfront hotel is next to the airport ferry dock, 7 minutes from downtown by water taxi. The sizable guest rooms have oversize work desks and a sophisticated no-frills style that contrasts with luxurious touches like pillow-top beds. Large windows afford dramatic views of the harbor and city skyline, especially from higher floors of the 14-story building. Guests have easy access to the airport and the Airport T stop (a 5-min. ride on the hotel or MBTA shuttle bus) and to downtown Boston by water. The airport Hilton is more centrally located and typically beats this hotel on price, but the views here are better.

101 Harborside Dr., Boston, MA 02128. www.harborside.hyatt.com. **800/233-1234** or 617/568-1234. Fax 617/567-8856. 270 units, some with shower only. High season $349–$599 double; low season $199–$259 double; year-round from $895 suite. Children 11 and under stay free in parent's room. Family packages available. AE, DC, DISC, MC, V. Valet parking $40; self-parking $34. T: Blue Line to Airport, then take shuttle bus. By car, follow signs to Logan Airport and take Harborside Dr. past car-rental area and tunnel entrance. **Amenities:** Restaurant and lounge w/seasonal outdoor seating; concierge; exercise room w/harbor view; Jacuzzi; 40-ft. indoor pool; room service; sauna. *In room:* A/C, TV, hair dryer, MP3 docking station, Wi-Fi ($13 per day).

PRACTICAL MATTERS: THE HOTEL SCENE

The Big Picture

As you plan, keep the city's size in mind, and check a map before you rule out a location. Especially downtown—in the neighborhoods defined in chapter 3 as the **Waterfront,** the **North End, North Station, Faneuil Hall Marketplace, Government Center,** the **Financial District, Downtown Crossing,** and **Beacon Hill**—the areas are so small and close together that the borders are somewhat arbitrary. The division to consider is **downtown vs. the Back Bay vs. Cambridge,** and not, for example, Faneuil Hall Marketplace vs. the adjacent Financial District.

Year-round, it's always a good idea to **make a reservation,** and the earlier you book, the better your chances of landing a (relative) bargain. Definitely reserve ahead for travel between April and November, when conventions, college graduations, and vacations increase demand. During foliage season, the busiest and priciest time of year—even more expensive than the summer—plan early. If you don't, you risk staying far from Boston, paying dearly, or both.

A Note About Smoking

The city of **Boston bans smoking** in all hotels, inns, and B&Bs, and the **Marriott, Sheraton, Westin,** and **Wyndham** chains forbid smoking in all their properties. Elsewhere, nonsmokers shouldn't assume that they'll get a nonsmoking room without requesting one. Hotels now squeeze smokers into fewer rooms, which often reek of smoke and air freshener, even in lodgings that are otherwise antiseptic. To avoid this disagreeable situation, be sure that everyone who handles your reservation knows that you need a completely nonsmoking room. And if you're a smoker or traveling with one, be sure you understand your hotel's smoking policy—lighting up in a nonsmoking room can subject you to a hefty cleaning fee.

Thanks to the mix of new construction and repurposed buildings, strict zoning laws and building codes, and varying market conditions at the time of construction, Boston hotels offer wildly **varying room sizes and amenities.** Don't assume that a certain hotel, even one that's part of your favorite chain, has every option you expect. If you must swim a mile every day, order food at 4am, or share a room with your dog, always check to see whether your hotel can accommodate you. If it can't, a comparable property almost certainly can.

Major chains operating in and around Boston include business-traveler magnets Hilton, Hyatt, Marriott (in all its incarnations, including Courtyard, Renaissance, and Residence Inn), Sheraton, and Westin; leisure-oriented Best Western, Holiday Inn, Radisson, Ramada, and Wyndham; boutique-hotel trendsetters Kimpton, Morgans, and W; and luxury operators Doyle Collection, Fairmont, Four Seasons, InterContinental, Le Méridien, Mandarin Oriental, Ritz-Carlton, and Sonesta. The scarcest lodging option in the immediate Boston area is the moderately priced chain motel, a category almost completely driven out by soaring real estate prices. And especially at busy times, brands that are bargains elsewhere may be pricey here—twice what you're used to paying, if not more.

Rates in this chapter are for a **double room** (except where noted); if you're traveling alone, single rates are almost always lower. The rates given here do not include the 5.7% state hotel tax. Boston and Cambridge add a 2.75% convention center tax on top of the 6% city tax, making the total tax 14.45%. Not all suburbs impose a local tax, so some towns charge only the state tax. These listings cover Boston, Cambridge, and Brookline. If you plan to visit a suburban town and want to stay overnight, see chapter 10 for suggestions.

Getting the Best Deal

The **rack rate** is the maximum rate that a hotel charges for a room. Hardly anybody pays it, however, except sometimes in high season. To cut costs:

- **Ask for a rate, then ask about special rates or other discounts.** You may qualify for corporate, student, military, senior/AARP, AAA, or other discounts. Nail down the standard rate before you ask for your discount.

- **Book online.** Many hotels offer Internet-only discounts or supply discounted rooms to Priceline, Hotwire, or Expedia. Some chains guarantee that the price on their websites is the lowest available; check anyway.

- **Dial direct.** When booking a room in a chain hotel, you'll often get a better deal from the hotel's reservation desk than from the chain's main number.

- **Remember the law of supply and demand.** Business-oriented hotels are busiest during the week, so you can expect weekend discounts. Leisure hotels are most crowded and expensive on weekends, so discounts may be available midweek.

- **Visit in the winter.** Boston-bound bargain hunters who don't mind cold and snow (sometimes *lots* of snow) aim for January through March, when hotels offer great deals, especially on weekends.

- **Avoid excess charges and hidden costs.** When you book a room, ask how much the hotel charges for parking and whether there's a charge for staying in the garage past room checkout time on the last day of your stay. Use your cellphone, prepaid phone cards, or pay phones instead of making expensive calls from hotel phones. If you know you'll be online a lot, seek out a hotel that includes Internet access in the room rate (many older properties and hotels that do a lot of expense-account business don't). And don't be tempted by the minibar: Prices for water, soda, and snacks tend to be outrageous. Finally, ask about local taxes, service charges, and energy surcharges, which can increase the cost of a room by 15% or more.

> ### 📎 Planning Pointer
>
> When you've narrowed down the list of hotels you find appealing, follow them on Twitter and friend them on Facebook. You may learn about special offers and receive early notification of events taking place during your trip.

- **Book an efficiency.** A room with a kitchenette allows you to shop for groceries and even cook. This is a big money saver, especially for families on long stays.

- **Enroll in frequent-traveler programs,** which court repeat customers. Guests can accumulate points or credits to earn free hotel nights, airline miles, in-room amenities, merchandise, concert and event tickets, and more. Fairmont, Kimpton, and Omni frequent guests enjoy free Wi-Fi access, saving as much as $15 a day. Many chains partner with other hotel chains, car-rental firms, airlines, and credit card companies to encourage repeat business.

For tips on surfing for hotel deals online, visit **www.frommers.com**.

Bed & Breakfasts

A bed-and-breakfast can be a good alternative to a chain hotel. B&Bs are usually less expensive than hotels and often more comfortable. Most are near public transportation. Because most B&Bs are small, they fill quickly. An agency can save you a lot of calling around and can match you with a lodging that accommodates your likes and dislikes, allergies, dietary restrictions, tolerance for noise and morning chitchat, and anything else you consider important. Reserve as soon as you start planning, especially for a visit during fall foliage season.

Expect to pay at least $85 a night for a double in the summer and fall, and more during special events. The room rate usually includes breakfast and often includes parking, but be sure to ask. Many lodgings require a minimum stay of at least 2 nights, and most offer good winter specials (discounts or 1-night-free deals).

The following organizations can help you find your ideal B&B in Boston, Cambridge, or the greater Boston area:

- **B&B Agency of Boston** (www.boston-bnbagency.com; ℭ **800/248-9262** or 617/720-3540, 0800/89-5128 from the U.K.)

- **Bed and Breakfast Associates Bay Colony** (www.bnbboston.com; ℭ **888/486-6018** or 617/720-0522)

- **Host Homes of Boston** (www.hosthomesofboston.com; ℭ **800/600-1308** outside MA or 617/244-1308)

- **Inn Boston Reservations** (www.innbostonreservations.com; ℭ **617/236-2227**)

Practical Matters: The Hotel Scene

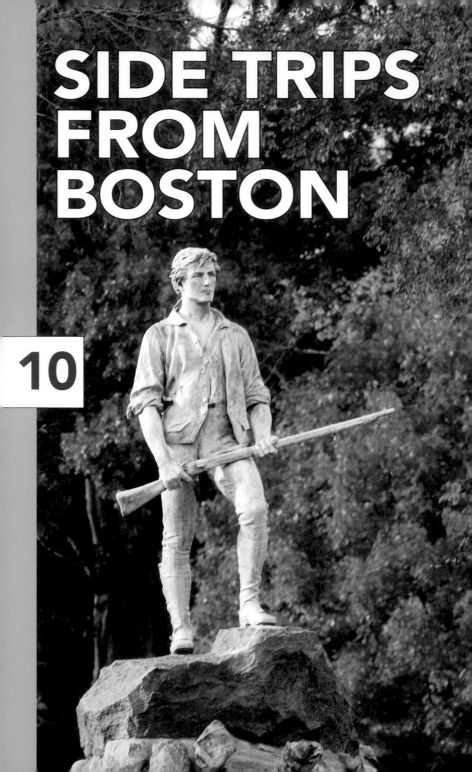

SIDE TRIPS FROM BOSTON

10

n addition to being, in Oliver Wendell Holmes's words, "the hub of the solar system," Boston is the hub of a number of delightful excursions. The destinations in this chapter—**Lexington** and **Concord,** the North Shore towns of **Marblehead** and **Salem,** the Cape Ann communities of **Gloucester** and **Rockport,** and **Plymouth**—make fascinating, manageable day trips and offer enough diversions to fill several days.

Like Boston, the suburbs are home to many attractions that rely heavily on aid from outside sources. Admission fees in this chapter are current at press time, but the double whammy of funding cuts and energy prices may have nudged them higher by the time you visit. In addition, some establishments have laid off staff (which means fewer guides), shortened open hours, and even stopped operating on the slowest day of the week, usually Monday. If you're on a tight budget or schedule, check ahead.

LEXINGTON

9 miles NW of Boston

A country village turned prosperous suburb, Lexington takes great pride in its history. The first skirmish of the Revolutionary War took place here, and parts of the town still look much as they did in April 1775, when the fight for independence began. Lexington is a pleasant place with some engaging destinations, but it lacks the atmosphere and abundant attractions of nearby Concord. Making sure to leave time for a tour of the **Buckman Tavern,** you can schedule as little as a couple of hours to explore Lexington center, possibly en route to Concord. A visit can also fill a half or full day, especially if you visit the **National Heritage Museum.** The town contains part of **Minute Man National Historical Park** (see "Exploring the Area" in the "Concord" section, below), which is definitely worth a visit.

British troops marched from Boston to Lexington late on April 18, 1775. Tipped off, Paul Revere and William Dawes rode ahead to sound the warning to

 You Do the Math

The **MBTA** (www.mbta.com; ☏ **800/392-6100** or 617/222-3200) serves most of the destinations in this chapter, but public transit isn't necessarily cheaper than renting a car for a day. For example, suppose you're visiting Gloucester with three other adults, each paying a total of $18.50 for the commuter rail. Even with summer gas prices, a good deal on a rental car will likely be cheaper than $74 in train fares. What's more, having a car allows you to make your own schedule instead of being tethered to the train's timetable—and you don't have to leave from North Station. Just make sure that the car-rental company accepts returns at the time you anticipate returning to Boston, so that you don't get stuck paying to park.

PREVIOUS PAGE: **The Lexington** *Minuteman* **statue.**

Minute Man National Historical Park.

their fellow rebellious colonists. Members of the local militia, known as minutemen for their ability to assemble quickly, were waiting at the Buckman Tavern. John Hancock and Samuel Adams, leaders of the revolutionary movement, were sleeping (or trying to) at the nearby **Hancock-Clarke House.** The warning came around midnight, followed about 5 hours later by some 700 British troops who stopped in Lexington en route to Concord, where they planned to destroy the rebels' military supplies. Ordered to disperse, the colonists—fewer than 100, and some accounts say 77—stood their ground. Nobody knows who started the shooting, but when it was over, eight militia members lay dead, including a drummer boy, and 10 were wounded.

Essentials

GETTING THERE From downtown Boston, take Storrow Drive or Memorial Drive to Route 2. Take Route 2 from Cambridge through Belmont, exit at Route 4/225, and follow signs to the center of Lexington. Or take Route 128 (I-95) to exit 31A and follow the signs. Massachusetts Avenue—the same Mass. Ave. you saw in Boston and Cambridge—runs through Lexington. There's metered parking on the street and in several municipal lots, and free parking at the National Heritage Museum and the National Historical Park.

The **MBTA** (www.mbta.com; ✆ **617/222-3200**) runs bus routes no. 62 (Bedford) and 76 (Hanscom) to Lexington from Alewife station, the last stop on the Red Line. The one-way fare is $1.50 with a CharlieCard or $2 with a CharlieTicket, and the trip takes about 25 minutes. Buses leave every hour during the day and every half-hour during rush periods, Monday through Saturday. There's no service on Sunday or holidays. The bus route passes the Munroe Tavern and the National Heritage Museum, if you prefer not to walk

Boston and Surrounding Areas

Touring Lexington & Concord

The **Liberty Ride** (www.libertyride.us; ☎ **781/862-0500**, ext. 702) is a 90-minute trolley tour, narrated by a costumed guide, that connects the attractions in Lexington and Concord. It operates from 10am to 4pm weekends in April and May, and daily from Memorial Day weekend through late October; check ahead for schedules. Tickets—$25 for adults, $10 for children 5 to 17, free for children 4 and under—are good for 24 hours and include admission to all three Lexington Historical Society houses. There's free parking at the National Heritage Museum and the national park, and your ticket entitles you to discounts at local attractions.

from the center of town. There's no public transit between Lexington and Concord, but the seasonal Liberty Ride tour connects the towns.

VISITOR INFORMATION   The **Chamber of Commerce Visitors Center,** 1875 Massachusetts Ave., Lexington, MA 02420 (www.lexingtonchamber.org; ☎ **781/862-1450**), on the Battle Green, distributes sketch maps and information. It's open daily from 9am to 5pm (Dec–Mar 10am–4pm). Information about Lexington is also available from the **Greater Merrimack Valley Convention & Visitors Bureau,** 40 French St., 2nd floor, Lowell, MA 01852 (www.merrimackvalley.org; ☎ **800/443-3332** or 978/459-6150).

Exploring Lexington

Minute Man National Historical Park is in Lexington, Concord, and Lincoln. At the Lexington end of the park is the **Minute Man Visitor Center ★**, 250 North Great Rd., Lincoln, off Route 2A, about a half-mile west of I-95 exit 30B (www.nps.gov/mima; ☎ **781/674-1920**). This area of the park, less than 10 minutes from Lexington center by car, includes the first 4 miles of the Battle Road, the route the defeated British troops took as they left Concord. Begin your visit by watching "The Road to Revolution," a fascinating multimedia program that explains Paul Revere's ride and the events of April 19, 1775. (This center is open Mar–Nov; winter visitors can start in Concord.) Also here are informational displays and a 40-foot mural illustrating the battle. From late May through October, rangers give talks and demonstrations daily; on summer weekends, they lead hiking tours of the park. Surf or call ahead for times. The **Battle Road Trail,** a 5-mile interpretive path, carries pedestrian, wheelchair, and bicycle traffic. Panels and granite markers along the trail display information about the military, social, and natural history of the area. In season (Mar–Nov), this center is open daily from 9am to 4 or 5pm; schedules vary. For open days and hours, check the website or call ahead (try the North Bridge Visitor Center, ☎ **978/369-6993,** if there's no answer here). For more information, see "Concord," below.

In the center of town, start at the **visitor center,** on the common, better known as the **Battle Green.** It's open daily from 9am to 5pm (Dec–Mar 10am–4pm). A **diorama** and accompanying narrative illustrate the Battle of Lexington. The **_Minuteman_ statue** on the Green is of Capt. John Parker, who commanded the militia. When the British confronted his troops, Parker called: "Stand your ground! Don't fire unless fired upon, but if they mean to have a war, let it begin here!" Allow about 30 minutes to look around the visitor center and the Green.

ATTRACTIONS
Battle Green **2**
Buckman Tavern **3**
Hancock-Clarke House **1**
Lexington Historical Society **7**
Minuteman Statue **4**
Munroe Tavern **15**
National Heritage Museum **16**

RESTAURANTS
Bertucci's **9**
Great Harvest Bread Co. **14**
Peet's Coffee & Tea **10**
Upper Crust **13**
Via Lago Café **6**

SHOPPING
Catch a Falling Star **8**
The Crafty Yankee **5**
Signature Stationers **11**
Sweet Breads **12**

Lexington Historical Society ★★ ☺ HISTORIC HOMES   The historical society's signature properties were among the country's first **historic houses** when restoration of the three buildings began around the turn of the 20th century. A guided tour (30–45 min. each) is the only way to see the houses.

Across from the Battle Green is the **Buckman Tavern** ★★, 1 Bedford St., built around 1710. If time is short and you have to pick just one house to visit, make it this one. The tour of the tavern, by a guide in period dress, is both educational and entertaining. The interior of the tavern has been restored to approximate its appearance on the day of the battle. The colonists gathered here to await word of British troop movements, and they brought their wounded here after the conflict.

Within easy walking distance, the **Hancock-Clarke House,** 36 Hancock St., is where Samuel Adams and John Hancock were staying when Paul Revere arrived. They fled to nearby Woburn. Visit the 1737 house, which contains some original furnishings as well as artifacts of the Battle of Lexington, to see an orientation film about the town.

The British took over the **Munroe Tavern** ★, 1332 Massachusetts Ave. (about 1 mile from the Battle Green), to use as their headquarters and, after the battle, as their field hospital. In this building (1690), you'll learn more about the royal troops and see furniture carefully preserved by the Munroe family, including the table and chair President George Washington used when he dined here in 1789. The historically accurate gardens in the rear (free admission) are beautifully planted and maintained.

The historical society makes its headquarters in the 1846 Lexington Depot, where changing exhibits on local history are open to the public.

Depot Square (off Mass. Ave. near the Battle Green). www.lexingtonhistory.org. ℭ **781/862-1703** or 781/862-5598 for information about group tours, offered by appointment only. Admission to all 3 houses $12 adults, $8 children 6–16; to individual houses $7 adults, $5 children. Free for children 5 and under. Buckman Tavern: Apr to late Nov daily 10am–4pm. Tours every 30 min. Hancock-Clarke House: Apr to late May Sat–Sun 10am–4pm; Memorial Day to Oct daily 10am–4pm. Tours on the hour. Munroe Tavern: Apr to late May Sat–Sun noon–4pm; Memorial Day to Oct daily noon–4pm. Tours on the hour. Buckman Tavern closed late Nov to Mar; Hancock-Clarke House and Munroe Tavern closed Nov–Mar.

National Heritage Museum ★★ ☺ 🔥 MUSEUM   The fascinating exhibits at this unusual museum explore American history and culture. The focus on daily life makes an entertaining complement to the Colonial-history focus of the rest of the town. The installations in the six exhibition spaces change regularly. You can start with the Revolution: the permanent exhibit **Sowing the Seeds of Liberty** tells the story of that tumultuous period through the lives of Lexington residents. Other topics of exhibits have ranged from early-20th-century postcards to photos of diners and movie theaters to America's national parks. Check ahead for the schedule of lectures, concerts, and family programs. The Scottish Rite of Freemasonry sponsors the museum.

33 Marrett Rd. (Rte. 2A), at Mass. Ave. www.nationalheritagemuseum.org. ℭ **781/861-6559.** Free admission. Wed–Sat 10am–4:30pm. Closed Jan 1, Thanksgiving, and Dec 24–25. From Lexington center, follow Mass. Ave. east to intersection with Rte. 2A; enter from Rte. 2A.

Where to Eat

If you're not continuing to Concord, which has more interesting dining options, you'll find some pleasant choices in Lexington. **Via Lago Café,** 1845 Massachusetts Ave. (www.vialagocatering.com; ℭ **781/861-6174**), is the retail arm of a popular local caterer. Its tasty international specialties, prepared from scratch, are available to stay or go. The town center has two excellent chain pizzerias: The Upper Crust, 41 Waltham St. (ℭ **781/247-0089**), and **Bertucci's,** 1777 Massachusetts Ave. (ℭ **781/860-9000**). **Peet's Coffee & Tea,** 1749 Massachusetts Ave. (ℭ **781/357-2090**), is a good place for a pick-me-up. For a muffin or scone and a hot drink, seek out Lexington's branch of **Great Harvest Bread Co.,** 1736 Massachusetts Ave. (ℭ **781/861-9990**).

 Poetry in Motion

Before you visit Lexington or Concord (or both), track down **"Paul Revere's Ride,"** Henry Wadsworth Longfellow's classic but historically questionable poem that dramatically chronicles the events of April 18 and 19, 1775.

Shopping

Mass. Ave. near the center of town is a retail hub. Check out **Catch a Falling Star,** 7 Depot Sq. (www.catchafallingstartoys.com; ℭ **781/674-2432**), for toys and games; **Sweet Beads,** 1792 Massachusetts Ave. (www.sweetbeads.us;

@ 781/860-7727), which sells jewelry and lets you make your own; high-end paper goods, journals, note cards, and travel accessories at **Signature Stationers,** 1800 Massachusetts Ave. (www.signaturestationers.com; @ **781/863-2777**); and jewelry and gifts at the **Crafty Yankee,** 1838 Massachusetts Ave. (www.craftyyankee.com; @ **781/861-1219**).

CONCORD

18 miles NW of Boston

Concord (say "conquered") revels in its legacy as a center of groundbreaking thought and its role in the country's political and intellectual history. A visit to this lovely town can easily fill a day; if your interests are specialized or time is short, a half-day excursion is reasonable. For an excellent overview, start at the **Concord Museum.**

The first official battle of the Revolutionary War took place in 1775 at Concord's **North Bridge** (now part of Minute Man National Historical Park); visitors can walk across a replica. In the 19th century, the town was an important center of literature and philosophy, and the heart of the Transcendentalist movement. Sightseers can tour the former homes of **Louisa May Alcott, Ralph Waldo Emerson, Nathaniel Hawthorne,** and **Henry David Thoreau,** and can visit their graves at **Sleepy Hollow Cemetery.** Thoreau's beloved **Walden Pond** looks much as it did when the contemplative writer roamed the countryside.

Essentials

GETTING THERE   From Boston and Cambridge, take Route 2 west into Lincoln and stay in the right lane. Where the main road makes a sharp left, go straight onto Cambridge Turnpike. Signs that point to HISTORIC CONCORD lead to downtown Concord, known as Concord Center. To go straight to Walden Pond, stay in the left lane on Route 2, take the main road (Rte. 2/2A) another mile or so, and turn left onto Route 126. There's parking throughout town and at the attractions.

The **commuter rail** (www.mbta.com; @ **617/222-3200**) takes about 45 minutes from North Station in Boston, with a stop at Porter Square in Cambridge. The round-trip fare is $16. There is no bus service from Boston to Concord, and no public transportation between Lexington and Concord. The **Liberty Ride** tour (p. 296) operates in the summer and fall. **Sunshine Taxi** (www.sunshine-taxi.com; @ **978/369-1752**) serves Concord.

VISITOR INFORMATION   The **Concord Chamber of Commerce,** 15 Walden St., Ste. 7, Concord, MA 01742 (www.concordchamberofcommerce.org; @ **978/369-3120**), maintains a visitor center at 58 Main St., next to Middlesex Savings Bank, 1 block south of Monument Square. It's open daily 10am to 4pm from April through October; public restrooms in the same building are open year-round. Ninety-minute guided walking tours ($20 adults, $12 seniors and students 13–18, $5 children 6–12, free for children 5 and under, $45 family [2 adults, 2 kids]) are available Friday through Monday from mid-April through October. Tours start at the visitor center. Group tours are available by appointment. The chamber office is open year-round Monday through Friday; hours vary, so call ahead.

Information about Concord is also available from the **Greater Merrimack Valley Convention & Visitors Bureau,** 40 French St., 2nd floor, Lowell, MA 01852 (www.merrimackvalley.org; ✆ **800/443-3332** or 978/459-6150). The town website, **www.concordma.gov**, has an area with visitor information.

GETTING AROUND   The train station is about three-quarters of a mile over flat terrain from the town center. Concord is relatively compact; if you plan to concentrate on attractions near the center of town, the commuter rail and your feet will get you there. If you plan to visit more than a couple of destinations, or if you can't miss the Old Manse, the North Bridge, or Walden Pond, seriously consider driving.

Exploring the Area

Concord Bike Tours (www.concordbiketours.com; ✆ **978/697-1897**) offers 2- to 3-hour guided excursions exploring various areas and themes related to Concord's history. Group tours and custom packages are also available. Prices, which include bike and helmet rental, start at $60 for adults, $45 for children 8 to 18.

Minute Man National Historical Park ★★ ☺ HISTORIC SITE   This 970-acre park preserves the scene of the first Revolutionary War battle at Concord on (all together now) April 19, 1775. After the skirmish at Lexington, royal troops continued to Concord in search of stockpiled arms (which militia members had already moved). Warned of the advance, the colonists prepared for a confrontation. The minutemen crossed the North Bridge, evading the "regulars" (soldiers) standing guard, and waited on a hilltop for reinforcements. The British searched nearby homes and burned any guns they found. The colonists saw the smoke and, mistakenly thinking that the troops were torching the town, mounted an attack at the bridge. The gunfire that ensued is remembered—in Ralph Waldo Emerson's words—as "the shot heard round the world," the opening salvo of the Revolution.

The park is open daily, year-round. A visit can take as little as half an hour for a jaunt to the North Bridge (a reproduction) or as long as half a day or more, if you stop at both visitor centers and perhaps participate in a ranger-led program. The rangers suggest beginning your visit at the Minute Man Visitor Center (see "Lexington," above), which is closed in the winter. Alternatively, start at the **North Bridge Visitor Center ★**, 174 Liberty St., off Monument Street (www.nps.gov/mima; ✆ **978/369-6993**), which overlooks the Concord River and the bridge. A diorama and video program illustrate the battle, and exhibits include uniforms, weapons, and tools of Colonial and British soldiers. Park rangers are on duty if you have questions. Picnicking is allowed, and the scenery is lovely, especially in the fall. The center is open daily from 9am to 5pm (11am–3pm in winter) and is closed January 1 and December 25.

⊙ Row, Row, Row Your Boat

Pretend you're Henry David Thoreau and take to the Concord River. The **South Bridge Boathouse,** 496–502 Main St. (www.canoeconcord.com; ✆ **978/369-9438**), just over half a mile west of the town center, will rent you a canoe for about $17 an hour on weekends, less on weekdays. The season runs from April through October. Single and double kayaks are available, too.

Concord

SHOPPING
Concord Bookshop **3**
The Grasshopper Shop **6**
Mascio-Ricci **8**
Toy Shop of Concord **4**
West Concord 5 & 10 **1**

Borden Pd.

Old
North
Bridge
Minute Man
National
Historical
Park

Sleepy
Hollow
Cem.

Concord
Visitors Center

Simon Willard Rd.

Lowell Rd.

Monument St.

Liberty St.

Bedford St.

Old Bedford Rd.

Park Ln.

Musketaquid Rd.

Elm St.

Concord R.

Main St.

Lexington Rd.

Nashoba Rd.

Belknap St.

Concord

Sudbury Rd.

Hubbard St.

Stow St.

Laurel St.

Everett St.

Walden St.

Cambridge Tpk.

Main St.

Concord Tpk.

Thoreau St.

Sudbury Rd.

Fairhaven Rd.

Crosby Pd.

Fairyland Pd.

Hapgood-
Wright
Forest

Concord Tpk.

Goose Pd.

Walden Pond
State
Reservation

Walden Pond

Concord Rd.

ATTRACTIONS
Concord Museum **12**
DeCordova Sculpture Park and
  Museum **15**
Gropius House **16**
North Bridge Visitor Center **9**
The Old Manse **10**
Orchard House **13**
Ralph Waldo Emerson House **11**
The Wayside **14**

HOTELS
Concord's Colonial Inn **7**

RESTAURANTS
Cheese Shop of Concord **5**
Nashoba Brook Bakery & Cafe **2**

0   1/2 mi
0   1/2 km

To go straight to the bridge, follow Monument Street out of Concord Center about half a mile until you see the parking lot on the right. Park and walk a short distance to the bridge, stopping along the unpaved path to read the narratives and hear the audio presentations. On one side of the bridge is a plaque marking the grave of the British soldiers who died here; on the other is Daniel Chester French's famed *Minute Man* statue.

IN & NEAR CONCORD CENTER

Concord Museum ★★ ☺ MUSEUM   Just when you're (understandably) suspecting that everything interesting in this area started on April 18, 1775, and ended the next day, this superb museum sets you straight. It's a great place to start your visit to the town.

The **History Galleries ★★** explore the question, Why Concord? Artifacts, murals, films, maps, documents, and other exhibits illustrate the town's changing roles. It has been a Native American settlement, Revolutionary War battleground, 19th-century intellectual center, and focal point of the 20th-century historic-preservation movement. Items on display include silver from Colonial churches, a fascinating collection of embroidery samplers, 19th-century clocks (Concord was a center of clock making), and rooms furnished with period furniture and textiles. Explanatory text places the objects in context. One of the **lanterns** immortalized by Longfellow in "Paul Revere's Ride" ("one if by land, two if by sea") is on display.

One of the Concord Museum's diverse exhibits.

You'll also see the contents of **Ralph Waldo Emerson's study,** arranged the way it was at his death in 1882, and a large collection of **Henry David Thoreau's belongings.**

Families and children will find plenty of hands-on activities, scavenger hunts, online previews, and other engaging ways to explore. The museum also mounts changing exhibits, offers special events such as living history performances and tea (winter only; call for reservations), and has an outstanding gift shop.

53 Cambridge Tpk. (at Lexington Rd.). www.concordmuseum.org. (℃ **978/369-9609** (recorded info) or 978/369-9763. Admission $10 adults, $8 seniors and students, $5 children 6–17, free for children 5 and under. June–Aug daily 9am–5pm (Thurs–Fri until 8pm late June to Aug); Apr–May and Sept–Dec Mon–Sat 9am–5pm, Sun noon–5pm (Thurs–Fri until 8pm 1st 3 weeks of Sept); Jan–Mar Mon–Sat 11am–4pm, Sun 1–4pm. Closed Easter, Thanksgiving, and Dec 25. Parking allowed on road. Follow Lexington Rd. out of Concord Center and bear right at museum onto Cambridge Tpk.; entrance is on left.

The Old Manse ★ HISTORIC HOME   The engaging history of this building touches on the military and the literary, but it's mostly the story of a family. The Rev. William Emerson built the Old Manse in 1770 and watched the Battle of Concord from the yard. He died during the Revolutionary War, and for almost 170 years the house was home to his widow, her second husband (Rev. Ezra Ripley), their descendants, and two famous friends. Nathaniel Hawthorne and his bride, Sophia Peabody, moved in after marrying in 1842 and stayed for 3 years. As a wedding present, Henry David Thoreau planted a vegetable garden; today, a re-creation of the garden is part of a self-guided tour of the grounds. William Emerson's grandson Ralph Waldo Emerson wrote the essay "Nature" here, in the same study where Hawthorne later toiled. On the guided tour (the only way to visit the house), you'll see mementos and memorabilia of the Emerson and Ripley families and of the Hawthornes, who scratched notes on two windows with Sophia's diamond ring.

The historic Old Manse.

269 Monument St. (at North Bridge). www.oldmanse.org. ℰ **978/369-3909.** Guided tour $8 adults, $7 seniors and students, $5 children 6–12, $25 families. House: Mid-Apr to Oct Mon–Sat 10am–5pm, Sun and holidays noon–5pm (last tour at 4:30pm); check ahead for winter hours. Grounds: Year-round daily sunrise to sunset. From Concord Center, follow Monument St. ½ mile; Old Manse is on left, North Bridge parking lot on right.

Orchard House ★★★ ☺ HISTORIC HOME   *Little Women* (1868), Louisa May Alcott's best-known and most popular work, was written and set at Orchard House. Seeing the Alcotts' home brings the beloved author and her family to life for legions of female visitors and their pleasantly surprised male companions. Fans won't want to miss the excellent tour (the only way to explore the house), copiously illustrated with heirlooms. Serious buffs can check ahead for information on the extensive schedule of special events and seasonal and holiday programs, some of which require reservations.

Louisa's father, Amos Bronson Alcott, was a writer, educator, philosopher, and leader of the Transcendentalist movement. He created Orchard House by joining and restoring two homes on 12 acres of land that he bought in 1857. Bronson and his wife, the social activist Abigail May Alcott, and their family lived here from 1858 to 1877, socializing in the same circles as Emerson, Thoreau, and Hawthorne.

Their daughters inspired the characters in *Little Women.* "Jo" was Louisa's alter ego; Anna ("Meg"), the eldest, was an amateur actress; and May ("Amy") was a talented artist. Elizabeth ("Beth"), a gifted musician, died before the family moved to this house, which has been open to the public since 1911.

399 Lexington Rd. www.louisamayalcott.org. ℰ **978/369-4118.** Guided tours $9 adults, $8 seniors and students, $5 children 6–17, free for children 5 and under, $25 families. Apr–Oct Mon–Sat 10am–4:30pm, Sun 1–4:30pm; Nov–Mar Mon–Fri 11am–3pm, Sat 10am–4:30pm, Sun 1–4:30pm. Closed Jan 1–2, Easter, Thanksgiving, Dec 25, and until noon Patriots' Day. Follow Lexington Rd. out of Concord Center and bear left at Concord Museum; house is on the left. Overflow parking lot is across the street.

Ralph Waldo Emerson House

HISTORIC HOME Emerson's stately home offers an instructive look at the days when a philosopher could attain the status we now associate with rock stars. Emerson, also an essayist and poet, lived here from 1835 until his death, in 1882. He moved in after marrying his second wife, Lydia Jackson, whom he called Lydian; she called him Mr. Emerson, as the staff still does. The tour (the only way to enter the house) gives an affectionate look at Emerson's personal side and at the fashionably ornate interior decoration of the time. You'll see original furnishings and some of Emerson's personal effects. The contents of his study from the time of his death are in the Concord Museum (p. 301).

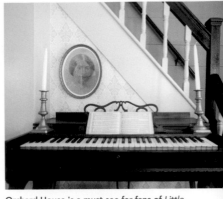
Orchard House is a must-see for fans of *Little Women*.

28 Cambridge Tpk. www.rwe.org/emersonhouse. (© **978/369-2236.** Guided tours $8 adults, $6 seniors and children 7–17, free for children 6 and under. Call to arrange group tours (10 people or more). Patriots' Day weekend to Oct Thurs–Sat 10am–4:30pm; Sun 1–4:30pm. Closed Nov to mid-Apr. Follow Cambridge Tpk. out of Concord Center; just before Concord Museum, house is on right.

Sleepy Hollow Cemetery ★

CEMETERY Follow the signs for author's ridge and climb the hill to the graves of some of the town's literary giants, including the Alcotts, Emerson, Hawthorne, and Thoreau. Emerson's bears no religious symbols; the marker is an uncarved quartz boulder. Thoreau is buried nearby; at his funeral, in 1862, his old friend Emerson concluded his eulogy with these words: ". . . wherever there is knowledge, wherever there is virtue, wherever there is beauty, he will find a home."

Entrance on Rte. 62 W. www.concordma.gov/pages/concordma_cemetery/sleepy. (© **978/318-3233.** Daily 7am to dusk, weather permitting. No buses allowed.

The Wayside ★

HISTORIC HOME The Wayside was Nathaniel Hawthorne's home from 1852 until his death, in 1864. The Alcotts also lived here (the girls called it "the yellow house"), as did Harriett Lothrop, who wrote the *Five Little Peppers* books under the pen name Margaret Sidney and owned most of the current furnishings. The Wayside is part of Minute Man National Historical Park, and the fascinating 45-minute ranger tour (the only way to see the house) illuminates the occupants' lives and the house's crazy-quilt architecture. The exhibit in the barn (free admission) consists of audio presentations and figures of Hawthorne, Louisa May and Bronson Alcott, and Sidney. Call ahead to double-check hours, which are subject to change.

> ### 💬 Military Intelligence
>
> Veterans' graves in Sleepy Hollow Cemetery bear small American flags from Memorial Day until just before Veterans Day. Of the famous occupants of Author's Ridge, only Louisa May Alcott (a Union Army nurse during the Civil War) qualifies.

The Wayside is a local home with a rich literary history.

455 Lexington Rd. www.nps.gov/mima. ☏ **978/318-7863** or 978/369-6993 (park headquarters). Guided tours $5 adults, free for children 16 and under. Late May to late Oct Wed–Sun 9:30am–5:30pm. Open hours and days subject to change; always call ahead. Closed late Oct to late May. Follow Lexington Rd. out of Concord Center past Concord Museum and Orchard House. Park across the street.

BEYOND CONCORD CENTER

deCordova Sculpture Park and Museum ★★ MUSEUM   Outdoors and in, this dramatic institution shows the work of American contemporary and modern artists, with an emphasis on living New England residents. The imaginative curatorial staff builds exhibits around themes as well as the work of individual artists. If you're interested in contemporary sculpture, deCordova is a can't-miss destination: The main building, on a leafy hilltop, overlooks the outdoor public sculpture park, and a sculpture terrace displays the work of one sculptor per year.

Allow at least half a day, perhaps including lunch. Year-round, free guided tours of the main galleries start Thursday at 1pm and Sunday at 2pm; sculpture-park tours run April through October on weekends at 1pm. Picnicking is allowed in the sculpture park; bring food or buy it at the cafe (open Tues–Fri 11am–3pm, Sat–Sun 11am–4pm). Be sure to check out the excellent museum store (☏ **781/259-8692;** Mon and Fri–Sat 9:30am–5:30pm, Tues–Thurs 9:30am–7:30pm, Sun 10:30am–5:30pm).

51 Sandy Pond Rd., Lincoln. www.decordova.org. ☏ **781/259-8355.** Admission $14 adults, $12 seniors, $10 students, free for children 12 and under. Free to all 1st Wed of every month. Admission to sculpture park free when museum is closed. Museum: Tues–Sun and some Mon holidays 10am–5pm. Closed Jan 1, July 4, Thanksgiving, and Dec 25. Sculpture park: Daily dawn to dusk. From Rte. 2 E., take Rte. 126 south to Baker Bridge Rd. (1st left after Walden Pond). When it ends, go right onto Sandy Pond Rd.; museum is on the left. From I-95, take exit 28B, follow Trapelo Rd. 2½ miles to Sandy Pond Rd., then follow signs.

Gropius House ★ HISTORIC HOME Architect Walter Gropius (1883–1969), founder of the Bauhaus school of design, built this hilltop home for his family in 1938 after accepting a job at the Harvard Graduate School of Design. He used traditional materials such as clapboard, brick, and fieldstone, with components then seldom seen in domestic architecture, including glass blocks and chrome (on the banisters). Marcel Breuer designed many of the furnishings, which were made for the family at the Bauhaus. Decorated as it was in the last decade of Gropius's life, the house affords a revealing look at his life, career, and philosophy. Call for information on workshops and special tours; evening tours (reservation required) take place throughout the year.

68 Baker Bridge Rd., Lincoln. www.historicnewengland.org. ✆ **781/259-8098.** Guided tours $10 adults, $9 seniors, $5 students with ID and children. Tours on the hour June–Oct 15 Wed–Sun 11am–4pm; Oct 16–May Sat–Sun 11am–4pm. From Rte. 2 E., take Rte. 126 south to Baker Bridge Rd. (1st left after Walden Pond); house is on the right. From I-95, take exit 28B, follow Trapelo Rd. to Sandy Pond Rd., go left onto Baker Bridge Rd.; house is on the left.

Walden Pond State Reservation ★★ HISTORIC SITE The conservation movement started here, in a small wooden structure where a misunderstood social activist moved to "live deliberately." A pile of stones marks the site of the cabin where Henry David Thoreau lived from July 1845 to September 1847; he captured the experience in the book *Walden.* Today the picturesque park is an extremely popular destination for walking (a path circles the pond), swimming, and fishing. Although crowded, the park's 462 acres are well preserved and insulated from development, making it less difficult than you might expect to imagine Thoreau's experience. Check ahead for the schedule of ranger-led interpretive programs. No dogs or bikes are allowed. In good weather, the parking lot fills early every day—call before setting out, because the rangers turn away visitors after the park reaches capacity (1,000).

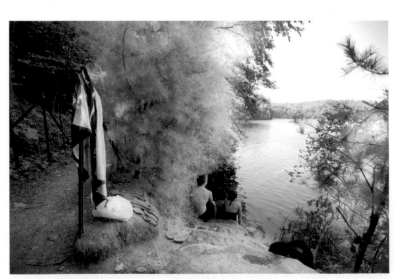

Walden Pond is still a great place to commune with nature.

Visitors Center: 915 Walden St. (Rte. 126). www.mass.gov/dcr/parks/walden. ☏ **978/369-3254.** Free admission. Parking $5 (cash only). Daily 8am to sunset. From Concord center, take Walden St. (Rte. 126) south, cross Rte. 2, and follow signs to the parking lot.

Where to Eat

Consider taking a **picnic** to the North Bridge, Walden Pond, or another spot that catches your eye. Stock up at **Nashoba Brook Bakery** (see below) or at the **Cheese Shop of Concord,** 29 Walden St. (www.concordcheeseshop.com; ☏ **978/369-5778**). The casual restaurant at **Concord's Colonial Inn** (see "Where to Stay," below) serves light meals and has outdoor seating with a view of the action on Monument Square. The inn serves afternoon tea on weekends ($30) and weekdays ($16); on weekends, reservations are required (☏ **978/369-2373**).

Nashoba Brook Bakery & Café ★★ AMERICAN   True story: A friend living in Australia recently returned home on vacation craving two things: a nap and a visit here. The enticing variety of fresh artisan breads, scrumptious baked goods and pastries, and made-from-scratch soups, salads, and sandwiches makes the airy cafe a popular destination throughout the day. It offers a good break from the sightseeing circuit. The industrial-looking building off West Concord's main street backs up to little Nashoba Brook, which is visible through the glass back wall. Order and pick up at the counter, and then grab a seat along the window or near the children's play area. You can also order takeout—this is great picnic food—or a loaf of crusty bread. On weekend mornings, the cafe serves homemade Belgian waffles.

152 Commonwealth Ave., West Concord. www.slowrise.com. ☏ **978/318-1999.** Sandwiches $7; other menu items $2–$8. MC, V. Mon–Fri 7am–5:30pm; Sat 7am–5pm; Sun 8am–5pm. From Concord Center, follow Main St. (Rte. 62) west, across Rte. 2; bear right at traffic light in front of train station and go 3 blocks. To reach overflow parking, turn right onto Commonwealth Ave. and take 1st right into lot on Winthrop St.; walk across bridge over brook.

Shopping

Concord center, off **Monument Square,** is a terrific shopping destination. Here you'll find the **Toy Shop of Concord,** 4 Walden St. (www.concordtoys.com; ☏ **978/369-2553**); the **Grasshopper Shop,** 36 Main St. (☏ **978/369-8295**), which carries women's clothing and accessories; jewelry at **Mascio-Ricci,** at Concord's Colonial Inn, 48 Monument Sq. (www.mascio-ricci.com; ☏ **978/371-1191**); and the **Concord Bookshop,** 65 Main St. (www.concordbookshop. com; ☏ **978/369-2405**). The compact shopping district in **West Concord,** along Route 62, is worth a visit just for the old-school **West Concord 5 & 10,** 106 Commonwealth Ave. (☏ **978/369-9011**). Opened in 1934, it carries everything from light bulbs to rubber duckies.

Where to Stay

Concord's Colonial Inn ★   The main building of the Colonial Inn has overlooked Monument Square since 1716. Modern amenities, the variety of rooms, and an accommodating staff make the inn popular with business travelers as well as vacationers, especially during foliage season. Like many historic inns, it's not luxurious, but it is comfortable, centrally located, and possibly haunted. The 15 original guest rooms are in great demand; the most popular, no. 24,

North Shore Information

If possible, explore the North Shore by car. Public transportation in this area is decent, but it doesn't go everywhere, and in some towns the train station isn't near the attractions. For the full day-trip experience, try to visit on a spring, summer, or fall weekday; traffic is brutal on warm weekends. Many areas are practically ghost towns from November through March, but all of the destinations in this chapter have enough of a year-round community to make an off-season excursion worthwhile.

The **North of Boston Convention & Visitors Bureau,** P.O. Box 5193, Salisbury, MA 01952 (www.northofboston. org; ℰ **800/742-5306** or 978/465-6555), publishes a map and a visitor guide that covers 34 municipalities, including Gloucester, Marblehead, Rockport, and Salem. It also coordinates **Escapes North** (www.escapesnorth.com), a clearinghouse for arts- and culture-oriented travel throughout the area.

---

supposedly is home to a ghost. Rooms in the 1970 Prescott House have country-style decor. Reserve early if you want to stay in the main inn, which is decorated in Colonial style.

48 Monument Sq., Concord, MA 01742. www.concordscolonialinn.com. ℰ **800/370-9200** or 978/369-9200. Fax 978/371-1533. 56 units, some with shower only. Apr to early Sept $179–$249 main inn, $149–$199 Prescott House; mid-Sept to Oct $199–$249 main inn, $169–$219 Prescott House; Nov–Mar from $159 main inn, from $129 Prescott House. Long-term rates available. AAA and AARP discounts available. AE, DC, DISC, MC, V. **Amenities:** 2 restaurants; bar w/live music on weekends; concierge; executive-level rooms; access to nearby health club ($10). *In room:* A/C, TV/DVD, hair dryer, Wi-Fi (free).

MARBLEHEAD

15 miles NE of Boston

Like an attractive person with a great personality, Marblehead has it all. Scenery, history, architecture, and shopping combine to make this one of the area's most popular day trips for locals and visitors alike. It's welcoming, manageable in size, and even polite—many speed-limit signs say please. Allow at least a full morning, but be flexible, because you might want to hang around.

One of the most picturesque neighborhoods in New England is **Old Town ★★★**, where narrow, twisting streets lead down to the magnificent harbor that helps make Marblehead the self-proclaimed "Yachting Capital of America." As you stroll the downtown historic district, you'll see plaques on the houses bearing the construction date and the names of the builder and original occupant—a history lesson without studying. Many of the houses have stood since before the Revolutionary War, when Marblehead was a center of merchant shipping. Two historic homes are open to the public (see "Exploring Marblehead," below).

Essentials

GETTING THERE   By car from Boston, take Route 1A north through Revere and Lynn; bear right at the signs for Nahant and Swampscott. Follow Lynn Shore Drive through Swampscott to Route 129, which runs into downtown

ATTRACTIONS
Abbot Hall **3**
Fort Sewall **17**
Jeremiah Lee Mansion **6**
King Hooper Mansion /
   Marblehead Arts
   Association **5**
Lafayette House **4**
Marblehead Museum &
   Historical Society **6**
Marblehead Neck Wildlife
   Sanctuary **1**
Old Town House **13**

HOTELS
Harbor Light Inn **15**

RESTAURANTS
Crosby's Marketplace **11**
Driftwood Restaurant **16**
Shubie's **2**

SHOPPING
Arnould Gallery **8**
Artists & Authors **12**
Candy Pop Sweet
   Shoppe **10**
Mud Puddle Toys **7**
St. Michael's Thrift Shop **9**
Scribe Paper & Gift **14**

Marblehead

Marblehead. Or take I-93 or Route 1 to Route 128, then follow Route 114 through Salem into Marblehead. Parking is tough, especially in Old Town—grab the first spot you see.

MBTA (www.mbta.com; ✆ **617/222-3200**) bus no. 441/442 runs from Haymarket (Orange or Green Line) to downtown Marblehead on weekdays; on weekends service is from Wonderland station at the end of the Blue Line. During rush periods on weekdays, the no. 448/449 connects Marblehead to Downtown Crossing. The trip takes about an hour, and the one-way fare is $3.50 with a CharlieCard, $4.50 with a CharlieTicket.

VISITOR INFORMATION The **Marblehead Chamber of Commerce,** 62 Pleasant St., Marblehead, MA 01945 (www.visitmarblehead.com; ✆ **781/ 631-2868**), is open weekdays from 9am to 5pm. The **information booth** (✆ **781/639-8469**), on Pleasant Street near Spring Street, is open mid-May through October, Monday to Friday 1 to 5pm, Saturday and Sunday 10am to 6pm. The chamber publishes a visitor guide and map that includes a calendar of events; before you visit, download a description of a walking tour as an MP3 file or document.

SPECIAL EVENTS Sailing regattas take place in the outer harbor all summer. The biggie, the **National Offshore One Design (NOOD) Regatta,** better known as Race Week, falls in late July and attracts enthusiasts from all over the country. The **Christmas Walk,** on the first weekend in December,

Marblehead Harbor has a rich maritime tradition.

incorporates music, arts and crafts, shopping, and Santa Claus, who arrives by lobster boat.

Exploring Marblehead

Marblehead is a wonderful place for aimless wandering; to add some structure, consult the walking tour available on the chamber of commerce's website. Whatever else you do, be sure to spend some time in **Crocker Park ★★**, on the harbor off Front Street. Especially in the warmer months, when boats jam the water nearly as far as the eye can see, the view is breathtaking. The park has benches and a swing, and it's a great place for a picnic. The view from **Fort Sewall,** at the other end of Front Street, is equally mesmerizing.

Just inland, the **Lafayette House** is at the corner of Hooper and Union streets. A corner of the private home was chopped off to make room for the passage of the Marquis de Lafayette's carriage when he visited the town in 1824. In Market Square on Washington Street, near the corner of State Street, is the **Old Town House,** in use for meetings and gatherings since 1727. The Marblehead Museum & Historical Society (see the listing for the Jeremiah Lee Mansion, below) maintains a small **Civil War museum** on the second floor. It's open every other Saturday in the summer, starting on Memorial Day weekend.

Abbot Hall GOVERNMENT BUILDING   A 5-minute stop here (look for the clock tower) is just the ticket if you want to be able to say you did some sightseeing. The town offices and historical commission share Abbot Hall with Archibald M. Willard's famous painting **_The Spirit of '76_ ★**, on display in the Selectmen's Meeting Room. The thrill of recognizing the drummer, drummer boy, and fife

---

 For the Birds

Across the causeway from Devereux Beach on Marblehead Neck, one of the ritziest neighborhoods on the North Shore, is the Massachusetts Audubon Society's **Marblehead Neck Wildlife Sanctuary** (www.massaudubon.org; ℭ **800/283-8266** or 978/887-9264). Turn east on Ocean Avenue south of downtown and follow it less than a mile until you see a little sign to the left at Risley Road. Park in the small lot to the left and

follow the path into the sanctuary, where you can see the varied species of birds that use the Atlantic flyway, especially in spring and fall. Admission is free, and the sanctuary is open daily from dawn to dusk. To return to Marblehead proper, continue on Ocean Avenue, which becomes Harbor Avenue and forms a loop. En route, at the end of "the Neck," you can park near the decommissioned lighthouse and take in a breathtaking view.

player is the main reason to stop here. Cases in the halls contain objects and artifacts from the collections of the Marblehead Historical Society and other organizations. The Maritime Room, which focuses on the town's naval history, is open weekday mornings in the summer.

Washington Sq. www.marblehead.org. ☎ **781/631-0528.** Free admission. Mon–Tues and Thurs 8am–5pm; Wed 8am–6pm; Fri 8am–12:30pm; check ahead for open days and hours in summer. From the historic district, follow Washington St. up the hill.

Jeremiah Lee Mansion/Marblehead Museum & Historical Society ★★

HISTORIC HOME   Built in 1768 for one of the wealthiest merchants in the colonies, the Lee Mansion is internationally recognized as an extraordinary example of pre-Revolutionary Georgian architecture. The attraction for aficionados is the excitement of seeing original hand-painted wallpaper in an 18th-century home, but the friendly, knowledgeable guides make visitors of all interest levels feel welcome. The tour touches on the history of the town as well as the home. Rococo woodcarving and other details complement historically accurate room arrangements, and ongoing restoration and interpretation by the Marblehead Museum & Historical Society place the 18th- and 19th-century furnishings and artifacts in context. The peaceful gardens are open to the public.

> ### Architectural Details
>
> On the hill between the Jeremiah Lee Mansion and Abbot Hall, notice the private homes at 185, 181, and 175 Washington St. Like the Lee Mansion—and hundreds of other residences in the tiny downtown area—these are good original examples of the architecture of the Colonial and early national period.

Across the street are two galleries (free admission) and administrative offices. One gallery shows paintings by the noted early-20th-century folk artist J.O.J. Frost, a Marblehead native who started painting when he was 70 years old; the other mounts changing exhibits that illustrate town history. Check ahead for the schedule of **summer walking tours** and other events.

161 Washington St. www.marbleheadmuseum.org. ☎ **781/631-1768.** Guided tours $5 adults, $4.50 seniors and students. June–Oct Tues–Sat 10am–4pm. Closed Nov–May. Galleries: 170 Washington St. Free admission; donations appreciated. June–Oct Tues–Sat 10am–4pm; Nov–May Tues–Fri 10am–4pm. From Abbot Hall, follow Washington St. down the hill; mansion is on left, galleries on right.

King Hooper Mansion/Marblehead Arts Association & Gallery

HISTORIC HOME   Shipping tycoon Robert Hooper got his nickname because he treated his sailors so well, but it's easy to think he was called "King" because he lived like royalty—his house has both a wine cellar and a ballroom. Around the corner from the home of Jeremiah Lee (whose sister-in-law was the second of Hooper's four wives), the 1728 mansion gained a Georgian addition sometime after 1745. The **Marblehead Arts Association** bought the building in 1938 and stages monthly exhibits in four galleries (with a public reception on the first Sunday of every month from 2–4pm), schedules special events, and sells members' work in the gift shop. The mansion has a lovely garden; enter through the gate at the right of the house.

8 Hooper St. www.marbleheadarts.org. ☎ **781/631-2608.** Free admission; donations welcome. Summer Sun and Tues–Wed noon–5pm, Thurs–Sat 10am–5pm; winter Sun and Tues–Fri

noon–5pm, Sat 10am–5pm; and by appointment. Where Washington St. curves at the foot of hill near Lee Mansion, look for the colorful sign.

Where to Eat

Marblehead has a number of serviceable dining options, plus a ton of bars that serve decent food. The tavern at the **Harbor Light Inn** (see listing below) offers a limited bar menu at dinner and lunch in a cozy 18th-century setting. You're probably better off heading to Salem if you want a fancier meal, but I prefer picnicking. You can stock up at a number of places in Old Town. **Crosby's Marketplace,** 118 Washington St. (www.crosbysmarkets.com; © 781/631-1741), is a full-service market with a large prepared-food section. **Shubie's,** 32 Atlantic Ave. (www.shubies.com; © 781/631-0149), carries a good selection of specialty foods. Hit the **Candy Pop Sweet Shoppe,** 152 Washington St. (www.facebook.com/candypopsweetshoppe; © 978/631-1519), for an impressive variety of dessert options, including penny candy. Another excellent option is to hit the road early and have breakfast near the harbor.

Driftwood Restaurant ★ 🦪 DINER/SEAFOOD At the foot of State Street, next to Clark Landing (the town pier), is an honest-to-goodness local hangout that serves excellent food. Join the crowd at a table or at the counter for a mug of strong coffee and breakfast (served all day) or lunch. Try pancakes or hash, chowder or a seafood roll—a hot dog bun filled with, say, fried clams or lobster salad. The house specialty, served on weekends and holidays, is fried dough, which is sort of a solid doughnut, as crispy as a good New Orleans beignet. At busy times, you may have to wait outside for a while.

63 Front St. © **781/631-1145.** Main courses $3–$12; breakfast items less than $7. No credit cards. Daily 6am–2pm.

Shopping

Marblehead is a legendary (or notorious, if you're on a budget) shopping destination. Shops, boutiques, and galleries abound in **Old Town** and on **Atlantic Avenue** and the east end of **Pleasant Street.** Good stops include **Arnould Gallery & Framery,** 111 Washington St. (© 781/631-6366); **Artists & Authors,** 108 Washington St. (www.artists-authors.com; © 781/639-0400), which carries rare books and fine art; **Mud Puddle Toys,** 1 Pleasant St. (© 781/631-0814; www.mudpuddletoys.com); and **Scribe Paper & Gift,** 84 Washington St. (www.scribepaper.com; © 781/631-7274). One of my favorite stops is the **St. Michael's Thrift Shop,** behind the Episcopal church at 20 Pleasant St. (www.stmichaels1714.org; © 781/631-0657; no credit cards). The gift shop at the Marblehead Arts Association (see above) sells members' creations.

Where to Stay

This is B&B heaven. Space considerations preclude listing the numerous small inns and bed-and-breakfasts, but the accommodations listings of the **Marblehead Chamber of Commerce** (www.visitmarblehead.com; © 781/631-2868) include many of them. Check the website, call or write for a visitor guide, or consult one of the B&B agencies listed on p. 290.

Harbor Light Inn ★★ Near the Old Town House, two Federal-era mansions make up this gracious inn, which is much bigger and more luxurious than its austere facade suggests. From the wood floors to the 1729 beams (in a third-floor room) to the swimming pool, it's both historic and relaxing. Rooms are comfortably furnished in period style, with some lovely antiques; most have canopy or four-poster beds. Eleven hold working fireplaces, and five have double Jacuzzis. The best rooms, on the top floor at the back of the building, away from the street, enjoy views of the harbor from a distance. The undeniably romantic inn, a popular honeymoon and weekend-getaway destination, also attracts weekday business travelers.

58 Washington St., Marblehead, MA 01945. www.harborlightinn.com. © **781/631-2186.** Fax 781/631-2216. 21 units, 7 with shower only. $145–$365 double; $195–$365 suite. Rates include breakfast buffet, afternoon refreshments, and use of bikes. Corporate rate available midweek. 2-night minimum stay weekends, 3-night minimum holiday and high-season weekends. AE, MC, V. Free parking. Children 7 and under not accepted. **Amenities:** Tavern; concierge; access to nearby health club ($5); Jacuzzi; heated outdoor pool. *In room:* A/C, TV/DVD, hair dryer, Wi-Fi (free).

SALEM

17 miles NE of Boston

Settled in 1626, 4 years before Boston, Salem later enjoyed international renown as a center of merchant shipping. Today it's a family-friendly destination that's worth at least a half-day visit (perhaps after a stop in Marblehead) and can easily fill a day

Salem is famous around the world because of a 7-month episode in 1692. The **witchcraft trial** hysteria led to 20 deaths, 3-plus centuries of notoriety, countless lessons on the evils of prejudice, and innumerable bad puns ("Stop by for a spell" is a favorite slogan). But there's much more to the city, which embraces its history as a thriving seaport, a literary inspiration, and a vital partner in the post–Revolutionary War China trade. Historic sites associated with **Nathaniel Hawthorne** complement the sorceresses and sailors, and one of the finest cultural institutions in New England, the **Peabody Essex Museum,** is a must-see for lovers of art and artifacts.

Essentials

GETTING THERE By car from Boston, take Route 1 or I-93 to Route 128 and then Route 114 into downtown Salem. You can also take Route 1A north to Salem, being careful in Lynn, where the road turns left and immediately right. The drive takes about 40 minutes in normal traffic. There's metered street parking and a reasonably priced municipal garage across the street from the National Park Service Regional Visitor Center.

From Boston, the **MBTA** (www.mbta.com; © **617/222-3200**) operates commuter trains from North Station and bus no. 450 from Haymarket (Orange or Green Line). The train is more comfortable than the bus but runs less frequently and is more expensive. It takes 30 to 35 minutes; the round-trip fare is $14. The station is about 5 blocks from the downtown area. The one-way fare for the 35- to 55-minute bus trip is $3.50 with a CharlieCard, $4.50 with a CharlieTicket.

The **Salem Ferry** (www.salemferry.com; © **978/741-0220**) operates daily from Memorial Day weekend through October. The 50-minute catamaran trip connects Central Wharf, next to Boston's New England Aquarium (T: Blue Line to Aquarium) to the Blaney Street Wharf, off Derby

Street, a 15-minute walk or quick hop on the Salem Trolley (see "Getting Around," below) from downtown Salem. The peak adult fare (late June to early Sept) is $13 one-way, $24 round-trip, with discounts for seniors, children, and families. The one-way off-season fare is $11 for adults.

VISITOR INFORMATION   A good place to start your visit is the **National Park Service Regional Visitor Center,** 2 New Liberty St. (www.nps.gov/sama; ✆ 978/740-1650), open daily from 9am to 5pm. Exhibits highlight early settlement, maritime history, and the leather and textiles industries in all of Essex County, not just Salem. The center also distributes brochures and pamphlets, including one that describes a **walking tour** of the historic district, and has an auditorium where a free film provides an overview of the region's history.

The city's Office of Tourism, **Destination Salem** (www.salem.org; ✆ 877/725-3662 or 978/744-3663), produces and distributes a free visitor guide that includes an excellent map. Visit the website to see the calendar of events. The **Salem Chamber of Commerce,** 265 Essex St., Ste. 101, Salem, MA 01970 (www.salem-chamber.org; ✆ 978/744-0004), maintains a large rack of brochures and pamphlets. Check with the helpful staff or visit the website for info on activities and events. The office is open weekdays from 9am to 5pm.

The city website (www.salem.com) and an excellent community site (www.salemweb.com) offer information for out-of-towners.

GETTING AROUND   In the congested downtown area, **walking** is the way to go, but you might not want to hoof it to all the sights, especially if it's hot. At the Essex Street side of the visitor center, you can board the **Salem Trolley ★** (www.salemtrolley.com; ✆ 978/744-5469) for a 1-hour narrated tour, and reboard as often as you like at any of the 13 stops. It's a good idea if you're spending the day and don't want to keep moving the car or carrying kids. The trolley operates daily April through October from 9:40am to 5pm (last tour at 4pm); check ahead for off-season hours and theme tours. Tickets ($15 adults, $14 seniors, $5 children 6–14, free for children 5 and under) are good all day; they're available onboard; from the Trolley Depot, 191 Essex St. (at Central St.), on the pedestrian mall; at the office, 8 Central St. (at Charter St.); and at other locations around town.

SPECIAL EVENTS   The city's month-long Halloween celebration, **Haunted Happenings ★★** (www.hauntedhappenings.org), includes parades, parties, tours, and a ceremony on the big day. In August, the 2-day **Salem Maritime Festival** fills the area around the Salem Maritime National Historic Site (see listing below) with live music, food, and demonstrations of nautical crafts. The festival is part of **Salem Heritage Days,** a weeklong celebration of the city's multicultural history, with musical and theatrical performances, a parade, and fireworks. Contact Destination Salem (see "Visitor Information," above) or Escapes North (www.escapesnorth.com) for details.

Exploring Salem

The historic district extends well inland from the waterfront. Many 18th-century houses, some with original furnishings, still stand. Ship captains lived near the water at the east end of downtown, in relatively small houses crowded close together. The captains' employers, the shipping company owners, built their

HOTELS
Coach House Inn **24**
Hawthorne Hotel **10**
The Salem Inn **1**
Salem Waterfront Hotel **11**

RESTAURANTS
A&J King Artisan Bakers **5**
Finz **12**
In a Pig's Eye **21**
Salem Beer Works **7**
Victoria Station **13**

SHOPPING
Boston Bead Company **3**
The Broom Closet **4**
Crow Haven Corner **8**
Harbor Sweets **25**
Pickering Wharf **14**
Seed Stitch Fine Yarn **2**

ATTRACTIONS
Custom House **16**
Derby House **18**
Friendship **20**
The House of the
    Seven Gables **22**
Peabody Essex Museum **6**
Salem Maritime National
    Historic Site **15**
Salem Willows **23**
Salem Witch Museum **9**
Scale House **17**
West India Goods Store **19**

Salem

homes away from the water (and the accompanying aromas). Many of them lived on **Chestnut Street ★★**, now a National Historic Landmark. Residents along the grand thoroughfare must, by legal agreement, adhere to Colonial style in their decorating and furnishings. Ask at the visitor center for the pamphlet that describes a walking tour of the historic district.

By car or trolley, the **Salem Willows** (www.salemwillows.com; ✆ 978/745-0251) amusements are 5 minutes away; many signs point the way. The strip of carnival-style diversions and snack bars has a retro honky-tonk air, and the waterfront park is a good place to bring a picnic and wander along the shore. There's no admission fee; meter parking is available. To enjoy the great view without the arcades and rides, have lunch one peninsula over at **Winter Island Park.**

Witch City Segway (www.witchcitysegway.com; ✆ 781/626-4000) offers guided tours on motorized stand-up scooters for people 14 and older. Prices start at $40 for a 1-hour excursion, which includes Segway instruction and helmet rental.

The House of the Seven Gables ★ ☺ HISTORIC HOME   Nathaniel Hawthorne's cousin lived here, and stories and legends of the house—formally the Turner-Ingersoll Mansion—and its inhabitants inspired the author's 1851 novel. If you don't know the eerie tale, don't let that keep you away; begin your visit with the audiovisual program, which tells the story. The house, built by Capt. John Turner in 1668, contains six rooms of period furniture, including pieces referred to in the book, and (spoiler alert) a secret staircase. Tours include a visit to Hawthorne's birthplace (built before 1750 and moved to the grounds) and describe what life was like for the house's 18th-century inhabitants. The enthusiastic costumed guides are well versed in the history of the buildings and artifacts. The site, a National Historic Landmark District overlooking Salem Harbor, also holds period gardens, the **Retire Beckett House** (1655), and a **counting house** (1830) where children and families find hands-on activities related to Salem's maritime legacy.

115 Derby St. www.7gables.org. ℂ **978/744-0991.** Guided tour of house and grounds $13 adults, $12 seniors and AAA members, $7.50 children 5–12, free for children 4 and under. Surcharges may apply for special exhibitions. July–Oct daily 10am–7pm; Nov–June daily 10am–5pm. Check ahead for extended Oct hours. Closed 1st 2 weeks of Jan, Thanksgiving, and Dec 25. From downtown, follow Derby St. east 3 blocks past Derby Wharf.

Peabody Essex Museum ★★★ ☺ MUSEUM   Now in its third century, the Peabody Essex Museum has grown into a national presence. All by itself, this captivating museum is reason enough to visit Salem. Allow at least half a day.

Impressive collections of art from New England and around the world are the Peabody Essex's calling card, but they're just part of the story. The museum owns 22 historic residences, including a well-preserved 18th-century Qing dynasty house, **Yin Yu Tang ★**, which was shipped to Salem from China and reassembled. The only example of Chinese domestic architecture outside that country, the house captures 2 centuries of rural life.

The museum's permanent collections hold nearly a million items. They blend contemporary acquisitions with "the natural and artificial curiosities" that Salem's sea captains and merchants brought back from around the world to the Peabody Museum (1799) and the local and domestic objects collected by the Essex Institute (1821), the county historical society. The displays help visitors understand the significance of each object, and interpretive materials (including interactive and hands-on activities) let children get involved. You might see

The House of the Seven Gables and its period gardens.

objects related to the history of the port of Salem (including gorgeous furniture) or to the whaling trade (such as amazing scrimshaw). Other noteworthy collections include American, African, Indian, Asian, and East Asian art and objects; photography; and the practical arts and crafts of East Asian, Pacific Island, and Native American peoples. Portraits of area residents include Charles Osgood's omnipresent rendering of Nathaniel Hawthorne.

Upcoming special exhibitions include *Ansel Adams: At the Water's Edge* (through Oct 8, 2012), and *Hats: An Anthology by Stephen Jones* (Sept 8, 2012–Jan 27, 2013).

To explore the museum, take a guided or self-guided gallery tour. The cafe in the atrium closes 30 minutes before the rest of the museum.

East India Sq., 161 Essex St. www.pem.org. ✆ **866/745-1876** or 978/745-9500. Admission $15 adults, $13 seniors, $11 students, free for children 16 and under. Yin Yu Tang admission $5 with museum admission. Tues–Sun and Mon holidays 10am–5pm. Take Hawthorne Blvd. to Essex St., following signs for visitor center. Enter on Essex St. or New Liberty St.

Salem Maritime National Historic Site ★ ☺ HISTORIC SITE An entertaining introduction to Salem's seagoing history, this complex includes an exciting attraction: a real ship. The *Friendship* **★★** is a full-size replica of a 1797 East Indiaman merchant vessel, a three-masted 171-footer that disappeared during the War of 1812. The tall ship is a faithful replica with some concessions to the modern era, such as diesel engines. The **guided ranger tour** includes a visit to the ship. You can also download one or more of the five available audio tours and set your own schedule.

With the decline of merchant shipping in the early 19th century, Salem's wharves fell into disrepair. In 1938, the National Park Service took over a small piece of the waterfront, **Derby Wharf.** It's now a finger of parkland extending into the harbor, part of the 9 acres that make up the historic site. On adjacent **Central Wharf** is a warehouse, built around 1800, that houses the orientation center. Tours, which vary seasonally, explore Salem's maritime history. Yours might include the **Derby House** (1762), a wedding gift to shipping magnate Elias Hasket Derby from his father, and the **Custom House** (1819). Legend—myth, really—has it that Nathaniel Hawthorne was working here when he found an embroidered scarlet *A*. If you prefer to explore on your own, you can see a free 18-minute orientation film and wander around **Derby Wharf,** the **West India Goods Store,** the **Bonded Warehouse,** the **Scale House,** and Central Wharf. Check ahead for lectures and other special events that focus on topics related to Salem's seagoing legacy.

> ### A Face in the Crowd
>
> On the traffic island across from the entrance to the **Salem Witch Museum** is a statue that's easily mistaken for a witch. It's really **Roger Conant,** who founded Salem in 1626.

193 Derby St. www.nps.gov/sama. ✆ **978/740-1660.** Free admission. Guided tours $5 adults, $3 seniors and children 6–16, free for children 5 and under. July–Oct daily 9am–5pm; Nov–June Mon–Fri 1–5pm, Sat–Sun 9am–5pm. Closed Jan 1, Thanksgiving, and Dec 25. Take Derby St. east; just past Pickering Wharf, Derby Wharf is on the right.

Salem Witch Museum ★★ ☺ MUSEUM This is one of the most memorable attractions in eastern Massachusetts—it's both interesting and scary. The main draw of the museum (a former church) is a three-dimensional audiovisual presentation with life-size figures. The show takes place in a huge room lined with displays that are lighted in sequence. The 30-minute narration tells the tale of the witchcraft trials and the accompanying hysteria. The well-researched presentation recounts the story accurately, with an enjoyable dash of drama. One of the victims was crushed to death by rocks piled atop a board on his chest—smaller kids might need a reminder that he's not real. The narration is available translated into Cantonese, French, German, Italian, Japanese, Mandarin, Russian, and Spanish. There's also a small exhibit that traces the history of witches, witchcraft, and witch hunts.

The Salem Witch Museum doesn't shy away from showing the gruesome reality of the witch trials.

19½ Washington Sq., on Rte. 1A. www.salemwitchmuseum.com. ℭ **978/744-1692.** Admission $9 adults, $7.50 seniors, $6 children 6–14. July–Aug daily 10am–7pm; Sept–June daily 10am–5pm; check ahead for extended Oct hours. Closed Jan 1, Thanksgiving, and Dec 25. Follow Hawthorne Blvd. to the northwest corner of Salem Common.

Where to Eat

The **Pickering Wharf** complex, 23 Congress St. (at Derby St.; www.pickering wharf.com; ℭ **978/740-6990**), has a food court as well as several restaurants with outdoor seating overlooking the marina: **Victoria Station** (www.victoriastation salem.com; ℭ **978/744-7644**) emphasizes seafood and traditional American dishes and has a huge salad bar, and **Finz** (www.hipfinz.com; ℭ **978/744-8485**) is known for innovative seafood preparations and creative drinks.

A block south of the Essex Street pedestrian mall is one of the best bakeries in the Boston area. **A & J King Artisan Bakers,** 48 Central St. (off Charter St.; www.ajkingbakery.com; ℭ **978-744-4881**), sells breads, pastries, coffee and tea, and fantastic sandwiches—great picnic fuel. **Salem Beer Works,** 278 Derby St. (www.beerworks.net; ℭ **978/745-BEER**), a sibling of Boston Beer Works (p. 234), serves a similar variety of pub grub and house-made brews. The cafe at the **Peabody Essex Museum** (p. 316) serves lunch.

In a Pig's Eye ★ AMERICAN/MEXICAN This neighborhood tavern near the House of the Seven Gables has a secret—the food is fantastic. Lunch features sandwiches, salads, and bar fare that's a step up from basic, with excellent seafood and several vegetarian and Mexican options. The dinner menu is mostly Mexican on Monday and Tuesday; Mexican pizzas (mounds of vegetables and salsa on flour tortillas) are terrific, as are the gigantic burritos. The regular dinner menu offers creative pasta dishes, beef, chicken, and at least half a dozen tasty seafood choices—my hyperpicky friend raved about the mussels. There's live music Wednesday through Monday; Sunday is jazz night.

148 Derby St. (at Daniels St.). www.inapigseye.com. ℭ **978/741-4436.** Reservations recommended at dinner in summer. Main courses $5–$8 at lunch, $7–$13 at dinner Wed–Sat, $6–$9 at dinner Mon–Tues. AE, DC, DISC, MC, V. Mon–Sat 11:30am–3pm and 6–10pm; Sun brunch 11:30am–4pm.

Shopping

Pickering Wharf, 23 Congress St. (at Derby St.; www.pickeringwharf.com; ℭ 978/740-6990), is a waterfront complex of shops, boutiques, restaurants, and condos. It's popular for strolling, snacking, and shopping, and the central location makes it a local landmark. Tiny Front Street, a block from the retail-rich **Essex Street pedestrian mall,** is home to several shops that cater to needlecrafters. I especially like **Seed Stitch Fine Yarn,** 21 Front St. (www.seedstitchfineyarn.com; ℭ 978/744-5557), which is across the street from the **Boston Bead Company,** 10 Front St. (www.bostonbeadcompany.com; ℭ **978/741-2323;** p. 205).

You can't go more than a couple of blocks downtown without passing a fortune-telling parlor, and several shops specialize in witchcraft accessories. Bear in mind that Salem is home to many practicing witches, mystics, and others who take their beliefs very seriously. **Crow Haven Corner,** 125 Essex St. (www.crowhaven corner.net; ℭ 978/745-8763), and the **Broom Closet,** 203 Essex St. (www. broomcloset.com; ℭ **978/741-9555**), stock everything from crystals to clothing.

Where to Stay

The busiest and most expensive time of year is Halloween week, followed closely by the rest of October; it's not unusual for the whole city to be sold out months in advance. The **Salem Waterfront Hotel,** 225 Derby St., at Pickering Wharf (www.salemwaterfronthotel.com; ℭ **888/337-2536** or 978/740-8788), is a large, modern establishment with an indoor pool. Double rates start at $139, which includes Wi-Fi and parking. There's a 2-night minimum on busy weekends.

Coach House Inn Far enough from downtown to feel like a getaway, this welcoming inn is in a historic district 2 blocks from the harbor and just 9 blocks from the major attractions—an easy walk in fine weather. The three-story mansion, set back from the street behind a well-kept lawn, is elegantly furnished in just-frilly-enough style. All the good-size rooms have high ceilings, period antiques, four-poster beds, and Oriental rugs, and most have (nonworking) fireplaces. Breakfast arrives at your door in a basket—a nice perk if dining-room chitchat isn't your thing. Built in 1879 for a ship's captain, the Coach House Inn is 20 minutes on foot or 5 minutes by car from the center of town, and just up the street from Salem State College.

 Confection Connection

Shops throughout New England sell the high-end chocolate creations of **Harbor Sweets ★★**, Palmer Cove, 85 Leavitt St., off Lafayette Street (www.harbor sweets.com; ℭ **800/243-2115** or 978/745-7648). The retail store overlooks the floor of the factory; tours begin Tuesday and Thursday at 11am (call ahead to confirm). The deliriously good sweets are expensive, but candy bars and small assortments are available. Closed Sunday except before candy-intensive holidays.

284 Lafayette St. (Rtes. 1A and 114), Salem, MA 01970. www.coachhousesalem.com. ℂ **800/688-8689** or 978/744-4092. Fax 978/745-8031. 11 units, 9 with bathroom, 2 with shower only. $138–$198 double; $205–$298 2-room suite. Rates include continental breakfast. Rates are higher in late Oct. Minimum 2- or 3-night stay weekends and holidays. AE, DISC, MC, V. Free parking. *In room:* A/C, TV, fridge, Wi-Fi (free).

Hawthorne Hotel ★ ☺   This historic hotel, built in 1925 in the heart of downtown, is both convenient and comfortable. It books business travelers as well as vacationers, and it's popular for functions. The six-story building holds well-kept guest rooms that vary in size from snug to spacious. All are attractively furnished with reproduction Federal-style pieces, but bathrooms can be small. The best units, on the Salem Common (north) side of the building, have better views than rooms that overlook the street. Whatever direction you face, ask to be as high up as possible, because the neighborhood is busy. If you're traveling with children, ask about "Family Fun" packages, which include discounted tickets to area museums.

18 Washington Sq. W. (at Salem Common), Salem, MA 01970. www.hawthornehotel.com. ℂ **800/729-7829** or 978/744-4080. Fax 978/745-9842. 89 units, 30 with shower only. $139–$220 double; $209–$344 suite. Extra person $12. Children 15 and under stay free in parent's room. 2-night minimum stay May–Oct weekends. Off-season, AAA, and AARP discounts, and weekend and other packages available. AE, DC, DISC, MC, V. Limited self-parking. Pets accepted ($100 deposit; $10 per day). **Amenities:** Restaurant (American); tavern; concierge; exercise room; access to nearby health club w/pool; room service. *In room:* A/C, TV, hair dryer, MP3 docking station, Wi-Fi (free).

The Salem Inn ★★   The Salem Inn occupies the comfortable niche between too-big hotel and too-small B&B. Its clientele includes honeymooners as well as sightseers and families, and the variety of rooms lets the innkeepers match guests with the right accommodations. The inn consists of three properties. The 1834 West House and the 1854 Curwen House, former homes of ship captains, are listed on the National Register of Historic Places. The best units are the honeymoon and family suites (which have kitchenettes) in the 1874 Peabody House. Guest rooms are large and tastefully decorated; some have fireplaces, canopy beds, and whirlpool baths. The peaceful rose garden at the rear of the main building is open to all guests.

7 Summer St. (Rte. 114), Salem, MA 01970. www.saleminnma.com. ℂ **800/446-2995** or 978/741-0680. Fax 978/744-8924. 40 units, some with shower only. Mid-Apr to Sept $159–$209 double; $209–$279 suite; Oct $210–$255 double, $255–$370 suite; Nov to mid-Apr $129–$169 double; $179–$239 suite. Rates include continental breakfast. Extra person $15–$25. 2- or 3-night minimum stay during special events and holidays. Winter and family packages available. AE, DC, DISC, MC, V. Free parking. Pets accepted by prior arrangement (Nov–Sept $15 per night, Oct $25 per night). *In room:* A/C, TV, hair dryer, Wi-Fi (free).

GLOUCESTER

33 miles NE of Boston

Gloucester (which rhymes with *roster*) is a working city, not a cutesy tourist town. It's home to one of the last commercial fishing fleets in New England, an internationally celebrated artists' colony, a large Portuguese-American community, and just enough historic attractions. Allow at least half a day, perhaps combined with a visit to the tourist magnet of Rockport; a full day would be better, especially if you plan a cruise or whale watch.

☼ A whale OF AN ADVENTURE

The depletion of New England's fishing grounds has led to the rise of another important seagoing industry, **whale-watching ★★**. The waters off the coast of Massachusetts are prime territory, and Gloucester is a center of whale-watching cruises. Stellwagen Bank, which runs from Gloucester to Provincetown about 27 miles east of Boston, is a rich feeding ground for the magnificent mammals. Species spotted in the area are mainly humpback, finback, and minke whales, which dine on sand eels and other fish that gather along the ridge. The whales often perform for their audience by jumping out of the water, and dolphins occasionally join the show. Naturalists onboard narrate the trip for the companies listed here, pointing out the whales—many of which they recognize and call by name—and describing birds and fish that cross your path.

Whale-watching is not particularly time- or cost-effective, especially if restless children are along, but it's so popular for a reason: The payoff is, literally and figuratively, huge. This is an "only in New England" experience that kids (and adults) will remember for a long time.

The season runs from April or May through October. Bundle up, even in the middle of summer—it's much cooler at sea than on land. Wear a hat, rubbersoled shoes, sunglasses, and sunblock, and be sure you have a camera. If you're prone to motion sickness, take precautions, because you'll be at sea for 3 to 5 hours. If you plan to take Dramamine, allow some time for it to kick in.

The North Shore whale-watch operators are for-profit businesses, and they're extremely competitive—they'd probably deny it, but the companies are virtually indistinguishable. Most guarantee sightings, offer a morning and an afternoon cruise as well as deep-sea fishing excursions and charters, honor other firms' coupons, and offer AAA and AARP discounts. Check ahead for sailing times, prices (at least $48 for adults, slightly less for seniors, students, and children), and reservations, which are strongly recommended. If you're on a tight budget, ask whether the company imposes a fuel surcharge, and double-check the cut-off ages for kids and seniors.

Cruises leave from downtown Gloucester. **Cape Ann Whale Watch** (www.seethewhales.com; ℂ **800/877-5110** or 978/283-5110) is the best-known operation; its main competitors are **Capt. Bill & Sons Whale Watch** (www.captbillandsons.com; ℂ **800/339-4253** or 978/283-6995) and **Seven Seas Whale Watch** (www.7seas-whalewatch.com; ℂ **888/283-1776** or 978/283-1776).

The ocean has been Gloucester's lifeblood since long before the first European settlement in 1623. The French explorer Samuel de Champlain called the harbor "Le Beauport" when he came across it in 1606, some 600 years after the Vikings. The harbor's configuration and proximity to good fishing helped Gloucester earn the reputation it enjoys to this day. If you read or saw *The Perfect Storm*, you'll have a sense of what to expect here.

Essentials

GETTING THERE   From Boston, take I-93 or Route 1 north to Route 128, which runs directly to Gloucester. To start your visit at the Stage Fort Park visitor center, use exit 14 and follow Route 133 east. There's street parking

Down by the Sea

On Stacy Boulevard west of downtown Gloucester is a reminder of the sea's danger. Leonard Craske's bronze statue *Memorial to the Gloucester Fisherman,* known as "the Man at the Wheel," bears the inscription "They That Go Down to the Sea in Ships, 1623–1923" (the phrase is from the 107th Psalm). A few hundred feet west is a memorial to the women and children who waited at home. As you take in the glorious view, consider this: More than 10,000 fishermen lost their lives during the city's first 300 years.

(metered and not) throughout the city, and a free lot on the causeway to Rocky Neck.

The **commuter rail** (www.mbta.com; ✆ 617/222-3200) runs from Boston's North Station. The trip takes about an hour; the round-trip fare is $19. The station is about 8 blocks from the waterfront area. The **Cape Ann Transportation Authority,** or CATA (www.canntran.com; ✆ 978/283-7916), runs buses from town to town on Cape Ann and operates special routes during the summer (except Sun). **Lighthouse Taxi** (✆ 978/281-6161) serves Gloucester.

VISITOR INFORMATION   The city maintains an information-packed website as well as the **Welcoming Center** (www.gloucesterma.com; ✆ 800/649-6839 or 978/281-8865) at Stage Fort Park, off Route 127 at Route 133. The center is open during the summer daily from 9am to 5pm (closed in winter). The **Cape Ann Chamber of Commerce,** 33 Commercial St., Gloucester, MA 01930 (www.capeannvacations.com; ✆ 978/283-1601), is open year-round (summer Mon–Thurs 9am–5pm, Fri 9am–6pm, Sat 10am–5pm, Sun 10am–4pm; winter Mon–Fri 9am–5pm). At either place, the helpful staff can offer insider tips and advice; be sure to grab a free copy of the annual *Cape Ann Guide.* For an entertaining look at the city through the eyes of a lobster dealer, visit **www.goodmorninggloucester.com**.

SPECIAL EVENTS   Gloucester holds festivals and street fairs on weekends throughout the summer. Check in advance to find out what's up when you'll be in town. The best-known event is **St. Peter's Fiesta,** a colorful 4-day celebration at the end of June. The Italian-American fishing colony's festival has more in common with a carnival midway than with a religious observation, but it's great fun. There are parades, games, music, food, sporting events, and, on Sunday, the blessing of the fleet. The **Schooner Festival,** a floating party with plenty of land-based revelry, including fireworks, takes place over Labor Day weekend.

Exploring Gloucester

Business isn't nearly what it once was, but fishing remains Gloucester's leading industry. Tourism is a very close second, and the city is an exceptionally

Gloucester

EAST GLOUCESTER

WEST GLOUCESTER

ROCKY NECK

Inner Harbor

GLOUCESTER HARBOR

Tenpound I.

Niles Pond

Cape Ann Chamber of Commerce

Bass Rocks Country Club

Marble Road Conservation Area

Annisquam R.

Ravenswood Park

Stage Fort Park

Lower Banjo Pd.

Upper Banjo Pd.

see inset

1/2 mi
1/2 km

Downtown Gloucester

Capt. Jacobs Park

Hidden Park

RESTAURANTS
The Crow's Nest **12**
The Cupboard **2**
Franklin Cape Ann **7**
Halibut Point Restaurant & Bar **11**
Latitude 43 Restaurant & Bar **6**
Lobsta Land **1**

SHOPPING
Cape Pond Ice **4**
Dogtown Book Shop **8**
Ménage Gallery **9**
Mystery Train **5**

ATTRACTIONS
Beauport (Sleeper-McCann House) **18**
Cape Ann Museum **10**
Gloucester Stage Company **15**
The Man at the Wheel **3**
Rocky Neck Art Colony **14**
Ryan & Wood, Inc. **18**

HOTELS
Atlantis Oceanfront Inn **17**
Bass Rocks Ocean Inn **16**

323

◯ The Perfect Storm

Long after the release of the blockbuster movie, Sebastian Junger's bestselling book *The Perfect Storm* remains a popular reason to visit Gloucester. The thrilling but tragic true account of the "no-name" hurricane of 1991 centers on the ocean and a neighborhood tavern. The **Crow's Nest,** 334 Main St. (www.crowsnestgloucester.com; ✆ **978/281-2965**), a bit east of downtown, is a no-frills place with a horseshoe-shaped bar and a crowd of regulars who continue to be amused that their hangout is a tourist attraction. The Crow's Nest plays a major role in Junger's story, but its ceilings weren't high enough to

accommodate a movie set, so the film crew built an exact replica nearby. If you admired the movie's wardrobe design, check out the shirts and caps at **Cape Pond Ice ★**, 104 Commercial St., near the chamber of commerce (www.capepondice.com; ✆ **978/283-0174**). "The Coolest Guys Around" have provisioned Gloucester's fishing fleet since 1848. The company offers 40-minute tours of its industrial facility, which is famous for its ice sculptures; bring (or buy) a sweatshirt. The price is $10 for adults, $6 for seniors and children 7 to 11; reservations are recommended.

---

welcoming destination—residents seem genuinely happy to see out-of-towners and to offer directions and insider info.

Stage Fort Park, off Route 127 at Route 133, offers a superb view of the harbor and has a busy snack bar (summer only) and a playground. It's a good spot for picnicking, barbecuing, swimming, or playing on the cannons in the Revolutionary War fort.

To reach **East Gloucester,** follow signs as you leave downtown or go directly from Route 128, exit 9. On East Main Street, you'll see signs for the world-famous **Rocky Neck Art Colony ★★**, headquartered in the Rocky Neck Gallery, 53 Rocky Neck Ave. (www.rockyneckartcolony.org; ✆ **978/282-0917**), the oldest continuously operating art colony in the country. Park in the lot on the tiny causeway and head west along Rocky Neck Avenue, which abounds with studios, galleries, restaurants, and people. The draw is the presence of working artists, not just shops that happen to sell art. Most galleries are open daily in the summer 10am to 10pm.

NARRATED CRUISES   For information on whale watches, see the box "A Whale of an Adventure," above.

The schooner *Thomas E. Lannon* ★★ (www.schooner.org; ✆ **978/281-6634**) is a gorgeous reproduction of a Gloucester fishing vessel. The 65-foot tall ship sails from Seven Seas Wharf downtown, off Rogers Street; 2-hour excursions ($40 for adults, $35 for seniors, $28 for children 16 and under) leave about four times daily from mid-June to mid-September, less often on weekends from mid-May to mid-June and mid-September to mid-October. On Saturday morning in July and August, kids (one per parent) sail free. The company also offers music and dining cruises, including sunset lobster dinners, and sails on nights when the moon is full. Reservations are recommended for all excursions.

The two-masted schooner *Adventure* ★ (www.schooner-adventure.org; ✆ **978/281-8079**) is a 122-foot fishing vessel built in Essex in 1926. It's being restored—a fascinating process—at Gloucester Marine Railways

10

Gloucester

SIDE TRIPS FROM BOSTON

at Rocky Neck, on the tip of the peninsula that's home to the artists' colony. *Adventure* will eventually resume regularly scheduled public sailing; meanwhile, the staff of the "living museum," a National Historic Landmark, offers dockside educational programs. Check ahead for details and schedules, open days and hours, and prices.

The **Gloucester Harbor Water Shuttle & Tour** (www.capeann harbortours.com; *©* **978/283-1979**) serves five stops around the harbor. It operates daily in summer and on weekends in the spring and fall. An all-day ticket ($10 adults, $5 children 6–12, free for children 5 and under) includes a 1-hour tour and unlimited reboarding.

Beauport, Sleeper-McCann House ★★ HISTORIC HOME   The rough-and-tumble fishing port of Gloucester has another face: exclusive summer community. Aficionados of house tours will want to build their schedules around a visit to this magnificent property on the stylish Back Shore, the product of a uniquely creative mind. Pioneering interior designer and antiquarian Henry Davis Sleeper created Beauport, transforming it into a repository for his vast collection of American and European decorative arts and antiques. From 1907 to 1934, he built and expanded the house, which has more than 40 rooms, and decorated many of the chambers to illustrate literary and historical themes. The entertaining tour concentrates more on the gorgeous house and rooms in general than on the countless objects on display, which remain virtually as Sleeper left them. You'll see architectural details rescued from other buildings, magnificent arrangements of colored glassware, secret staircases, the "Red Indian Room" (with a majestic view of the harbor), the "Master Mariner's Room" (overflowing with nautical items), and even the kitchen and servants' quarters. Explore the restored grounds, which look the way they did in the 1930s. Beauport, a National Historic Landmark, also schedules events such as afternoon tea, wine tastings, and specialty tours throughout the season.

Beauport's treasure-trove of antiques and beautifully restored grounds make it a popular stop for Gloucester visitors.

75 Eastern Point Blvd. www.historicnewengland.org. ✆ **978/283-0800.** Guided tour $10 adults, $9 seniors, $5 students and children 6–12. Tours on the hour June to mid-Oct Tues–Sat 10am–4pm. Closed July 4, mid-Oct to May, and Sun–Mon year-round. Take E. Main St. to Eastern Point Blvd. (a private road) and continue ½ mile to house; park on left.

Cape Ann Museum ★ MUSEUM   This meticulously curated museum makes an excellent introduction to Cape Ann's history and artists. An entire gallery holds extraordinary works by **Fitz Henry Lane ★★★** (formerly known as Fitz Hugh Lane), the Luminist painter whose light-flooded canvases show off the best of his native Gloucester. The nation's largest collection of his paintings and drawings is here. Other galleries feature works on paper by 20th-century artists such as Maurice Prendergast, Milton Avery, and Stuart Davis; work by other contemporary artists; and granite-quarrying tools and equipment. There's also an outdoor sculpture court. On display in the maritime and fisheries galleries are entire vessels (including one about the size of a minivan that crossed the Atlantic), exhibits on the fishing industry, ship models, and historic photographs and models of the Gloucester waterfront. Guided tours of the highlights of the collection (Tues–Sat 11am, Sat–Sun 2pm) include a look around the adjacent **Capt. Elias Davis House** (1804), decorated and furnished in Federal style with furniture, silver, and porcelains. Check ahead for information about touring the 1710 **White-Ellery House,** a rare example of First Period architecture about a mile away at 244 Washington St.

27 Pleasant St. (1 block from Main St.). www.capeannmuseum.org. ✆ **978/283-0455.** Admission $8 adults, $6 seniors and students, free for children 11 and under. Mar–Jan Tues–Sat 10am–5pm; Sun 1–4pm. Closed Feb. Follow Main St. west through downtown and turn right onto Pleasant St.; museum is on the right. Metered parking on street or in lot across street.

Ryan & Wood, Inc. DISTILLERY   Ryan & Wood is a family business that makes gin, rum, vodka, and rye in an industrial area not far from downtown Gloucester. The friendly, enthusiastic staff explains the distilling process, which uses a beautiful custom-built still. People of all ages can take the 1-hour tour.

15 Great Republic Dr. (off Blackburn Dr.). www.ryanandwood.com. ✆ **978/281-2282.** Tours free. Mon–Sat 10am and 1pm. From Rte. 128, go ¾ around Blackburn Circle rotary and exit onto Dory Rd. Go ½ mile and turn right onto Blackburn Dr.; Great Republic Dr. is the 1st left.

Where to Eat

See "A Detour to Essex," on p. 328, for information about the celebrated **Woodman's of Essex,** which is about 20 minutes from downtown Gloucester. The Stage Fort Park snack bar, the **Cupboard,** 41 Hough Ave. (✆ **978/281-1908**), serves excellent fried seafood and blue-plate specials in the summer. **Lobsta Land,** 10 Causeway St., near exit 12 off Route 128 (✆ **978/281-0415**), is a summer-only destination for familiar and unusual seafood dishes deftly prepared and served in a friendly atmosphere that belies the location, just off the busy highway. If you're

A guided tour of the Cape Ann Museum will help you make the most of your visit.

in town just for a day, consider sticking around for dinner at the **Franklin Cape Ann,** 118 Main St. (www.franklincafe.com; ✆ **978/283-7888**). It serves excellent bistro cuisine daily from 5pm to midnight (but unfortunately not at lunch).

Halibut Point Restaurant & Bar ★ SEAFOOD/AMERICAN   A local legend for its chowders and burgers, Halibut Point is a friendly tavern that serves generous portions of good food. The "Halibut Point Special"—a cup of chowder, a burger, and a beer—hits the high points. The clam chowder is terrific, and the spicy Italian fish chowder is so good that some people come to Gloucester just for that. There's also a raw bar. Main courses are simple (mostly sandwiches) at lunch and more elaborate at dinner. Be sure to check the specials board—you didn't come all this way to a fishing port not to have fresh fish, did you?

289 Main St. www.halibutpoint.com. ✆ **978/281-1900.** Main courses $7–$14 at lunch, $11–$20 at dinner. AE, DISC, MC, V. Daily 11:30am–11pm.

Latitude 43 Restaurant & Bar ★ SEAFOOD/CREATIVE AMERICAN/ SUSHI   A harborfront location is sometimes a red flag—a popular myth says water views make up for other deficiencies—but here the view just adds to the funky, laid-back atmosphere. Popular year-round (which means the picky locals eat here, too), "Lat 43" offers something for everyone. Clam and fish chowder, greaseless fried seafood, and tasty burgers and lobster rolls are terrific renditions of perennial favorites. More sophisticated dishes include salads overflowing with local produce, bistro favorites such as braised lamb shank, or excellent paella. You can even get sushi, an option inexplicably absent in many New England seaports. There's seating on the pleasant deck in good weather, and the staff can point out notable features of the certified-green building.

25 Rogers St. (½ block from Washington St.). www.latfortythree.com. ✆ **978/281-0223.** Reservations recommended at dinner. Main courses $7–$16 at lunch, $17–$25 at dinner; lobster market price. AE, DISC, MC, V. Sun–Thurs 11:30am–9pm; Fri–Sat 11:30am–10pm. Pub open until 1am (food served until midnight) daily.

Shopping

Rocky Neck (see "Exploring Gloucester," above) offers great browsing. Downtown, **Main Street** between Pleasant and Washington streets is a good destination. Agreeable stops include **Mystery Train,** 21 Main St. (www.mystery trainrecords.com; ✆ **978/281-8911**), which carries a huge variety of used music and films; the **Ménage Gallery,** 134 Main St. (www.menagegallery.com; ✆ **877/ 283-6030** or 978/283-6030), which shows varied works by artists and artisans, including gorgeous furniture; and the **Dogtown Book Shop,** 132 Main St. (www. dogtownbooks.com; ✆ **978/281-5599**), noted for its used and antiquarian selection. **Cape Pond Ice** (see box, *"The Perfect Storm,"* above) sells T-shirts, sweatshirts, and other merchandise bearing the company's distinctive logo.

Entertainment

Gloucester Stage Company ★   The Gloucester Stage, as it's known, is one of the best repertory troupes in New England. The air-conditioned theater schedules six plays a season (late May to early Sept) and occasional events—including a holiday program that features local child performers and an audience singalong—in the off season.

267 E. Main St. (at Mount Pleasant Ave.). www.gloucesterstage.org. ℂ **978/281-4433** (box office) or 978/281-4099. Tickets $40 adults, $35 seniors and students. From downtown, follow signs for E. Gloucester and take E. Main St. 1 mile; Gorton Theater is on the right.

Where to Stay

Gloucester abounds with B&Bs; for guidance, check with the Cape Ann Chamber of Commerce (www.capeannvacations.com; ℂ **978/283-1601**) or consult one of the agencies listed on p. 290.

Atlantis Oceanfront Inn   Across the street from the water, the Atlantis enjoys stunning views from every window. The property has an outdoor pool, a helpful staff, and good-size guest rooms. Decorated in comfortable, contemporary style, each well-maintained unit has a terrace or balcony with a small table and chairs. Second-floor guest rooms are slightly preferable owing to the better view. The Atlantis doesn't have the resort feel of its more expensive neighbor, the Bass Rocks Ocean Inn, but the million-dollar views are the same, and the on-premises cafe is a plus.

125 Atlantic Rd., Gloucester, MA 01930. www.atlantisoceanfrontinn.com. ℂ **800/732-6313** or 978/283-0014. Fax 978/281-8994. 40 units, 7 with shower only. Late June to Labor Day $180–$230 double; spring and fall $145–$195 double. Extra person $10. Rollaway or crib $15. Children 12 and under stay free in parent's room. Minimum stay may be required. Off-season midweek discounts available. AE, MC, V. Closed Nov to late Apr. Take Rte. 128 to the end (exit 9, East Gloucester), turn left onto Bass Ave. (Rte. 127A), and follow it ½ mile. Turn right and follow Atlantic Rd. **Amenities:** Cafe (breakfast only); heated outdoor pool. *In room:* A/C, TV, fridge, hair dryer, Wi-Fi (free).

Bass Rocks Ocean Inn   This inviting property offers gorgeous ocean views, an outdoor pool, and modern accommodations. Across the road from the rocky shore, the Bass Rocks feels like an old-fashioned resort, which distinguishes it from the neighboring Atlantis. Each room in the well-kept 1960s-era motel, has sliding glass doors that open onto a balcony or patio, and a king bed or two double beds. Second-floor rooms have slightly better views. A Colonial-revival mansion built in 1899 and known as the "wedding-cake house" holds three one-bedroom suites and the public areas, including a billiard room and a library. In the afternoon, the staff serves coffee, tea, lemonade, and chocolate-chip cookies.

107 Atlantic Rd., Gloucester, MA 01930. www.bassrocksoceaninn.com. ℂ **888/802-7666** or 978/283-7600. Fax 978/281-6489. 51 units. Summer $259–$360 double, $369 suite; spring and fall $179–$259 double, $299 suite. Extra person $10. Children 12 and under stay free in parent's room. Rollaway or crib $12. Rates include continental breakfast, afternoon refreshments, and use of bikes. Minimum 3-night stay summer weekends, some spring and fall weekends. AAA and AARP discounts available. AE, DC, DISC, MC, V. Closed Nov to late Apr. Follow Rte. 128 to the end (exit 9, East Gloucester), turn left onto Bass Ave. (Rte. 127A), and follow it ½ mile. Turn right and follow Atlantic Rd. **Amenities:** Heated outdoor pool. *In room:* A/C, TV/DVD, fridge, hair dryer, Wi-Fi (free).

A Detour to Essex

The beautiful little town of **Essex** is a quick trip from Gloucester or Rockport, and it makes a good detour as you approach or leave Cape Ann. From Route 128, take exit 14 and head west on Route 133. It's a beautiful little town known for Essex clams, salt marshes, a long tradition of shipbuilding, an incredible number of antiques shops, and one celebrated restaurant.

NORTH SHORE beaches

North of Boston, sandy beaches dot the predominantly rocky coastline. The water is cold—optimistic locals say "refreshing"—but typically not too rough. Parking can be scarce, especially on weekends, and lots often fill up despite costing as much as $25 per car. If you can't set out early, wait until midafternoon and hope that the people who arrived in the morning have had their fill. During the summer, lifeguards are on duty from 9am to 5pm at larger public beaches. Surfing is generally permitted outside of those hours. The beaches listed here all have bathhouses and snack bars. Whether or not you're swimming, watch out for greenhead flies in July and August. They don't sting—they take little bites of flesh. Bring or buy insect repellent.

The best-known North Shore beach is **Singing Beach ★★**, off Masconomo Street in Manchester-by-the-Sea. Because it's easily accessible by public transportation, it attracts the most diverse crowd—carless singles, local families, and other beach bunnies of all ages. They walk ½ mile on Beach Street from the train station to find sparkling sand and lively surf. Take the commuter rail (www.mbta.com; ℂ **617/222-3200**) from Boston's North Station.

Nearly as famous and popular is **Crane Beach ★**, off Argilla Road in Ipswich, part of a 1,400-acre barrier beach reservation. Fragile dunes and a white-sand beach lead down to Ipswich Bay. The surf is calmer than that at less sheltered Singing Beach, and quite chilly. Pick up Argilla Road south of Ipswich Center near the intersection of Routes 1A and 133, or take the Cape Ann Transportation Authority's summer-only, weekend-and-holidays-only **Ipswich Essex Explorer** bus service (www.ipswichessex explorer.com; ℂ **978/283-7916** or 978/356-8540) from the Ipswich train station. Also on Ipswich Bay is **Wingaersheek Beach ★**, on Atlantic Street off Route 133 in Gloucester. It has its own exit (no. 13) off Route 128, about 15 minutes away on winding roads with low speed limits. When you finally arrive, you'll find beautiful white sand, a glorious view, and more dunes. Because these beaches are harder to get to, they attract more locals—but also lots of day-tripping families. At the east end of Route 133, the beaches and snack bar in Gloucester's easily accessible **Stage Fort Park** are popular local hangouts.

Legend has it that **Woodman's of Essex ★★★**, 121 Main St. (www.woodmans.com; ℂ **800/649-1773** or 978/768-6057), was the birthplace of the fried clam in 1916. Today, the thriving family-owned eatery is a great spot to join legions of locals and visitors for lobster "in the rough," chowder, steamers, corn on the cob, onion rings, and (you guessed it) superb fried clams. In warm weather, people from all over the world flock here, especially on their way back from the beach. In the winter, the crowd is mostly locals desperate for a taste of summer (pass me a moist towelette, please). The line can be long, but it moves quickly and offers a good view of the regimented commotion in the food-prep area. Eat inside, upstairs on the deck, or out back at a picnic table. You'll want to be well fed before you set off to explore the numerous antiques shops along Main Street. The restaurant, which serves beer and wine and accepts credit cards, opens daily at 11am year-round (closing time changes seasonally); check the website or call ahead.

As with most cult-favorite foods, the fashion is to be contrarian and say that Woodman's is too crowded and too many people know about it. I disagree, but if you're interested in comparison shopping—in the interest of science, of course— two other excellent destinations are open in the summer only. **J. T. Farnham's,** 88 Eastern Ave., Essex (✆ **978768-6643**), lies about a mile east of Woodman's, and the **Clam Box,** 246 High St., Ipswich (www.ipswichma.com/clambox; ✆ **978/ 356-9707**), is a little over 7 miles northwest of Woodman's. Both accept cash only.

ROCKPORT

40 miles NE of Boston

This lovely little town at the tip of Cape Ann was settled in 1690. Over the years it has been an active fishing port, a center of granite excavation and cutting, and a thriving summer community whose specialty appears to be selling fudge and refrigerator magnets to out-of-towners. Rockport is an entertaining half-day trip, perhaps combined with a visit to Gloucester.

There's more to Rockport than just gift shops. It's home to a lovely state park, and it's popular with photographers, painters, jewelry designers, and sculptors. Winslow Homer, Fitz Henry Lane, and Childe Hassam are among the famous artists who have captured the local color. At times, especially on summer weekends, it can be tough to find much local color in this tourist-weary destination. But for every year-round resident who seems startled when legions of camera-wielding visitors descend on Rockport each June, there are dozens of gracious residents who are proud to show off their beautiful town.

Out of season, especially January through mid-April, Rockport is pretty but somewhat desolate. The year-round population is large enough that some businesses stay open, though many keep reduced hours.

Essentials

GETTING THERE From Boston, take I-93 or Route 1 north to Route 128, and follow it to the end. Turn left at the signs for Rockport to take Route 127, which is shorter but more commercial than Route 127A. To take Route 127A, which runs near (but not along) the east coast of Cape Ann, continue on Route 128 until you see the sign for East Gloucester and turn left. Parking is tough, especially on summer Saturday afternoons, but metered spots are available throughout downtown. Make one loop around downtown and then head to the free parking lot on Upper Main Street (Rte. 127), near the visitor information booth. The shuttle bus to or from downtown costs $1.

The **commuter rail** (www.mbta.com; ✆ 617/222-3200) runs from Boston's North Station. The trip takes 60 to 70 minutes, and the round-trip fare is $20. The station is about 6 blocks from the downtown waterfront. The **Cape Ann Transportation Authority,** or CATA (www.canntran.com; ✆ 978/283-7916), runs buses from town to town on Cape Ann Monday through Saturday.

VISITOR INFORMATION The **Rockport Chamber of Commerce,** 170 Main St. (www.rockportusa.com; ✆ 978/546-6575), is a division of the Cape Ann Chamber of Commerce (www.capeannvacations.com; ✆ 978/283-1601; see "Gloucester," earlier in this chapter). The chamber operates an information booth on Upper Main Street (Rte. 127) daily from July 1 through Labor

ATTRACTIONS
Halibut Point State Park **2**
Motif No. 1 **14**
Paper House **4**
Rockport Art Association **10**

HOTELS
Captain's Bounty
on the Beach **6**
Emerson Inn by the Sea **3**
Inn on Cove Hill (Caleb
Norwood Jr. House) **15**

RESTAURANTS
Helmut's Strudel **13**
The Lobster Pool **1**
Roy Moore Lobster
Company **12**

SHOPPING
Crackerjacks **5**
Tidal Edge Gallery **9**
Toad Hall Bookstore **7**
Tuck's Candy Factory **11**
Willoughby's **8**

Rockport

Day and on weekends from mid-May to June and early September through mid-October. It's about a mile from the town line and a mile from downtown—look for the WELCOME TO ROCKPORT sign on the right as you head north.

SPECIAL EVENTS   **Rockport Music** (www.rockportmusic.org; ℂ **978/546-7391**) organizes the **Rockport Chamber Music Festival** each June. It's a good excuse to see the town before the height of tourist season. In addition to performances by promising young musicians and family-oriented concerts, events include free lectures and discussions. The summer schedule highlights pop, folk, and world music artists as well as the **Rockport Jazz Festival,** in mid-August. Performances take place in the lovely **Shalin Liu Performance Center,** 37 Main St. Check ahead for the schedule of events in the 330-seat concert hall, noted for the two-story window overlooking the water at the back of the stage.

The annual **Christmas pageant,** on Main Street in December, is a crowded, kid-friendly event with carol singing and live animals.

Exploring Rockport

The most famous sight in Rockport has something of an "Emperor's New Clothes" aura—it's a wooden fish warehouse on the town wharf, or T-Wharf, in the harbor. The barn-red shack known as **Motif No. 1** is the most frequently painted and photographed object in a town filled with lovely buildings and

Motif No. 1 is the most frequently painted and photographed object in Rockport.

surrounded by breathtaking rocky coastline. The color certainly catches the eye against the neutrals of the seascape, but you might find yourself wondering what the big deal is. Originally constructed in 1884 and destroyed during the blizzard of 1978, Motif No. 1 was rebuilt using donations from residents and tourists. It stands on the same pier as the original, duplicated in every detail and reinforced to withstand storms.

Nearby is a phenomenon whose popularity is easier to explain. **Bearskin Neck,** named after an unfortunate ursine visitor who drowned and washed ashore in 1800, has perhaps the highest concentration of gift shops anywhere. It's a narrow peninsula with one main street (South Rd.) and several alleys crammed with galleries, snack and coffee bars, antiques shops, and ancient houses. The peninsula ends in a plaza with a magnificent water view.

Throughout the town, more than two dozen **art galleries** ★ display the works of local and nationally known artists. The **Rockport Art Association,** 12 Main St. (www. rockportartassn.org; ✆ **978/546-6604**), sponsors major exhibitions and special shows. It's open daily mid-morning to late afternoon in the summer (except on Sun, when it opens at noon); in the off season, it's open Wednesday through Saturday 10am to 4 or 5pm, and Sunday noon to 5pm.

To get a sense of the power of the sea, take Route 127 north of town to the tip of Cape Ann. Turn right on Gott

Bearskin Neck is home to a number of fun and funky shops.

Nature lovers should set aside time for a visit to Halibut Point State Park.

Avenue to reach **Halibut Point State Park** ★★ (www.mass.gov/dcr and www.thetrustees.org; ✆ **978/546-2997**). The park is a great place to wander around and admire the gorgeous scenery. On a clear day, you can see Maine. The park has a staffed visitor center, walking trails, and tidal pools. Swimming in the water-filled quarries is absolutely forbidden. You can climb around on giant boulders on the rocky beach or climb to the top of the World War II observation tower. To take a self-guided tour, pick up a brochure at the visitor center or the chamber of commerce. Check ahead for information about talks, guided tours, demonstrations, and other special programs; a good resource is the park **blog** (www.halibut point.wordpress.com). The park is open daily from Memorial Day to Labor Day 8am to 8pm, otherwise daily dawn to dusk; parking costs $2 year-round.

A genuinely wacky attraction between downtown and Halibut Point is the **Paper House,** 52 Pigeon Hill St., Pigeon Cove (www.paperhouserockport.com; ✆ **978/546-2629**). It was built beginning in 1922 entirely out of 100,000 newspapers—walls, furniture, even a newspaper-covered piano. Creator Elis Stenman made every item from papers of a different period. The house is open April through October daily from 10am to 5pm (closed Nov–Mar). Admission is $2 for adults, $1 for children 6 to 14. Follow Route 127 north out of downtown about 1½ miles, watching carefully until you see signs at Curtis Street pointing to the left, then go left on Pigeon Hill Street.

Where to Eat

Rockport's dining scene isn't nearly as varied or sophisticated as Gloucester's; if you're not ravenous, head there or to **Woodman's of Essex** (p. 329).

My top suggestion for food comes from the "would be an insider tip if it weren't so crowded" file. The **Roy Moore Lobster Company** ★★, 39 Bearskin Neck (✆ **978/546-6696**), is a fish market that specializes in ultrafresh lobster cooked in seawater and served with drawn butter and plenty of paper towels. The luscious crustaceans and a limited selection of other dishes (including clam chowder) are available to stay or go. Prices are exceptionally reasonable, thanks in part to the lack of atmosphere—the small dining area is outdoors, and drinks come from the soda machine—and the service at the counter is efficient and friendly. Roy Moore's is open daily from 8am until 6pm from late March through October.

Another seasonal favorite is the **Lobster Pool,** a classic clam shack at 329 Granite St. (www.lobsterpoolrestaurant.com; ✆ **978/546-7808**). Follow Route 127 north along the peninsula past Halibut Point State Park to this family-run self-service restaurant with picnic tables, spectacular water views, and huge weekend crowds. It serves seafood "in the rough" as well as soup, salads, sandwiches, and homemade desserts. It's open from April through November, weekends in the spring and daily in summer and fall from 11:30am to 8:30pm.

Helmut's Strudel, 49 Bearskin Neck (📞 **978/546-2824**), is known for its apple and cherry strudels—served warm and a la mode if you like. Helmut's offers a variety of other pastries and a good selection of beverages, including apple cider, hot chocolate, and fresh squeezed orange juice. The outdoor seating area enjoys a great view of the harbor. No credit cards.

Shopping

Bearskin Neck is the obvious place to start. Dozens of little shops stock clothes, gifts, toys, jewelry, souvenirs, inexpensive novelties, and expensive handmade crafts and paintings. Another enjoyable stroll is along **Main** and **Mount Pleasant streets.** Good stops include the nonprofit **Toad Hall Bookstore,** 47 Main St. (www.toadhallbooks.org; 📞 **978/546-7323**); **Tidal Edge Gallery,** 3 School St., off Main Street (www.tidaledgegallery.com; 📞 **978/546-3196**); and **Willoughby's,** 20 Main St. (📞 **978/546-9820**), a women's clothing and accessories shop.

Two of my favorite stops are retro delights. Downtown, you can watch taffy being made at **Tuck's Candy Factory,** 7 Dock Sq. (www.tuckscandy.com; 📞 **800/569-2767** or 978/546-6352), a local landmark that opened in 1929. There's a retail location at 15 Main St. Near the train station, **Crackerjacks,** 27 Whistlestop Mall, off Railroad Avenue (📞 **978/546-1616**), is an old-fashioned variety store with a great crafts department.

Where to Stay

When Rockport is busy, it's very busy, and when it's not, it's practically empty. The town's dozens of B&Bs fill in good weather and empty or even close in the winter. Make summer reservations well in advance or cross your fingers and call the chamber of commerce (p. 330) to ask about availability. The **Rockport Innkeepers Association** website (www.innsofrockport.com) consolidates information about member properties.

Two miles from downtown, the **Emerson Inn by the Sea,** 1 Cathedral Ave. (www.emersoninnbythesea.com; 📞 **800/964-5550** or 978/546-6321), is a miniresort with sweet views of the Atlantic and the rocky shore. Open year-round; rates for a double in high season run $159 to $379, which includes breakfast and Wi-Fi.

If you're traveling by train, call ahead to request pick-up at the Rockport commuter rail station, which most lodgings in town offer at no charge.

Captain's Bounty on the Beach   This modern, well-maintained motor inn is hardly plush, but the staff is welcoming and the location unbeatable. The Captain's Bounty is right on the beach, and is nearly as close to the center of town as to the harbor. Each room in the three-story building overlooks the water and has its own balcony and sliding glass door. Rooms are spacious and sound-proofed, with good cross-ventilation but no air-conditioning. Each has a micro-wave and fridge in case you want to eat some meals in; kitchenette units are available. The best rooms are on the adults-only top floor. All rooms and decks are nonsmoking.

1 Beach St., Rockport, MA 01966. www.captainsbountymotorinn.com. 📞 **978/546-9557.** Fax 978/546-9993. 24 units. Mid-June to mid-Sept $170 double, $180 efficiency, $210 efficiency suite; spring and fall $140 double, $145 efficiency, $160 efficiency suite. Extra adult $10; $5 for each child. 2-night minimum stay weekends, 3-night stay holiday weekends. MC, V. Closed Nov–Mar. Pets accepted ($10 per night). *In room:* TV/DVD, fridge, Wi-Fi (free).

Inn on Cove Hill (Caleb Norwood Jr. House) ★   This attractive Federal-style inn is just 2 blocks from the town wharf, but the building is set back from the street and has a delightful hideaway feel. The 1771 home was built using the proceeds of pirates' gold found nearby. Innkeeper Betsy Eck decorates the guest rooms in exquisite period style; most have Colonial furnishings and handmade quilts, and some have canopy beds. Water views from the windows and good-size decks at the back of the house are worth the climb to the third floor. The generous breakfast is served in the dining room or, in good weather, in the pleasant garden. Guests have the use of a phone in the living room. A harbor-view apartment across the street is available for stays of 1 week or more.

37 Mount Pleasant St., Rockport, MA 01966. www.innoncovehill.com. ✆ **888/546-2701** or 978/546-2701. Fax 978/546-1095. 6 units, some with shower only. $150–$165 double; $250 suite. Extra person $25. Rates include continental breakfast. 2-night minimum stay mid-May to mid-Oct and most weekends. MC, V. *In room:* A/C, TV, no phone.

PLYMOUTH

45 miles SE of Boston

Even though visitors jam the downtown area and waterfront in the summer, Plymouth is large enough to feel more like the working community it is than like a touristy day-trip destination. It's a manageable 1-day excursion from Boston, and particularly enjoyable if you're traveling with children. Plymouth also makes a good stop between Boston and Cape Cod.

Most people know at least a little of Plymouth's story—about how the Pilgrims, fleeing religious persecution, left Europe on the *Mayflower* and landed at Plymouth Rock in December 1620. Many also know that the Pilgrims endured disease and privation, and that just 53 people from the original group of 102 celebrated what we now call "the first Thanksgiving" in 1621 with Squanto, a Pawtuxet Indian associated with the Wampanoag people, and his cohorts.

What you won't know until you visit is how small everything was. The *Mayflower* (a reproduction) seems perilously tiny, and when you contemplate how dangerous life was at the time, it's hard not to marvel at the settlers' accomplishments. One of their descendants' accomplishments is this: Plymouth is in many ways a model destination, where the 17th century coexists with the 21st, and most historic attractions are both educational and fun.

Essentials

GETTING THERE   By car, follow the Southeast Expressway (I-93) south from Boston to Route 3. Take exit 6A to Route 44 east and follow signs to the historic attractions. The trip from Boston takes 45 to 60 minutes if it's not rush hour. Take exit 5 to the state **Tourist Information Center** (www.massvacation.com; ✆ **508/746-1150**) for maps, brochures, and information. To go directly to **Plimoth Plantation,** take exit 4. There's metered parking throughout town; visit **www.parkplymouth.com** for information.

Plymouth and Brockton **buses** (www.p-b.com; ✆ **508/746-0378**) serve Plymouth from South Station. The trip takes about 1 hour. Buses run more often than the train—and operate on weekends, which the commuter rail to Plymouth doesn't—and cost a little more ($14 one-way, $25 round-trip). Buses drop off and pick up passengers at the park-and-ride lot at

A worthwhile detour en route to Plymouth is the **Adams National Historical Park** in Quincy, about 10 miles south of Boston. The park preserves the birthplaces of presidents John Adams and John Quincy Adams, the house where four generations of the family lived, and other buildings associated with the political dynasty. A trolley connects the buildings, which are open for 2-hour guided tours—the only way to see the interiors—daily from 9am to 5pm in season (Apr 19–Nov 10). Admission is $5 for adults, free for children 15 and under. The grounds and the visitor center, 1250 Hancock St. (www.nps.gov/adam; ✆ **617/770-1175**), are across the street from the Quincy Center stop on the Red Line; call or surf ahead for driving directions.

Route 3, exit 5. The **commuter rail** (www.mbta.com; ✆ **617/222-3200**) serves Cordage Park, on Route 3A north of downtown, from Boston's South Station four times a day on weekdays only. The round-trip fare is $20. The **Plymouth Area Link** bus (www.gatra.org; ✆ **800/483-2500** or 508/747-1819) connects downtown with the park-and-ride lot and the train station. The fare is $1, free for children 6 and under.

VISITOR INFORMATION If you haven't visited the Tourist Information Center (above), pick up a map at the **Visitor Information Center** (✆ **508/747-7525**), open seasonally at 130 Water St., across from Town Pier. To plan ahead, contact **Destination Plymouth,** 134 Court St., Plymouth, MA 02360 (www.seeplymouth.com; ✆ **508/747-7533**).

GETTING AROUND The downtown attractions are easily accessible on foot. A shallow hill slopes from the center of town to the waterfront.

America's Hometown Shuttle (www.p-b.com/ahs.html; ✆ **508/746-0378**) covers a loop throughout the town. It operates from late June through Labor Day weekend, daily from 10am to 5pm. The fare ($15 adults, $7.50 children 6–18, $25 families) includes a narrated tour and unlimited reboarding. Check ahead for the schedule and route, which includes Plimoth Plantation.

Exploring Plymouth

The logical place to begin (good luck talking children out of it) is where the Pilgrims first set foot—at **Plymouth Rock ★★**. The rock, accepted as the

Seeing Plymouth Rock in person is a moving experience.

SHOPPING
British Imports **8**
Lily's Apothecary **12**
Main Street Antiques **9**
Pilgrim's Progress **7**

ATTRACTIONS
Mayflower II **5**
Pilgrim Hall Museum **4**
Plimoth Plantation **16**
Plymouth Rock **6**

HOTELS
Best Western Cold Spring **1**
John Carver Inn & Spa **14**
Pilgrim Sands on Long Beach **15**
Radisson Hotel Plymouth Harbor **2**

RESTAURANTS
Kiskadee Coffee Company **12**
Lobster Hut **3**
Persy's Place **11**
Sam Diego's **10**

Plymouth

landing place of the *Mayflower* passengers, was originally 15 feet long and 3 feet wide. It was moved on the eve of the Revolution and several times thereafter. In 1867, it assumed its present permanent position at tide level. The rock itself isn't much to look at, but the accompanying descriptions are interesting, and the atmosphere is curiously inspiring.

The Colonial Dames of America commissioned the portico around the rock, designed by McKim, Mead & White and erected in 1920. This property's formal name is **Pilgrim Memorial State Park** (www.mass.gov/dcr; © 508/747-5360); it's the smallest state park in Massachusetts.

The park just south of the Rock is **Brewster Gardens,** a lovely green space that traces Town Brook. This is a good shortcut to **Jenney Pond,** in Town Brook Park, across Summer Street from the John Carver Inn. A short distance from the bustle of the waterfront, the park has plenty of room to run around as well as a pond where ducks and geese live.

GUIDED TOURS To walk in the Pilgrims' footsteps, take a **Colonial Lantern Tour ★** (www.lanterntours.com; © 774/454-8126). Participants carry pierced-tin lanterns on a 90-minute walking tour of the original settlement, conducted by a knowledgeable guide. It might seem a bit hokey at first, but it's fascinating. Tours run nightly from April to Thanksgiving, rain or shine. The standard history tour begins at 7:30pm, the "Ghosts & Legends" tour at

Brewster Gardens is a lovely bit of greenery near the harbor.

8pm. Tickets are $12 for adults; $10 for seniors, AAA members, and children 6 to 16; free for children 5 and under. Check the meeting place when you make reservations. The company also offers special tours for Halloween and Thanksgiving.

Native Plymouth Tours (www.nativeplymouthtours.com; ℂ 774/454-7792) are guided walking tours that look at town history from the perspective of the original residents. The 90-minute excursions (Apr–Nov Fri–Sat 5:30pm, otherwise by reservation only) cost $15 for adults, $12 for seniors, $10 for children 5 to 18.

Narrated cruises run from April or May through November from State Pier and Town Wharf; check the departure point when you make reservations, which are always recommended and imperative at busy times. **Pilgrim Belle Cruises** (www.pilgrimbellecruises.com; ℂ 508/747-3434) offers 75-minute narrated **harbor tours** on a paddle wheeler ($17 adults, $15 seniors, $12 children 5–12) as well as sunset and dining cruises. The offerings of **Plymouth Cruises** (www.plymouthcruises.com; ℂ 508/746-5342) include **pirate cruises** ($18 per person), which allow kids aged 4 to 11 to don hats and face paint and "defend" the boat against marauding buccaneers, and **lobster excursions** ($16 adults, $14 seniors, $12 children 11 and under), which give passengers the chance to haul up traps and observe marine life. **Capt. John Boats** (www.captjohn.com; ℂ 800/242-2469 or 508/746-2643) offers **whale watches** ($45 adults, $37 seniors, $29 children 4–12, free for kids 3 and under).

Mayflower II ★ ☺ HISTORIC SITE   Berthed a few steps from Plymouth Rock, the *Mayflower II* is a full-scale reproduction of the type of ship that brought the Pilgrims from England to America in 1620. Even at full scale, the 107-foot vessel, constructed in England from 1955 to 1957, is remarkably small. Although little

Visitors are often surprised by just how small the *Mayflower II* is.

technical information about the original *Mayflower* survives, designer William A. Baker incorporated the few references in Governor Bradford's account of the voyage with other research to re-create the ship as authentically as possible.

Costumed guides provide interesting first-person narratives about the vessel and voyage, and other interpreters provide a contemporary perspective. Displays describe and illustrate the journey and the Pilgrims' experience. They include exhibits about 17th-century navigation techniques, stocking the ship with food and other provisions, and the history of the *Mayflower II*. Plimoth Plantation (below) owns and maintains the vessel and offers combined admission discounts. Alongside the ship are museum shops that replicate early Pilgrim dwellings.

State Pier. www.plimoth.org. © **508/746-1622.** Admission $10 adults, $9 seniors, $7 children 6–12, free for children 5 and under. Admission to both Plimoth Plantation (good for 2 consecutive days) and *Mayflower II* $30 adults, $27 seniors and students, $19 children 6–12, free for children 5 and under, $110 families (2 adults and up to 4 children 6–17; not available online). Late Mar to late Nov daily 9am–5pm (until 7pm July–Aug). Closed Dec to mid-Mar.

Pilgrim Hall Museum ★ ☺ MUSEUM   This is a great place to get a sense of the day-to-day lives of Plymouth's first European residents. Many original possessions of the early Pilgrims and their descendants are on display, including one of Myles Standish's swords, Governor Bradford's Bible, and an uncomfortable chair (you can sit in a replica) that belonged to William Brewster. Regularly changing exhibits explore aspects of the settlers' lives, such as the immigrant experience or children's embroidery, and hands-on activities such as treasure hunts get families interested. Built in 1824, the Pilgrim Hall Museum is the oldest public museum in the United States.

75 Court St. www.pilgrimhall.org. © **508/746-1620.** Admission $8 adults, $7 seniors, $6 AAA members, $5 children 6–15, $25 families. Feb–Dec daily 9:30am–4:30pm. Closed Jan and Dec 25. From Plymouth Rock, walk north on Water St. and up the hill on Chilton St.

Plimoth Plantation ★★ ☺ HISTORIC SITE   Allow at least half a day to explore this re-creation of a 1627 English village and 17th-century Native American extended-family home. Children and adults find the experience equally interesting. Although it can be a bit disorienting at first, visiting with the "Pilgrims" in their homes and gardens is great fun. They're role-players who, in speech, dress, and manner, assume the personalities of members of the original community. The interpreters who staff the Wampanoag Homesite aren't actors—they're Wampanoags and members of other tribes who show visitors native foodstuffs, agricultural practices, and crafts. Staff members throughout the plantation eagerly welcome questions.

The exhibits are as accurate as research can make them, constructed with careful attention to historical detail. The planners combined accounts of the original colony with archaeological research, old records, and the history written by the

LEFT: **The Pilgrim Hall Museum contains numerous artifacts ranging from the mundane to the military.** RIGHT: Plimoth Plantation provides modern visitors with a glimpse into the lives of the early settlers.

Pilgrims' leader, William Bradford (who often used the spelling "Plimoth"). You can watch the "Pilgrims" framing a house, splitting wood, shearing sheep, preserving foodstuffs, or cooking a pot of fish stew over an open hearth, all as it was done in the 1600s and using only the tools and cookware available then. Sometimes you can join the activities—perhaps planting, harvesting, witnessing a trial, or visiting a wedding party. There are daily militia drills with matchlock muskets that are fired to demonstrate the community's defense system. In fact, little defense was needed, because the Native Americans were friendly. **Note:** Wear comfortable shoes, because you'll be walking a lot.

At the main entrance are two modern buildings that house exhibits, a gift shop, a bookstore, a cafeteria, and an auditorium where visitors can view a film produced by the History Channel. There's also a picnic area. Call or surf ahead for information about the many special events, lectures, tours, workshops, theme dinners, and children's and family programs offered throughout the season.

137 Warren Ave. (Rte. 3). www.plimoth.org. ✆ **508/746-1622.** Admission (good for 2 consecutive days) $26 adults, $23 seniors, $15 children 6–12, free for children 5 and under. Admission to Plimoth Plantation and *Mayflower II* $30 adults, $27 seniors and students, $19 children 6–12, free for children 5 and under, $110 families (2 adults and up to 4 children 6–17; not available online). Late Mar to late Nov daily 9am–5pm. Closed Dec to mid-Mar. From Rte. 3, take exit 4, Plimoth Plantation Hwy.

Where to Eat

Plimoth Plantation (see above) has a cafeteria and a picnic area, and occasionally schedules theme dinners. Should you reach the "seafood again?" stage, a good destination downtown is **Sam Diego's,** 15 Main St. (www.samdiegos.com; ✆ **508/747-0048**), a cheerful Tex-Mex restaurant and bar in a renovated firehouse. It serves tasty renditions of exactly what you'd expect, and offers a kids' menu and seasonal outdoor seating. Hours are 11:30am to midnight daily. **Kiskadee Coffee Company,** 18 Main St. (www.kiskadeecoffee.com; ✆ **508/830-1410**), is a wonderful place to start the day or to stop in for a snack.

Lobster Hut ★ SEAFOOD   A busy self-service restaurant with a great view, the Lobster Hut is popular with both sightseers and, despite its touristy location, locals. Order and pick up at the counter, then head out onto the deck overlooking the bay (you can eat indoors, but the patio is nicer). This isn't an elegant place, but the food is ultrafresh and expertly prepared. To start, try clam chowder or lobster bisque. The seafood rolls (hot dog buns with your choice of filling) are excellent. The many fried seafood options include clams, scallops, shrimp, and haddock. You can also opt for broiled fish and shellfish, burgers, chicken tenders—or lobster, of course. Beer and wine are served, but only with meals.

25 Town Wharf. www.lobsterhutplymouth.com. 📞 **508/746-2270.** Reservations not accepted. Lunch specials (available Mon–Fri until 4pm) $9–$11, main courses $8–$21, sandwiches $3–$11 (most under $9), clams and lobster market price. MC, V. Summer daily 11am–9pm; winter daily 11am–7pm. Closed Jan.

Persy's Place AMERICAN   Part of a small local chain, Persy's Place is known for its menu, reputedly the largest in New England. Among the breakfast selections, served all day, you'll find the usual suspects, including an extensive selection of pancakes—try Cape Cod style, with cranberries and walnuts, for a taste of local flavor. They're yummy, but the magic here is in throwback dishes like baked beans (yes, for breakfast) and finnan haddie (smoked haddock cooked in cream), and oddities like biscuits and gravy, served Southern-style with sausage gravy or Northern-style with turkey gravy. Oh, and giant omelets. And a dozen variations on eggs Benedict. And crepes. And quiches. And perfectly good lunch food, too.

35A Main St. (at Middle St.). www.persysplace.com. 📞 **508/732-9876.** Breakfast items $4–$16, lunch items $6–$16. AE, MC, V. Daily 7am–3pm.

Shopping

Water Street, along the harbor, boasts an inexhaustible supply of souvenir and T-shirt shops. A less kitschy destination, just up the hill, is Route 3A, known as Court, Main, and Warren streets as it runs through town. **Lily's Apothecary,** 6 Main St. extension, in the old post office (www.lilysapothecary.com; 📞 **508/747-7546**), stocks a big-city-style selection of skin- and hair-care products for women and men. Closed Sunday and Monday except by appointment. **Main Street Antiques,** 46 Main St. (📞 **508/747-8887**), is home to dozens of dealers, and **Pilgrim's Progress,** 13 Court St. (www.pilgrimsprogressclothing.com; 📞 **508/746-6033**), carries stylish women's and men's clothing and accessories. **British Imports,** 1 Court St. (www.britishsupplies.com; 📞 **877/264-8586** or 508/747-2972), which specializes in English food, attracts homesick Marmite fans from miles around.

Where to Stay

On busy summer weekends, it's not unusual for every room in town to sell out. Make reservations well in advance.

The **Radisson Hotel Plymouth Harbor,** 180 Water St. (www.radisson.com/plymouthma; 📞 **800/395-7046** or 508/747-4900), is the only chain hotel downtown. The 175-unit hotel, on a hill across the street from the waterfront, offers all the usual chain amenities, including a swimming pool in the atrium lobby. Doubles in high season start at $159, which includes wireless Internet.

The **Hilton Garden Inn,** 4 Home Depot Dr. (www.hiltongardeninn.com; 📞 **877/782-9444** or 508/830-0200), is at Route 3 exit 5, about 10 minutes from downtown. The hotel has an indoor pool and extensive business features; doubles in high season go for $135 and up, which includes wireless Internet.

Best Western Plus Cold Spring ★★   The Cold Spring and its adjacent cottages surround landscaped lawns in a mostly residential neighborhood that makes a pleasant retreat from downtown's bustle. Rooms are attractively decorated and big enough for a family to spread out in. The fastidiously maintained property has a good-size outdoor pool. I especially like the location, a tolerable distance from the water; it's both quiet and convenient. The two-story complex is 1 long block inland, and set back from the street.

188 Court St. (Rte. 3A), Plymouth, MA 02360. www.bwcoldspring.com. (✆ **800/678-8667** or 508/746-2222. Fax 508/746-2744. 58 units, 10 with shower only, 2 2-bedroom cottages. Mar–Nov $99–$169 double; $139–$199 suite; $109–$159 cottage. Extra person $10. Rollaway $10, crib $5. Children 12 and under stay free in parent's room. Rates include continental breakfast buffet. Packages and AAA and off-season discounts available. AE, DC, DISC, MC, V. Closed Dec–Feb. Pets accepted ($10 fee). **Amenities:** Outdoor pool. *In room:* A/C, TV, hair dryer, high-speed Internet (free).

John Carver Inn & Spa ★ ☺ This centrally located hotel offers comfortable, modern accommodations and amenities, including a full-service spa, that appeal to both business and leisure travelers. The indoor "theme pool," a big hit with families, has a water slide and a Pilgrim ship model. The good-size guest rooms are regularly renovated and decorated in Colonial style. The best units are lavishly appointed two-room suites, with fireplaces and private Jacuzzis; I like the "four-poster" rooms, which have king beds. A three-story Colonial-style building with a landmark portico, the inn is on the edge of the downtown business district, within walking distance of the main attractions. Always check ahead for packages, which can be a great deal.

25 Summer St., Plymouth, MA 02360. www.johncarverinn.com. (✆ **800/274-1620** or 508/746-7100. Fax 508/746-8299. 80 units. Early Apr to mid-June and mid-Oct to Nov $119–$219 double; $259–$299 suite; mid-June to mid-Oct $159–$249 double; $299–$329 suite; Dec to early Apr $109–$199 double, $239–$279 suite. Extra person $20. Rollaway $20; cribs free. Children 18 and under stay free in parent's room. Packages and senior and AAA discounts available. AE, DC, DISC, MC, V. **Amenities:** Restaurant (American/seafood); concierge; fitness center; Jacuzzi; indoor pool; room service. *In room:* A/C, TV w/pay movies, hair dryer, Wi-Fi (free).

Pilgrim Sands on Long Beach ★★ ☺ This attractive motel sits directly on its own beach 3 miles south of town, within walking distance of Plimoth Plantation. An excellent choice if you want to avoid the busy downtown area, the well-maintained, regularly updated property also has indoor and outdoor pools. The good-size guest rooms are tastefully furnished and well maintained; most have two double or queen beds. The helpful staff and amenities make the Pilgrim Sands popular with business travelers as well as with vacationing families. In the afternoon, the breakfast room becomes the lounge, a local hangout with indoor and outdoor seating. If you can swing it, book a beachfront room for the view.

150 Warren Ave. (Rte. 3A), Plymouth, MA 02360. www.pilgrimsands.com. (✆ **800/729-7263** or 508/747-0900. Fax 508/746-8066. 64 units. Summer $159–$199 double; spring and early fall $114–$169 double; Apr and late fall $94–$134 double; Dec–Mar $84–$99 double. $159–$319 suite year-round. Extra person $6–$8 (suite $10–$15). Up to 2 children 6 and under stay free in parent's room. Rates include continental breakfast. Minimum 2-night stay holiday weekends. Rates may be higher on holiday weekends. AE, DC, DISC, MC, V. **Amenities:** Coffee shop and lounge (until 10pm daily in summer, Thurs–Sat off season); Jacuzzi; indoor and outdoor pools. *In room:* A/C, TV, fridge, hair dryer, Wi-Fi (free).

PLANNING YOUR TRIP TO BOSTON

A visit to Boston requires as much or as little forethought as you want, taking into account one important general rule: The later you plan, the more you'll pay. That isn't strictly true in the depths of winter, but for the other 44 or so weeks of the year, you'll most likely find yourself balancing spontaneity against thriftiness. This chapter provides a variety of planning tools, including information on how to get there, as well as quick, on-the-ground resources.

GETTING THERE

By Plane

The major domestic airlines serve **Logan International Airport,** or "Logan" (www.flylogan.com; ℭ **800/235-6426;** airport code BOS).

Boston is an increasingly popular direct destination for international travelers, although many itineraries from overseas still go through another American or European city. Because of fluctuating demand, international routes and schedules are subject to change; double-check details well in advance (especially if you're traveling in the winter).

Logan is in East Boston at the end of the Sumner, Callahan, and Ted Williams tunnels, 3 miles across the harbor from downtown. For a preview and real-time flight arrival and departure information, visit the website.

The airport has four terminals—A, B, C, and E (there's no D). Each has ATMs, Internet kiosks, free wireless Internet access, pay phones with dataports, fax machines, and an information booth (near baggage claim). Terminals C and E have bank branches that handle currency exchange. Terminals A and C have children's play spaces.

See the "Let's Make a Deal" box, below, for information on flying into Providence, Rhode Island, and Manchester, New Hampshire.

GETTING INTO TOWN FROM THE AIRPORT

The Massachusetts Port Authority, or **MassPort,** operates Logan Airport and coordinates ground transportation. The toll-free line (ℭ **800/235-6426;** staffed daily 7am–11:55pm) provides information about getting to the city and to many nearby suburbs, and the website (**www.flylogan.com**) has an application that lets you specify an origin point, destination, and mode or modes of travel, then returns suggestions for getting where you're going.

The trip into town takes 10 to 45 minutes, depending on traffic, your destination, and the time of day. Except at off-hours, such as early on weekend mornings, driving is usually the slowest way to reach central Boston. If you must travel during rush hours or on Sunday afternoon, allow plenty of extra time or plan to take the subway or water taxi (and pack accordingly).

PREVIOUS PAGE: **Boston's skyline viewed from the Charles River.**

You can get into town by bus, subway, cab, van, or boat. If you're taking the Silver Line bus or the subway, look for MBTA fare kiosks near the exits closest to the public transit pick-up area in each terminal. *Tip:* Paying your fare before boarding speeds up the trip for everyone.

The Silver Line **bus** stops at each airport terminal and runs directly to South Station, where you can connect to the Red Line subway and the commuter rail to the southern suburbs. It takes about 20 minutes, not including waiting time, and costs $2 (with a pass or CharlieCard) or $2.50 (with a CharlieTicket or cash)—a great deal if your final destination is near South Station or in Cambridge.

The **subway (the T)** arrives downtown in just 10 minutes, but first you have to reach the subway. Free **shuttle buses** run from each terminal to the Airport station on the Blue Line of the T from 4am to 1am every day, year-round. The Blue Line stops at Aquarium, State Street, and Government Center, downtown points where you can exit or transfer to the other lines. The fare is $2 (with a pass or CharlieCard) or $2.50 (with a CharlieTicket or cash).

Just getting into a **cab** at the airport costs a whopping $10.10 (don't blame the driver—that's $7.50 in fees plus the initial $2.60 fare). The total fare to downtown or the Back Bay usually runs $20 to $35, and may be as high as $45 in bad traffic. Depending on traffic, the driver might use the Ted Williams Tunnel for destinations outside downtown, such as the Back Bay. On a map, this doesn't look like the fastest route, but often it is.

The Logan Airport website (www.flylogan.com) lists numerous companies that operate **shuttle-van service** to local hotels. One-way prices start at $17 per person and are subject to fuel surcharges as gas prices fluctuate. Reservations are recommended.

 LET'S MAKE A deal

Major national carriers serve two airports less than 2 hours from Boston. They're not nearly as convenient as Logan Airport, but fares to either one can be considerably cheaper. For budget-conscious travelers, a quick check can pay off handsomely.

T. F. Green Airport (www.pvdairport.com; ☎ 888/268-7222; airport code PVD) is in the Providence, Rhode Island, suburb of Warwick, about 60 miles south of Boston. The **MBTA** commuter rail (www.mbta.com; ☎ 800/392-6100 or 617/222-3200) connects the airport station to South Station in Boston; the one-way fare at press time is $8.25. **Peter Pan/Bonanza** (www.peterpanbus.com; ☎ 800/343-9999) buses run to and from Boston; fares are $23 one-way, $42 round-trip. You can also take a cab or the local bus (www.ripta.com; ☎ 401/781-9400) to downtown Providence and transfer to **Amtrak** (www.amtrak.com; ☎ 800/872-7245). Allow at least 2 hours, and pack light.

Manchester–Boston Regional Airport (www.flymanchester.com; ☎ 603/624-6556; airport code MHT) is in southern New Hampshire, about 51 miles north of Boston. **Greyhound** (www.greyhound.com; ☎ 800/231-2222) runs buses to Boston's South Station and Logan Airport. The trip takes 60 to 90 minutes; fares start at $19 one-way, $37 round-trip. In addition, **Flight Line** (www.flightlineinc.com; ☎ 800/245-2525) operates van service to and from destinations in Massachusetts, including Logan Airport and suburban Woburn; one-way fares start at $29.

The trip to the downtown waterfront in a weather-protected **boat** takes about 7 minutes and costs $10 one-way. Service is available from early morning through early evening, with reduced schedules on weekends; at press time, all four providers are operating year-round. The free no. 66 shuttle bus connects the airport terminals to the Logan ferry dock. Leaving the airport, ask the shuttle driver to radio ahead for water-taxi pickup; on the way back, call ahead for service.

Two on-call water-taxi services serve the downtown waterfront and other points around Boston Harbor: **City Water Taxi** (www.citywatertaxi.com; ✆ 617/422-0392) and **Rowes Wharf Water Transport** (www.roweswharfwater transport.com; ✆ 617/406-8584). The MBTA (www.mbta.com; ✆ 800/392-6100 or 617/222-3200) contracts out scheduled ferry service to **Harbor Express** (www.harborexpress.com; ✆ 617/222-6999), which runs to Long Wharf, behind the Marriott Long Wharf hotel.

Some hotels have their own **shuttles** or **limousines;** ask about them when you make your reservation. To arrange private limo service, call ahead for a reservation, especially at busy times. Your hotel can recommend a company, or try **Boston Coach** (www.bostoncoach.com; ✆ 800/672-7676), **Carey Limousine** (www.carey.com; ✆ 800/336-4646), or **Commonwealth Limousine Service** (www.commonwealthlimo.com; ✆ 800/558-5466 or 617/787-1110). **PlanetTran** (www.planettran.com; ✆ 888/756-8876) is more expensive, but all of its vehicles are hybrids.

Seriously consider waiting to pick up your **rental car** until you're starting a day trip or other excursion. You'll avoid airport fees, tunnel tolls, hotel parking charges, and, most important, Boston traffic.

By Car

Renting a car to reach Boston will almost certainly be more expensive and less convenient than any other means of travel, and I can't recommend it. It's not that driving *to* Boston is difficult. But parking is scarce and wildly expensive, gasoline is pricey, traffic is terrible, and local drivers are famously reckless. If you're thinking of driving to Boston only because you want to use the car to get around town, think again.

If you have to drive, try to book a hotel or a special package that includes parking (see chapter 9). If you pay for parking, expect it to cost at least $30 a day downtown, and build that into your budget.

Three major highways converge in Boston. **I-90,** also known as the Massachusetts Turnpike ("Mass. Pike" to the locals), is an east-west toll road that originates at Logan Airport and links up with the New York State Thruway. **I-93/U.S. 1** extends north to Canada. **I-93/Route 3,** the Southeast Expressway, connects Boston with the south, including Cape Cod. To avoid driving downtown, exit the Massachusetts Turnpike at Cambridge/Allston or at the Prudential Center in the Back Bay. **I-95** (Massachusetts Rte. 128) is a beltway about 11 miles from downtown that connects Boston to highways in Rhode Island, Connecticut, and New York to the south, and New Hampshire and Maine to the north.

Note: The Massachusetts Turnpike is part of the **E-ZPass** system, and your E-ZPass transponder works in designated lanes. (You may see some signs bearing the name of the state's previous system, FastLane.) If you have a prepaid device from another system, check before you leave home to see whether you, too, can zip (at the speed limit, 15 mph) through the special lanes.

The approaches to Cambridge are **Storrow Drive** and **Memorial Drive,** which run along either side of the Charles River. Storrow Drive has a Harvard

Square exit that leads across the Anderson Bridge to John F. Kennedy Street and into the square. Memorial Drive intersects with Kennedy Street; turn away from the bridge to reach the square.

Boston is 218 miles from **New York City;** driving time is about 4½ hours. The 992-mile drive from **Chicago** to Boston takes around 21 hours; from **Washington, D.C.,** plan on 8 to 9 hours to cover the 468 miles.

In an emergency, you can call the **State Police** on a cellphone by dialing ℂ **911.** The **American Automobile Association** (**AAA;** www.aaa.com; ℂ **800/AAA-HELP** [222-4357]) provides members with maps, itineraries, and other travel information, and arranges free towing if you break down. The Massachusetts Turnpike is a privately operated road that arranges its own towing. If you break down there, ask the AAA operator for advice.

It's impossible to say this often enough: When you reach your hotel, **leave your car in the garage** and walk or use public transportation. Use the car for day trips, and before you set out, ask at the front desk for a route that avoids construction.

If you must drive, or if you rent a car for a day trip, budget for gas, tolls, and parking. International visitors should note that quoted rental-car rates in the U.S. almost never include insurance and taxes. Be sure to ask your rental agency about those additional fees, which can significantly increase your total cost.

For information on car rentals and gasoline (petrol) in Boston, see the "By Car" section under "Getting Around," later in this section. For a map of Boston and the surrounding area, see p. 38.

By Train

Boston has three rail centers: **South Station,** 700 Atlantic Ave. (at Summer St.), near the Waterfront and the Financial District, **Back Bay Station,** 145 Dartmouth St. (btw. Huntington and Columbus aves.), across from the Copley Place mall, and **North Station,** on Causeway Street under the TD Garden arena. **Amtrak** (www.amtrak.com; ℂ **800/872-7245** or 617/482-3660) serves all three, and each is also a stop on the MBTA **subway.** From South Station, you can take the Red Line to Cambridge or to Park Street, the system's hub, where you can make connections to the Green, Blue, and Orange lines. The Orange Line links Back Bay Station and Downtown Crossing, where there's a walkway to Park Street station. North Station is a Green and Orange Line stop.

Amtrak runs to South Station from New York and points south and in between, with stops at Route 128 and Back Bay. Its Downeaster service (www. amtrakdowneaster.com) connects North Station to Portland, Maine, with several stops en route. The MBTA **commuter rail** runs from North Station to Concord, Salem, Gloucester, and Rockport (see chapter 10), among other destinations, and from South Station to points south of Boston, including Plymouth (see chapter 10) and Providence, Rhode Island.

Especially on long trips, the train may not be cheaper than flying. Like the airlines, Amtrak adjusts fares depending on demand, so plan as far ahead as possible to get the lowest fares. Discounts are never available Friday or Sunday afternoon. Always remember to ask for the discounted rate.

Standard service from **New York** takes 4½ to just under 6 hours. If it's on schedule, high-speed Acela Express service takes just over 3 hours. From **Washington, D.C.,** count on a grueling 7½ to 8½ hours for the slowest service, 6 hours for the Acela.

By Bus

The bus is the only way out of many small New England towns. If you're coming from almost anywhere else, consider long-distance bus travel a last resort. The exception is the **New York** route, which is so desirable that numerous operators, including Greyhound and Peter Pan, offer service. It's frequent and relatively fast (4–4½ hr.), and the price is about half the regular train fare.

For bargain-hunters, the trip from South Station to midtown Manhattan can cost as little as $1—if you book at exactly the right moment—on **BoltBus** (www.boltbus.com; © **877/865-8287**) and **MegaBus** (www.megabus.com; © **877/462-6342**). Fares top out around $25, subject to fuel-price adjustments, and include on-board Wi-Fi access. Another option is the so-called Chinatown buses; the highest-profile operator is **Fung Wah** (www.fungwahbus.com; © **617/345-8000** or 212/925-8889), which connects South Station to Canal Street in New York's Chinatown for about $15 each way.

The bus terminal, formally the **South Station Transportation Center** (www.south-station.net; © 617/737-8040), is on Atlantic Avenue next to the train station. The major lines are **Greyhound** (www.greyhound.com; © 800/231-2222 or 617/526-1800) and **Peter Pan** (www.peterpanbus.com; © 800/343-9999). Other operators include **C & J** (www.ridecj.com; © 800/258-7111), **Concord Coach Lines/Dartmouth Coach/Boston Express** (www.concordcoachlines.com; © 800/639-3317), and **Plymouth & Brockton** (www.p-b.com; © 508/746-0378).

Business-oriented **LimoLiner** (www.limoliner.com; © **888/546-5469**) service connects the Back Bay Hilton, 40 Dalton St., to the Hilton New York, 1335 Ave. of the Americas (with an on-request stop in Framingham, Massachusetts). The luxury coach seats 28 and has Internet access, work tables, leather seats, and an on-board attendant. The one-way fare is $89, with occasional discounts for midweek, advance-purchase, and same-day round-trip travel.

World Wide Bus (www.worldwidebus.com; © **877/992-8797**) steers clear of Boston traffic. From New York, it serves Riverside station in Newton, which is also a Green Line stop, and Alewife station in Cambridge, the northern terminus of the Red Line. One-way fares start at $15.

By Cruise Ship

Cruise ships arrive at Cruiseport Boston's **Black Falcon Cruise Terminal,** 1 Black Falcon Ave., South Boston (www.massport.com; © 617/330-1500). Cabs are easy to find—the drivers know the cruise schedule—and a trolley shuttle operates when ships are in port. The terminal is about a mile from the nearest subway station, South Station; take the Silver Line SL2 bus from the Design Center Place stop if you don't feel like walking. Before heading out, make sure you have the number of a cab company programmed into your phone, and leave plenty of time for the trip back to the terminal.

GETTING AROUND

On Foot

If you can manage a fair amount of walking, this is the way to go. You can best appreciate Boston at street level, and walking the narrow, picturesque streets takes you past many gridlocked cars.

Even more than in a typical large city, be alert. Look both ways before crossing, even on one-way streets, where many bicyclists and some drivers blithely go against the flow. The "walk" cycle of many downtown traffic signals is brief, and a small but significant part of the driving population considers red lights optional anyway. Keep a close eye on the kids, especially in crosswalks. And you're wearing comfortable shoes, right?

By Public Transportation

The **Massachusetts Bay Transportation Authority,** or MBTA (www.mbta. com; 𝄢 **800/392-6100** or 617/222-3200), is known as "the T," and its logo is the letter T in a circle. It runs subways, trolleys, buses, and ferries in and around Boston and many suburbs, as well as the commuter rail, which extends as far as Providence, Rhode Island. The automated fare-collection system is a bit involved, but getting the hang of it is easy, and T employees who staff every station can answer questions.

For information on services and discounts for seniors and travelers with disabilities, see p. 365 and 358.

BY SUBWAY & TROLLEY

Subways and trolleys take you around Boston faster than any mode of transportation other than walking. The oldest system in the country, the T dates to 1897. Although it's generally reliable—the trolleys on the ancient Green Line are the most unpredictable—you should still leave extra time and carry cab fare if you're on the way to a vital appointment, because you may need to grab a taxi. The system is generally safe, but always watch out for pickpockets, especially during the holiday shopping season. And remember, downtown stops are so close together that it's often faster to walk.

The Red, Green, Blue, and Orange lines make up the subway system. The commuter rail to the suburbs is purple on system maps and is sometimes called

---

 The T's Fare-Collection System

"Charlie," hero of the Kingston Trio song "Charlie on the MTA," is the face of the T's automated fare-collection system. Passengers store prepaid fares on one of two different reloadable passes: The **CharlieTicket** is heavy paper with a magnetic strip, and the **CharlieCard** is a plastic "smart card" with an embedded chip. What's the difference? (1) Fares are higher if you pay with a CharlieTicket than if you use a CharlieCard; and (2) the bendable CharlieTicket goes into the front of the subway turnstile and pops out of the top (or in and out of the bus fare box), while the rigid CharlieCard registers when you hold it in front of the rectangular reader on the turnstile or

fare box. CharlieTickets are available from the self-service kiosks at the entrance to each subway station and in each terminal at the airport. To get a CharlieCard, ask a T employee, order one in advance, or visit a retail location (check **www.mbta.com** for a list of convenience stores, newsstands, and other outlets). In addition to dispensing CharlieTickets, kiosks allow you to add value onto CharlieTickets and CharlieCards, using cash or a credit or debit card. Consider ordering CharlieCards or CharlieTickets online before you leave home; at press time, shipping is free, and you won't have to buy one immediately upon arriving.

Ride & (Maybe) Save

The MBTA's 1-day and 7-day **LinkPasses** (www.mbta.com; *C* **888/844-0355** or 617/222-4545) can be a great deal—but only if you plan to use public transit enough. Passes cover unlimited travel on the subway and local buses, in commuter rail zone 1A, and on the Inner Harbor ferry. The cost for 24 hours is $11, which translates to an awful lot of riding before you start to save money. The 7-day pass, which costs $18, is more likely to pay off. At press time, passes must be loaded onto CharlieTickets. Check ahead to see whether you can put yours on a CharlieCard. You can order passes—long-term visitors may find one of the numerous commuter passes a better deal than a visitor-oriented LinkPass—in advance over the phone or on the Web (minimum 10; at press time, shipping is free), or buy them when you arrive at any kiosk or retailer that sells CharlieTickets and CharlieCards.

the Purple Line. The Silver Line is a fancy name for a bus line; route **SL1** runs from South Station to the airport via the South Boston waterfront, including the convention center and the Seaport Boston World Trade Center (the **SL2** stays on the downtown side of the harbor and serves the cruise ship terminal area). The fare on the subway and Silver Line routes SL1 and SL2 at press time is **$2** if you use a CharlieCard (transfers to local buses are free), **$2.50** with a CharlieTicket. Children 11 and under ride free with a paying adult. Route and fare information and timetables are available through the website (www.mbta.com) and at centrally located stations.

Service begins at around 5:15am and ends around 12:30am. (On New Year's Eve, or First Night, closing time is 2am and service is free after 8pm.) A sign in every station gives the time of the last train in either direction; if you're planning to be out late and don't see a sign, ask the attendant in the booth near the entrance.

BY BUS

The MBTA runs buses and "trackless trolleys" (buses with electric antennae) that provide service around town and to and around the suburbs. The local routes you're most likely to use are **no. 1,** along Massachusetts Avenue from Dudley Square in Roxbury through the Back Bay and Cambridge to Harvard Square; **no. 92** and **no. 93,** which connect Haymarket and Charlestown; and **no. 77,** along Mass. Ave. north of Harvard Square to Porter Square, North Cambridge, and Arlington. Two branches of the **Silver Line** run through the South End to Dudley Station in Roxbury and are part of the bus fare structure. Route **SL4** serves South Station (Essex St. at Atlantic Ave.), and Route **SL5** starts and ends on Temple Place, near Downtown Crossing between Washington and Tremont streets.

The fare on the local bus and Silver Line routes SL4 and SL5 at press time is **$1.50** with a CharlieCard, **$2** with a CharlieTicket or cash. Children 11 and under ride free with a paying adult. If you're paying cash, exact change is required.

BY FERRY

The MBTA Inner Harbor ferry connects **Long Wharf** (near the New England Aquarium) with the **Charlestown Navy Yard**—it's a good way to get back downtown from "Old Ironsides" and the Bunker Hill Monument. The fare is $3, or show your LinkPass. Visit www.mbta.com or call ✆ **617/227-4321** for more information, including schedules.

11

PLANNING YOUR TRIP TO BOSTON

By Taxi

Taxis are expensive and not always easy to hail—seek out a cabstand or call a dispatcher. Always ask for a receipt in case you have a complaint or lose something and need to call the company.

Cabs usually queue up near hotels. There are also busy cabstands at Faneuil Hall Marketplace (on North St. and in front of 60 State St.), South Station, and Back Bay Station, and on either side of Massachusetts Avenue in Harvard Square, near the Harvard Coop bookstore and Au Bon Pain.

To call ahead for a cab, try the **Independent Taxi Operators Association** (www.itoataxi.com; ✆ 617/426-8700), **Boston Cab** (www.bostoncab.us; ✆ 617/536-5010), **Top Cab/City Cab** (www.topcab.us; ✆ 617/266-4800 or 617/536-5100), or **Metro Cab** (www.boston-cab.com; ✆ 617/782-5500). In Cambridge, call **Ambassador Brattle/Yellow Cab** (www.ambassadorbrattle.com; ✆ 617/492-1100 or 617/547-3000) or **Checker Cab** (www.checkercabcambridge.com; ✆ 617/497-9000). Boston Cab will dispatch a wheelchair-accessible vehicle upon request; advance notice is recommended.

The Boston fare structure: The first ½ mile (when the flag drops) costs $2.60, and each additional ½ mile is 40¢. Wait time is extra, and the passenger pays all tolls. On trips leaving Logan Airport, you're on the hook for $10.10 in fare and fees, including the tunnel toll, before the cab goes an inch. Charging a flat rate is not allowed within the city; the police department (see below) publishes a list of flat rates for trips to the suburbs.

The city requires that Boston cabdrivers accept credit cards, and every vehicle has a card reader fastened to the divider. Drivers resisted the rule at first, and anecdotal evidence suggests that some "broken" card readers will suddenly come online if you say you don't have enough cash to pay up.

If you want to report a problem or have lost something in a Boston cab, contact the police department's **Hackney Unit** (www.cityofboston.gov/police/hackney; ✆ **617/343-4475**); visit the website for the list of suburban flat fares.

By Water Taxi

Water taxis serve stops around the waterfront, including the airport, in covered boats. They operate daily year-round, from 7am until at least 7pm (later in the summer). One-way fares start at $10. Reservations are recommended but not required; you can call from the dock for pick-up. The companies are **City Water Taxi** (www.citywatertaxi.com; ✆ **617/422-0392**), and **Rowes Wharf Water Taxi** (www.roweswharfwatertransport.com; ✆ **617/406-8584**).

By Car

If you plan to visit only Boston and Cambridge, there's absolutely no reason to have a car. With its pricey parking, narrow streets, and widespread construction, Boston in particular is a motorist's nightmare. If you arrive by car, park at the hotel and use the car for day trips. Drive from Boston to Cambridge only if you're feeling flush—you'll pay to park there, too. If you're not traveling to Boston by car and you decide to take a day trip (see chapter 10), you'll probably want to rent a vehicle. Here's the scoop:

RENTALS

Seriously consider waiting to pick up the car until you need it, to save yourself the hassle of driving and parking. The major car-rental firms have offices at Logan Airport and in Boston, and most have other area branches. Note that the Enterprise and Thrifty airport locations are nearby but not on the grounds, and allow time for the shuttle-bus ride. Rentals that originate in Boston carry a **$10 convention-center surcharge**—you can get around it by picking up your car in Cambridge, Brookline, Somerville, or another suburb.

> ### Impressions
>
> *Boston's freeway system was insane. It was clearly designed by a person who had spent his childhood crashing toy trains. Every few hundred yards I would find my lane vanishing beneath me and other lanes merging with it from the right or left, or sometimes both. This wasn't a road system, it was mobile hysteria.*
> —Bill Bryson, *The Lost Continent*, 1989 (but it's still true)

In general, Boston doesn't conform to the pattern of a big city that empties on weekends, when business travelers leave town and rental-car rates plummet. The parts of downtown Boston that aren't densely populated residential neighborhoods are near them, and at busy times—especially on summer weekends and during foliage season—you'll want to reserve a car well in advance or risk getting shut out.

Most major car-rental companies forbid smoking in their vehicles. Exceptions include Hertz, which allows customers to request no-smoking vehicles. To rent from the major national chains, you must be at least 25 years old and have a valid driver's license and credit card. Some companies allow drivers aged 21 to 24 to rent, subject to a steep daily fee. And some chains enforce a maximum age; if you're over 70, check ahead to avoid an unpleasant surprise.

If you're visiting from abroad and plan to rent a car in the United States, keep in mind that foreign driver's licenses are usually recognized in the U.S., but you may want to consider obtaining an international driver's license.

Money-saving tips: Rent the smallest car you're comfortable driving and you'll save on gas (petrol). The price per gallon at press time is nearly $4; the posted price includes taxes. One U.S. gallon equals 3.8 liters or .85 imperial gallons.

If you belong to **Zipcar** or another car-sharing service at home, check ahead to see whether your membership is good in the Boston area. And if you don't mind taking a short T ride to (potentially) save a bundle, check rates at Enterprise and Hertz neighborhood locations. Most branches will pick you up at the nearest train station or bus stop if the office isn't close to public transit.

Insurance

If you hold a private auto insurance policy, it probably covers you in the U.S. for loss of or damage to the rental car, and for liability in case a passenger is injured. The credit card you use to rent the car may also provide some coverage, but don't assume—check before you leave home.

International travelers should be aware that quoted rental car rates in the U.S. almost never include insurance and taxes. Be sure to ask your rental agency about these fees. They can add a significant cost to your car rental.

Car-rental insurance typically does not cover liability if you cause an accident. Check your own auto insurance policy, the rental company policy, and your credit

Boston Drivers: Beware

The incredibly sappy movie *Love Story* includes one hilarious observation: "This is Boston—everybody drives like a maniac." And that was before cell-phones. Boston drivers deserve their notoriety, and even though the truly reckless are a tiny minority, it pays to be careful. Never assume that another driver will behave as you might expect, especially when it comes to the rarely used turn signal. Watch out for cars that leave the curb and change lanes without signaling, double- and even triple-park, or travel the wrong way down one-way streets. And remember that most pedes-trians and bicyclists are just drivers with-out their protective covering.

card coverage for the extent of coverage: Is your destination covered? Are other driv-ers covered? How much liability is covered if a passenger is injured? If you rely on your credit card for coverage, you may want to bring a second card with you, because damages may be charged to your card, eating into your credit limit.

Car-rental insurance from rental-car companies starts at about $20 a day.

Package Deals

Many packages include airfare, accommodations, and a rental car with unlimited mileage. Compare these prices with the cost of booking airline tickets and rent-ing a car separately. Don't saddle yourself with a car for a long period if you won't be using it, though. And don't forget to account for parking fees, which can quickly wipe out any savings a package might represent.

Booking Online

For booking rental cars online, the best deals are usually on rental-car company websites. *Tip:* Sign up for e-mail alerts before you book, and you may land a deal. You can always cancel the alerts after you return home.

Check out **www.bnm.com**, which offers domestic car-rental discounts. Also worth visiting are Orbitz.com, Hotwire.com, Travelocity.com, and Priceline.com, all of which offer competitive rates.

PARKING

It's difficult to find your way around Boston, and practically impossible to find parking in some areas. Most spaces on the street are metered (and patrolled until at least 6pm Mon–Sat) or are open to nonresidents for 2 hours or less between 8am and 6pm. The penalty is a $45 ticket—the same as a full day at the most expensive garage. Read the sign or meter carefully. Some areas allow parking only at certain hours. Rates vary in different sections of the city (usually $1.25 per hour downtown); bring plenty of quarters. On some streets, you pay at a nearby machine and affix the receipt to the inside of the driver's-side window. Time lim-its range from 15 minutes to 2 hours.

If you blunder into a tow-away zone, retrieving the car will cost well over $100 and a lot of running around. The **city tow lot** (☏ **617/635-3900**) is at 200 Frontage Rd. in South Boston. Take a taxi, or ride the Red Line to Broadway and flag a cab.

It's best to leave the car in a garage or lot and walk, but be aware that Bos-ton's parking is the second-most expensive in the country (after Manhattan's). A full day at most garages costs no more than $30, but some downtown facilities charge as much as $45, and hourly rates typically are exorbitant. Many lots charge a lower flat rate if you enter and exit before certain times or if you park in the evening. Some restaurants offer reduced rates at nearby garages; ask when you call for reservations. Regardless of where you park, visit the attendant's booth as you exit on foot to ask whether any local businesses offer discounted parking with a purchase and validation; you may get lucky.

Enter the garage under **Boston Common** (www.mccahome.com/bcg.html; ☎ **617/954-2098**) from Charles Street between Boylston and Beacon streets. Access to the **CityPlace Garage,** in the state Transportation Building, 8 Park Plaza (www.pilgrimparking.com; ☎ **617/723-1488**), is from Charles Street South. The **Prudential Center** garage (www.prudentialcenter.com; ☎ **617/236-3060**) has entrances on Boylston Street, Huntington Avenue, and Exeter Street, and at the Sheraton Boston Hotel. Parking is discounted if you buy something at the Shops at Prudential Center and have your ticket validated. The garage at **Copley Place** (www.simon.com; ☎ **617/426-0604**), off Huntington Avenue, offers a similar deal. Many businesses in Faneuil Hall Marketplace validate parking at the **75 State St. Garage** (www.75statestreetgarage.com; ☎ **617/443-2817**).

Good-size garage facilities downtown include the **Government Center Garage,** 50 New Sudbury St., off Congress Street (www.governmentcentergarage. com; ☎ **617/227-0385**); **Parcel 7 Garage,** 136 Blackstone St., entrance on New Sudbury Street off Congress Street (☎ **617/973-0421**); and **Zero Post Office Square** in the Financial District (www.posquare.com; ☎ **617/423-1430**). In the Back Bay, there's a large facility near the Hynes Convention Center at **50 Dalton St.** (www.pilgrimparking.com; ☎ **617/723-1488**). The lots off **Northern Avenue** in the Seaport District are among the cheapest in town, but downtown proper is some distance away. Allow time for the walk or Silver Line bus ride.

DRIVING RULES

When traffic permits, drivers may turn right at a red light after stopping, unless a sign is posted saying otherwise (as it often is downtown). The speed limit on most city streets is 30 mph.

Seat belts are mandatory for adults and children, children 11 and under may not ride in the front seat, and infants and children 7 and under must be strapped into car seats in the back seat. You can be stopped just for having an unbelted child in the car, though not for traveling with an unsecured adult. Text-messaging while behind the wheel is against the law for drivers of all ages, and cellphone use of any kind by motorists 17 and under is illegal except in an emergency.

And be aware of two other state laws, if only because drivers break them so frequently it'll take your breath away: Pedestrians in the crosswalk have the right of way (most suburbs actually enforce this one), and vehicles already in a rotary (traffic circle or roundabout) have the right of way.

By Bicycle

Boston and Cambridge have bike lanes on many major streets and are striving to be more friendly to two-wheelers. However, I can't recommend biking as a sightseeing option for out-of-towners unfamiliar with the Boston area's maniacal drivers and oblivious pedestrians. Visit **www.cityofboston.gov/bikes** for information about biking in Boston; if you're going to be in Cambridge, visit **www.cambridgema.gov/cdd** and find "Bicycle Programs" under "Environmental and Transportation Planning."

For information about renting a bike and about recreational biking, see "Biking," on p. 117. If you bring or rent a bike, be sure to lock it securely when leaving it unattended, even for a short time.

SPECIAL-INTEREST TRIPS & TOURS

Academic Trips

Enormous college town that it is, Boston abounds with educational opportunities. Two nonprofit organizations—one large, one small—offer participants a chance to get comfortable with a destination or activity rather than trying to cram in as many attractions as possible.

Road Scholar programs offered by Elderhostel (www.roadscholar.org; *©* **800/454-5768**) no longer specifically target seniors, which is good news for younger travelers who appreciate their educational focus. Offerings include tours that highlight history, culture, science, and more; they incorporate scheduled activities led by local experts and free time for you to explore on your own.

Boston's beloved public-television station runs **WGBH LearningTours** (www.wgbh.org/support/learningtours; *©* **617/300-3505**), which draw on the know-how of both the station's producers and the experts who appear in PBS series about such topics as the national parks. They're mostly multiday excursions to destinations spotlighted in the station's programming, but some offerings are shorter trips to local points of interest.

Adventure Trips

The **Massachusetts Audubon Society** (www.massaudubon.org; *©* **800/ AUDUBON** [283-8266] or 781/259-9500), the largest conservation organization in New England, owns and operates wildlife sanctuaries across the state and offers programs that help people of all ages connect with nature. Classes, workshops, programs, and special events of all types, many designed specifically for children and families, take place throughout the year. Membership costs $48 per year for an individual, $65 for a family.

A good introduction to New England's diverse terrain is an excursion with the **Appalachian Mountain Club** (www.outdoors.org; *©* **800/372-1758** or 617/523-0636). The recreation and conservation organization is perhaps best known for its indispensable trail guides and maps, but it also coordinates volunteer-led activities that range from walking dogs on a beach to multiday backpacking tours. Though closely associated with New Hampshire's White Mountains, the AMC has chapters all over the Northeast and offers many activities in the Boston suburbs. First-time membership costs $50 for an individual, $75 for a family, or $25 if you're under 30 or over 69.

Guided Tours

Countless companies offer escorted tours that stop in Boston, especially during foliage season, when 5- to 10-day tours of New England are wildly popular with travelers from around the world. Few spend more than 2 days in Boston, however, meaning that you'll be rushing around trying to cram maximum action into minimum time, or skipping sights and activities you were looking forward to. If you plan to focus exclusively on Boston, most escorted tours won't meet your needs, but if a quick stop is all you can manage, most major tour operators can accommodate you.

Options include **Liberty Travel** (www.libertytravel.com; © 888/271-1584), **Collette Vacations** (www.collettevacations.com; © 800/340-5158), **Globus and Cosmos** (www.globusandcosmos.com; © 866/755-8581 or 800/276-1241), **Insight Vacations** (www.insightvacations.com; © 888/680-1241), **Tauck World Discovery** (www.tauck.com; © 800/788-7885), and **Trafalgar Tours** (www.trafalgar.com; © 866/544-4434).

Gray Line's New England presence is **Brush Hill Tours** (www.brushhill tours.com; © **800/343-1328** or 781/986-6100). Brush Hill operates Boston's Beantown Trolley and allows customers to build their own itineraries by choosing from a variety of half- and full-day escorted tours to destinations such as Plymouth, Salem, Cape Cod, and Newport, Rhode Island.

For more information on guided tours, including questions to ask before booking your trip, see **www.frommers.com/tips**.

Volunteer & Working Trips

The Greater Boston chapter of **Habitat for Humanity** (www.habitatboston.org; © **617/423-2223**) welcomes individual volunteers as well as groups to help construct and renovate affordable housing for low-income families. Be prepared and dress appropriately for up to 6½ hours of construction work, which can be strenuous. Volunteers are responsible for their own transportation and should bring lunch, drinks, and work gloves. The minimum age is 16 (16- and 17-year-olds must have an adult with them). There is no maximum age. Note that you must complete a 1-hour orientation before you can start work, and those sessions fill up quickly.

The **Massachusetts Audubon Society** and the **Appalachian Mountain Club** (see "Adventure Trips," above) rely heavily on volunteers. Most Mass Audubon activities are long-term commitments, but some are one-shot deals suitable for out-of-town visitors. AMC opportunities range from a day of trail clearing to leading a longer-term program.

[Fast FACTS] BOSTON

Area Codes Boston proper, **617** and **857**; immediate suburbs, **781** and **339**; northern and western suburbs, **978** and **351**; southern suburbs, **508** and **774**. *Note:* To make a local call, you must dial the three-digit area code and the seven-digit number.

Business Hours Offices are usually open weekdays from 9am to 5 or 6pm. Banks are open weekdays from 9am to 4pm or later and sometimes on Saturday morning; most offer 24-hour access to automated teller machines (ATMs). Stores typically open between 9 and 10am and close between 6 (neighborhood shops) and 9pm (mall and shopping center locations) from Monday through Saturday. Sunday hours (for stores that have them) are usually 11am or noon to 5 or 6pm. Some drugstores and grocery stores are open 24 hours a day, 7 days a week.

Car Rental   See the "By Car" section under "Getting Around," earlier in this chapter.

Cellphones   See "Mobile Phones," later in this section.

Crime   See "Safety," later in this section.

Customs   National customs agencies regulate what visitors to the United Stated may bring with them and what they may take home. For details regarding U.S. Customs and Border Protection, consult your nearest U.S. embassy or consulate, or visit **U.S. Customs and Border Protection** (www.cbp.gov).

Doctors   The front-desk staff at your hotel can often recommend a doctor, or you can use one of the referral services available through local hospitals. They include **Massachusetts General Hospital** (✆ **800/711-4644**) and **Brigham and Women's Hospital** (✆ **800/294-9999**). Also see "Hospitals," below.

Drinking Laws   The legal age for purchase and consumption of alcoholic beverages is 21. Proof of age is required and often requested at bars, nightclubs, and restaurants, particularly near college campuses (in the Boston area, that's everywhere), so it's always a good idea to bring ID when you go out. At sporting events, everyone buying alcohol must show ID. Liquor stores and some supermarkets and convenience stores sell alcohol Monday though Saturday during regular business hours; in communities where selling alcohol on Sunday is legal, sales begin at noon. Happy hours with discounted drinks are illegal, but discounted food is permitted. Most restaurants have full liquor licenses, but some serve only beer and wine or beer, wine, and cordials. Last call typically is 30 minutes before closing time (1am in bars, 2am in clubs).

Do not carry open containers of alcohol in your car or any public area that isn't zoned for alcohol consumption. The police can fine you on the spot. Don't even think about driving while intoxicated.

Driving Rules   See "Getting Around," earlier in this chapter.

Electricity   Like Canada, the United States uses 110–120 volts AC (60 cycles), compared to 220–240 volts AC (50 cycles) in most of Europe, Australia, and New Zealand. Downward converters that change 220–240 volts to 110–120 volts are difficult to find in the United States, so bring one with you.

Embassies & Consulates   All embassies are in the nation's capital, Washington, D.C. Some consulates are in major U.S. cities, and most nations have a mission to the United Nations in New York City. If your country isn't listed below, call directory assistance in Washington, D.C. (✆ **202/555-1212**), or check **www.embassy.org/embassies**.

The embassy of **Australia** is at 1601 Massachusetts Ave. NW, Washington, DC 20036 (www.usa.embassy.gov.au; ✆ **202/797-3000**).

The embassy of **Canada** is at 501 Pennsylvania Ave. NW, Washington, DC 20001 (www.canadainternational.gc.ca/washington; ✆ **202/682-1740**). The local Canadian consulate is at 3 Copley Place, Ste. 400, Boston, MA 02116 (www.boston.gc.ca; ✆ **617/247-5100**).

The embassy of **Ireland** is at 2234 Massachusetts Ave. NW, Washington, DC 20008 (www.embassyofireland.org; ✆ **202/462-3939**). The local Irish consulate is at 535 Boylston St., fifth floor, Boston, MA 02116 (www.consulategeneralofirelandboston.org; ✆ **617/267-9330**).

The embassy of **New Zealand** is at 37 Observatory Circle NW, Washington, DC 20008 (www.nzembassy.com/usa; ✆ **202/328-4800**). Contact the **honorary consul** to the New England area at P.O. Box 1318, 57 N. Main St., Concord, NH 03302 (nzconsulate@preti.com; ✆ **603/225-8228**).

The embassy of the **United Kingdom** is at 3100 Massachusetts Ave. NW, Washington, DC 20008 (http://ukinusa.fco.gov.uk/en; ✆ **202/588-6500**). The Boston-area **British consulate** is at 1 Broadway, Cambridge, MA 02142 (✆ **617/245-4500**).

Emergencies   Call ✆ **911** for fire, ambulance, or the police. This is a free call from pay phones. Dialing 911 on a cellphone connects you to a state police dispatcher, who transfers the call to the local authorities. The Boston police direct emergency number is ✆ **617/343-4911.**

Family Travel   Boston is a great family destination, with tons of activities that appeal to children and relatively few that don't. All area hotels, restaurants, and attractions have extensive experience meeting kids' needs.

The **Greater Boston Convention & Visitors Bureau** (www.bostonusa.com; ✆ **888/733-2678**) sells a *Kids Love Boston* guide ($5) filled with travel information for families. The **Boston Parents Paper** website (http://boston.parenthood.com) lists activities and events.

To locate accommodations, restaurants, and attractions that are particularly kid-friendly, look for the "Kids" icon throughout this guide. Also consult the "Family-Friendly Hotels" box (p. 274) and the sections "Family-Friendly Restaurants" (p. 179) and "Especially for Kids" (p. 113).

Gasoline   See the "By Car" section under "Getting Around," earlier in this chapter.

Health   Here's hoping you won't need to evaluate Boston's reputation for excellent medical care. The greatest threat to your health is the same as in most other North American cities: overexposure to the summer sun. Be sure to pack sunblock, sunglasses, and a hat, and remember to stay hydrated.

Hospitals   The closest hospitals to downtown are **Massachusetts General Hospital,** 55 Fruit St. (www.massgeneral.org; ✆ **617/726-2000**), and **Tufts Medical Center,** 800 Washington St. (www.tuftsmedicalcenter.org; ✆ **617/636-5000**). At the Harvard Medical Area on the Boston-Brookline border are **Beth Israel Deaconess Medical Center,** 330 Brookline Ave. (www.bidmc.org; ✆ **617/667-7000**), **Brigham and Women's Hospital,** 75 Francis St. (www.brighamandwomens.org; ✆ **617/732-5500**), and **Children's Hospital Boston,** 300 Longwood Ave. (www.childrenshospital.org; ✆ **617/355-6000**).

In Cambridge are **Mount Auburn Hospital,** 330 Mount Auburn St. (www.mountauburn hospital.org; ✆ **617/492-3500**), and **Cambridge Hospital,** 1493 Cambridge St. (www.cha. harvard.edu/cambridge; ✆ **617/665-1000**).

Nonemergency **MinuteClinics** (www.minuteclinic.com; ✆ **866/389-2727**) deal with ear infections, strep throat, and such, but not with dire emergencies. At press time, the closest one to downtown Boston is in the **CVS** at the Porter Square Shopping Center, 36 White St., off Mass. Ave., Cambridge (www.cvs.com; ✆ **617/876-5519**).

Insurance   Whether you choose to buy travel insurance depends on numerous factors, including how far you're traveling, how much you're spending, how set your schedule is, and your physical condition. For domestic travelers, most reliable healthcare plans provide coverage if you get sick away from home. International travelers should note that unlike many other countries, the United States does not usually offer free or low-cost medical care to visitors (or citizens).

For information on travel insurance, trip cancellation insurance, and medical insurance while traveling, please visit **www.frommers.com/tips**.

Internet & Wi-Fi   Internet access is widely available in the Boston area, where a wireless connection can be easier to come by than a wired one, and Wi-Fi is often (but not always) free. Most hotels and many businesses offer Wi-Fi access. (Paradoxically, high-end hotels tend to charge guests a daily fee for access, while many cheaper lodgings include Wi-Fi in their room rates.) Many coffee shops and fast-food restaurants, some lines of the commuter rail, and numerous other businesses have free wireless access. Wi-Fi is free at Logan Airport, on the Rose Kennedy Greenway, in and around the Quincy Market rotunda at Faneuil Hall Marketplace, and at Christopher Columbus Waterfront Park and Norman B. Leventhal Park at Post Office Square. Most businesses on upper Newbury Street provide free wireless thanks to **Tech Superpowers,** 252 Newbury St. (btw. Fairfield and Gloucester sts.), third floor (www.newburyopen.net; ✆ **617/267-9716**). The Digital Lounge offers wired access on Macs ($3 per 15 min. minimum; $49 per day). Find public Wi-Fi hot spots by searching **www.wififreespot.com**.

If you're traveling without a computer or other device, Boston's Logan and most other major airports have **Internet kiosks** that provide basic Web access; the per-minute fee can be steep. **FedEx Office** (www.fedexoffice.com) offers free access at some locations if you have a hand-held device and charges about 35¢ a minute to use a computer. Locations include 2 Center Plaza, Government Center (✆ **617/973-9000**); 10 Post Office Sq., Financial District (✆ **617/482-4400**); 575 Boylston St. (✆ **617/536-2536**) and 187 Dartmouth St. (✆ **617/262-6188**), Back Bay; and in Cambridge at 1 Mifflin Place (Mount Auburn St. and University Rd.), Harvard Square (✆ **617/497-0125**).

Legal Aid   While driving, if you are pulled over for a minor infraction (such as speeding), never attempt to pay the fine directly to a police officer; this could be construed as attempted bribery, a much more serious crime. Pay fines by mail, or directly into the hands of the clerk of the court. If accused of a more serious offense, say and do nothing before consulting a lawyer. In the U.S., the burden is on the state to prove a person's guilt beyond a reasonable doubt, and everyone has the right to remain silent, whether he or she is suspected of a crime or actually arrested. Once arrested, a person can make one telephone call to a party of his or her choice. The international visitor should call his or her embassy or consulate.

LGBT Travelers   The capital of the first state to legalize same-sex marriage, Boston is overall a gay- and lesbian-friendly destination, with a live-and-let-live attitude that long ago replaced the city's legendary Puritanism. The South End, Jamaica Plain, and Cambridge's Porter Square are home to many LGBT residents—as are plenty of other neighborhoods and suburbs. **Pride Week** (www.bostonpride.org), in early June, is so popular that it's actually 10 days, ending with a festive parade.

The free weekly *Bay Windows* (www.baywindows.com; ✆ **617/266-6670**) covers New England's LGBT community and features extensive entertainment listings. The alternative weekly *Boston Phoenix* publishes cultural and nightlife listings (www.bostonphoenix.com). A good online resource is **Edge Boston** (www.edgeboston.com).

An excellent guide to local gay-and-lesbian-owned-and-friendly businesses is the *Pink Pages* (www.pinkweb.com/boston.index.html). The website of the **Greater Boston Convention & Visitors Bureau** (www.bostonusa.com) has an LGBT traveler section; click "Visit Boston," then "Boston Insider." The state tourism department has a separate website, **www.lgbtmassvacation.com**, devoted to information about activities and attractions across Massachusetts. Other useful resources include the **Gay, Lesbian, Bisexual and Transgender Helpline** (✆ **888/340-4528** or 617/267-9001) and the **Peer Listening Line,** for people 25 and under (✆ **800/399-7337** or 617/267-2535), both operated by Fenway Community Health (www.fenwayhealth.org); the **Boston Alliance of Gay, Lesbian, Bisexual and Transgender Youth** (www.bagly.org; ✆ **617/227-4313**), which holds a general meeting every Wednesday evening; and the **Bisexual Resource Center** (www.biresource. net; ☎ **617/424-9595**).

Mail   At press time, domestic postage rates were 32¢ for a postcard and 45¢ for a letter. For international mail, a first-class letter of up to 1 ounce costs $1.05 (85¢ to Canada or Mexico); a first-class postcard costs the same as a letter. For more information, go to **www.usps.com**.

If you aren't sure what your address will be in the United States, mail can be sent to you, in your name, c/o General Delivery at the main post office of the city or region where you expect to be. (Call ☎ **800/275-8777** for information on the nearest post office.) The addressee must pick up mail in person and must produce proof of identity (driver's license or passport). Most post offices will hold mail for up to 1 month, and are open Monday to Friday from 8am to 6pm, and Saturday from 9am to 2pm.

Always include zip codes when mailing items in the U.S. If you don't know your zip code, visit **www.usps.com/zip4**.

Medical Requirements   Unless you're arriving from an area known to be suffering from an epidemic (particularly cholera or yellow fever), inoculations or vaccinations are not required for entry into the United States.

Mobile Phones   Most Americans call mobile phones "cellphones." The major North American service providers all cover Boston; in the suburbs, you'll encounter some dead spots. Don't count on reliable service in rural areas, especially if your phone is on the GSM network, which most of the world uses. Among major U.S. carriers, AT&T and T-Mobile are compatible with GSM, and Sprint and Verizon use CDMA. To see where GSM phones work in the U.S., check out www.t-mobile.com/coverage.

If you're traveling from overseas and haven't used your phone internationally before, call your provider before you leave home to determine whether your phone will work where you're going, whether you'll be able to send and receive SMS (text messages), and how much everything will cost.

If you plan to call home frequently, the cheapest option in many cases is **Skype** (www. skype.com). Sign up before you leave home, and you can place calls from a computer or mobile device. Calls to other Skype users are free; add credit to your account to call nonmembers.

If you want a phone just for emergencies and don't have to know your number ahead of time, I suggest heading straight to one of the Boston area's numerous freestanding cellphone stores or to **Radio Shack** (www.radioshack.com; ☎ **800/843-7422**) and buying a prepaid phone to use during your visit. Phones sell for as little as $15, but calling time can cost as much as 35¢ per minute. Make sure you're choosing a provider that allows you to activate international calling immediately (try making an international call while you're still in the store). Most important, be sure you understand all fees and per-minute charges and have enough money loaded onto the phone to cover the calls you're likely to make and receive.

A reliable outlet for "unlocked" cellphones—which recognize any carrier's SIM card—is **Mega Mobile,** 278 Washington St., Downtown Crossing (www.megamobileboston.com; ☎ **617/573-0073**). It also sells international SIM cards and does repairs. If you prefer to **rent** a phone, you can have it shipped to you before you leave from **InTouch Global** (www. intouchglobal.com; ☎ **800/872-7626** or 703/222-7161). Rates start at $29 a week, plus shipping.

WHAT THINGS COST IN BOSTON

	$
Taxi from airport to downtown or Back Bay	20.00–45.00
Water shuttle from airport to downtown	10.00
MBTA subway fare	2.00–2.50
Double at moderately priced hotel	159.00–259.00
Lunch for one at inexpensive restaurant	7.00–13.00
Three-course dinner for one, without wine, at moderately priced restaurant	20.00–29.00
Glass of beer	3.00 and up
Cup of coffee	1.50 and up
Adult admission to the Museum of Fine Arts	22.00
Child (17 and under) admission to the Museum of Fine Arts	free

THE VALUE OF THE U.S. DOLLAR VS. OTHER POPULAR CURRENCIES

US$	C$	£	€	A$	NZ$
1.00	1.00	0.63	0.76	.96	1.24

Money & Costs   Frommer's lists exact prices in the local currency. The currency conversions quoted above were correct at press time. However, rates fluctuate, so before departing, consult a currency exchange website such as **www.oanda.com/currency/ converter** or **www.xe.com/ucc** to check up-to-the-minute rates.

Like other large American cities, Boston can be an expensive destination. At the high end, it's nearly as costly as New York. The average hotel room rate in Boston and Cambridge is nearly $200—and that average includes deep off-season discounts. The area does offer numerous ways to offset the price of lodging. Some attractions offer free or discounted admission at certain times, and the performing arts provide options for every budget. Dining choices, from hole-in-the-wall noodle joints to acclaimed special-occasion restaurants, are equally diverse.

If you're visiting Boston from overseas, exchange enough petty cash to cover airport incidentals, tipping, and transportation to your hotel before you leave home, or withdraw money upon arrival at an airport ATM. Throughout eastern Massachusetts, you'll have little or no trouble finding ATMs (also known as "cash machines" or "cashpoints"); they're everywhere, even in some subway stations. **Cirrus** (www.mastercard.com; ✆ **800/ 4CIRRUS** [800/424-7787]) and **PLUS** (www.visa.com; ✆ **800/THE-PLUS** [843-7587]) are the major networks. The **NYCE** network (www.nyce.net) operates primarily in the eastern United States. NYCE administers the **SUM** network (www.sum-atm.com), which waives fees for customers of member banks using most ATMs belonging to other members. Look at the back of your bank card to see which network you're on, then call, check online, or download a smartphone app to find ATM locations in the Boston area.

Be sure you know your **personal identification number (PIN)** and your daily **withdrawal limit** before you depart. If you have a five- or six-digit PIN, ask your bank whether it will work; you may need to change it to a four-digit code. Also keep in mind that most banks impose a fee every time you use your card at a different bank's ATM, and the bank from which you withdraw cash may charge its own fee. At Massachusetts ATMs, a message should appear—onscreen or on a sticker near the keypad—specifying the amount of the charge.

Beware of hidden **credit card fees** while traveling. Check with your credit or debit card issuer to see what fees, if any, will be charged for overseas transactions. Recent reform legislation in the U.S., for example, has curbed some exploitative lending practices. But many banks have responded by increasing fees in other areas, including fees for customers who use credit and debit cards while out of the country—even if those charges were made in U.S. dollars. Fees can amount to 3% or more of the purchase price. Check with your bank before departing to avoid any surprise charges on your statement.

Stores and restaurants that accept credit cards generally accept **debit cards,** and some stores and most U.S. post offices enable you to receive "cash back" on your debit card purchases as well. If you don't keep a large checking balance, be aware that most banks "freeze" a portion of your account when you initiate a purchase without a definite total, such as a car rental or tank of gas.

Credit cards and debit cards are more popular, but **traveler's checks** are widely accepted in the U.S. In tourist-friendly Boston, you won't have much trouble using traveler's checks at any business. International visitors should make sure that they're denominated in U.S. dollars; foreign-currency checks are often difficult to exchange.

For help with currency conversions, tip calculations, and more, download the convenient Frommer's Travel Tools app for your mobile device. Go to **www.frommers.com/go/mobile** and click on the Travel Tools icon.

Newspapers & Magazines   The daily *Boston Globe, Boston Herald, New York Times, USA Today,* and *Wall Street Journal* are available at convenience stores, newsstands, some supermarkets, and sidewalk newspaper boxes all over the Boston area. The *Boston Phoenix,* a free weekly with extensive entertainment and restaurant listings, comes out on Thursday and is available from newspaper boxes.

Where, a monthly magazine available free at most hotels, lists information about shopping, nightlife, attractions, and current shows at museums and art galleries. Newspaper boxes dispense free copies of *Stuff@Night,* a biweekly *Phoenix* offshoot with selective listings and arts coverage; the irreverent *Weekly Dig,* which covers news, entertainment, and dining; the biweekly *Improper Bostonian,* packed with event and restaurant listings; and the weekly *Tab,* which lists neighborhood-specific event information. Available on newsstands, *Boston* magazine is a lifestyle-oriented monthly with cultural and restaurant listings.

Most large bookstores, including the local branches of Barnes & Noble, have extensive periodicals sections. Newsstands with good selections of international periodicals include **Out of Town News,** Zero Harvard Sq. (𝄐 **617/354-1441**), and **Crimson Corner,** 1394 Massachusetts Ave. (𝄐 **617/864-0700**), across the street from each other in the heart of Harvard Square.

Passports   Virtually every air traveler entering the U.S. is required to show a passport. All persons, including U.S. citizens, traveling by air between the United States and Canada, Mexico, Central and South America, the Caribbean, and Bermuda are required to present a valid passport. ***Note:*** U.S. and Canadian citizens entering the U.S. at land and seaports of entry from within the Western Hemisphere must now also present a passport or other documents compliant with the Western Hemisphere Travel Initiative (WHTI; see **www. getyouhome.gov** for details). Children 15 and under may continue entering with only a U.S. birth certificate, or other proof of U.S. citizenship.

Australia   Australian Passport Information Service (www.passports.gov.au; ✆ **131-232**).

Canada   Passport Canada, Foreign Affairs and International Trade Canada, Gatineau, QC K1A 0G3 (www.ppt.gc.ca; ✆ **800/567-6868**).

Ireland   Passport Office, Frederick Buildings, Molesworth Street, Dublin 2 (www.foreign affairs.gov.ie; ✆ **01/671-1633**).

New Zealand   Passport Office, Department of Internal Affairs, Level 3, 109 Featherston St., Wellington 6140 (www.passports.govt.nz; ✆ **0800/225-050** in New Zealand or 04/463-9360).

United Kingdom   Visit your nearest passport office, major post office, or travel agency, or contact the **Identity and Passport Service (IPS),** Globe House, 89 Eccleston Sq., London SW1V 1PN (www.ips.gov.uk; ✆ **0300/222-0000**).

United States   To find your regional passport office, check the U.S. State Department website (http://travel.state.gov/passport) or call the **National Passport Information Center** (✆ **877/487-2778**) for automated information.

Petrol   See the "By Car" section under "Getting Around," earlier in this chapter.

Police   Call ✆ **911** for emergencies. This is a free call from pay phones. From a cellphone, 911 connects you to the state police. To call the Boston police emergency line directly from a cellphone, use ✆ **617/343-4911.** The nonemergency number is ✆ **617/343-4200.**

Safety   Boston and Cambridge are generally safe, especially in the areas you're likely to visit. Nevertheless, you should take the same precautions you would in any other large North American city. Stash wallets and billfolds in your least accessible pocket, don't wave around your expensive camera or biggest map, and take off your headphones (or at least turn the volume way down) when you're wandering around alone. In general, trust your instincts—a dark, deserted street is probably deserted for a reason.

As in any city, stay out of parks (including Boston Common, the Public Garden, the Esplanade, the Rose Kennedy Greenway, and Cambridge Common) at night unless you're in a crowd. Specific areas to avoid at night include Boylston Street between Tremont and Washington streets, and Tremont Street from Stuart to Boylston streets. Try not to walk alone late at night in the Theater District or on the side streets around North Station. Public transportation in the areas you're likely to visit is busy and safe, but service stops between 12:30 and 1am. If you're going to be out late, carry cab fare and a charged phone programmed with the number of at least one cab company.

Senior Travel   Mention that you're a senior citizen when you make your travel reservations. Boston-area businesses offer many discounts to seniors with identification (a driver's license, passport, or other document that shows your date of birth). The cut-off age is usually 65, sometimes 62. Restaurants, museums, and movie theaters may offer special deals. Restaurants and theaters usually offer discounts only at off-peak times, but museums and other attractions offer reduced rates—usually the equivalent of the student price—at all times.

With a special photo ID card, seniors can ride the **MBTA** subways, local and express buses, commuter rail, and Inner Harbor ferries for at least half off the regular fare. You must have a Senior CharlieCard, available in person only from 8:30am to 5pm weekdays at Downtown Crossing and Back Bay stations. For more information, contact the Reduced Fare CharlieCard Office (www.mbta.com; ℂ **800/543-8287** or 617/222-5976; TTY 617/222-5854; under "Fares & Passes," click "Reduced Fare Programs").

Smoking   In a word, no. State law bans smoking in all workplaces, including restaurants, bars, and clubs, and the MBTA forbids smoking in subway stations. A growing number of hotel chains ban smoking in all guest rooms; in Boston, city law forbids smoking in hotels.

Student Travel   Students don't actually rule Boston—it just feels that way sometimes. Many museums, theaters, concert halls, and other establishments offer discounts for college and high school students with valid identification. Some restaurants near college campuses offer student discounts or other deals. Visiting students can check schools' and student groups' Facebook pages, relevant Twitter streams, and old-school campus bulletin boards for information about events and activities, many of which are open to them. The weekly *Boston Phoenix* also lists activities for students.

Taxes   The United States has no value-added tax (VAT) or other indirect tax at the national level. Every state, county, and city may levy its own local tax on all purchases, including hotel and restaurant checks and airline tickets. These taxes will *not* appear on price tags. The 6.25% Massachusetts sales tax does not apply to groceries, prescription drugs, newspapers, or clothing that costs less than $175. The tax on meals and takeout food varies by community; in Boston and Cambridge, it's 7%. The lodging tax is 14.45% in Boston and Cambridge.

Telephones   See "Mobile Phones," earlier in this section, for information about staying in touch when you're on the road. If you can't use your mobile phone, you may be able to find a public pay phone. Pay phones are increasingly scarce on the street, but they remain available in most hotel lobbies and all airport terminals. Some hotels include local calls in the room rate, but most impose astronomical surcharges on both local and long-distance calls; a quick trip to the lobby can spare you an unpleasant surprise at checkout.

Many convenience stores, drugstores, and packaging services sell **prepaid calling cards** in denominations up to $50. Many public pay phones at airports accept American Express, MasterCard, and Visa. **Local calls** made from pay phones in most locales cost 25¢ or 35¢ (no pennies, please). Most long-distance and international calls can be dialed directly from any phone.

To make calls within the United States and to Canada, dial 1 followed by the area code and the seven-digit number. **For other international calls,** dial 011 followed by the country code, city code, and the number you are calling. The country code for Australia is **61;** for Ireland, **353;** for New Zealand, **64;** and for the U.K., **44.** To place **international calls to the United States,** dial your country's international code plus the country code (1), the area code, and the local number.

Calls to area codes **800, 888, 877, 866,** and **855** are toll-free. However, calls to area codes **700** and **900** (chat lines, bulletin boards, "dating" services, and so on) can cost $3 or more per minute. Some numbers have minimum charges that can run $15 or more.

For **reversed-charge or collect calls,** and for person-to-person calls, dial the number 0, then the area code and number; an operator will come on the line, and you should specify whether you are calling collect, person-to-person, or both. If your operator-assisted call is international, ask for the overseas operator.

For **directory assistance** ("information"), dial 411 for local and national numbers in the U.S. and Canada. For dedicated long-distance information, dial 1, the appropriate area code, and 555-1212.

Time   Boston is in the Eastern time zone. The continental United States encompasses **four time zones:** Eastern Time (ET), Central Time (CT), Mountain Time (MT), and Pacific Time (PT). Alaska and Hawaii have their own zones. At noon in Boston and New York (ET), it's 7am in Honolulu (HT), 9am in Los Angeles (PT), 10am in Denver (MT), 11am in Chicago (CT), 5pm in London (GMT), and 2am the next day in Sydney.

Daylight saving time (summer time) is in effect from 1am on the second Sunday in March to 1am on the first Sunday in November, except in Arizona, Hawaii, the U.S. Virgin Islands, and Puerto Rico. Daylight saving time moves the clock 1 hour ahead of standard time.

For help with time translations and more, download our convenient Travel Tools app for your mobile device. Go to **www.frommers.com/go/mobile** and click on the Travel Tools icon.

Tipping   Tips are a very important part of some workers' income, and gratuities are the standard way of showing appreciation for services provided. (Tipping is certainly not compulsory if the service is poor!) In hotels, tip **bellhops** at least $1 per bag ($5 or more if you have a lot of luggage) and tip the **housekeeping staff** at least $2 per day (more if you've left a big mess). Tip the **doorman** or **concierge** only if he or she has provided you with some specific service (for example, calling a cab for you or obtaining difficult-to-get theater tickets). Tip the **valet-parking attendant** $1 or $2 every time you get your car.

In restaurants, bars, and nightclubs, tip **service staff** and **bartenders** 15% to 20% of the check, tip **checkroom attendants** $1 or $2 per garment, and tip **valet-parking attendants** $1 per vehicle.

Tip **cabdrivers** 15% to 20% of the fare; tip **skycaps** at airports at least $1 per bag ($5 or more if you have a lot of luggage); and tip **hairdressers** and **barbers** 15% to 20%.

For help with tip calculations, currency conversions, and more, download our convenient Travel Tools app for your mobile device. Go to **www.frommers.com/go/mobile** and click on the Travel Tools icon.

Toilets   You won't find public toilets or "restrooms" on the streets in most U.S. cities; seek them out in hotel lobbies, bars, restaurants, museums, department stores, railway and bus stations, and service stations. The visitor center in Faneuil Hall has a public restroom, as do the CambridgeSide Galleria, Copley Place, Prudential Center, and Quincy Market shopping areas. The central branch of the Boston Public Library, in Copley Square, has toilets in the basement. Large hotels and fast-food restaurants are often the best bet for clean facilities. Restaurants and bars in heavily visited areas, including Boston and Cambridge, may reserve their restrooms for patrons.

You'll find freestanding, self-cleaning **pay toilets** (25¢) at locations around downtown. These include City Hall Plaza, Congress Street behind City Hall; the plaza in front of the New England Aquarium; Christopher Columbus Waterfront Park; and Commercial Street at Snowhill Street, off the Freedom Trail in the North End. Check these facilities carefully before using them or sending a child in alone; despite regular patrols, IV-drug users have been known to take advantage of the generous time limits.

Travelers with Disabilities   Boston, like all other U.S. cities, has taken the required steps to provide access for people with disabilities. Hotels must provide accessible rooms, and museums and street curbs have ramps for wheelchairs. Some smaller accommodations, including most B&Bs, have not been retrofitted. In older neighborhoods (notably Beacon Hill and the North End), you'll find many narrow streets, cobbled thoroughfares, and brick sidewalks that can make getting around difficult.

Most stations on the Red, Blue, and Orange **subway** lines are wheelchair accessible. The Green Line, which uses trolleys, is problematic; some stops have ramps, lifts, or both; construction is under way or in the works at others; and some are inaccessible. Contact the **Massachusetts Bay Transportation Authority** (www.mbta.com; ✆ **800/392-6100** or 617/222-3200) for details about the stations you need and possible work-arounds. For service updates on elevators, escalators, and lifts, call the toll-free number and press 6, call ✆ **617/222-2828,** or visit the "Rider Tools" area of the website. All MBTA **buses** have lifts or ramps. To learn more, contact the **Office for Transportation Access,** 10 Park Plaza, Room 5750, Boston, MA 02116 (www.mbta.com; ✆ **800/533-6282** within Massachusetts or 617/222-5123; TTY 617/222-5415; under "Riding the T," click "Accessibility at the T").

One taxi company with wheelchair-accessible vehicles is **Boston Cab** (✆ **617/536-5010**); advance notice is recommended.

An excellent resource for out-of-towners with mobility issues is **VSA Arts Massachusetts,** 89 South St., Boston, MA 02111 (www.vsamass.org; ✆ **617/350-7713,** TTY 617/350-6536).

VAT   See "Taxes," earlier in this section.

Visas   The U.S. State Department has a **Visa Waiver Program (VWP)** allowing citizens of the following countries to enter the United States without a visa for stays of up to 90 days: Andorra, Australia, Austria, Belgium, Brunei, Czech Republic, Denmark, Estonia, Finland, France, Germany, Greece, Hungary, Iceland, Ireland, Italy, Japan, Latvia, Liechtenstein, Lithuania, Luxembourg, Malta, Monaco, the Netherlands, New Zealand, Norway, Portugal, San Marino, Singapore, Slovakia, Slovenia, South Korea, Spain, Sweden, Switzerland, and the United Kingdom. (***Note:*** This list was accurate at press time; for the most up-to-date list of countries in the VWP, consult **http://travel.state.gov/visa**.) Even though a visa isn't necessary, in an effort to help U.S. officials check travelers against terror watch lists before they arrive at U.S. borders, visitors from VWP countries must register online through the Electronic System for Travel Authorization (ESTA) before boarding a plane or a boat to the U.S. Travelers must complete an electronic application providing basic personal and travel eligibility information. The Department of Homeland Security recommends filling out the form at least 3 days before traveling. Authorizations will be valid for up to 2 years or until the traveler's passport expires, whichever comes first. Currently, there is a US$14 fee for the online application. Existing ESTA registrations remain valid through their expiration dates. ***Note:*** Any passport issued on or after October 26, 2006, by a VWP country must be an **e-Passport** for VWP travelers to be eligible to enter the U.S. without a visa. Citizens of these nations also need to present a round-trip air or cruise ticket upon arrival. E-Passports contain computer chips capable of storing biometric information, such as the required digital photograph of the holder. If your passport doesn't have this feature, you can still travel without a visa if the valid passport was issued before October 26, 2005, and includes a machine-readable zone; or if the valid passport was issued between October 26, 2005, and October 25, 2006, and includes a digital photograph. For more information, go to **http://travel.state.gov/visa**. Canadian citizens may enter the United States without visas, but they must show passports and proof of residence.

Citizens of all other countries must have (1) a valid passport that expires at least 6 months later than the scheduled end of their visit to the U.S.; and (2) a tourist visa.

For information about U.S. visas, go to **http://travel.state.gov/visa**. Or consult one of the following sources:

Australian citizens can obtain up-to-date visa information from the **U.S. Embassy Canberra,** Moonah Place, Yarralumla, ACT 2600 (http://canberra.usembassy.gov/visas.html; © **02/6214-5600**).

British subjects can obtain up-to-date visa information by calling the **U.S. Embassy Visa Information Line** (© **09042-450-100** from within the U.K. at £1.25 per minute; or © **866/382-3589** from within the U.S. at a flat rate of $16 [payable by credit card only]), or by visiting the "Visas" section of the American Embassy London's website, **http://london. usembassy.gov/visas.html**.

Irish citizens can obtain up-to-date visa information through the **U.S. Embassy Dublin,** 42 Elgin Rd., Ballsbridge, Dublin 4 (http://dublin.usembassy.gov; © **1580-47-VISA** [8472] from within the Republic of Ireland at €2.40 per minute).

Citizens of **New Zealand** can obtain up-to-date visa information by contacting the **U.S. Consulate General,** Citigroup Centre, 23 Customs St. E., Auckland CBD (www.ustravel docs.com/nz; © **649/915-1081**).

Visitor Information   The **Greater Boston Convention & Visitors Bureau** (www. bostonusa.com; © **888/733-2678** or 617/536-4100) offers a comprehensive visitor information kit ($10 plus postage) that includes a travel planner, a guidebook, a map, pamphlets, and information about discounts on shopping, dining, attractions, and nightlife. The free BostonUSA iPhone app allows users to buy e-tickets for attractions and tours and enter by just showing the screen. The bureau also publishes a *Kids Love Boston* guide ($5) and free smaller guides to specific seasons and special events

The bureau operates the **Boston Common Information Center,** 148 Tremont St., on Boston Common, which is open Monday through Friday from 8:30am to 5pm, Saturday from 9am to 5pm, and the **Prudential Information Center,** on the main level of the Prudential Center, 800 Boylston St. It's open Monday through Friday from 9am to 5:30pm, Saturday and Sunday from 10am to 6pm.

For information about Cambridge, contact the **Cambridge Office for Tourism** (www. cambridge-usa.org; © **800/862-5678** or 617/441-2884; fax 617/441-7736).

The office's **information kiosk** is in the heart of Harvard Square, near the T entrance at the intersection of Massachusetts Avenue, John F. Kennedy Street, and Brattle Street. It's open Monday through Friday from 9am to 5pm, Saturday and Sunday from 9am to 1pm.

The **Massachusetts Office of Travel & Tourism** (www.massvacation.com; © **800/227-6277** or 617/973-8500; fax 617/973-8525) distributes information about the whole state. Its free *Getaway Guide* magazine includes information about attractions and lodgings, a map, and a calendar.

National Park Service rangers staff the **Boston National Historical Park Visitor Center,** on the first floor of Faneuil Hall, Dock Square, North and Congress streets (www.nps.gov/bost; © **617/242-5642;** T: Blue or Orange Line to State St.), and lead seasonal free tours of the Freedom Trail. The center is open daily from 9am to 5pm. The ranger-staffed center at the Charlestown Navy Yard (© **617/242-5601**) keeps the same hours.

There's a small information booth at **Faneuil Hall Marketplace** between Quincy Market and the South Market Building. It's outdoors and staffed in the spring, summer, and fall Monday through Saturday from 10am to 6pm, Sunday from noon to 6pm.

To surf around for information about Boston before and during your visit, check out the following websites:

Boston.com (www.boston.com): A comprehensive source that includes some content from the *Boston Globe*.

National Park Service (www.nps.gov): An endlessly helpful resource for visitors to Boston and its history-rich suburbs.

MBTA (www.mbta.com): The go-to site for subway, trolley, bus, ferry, and commuter-rail schedules and route maps, plus fare and pass information and an interactive route planner.

HopStop (www.hopstop.com) and **Google Transit** (http://transit.google.com): These interactive sites are good backups to the MBTA route planner, which generally does a better job of accommodating local quirks.

Yelp (www.yelp.com/boston) and **Citysearch** (http://boston.citysearch.com): Exhaustive listings, including restaurants and clubs, accompanied by professional and hit-or-miss amateur reviews.

Boston-to-English Dictionary (www.universalhub.com/glossary): Hilarious yet useful lingo and slang.

Hammered.org (www.hammered.org): A good resource for students and others interested in alcohol-free entertainment and activities.

Twitter (www.twitter.com) and **Facebook** (www.facebook.com): Even social-networking novices can find plenty of useful information at these sites. If you're just getting your feet wet, pick out an appealing destination or two—museum, municipality, shop, whatever—to follow or friend. A good place to start is with the Greater Boston Convention & Visitors Bureau, **@BostonInsider**. To branch out, see what your chosen Twitterers recommend on "Follow Friday," and check out your Facebook friends' other friends.

iTunes App Store (http://itunes.apple.com): Hundreds of free iPhone apps deliver information about Boston. I'd start with the apps that put Frommer's and the Convention & Visitors Bureau in your hand, then check out the *Globe* and *Herald,* the MBTA, and at least a couple of local TV stations.

Wi-Fi See "Internet & Wi-Fi," earlier in this section.

Index

A

Abbot Hall, 310–311
Abercrombie & Fitch, 194
Abiel Smith School, 66, 67
Academic trips, 355
Accommodations, 252–291. *See also* Accommodations Index; *and specific neighborhoods*
  best, 252–254
  Concord, 307–308
  Gloucester, 328
  Marblehead, 312–313
  Plymouth, 341–342
  practical matters, 288–291
  price categories and rates, 252, 253
  Rockport, 334–335
  Salem, 319–320
Acme Fine Art, 197
Adams National Historical Park, 336
Adventure trips, 355
African-American History Month, 27
African Americans, 27
  Black Heritage Trail, 65–66
  Boston Black, 115
  Cambridge African American Heritage Trail, 110
  Museum of African American History, 67
  special events, 31
  54th Massachusetts Colored Regiment, 88
African Meeting House, 66, 67
Afternoon tea, 183
Air travel, 344–346
Alpha Gallery, 197
Ancient and Honorable Artillery Company of Massachusetts, 95
An Evening with Champions, 31
Annenberg Hall, 143
Antiques and collectibles, 196–197, 341
Appalachian Mountain Club, 355, 356
Apple Store, 214
Architecture tours, 110
Area codes, 356
Arlington Street Church, 131
Arnold Arboretum, 78, 103
Art & Architecture Tours, 71
Art galleries, 197, 332
Arthur M. Sackler Museum, 81–82, 143
Art lovers, suggested itinerary for, 53
Arts, crafts and museum stores, 199–200

ATMs (automated teller machines), 361–362
August Moon Festival, 30

B

The Back Bay, 41, 70–74
  accommodations, 270–279
  restaurants, 169–172
  shopping, 191–192
  walking tour, 127–133
Back Bay Bicycles, 118
Bank of America Pavilion, 227
The Bar at Taj Boston, 229
Barbara Krakow Gallery, 197
Bars and lounges, 229–235, 241–242
Bartholdi, Frédéric Auguste, 130
Baseball, 246–247
Basketball, 247–248
Battle of Bunker Hill Museum, 102
Bay State Cruise Company, 108–109
Beaches, 117, 329
Beacon Hill, 37
  accommodations, 263–264
  attractions, 65–68
  restaurants, 162
  shopping, 191
  tours, 104
Beacon Hill Skate Shop, 122
Beacon Street, 66
Beantown Trolley, 107
Bearskin Neck, 332, 334
Beauport, Sleeper-McCann House, 325–326
Beauty, cosmetics and perfume, 200
The Beehive, 229
Benjamin Franklin Statue, 91–92
Ben & Jerry's, 176
Berklee Beantown Jazz Festival, 238
Berklee Performance Center, 227
Big Apple Circus, 28
Bike Safe Boston, 118
Biking, 117–118, 300, 354–355
  tours, 110, 112
Bird-watching, 310
Black Heritage Trail, 65, 67
Black Nativity, 31
The Black Rose, 233
Bleacher Bar, 232
Blue Hills Trailside Museum, 114
Blue Man Group, 228
Boating (boat rentals), 123
Boat tours and cruises, 107–109, 120–121
Books, maps and stationery, 201–202

Boston African American National Historic Site, 65
Boston Athenæum, 66–67
Boston Ballet, 221
Boston Beer Works, 234
Boston Bikes, 118
Boston Black, 115
Boston Book Festival, 31
Boston Bruins, 248
Boston By Foot, 104, 114
Boston By Little Feet, 114
Boston Celtics, 247–248
Boston Center for Adult Education, 109
Boston Center for the Arts, 70, 227
Boston Children's Museum, 114–115
Boston City Hall, 64
Boston Common, 87–88
Boston Duck Tours, 105
Boston Film Festival, 30
Boston Harbor Cruises, 107, 109, 114
Boston Harborfest, 30
Boston Harbor Islands, 120–121
Boston Harbor Islands National Recreation Area, 121
Boston Harbor Islands Pavilion, 120
Bostonian Society's museum, 94
Boston Irish Tourism Association, 110
Boston Landmarks Orchestra, 226
Boston Light, 108, 121
Boston Marathon, 28, 249
Boston Massacre Site, 95
Boston Museum of Natural History, 131
Boston National Historical Park, 95
Boston National Historical Park Visitor Center, 86
Boston Pops, 221–222
Boston Pops Concert & Fireworks Display, 30
Boston Pride Parade, 29
Boston Public Library, 70–71, 132, 183
Boston Public Market, shopping, 194
Boston Red Sox, 113, 246–247
  Opening Day, 28
Boston Restaurant Week, 161
Boston Sailing Center, 123
Boston's Best Cruises, 120
Boston Sports Clubs, 119
Boston Symphony Orchestra, 222
Boston Tea Party, 93

Boston Tea Party Reenactment, 31
Boston Tea Party Ships & Museum, 68–69, 113
Boston Underfoot, 104
Boston University, 103
Boston University's Seminars, 112
Boston Vegetarian Society, 112
Boston Wine Festival, 27, 112
Boston Wine School, 112
Bowling, 245
Brattle Square, 146
Brattle Street, 80–81, 84
Brattle Theatre, 146, 147
Brewster Gardens, 337
Brimstone Corner, 89
Bristol Lounge, 112
The Bristol Lounge, 229
Brookline, 41–42, 79–80
Buckman Tavern, 297
Bunch of Grapes Tavern, 133
Bunker Hill Monument, 101–102
The Burren, 233
Busch-Reisinger Museum, 82
Business hours, 356
Bus travel, 348, 350

C
Cafe Vanille, 128
Calendar of events, 27–32
Cambridge, 42
  accommodations, 281–287
  restaurants, 175–184
  shopping, 192, 194
  sights and attractions, 80–85
Cambridge African American Heritage Trail, 110
Cambridge Bicycle, 118
Cambridge Brewing Company, 234
Cambridge Carnival International, 30
Cambridge Center for Adult Education, 109
Cambridge Common, 145
Cambridge Historical Commission, 110
Cambridge Office for Tourism, 80
Cambridge River Festival, 30
Cambridge School of Culinary Arts, 112
CambridgeSide Galleria, 194
Cantab Lounge, 238–239
Cape Ann Museum, 326
Carpenter Center for the Visual Arts, 142–143
Car travel, 346–347, 351–354
Casablanca, 229
Cask 'n Flagon, 232
Cellphones, 357, 360
Central Burying Ground, 87
Charles Hayden Planetarium, 62–63
Charles Playhouse, 228

Charles Riverboat Company, 107–108
Charles River Canoe & Kayak, 123
Charlestown, 37, 68
  accommodations, 265
CharlieTicket and CharlieCard, 349
Cheers (Beacon Hill), 128, 229–230
Cheers (Faneuil Hall Marketplace), 230
Chestnut Street, 315
Children, families with, 358
  accommodations, 274
  best family experiences, 5–6
  books about Boston, 23
  shopping, 205, 214–215
  sights and attractions, 113–116
  suggested itinerary, 51, 53
  theater, 225
Children's Museum, 27
Chinatown Market Tours, 112
Chinatown/Theater District, 40, 70
  accommodations, 267–269
  restaurants, 162–166
Chinese New Year, 27
Christ Church, 145
Christina's, 176
Christmas Revels, 31–32
Christopher Columbus Waterfront Park, 96
Church of the Covenant, 130
City Hall Plaza market, 194
CityPASS, 58
CityView Trolleys, 107
Classical music, opera and dance, 221
Climate, 26–27
Clothing and accessories, 202–208
Club and music scene, 235–239
Club Café, 242
Club Passim, 238
Codzilla cruise, 114
Coffeehouses, 243–245
College merchandise, 208
Colonnade Murals, 76
Comcast Center, 227
Comedy clubs, 240
Commonwealth Avenue Mall, 129–130
Commonwealth Shakespeare Company, 224
Community Boating, 123
Concert and performance series, 226
Concord, 299–308
Concord Museum, 301–302
Constitution, USS, 100–101, 107
Copley Place, 194
Copley Square, 131
Copp's Hill Burying Ground, 100
Crane Beach, 329

Credit cards, 362
Crocker Park, 310
Crow's Nest, 324
Cruise ships, 348
Custom House, 134
Customs regulations, 357
Cyclorama, 70

D
Dance clubs, 240–241
Darwin's Ltd., 171
Debit cards, 362
DeCordova Sculpture Park and Museum, 305
DeLux Cafe, 230
Department stores, 208
Dewey Square market, 194
Dim sum restaurants, 164
Dining, 149–188, 312. See also Restaurant Index; and specific neighborhoods
  afternoon tea, 183
  alfresco, 174
  best, 4, 149–150
  Boston Restaurant Week, 161
  breakfast and brunch, 159
  Cambridge, 175–184
  Concord, 307
  by cuisine, 187–188
  dim sum, 164
  family-friendly, 179
  food trucks, 154
  Gloucester, 326–327
  late-night, 231
  Lexington, 298
  Plymouth, 340–341
  practical matters, 185–187
  price categories, 150
  quick bites and picnic provisions, 171
  Rockport, 333–334
  Salem, 318–319
  steakhouse chains, 169
Disabilities, travelers with, 365
Discount shopping, 209
Discovering Justice, 110, 111
Doctors, 357
Dorchester, 77–78
Downtown Crossing, 37, 65
  accommodations, 261–263
  restaurants, 161–162
  shopping, 191
Dr. Paul Dudley White Charles River Bike Path, 118, 122–123
Dragon Boat Festival, 29–30
Drink, 3–4, 233
Drinking laws, 357
Driving rules, 357
Duck Tours, Boston, 105

E
Eastern Standard, 230
Electricity, 357
Elephant Walk cooking classes, 112

Emack & Bolio's, 176
Embassies and consulates, 357
Emerald Necklace, 102
Emergencies, 358
Emerson, Ralph Waldo, 302
    House, 304
Emmanuel Church, 131
Emmanuel Music, 226
Entertainment and nightlife, 217–250
    gay and lesbian, 241–243
    Gloucester, 327–328
    tickets, 220
The Esplanade, 122
Essex, 328–330
The Estate, 241
Exeter Street Theater, 130

F

Families with children, 358
    accommodations, 274
    best family experiences, 5–6
    books about Boston, 23
    shopping, 205, 214–215
    sights and attractions, 113–116
    suggested itinerary, 51, 53
    theater, 225
Faneuil Hall, 64, 95–96, 133
Faneuil Hall Marketplace, 37, 64, 96, 113, 134
    accommodations, 260–261
    restaurants, 159–161, 171, 174
    shopping, 190, 195
Farmers' markets, 195
The Fenway
    attractions, 74–77
    restaurants, 172–175
    shopping, 192
Fenway neighborhood, 42
Fenway Park, 246–247
Ferries, 350–351
    Charlestown Navy Yard to Long Wharf, 102, 107
    to Provincetown, 109
Ferris Wheels Bike Shop, 118
Fiedler, Arthur, 129
54th Massachusetts Colored Regiment, 88
Figs, 171
Films, 30
Financial District, 37, 190
    accommodations, 261–263
    restaurants, 159–161
First Baptist Church, 130
First Night, 32
First Public School, 91
Fogg Museum, 82, 143
Food and drink, 209–210
    tours, 112
Food trucks, 154
Football, 248
Fort Sewall, 310
The Fours, 232
Fourth of July, 101
Franklin, Benjamin
    birthplace, 93
    Statue, 91–92

Franklin Park Zoo, 116
Free and dirt-cheap things to do, 6–7, 226
Freedom Trail, 86–102
    audio tour narrative, 89
    guided walking tours, 104–105
Freedom Trail Foundation, 87, 89
Freedom Trail Players, 87
Freedom Trail Week, 28–29
French, Daniel Chester, 132, 136, 140
French Cultural Center, 110
Fresh Pond Golf Course, 119
Friends of Mount Auburn Cemetery, 85
Fritz, 242
Frog Pond, 87, 121

G

Galería Cubana, 197
Gallery NAGA, 197
Game On! Sports Cafe, 232
Gays and lesbians, 29, 241–243, 359
Georges Island, 120
Ghosts & Gravestones, 112
Gibson House Museum, 70, 71
Gifts and souvenirs, 210–212
GiGi Gelateria, 154
Glass Flowers, 82
Gloucester, 320–330
Gloucester Stage Company, 327–328
Go Boston Card, 58
Golf, 119, 250
Go Select Boston, 58
Government Center, 37, 64–65, 190
    accommodations, 260–261
Graduate School of Government, 147
Grafton Street, 230
Granary Burying Ground, 89–90
The Grand Canal, 233
Great Scott, 235–236
Greenway Open Market, 195
Grendel's Den, 230
Gropius House, 306
Gyms, 119–120

H

Halibut Point State Park, 333
Hall of the North American Indian, 83
Hancock-Clarke House, 294, 297
The Harborwalk, 86
Hard Rock Cafe, 240
Harvard, John, Statue, 140
Harvard Art Museums, 81–82
Harvard Book Store, 147
Harvard College Observatory, 103
Harvard Coop, 138
Harvard Hall, 139
Harvard Lampoon Castle, 147

Harvard Museum of Natural History, 82–83, 113, 143–144
Harvard Square, 80, 138
    restaurants, 175–179
    walking tour, 138–147
Harvard University, 81–83
Harvard Yard, 138–139
Harvard-Yenching Library, 144
Hatch Shell, 129, 227
Havana Club, 235
Haymarket, 96
Head of the Charles Regatta, 31, 250
Health concerns, 358
Healthworks, 119–120
Heart of the Freedom Trail tour, 104
Hiking, 120
Historic New England, 68, 110
History of Boston, 14–26
Hockey, 248–249
Holden Chapel, 139
Holidays, 32
Hollis Hall, 139
Holyoke Center, 146
Home design, furnishings and housewares, 212–213
The Hong Kong, 230
Horse racing, 249
Hospitals, 358
Hotels, 252–291. *See also* Accommodations Index
    best, 252–254
    Concord, 307–308
    Gloucester, 328
    Marblehead, 312–313
    Plymouth, 341–342
    practical matters, 288–291
    price categories and rates, 252, 253
    Rockport, 334–335
    Salem, 319–320
House of Blues Boston, 239
The House of the Seven Gables, 315–316
Huntington Avenue YMCA, 119

I

Ice cream, 176
Ice skating, 121
Il Panino Express, 171
IMAX movies, 60–62
Independent Film Festival of Boston, 29
InLine Club of Boston, 122
In-line skating, 122
Institute of Contemporary Art, 69
Insurance, 358
International Poster Gallery, 198
Internet and Wi-Fi, 358–359, 368
Isabella Stewart Gardner Museum, 74–75, 226, 234
Italian-American Feasts, 30
Itineraries, suggested, 43–53

J

Jacque's Cabaret, 242
Jamaica Plain, 78–79
Jamaica Pond, 78
James Rego Square (Paul
    Revere Mall), 99
Japanese House, 115
Jazz Week, 238
Jeremiah Lee Mansion/
    Marblehead Museum &
    Historical Society, 311
Jerry Remy's Sports Bar &
    Grill, 232
Jewelry, 205–206
Jillian's Boston, 245
Jogging, 122–123
John Adams Courthouse, 111
John F. Kennedy National
    Historic Site, 79–80
John F. Kennedy Park, 147
John F. Kennedy Presidential
    Library and Museum,
    77–78, 113
John Harvard's Brew House,
    234–235
John Harvard Statue, 140
John Joseph Moakley U.S.
    Courthouse, 110, 137
Johnny D's Uptown Restaurant
    & Music Club, 237
Johnny's Workbench, 115
JP Licks, 176

K

Kayaking, 123
Kendall Square, 83–84
Kendall Square Community
    Skating, 121–122
Kenmore Square, 41–42,
    74, 192
    accommodations, 279
    restaurants, 172–175
Kennedy, John F., 88
    John F. Kennedy National
      Historic Site, 79–80
    John F. Kennedy Presidential
      Library and Museum, 77–78
Kennedy, Rose Fitzgerald, 98
King Hooper Mansion/
    Marblehead Arts
    Association & Gallery,
    311–312
King's Chapel and Burying
    Ground, 90–91

L

L. A. Burdick Chocolates, 146
Lafayette House, 310
Legal aid, 359
Le Grand David and His Own
    Spectacular Magic
    Company, 225
Lexington, 293–299
Lexington Historical
    Society, 297
LGBT travelers, 29,
    241–243, 359

Liberty Ride, 296
Lilac Sunday, 29
LinkPasses, 350
List Visual Arts Center, 84
Little Brewster Island, 108
The Littlest Bar, 233
Lizard Lounge, 237
Lizzy's, 176
Lobsters, 213
Logan Airport, accommodations,
    287–288
Logan International Airport,
    344–345
Longfellow Bridge, 106
Longfellow House—Washington's
    Headquarters National
    Historic Site, 83
Long Wharf, 106, 134–135
Louisburg Square, 66

M

Machine, 242
McKim, Charles Follen, 70,
    132, 337
Macy's, 194
Made in Fort Point, 198
Mail, 359
Make Way for Ducklings, 128
Malls and markets, 194–196
Mapping Revolutionary Boston
    (website and iPhone
    app), 94
Marblehead, 308–313
Marblehead Neck Wildlife
    Sanctuary, 310
Martha Richardson Fine
    Art, 198
Martin Luther King, Jr., Birthday
    Celebration, 27
Mary Baker Eddy Library/
    Mapparium, 71–73
Massachusetts Audubon
    Society, 355, 356
Massachusetts Avenue, 41
Massachusetts Hall, 139
Massachusetts Historical
    Society, 73–74
Massachusetts Institute of
    Technology (MIT), 84
Massachusetts State House, 88
MassBike, 118
Mayflower II, 338–339
Media Lab (MIT), 84
Memorial Church, 141–142
Memorial Drive, 118, 122
Memorial Hall, 143
Memorial to the Gloucester
    Fisherman, 322
The Middle East, 236
Mike's Pastry, 61
Minuteman Bikeway, 118
Minute Man National Historical
    Park, 296, 300–301
Miracle of Science Bar + Grill,
    230–231
MIT (Massachusetts Institute of
    Technology), 84
MIT Museum, 84

Mobile phones, 360
Modern Pastry, 154, 156
Money and costs, 361–362
Motif No. 1, 331–332
Mount Auburn Cemetery, 84–85
Mount Vernon St., 66
Movies, 24, 30, 243
Mr. Dooley's Boston
    Tavern, 233
Mugar Omni Theater, 62
Munroe Tavern, 297–298
Museum of African American
    History, 66, 67
Museum of Fine Arts, 75–77,
    113, 226, 234
Museum of Science, 62, 113
Museums, best, 10
Music stores, 213–214
MyBike, 118

N

National Heritage Museum, 298
Navy Yard Visitor Center, 101
Neighborhoods, 35–42
New Balance Climb, 115
New Balance Hubway, 117–118
Newbury Street, 130, 198
New England Aquarium, 59–60,
    109, 113, 135
New England Holocaust
    Memorial, 96–97
New England Patriots, 248
Newspapers and magazines,
    362
Newton Commonwealth Golf
    Course, 119
New Yard, 140
Nichols House Museum, 67
Norman B. Leventhal Walk to
    the Sea, 86
North Bridge, 299, 300
The North End, 36, 61–64, 190
    accommodations, 254–259
    restaurants, 154–159
North End Market Tours, 112
Northern Avenue Bridge,
    136–137
North Shore, 308, 329
North Station/Science Park,
    36, 62
    accommodations, 259–260
The Nutcracker, 31

O

Oktoberfest, 31
Old Burying Ground, 145
Old City Hall, 92
Old Corner Bookstore
    Building, 92
The Old Manse, 302–303
Old North Church, 28, 99
Old South Meeting House,
    92–93
Old State House Museum,
    93–95, 133
Old Town House, 310
Old Town Trolley Tours, 107
Old Yard, 139

Olmsted, Frederick Law, 102, 103
On Location Tours, 112
Orchard House, 303
Orientation tours, 104–107
Orpheum Theatre, 227
Otis House, 67–68
Outdoor activities, 117–124
best, 11–12
Outlet shopping, 209
Out of Town News, 138

P

Panificio, 128
Paper House, 333
Paradise, 242
Paradise Rock Club, 236
Parking, 353–354
Parks and gardens, 102–103
Park Street Church, 89
Passports, 362–363
Patriots' Day, 28
Paul Revere House, 28, 97, 113
Paul Revere Mall (James Rego Square), 99
Peabody Essex Museum, 316–317
Peabody Museum of Archaeology & Ethnology, 82–83
Peep's World, 115
The Perfect Storm, 324
Performing arts, 217–228, 242–243
PhotoWalks, 112
Pierce/Hichborn House, 97
Pierre Lallement Bike Path, 118
Pilgrim Hall Museum, 339
Pilgrim Memorial State Park, 337
PlaySpace, 115
Plimoth Plantation, 339–340
The Plough & Stars, 234
Plymouth, 335–342
Plymouth Rock, 336–337
Police, 363
Pool, 245
Porter Exchange mall, food court, 184
Provincetown, day trips to, 108–109
Public Garden, 70, 103, 113, 127
Pucker Gallery, 199
Puerto Rican Festival & Parade, 30
Puppet Showplace Theatre, 225

Q

Quincy Market, 64, 96, 159

R

Radcliffe Yard, 145
Radius, 231
Ralph Waldo Emerson House, 304
Readings and lectures, 245

The Red Room @ Cafe 939, 237–238
Red Sox, 113, 246–247
Opening Day, 28
Regattabar, 239
Responsible tourism, 32–33
Restaurants, 149–188, 312. *See also* Restaurant Index; *and specific neighborhoods*
afternoon tea, 183
alfresco, 174
best, 4, 149–150
Boston Restaurant Week, 161
breakfast and brunch, 159
Cambridge, 175–184
Concord, 307
by cuisine, 187–188
dim sum, 164
family-friendly, 179
food trucks, 154
Gloucester, 326–327
late-night, 231
Lexington, 298
Plymouth, 340–341
practical matters, 185–187
price categories, 150
quick bites and picnic provisions, 171
Rockport, 333–334
Salem, 318–319
steakhouse chains, 169
Retire Beckett House, 316
Revere, Paul, House, 28, 97, 113
Richardson, H. H., 130, 131, 142
Rise, 242
Ritz-Carlton, 131
Robert Klein Gallery, 199
Rock of Ages, 236–237
Rockport, 330–335
Rockport Art Association, 332
Rocky Neck Art Colony, 324–325
Rose Fitzgerald Kennedy Greenway, 134
Rose Kennedy Greenway, 70
Rowes Wharf, 135–136
Royale Boston, 241
Royal Sonesta Hotel, restaurant patios at, 174
Ruth and Carl J. Shapiro Rotunda, 76
Ryan & Wood, Inc., 326
Ryles Jazz Club, 239

S

Sacred Cod, 88
Sacred Heart Church, 97–98
Safety, 363
Sailing, 123
St. Patrick's Day Celebrations, 27–28
St. Stephen's, 98
Salem, 313–320
Salem Haunted Happenings, 30–31

Salem Maritime National Historic Site, 317
Salem Willows, 315
Salem Witch Museum, 317–318
Sanders Theatre, 143
Sargent, John Singer, 76
Savenor's Market, 171
School Vacation Week, 27
Science Center, 144, 145
Science Playground, 115
Scullers Jazz Club, 239
Sears, 194
Seasons, 26
Semitic Museum, 144
Senior travel, 363
Sever Hall, 142
Shaw Memorial, 65–66, 87–88
Shear Madness, 228
Shoes and accessories, 206–207
Shopping, 190–215
best, 8–9
Concord, 307
Gloucester, 327
Lexington, 298–299
Marblehead, 312
Plymouth, 341
practical matters, 215
Rockport, 334
Salem, 319
The Shops at Prudential Center, 195–196
Shoreline of Colonial Boston, 134
Sights and attractions, 55–147. *See also specific neighborhoods*
Cambridge, 80–85
for kids, 113–116
by theme, 124–125
Silvertone Bar & Grill, 231
Simons IMAX Theatre, 60–61
Singing Beach, 329
Skywalk Observatory at the Prudential Center, 73–74, 113
Sleepy Hollow Cemetery, 304
Smoking, 364
Sonsie, 231
South Boston Waterfront (Seaport District), 40, 68–69
accommodations, 265–267
shopping, 191
South Bridge Boathouse, 300
The South End, 40–41, 70
accommodations, 269
restaurants, 166–169
shopping, 191
SoWa Open Market, 196
Spectacle Island, 120
Spectator sports, 245–250
Sports Museum of New England, 63, 113
Stage Fort Park, 324
Stata Center, 84
State Street, 133
Stoughton Hall, 139

Street Performers Festival, 29
Student travel, 364
Studio 73, 90
Subways, 349–350
Suffolk Downs, 249
Swan Boats, 28, 70, 103,
   113–114, 127
Symphony Hall, 104, 227

T

Tanglewood, 222
Tanner Rock Fountain, 144
Taxes, 364
Taxis, 351
TD Garden, 228
Telephones, 364–365
Tennis, 123
Tercentenary Theater, 140
Thanksgiving Celebration
   (Plymouth), 31
Theater, 222–228
Thompson Island, 120
Thoreau, Henry David, 302
   Walden Pond State Reservation,
      306–307
Tickets, online, 59
Time zones, 365
Tipping, 365
Toad, 237
Toilets, 365
Top of the Hub, 231
The Tortoise and Hare, 132
Tours, 355–356. *See also*
   Walking tours
Toys and games, 214–215
Trademark Tours, 104
Trader Joe's, 171
Train travel, 347
Transportation, public, 349–351
Trinity Church, 131
Trolleys, 349–350
Trolley tours, 106–107
T.T. the Bear's Place, 237
21st Amendment, 232

U

University Hall, 139
Upper Deck Trolley Tours, 107
Urban AdvenTours, 110,
   112, 118
USS *Constitution*, 100–101
   cruises, 107
USS *Constitution* Museum,
   101, 113

V

Vendome Memorial, 130
Via Matta, 232
Vintage and secondhand
   clothing, 207–208
Visas, 366–367
Visitor information, 367–368
Volle Nolle, 171
Volunteer and working
   trips, 356
Vose Galleries of Boston, 199

W

Wadsworth House, 138
Walden Pond State Reservation,
   306–307
Walking tours
   guided, 104–105
   self-guided, 127–147
      The Back Bay, 127–133
      Harvard Square, 138–147
      The Waterfront, 133–137
Wally's Cafe, 239
Wang YMCA of Chinatown, 119
Washington, George,
   equestrian statue of, 128
The Waterfront, 36, 190
   accommodations, 254–259
   attractions, 59–61
   restaurants, 150–151
   walking tour, 133–137
Water taxis, 351
The Wayside, 304–305
Weather, 26–27, 32
West Cambridge, 84–85
The West End Museum, 63–64
The Western Front, 238
Whale-watching, 109, 114, 321
Wheelock Family Theatre, 225
White House Black Market, 194
Widener Library, 140–141
Wilbur Theatre, 228
William J. Devine Golf
   Course, 119
Wingaersheek Beach, 329

Y

Yoga, 123–124

Accommodations

Ames, 260
Anthony's Town House, 280
Atlantis Oceanfront Inn, 328
The Back Bay Hotel, 273
Bass Rocks Ocean Inn, 328
Best Western Plus Boston/The
   Inn at Longwood
   Medical, 280
Best Western Plus Cold
   Spring, 341–342
Best Western Plus Hotel
   Tria, 286
Boston Common Hotel &
   Conference Center, 277
Boston Harbor Hotel, 254
Boston Marriott Copley Place,
   274–275
Boston Marriott Long
   Wharf, 258
The Boston Park Plaza Hotel &
   Towers, 275
Bulfinch Hotel, 259
Captain's Bounty on the
   Beach, 334
Chandler Inn Hotel, 269
The Charles Hotel, 281–282
Charlesmark Hotel, 277

Coach House Inn, 319–320
Colonnade Hotel Boston, 270
Comfort Inn & Suites Boston/
   Airport, 287
Concord's Colonial Inn, 307–308
Copley Square Hotel, 275–276
Courtyard Boston Brookline,
   279
Courtyard Boston
   Cambridge, 286
DoubleTree by Hilton Boston-
   Downtown, 268
DoubleTree Suites by Hilton
   Boston, 280–281
Eliot Hotel, 270–271
Embassy Suites Hotel Boston at
   Logan Airport, 287
Emerson Inn by the Sea, 334
Fairmont Battery Wharf,
   254–255
The Fairmont Copley Plaza, 271
40 Berkeley, 269
Four Seasons Hotel, 271
Hampton Inn Boston/
   Cambridge, 284
Hampton Inn Boston Logan
   Airport, 287
Harbor Light Inn, 312–313
Harborside Inn, 258–259
Harvard Square Hotel, 286–287
Hawthorne Hotel, 320
Hilton Boston Back Bay, 276
Hilton Boston Financial
   District, 262
Hilton Boston Logan Airport,
   287–288
Hilton Garden Inn, 341
Holiday Inn Boston at Beacon
   Hill, 264
The Holiday Inn Boston
   Brookline, 280
Holiday Inn Express Hotel &
   Suites, 285–286
Hostelling International-Boston,
   268–269
Hotel Commonwealth, 279
Hotel Marlowe, 284
Hotel 140, 277–278
Hotel Veritas, 282
Hyatt Harborside, 288
Hyatt Regency Boston Financial
   District, 262
The Hyatt Regency
   Cambridge, 284
The Inn at Harvard, 284–285
Inn on Cove Hill (Caleb
   Norwood Jr. House), 335
Inn @ St. Botolph, 273
InterContinental Boston,
   255, 258
John Carver Inn & Spa, 342
The Langham, Boston, 261
Le Méridien Cambridge, 285
The Lenox Hotel, 271–272
The Liberty Hotel, 264
Longwood Inn, 281
Mandarin Oriental, Boston,
   272–273

The MidTown Hotel, 278
Millennium Bostonian Hotel, 260–261
Newbury Guest House, 278–279
Nine Zero, 261–262
Omni Parker House, 262–263
Onyx Hotel, 259–260
Pilgrim Sands on Long Beach, 342
Radisson Hotel Plymouth Harbor, 341
Renaissance Boston Waterfront Hotel, 265–266
Residence Inn Boston Harbor on Tudor Wharf, 265
The Revere Boston, 267
The Ritz-Carlton, Boston Common, 267–268
Royal Sonesta Hotel, 282
The Salem Inn, 320
Seaport Hotel, 266
Sheraton Boston Hotel, 276
Sheraton Commander Hotel, 285
Taj Boston, 273
W Boston, 268
The Westin Boston Waterfront, 266–267
The Westin Copley Place Boston, 276–277
XV Beacon, 263–264

Restaurants

Abe & Louie's, 169
ArtBar, 174
Artú, 156–157, 162
Bangkok City, 172
Baraka Café, 182
The Barking Crab, 150–151
Bertucci's, 179, 298
Bond Restaurant & Lounge, 183
Border Café, 178
Boston Super Dog, 154
Bova's Bakery, 231
Brasserie Jo, 170–171
Bristol, 183
The Bristol Lounge, 171
Café Jaffa, 172
Cafe Mami, 184
Caffè dello Sport, 154
Caffé Pompei, 231
Caffè Vittoria, 154
Capital Grille, 169
Centre Street Café, 159
Chacarero, 162
Charlie's Sandwich Shoppe, 159
Chau Chow City, 164
China Pearl, 164

Citizen Public House & Oyster Bar, 173
Clover Food Lab, 178
Clover Food Truck, 150, 154, 184
Coppa, 166–167
Courtyard, 172
Courtyard (Boston Public Library), 183
Crema Cafe, 146
Daily Catch, 155
Dalí, 170, 180–181
Dante, 174
Davio's Northern Italian Steakhouse, 170
Driftwood Restaurant, 312
Durgin-Park, 160
East Coast Grill & Raw Bar, 180
Elephant Walk, 159, 180
The Elephant Walk, 173–174
Fajitas & 'Ritas, 161
Finale, 163, 228
Fleming's Prime Steakhouse & Wine Bar, 163, 169
Flour Bakery & Cafe, 168–169
Galleria Umberto Rosticceria, 158
Giacomo's Ristorante, 157–158
Great Taste Bakery & Restaurant, 164, 165–166
Grill 23 & Bar, 169, 170
Grotto, 162
Halibut Point Restaurant & Bar, 327
Hamersley's Bistro, 159, 166
Hei La Moon, 164
The Helmand, 182
Henrietta's Table, 174, 176
Hungry Mother, 181
In a Pig's Eye, 318–319
India Pavilion, 184
International House of Pancakes, 231
Island Creek Oyster Bar, 173
Ittyo Restaurant, 184
Jacob Wirth Company, 163–165
Japonaise Bakery, 184
Jasper White's Summer Shack, 170, 181
Johnny D's Uptown Restaurant & Music Club, 340
Kiskadee Coffee Company, 340
La Summa, 158
Latitude 43 Restaurant & Bar, 327
La Verdad Taqueria Mexicana, 174
Legal Sea Foods, 151, 163, 176, 180
Lobby Lounge (Mandarin Oriental), 183
Lobster Hut, 341

Lobster Pool, 333
Lounge (Taj Boston), 183
McCormick & Schmick's Seafood Restaurant, 159, 163
Maggiano's Little Italy, 163
Mamma Maria, 154–155
Map Room Café, 172
Market, 163
Miel, 174
Mike's Pastry, 154
Milk Street Cafe, 160
Morton's of Chicago, 169
Mr. Bartley's Burger Cottage, 178–179
Nashoba Brook Bakery & Café, 307
Neptune Oyster, 155–156
Oleana, 174, 180
Orinoco, 167
P. F. Chang's China Bistro, 163, 172
Palm, 169
Paramount, 159
Parish Cafe and Bar, 174
Peach Farm, 165
Persy's Place, 341
Picco Restaurant, 169
Pizzeria Regina, 158
Redbones, 182
Rowes Wharf Sea Grille, 183
Roy Moore Lobster Company, 333
Russell House Tavern, 176, 178
Ruth's Chris Steak House, 169
Sapporo Ramen, 184
Shay's Pub & Wine Bar, 174
Smith & Wollensky, 169
South End Buttery, 167–168
South Street Diner, 231
S&S Restaurant, 159, 184
Stephanie's on Newbury, 174
Sultan's Kitchen, 160
Swans, 183
Tampopo, 184
Tapéo, 170
Taranta Cucina Meridionale, 155
Tasty Burger, 175
Tealuxe, 183
Teranga, 168
Toro, 168
Trade, 151
Union Oyster House, 160–161
UpStairs on the Square, 175, 183
Veggie Galaxy, 179
Veggie Planet, 179
Volle Nolle, 159
Winsor Dim Sum Cafe, 164
Woodman's of Essex, 326, 329–330
Xinh Xinh, 166

PHOTO CREDITS